HP-UX 11i Version 2
System Administration

Hewlett-Packard® Professional Books

HP-UX

Cooper/Moore	HP-UX 11i Internals
Fernandez	Configuring CDE
Keenan	HP-UX CSE: Official Study Guide and Desk Reference
Madell	Disk and File Management Tasks on HP-UX
Olker	Optimizing NFS Performance
Poniatowski	HP-UX 11i Virtual Partitions
Poniatowski	HP-UX 11i System Administration Handbook and Toolkit, Second Edition
Poniatowski	The HP-UX 11.x System Administration Handbook and Toolkit
Poniatowski	HP-UX 11.x System Administration "How To" Book
Poniatowski	HP-UX 10.x System Administration "How To" Book
Poniatowski	HP-UX System Administration Handbook and Toolkit
Poniatowski	Learning the HP-UX Operating System
Rehman	HP-UX CSA: Official Study Guide and Desk Reference
Sauers/Ruemmler/Weygant	HP-UX 11i Tuning and Performance
Weygant	Clusters for High Availability, Second Edition
Wong	HP-UX 11i Security

UNIX, LINUX

Mosberger/Eranian	IA-64 Linux Kernel
Poniatowski	Linux on HP Integrity Servers
Poniatowski	UNIX User's Handbook, Second Edition
Stone/Symons	UNIX Fault Management

COMPUTER ARCHITECTURE

Evans/Trimper	Itanium Architecture for Programmers
Kane	PA-RISC 2.0 Architecture
Markstein	IA-64 and Elementary Functions

NETWORKING/COMMUNICATIONS

Blommers	Architecting Enterprise Solutions with UNIX Networking
Blommers	OpenView Network Node Manager
Blommers	Practical Planning for Network Growth
Brans	Mobilize Your Enterprise
Cook	Building Enterprise Information Architecture
Lucke	Designing and Implementing Computer Workgroups
Lund	Integrating UNIX and PC Network Operating Systems

SECURITY

Bruce	Security in Distributed Computing
Mao	Modern Cryptography: Theory and Practice
Pearson et al.	Trusted Computing Platforms
Pipkin	Halting the Hacker, Second Edition
Pipkin	Information Security

WEB/INTERNET CONCEPTS AND PROGRAMMING

Amor	E-business (R)evolution, Second Edition
Apte/Mehta	UDDI
Chatterjee/Webber	Developing Enterprise Web Services: An Architect's Guide
Kumar	J2EE Security for Servlets, EJBs, and Web Services

About Prentice Hall Professional Technical Reference

With origins reaching back to the industry's first computer science publishing program in the 1960s, and formally launched as its own imprint in 1986, Prentice Hall Professional Technical Reference (PH PTR) has developed into the leading provider of technical books in the world today. Our editors now publish over 200 books annually, authored by leaders in the fields of computing, engineering, and business.

Our roots are firmly planted in the soil that gave rise to the technical revolution. Our bookshelf contains many of the industry's computing and engineering classics: Kernighan and Ritchie's *C Programming Language*, Nemeth's *UNIX System Administration Handbook*, Horstmann's *Core Java*, and Johnson's *High-Speed Digital Design*.

PH PTR acknowledges its auspicious beginnings while it looks to the future for inspiration. We continue to evolve and break new ground in publishing by providing today's professionals with tomorrow's solutions.

HP-UX 11i Version 2 System Administration

HP Integrity and HP 9000 Servers

Marty Poniatowski

Upper Saddle River, NJ • Boston• Indianapolis • San Francisco

New York • Toronto • Montreal • London • Munich • Paris • Madrid

Capetown • Sydney • Tokyo • Singapore • Mexico City

The publisher offers excellent discounts on this book when ordered in quantity for bulk purchases or special sales, which may include electronic versions and/or custom covers and content particular to your business, training goals, marketing focus, and branding interests. For more information, please contact:

U. S. Corporate and Government Sales
(800) 382-3419
corpsales@pearsontechgroup.com

For sales outside the U. S., please contact:

International Sales: international@pearsoned.com
Visit us on the Web: www.phptr.com

Library of Congress Number: 2005923195

Pearson Education, Inc.
Rights and Contracts Department
One Lake Street
Upper Saddle River, NJ 07458

ISBN 0-13-192759-0
Text printed in the United States on recycled paper at R.R. Donnelley in Crawfordsville, Indiana.
First printing, May 2005

Contents

Preface

About This Book

HP-UX 11i System Administration Handbook covers HP-UX for both Intel Itanium servers, called Integrity Servers, and Precision Architecture (PA-RISC) servers, called the HP 9000 Servers. There were different versions of HP-UX that ran on HP Integrity and HP 9000 server families in the past, but now HP-UX 11i version 2 runs on both server families; that is, the same source code base is used for both server families. Many differences exist between version 1 and version 2, such as the commands used to configure the kernel. The following is a partial list of features of version 2, some of which are comparisons to version 1, that are important to the operation of HP-UX 11i. Keep in mind that this list is being enhanced continuously and that these are some features available at the time of this writing.

Version 2 Update 2 Features

- 1 to 128-way processor scalability under the same operating system.
- Huge file system size of 32 TB, file size of 2 TB, and many other advanced file system-related features.
- Up to four different 64-bit operating systems can run simultaneously on the same HP Integrity Server including HP-UX 11i (which is cov-

ered extensively throughout this book), Windows Server 2003 and Linux, and OpenVMS.

- Multi-operating-system management with HP System Insight Manager (HP SIM), which is covered in Chapter 11.

- Electrically isolated hard partitions (nPartitions), which is covered in Chapter 17.

- Virtual Partitions (vPars) that provide full software isolation which is covered in Chapter 16.

- In-chassis upgrade from PA-RISC to Itanium with version 2 being the same source code base for both architectures.

- ServiceGuard support for mixed environments with both HP Integrity and HP 9000 servers.

- Instant Capacity (iCAP) and numerous variants of iCAP.

- Substantial performance increase of version 2 over version 1.

This is only a partial list of the many advanced features of HP-UX 11i.

HP-UX has come a long way since the early days of the operating system. The speed of the operating system has increased along with the speed of the hardware. Functionality such has both hard and soft partitions and manageability with HP SIM has changed the way that systems are laid out and managed.

For enterprise applications, HP-UX has truely reached the level of a fully functional data center operating system that can run any application vital to the operation of a business.

I crafted this book in such a way that the major HP-UX topics are covered in such a way to help you get up-and-running quickly using some of HP-UX's advanced features, such as partitioning.

This book starts out with extensive coverage of booting HP Integrity and HP 9000 servers. Much of the firmware related to booting differs on these two server families, so I cover booting these systems in detail in Chapters 1 and 2 for Integrity and HP 9000, respectively. The Extensible Firmware Interface (EFI) is an important part of booting HP Integrity servers, which can run different operating systems in different partitions, so I spend a significant amount of time covering this topic in Chapter 1.

There are many new functions in HP-UX 11i version 2 that have been introduced and have become mainstream since the previous revision of this book. Most HP-UX installations now make liberal use of Virtual Partitions (vPars) and hard partitions (called Node Partitions or nPartitions). I cover these technologies extensively in this book since this is currently the most sought after topic related to HP-UX. Many other topics are covered in additional chapters as you would expect in one of my HP-UX system adminstration books.

I hope you enjoy reading this book and learning the material as much as I did writing it.

Marty Poniatowski

marty.poniatowski@hp.com

Relevant URLs

There are many Web sites that can assist you in your HP-UX system administration endeavors. Here are some of the more prominent HP-UX-related Web sites below as they existed at the time of this writing:

HP Developer and Solution Partner Portal (DSPP). This Web site has a lot of good software developer information and tools such as the Software Transition Kit (STK). You can download the STK to test your application when moving from one revision of HP-UX to another:
http://www.hp.com/dspp

The Extended Firmware Interface (EFI). This is firmware on Itanium-based systems that sits between the operating system and platform firmware:
http://www.intel.com/technology/efi/index.htm

IT Resource Center (ITRC) has valuable hardware, software, network, and other kinds of information for HP system administrators:
http://www.itrc.com

Technical documentation, including most all HP-UX documents:
http://www.docs.hp.com

Software depot home page for HP:
http://www.software.hp.com

HP education Web site:
http://www.education.hp.com

vPar product information:
http://www.hp.com/go/servicecontrol

HP-UX documentation:
http://docs.hp.com/hpux/

Instant Capacity on Demand (iCOD):
http://www.hp.com/go/icod

The International Association of HP Computing Professionals:
http://www.interex.org

Information on Intel's Itanium Processor:
http://www.hp.com/go/itanium

Register name servers:
http://www.icann.org/registrars/accredited-list.html

Excellent unsupported system administration scripts:
ftp://contrib:9unsupp8@hprc.external.hp.com/sysadmin/

Ximian GNOME on HP-UX:
http://www.hp.com/workstations/support/software/hpux/gnome/index.html

Open Source and Other Sites of Interest

Information on Perl, including sites to download Perl:
http://www.perl.com

The Perl Journal:
http://www.tpj.com

Information about the GNOME desktop environment:
http://www.gnome.org

Public-domain software that has been ported to HP-UX:
http://hpux.connect.org.uk

Site devoted to managing and promoting Open Source:
http://www.opensource.org

Linux documentation site:
http://www.linuxdoc.org

Acknowledgments

So many people were involved in helping me with this book that it is impossible to list each and every one. I have, therefore, decided to formally thank those who wrote sections of the book and those who took time to review it. I'm still not sure whether it takes more time to write something or review something that has been written to ensure that it is correct.

The Author: Marty Poniatowski

Marty has been a Solution Architect with Hewlett-Packard Company for 18 years in the New York area. He has worked with hundreds of Hewlett-Packard customers in many industries, including media and entertainmet, consulting, Internet startups, financial services, and manufacturing.

Marty has been widely published in computer-industry trade publications. He has published more than 50 articles on various computer-related topics. In addition to this book, he is the author of 13 other Prentice Hall books. Marty holds an M.S. in Information Systems from Polytechnic University (Brooklyn, NY), an M.S. in Management Engineering from the University of Bridgeport (Bridgeport, CT), and a B.S. in Electrical Engineering from Roger Williams University (Bristol, RI).

Martin Whittaker

Martin Whittaker is the Director of System Software Engineering in the Enterprise UNIX Division (EUD) of Hewlett-Packard. Martin is responsible for the core kernel, commands, and libraries in the HP-UX operating system and for HP-UX performance and scalability, Linux affinity, and ISV enablement.

Martin has been with Hewlett-Packard for more than twenty years in a variety of senior technical and management positions in areas including mass storage, Itanium architecture, x86 server performance, I/O systems, the 5Nines:5Minutes high availability program, and operating systems.

He holds a Bachelor's degree in Electrical and Electronic Engineering from the University of Nottingham in England and a Master's degree in Microprocessor Engineering and Digital Electronics from the University of Manchester Institute of Science and Technology in England.

Steven M. Wolff

Steven supplied the tear-out card for this book.

Steven came to HP as a result of HP's acquisition of Convex. He has been supporting high-end Servers since 1989. He is currently in the Remote/E-Delivery Organization working for the Superdome Support Team supporting North American Superdome customers. Steven is also a certified HP-UX system administrator and is Linux Professional Institute (LPI) certified.

Brian Hackley

Brian supplied material on DNS and BIND, NFS performance assessment, and NIS background used in various sections throughout this book. Brian is a member of the Hewlett Packard Global Customer Solution Center UNIX Network Team (NETUX.)

Brian came to Hewlett Packard as a result of the HP-Apollo merger in 1989. Until 1993, he was an Offline Technical Marketing Support Engineer, responsible for New Product Introduction for Apollo Domain/OS and HP-UX network products. Brian moved into the Chelmsford Response Center in 1993, where he worked as a Senior NETUX Engineer supporting Apollo and HP network products. After a 2-year hiatus at Sun Microsystems in 1995 and 1996, he returned to HP and re-joined the HP Customer Solution Center NETUX team in early 1997. Assignments since that time include a variety of roles supporting HP-UX Network Products as a Senior Support Engineer and as a Support Consultant for Mission-Critical customers.

Brian lives and works in Lexington, Massachusetts and is married to Wendy Carter, a Registered Pharmacist. They have a son, Steve, who is an IT Director at the BPS Center in Birmingham, Michigan.

Glenn Miller

Glenn Miller has worked in a variety of functional areas in HP over the last 23 years. The majority of these years were spent in HP-UX related positions including marketing, strategy, R&D, and program management. He is currently in the HP-UX 11i Planning group in the Enterprise Unix Division responsible for software deployment tools and HP-UX 11i Operating Environments.

Reviewers and Other Contributors

In all, there were about 25 reviewers and additional contributors to this book. I'm not sure what makes someone agree to review a book. You don't get the glory of a contributing author, but it is just as much work. I would like to thank the many people who devoted a substantial amount of time to reviewing this book to ensure that I included topics important to new system administrators and accurately covered those topics.

Among the additional contributors and reviewers who agreed to help me are Joe Lucas (operating environments), Claudia Peters and Paul Vetter (HP SIM), Steven Roth (kernel), Bruce Henderson (patch), Aparna Das-Caro, Wade Satterfield, Gary Thomsen, and Erik Bostrom (SAM), David Soper and Adam Schwartz (EFI), Myron Stowe (booting), and Alan Hymes (vPars chapter and the vPars portion of the Startup chapter).

Several Prentice Hall reviewers who scoured the entire manuscript are Marty Paul, Tracy Hendler, Rick DeAngelis, Edward Karasinski, and Sree Grish.

Conventions Used in This Book

I don't use a lot of complex notations in this book. Here are a few simple conventions I've used to make the examples clear and the text easy to follow:

$ and #
: The HP-UX command prompt. Every command issued in the book is preceded by a command prompt. Either one of these two will be used or a system name are usually used as prompts.

italics
: Italics are used for variable values and when referring to functional areas and menu picks in the System Administration Manager (SAM).

bold and " "
: Bold text is the information you would type, such as the command you issue after a prompt or the information you type when running a script. Sometimes information you would type is also referred to in the text explaining it, and the typed information may appear in quotes.

<----
: When selections have to be made, this convention indicates the one chosen for the purposes of the example.

[ ]
: Brackets indicate optional items and command descriptions.

{ }
: Curly braces indicate a list from which you must choose.

|
: A vertical bar separates items in a list of choices.

<Enter>
: Indicates the "Enter" key has been pressed on the keyboard. Sometimes <Return> is used to indicate the return key has been pressed.

One additional convention is that used for command formats. I don't use command formats more than I have to because I could never do as thorough a job of describing commands as the HP-UX manual pages. The manual pages go into detail on all HP-UX commands. Here is the format I use when I cover commands:

form 1   command [option(s)] [arg(s)]
form 2   command [option(s)] [arg(s)]
form n   command [option(s)] [arg(s)]

I try not to get carried away with detail when covering a command, but there are sometimes many components that must be covered in order to understand a command. Here is a brief description of the components listed above:

form # -There are sometimes many forms of a command. If there is more than one form of a command that requires explanation, then I will show more than one form.

command - The name of the executable.

option(s) - Several options may appear across a command line.

cmd_arg(s) - Command arguments such as path name.

Chapter 1

Booting HP Integrity Servers

Introduction

This chapter covers booting an HP Integrity (Itanium-based) server and Chapter 2 covers HP 9000 (PA-RISC) server booting. Booting an Integrity server requires that you become familiar with two levels of firmware. The first level is HP's implementation of Intel's EFI (Extensible Firmware Interface), *POSSE* (Pre-OS System Environment). The second is HP's independent support processor for the system console, the *Management Processor* (MP), which is covered along with Node Partitions (nParitions) in Chapter 17. The MP is integral to booting both HP Integrity and HP 9000 servers. Although functionality varies from one platform to another, the topics in this chapter apply to all HP Integrity servers at the time of this writing. The systems used throughout this chapter include a variety of two, and four-way Integrity servers.

This chapter covers the following topics:

• High-level boot process overview on HP Integrity servers

• EFI and POSSE

In addition to providing background on these topics, this chapter also provides many examples of running commands and analyzing output for both POSSE and MP.

The trifold included with this book is a quick reference for many boot-related commands.

High-Level Boot Process Overview on HP Integrity Servers

The boot process on HP Integrity Servers is much different than that on HP 9000 servers. Figure 1-1 summarizes the Integrity boot process.

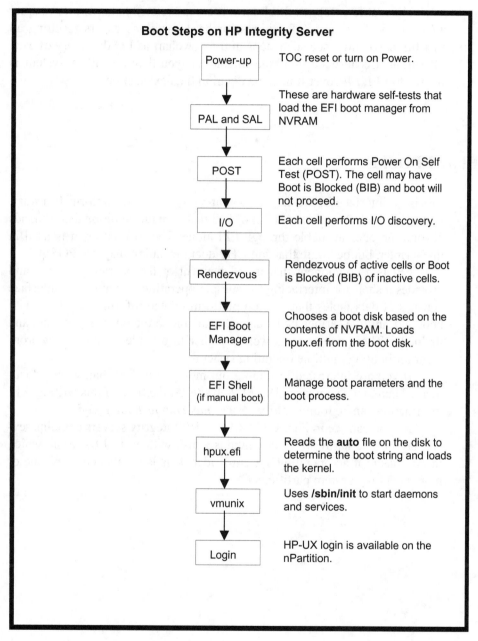

Boot Steps on HP Integrity Server

Step	Description
Power-up	TOC reset or turn on Power.
PAL and SAL	These are hardware self-tests that load the EFI boot manager from NVRAM
POST	Each cell performs Power On Self Test (POST). The cell may have Boot is Blocked (BIB) and boot will not proceed.
I/O	Each cell performs I/O discovery.
Rendezvous	Rendezvous of active cells or Boot is Blocked (BIB) of inactive cells.
EFI Boot Manager	Chooses a boot disk based on the contents of NVRAM. Loads hpux.efi from the boot disk.
EFI Shell (if manual boot)	Manage boot parameters and the boot process.
hpux.efi	Reads the **auto** file on the disk to determine the boot string and loads the kernel.
vmunix	Uses **/sbin/init** to start daemons and services.
Login	HP-UX login is available on the nPartition.

Figure 1-1   Boot Steps on HP Integrity Servers

The first few steps of this boot process are related to hardware. Chapter 17 on Node Partitions (nPartitions) or hard partitions covers resetting an nPartition, so you'll see such steps in the flowchart as I/O discovery of each nPartition. Because most of the interaction you'll have with a system is related to EFI, I'll cover it in some detail in the next section.

EFI and POSSE

EFI is an interface between your operating system and platform firmware. POSSE is the HP implementation of EFI that contains additional commands beyond the ones available through EFI alone. The EFI acronym is used in this chapter, but be aware that some HP documentation may use POSSE.

EFI is a component that is independent of the operating system and provides a shell for interfacing to multiple operating systems. The interface consists of data tables that contain platform-related information along with boot and runtime service calls that are available to the operating system and its loader. These components work together to provide a standard environment for booting multiple operating systems.

If you are interested in finding out more about EFI than what's documented here, take a look Intel's EFI Web site. At the time of this writing, EFI information can be found at *http://www.intel.com/technology/efi.*

As you can see in Figure 1-2, EFI on HP Integrity servers contains several layers. The hardware layer contains a disk with an EFI partition, which in turn has in it an operating system loader. This layer also contains one or more operating system partitions.

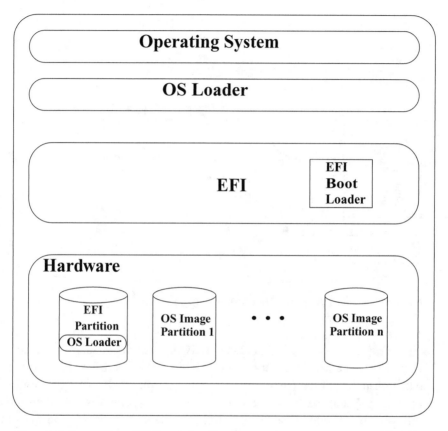

Figure 1-2   EFI on HP Integrity Servers

In addition, the EFI system partition itself consists of several different components, as shown in Figure 1-3.

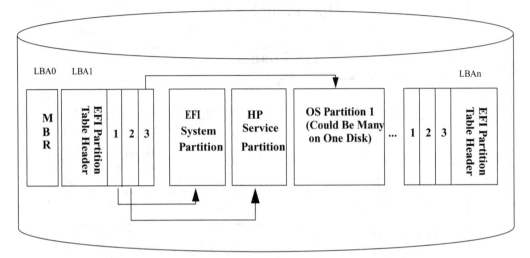

Figure 1-3   EFI System Partition

The Logical Block Addresses (LBAs) are shown across the top of Figure 1-3. The Master Boot Record (MBR) is the first LBA. There is then a partition table. Three partitions are shown on this disk. Note that multiple operating system partitions can be loaded on the same disk. At the time of this writing, Windows Server 2003 and Linux can be loaded on the same disk. The EFI partition table on the right is a backup partition table.

Booting an operating system with EFI on an Integrity server involves several steps. Figure 1-4 depicts the high-level steps.

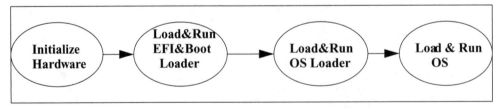

Figure 1-4   Load and Run an Operating System

The first step is to initialize the hardware. This takes place at the lowest level (BIOS) before EFI or the operating systems play any part in the process. Next, the EFI and boot loader are loaded and run. After an operating system is chosen, the operating system loader is loaded and run for the specific operating system being booted. Finally, the operating system itself is loaded and run. There are no specific operating systems cited in Figure 1-4 because the process is the same regardless of the operating system being loaded. In the examples in this book, Linux, HP-UX, and Windows are used and all these operating systems would load in the same manner.

Working with EFI

Traversing the EFI menu structure and issuing commands is straight forward. You make your desired selections and then traverse a menu hierarchy. To start EFI, when the system self-test is complete, use the "v" key to stop the countdown timer. The main EFI screen appears. The following output shows the EFI Boot Administration main screen, which is where you can make various boot-related selections:

```
EFI Boot Manager ver 1.10 [14.60]

Please select a boot option

    HP-UX Primary Boot: 1/0/0/2/0.6.0
    Acpi(000222F0,0)/Pci(1|0)/Mac(00306E4B9AD9)
    Acpi(000222F0,100)/Pci(1|0)/Mac(00306E4BAA28)
    EFI Shell [Built-in]
    LAN1boot
    Boot option maintenance menu


    Use ^ and v to change option(s). Use Enter to select an option
```

This output shows the primary HP-UX boot device and two LAN cards with their MAC addresses. From the main screen, you can also choose either *EFI Shell [Built-in]*, *LAN1boot* (which is a customer boot selection I created), or *Boot option maintenance menu*. The first item shown in the EFI main screen is the default. Use the arrow keys to scroll and highlight a selection. After the item you need is highlighted, press *Enter* to select it. For example, if you were to select *Boot option maintenance menu*, you would see a screen resembling the one shown in the following output:

```
EFI Boot Maintenance Manager ver 1.10 [14.60]

Main Menu. Select an Operation
```

```
Boot from a File
Add a Boot Option
Delete Boot Option(s)
Change Boot Order

Manage BootNext setting
Set Auto Boot TimeOut

Select Active Console Output Devices
Select Active Console Input Devices
Select Active Standard Error Devices

Cold Reset
Exit


Timeout-->[10] sec SystemGuid-->[0C8E34C2-3F1E-11D8-9D70-F907BCE0A36D]
SerialNumber-->[USE43499VC]
```

Table 1-1 summarizes many of the frequently used EFI commands. I cover many of these commands in the next section.

Table1-1   Commonly Used EFI Commands

EFI Command	Description
Commands Found in All Menus	
map	Produces a device map list (**map -r** rescans the bus).
info boot	Boots from a specified path.
help *command*	Displays help for specified command or menu (**help bch** is handy).
reset	Resets the system (to allow reconfiguration of Complex).
exit (at the EFI shell)	Returns you to the Main Menu.
Commands Found on the MAin Menu	
EFI Boot Manager "Change Boot Order"	Displays or modifes a path. (In "Boot option maintenance menu" and then "Change Boot Order," select the desired boot path and use "u" or "d" to move up or down.)
bcfg	Searches for boot devices.
more, plus many commands offer a [-b] parameter to cause 25 line breaks	Displays or changes scrolling capability.

EFI Command	Description
Commands Found on the Configuration Menu	
autoboot	Displays or starts the auto start flag.
info boot	Displays or sets processor Boot Identifier.
EFI Boot Manager	Display boot-related information.
autoboot	Seconds allowed for boot attempt.
cpuconfig	Config/Deconfig Processor.
autoboot	Displays or sets boot tests execution.
time	Reads or sets the real time clock.
Commands Found on the Information Menu	
info all	Displays all system information.
info boot	Displays boot-related information.
info cache	Displays cache information.
info chiprev	Displays revision number of major VLSI.
MP command <df>	Displays FRU information.
info fw	Displays firmware version for PDC, ICM, and Complex.
info io	Displays information about components in the partition.
info mem	Displays memory information.
info cpu	Displays processor information.
SERvice	Service-related commands.
errdump clear	Clears (zero) the contents of PIM.
mm	Reads memory locations scope of page deallocations.
PDT	Displays or clears the Page Deallocation (Processor Internal Memory).
errdump mca	Displays PIM information (Processor Internal Memory).
more [-b]	Displays or changes scrolling capability.

An interesting aspect of the EFI commands is that you can accomplish many of the same functions running BCH commands on HP 9000 (PA-

RISC) systems. To those of you who have PA-RISC system experience, you'll see many of the same functions performed in EFI.

Using EFI, you can control the boot-related setup on your Integrity server. Because of the number of operating systems you can run on Integrity servers, you use this interface often to coordinate and manage them.

EFI Command Examples

As previously mentioned, traversing the EFI menu structure and issuing commands is straightforward. When the system boots, you are given the option to interrupt the autoboot. (If you don't interrupt it, the autoboot loads the first operating system listed, which, in our case, is *HP-UX Primary Boot.* At system startup, the EFI Boot Manager presents the boot option menu (as shown in the following output). Here, you have 10 seconds to enter a selection before *HP-UX Primary Boot* is selected:

```
EFI Boot Manager ver 1.10 [14.60]

Please select a boot option

    HP-UX Primary Boot: 1/0/0/2/0.6.0
    Acpi(000222F0,0)/Pci(1|0)/Mac(00306E4B9AD9)
    Acpi(000222F0,100)/Pci(1|0)/Mac(00306E4BAA28)
    EFI Shell [Built-in]
    LAN1boot
    Boot option maintenance menu


    Use ^ and v to change option(s). Use Enter to select an option
```

You can use the arrow, or the *u* and *d* keys, to move up and down respectively. I used the ↓ key (down arrow) to select *EFI Shell [Built-in]*. This brought me to the *Shell>* prompt. From there, you can issue EFI commands. Similarly, once you're at the *Shell>* prompt, help is always available. To get a listing of the classes of commands available in *Shell>*, simply enter **help** and press Enter as shown in the following output:

```
Shell> help
List of command classes:

boot           -- Boot related commands
configuration  -- Changing and retrieving system information
device         -- Device, driver and handle related commands
filesystem     -- Filesystem related commands
memory         -- Memory related commands
shell          -- Basic shell navigation and customization
scripts        -- EFI shell-script commands
```

```
Type 'help' followed by a class name for a list of commands in that class.
Type 'help' followed by a command name for full documentation.
Type 'help -a' for a list of all available commands.

Shell>
```

When using a network connection from another system, you may have
to use the ^ and *v* to move up and down the menu structure respectively.

You can also issue *help* requests for any EFI commands at any level.
For example, if you want to know more about your current CPU configuration, you would start with **help configuration** to determine the help command for CPU configuration, and then use the **help cpuconfig** command:

```
Shell> help configuration
Configuration commands:

acpiconfig -- Set/View ACPI configuration mode
cellconfig -- Deconfigure/Reconfigure cells
cpuconfig  -- Deconfigure/Reconfigure cpus
date       -- Display the current date or set the date of the system
dimmconfig -- Deconfigure/Reconfigure dimms
err        -- Display/Change the error level
errdump    -- View/Clear logs
fru        -- View Fru data
info       -- Display hardware information
monarch    -- Set/View a monarch processor
palproc    -- Make a PAL call.
romdrivers -- Enable/Disable PCI expansion ROM drivers
rootcell   -- Set/View preferred root cells
salproc    -- Make a SAL call
tftp       -- Performs tftp operation to a bootp/dhcp enabled unix boot server
time       -- Display the current time or set the time of the system
variable   -- Save/Restore specific EFI variables
ver        -- Display the version information

Type 'help' followed by a command name for full documentation.

Shell>
```

As a result of having issued **help cpuconfig**, you now know how to
manipulate the CPUs in your system. The following output shows what happens when you issue the **cpuconfig** command with a few options:

```
Shell> help cpuconfig
CPUCONFIG [cell] [module] [on|off]

    cell   : Specifies which cell to use
    module : Specifies which cpu module to configure
    on|off : Specifies to configure or deconfigure a cpu module

    Note:
        1. CPU status will not change until next boot.
```

```
Examples:
    * To deconfigure CPU Module 0 on Cell 0:
      Shell> cpuconfig 0 0 off

    * To display configuration status of CPUs on all Cells:
      Shell> cpuconfig

    * To display configuration status of CPUs on Cell 0:
      Shell> cpuconfig 0
```

```
Shell> cpuconfig

PROCESSOR INFORMATION

        Cab/  Mod/                 Proc                Arch  Processor
   Cell Slot  CPU    Speed         Rev  Model Family   Rev   State
   ---- ----- ----   ----------    ---- ----- ------   ----  -------------
      1 0/1   0/0    1500 MHz      B1   1     31       0     Active
      1 0/1   1/0    1500 MHz      B1   1     31       0     Active
      1 0/1   2/0    1500 MHz      B1   1     31       0     Active
      1 0/1   3/0    1500 MHz      B1   1     31       0     Active
```

```
Shell> cpuconfig 1 3 off

CPU Module will be deconfigured on next boot.
```

```
Shell> cpuconfig

PROCESSOR INFORMATION

        Cab/  Mod/                 Proc                Arch  Processor
   Cell Slot  CPU    Speed         Rev  Model Family   Rev   State
   ---- ----- ----   ----------    ---- ----- ------   ----  -------------
      1 0/1   0/0    1500 MHz      B1   1     31       0          Active
      1 0/1   1/0    1500 MHz      B1   1     31       0          Active
      1 0/1   2/0    1500 MHz      B1   1     31       0          Active
      1 0/1   3/0    1500 MHz      B1   1     31       0     Sched Deconf
```

```
Shell>
```

I used **cpuconfig** to view the current CPU configuration, showing that all four processors are *Active*. I then turned *off* processor *3* on cell board 1 (**cpuconfig 1 3 off**). Finally, I viewed the CPU configuration again to confirm that processor *3* had been turned off as indicated by the *Sched Deconf* (**cpuconfig**).

As you can see, by using EFI, you can get a lot of useful configuration information about your system. In addition to **cpuconfig**, you can also use **info** to get important system information. The following listing first shows the results of the **info** command. **info**, with no argument, lists all the differing information options available (such as **all**, **boot**, **cache**, and so on). After you see all the **info** options, use **info all** to get a complete rundown on your system:

```
Shell> info

Usage:
INFO [cell] target [target...]

target : all, boot, cache, cell, chiprev,
         cpu, fabric, fw, io, mem, sys

Execute 'help info' for more help.

Shell> info all

SYSTEM INFORMATION

   Date/Time:  Nov 14, 2004  22:34:51  (20:04:11:14:22:34:51)

   Partition : 1
      Active Cell List       : 1
      Total Active CPUs      : 4
      Total Active Memory    : 16384 MB
        Interleaved Memory    : 16352 MB
        NonInterleaved Memory :    32 MB


PROCESSOR INFORMATION

        Cab/  Mod/              Proc                  Arch  Processor
  Cell  Slot  CPU    Speed      Rev   Model Family    Rev   State
  ----  ----- ----   ---------- ----  ----- ------    ----  -------------
     1  0/1   0/0    1500 MHz   B1    1     31        0        Active
     1  0/1   1/0    1500 MHz   B1    1     31        0        Active
     1  0/1   2/0    1500 MHz   B1    1     31        0        Active
     1  0/1   3/0    1500 MHz   B1    1     31        0     Sched Deconf


CACHE INFORMATION for CELL 1

  Cab/  Mod/                 Cache Sizes
  Slot  CPU    L1i     L1d      L2        L3
  ----- ----   ------- ------- --------  ---------
  0/1   0/0    16 KB   16 KB   256 KB    6144 KB
  0/1   1/0    16 KB   16 KB   256 KB    6144 KB
  0/1   2/0    16 KB   16 KB   256 KB    6144 KB
  0/1   3/0    16 KB   16 KB   256 KB    6144 KB


MEMORY INFORMATION

        Cab/   Total     Active    Failed SW Deconf HW Deconf
  Cell  Slot   Mem       Mem       DIMMs  DIMMs     DIMMs     Unknown
  ----  -----  --------- --------- ------ --------- --------- -------
     1  0/1    16384 MB  16384 MB    0        0         0        0

  Active Memory                : 16384 MB
    Interleaved Memory         : 16352 MB
    NonInterleaved Memory      :    32 MB
  Installed Memory             : 16384 MB


CHIP REVISION INFORMATION

        Module      Cell    Revision
        ----------  ----    --------
            cc        1     0x2
           sba        1     0x01
           ioc        1     0x01
          lba0        1     0x05
          lba1        1     0x32
          lba2        1     0x32
          lba4        1     0x32
          lba6        1     0x32
           ioc        1     0x01
          lba8        1     0x32
         lba10        1     0x32
         lba12        1     0x32
```

```
        lba14      1    0x32
        crossbar   1    0x2
```

I/O INFORMATION

   I/O CHASSIS INFORMATION

```
     Cell Info                   I/O Chassis Info
     Cell  Cab/Slot      Cabinet  Bay  Chassis  Type
     ----  --------      -------  ---  -------  -----
      1     0/1             0      0      1     PCI-X
```

   IO MODULE INFORMATION for Root CELL 1

```
                          Slot   Rope
     Type                  #      #
     ----                 ----  -----
     System Bus Adapter
     Local Bus Adapter     0      0
     Local Bus Adapter     1     8/9
     Local Bus Adapter     2    10/11
     Local Bus Adapter     3    12/13
     Local Bus Adapter     4    14/15
     Local Bus Adapter     5     6/7
     Local Bus Adapter     6     4/5
     Local Bus Adapter     7     2/3
     Local Bus Adapter     8      1
```

   PCI DEVICE INFORMATION

```
 Seg Bus Dev Fnc Vendor Device Slot
  #   #   #   #    ID     ID    #   Description
 --- --- --- --- ------ ------ ---- -----------
 01  00  00  00  0x103C 0x1290  00  Simple Communications Controllers - Other
 01  00  00  01  0x103C 0x1048  00  Simple Communications Controllers - Serial
 01  00  00  02  0x0000 0x0000  00  Serial Bus Controllers - UNDEFINED
 01  00  01  00  0x14E4 0x1645  00  Network Controller - Ethernet controller
 01  00  02  00  0x1000 0x0021  00  Mass Storage Controller - SCSI controller
 01  00  02  01  0x1000 0x0021  00  Mass Storage Controller - SCSI controller
 01  00  03  00  0x1000 0x0021  00  Mass Storage Controller - SCSI controller
 01  00  03  01  0x1000 0x0021  00  Mass Storage Controller - SCSI controller
 01  30  01  00  0x1000 0x0021  05  Mass Storage Controller - SCSI controller
 01  30  01  00  0x1000 0x0021  05  Mass Storage Controller - SCSI controller
 01  40  01  00  0x103C 0x1029  01  Serial Bus Controllers - Fibre Channel
 01  50  01  00  0x103C 0x1029  02  Serial Bus Controllers - Fibre Channel
 01  60  01  00  0x14E4 0x1645  03  Network Controller - Ethernet controller
 01  70  01  00  0x14E4 0x1645  04  Network Controller - Ethernet controller
```

BOOT INFORMATION

   Monarch CPUs:

```
          Current  Preferred
          Monarch  Monarch
     Cell  Mod/CPU  Mod/CPU   Warnings
     ----  -------  ---------  --------
      1     0/0       0/0
```

   The current root cell is 1.
   The preferred root cell is 1.

   AutoBoot: ON - Timeout is : 10 sec

   Boottest:

   BOOTTEST Settings Default Variable

   OS is not speedy boot aware.

```
    Selftest        Setting
    ---------       --------------
    early_cpu       Run this test
    late_cpu        Run this test
    platform        Run this test
    chipset         Run this test
    io_hw           Skip this test
    mem_init        Run this test
    mem_test        Run this test

    LAN Address Information:

    LAN Address         Path
    -----------------   ----------------------------------------
    Mac(00306E4BAA28)   Acpi(000222F0,100)/Pci(1|0)/Mac(00306E4BAA28))


FIRMWARE INFORMATION

    Firmware Revision:
          All CELLS - 000.018 Thu Aug 14 10:34:10 2003

    PAL_A Revision:
          All CELLS - 7.31/5.37
    PAL_B Revision:
          All CELLS - 5.37

    SAL Spec Revision:
          All CELLS - 3.1
    SAL_A Revision:
          All CELLS - 0.18
    SAL_B Revision:
          All CELLS - 0.18

    EFI Spec Revision:
          All CELLS - 1.10
    EFI Intel Drop Revision:
          All CELLS - 14.60
    EFI Build Revision:
          All CELLS - 000.018

    POSSE Revision:
          All CELLS - 000.018

    ACPI Revision:
          All CELLS - 2.0a


FABRIC INFORMATION

    Fabric Topology:

    Cabinets        Backplane Configuration
    --------        -------------------------
    0                       OlympiaTopology

    Fabric Links:

        Start           End           Link Status Fields
                  P             P
    C    L    o  C    L    o
    a    o    r  a    o    r   Pre  Prev Veri      SW   HW
    b Type c ID t  b Type c ID t  sent Err  fied FE Link Link
    - ---- - -- -  - ---- - -- -  ---- ---- ---- -- ---- ----
    0  XBC 0  0 0  0   CC 0  0 0   1    0    1   0   1    1
    0  XBC 0  0 1      NONE        0    0    1   0   0    0
    0  XBC 0  0 2      NONE        0    0    1   0   0    0
    0  XBC 0  0 3  0   CC 3  3 0   1    0    1   0   1    1
    0  XBC 0  0 4      NONE        0    0    1   0   0    0
    0  XBC 0  0 5      NONE        0    0    1   0   0    0
    0  XBC 0  0 6  0   CC 2  2 0   1    0    1   0   1    1
    0  XBC 0  0 7  0   CC 1  1 0   1    0    1   0   1    1


Shell>
```

As you can see, **info all** produces a great overview of the system configuration. You get information on the processors and cache sizes (including the one that is scheduled to be reconfigured), the 16 GB of memory, firmware revisions, PCI device information, the LBAs, Slots, and Ropes. (These are described in Chapter 6.)

Of particular interest in this listing is the LBA-slot-rope information. Chapter 6 details device files and mapping an LBA to a slot. I recommend you save the **info all** output so that you have this information about all of your partitions for future reference.

In addition to selecting the *EFI Shell,* which I have been using in the examples to this point, I also have other options. Selecting *Boot option maintenance menu* produces the selections shown here:

```
EFI Boot Maintenance Manager ver 1.10 [14.60]

Main Menu. Select an Operation


        Boot from a File
        Add a Boot Option
        Delete Boot Option(s)
        Change Boot Order

        Manage BootNext setting
        Set Auto Boot TimeOut

        Select Active Console Output Devices
        Select Active Console Input Devices
        Select Active Standard Error Devices

        Cold Reset
        Exit


    Timeout-->[10] sec SystemGuid-->[0C8E34C2-3F1E-11D8-9D70-F907BCE0A36D]
    SerialNumber-->[USE43499VC]
```

At this point, you could perform a variety of functions. The *Select the Console Output Device(s)* menu appears listing all possible console devices. The first device with an * is the serial port that was selected by default:

```
EFI Boot Maintenance Manager ver 1.10 [14.60]

Select the Console Output Device(s)


  Acpi(000222F0,100)/Pci(0|1)/Uart(9600 N81)/VenMsg(PcAnsi)
  Acpi(000222F0,100)/Pci(0|1)/Uart(9600 N81)/VenMsg(Vt100)
```

```
  * Acpi(000222F0,100)/Pci(0|1)/Uart(9600 N81)/VenMsg(Vt100+)
    Acpi(000222F0,100)/Pci(0|1)/Uart(9600 N81)/VenMsg(VtUtf8)
Save Settings to NVRAM
Exit
```

The server on which I'm working does not have a graphics card installed, so there is not one shown in the output. The next output is from a system with a graphics card. To enable the graphics as well, you would select the last console device. You know that this is the graphics device port because it does not contain *Uart* as part of the selection. Note that *Uart* devices are always serial devices. Also note that in the following example, the graphical device port is already selected (indicated by an *). Select *Save Settings to NVRAM,* which saves the console device settings, and then exit:

```
EFI Boot Maintenance Manager ver 1.10 [14.60]

Select the Console Output Device(s)


      Acpi(PNP0501,0)/Uart(9600 N81)/VenMsg(PcAnsi)
      Acpi(PNP0501,0)/Uart(9600 N81)/VenMsg(Vt100)
      Acpi(PNP0501,0)/Uart(9600 N81)/VenMsg(Vt100+)
      Acpi(PNP0501,0)/Uart(9600 N81)/VenMsg(VtUtf8)
      Acpi(HWP0002,700)/Pci(1|1)/Uart(9600 N81)/VenMsg(PcAnsi)
      Acpi(HWP0002,700)/Pci(1|1)/Uart(9600 N81)/VenMsg(Vt100)
    * Acpi(HWP0002,700)/Pci(1|1)/Uart(9600 N81)/VenMsg(Vt100+)
      Acpi(HWP0002,700)/Pci(1|1)/Uart(9600 N81)/VenMsg(VtUtf8)
    * Acpi(HWP0002,700)/Pci(2|0)
Save Settings to NVRAM
Exit
```

This setting enables both the serial and graphics consoles. The early boot messages go to the serial console. If you were to install a graphics-based operating system, such as Linux or Windows, the graphics server would start.

The first four entries with *PNP0501* in them are on the nine pin serial port. The next four entries with *HWP0002* in them are on the three-cable device that fits into the 25 pin connector.

An additional topic about which you might need to know is a given system's device mappings. Device mapping are peculiar to the system on which you're working. To view mappings using EFI, you need to get to a console-like EFI *Shell>* prompt. To do so, you must select *EFI Shell.* Once at the prompt, there are a variety of commands that you can run, including **map**. See Chapter 6 for additional ACPI and device mapping information.

Much of the information is intended for programmers and technicians. As a system administrator, however, you need to know which entries correspond to which devices and which entries are for your partitions and file systems. To determine that, let's take a look at each entry.

At the time of initial installation, you might issue **map** to see the path of a peripheral in which you have operating system media loaded. After issuing the **map** command, you then select the device in which the media is loaded with **fs2:** as shown in the following listing:

```
Shell> map
Device mapping table
   fs0  : Acpi(HWP0002,100)/Pci(3|0)/Scsi(Pun6,Lun0)/HD(Part1,Sig9A3F1F4A-401A-11
D9-8002-D6217B60E588)
   fs1  : Acpi(HWP0002,100)/Pci(3|0)/Scsi(Pun6,Lun0)/HD(Part3,Sig9A3F1F86-401A-11
D9-8004-D6217B60E588)
   fs2  : Acpi(HWP0002,100)/Pci(3|1)/Scsi(Pun2,Lun0)/CDROM(Entry0)
   blk0 : Acpi(HWP0002,100)/Pci(3|0)/Scsi(Pun6,Lun0)
   blk1 : Acpi(HWP0002,100)/Pci(3|0)/Scsi(Pun6,Lun0)/HD(Part1,Sig9A3F1F4A-401A-11
D9-8002-D6217B60E588)
   blk2 : Acpi(HWP0002,100)/Pci(3|0)/Scsi(Pun6,Lun0)/HD(Part2,Sig9A3F1F68-401A-11
D9-8003-D6217B60E588)
   blk3 : Acpi(HWP0002,100)/Pci(3|0)/Scsi(Pun6,Lun0)/HD(Part3,Sig9A3F1F86-401A-11
D9-8004-D6217B60E588)
   blk4 : Acpi(HWP0002,100)/Pci(3|1)/Scsi(Pun2,Lun0)
   blk5 : Acpi(HWP0002,100)/Pci(3|1)/Scsi(Pun2,Lun0)/CDROM(Entry0)
   blk6 : Acpi(HWP0002,100)/Pci(3|1)/Scsi(Pun2,Lun0)/CDROM(Entry1)
   blk7 : Acpi(HWP0002,108)/Pci(1|0)/Pci(1|1)/Scsi(Pun6,Lun0)

Shell> fs2:

fs2:\> dir
Directory of: fs2:\

   09/02/04  10:41p <DIR>           1,024   EFI
   09/02/04  10:41p               521,494   INSTALL.EFI
   09/02/04  10:41p                    16   AUTO
   09/02/04  10:41p                   174   STARTUP.NSH
            3 File(s)    521,684 bytes
            1 Dir(s)


fs2:\> install.efi

(C) Copyright 2004 Hewlett-Packard Development Company, L.P.All rights reserved

HP-UX Boot Loader for IPF  --  Revision 2.018

Press Any Key to interrupt Autoboot
\AUTO ==> boot :IINSTALL
```

After selecting path **fs2:** and issuing **dir**, the information on the DVD-ROM is displayed. I execute the **install.efi** command, which brings up the installation program. Chapter 3, which covers installing HP-UX, details the process of installation.

Keep in mind my comment at the beginning of this chapter related to working with the Management Processor (MP), which is covered along with Node Partitions, or nPartitions, in Chapter 17.

Chapter 2

Booting on HP 9000 Servers (PDC, ISL, hpux)

Introduction

The following topics are covered in this chapter:

- An overview of the boot process on HP 9000 (PA-RISC) servers

- Boot Control Handler (BCH) and Processor Dependent Code (PDC)

- Initial System Load (ISL)

Another important topic is HP's independent support processor for the system console, the *Management Processor* (MP), which is covered along with Node Partitions, or nPartitions, in Chapter 17.

Most of the examples in this chapter were run on nPartions on an rp7420 server. Because this is a partitioned system, you see only the information related to the partition on which I'm working in the examples and not the other partition.

The next section provides an overview of the boot process.

Boot Process Overview

The boot process on a PA-RISC system can be reduced in its simplest form to three steps. I provide a quick description of the three steps and then look at some example boot processes so that you can see these three steps in action. The following is a description of the three steps:

PDC   HP-UX systems come with firmware installed called Processor Dependent Code. After the system is powered on or the processor is RESET, the PDC runs self-test operations and initializes the processor. PDC also identifies the console path so it can provide messages and accept input. PDC would then begin the "auto-boot" process unless you interrupt it during the 10-second interval that is supplied. If you interrupt the "autoboot" process, you can issue a variety of commands. The interface to PDC commands is called the Boot Console Handler (BCH). This is sometimes a point of confusion; that is, are we issuing PDC commands or BCH commands? The commands are normally described as PDC commands, and the interface through which you execute them is the BCH.

ISL   The Initial System Loader is run after PDC. You would normally just run an "autoboot" sequence from ISL; however, you can run a number of commands from the ISL prompt.

hpux   The hpux utility manages loading the HP-UX kernel and gives control to the kernel. ISL can have hpux run an "autoexecute" file, or commands can be given interactively. In most situations, you would just want to automatically boot the system; however, I cover some of the hpux commands you can execute. This is sometimes called the Secondary System Loader (SSL).

I find that there is a lot of confusion related to the boot process for new system administrators. To begin with, there is not much documentation that comes with new systems related to HP system boot. Second, without any background on the boot process, it is difficult to determine at which phase of the boot your system is at any given time. Table 2-1 shows some system states and the corresponding prompts that you can expect for each state in roughly the order you might see them at the time of system boot.

Table 2-1 System Boot Prompts

Boot State of System	Prompt
Boot Console Handler (BCH) Seen when you discontinue boot within 10 seconds. Used to perform PDC-related work.	`Main Menu: Enter command or menu >`
Initial System Loader (ISL) Seen after PDC-related work.	`ISL> ?`
hpux Prompt varies. You usually issue **hpux** command at ISL prompt to boot. This is sometimes called the Secondary System Loader (SSL).	Varies depending on the state of the system.
Management Processor (MP)	`MP>`

There is only one way to describe the boot process and that is through example. The boot of a system with minimal hardware will be covered in the upcoming sections. I choose the boot of a system with minimal hardware so we're not bogged down in hardware-related details, but focus on the boot process. The messages supplied as a result of booting this modest system allows us to focus on the boot process rather than on the many hardware components. The boot process consists of mostly the same steps for any HP system, so you can apply this information to your system. It may be, however, that you have a much larger system with more components that will produce more lengthy boot messages.

Because you may be working with the boot process on a system with multiple partitions, you'll want to see the material related to the Management Processor in Chapter 17 as well.

The BCH Commands Including PathFlags on PA-RISC

The Boot Console Handler (BCH) is an important part of working with nPartitions and HP-UX on PA-RISC systems. Many commands can be issued through BCH, but I cover just a couple of the most commonly used commands. Figure 2-1 shows the high-level steps involved in booting an nPartition on an HP 9000 (PA-RISC system). The figure depicts the progression of steps starting at the top and working it's way down to the bottom.

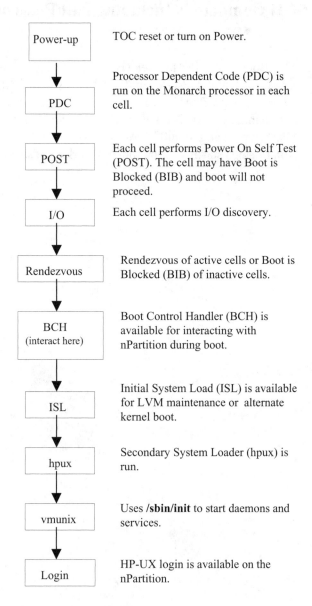

Power-up	TOC reset or turn on Power.
PDC	Processor Dependent Code (PDC) is run on the Monarch processor in each cell.
POST	Each cell performs Power On Self Test (POST). The cell may have Boot is Blocked (BIB) and boot will not proceed.
I/O	Each cell performs I/O discovery.
Rendezvous	Rendezvous of active cells or Boot is Blocked (BIB) of inactive cells.
BCH (interact here)	Boot Control Handler (BCH) is available for interacting with nPartition during boot.
ISL	Initial System Load (ISL) is available for LVM maintenance or alternate kernel boot.
hpux	Secondary System Loader (hpux) is run.
vmunix	Uses **/sbin/init** to start daemons and services.
Login	HP-UX login is available on the nPartition.

Figure 2-1   Boot Steps on the HP 9000 Server From the Top Down

BCH is the primary way to interact with an nPartition at boot time. The steps and interfaces of the boot process meld together. There are a few different interfaces and levels of boot through which you work. When you get to the main menu of the Management Processor and issue commands you are using BCH. When you get past BCH, you reach ISL, which is considered the next step of the boot process beyond BCH. Then, you reach the Secondary System Loader by issuing the **hpux** command, which attempts to load the kernel. You need to know at what level of the boot process you are working so you can issue the appropriate commands.

I'll connect to BCH, after rendezvous, through *Consoles* in the following examples. Because this is done through the console the information provided is for the specific processor nPartition to which the console is connected.

In the first example, I issue **in** to go to the information menu and then get information on the **io** and **pr** and then go back to the *Main Menu* with **ma** from BCH:

```
Main Menu: Enter command or menu > in   <-- Select information menu at BCH

---- Information Menu ------------------------------------------------

    Command                          Description
    -------                          -----------
    ALL [<cell>]                     Display all of the information
    BootINfo                         Display boot-related information
    CAche [<cell>]                   Display cache information
    ChipRevisions [<cell>]           Display revisions of major VLSI
    ComplexID                        Display Complex information
    FwrVersion [<cell>]              Display version for PDC, ICM, and Complex

    IO [<cell>]                      Display I/O interface information
    MEmory [<cell>]                  Display memory information
    PRocessor [<cell>]               Display processor information

    BOot [PRI|HAA|ALT|<path>]        Boot from specified path
    DIsplay                          Redisplay the current menu
    HElp [<command>]                 Display help for specified command
    REBOOT                           Restart Partition
    RECONFIGRESET                    Reset to allow Reconfig Complex Profile
    MAin                             Return to Main Menu
----
Information Menu: Enter command > io          <-- Obtain I/O information

I/O CHASSIS INFORMATION

    Cell Info            I/O Chassis Info

Cell  Cab/Slot       Cab   Bay   Chassis
----  --------       ---   ---   -------
  0     0/0           0     0      0


I/O MODULE INFORMATION

                     Path       Slot  Rope                         IODC
Type                 (dec)      #     #     HVERSION   SVERSION     Vers
----                 -----      ----  ----  --------   --------     ----
System Bus Adapter   0/0                    0x8050     0x0c18       0x00
```

```
Local Bus Adapter    0/0/0         0     0    0x7820   0x0a18   0x00
Local Bus Adapter    0/0/1         8     1    0x7830   0x0a18   0x00
Local Bus Adapter    0/0/2         7     2    0x7830   0x0a18   0x00
Local Bus Adapter    0/0/4         6     4    0x7830   0x0a18   0x00
Local Bus Adapter    0/0/6         5     6    0x7830   0x0a18   0x00
Local Bus Adapter    0/0/8         1     8    0x7830   0x0a18   0x00
Local Bus Adapter    0/0/10        2    10    0x7830   0x0a18   0x00
Local Bus Adapter    0/0/12        3    12    0x7830   0x0a18   0x00
Local Bus Adapter    0/0/14        4    14    0x7830   0x0a18   0x00


PCI DEVICE INFORMATION

                          Path            Bus    Slot      Vendor   Device
Description               (dec)           #      #         Id       Id
-----------               -----           ---    ------    ------   ------
Communications dev        0/0/0/0/0       0      Built-In  0x103c   0x1290
Comm. serial cntlr        0/0/0/0/1       0      Built-In  0x103c   0x1048
SCSI bus cntlr            0/0/0/3/0       0      Built-In  0x1000   0x0021
SCSI bus cntlr            0/0/0/3/1       0      Built-In  0x1000   0x0021
PCI-to-PCI bridge         0/0/8/1/0       64     1         0x1014   0x01a7
SCSI bus cntlr            0/0/8/1/0/1/0   65     1         0x1000   0x0021
SCSI bus cntlr            0/0/8/1/0/1/1   65     1         0x1000   0x0021
Ethernet cntlr            0/0/8/1/0/4/0   65     1         0x14e4   0x1645
PCI-to-PCI bridge         0/0/10/1/0      80     2         0x1014   0x01a7
Fibre channel             0/0/10/1/0/4/0  81     2         0x1077   0x2312
Ethernet cntlr            0/0/10/1/0/6/0  81     2         0x14e4   0x16c7
PCI-to-PCI bridge         0/0/12/1/0      96     3         0x1014   0x01a7
Fibre channel             0/0/12/1/0/4/0  97     3         0x1077   0x2312
Ethernet cntlr            0/0/12/1/0/6/0  97     3         0x14e4   0x16c7


Information Menu: Enter command > pr    <-- Obtain processor information

PROCESSOR INFORMATION
         Cab/                                                   Processor
Cell     Slot    CPU    Speed      HVERSION   SVERSION  CVERSION State
----     ----    ---    --------   --------   --------  -------- --------------
  0      0/0     0A     1000 MHz   0x8830     0x0491    0x0302   Active
                 0B     1000 MHz   0x8830     0x0491    0x0302   Idle

              Partition Total Cells: 1
         Partition Total Processors: 2
        Partition Active Processors: 2
    Partition Deconfigured Processors: 0

Information Menu: Enter command > ma       <-- Return to the Main Menu

---- Main Menu -------------------------------------------------------------

     Command                    Description
     -------                    -----------
     BOot [PRI|HAA|ALT|<path>]  Boot from specified path
     PAth [PRI|HAA|ALT] [<path>] Display or modify a path
     SEArch [ALL|<cell>|<path>] Search for boot devices
     ScRoll [ON|OFF]            Display or change scrolling capability

     COnfiguration menu         Displays or sets boot values
     INformation menu           Displays hardware information
     SERvice menu               Displays service commands

     DIsplay                    Redisplay the current menu
     HElp [<menu>|<command>]    Display help for menu or command
     REBOOT                     Restart Partition
     RECONFIGRESET              Reset to allow Reconfig Complex Profile
----
```

One I/O chassis (0/0) in this nPartition has several cards in it, as shown in the **io** command. The I/O chassis connected to a cell board is fully devoted to that nPartition. This means that all the cards in the I/O chassis are used by the nPartition. With Virtual Partitions the cards within an I/O chassis can be used for different vPars. vPars are covered in Chapter 16. In addition, device files and the mapping of a slot to a Local Bus Adapter (LBA), which is important to know, is covered extensively in Chapter 6, which covers devices.

There are two processors in the nPartition, one of which is idle, as shown in the **pr** output. As you can see, a lot of additional information can be obtained from the *Information Menu*. I always issue the commands shown to get information on the hardware of the system to include as part of the partition documentation.

Next, I go to the *Configuration Menu* with **co** and issue a variety of commands related to booting:

```
Configuration Menu: Enter command > co  <-- Go to the configuration menu

---- Configuration Menu -----------------------------------------------------

    Command                          Description
    -------                          -----------
    BootID [<cell>[<cpu>[<bootid>]]]  Display or set Boot Identifier
    BootTimer [0-200]                Seconds allowed for boot attempt
    COreCell [<choice> <cell>]       Display or set core cell
    CPUconfig [<cell>[<cpu>[ON|OFF]]] Config/Deconfig processor
    DataPrefetch [ENABLE|DISABLE]    Display or set data prefetch behavior
    DEfault                          Set the Partition to predefined values
    FastBoot [test][RUN|SKIP]        Display or set boot tests execution
    KGMemory [<value>]               Display or set KGMemory requirement
    PathFlags [PRI|HAA|ALT] [<value>] Display or set Boot Path Flags
    PD [<name>]                      Display or set Partition name values
    ResTart [ON|OFF]                 Set Partition Restart Policy
    TIme [cn:yr:mo:dy:hr:mn:[ss]]    Read or set the real time clock
    ZLco [ON|OFF]                    Display or set ZLCO behavior

    BOot [PRI|HAA|ALT|<path>]        Boot from specified path
    DIsplay                          Redisplay the current menu
    HElp [<command>]                 Display help for specified command
    REBOOT                           Restart Partition
    RECONFIGRESET                    Reset to allow Reconfig Complex Profile
    MAin                             Return to Main Menu
----
Configuration Menu: Enter command > FastBoot skip        <-- Employ fastboot

Selftest     Setting
-----------  -------
PDH          SKIP
EARLY cpu    SKIP
LATE cpu     SKIP

Configuration Menu: Enter command > PathFlags           <-- View PathFlags

    Primary Boot Path Action
        Boot Actions:  Skip this path.
                       Go to next path.

HA Alternate Boot Path Action
        Boot Actions:  Skip this path.
                       Go to next path.

    Alternate Boot Path Action
        Boot Actions:  Skip this path.
                       Go to BCH.

Configuration Menu: Enter command > PathFlags PRI 2     <-- Boot primary,
                                                        go to next on failure
```

```
        Primary Boot Path Action
            Boot Actions:  Boot from this path.
                           If unsuccessful, go to next path.

Configuration Menu: Enter command > PathFlags HAA 2<-- Boot HA alternate,
                                                     go to next on failure

HA Alternate Boot Path Action
            Boot Actions:  Boot from this path.
                           If unsuccessful, go to next path.

Configuration Menu: Enter command > PathFlags ALT 1<-- Boot alternate,
                                                   go to BCH on failure

     Alternate Boot Path Action
            Boot Actions:  Boot from this path.
                           If unsuccessful, go to BCH.

Configuration Menu: Enter command > PathFlags          <-- View PathFlags

        Primary Boot Path Action
            Boot Actions:  Boot from this path.
                           If unsuccessful, go to next path.

HA Alternate Boot Path Action
            Boot Actions:  Boot from this path.
                           If unsuccessful, go to next path.

     Alternate Boot Path Action
            Boot Actions:  Boot from this path.
                           If unsuccessful, go to BCH.

Configuration Menu: Enter command > ma                 <-- Go to main menu

---- Main Menu --------------------------------------------------------------

        Command                        Description
        -------                        -----------
        BOot [PRI|HAA|ALT|<path>]      Boot from specified path
        PAth [PRI|HAA|ALT] [<path>]    Display or modify a path
        SEArch [ALL|<cell>|<path>]     Search for boot devices
        ScRoll [ON|OFF]                Display or change scrolling capability

        COnfiguration menu             Displays or sets boot values
        INformation menu               Displays hardware information
        SERvice menu                   Displays service commands

        DIsplay                        Redisplay the current menu
        HElp [<menu>|<command>]        Display help for menu or command
        REBOOT                         Restart Partition
        RECONFIGRESET                  Reset to allow Reconfig Complex Profile
----
```

Many more commands can be issued from the *Configuration Menu* beyond the selections that I made. The first command that I issued was to employ *Fastboot skip,* which skips tests at boot time.

The next series of commands set boot flags. The process of setting up the boot options is important. If your primary boot devices is not available, it is important for you to specify the alternate devices you have set up. Table 2-2 summarizes some of the settings that you can issue related to boot flags.

Table 2-2 MP and HP-UX Boot Paths

Command	Description
PathFlags PRI 2	Set the primary to *2*. The following are definitions of the numbers: *0* - Go directly to BCH without trying to boot. *1* - Boot from this path and go to BCH on a failure. *2* - Boot from this path and go to the next boot path, if one is defined, on a failure. If not, go to BCH. *3* - Skip this path and go to the next boot path, if one is defined. If not, go to BCH.
PathFlags HAA 2	Set the High Availability Alternative (HAA) to *2*.
PathFlags ALT 1	Set the Alternate to *1*.
nPartition equivalents to the BCH definitions: PRI = -b (primary) HAA = -t (alternate) ALT = -s (secondary)	The -b, -t, and -s are used by HP-UX commands such as **parcreate** and **parmodify** to specify the *primary, alternate,* and *secondary* boot paths. Note that these are different than the names used by BCH.
setboot equivalents to the BCH definitions: primary = -p (primary) high availability = -h (alternate-path) alternate = -a (alternate) autoboot = -b on|off autosearch = -s on|off tests = -t testname on|off verbose output = -v	The -p, -a, and -b are used by **setboot** at the HP-UX prompt to control the *primary, alternate,* and *autoboot* parameters. Run **setboot -v** to see the current settings.

For more detailed information on the **setboot** command, including examples, see Chapter 8.

The setboot Command

The **setboot** command allows you to display and modify boot variables. You can set a variety of parameters with **setboot**. The following command shows displaying the current settings with **setboot -v** on an Integrity server:

```
# setboot -v
Primary bootpath : 0/0/0/3/0.6.0
Alternate bootpath : 0/0/0/0/0.0.0

Autoboot is ON (enabled)
Autosearch is ON (enabled)

Note: The interpretation of Autoboot and Autosearch has changed for
systems that support hardware partitions. Please refer to the manpage.
TEST            CURRENT      SUPPORTED      DEFAULT      NEXT BOOT
----            -------      ---------      -------      ---------
all             off          partial        partial      off
  SELFTESTS     off          yes            on           off
    early_cpu   off          yes            on           off
    late_cpu    off          yes            on           off
  FASTBOOT      off          partial        partial      off
    full_memory off          no             off          off
    PDH         off          yes            on           off
  CEC           off          no             off          off
```

This output shows the values of many parameters that are in stable storage.

Boot Console Handler (BCH) and Processor Dependent Code (PDC)

As mentioned earlier, PA-RISC systems come with firmware installed called Processor Dependent Code (PDC). After the system is powered on or the processor is RESET, the PDC runs self-test operations and initializes the processor. PDC also identifies the console path so that it can provide messages and accept input. PDC would then begin the "autoboot" process, unless you interrupt it during the 10-second interval that is supplied. If you interrupt the "autoboot" process, you can issue a variety of commands.

Chapter 17, which covers Node Partitions, provides background on the Management Process (MP). There are several areas to the MP in which you can work such as the Command Menu, Virtual Front Panel (VFP), and the console. See Chapter 17 if you are not familiar with working with the MP.

The following example shows resetting a partition at the Command Menu, seeing log files generated at the VFP, and then switching back to the console to work with PDC commands:

```
MP MAIN MENU:

    CO: Consoles
   VFP: Virtual Front Panel (partition status)
    CM: Command Menu
    CL: Console Logs
    SL: Show Event Logs
    HE: Help
     X: Exit Connection

[otcapmp] MP> cm               <-- Go CM


        Enter HE to get a list of available commands


[otcapmp] MP:CM> rs            <-- Reset nPartition
This command resets the selected partition.

WARNING: Execution of this command irrecoverably halts all system
         processing and I/O activity and restarts the selected
         partition.

  Part#  Name
  -----  ----
    0)   Partition 0
    1)   nPar1cell0

  Select a partition number: 1     <-- Select nPartition 1

  Do you want to reset partition number 1? (Y/[N]) y

  -> The selected partition will be reset.

[otcapmp] MP:CM> ma

        V-- Select VFP from main menu to see progress


  #  Partition state          Activity
  -  ---------------          --------
  1  Cell(s) Booting:                                378 Logs

  #  Cell state               Activity
  -  ----------               --------
  0  Memory discovery         MEM_TEST_READ_BARGRAPH    378 Logs
```

After the "early" boot is complete, you get a brief system summary, including the firmware revision on your system, and are then given the option to automatically boot off the primary path or press any key to stop the boot process. Under normal system operation, you would autoboot; however, in this case, we interrupt the boot process to see what commands are available in the PDC.

As was done earlier, I return to the *Main* menu and then type *IN* to get access to the *INformation* menu and then view *all*:

```
Configuration Menu: Enter command > main

---- Main Menu ----------------------------------------------------------

        Command                         Description
        -------                         -----------
        BOot [PRI|HAA|ALT|<path>]       Boot from specified path
        PAth [PRI|HAA|ALT] [<path>]     Display or modify a path
        SEArch [ALL|<cell>|<path>]      Search for boot devices
        ScRoll [ON|OFF]                 Display or change scrolling capability

        COnfiguration menu              Displays or sets boot values
        INformation menu                Displays hardware information
        SERvice menu                    Displays service commands

        DIsplay                         Redisplay the current menu
        HElp [<menu>|<command>]         Display help for menu or command
        REBOOT                          Restart Partition
        RECONFIGRESET                   Reset to allow Reconfig Complex Profile
----
Main Menu: Enter command or menu > in

---- Information Menu ----------------------------------------------------

        Command                         Description
        -------                         -----------
        ALL [<cell>]                    Display all of the information
        BootINfo                        Display boot-related information
        CAche [<cell>]                  Display cache information
        ChipRevisions [<cell>]          Display revisions of major VLSI
        ComplexID                       Display Complex information
        FwrVersion [<cell>]             Display version for PDC, ICM, and Complex

        IO [<cell>]                     Display I/O interface information
        MEmory [<cell>]                 Display memory information
        PRocessor [<cell>]              Display processor information

        BOot [PRI|HAA|ALT|<path>]       Boot from specified path
        DIsplay                         Redisplay the current menu
        HElp [<command>]                Display help for specified command
        REBOOT                          Restart Partition
        RECONFIGRESET                   Reset to allow Reconfig Complex Profile
        MAin                            Return to Main Menu
----


Information Menu: Enter command > all

BOOT INFORMATION

        Primary Boot Path:      0/0/0/3/0.6
                                0/0/0/3/0.6     (hex)
             Boot Actions:      Boot from this path.
                                If unsuccessful, go to next path.

HA Alternate Boot Path:         0/0/0/0/0.0
                                0/0/0/0/0.0     (hex)
             Boot Actions:      Boot from this path.
                                If unsuccessful, go to next path.

   Alternate Boot Path:         0/0/0/0/0.0
                                0/0/0/0/0.0     (hex)
             Boot Actions:      Boot from this path.
                                If unsuccessful, go to BCH.

    Software ID (hex):          0x3e1139bc594121c9

   Software Capability:         0x0


          Boot Timer :    0
```

```
CACHE INFORMATION

            Cab/           Instruction Cache     Data Cache
     Cell   Slot   CPU           Size               Size
     ----   ----   ---    -----------------    ---------------
      0     0/0    0A          32 MB               32 MB
                   0B          32 MB               32 MB


CHIP REVISION INFORMATION

            Cab/
     Cell   Slot   Module    Revision
     ----   ----   -------   ----------
      0     0/0    PDC        21.3
                   CPU(0A)    PA8800 3.2
                   CPU(0B)    PA8800 3.2
                   CC         1.0
                   SBA        1.0
                   LBA        3.2
                   PDH        2.0


COMPLEX ID INFORMATION

                Complex Name: Complex 01
                Model String: 9000/800/rp7420
     Original Product Number: A7025A
      Current Product Number: A7025A
              Serial Number: USE4440F97
     Number of Supported Cells: 2
     Complex Revision Number: 1.0


FIRMWARE INFORMATION

                                              PDC ICM       PDC Utils
     Cell   Cab/Slot   PDC Ver   PDC Date Code   Layout Rev   XFace Rev
     ----   --------   -------   -------------   ----------   ---------
      0       0/0      021.003      44.19          008          008


I/O CHASSIS INFORMATION

     Cell Info              I/O Chassis Info

     Cell   Cab/Slot     Cab   Bay   Chassis
     ----   --------     ---   ---   -------
      0       0/0         0     0       0


I/O MODULE INFORMATION

                        Path        Slot  Rope                           IODC
     Type               (dec)        #     #    HVERSION   SVERSION      Vers
     ----               -----       ----  ----  --------   --------      ----
     System Bus Adapter 0/0                      0x8050     0x0c18       0x00
     Local Bus Adapter  0/0/0        0     0     0x7820     0x0a18       0x00
     Local Bus Adapter  0/0/1        8     1     0x7830     0x0a18       0x00
     Local Bus Adapter  0/0/2        7     2     0x7830     0x0a18       0x00
     Local Bus Adapter  0/0/4        6     4     0x7830     0x0a18       0x00
     Local Bus Adapter  0/0/6        5     6     0x7830     0x0a18       0x00
     Local Bus Adapter  0/0/8        1     8     0x7830     0x0a18       0x00
     Local Bus Adapter  0/0/10       2    10     0x7830     0x0a18       0x00
     Local Bus Adapter  0/0/12       3    12     0x7830     0x0a18       0x00
     Local Bus Adapter  0/0/14       4    14     0x7830     0x0a18       0x00
```

```
PCI DEVICE INFORMATION

                          Path            Bus    Slot     Vendor   Device
Description               (dec)           #      #        Id       Id
-----------               -----           ---    ------   ------   ------
Communications dev        0/0/0/0/0       0      Built-In 0x103c   0x1290
Comm. serial cntlr        0/0/0/0/1       0      Built-In 0x103c   0x1048
SCSI bus cntlr            0/0/0/3/0       0      Built-In 0x1000   0x0021
SCSI bus cntlr            0/0/0/3/1       0      Built-In 0x1000   0x0021
PCI-to-PCI bridge         0/0/8/1/0       64     1        0x1014   0x01a7
SCSI bus cntlr            0/0/8/1/0/1/0   65     1        0x1000   0x0021
SCSI bus cntlr            0/0/8/1/0/1/1   65     1        0x1000   0x0021
Ethernet cntlr            0/0/8/1/0/4/0   65     1        0x14e4   0x1645
PCI-to-PCI bridge         0/0/10/1/0      80     2        0x1014   0x01a7
Fibre channel             0/0/10/1/0/4/0  81     2        0x1077   0x2312
Ethernet cntlr            0/0/10/1/0/6/0  81     2        0x14e4   0x16c7
PCI-to-PCI bridge         0/0/12/1/0      96     3        0x1014   0x01a7
Fibre channel             0/0/12/1/0/4/0  97     3        0x1077   0x2312
Ethernet cntlr            0/0/12/1/0/6/0  97     3        0x14e4   0x16c7


PARTITION MEMORY INFORMATION

Cell   Echelon 0-3        Echelon 4-7        Echelon 8-B        Echelon C-F
       Size   Status      Size   Status      Size   Status      Size   Status
----   ------ ---------   ------ ---------   ------ ---------   ------ ---------
  0    4096MB Active       ---                ---                ---
       4096MB Active       ---                ---                ---
        ---                ---                ---                ---
        ---                ---                ---                ---

         Partition Total Memory:        8192 MB
         Partition Active Memory:       8192 MB
  Partition Deconfigured Memory:           0 MB

* status is scheduled to change on next boot.


PROCESSOR INFORMATION
         Cab/                                                     Processor
  Cell   Slot   CPU   Speed     HVERSION   SVERSION   CVERSION     State
  ----   ----   ---   --------  --------   --------   --------   ---------------
    0    0/0    0A    1000 MHz  0x8830     0x0491     0x0302     Active
                0B    1000 MHz  0x8830     0x0491     0x0302     Idle

              Partition Total Cells: 1
         Partition Total Processors: 2
        Partition Active Processors: 2
  Partition Deconfigured Processors: 0
```

This report would be an excellent addition to a system administration notebook. Knowing such information as the firmware revision levels and the settings of the boot flags is valuable.

In the previous example, I used the BCH to issue the PDC commands *INformation* and then *ALL*. Both *INformation* and *ALL* are PDC commands issued through the BCH interface. Sometimes PDC and BCH are used interchangeably in documentation, however, knowing that BCH is the interface through which PDC commands are issued will usually serve you well when looking for information on specific commands.

I'll now go back to the *Main* menu and then look at the *SERvice* menu:

```
Information Menu: Enter command > main

---- Main Menu -----------------------------------------------------------

      Command                      Description
      -------                      -----------
      BOot  [PRI|HAA|ALT|<path>]   Boot from specified path
      PAth  [PRI|HAA|ALT] [<path>] Display or modify a path
      SEArch [ALL|<cell>|<path>]   Search for boot devices
      ScRoll [ON|OFF]              Display or change scrolling capability

      COnfiguration menu           Displays or sets boot values
      INformation menu             Displays hardware information
      SERvice menu                 Displays service commands

      DIsplay                      Redisplay the current menu
      HElp [<menu>|<command>]      Display help for menu or command
      REBOOT                       Restart Partition
      RECONFIGRESET                Reset to allow Reconfig Complex Profile
----
Main Menu: Enter command or menu > ser

---- Service Menu --------------------------------------------------------

      Command                      Description
      -------                      -----------
      BAttery [<cell>]             Display Cell Battery Status
      CLEARPIM [<cell>]            Clear the Partition's NVM PIM data
      DimmDealloc [<cell>] [<dimm>] Display or Deallocate a DIMM
                  [ON|OFF]
      ErrorLog [<cell>]            Display Error log information
               [MEMORY|IO|FABRIC|CELL]
      LanAddress                   Display Core LAN station address
      MemRead <address> [<len>]    Read memory locations scope of Partition
      PDT [<cell>] [CLEAR]         Display or clear the PDT
      PIM [<cell>[<cpu>]][HPMC|LPMC|TOC] Display PIM information
      SCSI [<cell>] [<path>]       Display or set SCSI device parameters
           [INIT|RATE|TERM|WIDTH <value>] [DEFAULT] [DELETE]

      BOot  [PRI|HAA|ALT|<path>]   Boot from specified path
      DIsplay                      Redisplay the current menu
      HElp [<command>]             Display help for specified command
      REBOOT                       Restart Partition
      RECONFIGRESET                Reset to allow Reconfig Complex Profile
      MAin                         Return to Main Menu
----
```

Among the options you have in the *SERvice* menu is to manipulate the Processor Internal Memory, display SCSI controller values, and enable and disable self-tests. In the following example, we run *scsi* to get information on our SCSI interfaces and then return to the *Main* menu:

```
Service Menu: Enter command > scsi

    This may take a while.  Please wait...

Cell: 0
=========
    Path (dec)            Initiator ID  SCSI Rate  Auto Term  Bus Width
    -----------------     ------------  ---------  ---------  ---------
    0/0/0/3/0                   7          MAX      UNKNOWN      MAX
    0/0/0/3/1                   6          MAX      UNKNOWN      MAX
    0/0/8/1/0/1/0               7          MAX      UNKNOWN      MAX
    0/0/8/1/0/1/1               7          MAX      UNKNOWN      MAX


Note: Only displaying SCSI parameters as stored in PDH NVRAM.
Mismatches between PDH NVRAM and card NVRAM SCSI values will not be reported.
To check PDH NVRAM against I/O card values, run 'SER SCSI <PATH>'

Service Menu: Enter command > main

---- Main Menu -------------------------------------------------------------

    Command                              Description
    -------                              -----------
    BOot [PRI|HAA|ALT|<path>]            Boot from specified path
    PAth [PRI|HAA|ALT] [<path>]          Display or modify a path
    SEArch [ALL|<cell>|<path>]           Search for boot devices
    ScRoll [ON|OFF]                      Display or change scrolling capability

    COnfiguration menu                   Displays or sets boot values
    INformation menu                     Displays hardware information
    SERvice menu                         Displays service commands

    DIsplay                              Redisplay the current menu
    HElp [<menu>|<command>]              Display help for menu or command
    REBOOT                               Restart Partition
    RECONFIGRESET                        Reset to allow Reconfig Complex Profile
----
```

Now that I've covered some of the PDC commands, let's return to the process of booting by looking at the first three commands under *Main* menu.

BOot allows you to specify the path from which you'll boot your system. *PAth* allows you to display or modify the boot paths. *SEArch* will display boot paths. In the following example, I *SEArch* to show all potential boot devices on the nPartition, run *PAth* to display the existing boot path, and then specify the device from which I want to boot the system:

```
Main Menu: Enter command or menu > main

---- Main Menu -------------------------------------------------------------

    Command                              Description
    -------                              -----------
    BOot [PRI|HAA|ALT|<path>]            Boot from specified path
    PAth [PRI|HAA|ALT] [<path>]          Display or modify a path
    SEArch [ALL|<cell>|<path>]           Search for boot devices
    ScRoll [ON|OFF]                      Display or change scrolling capability

    COnfiguration menu                   Displays or sets boot values
    INformation menu                     Displays hardware information
    SERvice menu                         Displays service commands

    DIsplay                              Redisplay the current menu
    HElp [<menu>|<command>]              Display help for menu or command
    REBOOT                               Restart Partition
    RECONFIGRESET                        Reset to allow Reconfig Complex Profile
----
```

```
Main Menu: Enter command or menu > sea

Searching for potential boot device(s) on the core cell
This may take several minutes.

To discontinue search, press any key (termination may not be immediate).


                                                                    IODC
       Path#  Device Path (dec)              Device Type           Rev
       -----  -----------------              -----------           ----
       P0     0/0/0/3/0.6                    Random access media   3
       P1     0/0/0/3/0.5                    Random access media   3
              0/0/10/1/0/4/0.0               Fibre Channel Protocol 13
              0/0/12/1/0/4/0.0               Fibre Channel Protocol 13


Main Menu: Enter command or menu > pa

    Primary Boot Path:    0/0/0/3/0.6
                          0/0/0/3/0.6      (hex)

HA Alternate Boot Path:   0/0/0/0/0.0
                          0/0/0/0/0.0      (hex)

   Alternate Boot Path:   0/0/0/0/0.0
                          0/0/0/0/0.0      (hex)

Main Menu: Enter command or menu > bo p0

 BCH Directed Boot Path: 0/0/0/3/0.6
```

The *SEArch* command shows two internal disks and two fibre interfaces off of which this nPartition could boot. The path of the two internal
boot devices is composed of numbers separated by slashes (/), which indicate bus converters, and dots (.), which indicate cards, slot numbers, and
addresses. The paths of the fibre cards are similar, but they have more entries
for the external storage device to which they're connected. You sometimes
end up decoding these paths to figure out what boot devices map to what
hardware devices on your system.

When I issued the *BOot* command in the previous example, I specified
a device of *p0,* which corresponds to the disk on internal bus1, shown in the
SEArch command results. I responded that I did indeed want to interact with
IPL, which would normally not be the case when booting the system; however, I want to look briefly at IPL in the upcoming IPL section.

PDC commands issued through BCH are a mystery to many new system administrators. I covered enough in this section to get you comfortable
enough on your system to look at the non-intrusive commands, that is, those
that supply useful information without changing the settings on your system.
Be careful if you issue commands that change your configuration.

Under

MAIN-CON-CPU

for instance, you can configure and reconfigure processors. You would not want to experiment with this command unless your system is unused.

PDC Commands

Table 2-3 is a list of PDC commands available. These commands vary somewhat on different systems and are updated on a regular basis, so check *IT Resource Center (itrc.hp.com)* for updates.

Table 2-3   PDC Commands

Command	Explanation
ALL	Displays the collection of all information provided by other display commands typically resident in the INFORMATION menu.
AUTO	Displays or sets status of AUTOBOOT, AUTOSEARCH, or AUTOSTART flags.
BOOT	Initiates boot sequence.
BOOTID	Displays or modifies boot *id* for the processors present.
BOOTINFO	Displays PDC-level information about the configured parameters used for system boot.
BOOTTIMER	Sets a delay value in the system to wait for external mass storage devices to come online.
CACHE	Displays information about the cache memory portion of all installed processors.
CHASSISCODES	Displays a queue of the most recent chassis codes.
CHIPREVISIONS	Displays the revisions of major Very Large Scale Integration (VLSI) in the system.
CLEARPIM	Clears (zero) the contents of the Processor Internal Memory (PIM).
CONFIGURATION	Used to enter the Configuration sub-menu.
COPROCESSOR	Displays information about all installed coprocessors.

Command	Explanation
CPUCONFIG	Allows the user to configure or deconfigure processors in the system.
DEFAULT	Sets the system to predefined defaults.
DISPLAY	Redisplays the current menu.
FAN	Displays or sets the speed of system internal fans.
FASTBOOT	Displays or sets the fastboot flag.
FWRVERSION	Displays the revision of currently installed firmware.
HELP	Returns help information for the specified command, menu, or the system itself.
INFORMATION	Accesses the Information menu.
IO	Displays I/O interface on all I/O modules in the system.
LANADDRESS	Allows the user to display station address.
LANCONFIG	Configures the LAN card.
MAIN	User interface for PDC.
MEMORY	Displays memory information for total amount of physical memory as well as configured memory in a system.
MEMREAD	Reads memory locations.
MONITOR	Allows the user to view and change the monitor type for graphic cards.
PATH	Sets and/or displays the system paths from Stable Storage.
PDT	Displays or clears the Page Deallocation Table (PDT).
PIM	Displays Processor Internal Memory (PIM) Information.
PROCESSOR	Displays information about the processor(s) in the system.
RESET	Resets the machine state.
SEARCH	Searches for boot devices in the system.
SECURE	Displays or sets the secure mode flag.
SERVICE	Allows the user to go to the Service menu.
TIME	Reads or sets the real time clock in GMT.
WARNINGS	Display any warning messages that may have resulted from the previous PDC self-test execution.

Initial System Loader

As previously mentioned, the Initial System Loader (ISL) is run after the PDC. You would normally just run an "autoboot" sequence from ISL; however, you could run a number of commands from the ISL prompt.

Picking up where we left off in the previous example, I chose to *BOot* off device *p0* and interact with IPL, as shown in the following example:

```
Main Menu: Enter command or menu > bo p0

 BCH Directed Boot Path: 0/0/0/3/0.6


 Do you wish to stop at the ISL prompt prior to booting? (y/n) >> y

Initializing boot Device.


Boot IO Dependent Code (IODC) Revision 3


Boot Path Initialized.


HARD Booted.

ISL Revision A.00.43  Apr 12, 2000

ISL>

ISL> ?
        HELP          Help Facility
        LS            List ISL utilities
        AUTOBOOT      Set or clear autoboot flag in stable storage
        AUTOSEARCH    Set or clear autosearch flag in stable storage
        PRIMPATH      Modify primary boot path in stable storage
        ALTPATH       Modify alternate boot path in stable storage
        CONSPATH      Modify system console path in stable storage
        DISPLAY       Display boot and console paths in stable storage
        LSAUTOFL      List contents of autoboot file
        FASTSIZE      Sets or displays FASTSIZE
        800SUPPORT    Boots the s800 Support Kernel from the boot device
        700SUPPORT    Boot the s700 Support Kernel from the boot device
        READNVM       Displays contents of one word of NVM
        READSS        Displays contents of one word of stable storage
        LSBATCH       List contents of batch file
        BATCH         Execute commands in batch file
        LSEST         List contents of EST (Extended Self Test) file
        EST           Execute commands in EST (Extended Self Test) file
        EXIT          Return to the Boot Console Handler

Enter 'LS' to see a list of the ISL utilities.
```

Issuing a *?* produces a list of ISL commands that I could issue. Issuing the *DISPLAY* command shows the boot and console paths, and *LS* lists the ISL utilities available, as shown in the following example:

```
ISL>    display

    Autoboot is ON (enabled)

    Autosearch is OFF (disabled)

    Primary boot path is 0/0/0/3/0.100663296.0.0.0.0.0
    Primary boot path is (hex) 0/0/0/3/0.6000000.0.0.0.0.0

    Alternate boot path is 0/0/0/0/0.0.0.0.0.0.0
    Alternate boot path is (hex) 0/0/0/0/0.0.0.0.0.0.0

    System console path is 0/0/0/0/0/0/0/0.0.0.0.0.0.0
    System console path is (hex) 0/0/0/0/0/0/0/0.0.0.0.0.0.0
ISL> ls

    Utilities on this system are:

filename   type    start    size     created
=====================================================
ODE        -12960  584      880      04/05/13 13:12:43
HPUX       -12928  4616     848      02/05/10 16:25:44
```

DISPLAY produced the information we expected based on what we saw PDC produce in the previous section. *LS* produced two utilities available to us: *ODE* and *HPUX* (*ODE* is the Offline Diagnostics Environment.) The following example shows listing the *ODE* utilities available on the system by running *ODE*, the *HELP* command to see what commands are available, and *LS* to list the *ODE* utilities:

```
ISL> ode


*****************************************************************
******                                                     ******
******           Offline Diagnostic Environment            ******
******                                                     ******
****** (C) Copyright Hewlett-Packard Co 1993-2004          ******
******              All Rights Reserved                    ******
******                                                     ******
****** HP shall not be liable for any damages resulting from the ******
****** use of this program.                                ******
******                                                     ******
******             TC  Version A.02.26                     ******
******             SysLib Version A.00.78                  ******
******             Loader Version A.00.62                  ******
******             Mapfile Version A.01.59                 ******
******                                                     ******
*****************************************************************
```

```
Type HELP for command information.
ODE> help

ODE Help

    Basic Commands
    --------------
    HELP -- Prints detailed information to the screen, when "help <command>"
            or "help <var>" is typed
    LS -- List modules available on boot medium
    <Module_Name> -- Load and initialize a module by typing its name
                     (For more help, type "help module_name")
    MENU -- Launch ODE's ease-of-use interface
    RUN -- Run a module (after setting desired environment variables)
    Control-Y|Control-C -- Abort an ODE command; pause a module run
    RESUME -- Restart a paused module
    DISPLOG -- After running a module, display contents of a log
    EXIT -- Return to next higher level prompt

    Environmental Variables
    -----------------------
    SHOWSTATE -- Display the value of the following environment variables:
        LOOP -- Run a test this many times
        ERRPRINT [ON|OFF] -- Print low-level error messages to console
                             (primarily for manufacturing use)
        ERRNUM [ON|OFF] -- Print one-line, numbered errors to the console

Continue ([y]/n)? y

        ERRPAUSE [ON|OFF] -- Pause module upon error detection
        ERRONLY [ON|OFF] -- Print ONLY error messages; disable non-error
                            and isolation message printing
        INFOPRINT [ON|OFF] -- Print informational messages to the console
        ISOPRINT [ON|OFF] -- Print fault isolation messages to the console
        ISOPAUSE [ON|OFF] -- Pause module when isolation message is generated
    LOGSIZE -- Set the size of a message log
    DEFAULT -- Reset environment variables to default state

ODE> ls

        Modules on this boot media are:

filename    type    size    created    description
------------------------------------------------------------------------------
MAPPER2     TM      146     04/05/13   64 bit version of the system mapping ut
IOTEST2     TM      880     04/05/13   64 bit version that runs ROM-based self
PERFVER2    TM      126     04/05/13   64 bit version that runs ROM-based self
```

When I ran *ODE* and issued *LS,* the three utilities at the end of the example were listed. I always load *ODE* as a part of system installations to help in the event of a possible system hardware problem that an HP Customer Engineer may need to come onsite to diagnose.

Next, I'll proceed with the boot process by running the *HPUX* utility.

HPUX Secondary System Loader (hpux)

As previously mentioned, the *hpux* utility manages loading the HP-UX kernel and gives control to the kernel. ISL can have **hpux** run an "autoexecute" file, or commands can be given interactively. In most situations, you just want to automatically boot the system, however, in this example so far, I decided to interact with IPL in the interest of looking at some of the functionality in ISL. I proceed with the boot process by simply issuing the *HPUX* utility name, as shown in the following example:

```
ISL> hpux

Boot
: disk(0/0/0/3/0.6.0.0.0.0.0;0)/stand/vmunix
10739712 + 2048000 + 4545792 start 0x1fdf68


gate64: sysvec_vaddr = 0xc0002000 for 2 pages
NOTICE: autofs_link(): File system was registered at index 3.
NOTICE: cachefs_link(): File system was registered at index 5.
NOTICE: nfs3_link(): File system was registered at index 6.

    System Console is on the Built-In Serial Interface
igelan0: INITIALIZING HP A6794-60001 PCI 1000Base-T at hardware path 0/0/8/1/0/4
/0
igelan1: INITIALIZING HP A9784-60001 PCI/PCI-X 1000Base-T FC/GigE Combo Adapter
at hardware path 0/0/10/1/0/6/0
igelan2: INITIALIZING HP A9784-60001 PCI/PCI-X 1000Base-T FC/GigE Combo Adapter
at hardware path 0/0/12/1/0/6/0
Logical volume 64, 0x3 configured as ROOT
Logical volume 64, 0x2 configured as SWAP
Logical volume 64, 0x2 configured as DUMP
    Swap device table:  (start & size given in 512-byte blocks)
        entry 0 - major is 64, minor is 0x2; start = 0, size = 8388608
Starting the STREAMS daemons-phase 1
Checking root file system.
file system is clean - log replay is not required
Root check done.
Create STCP device files
Starting the STREAMS daemons-phase 2
        $Revision: vmunix:    vw: -proj    selectors: CUPI80_BL2000_1108 -c 'V
w for CUPI80_BL2000_1108 build' -- cupi80_bl2000_1108 'CUPI80_BL2000_1108'  Wed
Nov  8 19:24:56 PST 2000 $
Memory Information:
    physical page size = 4096 bytes, logical page size = 4096 bytes
    Physical: 8360960 Kbytes, lockable: 6429056 Kbytes, available: 7385176 Kbytes

/sbin/ioinitrc:
insf: Installing special files for ipmi instance 1 address 0/6
/sbin/krs_sysinit:


/sbin/bcheckrc:
Checking for LVM volume groups and Activating (if any exist)
Volume group "/dev/vg00" has been successfully changed.
Activated volume group
Volume group "/dev/vg01" has been successfully changed.
Resynchronized volume group /dev/vg00
vxfs fsck: sanity check: root file system OK (mounted read/write)
Checking hfs file systems
/sbin/fsclean: /dev/vg00/lvol1 (mounted) ok
HFS file systems are OK, not running fsck
```

```
Checking vxfs file systems
/dev/vg00/lvol8 :
vxfs fsck: sanity check: /dev/vg00/lvol8 OK
/dev/vg01/lvol1 :
vxfs fsck: sanity check: /dev/vg01/lvol1 OK
/dev/vg01/lvol2 :
vxfs fsck: sanity check: /dev/vg01/lvol2 OK
/dev/vg01/lvol3 :
vxfs fsck: sanity check: /dev/vg01/lvol3 OK
/dev/vg01/lvol4 :
vxfs fsck: sanity check: /dev/vg01/lvol4 OK
/dev/vg00/lvol3 :
vxfs fsck: sanity check: root file system OK (mounted read/write)
/dev/vg00/lvol4 :
vxfs fsck: sanity check: /dev/vg00/lvol4 OK
/dev/vg00/lvol5 :
vxfs fsck: sanity check: /dev/vg00/lvol5 OK
/dev/vg00/lvol6 :
Resynchronized volume group /dev/vg01
vxfs fsck: sanity check: /dev/vg00/lvol6 OK
/dev/vg00/lvol7 :
vxfs fsck: sanity check: /dev/vg00/lvol7 OK

Cleaning /etc/ptmp...
```

```
/sbin/auto_parms: DHCP access is disabled (see /etc/auto_parms.log)


    HP-UX Start-up in progress                                       Status
    ───────────────────────                                         ──────

    Configure system crash dumps ................................... [ OK ]
    VxVM device node check ......................................... [ OK ]
    VxVM general startup ........................................... [ OK ]
    VxVM reconfiguration recovery .................................. [ OK ]
    Mount file systems ............................................. [ OK ]
    Update kernel and loadable modules ............................ [N/A ]
    Initialize loadable modules ................................... [ OK ]
    Setting hostname .............................................. [ OK ]
    Start Kernel Logging facility ................................. [N/A ]
    Set privilege group ........................................... [N/A ]
    Display date .................................................. [N/A ]
    Copy processor logs to /var/tombstones ........................ [ OK ]
    Save system crash dump if needed .............................. [N/A ]
    Enable auxiliary swap space ................................... [ OK ]
    Start syncer daemon ........................................... [ OK ]
```

```
        .
        .
        .

The system is ready.

GenericSysName [HP Release B.11.11] (see /etc/issue)
```

I abbreviated this listing where the three dots appear before the *Console Login:* prompt.

There are several volumes on an external HP storage unit on which **fsck** is run to perform a sanity check. Many HP-UX startup scripts are run, so I omitted most of them, that you can read more about in Chapter 8.

I can issue with the *HPUX* utility. Table 2-4 shows examples of some common *HPUX* utility booting options.

TABLE 2-4   hpux Examples

Command (All at *ISL>* Prompt)	**Comments**
Automatic Boot	No interaction - autoboot sequence.
hpux -is	Brings up system at run level *s* for single user mode.
hpux	Default boot sequence from **autoexecute**, normally, object file is **/stand/vmuinx**.
hpux vmunix.test	Boots object file **vmunix.test**.
hpux (52.5.0.0) /stand/vmunix	Boots from **/stand/vmunix** on the disk at the path *52.5.0.0*.
hpux lan(32) /stand/vmunix	Boots from LAN.
hpux -v	Gets HP-UX version numbers.
hpux ll /stand	Lists contents of **/stand** on root disk.

The part of the boot that takes place after the **hpux** command is issued is in four parts:

1. HP-UX initializes the system hardware and devices - The HP-UX kernel locates and initializes system hardware such as memory, I/O busses and devices, and so on. Kernel device drivers are associated with I/O devices at this time. You see many messages fly-by on the system console as this process is taking place.

2. HP-UX kernel data structures are created and initialized - Many tables for system processes and memory, file systems, and so on are created. You also see the status of this part of the boot on the system console.

3. HP-UX searches for the root file system - The base file system contains critical system files and is usually found on the disk from which HP-UX boots. Many commands are run as part of this process.

4. HP-UX starts the init process called **/sbin/init** - The init process, which has an ID of one, starts all other processes on the system. The init process reads **/etc/inittab** for direction. There is a detailed description of the contents of **/etc/inittab** in Chapter 7.

I encourage you to issue some of the PDC, ISL, and hpux utility commands covered earlier, especially those that do not modify your system in any way but only provide information about the system.

Keep in mind my comment at the beginning of this chapter, related to working with the Management Processor (MP). MP is covered along with nPartitions in Chapter 17.

Chapter 3

Installing HP-UX

Topics Covered in this Chapter

This chapter covers several topics related to installing HP-UX. These topics are covered in the order you would install the software when initially loading your system:

- Background on HP-UX 11i *Operating Environments*

- Installing the HP-UX 11i *Operating Environment*

- Setting system parameters at the time of first boot after loading HP-UX 11i with **set_parms**

- Viewing *Mission Critical Operating Environment* components and installing additional software with Software Distributor

- Download and install select patches on your system

- Software Distributor background

You would typically load software in this order: install the base *Operating Environment*; boot your system and use **set_parms**; load application software; and finally, download and install select patches.

Background on HP-UX 11i Operating Environments

HP-UX 11i version 2 is organized into *Operating Environments*. These are software groupings provided by HP that are integrated, tested, and supported by HP. There are the five operating environments at the time of this writing:

- Basic HP-UX OE
- Enterprise HP-UX OE
- Mission Critical HP-UX OE
- Minimal Technical OE
- Technical Computing OE

You can expect these OEs to change over time as the needs of 11i users change. Tables 3-1 and 3-2 show high-level contents of the three commercial OEs and two technical OEs respectively.

Table 3-1   HP-UX 11i Commercial OEs

HP-UX 11i v2 Base OE	HP-UX 11i v2 Foundation OE	HP-UX 11i v2 Enterprise OE	HP-UX 11i v2 Mission Critical OE
Customer Selectable Software (Can be selected at installation) ATM (PCI) HyperFabric (PCII) MUX (PCI) TokenRing (PCI) HP-UX Install Utilities (many versions) IDS 9000 Servers only RAID Utilities Mobile IPV6 PkgBuilder PayPerUse JavaOOB Security Level 10, 20, and 30 iSCSI Netscape Directory Server (LDAP) **Default Installed Software** (Can be deselected at installation) Perl MySQL Security Tools ServiceControl Manager Judy Libraries GNOME GTK+Lib Bastille, Secure Shell Mozilla, Mozilla Source OpenSSL, IP Filter, ISEE Secure Path Check ParManager Java JRE, SDK (several revisions) HPUX Apache Web Server HPUX TOMCAT, HPUX Webmin HPUX XML **Always Installed Stand Alone** Online Diagnostics iCOD, OpenSSL WBEM Services, WBEM LAN Base-VXVM nPartition Provider **Always-Installed Standalone Network Drivers** USB, Gigabit Ethernet (PCI) FDDI (PCI) FibreChannel (PCI) RAID, scsiU320 IEther(PCI) **Obsolesence Bundle** Many obs* products **Base AUX Contents** Casey, ONC UpdateUX EMS Framework SWGETTOOLS Software Distributor Peripheral Device Tool SysMgmtBase	All items in *Base* plus the following: **Foundation HP-UX 11i OE** CIFS/9000 Server, CIFS/9000 Client Java JPI v1.3 and 1.4 PAM Kerberos, PAM Libraries	All items in *Base* plus *Foundation* plus the following: EMS HA Monitors MirrorDisk/UX Online JFS (v3.3) OV GlancePlus Pak (English) OV GlancePlus Pak (Japanese) Process Resource Manager	All items in *Base* plus *Foundation* and *Enterprise* plus the following: ECM Toolkit ServiceGuard (v11.16) ServiceGuard NFS Cluster Object Manager Workload Manager Workload Manager Toolkit

Table 3-2   HP-UX 11 Technical OEs

HP-UX 11i v2 Minimal Technical OE	HP-UX 11i v2 Technical Computing OE
All items in *Base* plus the following: 3D Graphics Developers Kit and Runtime Env TechSysConf	All items in *Base* plus *Minimal Technical OE* plus the following: CIFS/9000 Server CIFS/9000 Client Java 3D Java JPI MLIB MPI PAM Kerberos

Keep in mind that the contents of the OEs shown in the tables will be adjusted over time, and the OEs themselves may change, but these OEs and their contents are accurate at the time of this writing. In the installation example in this chapter we install the Mission Critical OE.

At the time of this writing, HP-UX 11i version 2 media consists of the operating system DVD, and applications DVD, Instant Information DVD, Internet Express DVD (which are a collection of open source tools that have been tested by HP,) and some documentation related to 11i version 2.

The next section covers installing HP-UX 11i version 2; however, there is also the **update-ux** utility to update from a previous version of HP-UX to 11i version 2. I suggest you look at the man page (1M) for this command and see documents on *www.docs.hp.com*, such as *HP-UX 11i Version 1 Installation and Update Guide*, if you are considering updating HP-UX to 11i version 2. Updates to 11i version 2 are supported for some older releases of HP-UX, such as 11i version 1.6. At the time of this writing, there are several recent releases of HP-UX about which you want to be aware, including the following:

B.11.11 HP-UX 11i version 1 for PA-RISC only

B.11.20 HP-UX 11i version 1.5 for Itanium only

B.11.22 HP-UX 11i version 1.6 for Itanium only

B.11.23 HP-UX 11i version 2 for Itanium only

B.11.23 HP-UX 11i version 2 update 2 for Itanium and PA-RISC, which is the focus of this book

The next section covers loading HP-UX 11i version 2 update 2 on an Itanium system.

Installing the HP-UX 11i Operating Environment

Installing HP-UX means installing one of the 11i *Operating Environments*, and later building your complete, fully functional HP-UX system by installing both HP and non-HP applications. The initial system is loaded from the 11i media, or from another system on the network using Ignite-UX. Later in this chapter, there is an example of mounting a DVD-ROM to begin loading software, as well as the complete process of selecting the Ignite-UX server as a source and loading software from it.

You can have your system delivered with instant ignition, which means that HP-UX is loaded on your system and you only have to add to it the application software that you need. I cover the complete installation process so you can see the process from start to finish. If you have instant ignition on your system, you may need to install additional software on your system in the future and can, therefore, use some of the techniques described in this section to load that software.

Integrity Early Boot and Begin Loading HP-UX from an Ignite-UX Server

On an Integrity (Itanium) server, the boot process is done with selections in EFI. On partitioned systems, it is common to have no DVD from which to load software, in which case you'd load HP-UX from an Ignite-UX server. In the first part of this section, I begin the boot process from an Ignite-UX server and then show loading from a DVD-ROM in the next section. Chapter 11 covers the Ignite-UX process in detail. The following listing shows two LAN cards: One is the built-in LAN on the Core I/O board, and the other is an independent LAN card. The Core I/O LAN card is shown in EFI in the following listing:

```
EFI Boot Manager ver 1.10 [14.60]

Please select a boot option

    HP-UX Primary Boot: 1/0/0/2/0.6.0
    Acpi(000222F0,0)/Pci(1|0)/Mac(00306E4B9AD9)
    Acpi(000222F0,100)/Pci(1|0)/Mac(00306E4BAA28) <- Core I/O LAN
    EFI Shell [Built-in]
```

```
LAN1boot
Boot option maintenance menu


Use ^ and v to change option(s). Use Enter to select an option
```

You can also create a custom boot option, as I had done for LAN1boot in the previous listing, using the Boot option maintenance menu, but this is not required because you can just select the LAN interface.

After the boot process begins, information is downloaded from the Ignite-UX server to the client, as shown in the following listing:

```
Booting from Lan
Downloading file AUTO   (26 bytes)
Press Any Key to interrupt Autoboot
AUTO ==> boot Rel_B.11.23/IINSTALL
Seconds left till autoboot -   0
AUTOBOOTING...
AUTO BOOT> boot Rel_B.11.23/IINSTALL
Downloading file Rel_B.11.23/IINSTALL   (52628816 bytes)
> System Memory = 16351 MB
loading section 0
............................................. (complete)
loading section 1
........... (complete)
loading symbol table
Downloading file Rel_B.11.23/IINSTALLFS   (29753344 bytes)
loading ram disk file (Rel_B.11.23/IINSTALLFS).
.............................................
 (complete)
Launching Rel_B.11.23/IINSTALL
SIZE: Text:24913K + Data:5919K + BSS:5356K = Total:36189K

Console is on a Serial Device
Booting kernel...
```

The installation file is downloaded from the Ignite-UX server to this client.

After the installation file is downloaded and invoked, the standard HP-UX installation screen appears, as shown in the following listing:

```
                    Welcome to Ignite-UX!

  Use the <tab> key to navigate between fields, and the arrow keys
  within fields.  Use the <return/enter> key to select an item.
  Use the <return/enter> or <space-bar> to pop-up a choices list.  If the
  menus are not clear, select the "Help" item for more information.



  Hardware Summary:       System Model: ia64 hp server rx8620
  +--------------------+-----------------+------------------+ [ Scan Again  ]
  | Disks: 2  (205.1GB) | Floppies: 0    | LAN cards:   3   |
  | CD/DVDs:          0 | Tapes:    1    | Memory:  16351Mb |
  | Graphics Ports: 0   | IO Buses: 6    | CPUs:        4   | [ H/W Details ]
  +--------------------+-----------------+------------------+
```

```
        [      Install HP-UX      ]

        [   Run a Recovery Shell  ]

        [    Advanced Options     ]


   [  Reboot  ]                                   [  Help  ]
```

From this point on a standard HP-UX installation takes place if you select *Install HP-UX* which is covered in the "Loading HP-UX" section.

Integrity Early Boot and Begin Loading HP-UX from Media

To load from a DVD-ROM on Integrity, you select the EFI shell, pick the DVD-ROM device (in this case, **fs0:**) and then run the **install.efi** program as shown in the following listing:

```
EFI Boot Manager ver 1.10 [14.61]

Please select a boot option

     HP-UX Primary Boot: 0/0/0/3/0.6.0
     Acpi(HWP0002,108)/Pci(1|0)/Pci(4|0)/Mac(000F202B33BC)
     EFI Shell [Built-in]
     Boot option maintenance menu


     Use ^ and v to change option(s). Use Enter to select an option
Loading.: EFI Shell [Built-in]
EFI Shell version 1.10 [14.61]
Device mapping table
  fs0  : Acpi(HWP0002,100)/Pci(3|1)/Scsi(Pun2,Lun0)/CDROM(Entry0)
  blk0 : Acpi(HWP0002,100)/Pci(3|0)/Scsi(Pun6,Lun0)
  blk1 : Acpi(HWP0002,100)/Pci(3|1)/Scsi(Pun2,Lun0)
  blk2 : Acpi(HWP0002,100)/Pci(3|1)/Scsi(Pun2,Lun0)/CDROM(Entry0)
  blk3 : Acpi(HWP0002,100)/Pci(3|1)/Scsi(Pun2,Lun0)/CDROM(Entry1)
  blk4 : Acpi(HWP0002,108)/Pci(1|0)/Pci(1|1)/Scsi(Pun6,Lun0)

startup.nsh> echo -off

Welcome to HP-UX Install Media


(C) Copyright 2004 Hewlett-Packard Development Company, L.P.All rights reserved

HP-UX Boot Loader for IPF  --  Revision 2.018

Press Any Key to interrupt Autoboot
```

```
AUTO ==> boot :IINSTALL
Seconds left till autoboot -    9
   Type 'help' for help

HPUX> exit
Exiting bootloader.

Shell> fs0:

fs0:\> dir
Directory of: fs0:\

   09/02/04  10:41p <DIR>            1,024   EFI
   09/02/04  10:41p             521,494   INSTALL.EFI
   09/02/04  10:41p                  16   AUTO
   09/02/04  10:41p                 174   STARTUP.NSH
           3 File(s)     521,684 bytes
           1 Dir(s)


fs0:\> install.efi

(C) Copyright 2004 Hewlett-Packard Development Company, L.P.All rights reserved

HP-UX Boot Loader for IPF  --  Revision 2.018

Press Any Key to interrupt Autoboot
\AUTO ==> boot :IINSTALL
Seconds left till autoboot -    0
AUTOBOOTING...
AUTO BOOT> boot :IINSTALL
> System Memory = 16367 MB
loading section 0
............................................. (complete)
loading section 1
........... (complete)
loading symbol table
loading ram disk file (:IINSTALLFS).
............................................
  (complete)
Launching :IINSTALL
SIZE: Text:24784K + Data:5919K + BSS:5364K = Total:36068K

Console is on a Serial Device
Booting kernel...

HP-UX will call firmware in physical-addressing mode

Memory Class Setup
-------------------------------------------------------------------------
Class     Physmem          Lockmem          Swapmem
-------------------------------------------------------------------------
System :  16367 MB         16367 MB         16367 MB
Kernel :  16367 MB         16367 MB         16367 MB
User   :  15341 MB         13368 MB         13421 MB
-------------------------------------------------------------------------

Loaded ACPI revision 2.0 tables.
krs_read_mfs: Error 5 opening MFS.
WARNING: GIO: read_ioconfig_file(): /stand/ioconfig read error.
        ioconfig = NULL
NOTICE: cachefs_link(): File system was registered at index 4.
NOTICE: nfs3_link(): File system was registered at index 7.

    System Console is on the Built-In Serial Interface
igelan0: INITIALIZING HP A6794-60001 PCI 1000Base-T at hardware path 1/0/1/1/0/4
/0
    Swap device table:  (start & size given in 512-byte blocks)
        entry 0 - auto-configured on root device; ignored - no room
WARNING: no swap device configured, so dump cannot be defaulted to primary swap.
WARNING: No dump devices are configured.  Dump is disabled.
Starting the STREAMS daemons-phase 1
execve("/sbin/sh") failed, errno 0xffffffff
execve("/bin/sh") failed, errno 0xffffffff
Create STCP device files
```

```
Starting the STREAMS daemons-phase 2
     $Revision: vmunix:    B11.23_LR FLAVOR=perf Fri Aug 29 22:35:38 PDT 2003 $
Memory Information:
 physical page size = 4096 bytes, logical page size = 4096 bytes
 Physical: 16760080 Kbytes, lockable: 12555548 Kbytes, available: 14605548 Kbytes

======= 11/26/04 20:02:55 EST  HP-UX Installation Initialization. (Fri Nov 26
        20:02:55 EST 2004)
        @(#) Ignite-UX Revision C.6.0.109
        @(#) install/init (opt) $Revision: 10.303 $
      * Scanning system for IO devices...
      * Querying disk device: 1/0/0/3/0.6.0 ...
      * Querying disk device: 1/0/1/1/0/1/1.6.0 ...
NOTE:    Primary path not currently set to an existing disk device.
      * Setting keyboard language.


           Welcome to the HP-UX installation/recovery process!

     Use the <tab> key to navigate between fields, and the arrow keys
     within fields.  Use the <return/enter> key to select an item.
     Use the <return/enter> or <space-bar> to pop-up a choices list.  If the
     menus are not clear, select the "Help" item for more information.

     Hardware Summary:         System Model: ia64 hp server rx7620
     +--------------------+----------------+-------------------+ [ Scan Again  ]
     | Disks: 2  (136.7GB) | Floppies: 0    | LAN cards:    1   |
     | CD/DVDs:          1 | Tapes:    0    | Memory:   16367Mb |
     | Graphics Ports: 0   | IO Buses: 8    | CPUs:         2   | [ H/W Details ]
     +--------------------+----------------+-------------------+

                    [     Install HP-UX      ]

                    [  Run a Recovery Shell  ]

                    [    Advanced Options     ]


         [  Reboot  ]                        [  Help  ]
```

Selecting Install HP-UX brings up the installation screen shown in the next section. From there you can complete the installation.

Loading HP-UX

With the section of the Ignite-UX server, or DVD-ROM if you load from media, having been run, complete the installation by first selecting all the basic information, as shown in Figure 3-1.

```
≠                                                                                    ≠
≠ +--------++----------++--------++-------------++----------+                        ≠
≠ ≠ Basic ≠≠ Software ≠≠ System ≠≠ File System ≠≠ Advanced ≠                        ≠
≠ ≠       \------------------------------------------------------------------+≠
≠ ≠                                                                          ≠≠
≠ ≠ Configurations:  [ HP-UX B.11.23 Default    ->] [ Description... ]        ≠≠
≠ ≠                                                                          ≠≠
≠ ≠ Environments:    [ Mission Critical OE-64bit ->] (HP-UX B.11.23)          ≠≠
≠ ≠                                                                          ≠≠
≠ ≠ [ Root Disk... ] HP_146_GMAP3147NC, 1/0/0/2/0.6.0, 140014                 ≠≠
≠ ≠                                                                          ≠≠
≠ ≠ File System:     [ Logical Volume Manager (LVM) with VxFS  ->]            ≠≠
≠ ≠                                                                          ≠≠
≠ ≠ [ Root Swap (MB)... ] 4096      Physical Memory (RAM) =  16351 MB         ≠≠
≠ ≠                                                                          ≠≠
≠ ≠ [ Languages...  ] English           [ Keyboards... ] [ Additional... ]≠≠
≠ ≠                                                                          ≠≠
≠ +------------------------------------------------------------------------+≠
≠     [ Show Summary... ]                      [ Reset Configuration ]  ≠
≠------------------------------------------------------------------------≠
≠ [ Go! ]                   [ Cancel ]                 [ Help ] ≠
+--------------------------------------------------------------------------+
```

Figure 3-1   Ignite-UX Display *Basic* Tab Area Using CLI

The *Advanced Installation* menu lets you choose from among the menu tab areas with the ability of going back and forth among them until you are satisfied with your choices.

Across the top of the menu display are five tab areas: *Basic*, *Software*, *System*, *File System*, and *Advanced*. By pressing the Tab key, each area can be highlighted. To select the highlighted tab area, press the Enter/Return key. This causes that tab area's screen to appear. Within each of these areas are several parameters that can be modified for your specific system. Here are the main features of each tab area:

• *Basic* - configuration and environment information.

• *Software* - ability to choose optional software to be installed. Mostly the same options that appear under *Guided Installation*.

• *System* - networking parameters. Also configurable via the **set_parms** command.

• *File System* - disk space allocation.

• *Advanced* - advanced disk, file system, logical volume, and volume group parameters.

I'll begin to configure the system beginning with the *Basic* screen, as shown in Figure 3-1.

Here are the items of particular importance:

• Configuration - I selected *HP-UX B.11.23 Default*. HP-UX 11i version 2 update 2 is called by its original name, 11.23, in some cases. I could select other operating systems from the Ignite-UX server, including a recovery archive, which was earlier produced for this partition.

• Environments - *Mission Critical OE-64bit* is selected in the example. The four OE selections are as follows:

```
Mission Critical OE-64bit .>]  (HP-UX B.11.23)
                               Enterprise OE-64bit
                               Foundation OE-64bit
                               HP-UX 11i Base OS-64bit
```

• Root Disk - the default selection for the root disk is the first internal disk drive. There are two internal drives available to this partition.

• File System - There are the three following options available in this area the first of which is selected:

```
Veritas Volume Manager (VxVM) with VxFS
Whole disk with VxFS
Logical Volume Manager (LVM) with VxFS
```

• Root Swap - the system automatically selects an amount twice the size of your main memory, or a maximum of 4,096 MB. Consider your primary swap space very carefully. The partition has 16 GB of memory so the maximum of 4,096 is selected.

• Languages - I'll install English on this system; however, many languages are available for 11i systems.

• Additional - this is the pick at the bottom-right corner of the screen, not the tab area. Here, you can configure such things as creating an   / **export** volume, create a EFI partition since this is an Integrity server, create second swap area, add disk drives to the root volume, and disabling Dynamic Host Configuration Protocol (DHCP.) With 11i, DHCP, Dynamic Host Configuration Protocol, works with an Ignite-UX server that automatically assigns system name, IP address, and so on.

Moving to the *Software* tab area, you see a small portion of the software listing on the Ignite-UX server for 11i that has been marked for installation as part of *Mission Critical Operating Environment* shown in Figure 3-2.

```
≠                                                                          ≠
≠ +-------++----------++--------++-------------++----------+                ≠
≠ ≠ Basic ## Software ## System ## File System ## Advanced ≠                ≠
≠ +--------/           \----------------------------------------------------+≠
≠ ≠                                                                         ≠≠
≠ ≠  Category          Marked ?  Product          Description              ≠≠
≠ ≠+----------------+ +--------------------------------------------------+ ≠≠
≠ ## All              ^ ≠ Yes    IEther-00        PCI IEther;Supptd HW=A6 ^ ≠≠
≠ ## SecurityChoices    ≠ Yes    ISEEPlatform     ISEE Platform            ≠≠
≠ ## OrderedApps        ≠ No     Ignite-IA-11-22  HP-UX Installation Util  ≠≠
≠ ## HPUXAdditions      ≠ No     Ignite-UX-11-00  HP-UX Installation Util  ≠≠
≠ ## Uncategorized      ≠ No     Ignite-UX-11-11  HP-UX Installation Util  ≠≠
≠ ##                    ≠ No     J4258CA          Netscape Directory Serv  ≠≠
≠ ##                  v ≠ No     JAVAOOB          Java2 Out-of-box for HP v ≠≠
≠ ≠+----------------+ +<                                             >+ ≠≠
≠ ≠                                                                         ≠≠
≠ ≠ [ Change Depot Location...  ]                                          ≠≠
≠ +-------------------------------------------------------------------------+≠
≠     [ Show Summary...  ]                          [ Reset Configuration ]  ≠
≠---------------------------------------------------------------------------≠
≠ [  Go!   ]                        [ Cancel ]                    [  Help  ] ≠
+-----------------------------------------------------------------------------+
```

Figure 3-2   *Software* Tab Area with *Category All*

Although you can't see it in Figure 3-2, the *Category* of software selected is *All*. Other software that you may want to install can be selected from the installation source. In this figure the first two items have been selected automatically as part of the *Mission Critical Operating Environ-*

ment. At this point, you could select additional software, such as *Ignite,* which you want to load for all operating systems on your Ignite-UX server, and *Netscape Directory Server* in this window. The full Mission Critical OE is available for selection. If you were installing from a DVD, you might have additional media from which to load and select software. This is done using Software Distributor. (An overview of the Software Distributor product used for installing all HP-UX 11i software appears later in this chapter.) You may want to look at this overview to get a feeling for the type of functionality that Software Distributor offers. The **swinstall** program is the Software Distributor program used to install software.

You could select one of the other categories, such as *HPUXAdditions,* which would show software such as *Bundle11i.*

The *System* tab area, shown in Figure 3-3, is where system identification-related configuration information can be found. Because I want to configure networking and related information after the installation is complete, I change only the first item on this screen. The options for the first item are as follows:

```
Final system parameters: [Set parameters now]
                         [Ask at first boot]
```

I select *Set Parameters Now.*

```
≠ +-------++----------++--------++--------------++----------+                    ≠
≠ ≠ Basic ≠≠ Software ≠≠ System ≠≠ File System ≠≠ Advanced ≠                     ≠
≠ +-------------------/          \-------------------------------------------+≠
≠ ≠                                                                           ≠≠
≠ ≠  Final System Parameters:  [ Set parameters now   ->]                     ≠≠
≠ ≠                                                                           ≠≠
≠ ≠ +----------------------------------------------------------------------+  ≠≠
≠ ≠ ≠  Hostname:  npar2                                              ≠        ≠≠
≠ ≠ ≠                                                                ≠        ≠≠
≠ ≠ ≠IP Address:  192.6.174.67    Subnet Mask:  255.255.255.240      ≠        ≠≠
≠ ≠ ≠                                                                ≠        ≠≠
≠ ≠ ≠     Time:  22:28  Day:  11  Month:  [ November  ->] Year:  2004 ≠       ≠≠
≠ ≠ +----------------------------------------------------------------------+  ≠≠
≠ ≠   [ Set Time Zone (EST5EDT)... ]   [     Network Services...    ]         ≠≠
≠ ≠   [    Set Root Password...    ]   [ Additional Interface(s)... ]         ≠≠
≠ ≠                                                                           ≠≠
≠ +--------------------------------------------------------------------------+≠
≠      [ Show Summary... ]                              [ Reset Configuration ]  ≠
≠--------------------------------------------------------------------------------≠
≠ [  Go!  ]                         [ Cancel ]                      [  Help  ] ≠
 +------------------------------------------------------------------------------+
```

Figure 3-3   *System* Tab Area

     The *File System* tab area, shown in Figure 3-3, is of particular importance. Here, you can change file system sizes. You probably won't be satisfied with the default sizes of some of the logical volumes. I normally spend some time in this tab area increasing the sizes of some of the logical volumes. Figure 3-4 also shows the layout of the *File System* screen and the values of three of the logical volumes. **/stand** is highlighted in this example, so the parameters related to it appear under *Usage, Size,* and so on.

```
≠ +-------++----------++--------++-------------++----------+              ≠
≠ ≠ Basic ≠≠ Software ≠≠ System ≠≠ File System ≠≠ Advanced ≠              ≠
≠ +----------------------------/              \---------------------------+≠
≠ ≠    Mount Dir    Usage   Size(MB)   % Used  Group    S                ≠≠
≠ ≠  +--------------------------------------------------+                 ≠≠
≠ ≠  ≠ /stand       VxFS    300        7       rootdg  F ^ [ Add     ]    ≠≠
≠ ≠  ≠ primary      SWAP+D  4096       0       rootdg  R   [ Modify  ]    ≠≠
≠ ≠  ≠ /            VxFS    299        81      rootdg  F v [ Remove  ]    ≠≠
≠ ≠  +<                                             >+                    ≠≠
≠ ≠                                                                       ≠≠
≠ ≠  Usage:  [ VxFS      ->]  Group:  [ root ->]  Mount Dir:  /stand      ≠≠
≠ ≠                                                                       ≠≠
≠ ≠  Size:  [ Fixed MB    ->]  300     Avail: 121781 M                    ≠≠
≠ ≠                                                                       ≠≠
≠ ≠  [ Add/Remove Disks... ]   [ ---- Additional Tasks ----  ->]          ≠≠
≠ ≠                                                                       ≠≠
≠ +-----------------------------------------------------------------------+≠
≠     [ Show Summary... ]                        [ Reset Configuration ]  ≠
≠------------------------------------------------------------------------≠
≠ [  Go!  ]                     [ Cancel ]                 [  Help  ] ≠
```

Figure 3-4   *File System* Tab Area

To make logical volume size changes, select the mount directory of the logical volume, tab down to *Size,* and enter the desired new size. In addition to *Size,* several other parameters are related to the logical volume that you can change.

Notice that *Avail* shows you how much disk space is left to be allocated on your disk drive. It is perfectly all right to leave some disk space unallocated. This gives you a cushion for when you need to increase disk space down the road.

After making all the volume size-related modifications, you are ready to install the system. However, you first want to choose the *Show Summary* option, which is toward the bottom of the screen. This option shows you a summary of all the changes you made. This gives you a chance to make sure that you didn't forget something. Figure 3-5 shows the *General Summary* screen.

```
++                          Summary View                         ++
≠≠                                                               ≠≠
≠≠ +----------------++--------------------+                      ≠≠
≠≠ ≠ General Summary ≠≠ Hardware Inventory ≠                     ≠≠
≠≠ ≠               \----------------------------------------------+≠≠
≠≠ ≠                             Operating System: HP-UX B.11.23  ≠##
≠≠ ≠   Product             Description                            ≠##
≠≠ ≠   +-----------------------------------------------------+    ≠##
≠≠ ≠   ≠ B6848BA             Ximian GNOME 1.4 GTK+ Libraries for ^ ≠##
≠≠ ≠   ≠ B6849AA             Bastille Security Hardening Tool      ≠##
≠≠ ≠   ≠ B8339BA             servicecontrol manager Server and A v ≠##
≠≠ ≠   +<                                                 >+       ≠##
≠≠ ≠                                                               ≠##
≠≠ ≠   Grp Name  Usage   Size(MB)  % Used  Mount Dir             ≠##
≠≠ ≠   +-------------------------------------------------------+  ≠##
≠≠ ≠   ≠ rootdg   VxFS    300       7       /stand          ^     ≠##
≠≠ ≠   ≠ rootdg   SWAP+D  4096      0       primary               ≠##
≠≠ ≠   ≠ rootdg   VxFS    299       81      /                     ≠##
≠≠ ≠   ≠ rootdg   VxFS    200       0       /tmp            v     ≠##
≠≠ ≠   +-------------------------------------------------------+  ≠##
≠≠ +----------------------------------------------------------------+≠##
≠#----------------------------------------------------------------≠≠
+≠ [   OK   ]                                         [  Help  ]
```

Figure 3-5   *General Summary* Screen

This screen provides information on the software you have selected to
load and information on your logical volumes. Although you can view items
on this screen, you'd have to go back to previous screens to make modifications to the items.

Figure 3-6 shows the *Hardware Inventory Summary* screen.

```
##                                                                          ##
## +-----------------++-------------------+                                 ##
## ≠ General Summary ## Hardware Inventory ≠                                ##
## +-----------------/                      \----------------------------+##
## ≠  +------------------------------------------------------------------+  ###
## ≠  ≠    Hardware Summary:       System Model: ia64 hp server rx8620  ^  ###
## ≠  ≠    +--------------------+---------------+------------------+        ###
## ≠  ≠    | Disks: 2  (205.1GB) | Floppies: 0  | LAN cards:   3   |        ###
## ≠  ≠    | CD/DVDs:         0  | Tapes:    1  | Memory:   16351Mb |       ###
## ≠  ≠    | Graphics Ports: 0   | IO Buses: 6  | CPUs:          4  |       ###
## ≠  ≠    +--------------------+---------------+------------------+        ###
## ≠  ≠                                                                     ###
## ≠  ≠ Disk Drives:                                                        ###
## ≠  ≠    H/W Path            Capacity(Mb)     Model                       ###
## ≠  ≠    1/0/0/2/0.6.0        140014          HP_146_GMAP3147NC           ###
## ≠  ≠    1/0/0/3/0.6.0         70007          HP_73.4GMAS3735NC           ###
## ≠  ≠                                                              v      ###
## ≠  +<                                                            >+      ###
## ≠                                                                        ###
## +-------------------------------------------------------------------+##
##--------------------------------------------------------------------------##
+≠ [   OK   ]                                                    [  Help  ]
```

Figure 3-6   *Hardware Inventory* Screen

The *Hardware Inventory* screen information provides a summary of system hardware.

Becasue I am satisfied with all the modifications I have made, I'm ready to load the operating system. I choose *OK,* which appears at the bottom of all the tab area screens. The screen in Figure 3-7 appears.

```
## All data will be destroyed on the following disks:              ##

##                                                                 ##

##   Addr          Disk Size(MB)  Description                      ##

## +------------------------------------------------------------+  ##

## ≠ 1/0/0/2/0.6.0  140014 MB      HP_146_GMAP3147NC         ^     ##

## ≠                                                              ##

## ≠                                                        v     ##

## +------------------------------------------------------------+  ##

##                                                                 ##

## The results of the pre-install analysis are:                   ##

##                                                                 ##

## +-------------------------------------------------------------+ ##

## ≠ NOTE: Dump space (4194304KB) is less than 50% of system  ^   ##

## ≠ memory (16743584KB). There is a possibility that the system  ##

## ≠ dump will be truncated with a failure to capture important   ##

## ≠ system information in the event of a system crash. You can    ##

## ≠ increase the size of the dump volumes or add additional dump ##

## ≠ volumes on the                                               ##

"File System

" tab when using the advanced     v            ##

## +-------------------------------------------------------------+ ##

##-----------------------------------------------------------------##

+≠ [  Go!  ]                  [ < Back ]              [  Help  ]
```

Figure 3-7   *Go!* Screen

The screen in Figure 3-7 warns me that there is an operating system already present my our target disk, but I want to proceed with the installation anyway, so select *Go!*. The load of the HP-UX is automatic at this point, and you can come back in an hour or so to check the log file to see if loading the operating system completed successfully.

It may be that your HP-UX 11i *Operating Environment* requires more than one DVD-ROM to complete the installation. In this case, you are prompted to insert the additional media. This is an additional reason to set up an Ignite-UX server to accomplish much faster and efficient initial loads of operating systems, as well as add-on loads of applications, patches, and so on. I almost invariably set up Ignite-UX servers in environments in which many partitions need to be installed and maintained. The initial system load needs to take place from media.

As part of the operating system load process under the *System* tab, I specify a system name, IP address, subnet mask, and some other information. You would specify this information after the load takes place if you choose not to enter it when the initial load occurs.

The next section covers the **set_parms** program that runs after system installation if you do not enter Network Configuration during system installation.

HP 9000 Early Boot and Beginning the Load of HP-UX

The process of loading an HP 9000 (PA-RISC) is nearly identical to loading HP-UX on an HP Integrity server. The early boot process is different on Integrity and HP 9000. Chapter 1 covers Integrity, and Chapter 2 covers HP 9000 early boot in detail. The example of loading HP-UX in the previous sections took place on an Integrity server. This section covers just enough of the HP 9000 boot to get to the menu for loading HP-UX. Chapter 2 supplies more detail on the HP 9000 boot if you need to see it.

The following example begins at the end of early boot, which is the first part of the load process from media. There were many early boot-related messages that appeared before the point where this example begins. I discontinued the boot process by pressing a key. After discontinuing the boot, I run *SEArch* to find bootable devices. Among the devices shown is the DVD-ROM drive containing the operating system media. I select *p1* to boot off with the **bo p1** command. I then choose not to interact with IPL:

```
Cells have been reset (Boot Is Blocked (BIB) is not set).


Firmware Version  21.3

Duplex Console IO Dependent Code (IODC) revision 2
------------------------------------------------------------------------
   (c) Copyright 1995-2002, Hewlett-Packard Company, All rights reserved
------------------------------------------------------------------------

          Cab/    Cell      ------- Processor --------   Cache Size
   Cell   Slot    State      #    Speed       State      Inst   Data
   ----   ----    --------- ---   --------   ---------   ------ ------
    1     0/1     Active     0A   1000 MHz   Active      32 MB  32 MB
                             0B   1000 MHz   Idle        32 MB  32 MB
```

```
            Primary Boot Path:   1/0/0/3/0.6
                 Boot Actions:   Go to BCH.

   HA Alternate Boot Path:   1/0/1/1/0/1/1.6
                 Boot Actions:   Go to BCH.

      Alternate Boot Path:   1/0/1/1/0/1/1.6
                 Boot Actions:   Go to BCH.

             Console Path:   1/0/0/0/1.0


Attempting to boot using the primary path.
--------------------------------------------------------------

The Boot Action for this path specifies that PDC stop at BCH.


---- Main Menu ----------------------------------------------------------

     Command                         Description
     -------                         -----------
     BOot [PRI|HAA|ALT|<path>]       Boot from specified path
     PAth [PRI|HAA|ALT] [<path>]     Display or modify a path
     SEArch [ALL|<cell>|<path>]      Search for boot devices
     ScRoll [ON|OFF]                 Display or change scrolling capability

     COnfiguration menu             Displays or sets boot values
     INformation menu               Displays hardware information
     SERvice menu                   Displays service commands

     DIsplay                        Redisplay the current menu
     HElp [<menu>|<command>]        Display help for menu or command
     REBOOT                         Restart Partition
     RECONFIGRESET                  Reset to allow Reconfig Complex Profile


Main Menu: Enter command or menu > search

Searching for potential boot device(s) on the core cell
This may take several minutes.

To discontinue search, press any key (termination may not be immediate).

                                                                      IODC
     Path#  Device Path (dec)            Device Type              Rev
     -----  -----------------            -----------              ----
     P0     1/0/0/3/0.6                  Random access media      3
     P1     1/0/0/3/1.2                  Random access media      3
     P2     1/0/1/1/0/1/1.6              Random access media      3
            1/0/2/1/0/4/0.0              Fibre Channel Protocol   13
            1/0/4/1/0/4/0.0              Fibre Channel Protocol   13

Main Menu: Enter command or menu > bo p1

  BCH Directed Boot Path: 1/0/0/3/1.2
```

The *SEArch* command in the previous listing shows the bootable devices for this specific nPartition. There are five possible boot devices. The last two are the fibre cards connected to external storage.

To boot off the media and not interact with IPL (for more information on IPL, see Chapter 2), issue the following command:

```
Main Menu: Enter command or menu > bo p1
Interact with IPL (Y or N)?> N
```

After booting off *P1*, the *Welcome to the HP-UX installation/recovery process!* menu appears as shown in the following example:

```
        Welcome to the HP-UX installation/recovery process!

Use the <tab> key to navigate between fields, and the arrow keys
within fields.  Use the <return/enter> key to select an item.
Use the <return/enter> or <space-bar> to pop-up a choices list.  If the
menus are not clear, select the "Help" item for more information.

Hardware Summary:        System Model: 9000/800/rp7420
+--------------------+---------------+------------------+ [ Scan Again  ]
| Disks: 54 (815.3GB) | Floppies: 0  | LAN cards:   3   |
| CD/DVDs:         1  | Tapes:    0  | Memory:    8165Mb|
| Graphics Ports: 0   | IO Buses: 10 | CPUs:        2   | [ H/W Details ]
+--------------------+---------------+------------------+

              [      Install HP-UX       ]

              [   Run a Recovery Shell   ]

              [   Advanced Options       ]


    [ Reboot  ]                          [ Help  ]
```

This menu summarizes the hardware in this nPartition. If you want to see more details, select the *H/W Details* option on the right side of the screen. This takes you to a detailed listing of your hardware. It includes items such as hardware paths, disk drive capacities, and LAN addresses.

From this point on, the process of loading HP-UX is identical to the process on an Integrity server, so you can follow the previous section to see this process.

Setting the System Parameters After Booting

When the system comes up after installation, a series of windows appear that allow you to configure your system name, time zone, root password, Internet Protocol (IP) address, subnet mask, and other networking settings if you don't enter them under the *System* tab at the time of installation. (IP address and subnet mask background are provided in Chapter 12.) One of the first questions you are asked is whether you want to use DHCP to obtain networking information. Dynamic Host Configuration Protocol works with an Ignite-UX server that automatically assigns system name, IP address, and so on. Because the installation does not use this, I answered "no" which means that I have to manually enter all the information.

The system-specific information to be entered next can also be entered, after your system boots, by running **/sbin/set_parms**. This program can be used to set an individual system parameter or all the system parameters that would be set at boot time. **/sbin/set_parms** uses one of the arguments in Table 3-3, depending on what you would like to configure.

Table 3-3   /sbin/set_parms Arguments

set_parms Argument	Comments
hostname	Sets hostname.
timezone	Sets time zone.
date_time	Sets date and time.
ip_address	Sets Internet Protocol address. (See Chapter 12 for networking background.)
addl_network	Configures subnet mask, Domain Name System, and Network Information Service.
initial	Goes through the entire question-and-answer session you would experience at boot time.

If you use the **initial** argument, various dialog boxes ask you for information. The System Hostname is requested in the following listing:

```
For the system to operate correctly, you must assign it a unique
system name or "hostname".  The hostname can be a simple name
(example: widget) or an Internet fully-qualified domain name
(example: widget.region.mycorp.com).

A simple name, or each dot (.) separated component of a domain name, must:

    * Start and end with a letter or number.
    * Contain no more than 8 characters per component.
    * Contain no more than 63 total characters.
    * Contain only letters, numbers, underscore (_), or dash (-).
      The underscore (_) is not recommended.

NOTE: The first or only component of a hostname should contain no more
      than 8 characters and the full hostname should contain no more
      than 63 characters for maximum compatibility with HP-UX software.

The current hostname is npar2.
```

```
Enter the system name, then press [Enter] or simply press [Enter]
to retain the current host name (npar2):
```

Next, you're asked about the time zone and root password. After these are entered, you're asked for the IP address as shown in the following listing:

```
If you wish networking to operate correctly, you must assign the
system a unique Internet Protocol (IP) address.  The IP address must:

    * Contain 4 numeric components.

    * Have a period (.) separating each numeric component.

    * Contain numbers between 0 and 255.

    For example:  134.32.3.10

Warning: Leading zeros within a component are not allowed!

Your current address is 192.6.174.67.  To retain this address,
just press [Enter].
```

```
Enter your IP address, then press [Enter] or press [Enter] to select
the current address (192.6.174.67):
```

You can now configure your subnet mask and other networking parameters.

Configuration includes the items shown in this listing:

```
You may configure some additional network parameters at this time:

  * Subnetwork Mask and Default Gateway

  * Domain Name System (DNS)

  * Network Information Service (NIS)

Your local network administrator can tell you which if any of these
parameters should be configured for your system, and provide you the
appropriate values.

If you do not have these values now, you can configure them later.
```
```
Do you want to configure these additional network parameters?

Press [y] for yes or [n] for no, then press [Enter]
```

Running **set_parms initial** or **set_parms** with other options allows
you to specify all the initial information related to your system setup. This
saves you the trouble of finding all the relevant files in which you'd have to
place the information you provide to **set_parms**.

Among the information that is updated is the contents of **/etc/rc.con-
fig.d/netconf**, which contains the IP address of the LAN card, netmask, and
default router you just entered. The **/etc/hosts** file is updated with the name
and IP address of this host. These files and their configuration are described
in Chapter 12, which covers networking.

Software Distributor Example: Load Additional Software

In this section, I use some Software Distributor commands to view existing loaded software and use the Character Line Interface (CLI) to **swinstall** to load additional software. The *Mission Critical Operating Environment* and some additional software products were loaded on the system on which the following examples are run. I check the operating system revision with **uname -a** and software bundles that have been loaded on the system with **swlist** in the following listing:

```
# uname -a
HP-UX npar2 B.11.23 U ia64 0210646210 unlimited-user license

# swlist
# Initializing...
# Contacting target "npar2"...
#
# Target: npar2:/
#

#
# Bundle(s):
#

  B5725AA              C.6.0.57        HP-UX Installation Utilities (Ignite-UX)

  B6848BA              1.4.gm.46.9     Ximian GNOME 1.4 GTK+ Libraries for HP-UX

  B6849AA              B.02.01.02      Bastille Security Hardening Tool
  B8339BA              B.03.00.09      servicecontrol manager Server and Agent Bundle
  B8465BA              A.02.00.04.%71Q HP WBEM Services for HP-UX
  B9073BA              B.11.23.06.03.%IC7IO HP-UX iCOD (Instant Capacity on Demand)
  B9788AA              1.3.1.13.01     Java2 1.3 SDK for HP-UX
  B9789AA              1.3.1.13.01     Java2 1.3 RTE for HP-UX
  B9901AA              A.03.05.10.%71P HP IPFilter 3.5alpha5
  BUNDLE11i            B.11.23.040713  CH PI IC Bundle for 11.23 040713
  Base-VXVM            B.03.50.IA.008  Base VERITAS Volume Manager Bundle 3.5 for HP-UX
  CDE-English          B.11.23         English CDE Environment
  FDDI-00              B.11.23.01.%71Q PCI FDDI;Supptd HW=A3739B;SW=J3626AA
  FibrChanl-00         B.11.23.03.%71Q PCI FibreChannel;Supptd HW=A6795A,A5158A

  FibrChanl-01         B.11.23.02.%71Q PCI-X FibreChannel;Supptd HW=A6826A,
                       A9782A,A9784A
  GigEther-00          B.11.23.05.%1Q PCI GigEther;Supptd HW=A4926A/A4929A/
                       A6096A;SW=J1642AA
  GigEther-01          B.11.23.05.%1Q PCI GigEther;Supptd HW=A6825A/A6794A/
                       A6847A/A8685A/A9782A/A9784A/A7109A
  HPUX11i-OE-MC        B.11.23.0409.%1Q HP-UX Mission Critical Operating Environment
                       Component
  HPUXBaseAux          B.11.23.0409.%1Q HP-UX Base OS Auxiliary
  HPUXBaseOS           B.11.23         HP-UX Base OS
  IEther-00            B.11.23.05.%1Q PCI IEther;Supptd HW=A6974A
  ISEEPlatform         A.03.90.001     ISEE Platform
  Ignite-IA-11-22      C.6.0.57        HP-UX Installation Utilities for Installing 11.22
                       IPF Systems
  Ignite-UX-11-11      C.6.0.57        HP-UX Installation Utilities for Installing 11.11
                       Systems
  Judy                 B.11.11.04.15   Judy Library - development and runtime libraries
                       for handling dynamic arrays
  MOZILLA              1.4.0.01.04     Mozilla 1.4 for HP-UX
  MOZILLAsrc           1.4.0.01.04     Mozilla 1.4 Source distribution
  MySQL                3.23.54a.01     MySQL open-source database
  NPar                 B.11.23.01.03.00.05 nPartition Provider - HP-UX
  OnlineDiag           B.11.23.03.14.%ic71Q HPUX 11.23 Support Tools Bundle, Sep 2004
```

```
OpenSSL              A.00.09.07-d.009%ic71Q Secure Network Communications Protocol
ParMgr               B.11.23.02.00.03.03 Partition Manager - HP-UX
RAID-01              B.11.23.01.5.%ic71Q RAID SA; Supptd HW=A7143A/A9890A/A9891A
Sec00Tools           B.01.02.00    Install-Time security infrastructure.
SecPatchCk           B.02.01       HP-UX Security Patch Check Tool
T1456AA              1.4.2.03.04   Java2 1.4 SDK for HP-UX
T1456AAaddon         1.4.2.03.04   Java2 1.4 SDK -AA addon for HP-UX
T1457AA              1.4.2.03.04   Java2 1.4 RTE for HP-UX
T1457AAaddon         1.4.2.03.04   Java2 1.4 RTE -AA addon for HP-UX
T1471AA              A.03.71.006.%ic71P HP-UX Secure Shell
USB-00               B.11.23.02.%ic71P Object Oriented USB Driver
WBEMP-LAN-00         B.11.23.00.%71P LAN Provider for Ethernet LAN interfaces

hpuxwsApache         B.2.0.49.03.%71P HP-UX Apache-based Web Server
hpuxwsTomcat         B.4.1.29.02.%71P HP-UX Tomcat-based Servlet Engine
hpuxwsWebmin         A.1.070.01.%71P HP-UX Webmin-based Admin
hpuxwsXml            A.2.00.%71P   HP-UX XML Web Server Tools
perl                 D.5.8.0.C.%71P Perl Programming Language
scsiU320-00          B.11.23.1.%ic71Q PCI SCSI U320; Supptd HW=A7173A
```

This listing shows that HP-UX 11i version 2 update 2 has been loaded, shown as 11.23 in the listing, and that several software bundles that we selected have been loaded as well, including the *Mission Critical Operating Environment,* which is shown as *HPUX11I-OE-MC* in roughly the middle of the **swlist** output.

Many products are loaded as part of the *Mission Critical Operating Environment.* The following **swlist** shows the components of which *Mission Critical Operating Environment* is comprised at the time of this writing:

```
# swlist -l product HPUX11i-OE-MC
# Initializing...
# Contacting target "npar2"...
#
# Target:  npar2:/
#

# HPUX11i-OE-MC                    B.11.23.0409.%1Q HP-UX Mission Critical
Operating Environment Component
  HPUX11i-OE-MC.OE                 B.11.23.0409.%1Q HP-UX OE control script
                                   product
  HPUX11i-OE-MC.Glance             C.03.85.%ic71Q HP GlancePlus/UX
  HPUX11i-OE-MC.MeasureWare        C.03.85.%ic71Q MeasureWare Software/UX
  HPUX11i-OE-MC.MeasurementInt     C.03.85.%ic71Q HP-UX Measurement Interface
                                   for 11.23
  HPUX11i-OE-MC.LVM                B.11.23       LVM
  HPUX11i-OE-MC.SG-Tomcat-Tool     B.02.11.%71O  Serviceguard Tomcat Script
                                   Templates
  HPUX11i-OE-MC.SG-Samba-Tool      B.02.11.%71O  Serviceguard Samba Script
                                   Templates
  HPUX11i-OE-MC.SG-Apache-Tool     B.02.11.%71O  Serviceguard Apache Script
                                   Templates
  HPUX11i-OE-MC.SG-Oracle-Tool     B.02.11.%71O  Serviceguard Oracle Script
                                   Templates
  HPUX11i-OE-MC.WLM-Toolkits       A.01.07.%q06  HP-UX Workload Manager Toolkits
  HPUX11i-OE-MC.OPS-Provider-MOF   B.03.00.01.%71Q OPS Provider and MOF
  HPUX11i-OE-MC.CM-Provider-MOF    B.03.00.01.%71Q CM Provider and MOF
  HPUX11i-OE-MC.Cluster-OM         B.03.00.01.%71Q HP Cluster API
  HPUX11i-OE-MC.Jpi13              1.3.1.13.01   Java2 1.3 Netscape Plugin
  HPUX11i-OE-MC.Package-Manager    A.11.16.00    HP Package-Manager
  HPUX11i-OE-MC.Cluster-Monitor    A.11.16.00    HP Cluster Monitor
  HPUX11i-OE-MC.ServiceGuard       A.11.16.00    ServiceGuard
```

```
HPUX11i-OE-MC.PRM-Sw-Lib          C.02.03.%11    Process Resource Manager
                                  PRM-Sw-Lib product
HPUX11i-OE-MC.Proc-Resrc-Mgr      C.02.03.%11    Process Resource Manager
                                  Proc-Resrc-Mgr product
HPUX11i-OE-MC.WLM-Monitor         A.02.03.%q17   HP-UX Workload Manager Utilities
HPUX11i-OE-MC.Workload-Mgr        A.02.03.%q17   HP-UX Workload Manager
HPUX11i-OE-MC.PAM-Kerberos        C.01.23.%71N   PAM-Kerberos Version 1.23

HPUX11i-OE-MC.Jpi14               1.4.2.03.04    Java2 1.4 Netscape Plugin

HPUX11i-OE-MC.CIFS-Server         A.01.11.01.%71N HP CIFS Server (Samba) File and
                                  Print Services
HPUX11i-OE-MC.CIFS-Development    A.01.11.01.%71N HP CIFS Ser Source Code Files
HPUX11i-OE-MC.EMS-DBMon           A.04.10.%ic71p EMS Database Monitor
HPUX11i-OE-MC.EMS-DskMon          A.04.10.%ic71p EMS Disk Resource Monitor

HPUX11i-OE-MC.EMS-MIBMon          A.04.10.%ic71p EMS MIB Resource Monitor Product
HPUX11i-OE-MC.SG-NFS-Tool         A.11.23.02     MC/ServiceGuard NFS Script
                                  Templates
HPUX11i-OE-MC.PAM-NTLM            A.01.09.02.%711 HP NTLM Pluggable
                                  Authentication Module
HPUX11i-OE-MC.CIFS-Client         A.01.09.02.%711 CIFS Client
HPUX11i-OE-MC.PRM-Sw-Krn          C.01.02        Process Resource Manager
                                  PRM-Sw-Krn product
HPUX11i-OE-MC.OnlineJFS           B.11.23.05.%1Q Online features of the VxFS
                                  File System
#
```

The initial **swlist** output is deceiving in that the *Mission Critical Operating Environment* is shown as only one entry. You can see from the display of the *product* level details of *Mission Critical Operating Environment* in the last listing that many products are included in this OE, including Service-Guard, Process Resource Manager, GlancePlus/UX, CIFS/9000, and many other products.

Now that we know the initial software that has been loaded, let's move on to load additional products. Software Distributor-HP-UX (I call this Software Distributor throughout this book; HP documentation typically uses SD-UX) is the program used in HP-UX 11i to perform all tasks related to software management. Software Distributor is used in an example to install software on the same system on which we loaded our operating system earlier in this chapter. Software Distributor is a standards-based way to perform software management. It conforms to the Portable Operating System Interface (POSIX), which is the standard for packaging software and utilities related to software management. The Software Distributor product described in this section comes with your HP-UX system.

Software Distributor can be invoked using the commands described in this section, by using SAM (covered in Chapter 12), or by installing software for the first time as described earlier in this chapter.

The following four phases of software installation are performed with Software Distributor:

• Selection(1) - You can select the source and software you wish to load during this phase. In the upcoming example, the Graphical User Interface of Software Distributor is used, and you see how easily you can select these.

• Analysis(2) - All kinds of checks are performed for you, including free disk space, dependencies, compatibility, mounted volumes, and others. One of the useful outputs of this phase is the amount of space the software you wish to load consumes on each logical volume. This will be shown in the example.

• Load(3) - After you are satisfied with the analysis, you can proceed with loading the software.

• Configuration(4) - The software you load may require kernel rebuilding and a system reboot. Startup and shutdown scripts may also need to be modified.

I tend to use some terminology associated with Software Distributor somewhat loosely. I have nothing but good things to say about Software Distributor, but I don't conform to the official Software Distributor terminology as much as I should. For instance, I use the word "*system*" a lot, which could mean many different things in the Software Distributor world. For instance, Software Distributor uses "*local host*" (a system on which Software Distributor is running or software is to be installed or managed by Software Distributor), "*distribution depot*" (a directory that is used as a place for software products), and "*development system*" (a place where software is prepared for distribution). I will use the word *system* to mean the system on which we are working in the examples, because software is loaded onto the system from media.

The example of Software Distributor in this section describes the process of loading software from a DVD-ROM to the local system. What I show here only begins to scratch the surface of functionality you have with Software Distributor, but because I want to get you up and running quickly, this overview should help. You can load software from various media as well as across the network. You can run **swinstall** through the graphical interface, the Character Line Interface (CLI) used throughout this section, or the command line. You can use the **swinstall** command from the command line specifying source, options, target, and so on. I like using the CLI because you don't need any graphics capability, and you get full functionality. If, however, you like to do things the "traditional UNIX" way, you can issue the **swinstall** command with arguments. You can look at the manual page for **swinstall** to understand its arguments and options and use this command from the command line. There are many Software Distributor commands, including **sd**, **swjob -i**, **swcopy**, **swremove**, **swlist**, and **swinstall**.

To load software from a DVD-ROM, you must first mount the DVD-ROM. This can be done at the command line or in SAM. Figure 3-8 shows the SAM log file after the DVD-ROM was mounted and the directory **dvdrom** was searched for in the SAM log file.

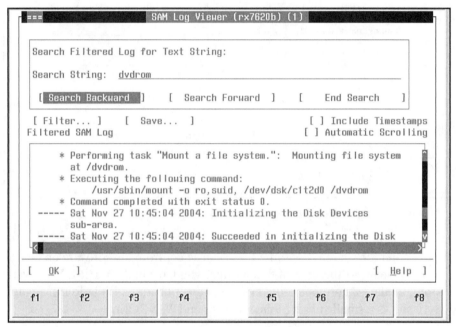

Figure 3-8   SAM Log Viewer Showing Mount of **dvdrom**

Figure 3-8 shows the **mount** command of the DVD-ROM that could have been issued at the command line. If you're not sure of the device file of the DVD-ROM, you would issue **ioscan -funC disk** and all the disk devices including the DVD-ROM would be listed.

After the DVD-ROM has been mounted, run **swinstall** and select the source, as shown in Figure 3-9.

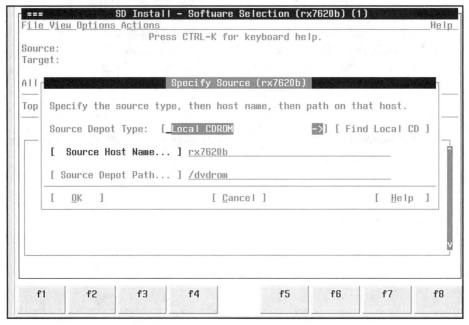

```
=== ▬▬▬▬▬▬▬   SD Install - Software Selection (rx7620b) (1) ▬▬▬▬▬▬
File View Options Actions                                                Help
                        Press CTRL-K for keyboard help.
Source:
Target:

All ┌▬▬▬▬▬▬▬▬▬▬▬▬▬▬  Specify Source (rx7620b) ▬▬▬▬▬▬▬▬▬▬▬▬▬
    │
Top │ Specify the source type, then host name, then path on that host.
    │
    │ Source Depot Type:   [ Local CDROM          →] [ Find Local CD ]
    │
    │ [  Source Host Name... ]  rx7620b
    │
    │ [ Source Depot Path... ]  /dvdrom
    │
    │ [    OK    ]                  [ Cancel ]              [  Help   ]
    │
    │
    │
    │
    │
    └▬▬▬▬▬▬▬▬▬▬▬▬▬▬▬▬▬▬▬▬▬▬▬▬▬▬▬▬▬▬▬▬▬▬▬▬▬▬▬▬▬▬▬▬▬▬▬▬▬▬
    ┌──────┬──────┬──────┬──────┐    ┌──────┬──────┬──────┬──────┐
    │  f1  │  f2  │  f3  │  f4  │    │  f5  │  f6  │  f7  │  f8  │
    └──────┴──────┴──────┴──────┘    └──────┴──────┴──────┴──────┘
```

Figure 3-9   Specify Source in **swinstall**

After the source is specified, you can select from the software on DVD-ROM to load. At the time of this writing, you have both an HP-UX 11i version 2 update 2 core operating system and applications DVD-ROM. Figure 3-10 shows a small subset of the software on DVD-ROM.

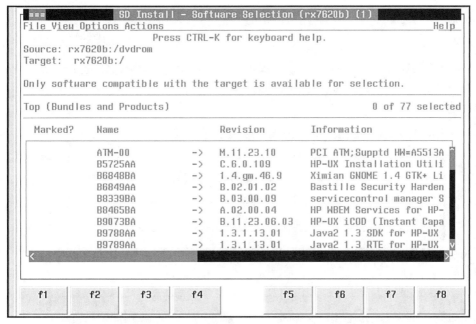

Figure 3-10   Software on DVD-ROM

From this screen, you can view and select software to load from a DVD-ROM. The process of selecting software to load is covered next for loading from an Ignite-UX server, but the process is the same for a DVD-ROM.

This process is not much different than the process of loading software from an Ignite-UX server, as described next, other than the source being DVD-ROM, in this case, rather than the Ignite-UX server.

An alternative to loading software from a DVD is to access an Ignite-UX server, as covered in Chapter 11, and load software from one or more of the software depots on the Ignite-UX server. Figure 3-11 shows accessing software on an Ignite-UX server.

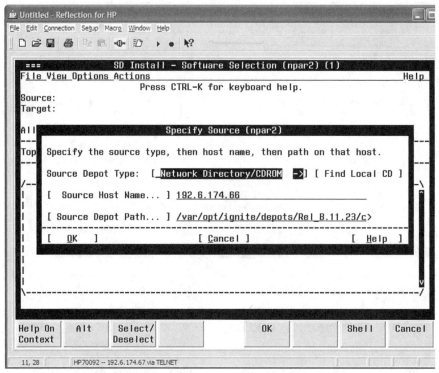

Figure 3-11   **swinstall** Core OS Load From Ignite-UX Server Depot

This figure shows the **swinstall** screen contents you would enter after HP-UX is running to load additional software. Ignite-UX server IP address is specified and so is the full path of the depot **/var/opt/ignite/depots/ Rel_B.11.23/core** (which can't be fully seen in the figure). I also have an applications depot that I could have selected as the source of this load. The next screen you see after this are the contents of the Core OS components, as shown in Figure 3-12:

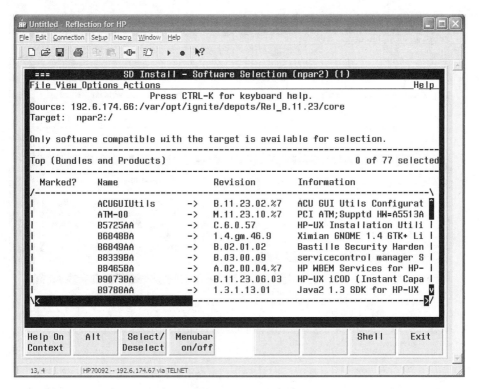

Figure 3-12   **swinstall** Core OS Components

Figure 3-12 shows the contents of **/var/opt/ignite/depots/
Rel_B.11.23/core**. From this depot, you can load any of its components.

Among the advantages of booting and installing software from an
Ignite-UX server are media is not required when software is loaded on the
clients, and multiple clients can boot from a single Ignite-UX server simultaneously. I install many systems, so this is a big advantage for me.

When you select *Match What Target Has* under the *Actions* menu, you
can view the software currently loaded on your system. You may receive a
"Yes" in the "Marked?" column or a "Partial." "Yes" means that all the
filesets associated with your selection will be loaded, and "Partial" means
only some will be loaded. Figure 3-13 shows "Yes" in the "Marked?" column
for software that has been selected.

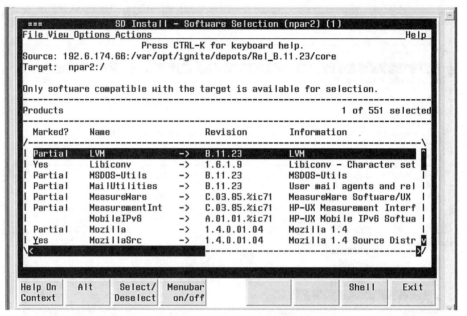

Figure 3-13   Software Selection Software Distributor Screen

A bundle of software you select to install may be composed of products, subproducts, and filesets. You can select any item you have "Marked" for loading to see of what filesets it is comprised. I have done this for Pay Per Use to see the software of which it is comprised in Figure 3-14.

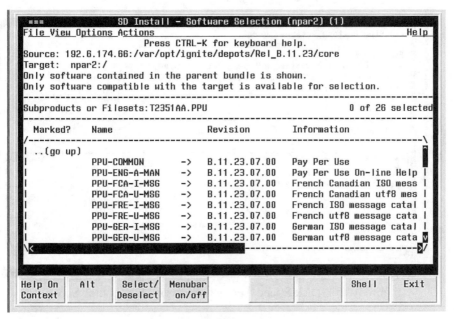

```
===            SD Install - Software Selection (npar2) (1)
File View Options Actions                                          Help
                   Press CTRL-K for keyboard help.
Source: 192.6.174.66:/var/opt/ignite/depots/Rel_B.11.23/core
Target:  npar2:/
Only software contained in the parent bundle is shown.
Only software compatible with the target is available for selection.
------------------------------------------------------------------
Subproducts or Filesets:T2351AA.PPU                  0 of 26 selected
------------------------------------------------------------------
  Marked?   Name                 Revision        Information
/------------------------------------------------------------------\
| ..(go up)                                                        ^
|           PPU-COMMON      ->  B.11.23.07.00  Pay Per Use          |
|           PPU-ENG-A-MAN   ->  B.11.23.07.00  Pay Per Use On-line Help |
|           PPU-FCA-I-MSG   ->  B.11.23.07.00  French Canadian ISO mess |
|           PPU-FCA-U-MSG   ->  B.11.23.07.00  French Canadian utf8 mes |
|           PPU-FRE-I-MSG   ->  B.11.23.07.00  French ISO message catal |
|           PPU-FRE-U-MSG   ->  B.11.23.07.00  French utf8 message cata |
|           PPU-GER-I-MSG   ->  B.11.23.07.00  German ISO message catal |
|           PPU-GER-U-MSG   ->  B.11.23.07.00  German utf8 message cata v
\<------------------------------------------------------------------>/

 Help On    Alt    Select/  Menubar                      Shell    Exit
 Context           Deselect  on/off
```

Figure 3-14   Components of a Software Product

Figure 3-14 shows that the Pay Per Use software is indeed composed of many components. To go back to the top, select *(go up)*.

Selecting *Install* runs analysis (Step 2 - Analysis) on the software you select to load. After the analysis is completed, you can take a look at the log-file, view the disk space analysis, and perform other tasks. I normally take a look at the disk space analysis just to see the impact the software I am loading is having on free disk space, as shown in Figure 3-15.

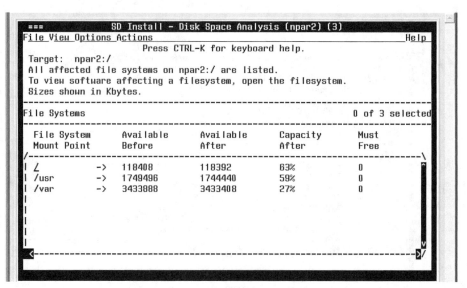

Figure 3-15   Disk Space Analysis Software Distributor Screen

You can see in Figure 3-15 that Pay Per Use consumes minimal disk space.

I also look at the products to ensure that I'm loading the software I expect to load, as shown in Figure 3-16 for Pay Per Use.

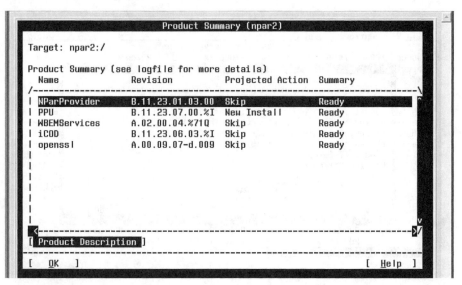

Figure 3-16   Product Summary Software Distributor Screen

After you are satisfied with the analysis, you can proceed with the installation (Step 3 - Load). Figure 3-17 shows the type of status you are provided as software is loaded on the system.

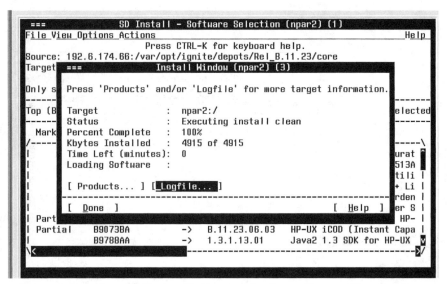

Figure 3-17   Install Window Software Distributor Screen Showing Status

In this case, all the software has been loaded. I could view the logfile to check for errors or warnings.

After the load of your software is complete, you can either exit the session or you are given a message indicating that a reboot is required to complete the configuration (Step 4 - Configuration). Not all software requires a reboot in order for configuration to take place. Most software will run configuration routines after the software is loaded without the need for a reboot. If a reboot is required, you are asked if you wish to reboot; but it could be a bad time to reboot, so you may want to wait or delay the reboot.

The process of loading software from media using Software Distributor is easy and thorough. The user interface to Software Distributor makes it easy to select and load software from media.

Loading Patches

HP-UX patches can be obtained from a variety of sources. Most people start at *IT Resource Center (itrc.hp.com)*, commonly called ITRC, because a variety of useful HP-UX information can be found there. With the proper level of support, you also receive media with tested patch bundles on a regular basis. These bundles, whether you load them from media or ITRC, have the following contents in them (at the time of this writing):

   • Quality Pack - Latest recommended defect fixes. Recommended means level 3 patches (levels are described shortly), or if none exists, level 2. It is divided into two bundles: a base bundle that contains core patches and an application bundle that contains patches for the Operating Environment products (applications). This bundle rolls every 6 months for its respective OS stream.

   • Hardware Enablement - Patches required to enable a new hardware product or fix some defect that would have rendered a hardware product unusable. Many times, the actual enablement requires more than the patch bundle. Device drivers, diagnostics, firmware, specific Ignite/UX versions may also be required. This specific information is contained in the individual product readme files. Patches in the this bundle are not necessarily level 3 or level 2. They may be brand new patches.This bundle rolls every 6 months for its respective OS stream.

   • Bundle11i - These patches are required for everyone to install on their systems, no questions asked! Each bundle, and sometimes specific patches within the bundle, has different reasons for being required, but everyone should install them. Typically, this bundle does not change often.

There are significant differences in patch levels which are in the following descriptions:

   • Level 1 - The patch has gone through its normal development and test process. Testing includes validation that the patch fixes the problems it is intended to fix, does not introduce new problems, and cleanly installs and de-installs. Almost all General Release patches are level 1 at initial release. You would use a level 1 patch typically for a reactive situation, where there is no higher level patch available to fix the problem. If you are more risk tolerant, you may choose to select level 1 patches for pro-active patching. If you are conservative, you would never choose level 1 for proactive work, unless there was some extenuating circumstance.

• Level 2 - These patches have met minimum criteria based on the number of days available to customers and the number of times down-loaded with no problems reported. The number of days and number of downloads criteria is statistically derived to minimize customer risk. The specific criteria changes as needed. Level 2 patches are used for both reactive and proactive patching. They are proactive when no level 3 is available. The ITRC label of "recommended" is given to a level 2 patch when no level 3 is available. Patches are promoted to a level 2 rating as applicable.

• Level 3 - Rating three is the highest level HP assigns to a patch. These patches represent the lowest level of risk. HP recommends these patches whenever possible for both proactive and reactive patching.

Knowing these patch levels is important so you can make informed decisions when considering what patches to load.

Because installing HP-UX from media has already been covered and because you may urgently need a patch that has just been released and is not on your media I cover the process of installing patches from ITRC in this section.

From ITRC, you can download "standard" HP-UX patch bundles or select individual patches for what I call "surgical" loading of patches to fix specific problems or support third-party applications.

The high-level steps of downloading and installing patches include the following:

• Select patches for download on ITRC (either bundles or individual).

• Select the format of the patch file for download from ITRC, such as **tar** format.

• Download the patch file to your HP-UX system. (This may involve downloading the patch file to another system and then copying it to your HP-UX system.)

• Unarchive the file, if it is in **tar** format, and run the embedded script that creates a depot.

• Run **swinstall**, specifying the directory to be the depot produced by the script in the previous bullet.

The patch work begins when you set up your account initially with *IT Resource Center.* You want to enter your system handle, and the serial number of one of your systems if you have it to get full access to all of the information on the site.

The process of viewing individual patches on *IT Resource Center* is self-explanatory when you log into the site. When you select *patch/firmware database,* you are asked to log in and you can select an operating system for which you want to select patches and select the patch(es) you want to load on your system.

When you select the patch(es) that you want to download, you may be given updated patch information. Figure 3-18 shows the original patch I selected, PHSS_31087, and a newer patch.

Figure 3-18   Original, Recommended, and Newest Patch

Figure 3-18 shows the recommended and most recent patches. You may see other categories, such as the original patch you specified if it is not the recommended or most recent. The newest one may not be recommended because it may not have been thoroughly tested.

The legend that appears on the figure indicates information such as whether the patch is critical, if it requires a reboot, if special instructions are used, and other relevant information.

After opening up the newest patch, several categories of information related to the patch are displayed, as shown in Figure 3-19.

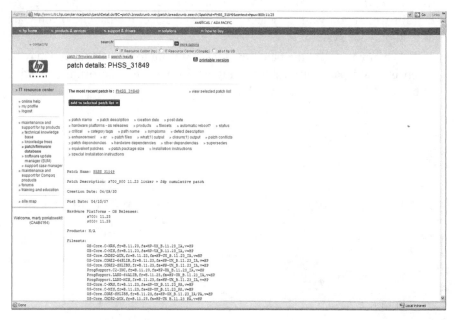

Figure 3-19   Patch-Related Information Details

Figure 3-19 shows a series of categories related to the patch that you can view to get detailed information about the patch including the following:

patch name
patch description
creation date
post date
hardware platforms: OS releases
products
filesets
automatic reboot
status
critical
category tags

path name
symptoms
defect description
enhancement
sr
patch files
what(1) output
cksum(1) output
patch conflicts
patch dependencies
hardware dependencies
other dependencies
supersedes
equivalent patches
patch package size
installation instructions
special installation instructions

When you add the selected patch to the list of patches you want to download, many dependencies may be added as well. Therefore, the list of patches you download may be substantially greater than your original list of patches.

When you download the patches, you are given options for the type of file you want to download, such as **zip**, **gzip**, **tar**, or a script that will FTP the patches. I normally select **tar** format. The filename will have embedded in it the HP-UX release such as 11.23, in the case of this patch.

After the **tar** file is on your system, view the README file to get instructions on how to create a depot. I issue **tar xvf** *filename* to extract the files. Among the files present is one to create a depot. You simply run this script, which usually begins with *create*, without any command-line arguments, and it produces a depot in the directory that extracted the files. I typically do all this work in one directory. A directory called **depot** is created in the directory where the script was run to create the depot.

In the following example, there is a **tar** patch bundle present in the directory **/tmp/patch** that I downloaded from ITRC in the patch bundles index. I run **tar xvf** on this file, which produces several files, including the *create* file that creates the directory **/tmp/patch/depot** in which a group of patches are located (use **gunzip** if you download a zip file). This procedure is shown in the following listing:

```
[rx8620b{root}:/tmp/patch] >pwd
```

```
/tmp/patch
[rx8620b{root}:/tmp/patch]>ls
hpux_800_11.23_10150451.tar
[rx8620b{root}:/tmp/patch]>tar -xvf hpux*
x patch_manifest, 109 bytes, 1 tape blocks
x README_hp-ux, 1780 bytes, 4 tape blocks
x create_depot_hp-ux_11, 5768 bytes, 12 tape blocks
x BUNDLE11i_B.11.23.0408.1.depot, 675840 bytes, 1320 tape blocks

[rx8620b{root}:/tmp/patch]>ls
BUNDLE11i_B.11.23.0408.1.depot   hpux_800_11.23_10150451.tar
README_hp-ux                     patch_manifest
create_depot_hp-ux_11
[rx8620b{root}:/tmp/patch]>./create*
DEPOT: /tmp/patch/depot
BUNDLE: BUNDLE
TITLE: Patch Bundle
UNSHAR: y
PSF: depot.psf
Expanding patch shar files...
list of SD installable patches =  BUNDLE11i_B.11.23.0408.1
Copying BUNDLE11i_B.11.23.0408.1 into depot /tmp/patch/depot

=======  10/17/04 22:20:22 EDT  BEGIN swcopy SESSION (non-interactive)
         (jobid=rx8620b-0009)

      * Session started for user "root@rx8620b".

      * Beginning Selection
      * "rx8620b:/tmp/patch/depot":  This target does not exist and
        will be created.
      * Source:
        /tmp/patch/BUNDLE11i_B.11.23.0408.1.depot
      * Targets:             rx8620b:/tmp/patch/depot
      * Software selections:
BUNDLE11i,r=B.11.23.0408.1,a=HP-UX_B.11.23_IA/PA,v=HP
PHCO_30440.UX2-CORE,r=1.0,a=HP-UX_B.11.23_IA,v=HP,fr=1.0,fa=HP-UX_B.11.23_IA
PHKL_30442.CORE2-KRN,r=1.0,a=HP-UX_B.11.23_IA,v=HP,fr=1.0,fa=HP-UX_B.11.23_IA
PHKL_30443.VXFS-BASE-KRN,r=1.0,a=HP-UX_B.11.23_IA,v=HP,fr=1.0,fa=HP-UX_B.11.23_IA
PHKL_30444.CORE2-KRN,r=1.0,a=HP-UX_B.11.23_IA,v=HP,fr=1.0,fa=HP-UX_B.11.23_IA
PHKL_30471.CORE2-KRN,r=1.0,a=HP-UX_B.11.23_IA,v=HP,fr=1.0,fa=HP-UX_B.11.23_IA
PHKL_30506.CORE2-KRN,r=1.0,a=HP-UX_B.11.23_IA,v=HP,fr=1.0,fa=HP-UX_B.11.23_IA
PHKL_31151.CORE2-KRN,r=1.0,a=HP-UX_B.11.23_IA,v=HP,fr=1.0,fa=HP-UX_B.11.23_IA
      * Selection succeeded.


      * Beginning Analysis and Execution
      * Session selections have been saved in the file
        "/roothome/.sw/sessions/swcopy.last".
      * "rx8620b:/tmp/patch/depot":  There will be no attempt to mount
        filesystems that appear in the filesystem table.
      * The execution phase succeeded for "rx8620b:/tmp/patch/depot".
      * Analysis and Execution succeeded.

NOTE:    More information may be found in the agent logfile using the
         command "swjob -a log rx8620b-0009 @
         rx8620b:/tmp/patch/depot".

=======  10/17/04 22:20:24 EDT  END swcopy SESSION (non-interactive)
         (jobid=rx8620b-0009)

Bundling patches in depot

=======  10/17/04 22:20:24 EDT  BEGIN swpackage SESSION

      * Session started for user "root@rx8620b".

      * Source:         rx8620b:depot.psf
      * Target:         rx8620b:/tmp/patch/depot
      * Software selections:
             *


      * Beginning Selection Phase.
```

```
                   * Reading the Product Specification File (PSF) "depot.psf".
                   * Reading the bundle "BUNDLE" at line 13.
        NOTE:        Adding unrecognized keyword "PHKL_30442" at line 27.
        NOTE:        Adding unrecognized keyword "PHKL_30443" at line 28.
        NOTE:        Adding unrecognized keyword "PHKL_30444" at line 29.
        NOTE:        Adding unrecognized keyword "PHKL_30471" at line 30.
        NOTE:        Adding unrecognized keyword "PHKL_30506" at line 31.
        NOTE:        Adding unrecognized keyword "PHKL_31151" at line 32.

                   * Selection Phase succeeded.


                   * Beginning Analysis Phase.
                   * Analysis Phase succeeded.


                   * Beginning Package Phase.

                   * Packaging the bundle
                     "BUNDLE,r=B.11.23,a=HP-UX_B.11.23_32/64,v=HP".
                   * Package Phase succeeded.

======= 10/17/04 22:20:25 EDT   END swpackage SESSION

Verifying the depot.

======= 10/17/04 22:20:25 EDT   BEGIN swverify SESSION
        (non-interactive) (jobid=rx8620b-0010)

                   * Session started for user "root@rx8620b".

                   * Beginning Selection
                   * Target connection succeeded for "rx8620b:/tmp/patch/depot".
                   * Software selections:
        BUNDLE,r=B.11.23,a=HP-UX_B.11.23_32/64,v=HP
        BUNDLE11i,r=B.11.23.0408.1,a=HP-UX_B.11.23_IA/PA,v=HP
        PHCO_30440.UX2-CORE,r=1.0,a=HP-UX_B.11.23_IA,v=HP,fr=1.0,fa=HP-UX_B.11.23_IA
        PHKL_30442.CORE2-KRN,r=1.0,a=HP-UX_B.11.23_IA,v=HP,fr=1.0,fa=HP-UX_B.11.23_IA
        PHKL_30443.VXFS-BASE-KRN,r=1.0,a=HP-UX_B.11.23_IA,v=HP,fr=1.0,fa=HP-UX_B.11.23_IA
        PHKL_30444.CORE2-KRN,r=1.0,a=HP-UX_B.11.23_IA,v=HP,fr=1.0,fa=HP-UX_B.11.23_IA
        PHKL_30471.CORE2-KRN,r=1.0,a=HP-UX_B.11.23_IA,v=HP,fr=1.0,fa=HP-UX_B.11.23_IA
        PHKL_30506.CORE2-KRN,r=1.0,a=HP-UX_B.11.23_IA,v=HP,fr=1.0,fa=HP-UX_B.11.23_IA
        PHKL_31151.CORE2-KRN,r=1.0,a=HP-UX_B.11.23_IA,v=HP,fr=1.0,fa=HP-UX_B.11.23_IA
                   * Selection succeeded.


                   * Beginning Analysis
                   * Session selections have been saved in the file
                     "/roothome/.sw/sessions/swverify.last".
                   * "rx8620b:/tmp/patch/depot":  There will be no attempt to mount
                     filesystems that appear in the filesystem table.
                   * Verification succeeded.


        NOTE:    More information may be found in the agent logfile using the
                 command "swjob -a log rx8620b-0010 @
                 rx8620b:/tmp/patch/depot".

======= 10/17/04 22:20:25 EDT   END swverify SESSION (non-interactive)
        (jobid=rx8620b-0010)

[rx8620b{root}:/tmp/patch]>ls
BUNDLE11i_B.11.23.0408.1.depot   depot.psf
README_hp-ux                     hpux_800_11.23_10150451.tar
create_depot_hp-ux_11            patch_manifest
depot
[rx8620b{root}:/tmp/patch]>cd depot


[rx8620b{root}:/tmp/patch/depot]>ll
total 32
dr-x------   2 root      sys           96 Oct 17 22:20 BUNDLE
dr-x------   2 root      sys           96 Oct 17 22:20 BUNDLE11i
dr-x------   3 root      sys           96 Oct 17 22:20 PHCO_30440
dr-x------   3 root      sys           96 Oct 17 22:20 PHKL_30442
```

```
dr-x------    3 root        sys              96 Oct 17 22:20 PHKL_30443
dr-x------    3 root        sys              96 Oct 17 22:20 PHKL_30444
dr-x------    3 root        sys              96 Oct 17 22:20 PHKL_30471
dr-x------    3 root        sys              96 Oct 17 22:20 PHKL_30506
dr-x------    3 root        sys              96 Oct 17 22:20 PHKL_31151
dr-x------   12 root        sys            8192 Oct 17 22:20 catalog
-rw-r--r--    1 root        sys            4130 Oct 17 22:20 swagent.log
[rx8620b{root}:/tmp/patch/depot]>
```

Running the *create* script produced several directories in **/tmp/patch/
depot** including **BUNDLE11i**, that I want to load. The **swinstall** window in
Figure 3-20 shows the patches in **BUNDLE11i** that I want to load on the
system with **/tmp/patch/depot** selected as the source directory.

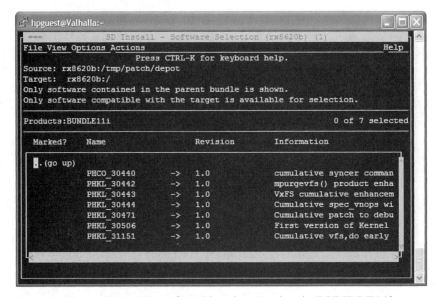

Figure 3-20   **swinstall** Interface Showing Patches in BUNDLE11i

This patch bundle requires a reboot because kernel patches in the bundle. After the reboot, I view the PHKL patches to ensure the patches in this
bundle have been loaded:

```
[rx8620b{root}:/roothome]>swlist -l fileset | grep PHKL
# PHKL_29562                     1.0            HW enablement: gvid graphics multicard
  PHKL_29562.CORE2-KRN           1.0            OS-Core.CORE2-KRN
# PHKL_29681                     1.0            SCSI c8xx Dump Driver Cumulative Patch
  PHKL_29681.CORE2-KRN           1.0            OS-Core.CORE2-KRN
# PHKL_29881                  1.0            New audio h/w support and cumulative fixes
  PHKL_29881.C-INC               1.0            ProgSupport.C-INC
  PHKL_29881.CORE2-KRN           1.0            OS-Core.CORE2-KRN
```

```
# PHKL_30155                    1.0              enables PAL calls with 64-bit indices
  PHKL_30155.CORE2-KRN              1.0                OS-Core.CORE2-KRN
# PHKL_30165                    1.0              enables diag2 driver 64-bit PAL calls
  PHKL_30165.CORE2-KRN              1.0                OS-Core.CORE2-KRN
# PHKL_30289                1.0              Removes unwanted confusing CMC & CPE Message
  PHKL_30289.CORE2-KRN              1.0                OS-Core.CORE2-KRN
# PHKL_30442                    1.0              mpurgevfs() product enhancement
  PHKL_30442.CORE2-KRN              1.0                OS-Core.CORE2-KRN
# PHKL_30443                    1.0              VxFS cumulative enhancements
  PHKL_30443.VXFS-BASE-KRN          1.0                JFS.VXFS-BASE-KRN
# PHKL_30444            1.0              Cumulative spec_vnops with closed() change
  PHKL_30444.CORE2-KRN              1.0                OS-Core.CORE2-KRN
# PHKL_30471                    1.0              Cumulative patch to debugging info
  PHKL_30471.CORE2-KRN              1.0                OS-Core.CORE2-KRN
# PHKL_30506                    1.0              First version of Kernel Syncer
  PHKL_30506.CORE2-KRN              1.0                OS-Core.CORE2-KRN
# PHKL_31151                1.0              Cumulative vfs,do early escapes,buffer
flush
  PHKL_31151.CORE2-KRN              1.0                OS-Core.CORE2-KRN
[rx8620b{root}:/roothome] >
```

This listing verifies that the patches from the bundle just loaded are indeed present after the reboot.

To display installed patches at the command line you would issue the following command:

```
# swlist -l patch \*.\*,c=patch | more
# Initializing...
# Contacting target "rx7620a"...
#
# Target:  rx7620a:/
#

# PHCO_30312.Q4                 1.0      OS-Core.Q4                applied
# PHCO_31540.SECURITY           1.0      SecurityMon.SECURITY      applied
# PHCO_31540.SECURITY2          1.0      SecurityMon.SECURITY2     applied
# PHCO_31540.UX-FRE-I-MSG       1.0      OS-Core.UX-FRE-I-MSG      applied
# PHCO_31540.UX-FRE-U-MSG       1.0      OS-Core.UX-FRE-U-MSG      applied
# PHCO_31540.UX-GER-I-MSG       1.0      OS-Core.UX-GER-I-MSG      applied
# PHCO_31540.UX-GER-U-MSG       1.0      OS-Core.UX-GER-U-MSG      applied
# PHCO_31540.UX-ITA-I-MSG       1.0      OS-Core.UX-ITA-I-MSG      applied
# PHCO_31540.UX-ITA-U-MSG       1.0      OS-Core.UX-ITA-U-MS#
```

(This is a truncated output of the complete patch list output.)

To remove a patch, issue the following command:

```
# swremove -p patch_name1 patch_name2 ...
```

This results in the specified patches being removed.

The next section covers an important monitoring topic ISEE.

Remote Support (Instant Support Enterprise Edition)

Instant Support Enterprise Edition (ISEE) provides remote hardware event management. Diagnostic software monitors hardware status and generates alerts for servers, connected peripherals, and storage devices. Alerts are received at your site and then automatically forwarded to HP. You must have the ability to browse from the subnet on which your system is located, which usually means that port 80 is open on your system for outbound traffic, so the alerts can be sent to HP. You need to have the proper support level for ISEE and, with higher levels of support, there is an advanced configuration of ISEE. This is a fantastic support tool so be sure to talk to your HP support team if you're not now running ISEE.

ISEE configuration is performed by an HP support representative. I provide a quick overview of ISEE in this section.

Online Diagnostics are a prerequisite to having ISEE installed. The following listing shows the ISEE platform, installed by the HP support representative, and the Online Diagnostics, which are provided with HP-UX 11i, are installed:

```
# swlist | grep -i ISEE
  ISEEPlatform              A.03.50.854    ISEE Platform
#


# swlist | grep -i diag
  OnlineDiag                B.11.23.02.22  HPUX 11.23 Support Tools Bundle,
Mar 2004
#
```

After ISEE is installed, ISEE is configured through a browser window with http://*ip_address*:5060/start.html, which opens the initial window shown in Figure 3-21.

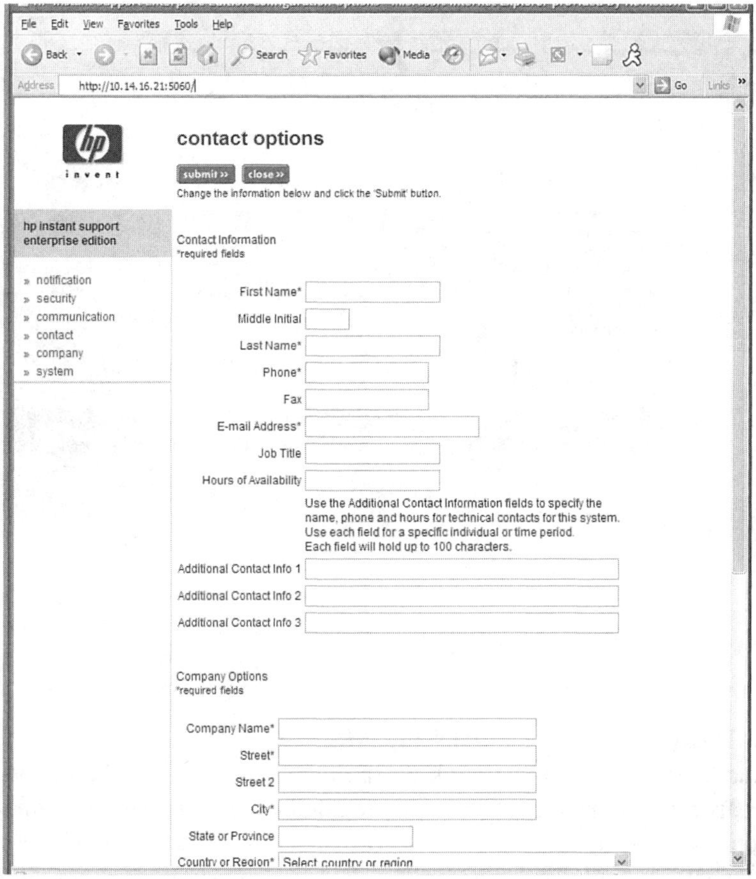

Figure 3-21   ISEE Contact Screen

In this window, all the initial contact information is entered and submitted. After this information is entered and the same URL is again opened, you see the main ISEE screen, as shown in Figure 3-22.

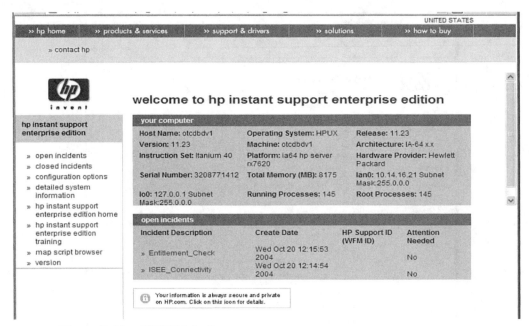

Figure 3-22   ISEE Main Screen

This screen has the initial setup information on the right and a series of menus from which you can pick on the left. You can view the incidents on this partition, both open and closed, detailed system information, and other selections. The detailed system information is really detailed, including every package loaded on your system. This is a great way to access information related to your system.

As part of the setup, a **cron** job is created, as shown in the following listing:

```
# /opt/hpservices/contrib/SysInfo/bin/setSysInfoCronEntry.sh -i

Welcome to setSysInfoCronEntry utility script, version 1.00.
Copyright 2002 Hewlett-Packard Company.
All rights reserved.
Wed Oct 20 12:32:00 EDT 2004

Please enter day of the week, 0-6, 0=Sunday? >> 0

Please enter time of day, 24 hr time, 2300 for 11:00pm >>
```

```
entry for SysInfoRunMap.sh DOES NOT exist in the cron file, will create a new en
try.
00 00 * * 0 /opt/hpservices/contrib/SysInfo/bin/SysInfoRunMap.sh 1>> /var/opt/hp
services/contrib/SysInfo/adm/SysInfoRunMap.cronlog 2>&1 &

# crontab -l root
# Entry(s) in /opt/hpservices/RemoteSupport are for HP Instant Support Enterprise
Edition
0  0  *  *  1  /opt/hpservices/RemoteSupport/config/pruneIncidents.sh
00 00 * * 0 /opt/hpservices/contrib/SysInfo/bin/SysInfoRunMap.sh 1>> /var/opt/hp
services/contrib/SysInfo/adm/SysInfoRunMap.cronlog 2>&1 &
```

This listing shows that the ISEE cron job was indeed created.

If you have Critical Support (CS) there is an advanced configuration of ISEE and many other support services.

Software Distributor Background

You need to have some background on the way software is organized in Software Distributor. There are the four following types of objects into which software is grouped in Software Distributor: bundle, product, subproduct, and fileset. Figure 3-23 shows the hierarchy of Software Distributor objects.

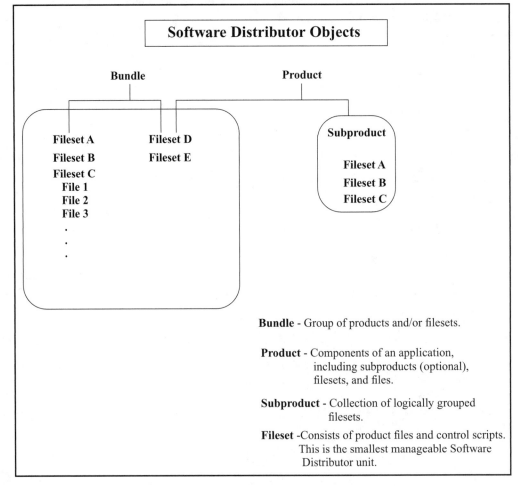

Figure 3-23   Software Distributor Objects

You can look at the bundle in Figure 3-23 as a group of software. This can be products, subproducts, and filesets, as shown in the diagram. The concept here is to organize software in such a way that it is easy to manage. The diagram shows that some filesets are shared between different bundles and products. This hierarchical organization and sharing makes managing software with Software Distributor flexible.

Here are some of the common software management-related tasks you can perform with Software Distributor.

Installing and Updating Software (Command Line or GUI)

The **swinstall** command is used to install and update software. The source of the software you are loading can come from a variety of places, including, CD-ROM, magnetic tape, or a "depot" directory from which software can be distributed. Using the depot, you can load software into a directory and then install and update software on other nodes from this directory. Software loaded from CD-ROM with Software Distributor must be loaded onto the local system; this technique is used in the upcoming example. You have a lot of flexibility with SD-OV when selecting the target system onto which you want to load software and the source from which you will load the software. You can, for instance, load software from a depot that is on another system on your network. This command can be run at the command line or with the Graphical User Interface.

Copying Software to a Depot (Command Line or GUI)

The **swcopy** command is used to copy software from one depot to another. The depot used in the upcoming examples is a CD-ROM. By setting up depots, you can quickly install or update software to other nodes simultaneously with SD-OV. This command can be run at the command line or with the Graphical User Interface.

Removing Software from a System (Command Line or GUI)

The **swremove** command is used to remove software from a system that has had software loaded with Software Distributor. This includes removing installed and configured software from a system or removing software from a depot. This command can be run at the command line or with the Graphical User Interface.

List Information About Installation Software

The **swlist** command provides information about the depots that exist on a system, the contents of a depot, or information about installed software. Examples of using this command are provided shortly. This command can be run at the command line or with the Graphical User Interface.

Configure Installed Software

The **swconfig** command configures or unconfigures installed software. Configuration of software normally takes place as part of **swinstall**, but configuration can be deferred until a later time.

Verify Software

The **swverify** command confirms the integrity of installed software or software stored in a depot.

Package Software That Can Later Be Installed (Local Sys Only)

You may want to produce "packages" of software that you can later put on tape or in a depot with the **swpackage** command. This packaged software can then be used as a source for **swinstall** and be managed by other Software Distributor commands.

Control Access to Software Distributor Objects

You may want to apply restricted access to Software Distributor objects such as packaged software. Using the **swacl** command, you can view and change the Access Control List (ACL) for objects.

Modify Information about Loaded Software (Local System Only)

The Installed Products Database (IPD) and associated files are used to maintain information about software products you have loaded. **swmodify** can be run at the command line to modify these files.

Register or Unregister a Depot

A software depot can be registered or unregistered with **swreg**. This means you don't have to remove a depot; if you temporarily don't want it used, you can unregister it.

Manage Jobs (Command Line or GUI, this is SD-OV only)

Software Distributor jobs can be viewed and removed with **swjob**. The graphical user interface version of this command can be invoked with **sd** or **swjob -i**.

Listing Software

Although I like the Graphical User Interface of **swinstall,** you can also issue Software Distributor commands at the command line. One example is the **swlist** command. The **swlist** command is useful for viewing the software you have loaded on your system, viewing the software you have loaded in a depot, or producing a list of depots. A Graphical User Interface to the **swlist** command can be invoked with the *-i* option and is also available in SAM. With the **swlist** command, you perform many functions, including the following:

• List the software you have at the specified level with the **-l** option. I will show several examples shortly. The levels you can specify are:
    root
    depot
    bundle
    product
    subproduct
    fileset
    file

Levels are delineated by "." so you will see *bundle.[product].[sub-product].[fileset]*. You can get all kinds of useful information out of **swlist** and use this for other purposes. Some of the things you can do with **swlist** are:

• Display the table of contents from a software source.
• Specify which attributes you wish to see for a level of software such as name, size, revision, etc.
• Create a list of products that can be used as input to other Software Distributor commands, such as **swinstall** and **swremove**.

When you run **swlist** with no options, you get a list of the software products installed on your system. Let's try a few **swlist** commands with the **-l** option to view software installed on a system (by default, **swlist** will list installed products; you can use the **-s** option to specify a software depot or other source). The following example shows listing software at the *bundle* level.

```
$ swlist -l bundle

# various header information
#              .
B2491BA        B.11.00 MirrorDisk/UX
B3701AA_TRY    B 11.00.31 Trial HP GlancePlus/UX Pak s800
B3929BA        B11.00  HP   OnLineJFS (Advanced VxFS)
B3947BA        B.11.00 HP Process Resource Manager
B5725AA        B.1.4   HP-UX Installation Utilities (Ignite-UX)
HPUXEng32RT    B 11.00 English HP-UX 32-bit Runtime Environment
```

This system has the HP-UX runtime environment, GlancePlus/UX trial software, HP OnLineJFS, and MirrorDisk/UX.

If we run **swlist** at the product level, the following is produced for GlancePlus/UX trial software:

```
$ swlist -l product B3701AA_TRY

# various header information
#              .
#              .
#              .
B3701AA_TRY                    B.11.00.31  Trial HP GlancePlus/UX Pak for s800 11.00
B3701AA_TRY.MeasurementInt     B.11.00.31 HP-UX Measurement Interface for 11.00
B3701AA_TRY.MeasureWare        B.11.00.31  MeasureWare Software/UX
B3701AA_TRY.Glance             B.11.00.31  HP GlancePlus/UX

 (bundle)   (product)
```

GlancePlus/UX is comprised of the two products shown in this example. Are there any subproducts of which GlancePlus/UX is comprised? The following example will help us determine the answer.

```
$ swlist -l subproduct B3701AA_TRY

# various header information
#              .
#              .
#              .
B3701AA_TRY                    B.11.00.31  Trial HP GlancePlus/UX Pak for s800 11.00
B3701AA_TRY.MeasurementInt     B.11.00.31 HP-UX Measurement Interface for 11.00
B3701AA_TRY.MeasureWare        B.11.00.31 MeasureWare Software/UX
B3701AA_TRY.Glance             B.11.00.31 HP GlancePlus/UX

(bundle)   (product)
```

The output of the products and subproducts levels is the same; therefore, there are no subproducts in GlancePlus/UX. We can go one step further and take this to the fileset level, as shown in the following example:

```
$ swlist -l fileset B3701AA_TRY

# various header information
#          .
#          .
#          .
B3701AA_TRY                        B.11.00.31  Trial HP GlancePlus/UX Pak for s800 11.00
B3701AA_TRY.MeasurementInt          B.11.00.31  HP-UX Measurement Interface for 11.00
B3701AA_TRY.MeasurementInt.ARM      B.11.00.31  HP-UX Application Response Measurement
for 11.00
B3701AA_TRY.MeasurementInt.MI       B.11.00.31 HP-UX Measurement Interface for 11.00
B3701AA_TRY.MeasureWare             B.11.00.31 MeasureWare Software/UX
B3701AA_TRY.MeasureWare.MWA         B.11.00.31 MeasureWare Software files
B3701AA_TRY.MeasureWare.MWANO       B.11.00.31 MeasureWare NOS Connectivity Module
Software files
B3701AA_TRY.MeasureWare.PERFDSI     B.11.00.31 HP PCS Data Source Integration
B3701AA_TRY.Glance                  B.11.00.31 HP GlancePlus/UX
B3701AA_TRY.Glance.GLANC            B.11.00.31 HP GlancePlus files
B3701AA_TRY.Glance.GPM              B.11.00.31   HP GlancePlus Motif interface files

(bundle)   (product) (fileset)
```

With the **swlist** command and the *-l* option, we have worked our way down the hierarchy of HP GlancePlus/UX. Going down to the file level with the *-l file* option produces a long list of files associated with this product.

Table 3-4 shows some of the *-l* options to **swlist** that I use:

Table 3-4   **Some swlist -l Options**

Command	Explanation
swlist -l root	Shows the root level.
swlist -l shroot	Shows the shared roots.
swlist -l prroot	Shows the private roots.
swlist -l bundle	Shows bundles only.
swlist -l product	Shows products only.
swlist -l subproduct	Shows both products and subproducts.
swlist -l fileset	Shows products, subproducts, and filesets.
swlist -l file	Shows products, subproducts, filesets, files and numbers.
swlist -l category	Shows all categories of available patches if they have category in their definition.
swlist -l patch	Shows all applied patches.
swlist -l depot	Shows all depots on the local host.
swlist -l depot @ sys	Shows all depots on *sys*.

I also like to use the -*a* option with **swlist.** -*a* specifies that you would like to see a specific attribute associated with the software you are listing. You can look at the **sd** manual page on your HP-UX system to get a complete list of attributes. One attribute I often look at is *size*. To get a list of the *subproducts* in *NETWORKING* and their *size* in KB you would issue the following command:

```
$ swlist -l subproduct -a size NETWORKING
```

Another attribute I often view is *revision,* which you can view with the following command:

```
$ swlist -l subproduct -a revision NETWORKING
```

Sometimes, the brief descriptions of filesets that are given are insufficient to really understand the fileset. The *title* attribute provides a descriptive title, which you can see with the following command for the fileset level:

```
$ swlist -l fileset -a title NETWORKING
```

Table 3-5 is a list of some attributes that you may find of interest.

Table 3-5   Some Attributes of Interest

Attribute	Explanation
architecture	Shows the target systems supported by the software.
category	Shows the type of software.
description	Shows more detailed description of software.
title	Shows the official name of the software.
owner	Shows the owner of the file.
path	Shows the full pathname of the file.
revision	Shows the revision number of the software object.
size	Shows the size of all filesets.
state	Shows the state of the fileset.

The other Software Distributor commands listed earlier can also be issued at the command line. You may want to look at the manual pages for these commands as you prepare to do more advanced Software Distributor work than loading software from DVD, CD-ROM, or tape.

Chapter 4

Logical Volume Manager

Introduction

Because this is a "how to" book, this chapter focuses on some commonly performed Logical Volume Manager (LVM):

> • Logical Volume Manager (LVM) - You will probably use LVM to manage the data on your system. This section provides background information on LVM.

> • Example of adding external disk capacity on an Integrity server. This thorough section shows the commands used to recognize the external storage, the commands used to configure the external storage and mount the file systems, and the scripts I use to accomplish some of the configuration automatically.

> • A summary of some commonly used LVM procedures.

> • Some additional file system commands.

Logical Volume Manager Background

Logical Volume Manager is a disk-management subsystem that allows you to manage physical disks as logical volumes which means that a file system can span multiple physical disks. You can view Logical Volume Manager as a flexible way of defining boundaries of disk space that are independent of one another. Not only can you specify the size of a logical volume, but you can also change its size if the need arises. This possibility is a great advancement over dedicating a disk to a files ystem or having fixed-size partitions on a disk. Logical volumes can hold file systems, raw data, or swap space. You can now specify a logical volume to be any size you wish, have logical volumes span multiple physical disks, and change the size of the logical volume if you need to!

So what do you need to know to set up Logical Volume Manager and realize all these great benefits? First, you need to know the terminology, and second, you need to know Logical Volume Manager commands. As with many other system administration tasks, you can use graphical management tools which are covered in Chapter 12. But, as usual, I recommend that you read this section first so you understand the basics of Logical Volume Manager.

For use with the Journaled File System (JFS), Hewlett-Packard has an add-on product called HP OnLineJFS. This product allows you to perform many of the LVM functions without going into single-user mode. For example, when a file system needs to be expanded, the logical volume on which it resides needs to be unmounted before the expansion takes place. Normally, that unmounting would mean shutting the system down into single-user mode so that no user or process could access the volume and it could then be unmounted. With OnLineJFS, the logical volumes and file systems are simply expanded with the system up and running and no interruption to users or processes. Even without OnLineJFS, there are some file systems that can be unmounted when not in single-user mode.

With both JFS and OnLineJFS, an *intent log*, or *journal*, is used to keep track of metadata (structural information) that would be written synchronously on a traditional HFS-based system. The journal information is used to complete an operation if a crash occurs, thereby making system recovery with **fsck** much faster.

With both the base JFS and OnLineJFS products, you can specify a file system as *vxfs* rather than *hfs*. With the **newfs** or **mount** commands, for example, you can specify *-F vxfs*. There are many options that you can specify with *-o* when working with JFS. One of the most common is *-o largefiles,* which allows files larger than 2 GB in size.

Logical Volume Manager Terms

The following terms are used when working with Logical Volume Manager. They are only some of the terminology associated with Logical Volume Manager, but they'll get you started with Logical Volume Manager. It is a good idea to read the following brief overview of these terms:

Volume	A device used for a file system, swap, or raw data. Without Logical Volume Manager, a volume would be either a disk partition or an entire disk drive.
Physical Volume	A disk that has not been initialized for use by Logical Volume Manager. An entire disk must be initialized if it is to be used by Logical Volume Manager; that is, you can't initialize only part of a disk for Logical Volume Manager use and the rest for fixed partitioning.
Volume Group	A collection of logical volumes that are managed by Logical Volume Manager. You would typically define which disks on your system are going to be used by Logical Volume Manager and then define how you wish to group these into volume groups. Each individual disk may be a volume group, or more than one disk may form a volume group. At this point, you have created a pool of disk space called a *volume group*. A disk can belong to only one volume group. A volume group may span multiple physical disks.

Logical Volume | This is space that is defined within a volume group. A volume group is divided up into logical volumes. This is similar to a disk partition, which is of a fixed size, but you have the flexibility to change its size. A logical volume is contained within a volume group, but the volume group may span multiple physical disks. You can have a logical volume that is bigger than a single disk.

Physical Extent | A set of contiguous disk blocks on a physical volume. If you define a disk to be a physical volume, the contiguous blocks within that disk form a physical extent. Logical Volume Manager uses the physical extent as the unit for allocating disk space to logical volumes. If you use a small physical extent size, such as 1 MB, you have a fine granularity for defining logical volumes. If you use a large physical extent size, such as 256 MB, then you have a coarse granularity for defining logical volumes. The default size is 4 MB. The physical extent is a function of the size of the disk by default.

Logical Extents | A logical volume is made up of logical extents. Logical extents and physical extents are the same size within a volume group. Although logical and physical extents are the same size, this doesn't mean that two logical extents map to two contiguous physical extents. It may be that you have two logical extents that end up being mapped to physical extents on different disks!

/etc/lvmtab | This file has in it the device file associated with each disk in a volume group. **/sbin/lvmrc** starts each volume group by reading the contents of this file at boot time. This file can be rebuilt with **vgscan**. This is not an ascii file, so **strings /etc/lvmtab** is used to see its contents.

PV Links   Physical Volume Links (PV Links) provide dual
                          SCSI or Fibre Links to the same disk. If one of
                          the links were to fail, the other link automatically
                          takes over routing I/O to the disk.

Figure 4-1 graphically depicts some of the logical volume terms just
covered. In this figure, you can see clearly that logical extents are not
mapped to contiguous physical extents, because some of the physical extents
are not used.

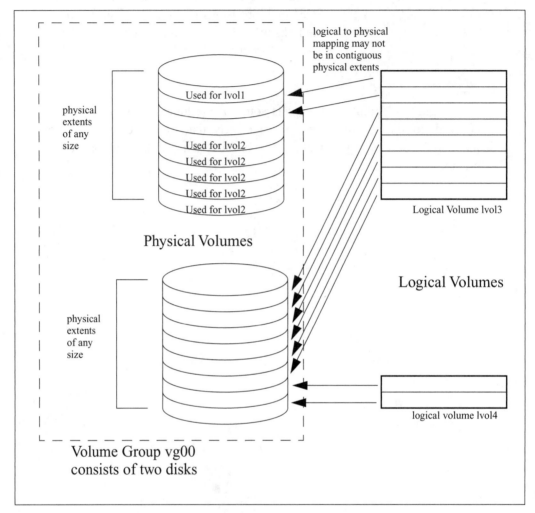

Figure 4-1   Logical Volume Manager Partial Logical to Physical Mapping

Another diagram that is helpful in understanding LVM is Figure 4-2 which shows some of the important components of which an LVM boot disk is comprised on an HP server.

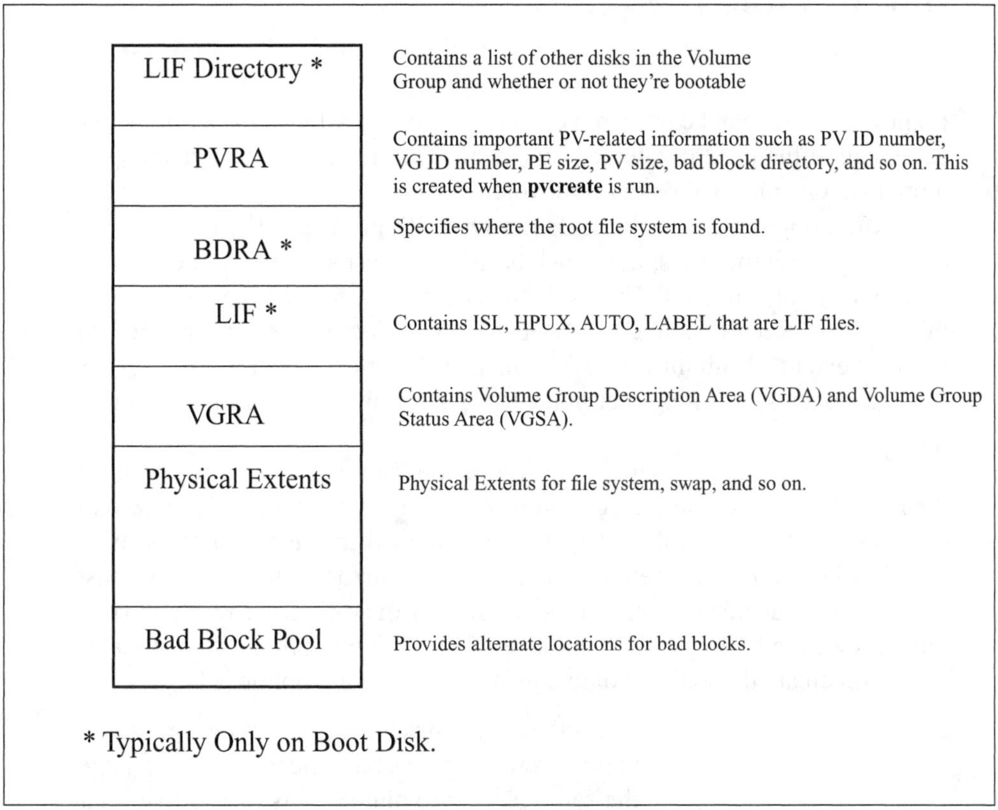

LIF Directory *	Contains a list of other disks in the Volume Group and whether or not they're bootable
PVRA	Contains important PV-related information such as PV ID number, VG ID number, PE size, PV size, bad block directory, and so on. This is created when **pvcreate** is run.
BDRA *	Specifies where the root file system is found.
LIF *	Contains ISL, HPUX, AUTO, LABEL that are LIF files.
VGRA	Contains Volume Group Description Area (VGDA) and Volume Group Status Area (VGSA).
Physical Extents	Physical Extents for file system, swap, and so on.
Bad Block Pool	Provides alternate locations for bad blocks.

* Typically Only on Boot Disk.

Figure 4-2   Boot Disk Components on HP 9000

Some of these components exist only on a boot disk (as noted), and others exist on all LVM disks. The components in *LIF* are put there when the **mkboot** and **lvlnboot** commands are run.

Disk Mirroring

Logical volumes can be mirrored one or more times, which creates an identical image of the logical volume. This means that a logical extent can map to more than one physical extent if mirrored.

Mirroring is done with the *MirrorDisk/UX* product. Mirroring is done on a logical volume basis, not a disk basis. You must specify the logical volumes you want mirrored. This is demonstrated in several examples later in this chapter. Recall Figure 4-1, which showed logical extents mapped to physical extents. With mirroring, you map each logical extent to two or more physical extents, meaning that your data physically resides in two or more places.

You may have an environment where you want to mirror some or all of the logical volumes. You can configure your mirroring manually (as shown in some examples later in this chapter), or graphical management tools (covered in Chapter 12) can be used to set up disk mirroring for you. You must first, however, decide the characteristics of your mirroring. There is a mirroring policy called *strict*. You define one of the following three strict policies when you create the logical volume using the following options:

n	No, this is not a strict allocation policy, meaning that mirrored copies of a logical extent can share the same physical volume. This means that your original data and mirrored data may indeed be on the same physical disk. If you encounter a disk mechanism problem of some type, you may lose both your original and mirrored data.
y	Yes, this is a strict allocation policy, meaning that mirrored copies of a logical extent may not share the same physical volume. This is safer than allowing mirrored copies of data to share the same physical volume. If you have a problem with a disk in this scenario, you are guaranteed that your original data is on a different physical disk from your mirrored data. Original data and mirrored data are always part of the same volume group even if you want them on different physical volumes.

g   Mirrored data will not be on the same Physical Volume Group (PVG) as the original data. This policy is called a PVG-strict allocation policy.

The strict allocation policy depends on your environment. Most installations that employ mirroring buy sufficient disk drives to mirror all data. In an environment such as this, I would create two volume groups, one for the original data and one for the mirrored data, and use the *strict -g* option when creating logical volumes so that the original data is on one volume group and the mirrored data on the other.

Logical Volume Manager Commands

The following definitions are of some of the more common LVM commands. This section describes these commands so that when you see them, you have an idea of each command's use. Although these are not all of the Logical Volume Manager commands, these are the ones I use most often and are the commands you should have knowledge of when using Logical Volume Manager. The commands are grouped by physical volume (pv) commands, volume group (vg) commands, and logical volume (lv) commands. There are *usage* summaries of some of the commands included with the descriptions, and details can be found in the online manual pages. Some of the commands, such as **vgdisplay**, **pvdisplay**, and **lvdisplay**, were issued so that you could see examples of these. The following output of **bdf** will be helpful to you when you view the output of Logical Volume Manager commands that are issued. The output of **bdf** shows several logical volumes mounted (**lvol1**, **lvol3**, **lvol4**, **lvol5**, **lvol6**, **lvol7**, and **lvol8**), all of which are in volume group **vg00** (see the **bdf** command overview later in this chapter).

$ bdf

File system	kbytes	used	avail	%used	Mounted on
/dev/vg00/lvol3	47829	18428	24618	43%	/
/dev/vg00/lvol1	67733	24736	36223	41	/stand
/dev/vg00/lvol8	34541	8673	22413	28%	/var
/dev/vg00/lvol7	299157	149449	119792	56%	/usr
/dev/vg00/lvol4	23013	48	20663	0%	/tmp
/dev/vg00/lvol6	99669	32514	57188	36%	/opt
/dev/vg00/lvol5	19861	9	17865	0%	/home
/dev/dsk/c0t6d0	802212	552120	169870	76%	/mnt/9.x

For these logical volumes to be mounted, you must manually mount them with the **mount** command or have them automatically mounted by placing entries in **/etc/fstab**.

The **/usr/sbin/mount** (1M) command has many options so consult the man page for it. The -a option, which I use in the command file in the upcoming section, mounts all files in **/etc/fstab**. I also show an example of **/etc/fstab** in this section. The *-r* option to **mount** mounts the file system as read only. The -f *FStype* allows you to specify the type of file system to mount, such as vxfs, cdfs, and others.

Physical Volume Commands

Here is a list of the **pv** commands:

pvchange	Changes a physical volume in some way. For example, you may want to allow additional physical extents to be added to a physical volume if they are not permitted, or prohibit additional physical extents from being added to a physical volume if, indeed, they are allowed:

```
/usr/sbin/pvchange [-A autobackup] -s pv_path

/usr/sbin/pvchange [-A autobackup] -S autoswitch pv_path

/usr/sbin/pvchange [-A autobackup] -x extensibility pv_path

/usr/sbin/pvchange [-A autobackup] -t IO_timeout pv_path

/usr/sbin/pvchange [-A autobackup] -z sparepv pv_path
```

pvcreate   Creates a physical volume that will be part of a
                      volume group. Remember that a volume group
                      may consist of several physical volumes. The
                      physical volumes are the disks on your system:

```
/usr/sbin/pvcreate [-b] [-B] [-d soft_defects] [-s disk_size]
                   [-f] [-t disk_type] pv_path
```

pvdisplay   Shows information about the physical volumes
                      you specify. You can get a lot of information
                      about the logical to physical mapping with this
                      command if you use the verbose (-v) option.
                      With -v **pvdisplay** shows you the mapping of
                      logical to physical extents for the physical vol-
                      umes specified:

```
/usr/sbin/pvdisplay [-v] [-b BlockList] pv_path ...
```

                      You get a lot of other useful data from this com-
                      mand, such as the name of the physical volume;
                      the name of the volume group to which the phys-
                      ical volume belongs; the status of the physical
                      volume; the size of physical extents on the physi-
                      cal volume; the total number of physical extents;
                      and the number of free physical extents.

pvmove   You can move physical extents from one physical
                      volume to other physical volumes with this com-
                      mand. By specifying the source physical volume
                      and one or more destination physical volumes,
                      you can spread data around to the various physi-
                      cal volumes you wish with this command. In this

example, if the lvol had been left off, the entire disk would have been moved.

```
/usr/sbin/pvmove [-A autobackup] [-n lv_path] source_pv_path
                 [dest_pv_path ... | dest_pvg_name ...]
```

```
# pvmove -n /dev/vg01/lvol1 /dev/dsk/c0t2d0 /dev/dsk/c0t4d0
```

mknod   Although this is not an LVM command exclusively, it is used often when creating volume groups, as shown in this example:

```
# cd /dev
# mkdir vg01
# cd vg01
# mknod group c 64 0x010000
```

Volume Group Commands

vgcfgbackup   Saves the configuration information for a volume group. Remember that a volume group is made up of one or more physical volumes:

```
/usr/sbin/vgcfgbackup [-f vg_conf_path] [-u] vg_name
```

vgcfgrestore   Restores the configuration information for a volume group:

```
/usr/sbin/vgcfgrestore -n vg_name -l
```

```
/usr/sbin/vgcfgrestore [-R] [-F] -n vg_name [-o old_pv_path]
                       pv_path
```

```
/usr/sbin/vgcfgrestore -f vg_conf_path -l
```

```
/usr/sbin/vgcfgrestore [-R] [-F] -f vg_conf_path
                       [-o old_pv_path] pv_path
```

vgchange   Makes a volume group active or inactive. With the -a option, you can deactivate (-a n) a volume group or activate (-a y) a volume group:

```
/usr/sbin/vgchange -a availability [-l] [-p] [-q quorum] [-s]
                   [-P resync_daemon_count] [vg_name...]
```

vgcreate   You can create a volume group and specify all of its parameters with this command. You specify a volume group name and all the associated parameters for the volume group when creating it. You can specify many physical volume block devices on the same command line if you want. *ex2* below shows creating a PV link. The second path in the **vgcreate** command is the *alternate* link:

```
/usr/sbin/vgcreate [-f] [-A autobackup] [-x extensibility]
                   [-e max_pe] [-l max_lv] [-p max_pv]
                   [-s pe_size] [-g pvg_name] vg_name
                   pv_path ...
```

ex1: **vgcreate /dev/vg01 /dev/dsk/c0t2d0**

ex2: **pvcreate /dev/rdsk/c0t1d0**
     vgcreate /dev/vg01 /dev/dsk/c0t1d0 /dev/dsk/c2t1d0

vgdisplay   Displays all information related to the volume group if you use the verbose (*-v*) option, including the volume group name; the status of the volume group; the maximum, current, and open logical volumes in the volume group; the maximum, current, and active physical volumes in the volume group; and physical extent-related information:

```
/usr/sbin/vgdisplay [-v] [vg_name ...]
```

vgexport   Removes a logical volume group from the system, but does not modify the logical volume information on the physical volumes. These physical volumes can then be imported to another system using **vgimport**. Use *-s* for sharable option in ServiceGuard environments:

```
/usr/sbin/vgexport [-m mapfile] [-p] [-v] [-f outfile] vg_name

/usr/sbin/vgexport -m mapfile -s -p -v vg_name
```

```
# vgchange -a n /dev/vg01
# vgexport -v -m /etc/lvmconf/vg01.map /dev/vg01
```

vgextend   Physical volumes can be added to a volume
                    group with this command by specifying the
                    physical volume to be added to the volume
                    group. After the summary of the command is an
                    example:

```
/usr/sbin/vgextend [-f] [-A autobackup] [-g pvg_name]
        [-x extensibility] [-z sparepv] vg_name pv_path ...
```

```
# vgextend /dev/vg01 /dev/dsk/c0t2d0
```

vgimport   Can be used to import a physical volume to
                    another system. Note in the example below that
                    several disks could have been specified on the
                    vgimport line:

```
/usr/sbin/vgimport [-m mapfile] [-p] [-v] [-f infile]
                vg_name pv_path ...
```

```
/usr/sbin/vgimport -m mapfile -s -v vg_name
```

```
# mkdir /dev/vg01
# mknod /dev/vg01/group c 64 0x010000
# vgimport -v -m /dev/lvmconf/vg01.map /dev/vg01 /dev/dsk/c0t2d0
# vgchange -a y /dev/vg01
# vgcfgbackup vg01
```

vgreduce   The size of a volume group can be reduced with
                    this command by specifying which physical vol-
                    ume(s) to remove from a volume group. Make
                    sure that the physical volume to be removed has
                    no data on it before doing this:

```
/usr/sbin/vgreduce [-A autobackup] vg_name pv_path ...
```

```
/usr/sbin/vgreduce [-A autobackup] [-l] vg_name pv_path
```

```
/usr/sbin/vgreduce [-A autobackup] [-f] vg_name
```

    vgremove   A volume group definition can be completely removed from the system with this command. The entry for the volume group in **/dev** is not removed. An example of removing a volume group is shown below also:

```
/usr/sbin/vgremove vg_name ...
```

```
# vgchange -a n /dev/vg01
# lvremove /dev/vg01/lvol1          ;run for all lvols in vg
# vgremove /dev/vg01
```

    vgscan   In the event of a catastrophe of some type, use this command to scan your system in an effort to rebuild the **/etc/lvmtab** file. The *-p* option performs a *preview* of **vgscan**:

```
/usr/sbin/vgscan [-a] [-p] [-v]
```

    vgsync   There are times when mirrored data in a volume group becomes "stale" or out-of-date. **vgsync** synchronizes the physical extents in each mirrored logical volume in a volume group:

```
/usr/sbin/vgsync vg_name ...
```

Logical Volume Commands

Here is a list of **lv** commands:

    lvcreate   Creates a new logical volume. A logical volume is created within a volume group. A logical volume may span multiple disks, but must exist within a volume group. Many options exist for this command, and two that you would often use are *-L* to define the size of the logical volume and *-n* to define the name of the logical volume:

```
/usr/sbin/lvcreate [-A autobackup] [-c mirror_consistency]
        [-C contiguous] [-d schedule] [-D distributed]
        [-i stripes -I stripe_size] [-l le_number | -L lv_size]
        [-m mirror_copies] [-M mirror_write_cache] [-n lv_name]
        [-p permission] [-r relocate] [-s strict] vg_name
```

An interesting nuance to **lvcreate** is that you can't specify a physical volume on which to create the logical volume. If you want a logical volume and its mirror on specific disks, you first run **lvcreate** specifying no size, then two **lvextend** commands for the original and mirror copies as shown below:

```
# lvcreate /dev/vg03/lvol3
# lvextend -L 400 /dev/vg03/lvol3 /dev/dsk/c0t2d0
# lvextend -m 1 /dev/vg03/lvol3 /dev/dsk/c2t2d0
```

lvchange   Changes the logical volume in some way. For example, you may wish to change the permission on a logical volume to read-write (w) or read (r) with the *-p* option. The *-C* is used to specify contiguous. Or you may want to change the strict policy (described under "Disk Mirroring") to strict (y), not strict (n), or PVG strict (g):

```
/usr/sbin/lvchange [-a availability] [-A autobackup]
     [-c mirror_consistency] [-C contiguous]
     [-d schedule] [-D distributed] [-M mirror_write_cache]
     [-p permission] [-r relocate] [-s strict]
     [-t IO_timeout] lv_path
```

lvdisplay   Shows the status and characteristics of every logical volume that you specify. If you use the verbose (*-v*) option of this command, you get a lot of useful data in many categories, including the following:

1) Information about the way in which the logical volumes are set up, such as the physical volume on which the logical extents appear; the number of local extents on a physical volume; and the number of physical extents on the physical volume.

2) Detailed information for logical extents, including the logical extent number and some information about the physical volume and physical extent for the logical extent:

```
/usr/sbin/lvdisplay [-k] [-v] lv_path ...
```

lvextend   Increases the number of physical extents allocated to a logical volume. We sometimes underestimate the size required for a logical volume and with this command, you can easily correct this problem. You may want to extend a logical volume to increase the number of mirrored copies (using the -*m* option), to increase the size of the logical volume (using the -*L* option), or to increase the number of logical extents (using the -*l* option). You can specify the disk on which you want the logical volume extended and the *size* is the new size, not an amount by which you want the logical volume extended:

```
/usr/sbin/lvextend [-A autobackup] {-l le_number | -L lv_size
        | -m mirror_copies} lv_path [pv_path ... | pvg_name ...]
# lvextend -L 300 /dev/vg01/lvol1
```

extendfs   Use this command after **lvextend**. Whereas the **lvextend** command expands the logical volume, **extendfs** expands the file system within the logical volume. Use **fsadm** if you have OnLineJFS installed rather than this procedure:

```
/usr/sbin/extendfs [-F FStype] [-q] [-v] [-s size] special
# umount /dev/vg01/lvol1          ;use fsadm if online
# extendfs -f vxfs /dev/vg01/rlvol1   ;JFS installed
# mount /dev/vg01/lvol1 /backup
```

mkboot   Places boot utilities in boot area:

```
/usr/sbin/mkboot  [-b boot_file_path]   [-c [-u] | -f | -h | -u]
   [-i included_lif_file]  [-p preserved_lif_file]
   [-l | -H | -W] [-v] device

/usr/sbin/mkboot [-a auto_file_string] [-v] device

/usr/sbin/rmboot device
```

lvlnboot   Use this to set up a logical volume to be a root, boot, primary swap, or dump volume (which can be undone with **lvrmboot**). Issuing the **lvlnboot** command with the -*v* option gives the current settings:

```
/usr/sbin/lvlnboot [[-A autobackup { -b boot_lv |
   -d dump_lv | -r root_lv | -R | -s swap_lv }] [-v] [vg_name]
```

lvsplit and **lvmerge**

          Split and merge mirrored logical volumes, respectively. If you have a mirrored logical volume, **lvsplit** splits this into two logical volumes. **lvmerge** merges two logical volumes of the same size, increasing the number of mirrored copies. In the following example below, two logical volumes are split and the name *backup* is appended to each. **fsck** is run on the split volumes, and they are mounted under separate names. **lvsplit** performs an *atomic* split, which means that the split takes place at the same time for all logical volumes that appear on the command line. In the **lvmerge** example, the primary, or master copy, is specified first, and the logical volume to be synchronized with the primary is specified second:

```
/usr/sbin/lvsplit [-A autobackup] [-s suffix]
                  [-g PhysicalVolumeGroup] lv_path ...
```

```
# lvsplit -s backup /dev/vg01/lvol1 /dev/vg01/lvol4
# fsck -f vxfs -p /dev/vg01/rlvol1backup
# fsck -f vxfs -p /dev/vg01/rlvol4backup
# mount /dev/vg01/lvol1 backuplvol1
# mount /dev/vg01/rlvol4 backuplvol4
```

/usr/sbin/lvmerge [-A autobackup] dest_lv_path src_lv_path

```
# lvmerge /dev/vg00/lvol1backup /dev/vg00/lvol1
```

lvmmigrate   Prepares a root file system in a disk partition for
                         migration to a logical volume. Use this if you
                         had a partition to convert into a logical volume.

lvreduce   Use this command to decrease the number of
                         physical extents allocated to a logical volume.
                         When creating logical volumes, we sometimes
                         overestimate the size of the logical volume. This
                         command can set the number of mirrored copies
                         (with the -*m* option), decrease the number of log-
                         ical extents (with the -*l* option), or decrease the
                         size of the logical volume (with the -*L* option).
                         Be careful when decreasing the size of a logical
                         volume, however, you may make it smaller than
                         the data in it. If you choose to do this, make sure
                         that you have a good backup of your data.

/usr/sbin/lvreduce [-A autobackup] [-f] -l le_number lv_path

/usr/sbin/lvreduce [-A autobackup] [-f] -L lv_size lv_path

/usr/sbin/lvreduce [-A autobackup] -m mirror_copies lv_path
[pv_path ...]

/usr/sbin/lvreduce [-A autobackup] -k -m mirror_copies lv_path
                    pv_key ...

lvremove   After emptying a logical volume, you can use
                         this command to remove logical volumes from a
                         volume group:

/usr/sbin/lvremove [-A autobackup] [-f] lv_path ...

lvrmboot   Use this command if you don't want a logical
                    volume to be root, boot, primary swap, or a
                    dump device. (This is the converse of the **lvln-
                    boot** command.) However, unless you have a
                    disk partition to boot from, don't leave the sys-
                    tem without a root or boot device designated
                    with the **lvlnboot** command, or the system won't
                    know where to boot from:

```
/usr/sbin/lvrmboot [-A autobackup] [-d dump_lv] [-r] [-s]
                   [-v] vg_name
```

lvsync   There are times when mirrored data in a logical
                    volume becomes "stale" or out-of-date. **lvsync**
                    synchronizes the physical extents in a logical
                    volume:

```
/usr/sbin/lvsync lv_path ...
```

newfs   Although this is not exclusively an LVM com-
                    mand, it is often used to place a file system on a
                    newly created logical volume. The following
                    example shows placing a file system on new log-
                    ical volume and mounting it:

```
/usr/sbin/newfs [-F FStype] [-o specific_options] [-V] special
```

```
# newfs -F vxfs -o largefiles /dev/vg01/rlvol1
# mount /dev/vg01/lvol1 /backup
```

JFS and OnLineJFS Commands

fsck   Because of the intent log, you can run **fsck** much
                    faster with JFS than without it. If you specify *-F
                    vxfs,* your **fsck** runs faster and you can specify
                    many additional options with *-o:*

```
/usr/sbin/fsck [-F FSType] [-m] [-V] [special ...]
```

```
/usr/sbin/fsck [-F FSType] [-o FSspecific-options] [-V]
               [special ...]
```

      fsadm   Performs a variety of operations when using OnLineJFS, such as defragmentation, resizing, online backup, and so on:

```
/usr/sbin/fsadm [-F FStype] [-V] [-o specific_options] special
```

For defragmentation:
```
fsadm -F vxfs [-d] [-D] [-d] [-E] /mount_point
```

To increase OnlineJFS file system:
```
fsadm -F vxfs -b new_size /mount_point
```

```
# lvextend -L 400 /dev/vg01/lvol3
# fsadm -F vxfs 400 /backup
```

To reduce OnlineJFS file system:
```
fsadm -f vxfs -b new_size /mount_point
```

```
# fsadm -F vxfs -d -D -e -E /backup
# fsadm -f vxvs -b 300 /backup
```

Example of Adding External Disks

One commonly performed task, that encompasses almost all LVM-related concepts, is adding disks from external storage units to your server. The following detailed example covers this process start to finish, including shell programs to help accomplish this. I performed this example for one of my clients on an Oracle database development server. This example uses HP's XP storage unit for external storage, but the process works for any external storage devices that presents Logical UNits (LUNs) to a server.

You don't want to use the volume information sizes, mount points, and other information in this section because they were unique to a specific installation. This example does, however, provide an excellent overview of this process, including the commands issued to set up all the specified volumes as well as performing some automation.

Fibre Interface Worldwide Names

For a storage expert to present LUNs to your server, they need to know the worldwide name on the fibre interfaces for each partition. The LUNs are presented to the specific partition from which they'll be accessed. Each partition has storage configured as if it were server. The partitions have a hostname, IP address, and other configured parameters so the storage LUNs must be presented to and configured on each partition.

The following commands are issued on a system to get information about the fibre cards with **ls** (in this case, two cards) and then obtain the worldwide names with **fcdutil**:

```
# ll /dev | grep fc
crw-rw-rw-  1 bin       bin        49 0x000000 Oct  6 14:32 fcd0
crw-rw-rw-  1 bin       bin        49 0x010000 Oct  6 14:32 fcd1
#
# fcdutil /dev/fcd0
                        Vendor ID is = 0x001077
                        Device ID is = 0x002312
          PCI Sub-system Vendor ID is = 0x00103c
                PCI Sub-system ID is = 0x0012c7
                        PCI Mode = PCI-X 133 MHz
                  ISP Code version = 3.2.168
                  ISP Chip version = 3
                        Topology = PRIVATE_LOOP
                        Link Speed = 2Gb
              Local N_Port_id is = 0x000001
            Previous N_Port_id is = 0x000001
                Local Loop_id is = 125
        N_Port Node World Wide Name = 0x50060b000029976f
        N_Port Port World Wide Name = 0x50060b000029976e    <- Port Name
        Switch Port World Wide Name = N/A
```

```
                Switch Node World Wide Name = N/A
                              Driver state = ONLINE
                         Hardware Path is = 1/0/2/1/0/4/0
                       Maximum Frame Size = 2048
            Driver-Firmware Dump Available = NO
            Driver-Firmware Dump Timestamp = N/A
                            Driver Version = @(#) libfcd.a HP Fibre Channel ISP 23x
x Driver B.11.23.01 /ux/kern/kisu/FCD/src/common/wsio/fcd_init.c:Jan 15,12:44:56


# fcdutil /dev/fcd1

                          Vendor ID is = 0x001077
                          Device ID is = 0x002312
            PCI Sub-system Vendor ID is = 0x00103c
                   PCI Sub-system ID is = 0x0012c7
                              PCI Mode = PCI-X 133 MHz
                     ISP Code version = 3.2.168
                     ISP Chip version = 3
                              Topology = PRIVATE_LOOP
                            Link Speed = 2Gb
                  Local N_Port_id is = 0x000001
               Previous N_Port_id is = None
                    Local Loop_id is = 125
        N_Port Node World Wide Name = 0x50060b0000299775
        N_Port Port World Wide Name = 0x50060b0000299774         <- Port Name
         Switch Port World Wide Name = N/A
         Switch Node World Wide Name = N/A
                        Driver state = ONLINE
                   Hardware Path is = 1/0/4/1/0/4/0
                 Maximum Frame Size = 2048
      Driver-Firmware Dump Available = NO
      Driver-Firmware Dump Timestamp = N/A
                      Driver Version = @(#) libfcd.a HP Fibre Channel ISP 23x
x Driver B.11.23.01 /ux/kern/kisu/FCD/src/common/wsio/fcd_init.c:Jan 15,12:44:56
```

The *Port World Wide Name* is used by a storage expert when setting up external storage.

Install Special Files and Work with Disk Devices

To have disk devices built for you after the external storage device is configured, run **ioscan** and **insf** to have the special files or the disk built for you. This results in many additional disk devices on your system. We'll be working with these device files as we go about configuring them in this section.

Example Volume Layout Table

Table 4-1 shows the storage layout that I will be using. This is only an example on which I have worked, so you should not use this layout on your system. It does, however, serve as an excellent example.

Table 4-1   Example Volume Layout

Volume Group Name	Logical Volume Name	Mount Point (fs Replaced raw)	Logical Volume Size
vg01 (changed from vg_system)	lvol1 lvol2 lvol2	lv_fs_system_400 lv_fs_temp_100 lv_fs_ctl1_110	400 100 110
vg02 (changed from vg_undo)	lvol1 lvol2	lv_fs_undo_500 lv_fs_ctl2_110	500 110
vg03 (changed from vg_logA)	lvol1 lvol2 lvol3	lv_fs_logA1 lv_fs_logA1 lv_fs_logA1	120 120 120
vg04 (changed from vg_logB)	lvol1 lvol2 lvol3	lv_fs_logB1 lv_fs_logB1 lv_fs_logB1	120 120 120
vg05 (changed from vg_data1)	lvol1 lvol2 lvol3 lvol4 lvol5 lvol6 lvol7 lvol8	lv_fs_users_data1_250 lv_fs_users_data2_250 lv_fs_users_data3_250 lv_fs_users_data4_250 lv_fs_users_data5_250 lv_fs_users_data6_250 lv_fs_users_data7_250 lv_fs_users_data8_250	251 251 251 251 251 251 251 251
vg06 (changed from vg_data2)	lvol1 lvol2 lvol3 lvol4 lvol5 lvol6 lvol7 lvol8	lv_fs_data1_250 lv_fs_data2_250 lv_fs_data3_250 lv_fs_data4_250 lv_fs_data5_250 lv_fs_data6_250 lv_fs_data7_250 lv_fs_data8_250	251 251 251 251 251 251 251 251

Volume Group Name	Logical Volume Name	Mount Point (fs Replaced raw)	Logical Volume Size
vg07 (changed from vg_indx)	lvol1	lv_fs_indx1_250	251
	lvol2	lv_fs_indx2_250	251
	lvol3	lv_fs_indx3_250	251
	lvol4	lv_fs_indx4_250	251
	lvol5	lv_fs_indx5_250	251
	lvol6	lv_fs_indx6_250	251
	lvol7	lv_fs_indx7_250	251
	lvol8	lv_fs_indx8_250	251

The information shown in Table 4-1 is only an example, but it serves as a good one for covering LVM.

Steps to Add External Storage to Partitions

Based on the information shown in Table 4-1, the following file shows the primary and alternate disk devices that will be automatically configured by some scripts that I show shortly. For the purposes of walking through the procedure please focus on volume group 07, the last group of devices in both files, and the disks in the group. The first field in each line is the name of the script that is called for every line in the files and the second field is the volume group number:

```
# cat primary_devices
/home/marty/scripts/oracle_primary 01 c7t0d0 c7t0d1 c7t0d2 c7t0d3
/home/marty/scripts/oracle_primary 02 c7t0d4 c7t0d5 c7t0d6 c7t0d7
/home/marty/scripts/oracle_primary 03 c7t1d0 c7t1d1 c7t1d2 c7t1d3
/home/marty/scripts/oracle_primary 04 c7t1d4 c7t1d5 c7t1d6 c7t1d7
/home/marty/scripts/oracle_primary 05 c7t2d0 c7t2d1 c7t2d2 c7t2d3
/home/marty/scripts/oracle_primary 06 c7t2d4 c7t2d5 c7t2d6 c7t2d7
/home/marty/scripts/oracle_primary 07 c7t3d0 c7t3d1 c7t3d2 c7t3d3
```

The following steps are performed to create disks, make the volume group, and add both the primary and alternate disks to the volume group. Some of these steps are performed on the volume group and others on the disks on the volume group. All the steps in this group are done by the "primary" script, which is covered in the next section except for the last step in the group that is performed by the "alternate" script:

1) pvcreate /dev/rdsk/c7t3d0 for every disk in the primary volume group.

2) mkdir /dev/vg07 for every volume group.

3) mknod /dev/vg07 c 64 0x070000 for every volume group.

4) vgcreate -s 4 -p 128 -g PVG07 /dev/vg07 /dev/dsk/c7t3d0 for the first disk in the volume group

5) vgextend -g PVG07 /dev/vg07 /dev/dsk/c7t3d1 for every additional disk in the volume group.

1alt) vgextend -g PVG07_ALT /dev/vg07 /dev/dsk/c10t3d0 for every alternate disk in the volume group. (This step is performed by the "alternate" script.)

These steps are required to get the devices and volume groups in place. I have two separate scripts to automate this procedure for the primary and alternate devices that I show shortly. The first line in the two files shown earlier calls the script for each line.

Next, the work related to the logical volumes and file systems is performed as shown in the following steps, which are performed in an "fstab" script covered in the next section:

1) lvcreate -L 250 -n lvol1 -r n -D y -s g /dev/vg07 for each logical volume. The size of the logical volume, in this case 250MB, may vary for each lvol in the volume group. The name is lvol1. Bad block relocation is set to no. Distributed allocation policy is used, which allocates free extents over multiple physical volumes. The strict allocation policy is set such that mirrors will not reside on the same physical volume. All these options appear in the man page for **lvcreate**, and you need to review these when determining what options to use when issuing the **lvcreate** command.

2) newfs -F vxfs -o largefiles /dev/vg07/rlvol1 to build the file systems for all lvols in the volume group.

3) mkdir /u01/dev/oracle/lv_fs_indx1_250 for every directory under which an lvol will be mounted. For seven lvols, for example, seven directories are created.

4) /dev/vg07/lvol1 /u01/dev/oracle/lv_fs_indx1_250 vxfs delaylog 02 in
/etc/fstab for every lvol to be automatically mounted.

5) mount -a to manually mount the file systems that have been created in the
steps.

As you can see, many steps are involved in this process. If you have a
lot of volume groups and a lot of disks in each volume group, automating
some of the steps of the process helps reduce the number of possible errors
immensely. The following sections cover the scripts that automate some of
the steps.

Scripts to Handle pv and vg Work

The following file, shown earlier in this chapter, has a line for every primary
disk:

```
# cat primary_devices
/home/marty/scripts/oracle_primary 01 c7t0d0 c7t0d1 c7t0d2 c7t0d3
/home/marty/scripts/oracle_primary 02 c7t0d4 c7t0d5 c7t0d6 c7t0d7
/home/marty/scripts/oracle_primary 03 c7t1d0 c7t1d1 c7t1d2 c7t1d3
/home/marty/scripts/oracle_primary 04 c7t1d4 c7t1d5 c7t1d6 c7t1d7
/home/marty/scripts/oracle_primary 05 c7t2d0 c7t2d1 c7t2d2 c7t2d3
/home/marty/scripts/oracle_primary 06 c7t2d4 c7t2d5 c7t2d6 c7t2d7
/home/marty/scripts/oracle_primary 07 c7t3d0 c7t3d1 c7t3d2 c7t3d3
```

The first field in each line calls the script that handles the **pv** and **vg**
work for every disk device across the line. The second field is the volume
group number. The remaining fields are the primary disks in the volume
group.

The following listing shows the script that is called in each line of the
primary_devices file:

```
# cat oracle_primary

#/bin/ksh
# oracle_primary
# This script reads in lines (in this specific case 7) that start with a
# volume group number and then have the disk names. A volume group is created
# for each line.
# 1) Get the volume group number in each line (vgnum variable).
# 2) Shift to get the first disk name in the line.
# 3) Run pvcreate for every disk in the line (loop).
# 4) Pause to view what has been run.
# 5) mkdir for the volume group.
# 6) mknod for the volume group.
```

```
# 7) vgcreate for first disk in the vg (other disks in vg included in step9).
# 8) Shift to the second disk.
# 9) vgextend the volume group to include all remaining disks (loop).

# oracle_alternate script creates alternate paths.
# oracle_fstab file has manual commands to create lvols, run newfs, mount lvols,
# and update /etc/fstab.

set -x                            #set tracing on

      vgnum=$1                    #first item in each line is vg number
      shift                       #shift to get first disk of first vg
# pvcreate for primary
      for i in $*                 #run pvcreate for every disk in 1st line

      do
            pvcreate -f /dev/rdsk/$i
      done

      read a                      #pause program to view what has been run


      mkdir /dev/vg$vgnum                      #mkdir for the volume group
      mknod /dev/vg$vgnum/group c 64 0x"$vgnum"0000 #mknod for the volume group
      vgcreate -s 4 -p 128 -g PVG$vgnum /dev/vg$vgnum /dev/dsk/$1 #vgcreate 1st
                                               # disk in volume group

      shift   #shift to the second disk in vg

# vgextend for primary only (note that these are dsk, not rdsk)
      for i in $*    #extend the volume group to include the remaining disks
      do
            vgextend -g PVG$vgnum /dev/vg$vgnum /dev/dsk/$i
      done
```

This script performs all the steps previously listed for the primary devices. I like to set tracing on as well as have the **read** lines in the script so I can view what is taking place and have pauses in the execution of the script where I have to enter a key to proceed.

There are loops for the **pvcreate** commands on all the disks and a loop for **vgextend** because these commands must be performed on all disks.

Keep in mind that this script is called for each line in the **primary_devices** file.

vgextend must be run for all the alternate devices in a volume group. The **alternate_devices** file is shown here:

```
# cat alternate_devices
/home/marty/scripts/oracle_alternate 01 c10t0d0 c10t0d1 c10t0d2 c10t0d3
/home/marty/scripts/oracle_alternate 02 c10t0d4 c10t0d5 c10t0d6 c10t0d7
/home/marty/scripts/oracle_alternate 03 c10t1d0 c10t1d1 c10t1d2 c10t1d3
/home/marty/scripts/oracle_alternate 04 c10t1d4 c10t1d5 c10t1d6 c10t1d7
/home/marty/scripts/oracle_alternate 05 c10t2d0 c10t2d1 c10t2d2 c10t2d3
/home/marty/scripts/oracle_alternate 06 c10t2d4 c10t2d5 c10t2d6 c10t2d7
/home/marty/scripts/oracle_alternate 07 c10t3d0 c10t3d1 c10t3d2 c10t3d3
#
```

This file calls the "alternate" script on each line. The second field in a line is the volume group and the remaining fields are the alternate devices for the volume group.

The following script is called by **alternate_devices**:

```
# cat oracle_alternate
#!/bin/ksh

# This script reads in lines (in this specific case 7) that start with a
# volume group number and then have the disk names. The existing volume group
# is extended to include the alternate path for every disk
# 1) Get the volume group number in each line (vgnum variable).
# 2) Shift to get the first disk name in the line.
# 3) vgextend the volume group to include all remaining disks (loop).

# oracle primary script creates the phys volumes, vg, and primary paths.
# oracle_fstab has commands to create lvols, run newfs, mount lvols, and
# update /etc/fstab.

set -x                          #set tracing on

    vgnum=$1                    #first item in each line is vg number
    shift                       #shift to get first disk of first vg

# vgextend for secondary disks only (note that these are rdsk)
    for i in $*     #extend the volume group to include the remaining disks
    do
            vgextend -g PVG"$vgnum"_ALT /dev/vg$vgnum /dev/dsk/$i
    done
```

This script runs **vgextend** for every alternate device in the volume
group. The results of having run the "primary" and "alternate" scripts are
shown in the following output:

The following listing shows the volume groups and their contents after
this script is run:

```
# strings /etc/lvmtab
/dev/vg00
/dev/dsk/c0t6d0s2
/dev/vg01
/dev/dsk/c7t0d0
/dev/dsk/c7t0d1
/dev/dsk/c7t0d2
/dev/dsk/c7t0d3
/dev/dsk/c10t0d0
/dev/dsk/c10t0d1
/dev/dsk/c10t0d2
/dev/dsk/c10t0d3
/dev/vg02
/dev/dsk/c7t0d4
/dev/dsk/c7t0d5
/dev/dsk/c7t0d6
/dev/dsk/c7t0d7
/dev/dsk/c10t0d4
/dev/dsk/c10t0d5
/dev/dsk/c10t0d6
/dev/dsk/c10t0d7
/dev/vg03
/dev/dsk/c7t1d0
/dev/dsk/c7t1d1
/dev/dsk/c7t1d2
/dev/dsk/c7t1d3
/dev/dsk/c10t1d0
/dev/dsk/c10t1d1
/dev/dsk/c10t1d2
/dev/dsk/c10t1d3
/dev/vg04
/dev/dsk/c7t1d4
/dev/dsk/c7t1d5
```

```
/dev/dsk/c7t1d6
/dev/dsk/c7t1d7
/dev/dsk/c10t1d4
/dev/dsk/c10t1d5
/dev/dsk/c10t1d6
/dev/dsk/c10t1d7
/dev/vg05
/dev/dsk/c7t2d0
/dev/dsk/c7t2d1
/dev/dsk/c7t2d2
/dev/dsk/c7t2d3
/dev/dsk/c10t2d0
/dev/dsk/c10t2d1
/dev/dsk/c10t2d2
/dev/dsk/c10t2d3
/dev/vg06
/dev/dsk/c7t2d4
/dev/dsk/c7t2d5
/dev/dsk/c7t2d6
/dev/dsk/c7t2d7
/dev/dsk/c10t2d4
/dev/dsk/c10t2d5
/dev/dsk/c10t2d6
/dev/dsk/c10t2d7
/dev/vg07
/dev/dsk/c7t3d0
/dev/dsk/c7t3d1
/dev/dsk/c7t3d2
/dev/dsk/c7t3d3
/dev/dsk/c10t3d0
/dev/dsk/c10t3d1
/dev/dsk/c10t3d2
/dev/dsk/c10t3d3
#
```

For each volume group, there are four primary and alternate devices shown that were produced by the scripts.

Although the pv and vg work is done, there are still logical volumes to be created, **newfs** to be run, and mount points to be created and mounted. These steps are covered in the next section.

Command File to Perform Logical Volume-Related Work

The following five steps, shown in an earlier section, are performed for all the seven volume groups:

1) lvcreate -L 250 -n lvol1 -r n -D y -s g /dev/vg07 for each logical volume. The size of the logical volume (in this case 250MB) may vary for each lvol in the volume group.

2) newfs -F vxfs -o largefiles /dev/vg07/rlvol1 to build the file systems for all lvols in the volume group.

3) mkdir /u01/dev/oracle/lv_fs_indx1_250 for every directory under which an lvol will be mounted. For seven lvols, for example, seven directories are created.

4) /dev/vg07/lvol1 /u01/dev/oracle/lv_fs_indx1_250 vxfs delaylog 02 in **/etc/fstab** for every lvol to be automatically mounted.

5) mount -a to manually mount the filesystems that have been created in the steps.

In this section's example with seven volume groups, there are different logical volumes and sizes in all seven of the groups. This means that minimal automation can be employed so I created a command file that has the commands in it for all seven volume groups but doesn't have any loops or efficient automation in it. The following command file contains the lines to be executed for each of the seven volume groups:

```
# cat oracle_fstab_full
#!/bin/ksh
set -x

# This file contains manual commands to create logical volumes, run newfs,
# mount logical volumes, and update /etc/fstab based on scripts
# oracle_primary and oracle_alternate that created oracle DB file systems.
# 1) Manually create each logical volume in the vg since they're unique.
# 2) Manually run newfs on each logical volume
# 3) Manually mount each logical volume.
# 4) Manaully update fstab to include each logical volume

#  vg01 logical volumes, newfs, mount, and mkdir
#       lvcreate -L 400 -n lvol1 -r n -D y -s g /dev/vg01
#       lvcreate -L 100 -n lvol2 -r n -D y -s g /dev/vg01
#       lvcreate -L 110 -n lvol3 -r n -D y -s g /dev/vg01
# Run newfs on all new logical volumes in vg01
#       newfs -F vxfs -o largefiles /dev/vg01/rlvol1
#       newfs -F vxfs -o largefiles /dev/vg01/rlvol2
#       newfs -F vxfs -o largefiles /dev/vg01/rlvol3
# mkdir all in /u01/dev/oracle
#       mkdir /u01/dev/oracle/lv_fs_system_400
#       mkdir /u01/dev/oracle/lv_fs_temp_100
#       mkdir /u01/dev/oracle/lv_fs_ctl1_110
# fstab entry for all in vg01
#       print "/dev/vg01/lvol1 /u01/dev/oracle/lv_fs_system_400 vxfs delaylog 0
2" >> /etc/fstab
#       print "/dev/vg01/lvol2 /u01/dev/oracle/lv_fs_temp_100 vxfs delaylog 0 2"
 >> /etc/fstab
#       print "/dev/vg01/lvol3 /u01/dev/oracle/lv_fs_ctl1_110 vxfs delaylog 0 2"
 >> /etc/fstab
#mount -a

#  vg02 logical volumes, newfs, mount, and mkdir
#       lvcreate -L 500 -n lvol1 -r n -D y -s g /dev/vg02
#       lvcreate -L 110 -n lvol2 -r n -D y -s g /dev/vg02
# Run newfs on all new logical volumes in volume group
#       newfs -F vxfs -o largefiles /dev/vg02/rlvol1
#       newfs -F vxfs -o largefiles /dev/vg02/rlvol2
# mkdir all in volume group
#       mkdir /u01/dev/oracle/lv_fs_undo_500
#       mkdir /u01/dev/oracle/lv_fs_ctl2_110
# fstab entry for all in vg01
```

```
#       print "/dev/vg02/lvol1 /u01/dev/oracle/lv_fs_undo_500 vxfs delaylog 0 2"
>> /etc/fstab
#       print "/dev/vg02/lvol2 /u01/dev/oracle/lv_fs_ctl2_110 vxfs delaylog 0 2"
>> /etc/fstab
#mount -a

#  vg03 logical volumes, newfs, mount, and mkdir
#       lvcreate -L 120 -n lvol1 -r n -D y -s g /dev/vg03
#       lvcreate -L 120 -n lvol2 -r n -D y -s g /dev/vg03
#       lvcreate -L 120 -n lvol3 -r n -D y -s g /dev/vg03
# Run newfs on all new logical volumes in volume group
#       newfs -F vxfs -o largefiles /dev/vg03/rlvol1
#       newfs -F vxfs -o largefiles /dev/vg03/rlvol2
#       newfs -F vxfs -o largefiles /dev/vg03/rlvol3
# mkdir all in volume group
#       mkdir /u01/dev/oracle/lv_fs_logA1_120
#       mkdir /u01/dev/oracle/lv_fs_logA2_120
#       mkdir /u01/dev/oracle/lv_fs_logA3_120
# fstab entry for all in vg01
#       print "/dev/vg03/lvol1 /u01/dev/oracle/lv_fs_logA1_120 vxfs delaylog 0 2
" >> /etc/fstab
#       print "/dev/vg03/lvol2 /u01/dev/oracle/lv_fs_logA2_120 vxfs delaylog 0 2
" >> /etc/fstab
#       print "/dev/vg03/lvol3 /u01/dev/oracle/lv_fs_logA3_120 vxfs delaylog 0 2
" >> /etc/fstab
#mount -a

#  vg04 logical volumes, newfs, mount, and mkdir
#       lvcreate -L 120 -n lvol1 -r n -D y -s g /dev/vg04
#       lvcreate -L 120 -n lvol2 -r n -D y -s g /dev/vg04
#       lvcreate -L 120 -n lvol3 -r n -D y -s g /dev/vg04
# Run newfs on all new logical volumes in volume group
#       newfs -F vxfs -o largefiles /dev/vg04/rlvol1
#       newfs -F vxfs -o largefiles /dev/vg04/rlvol2
#       newfs -F vxfs -o largefiles /dev/vg04/rlvol3
# mkdir all in volume group
#       mkdir /u01/dev/oracle/lv_fs_logB1_120
#       mkdir /u01/dev/oracle/lv_fs_logB2_120
#       mkdir /u01/dev/oracle/lv_fs_logB3_120
# fstab entry for all in vg01
#       print "/dev/vg04/lvol1 /u01/dev/oracle/lv_fs_logB1_120 vxfs delaylog 0 2
" >> /etc/fstab
#       print "/dev/vg04/lvol2 /u01/dev/oracle/lv_fs_logB2_120 vxfs delaylog 0 2
" >> /etc/fstab
#       print "/dev/vg04/lvol3 /u01/dev/oracle/lv_fs_logB3_120 vxfs delaylog 0 2
" >> /etc/fstab
#mount -a

#  vg05 logical volumes, newfs, mount, and mkdir
#       lvcreate -L 250 -n lvol1 -r n -D y -s g /dev/vg05
#       lvcreate -L 250 -n lvol2 -r n -D y -s g /dev/vg05
#       lvcreate -L 250 -n lvol3 -r n -D y -s g /dev/vg05
#       lvcreate -L 250 -n lvol4 -r n -D y -s g /dev/vg05
#       lvcreate -L 250 -n lvol5 -r n -D y -s g /dev/vg05
#       lvcreate -L 250 -n lvol6 -r n -D y -s g /dev/vg05
#       lvcreate -L 250 -n lvol7 -r n -D y -s g /dev/vg05
#       lvcreate -L 250 -n lvol8 -r n -D y -s g /dev/vg05
# Run newfs on all new logical volumes in volume group
#       newfs -F vxfs -o largefiles /dev/vg05/rlvol1
#       newfs -F vxfs -o largefiles /dev/vg05/rlvol2
#       newfs -F vxfs -o largefiles /dev/vg05/rlvol3
#       newfs -F vxfs -o largefiles /dev/vg05/rlvol4
#       newfs -F vxfs -o largefiles /dev/vg05/rlvol5
#       newfs -F vxfs -o largefiles /dev/vg05/rlvol6
#       newfs -F vxfs -o largefiles /dev/vg05/rlvol7
#       newfs -F vxfs -o largefiles /dev/vg05/rlvol8
# mkdir all in volume group
#       mkdir /u01/dev/oracle/lv_fs_users_data1_250
#       mkdir /u01/dev/oracle/lv_fs_users_data2_250
#       mkdir /u01/dev/oracle/lv_fs_users_data3_250
#       mkdir /u01/dev/oracle/lv_fs_users_data4_250
#       mkdir /u01/dev/oracle/lv_fs_users_data5_250
#       mkdir /u01/dev/oracle/lv_fs_users_data6_250
#       mkdir /u01/dev/oracle/lv_fs_users_data7_250
#       mkdir /u01/dev/oracle/lv_fs_users_data8_250
```

```
# fstab entry for all in vg01
#     print "/dev/vg05/lvol1 /u01/dev/oracle/lv_fs_users_data1_250 vxfs
          delaylog 0 2" >> /etc/fstab
#     print "/dev/vg05/lvol2 /u01/dev/oracle/lv_fs_users_data2_250 vxfs
          delaylog 0 2" >> /etc/fstab
#     print "/dev/vg05/lvol3 /u01/dev/oracle/lv_fs_users_data3_250 vxfs
          delaylog 0 2" >> /etc/fstab
#     print "/dev/vg05/lvol4 /u01/dev/oracle/lv_fs_users_data4_250 vxfs
          delaylog 0 2" >> /etc/fstab
#     print "/dev/vg05/lvol5 /u01/dev/oracle/lv_fs_users_data5_250 vxfs
          delaylog 0 2" >> /etc/fstab
#     print "/dev/vg05/lvol6 /u01/dev/oracle/lv_fs_users_data6_250 vxfs
          delaylog 0 2" >> /etc/fstab
#     print "/dev/vg05/lvol7 /u01/dev/oracle/lv_fs_users_data7_250 vxfs
          delaylog 0 2" >> /etc/fstab
#     print "/dev/vg05/lvol8 /u01/dev/oracle/lv_fs_users_data8_250 vxfs
          delaylog 0 2" >> /etc/fstab
#mount -a

#  vg06 logical volumes, newfs, mount, and mkdir
#       lvcreate -L 250 -n lvol1 -r n -D y -s g /dev/vg06
#       lvcreate -L 250 -n lvol2 -r n -D y -s g /dev/vg06
#       lvcreate -L 250 -n lvol3 -r n -D y -s g /dev/vg06
#       lvcreate -L 250 -n lvol4 -r n -D y -s g /dev/vg06
#       lvcreate -L 250 -n lvol5 -r n -D y -s g /dev/vg06
#       lvcreate -L 250 -n lvol6 -r n -D y -s g /dev/vg06
#       lvcreate -L 250 -n lvol7 -r n -D y -s g /dev/vg06
#       lvcreate -L 250 -n lvol8 -r n -D y -s g /dev/vg06
# Run newfs on all new logical volumes in volume group
#       newfs -F vxfs -o largefiles /dev/vg06/rlvol1
#       newfs -F vxfs -o largefiles /dev/vg06/rlvol2
#       newfs -F vxfs -o largefiles /dev/vg06/rlvol3
#       newfs -F vxfs -o largefiles /dev/vg06/rlvol4
#       newfs -F vxfs -o largefiles /dev/vg06/rlvol5
#       newfs -F vxfs -o largefiles /dev/vg06/rlvol6
#       newfs -F vxfs -o largefiles /dev/vg06/rlvol7
#       newfs -F vxfs -o largefiles /dev/vg06/rlvol8
# mkdir all in volume group
#       mkdir /u01/dev/oracle/lv_fs_data1_250
#       mkdir /u01/dev/oracle/lv_fs_data2_250
#       mkdir /u01/dev/oracle/lv_fs_data3_250
#       mkdir /u01/dev/oracle/lv_fs_data4_250
#       mkdir /u01/dev/oracle/lv_fs_data5_250
#       mkdir /u01/dev/oracle/lv_fs_data6_250
#       mkdir /u01/dev/oracle/lv_fs_data7_250
#       mkdir /u01/dev/oracle/lv_fs_data8_250
# fstab entry for all in vg06
#       print "/dev/vg06/lvol1 /u01/dev/oracle/lv_fs_data1_250 vxfs delaylog 0 2
" >> /etc/fstab
#       print "/dev/vg06/lvol2 /u01/dev/oracle/lv_fs_data2_250 vxfs delaylog 0 2
" >> /etc/fstab
#       print "/dev/vg06/lvol3 /u01/dev/oracle/lv_fs_data3_250 vxfs delaylog 0 2
" >> /etc/fstab
#       print "/dev/vg06/lvol4 /u01/dev/oracle/lv_fs_data4_250 vxfs delaylog 0 2
" >> /etc/fstab
#       print "/dev/vg06/lvol5 /u01/dev/oracle/lv_fs_data5_250 vxfs delaylog 0 2
" >> /etc/fstab
#       print "/dev/vg06/lvol6 /u01/dev/oracle/lv_fs_data6_250 vxfs delaylog 0 2
" >> /etc/fstab
#       print "/dev/vg06/lvol7 /u01/dev/oracle/lv_fs_data7_250 vxfs delaylog 0 2
" >> /etc/fstab
#       print "/dev/vg06/lvol8 /u01/dev/oracle/lv_fs_data8_250 vxfs delaylog 0 2
" >> /etc/fstab
#mount -a

#  vg07 logical volumes, newfs, mount, and mkdir
        lvcreate -L 250 -n lvol1 -r n -D y -s g /dev/vg07
        lvcreate -L 250
 -n lvol2 -r n -D y -s g /dev/vg07
        lvcreate -L 250 -n lvol3 -r n -D y -s g /dev/vg07
        lvcreate -L 250 -n lvol4 -r n -D y -s g /dev/vg07
        lvcreate -L 250 -n lvol5 -r n -D y -s g /dev/vg07
        lvcreate -L 250 -n lvol6 -r n -D y -s g /dev/vg07
        lvcreate -L 250 -n lvol7 -r n -D y -s g /dev/vg07
        lvcreate -L 250 -n lvol8 -r n -D y -s g /dev/vg07
```

```
# Run newfs on all new logical volumes in volume group
        newfs -F vxfs -o largefiles /dev/vg07/rlvol1
        newfs -F vxfs -o largefiles /dev/vg07/rlvol2
        newfs -F vxfs -o largefiles /dev/vg07/rlvol3
        newfs -F vxfs -o largefiles /dev/vg07/rlvol4
        newfs -F vxfs -o largefiles /dev/vg07/rlvol5
        newfs -F vxfs -o largefiles /dev/vg07/rlvol6
        newfs -F vxfs -o largefiles /dev/vg07/rlvol7
        newfs -F vxfs -o largefiles /dev/vg07/rlvol8
# mkdir all in volume group
        mkdir /u01/dev/oracle/lv_fs_indx1_250
        mkdir /u01/dev/oracle/lv_fs_indx2_250
        mkdir /u01/dev/oracle/lv_fs_indx3_250
        mkdir /u01/dev/oracle/lv_fs_indx4_250
        mkdir /u01/dev/oracle/lv_fs_indx5_250
        mkdir /u01/dev/oracle/lv_fs_indx6_250
        mkdir /u01/dev/oracle/lv_fs_indx7_250
        mkdir /u01/dev/oracle/lv_fs_indx8_250
# fstab entry for all in vg07
        print "/dev/vg07/lvol1 /u01/dev/oracle/lv_fs_indx1_250 vxfs delaylog 0 2
" >> /etc/fstab
        print "/dev/vg07/lvol2 /u01/dev/oracle/lv_fs_indx2_250 vxfs delaylog 0 2
" >> /etc/fstab
        print "/dev/vg07/lvol3 /u01/dev/oracle/lv_fs_indx3_250 vxfs delaylog 0 2
" >> /etc/fstab
        print "/dev/vg07/lvol4 /u01/dev/oracle/lv_fs_indx4_250 vxfs delaylog 0 2
" >> /etc/fstab
        print "/dev/vg07/lvol5 /u01/dev/oracle/lv_fs_indx5_250 vxfs delaylog 0 2
" >> /etc/fstab
        print "/dev/vg07/lvol6 /u01/dev/oracle/lv_fs_indx6_250 vxfs delaylog 0 2
" >> /etc/fstab
        print "/dev/vg07/lvol7 /u01/dev/oracle/lv_fs_indx7_250 vxfs delaylog 0 2
" >> /etc/fstab
        print "/dev/vg07/lvol8 /u01/dev/oracle/lv_fs_indx8_250 vxfs delaylog 0 2
" >> /etc/fstab
mount -a
```

This command file has seven sections, one for every volume group, that I execute one at a time. In the example the first six volume groups are commented and only the last volume group is uncommented. When I run this command file-only the uncommented section is executed.

Although this is a long command file the five logical volume-related commands shown earlier are executed.

When this command file is run for only the last volume group (07), the following detailed output is produced because I set tracing on in the command file:

```
# ./oracle_fstab_full
+ lvcreate -L 250 -n lvol1 -r n -D y -s g /dev/vg07
Warning: rounding up logical volume size to extent boundary at size "252" MB.
Logical volume "/dev/vg07/lvol1" has been successfully created with
character device "/dev/vg07/rlvol1".
Logical volume "/dev/vg07/lvol1" has been successfully extended.
Volume Group configuration for /dev/vg07 has been saved in /etc/lvmconf/vg07.conf
+ lvcreate -L 250 -n lvol2 -r n -D y -s g /dev/vg07
Warning: rounding up logical volume size to extent boundary at size "252" MB.
Logical volume "/dev/vg07/lvol2" has been successfully created with
character device "/dev/vg07/rlvol2".
Logical volume "/dev/vg07/lvol2" has been successfully extended.
Volume Group configuration for /dev/vg07 has been saved in /etc/lvmconf/vg07.conf
+ lvcreate -L 250 -n lvol3 -r n -D y -s g /dev/vg07
Warning: rounding up logical volume size to extent boundary at size "252" MB.
Logical volume "/dev/vg07/lvol3" has been successfully created with
```

```
character device "/dev/vg07/rlvol3".
Logical volume "/dev/vg07/lvol3" has been successfully extended.
Volume Group configuration for /dev/vg07 has been saved in /etc/lvmconf/vg07.conf
+ lvcreate -L 250 -n lvol4 -r n -D y -s g /dev/vg07
Warning: rounding up logical volume size to extent boundary at size "252" MB.
Logical volume "/dev/vg07/lvol4" has been successfully created with
character device "/dev/vg07/rlvol4".
Logical volume "/dev/vg07/lvol4" has been successfully extended.
Volume Group configuration for /dev/vg07 has been saved in /etc/lvmconf/vg07.conf
+ lvcreate -L 250 -n lvol5 -r n -D y -s g /dev/vg07
Warning: rounding up logical volume size to extent boundary at size "252" MB.
Logical volume "/dev/vg07/lvol5" has been successfully created with
character device "/dev/vg07/rlvol5".
Logical volume "/dev/vg07/lvol5" has been successfully extended.
Volume Group configuration for /dev/vg07 has been saved in /etc/lvmconf/vg07.conf
+ lvcreate -L 250 -n lvol6 -r n -D y -s g /dev/vg07
Warning: rounding up logical volume size to extent boundary at size "252" MB.
Logical volume "/dev/vg07/lvol6" has been successfully created with
character device "/dev/vg07/rlvol6".
Logical volume "/dev/vg07/lvol6" has been successfully extended.
Volume Group configuration for /dev/vg07 has been saved in /etc/lvmconf/vg07.conf
+ lvcreate -L 250 -n lvol7 -r n -D y -s g /dev/vg07
Warning: rounding up logical volume size to extent boundary at size "252" MB.
Logical volume "/dev/vg07/lvol7" has been successfully created with
character device "/dev/vg07/rlvol7".
Logical volume "/dev/vg07/lvol7" has been successfully extended.
Volume Group configuration for /dev/vg07 has been saved in /etc/lvmconf/vg07.conf
+ lvcreate -L 250 -n lvol8 -r n -D y -s g /dev/vg07
Warning: rounding up logical volume size to extent boundary at size "252" MB.
Logical volume "/dev/vg07/lvol8" has been successfully created with
character device "/dev/vg07/rlvol8".
Logical volume "/dev/vg07/lvol8" has been successfully extended.
Volume Group configuration for /dev/vg07 has been saved in /etc/lvmconf/vg07.conf
+ newfs -F vxfs -o largefiles /dev/vg07/rlvol1
    version 5 layout
    258048 sectors, 258048 blocks of size 1024, log size 1024 blocks
    unlimited inodes, largefiles supported
    258048 data blocks, 256896 free data blocks
    8 allocation units of 32768 blocks, 32768 data blocks
    last allocation unit has 28672 data blocks
+ newfs -F vxfs -o largefiles /dev/vg07/rlvol2
    version 5 layout
    258048 sectors, 258048 blocks of size 1024, log size 1024 blocks
    unlimited inodes, largefiles supported
    258048 data blocks, 256896 free data blocks
    8 allocation units of 32768 blocks, 32768 data blocks
    last allocation unit has 28672 data blocks
+ newfs -F vxfs -o largefiles /dev/vg07/rlvol3
    version 5 layout
    258048 sectors, 258048 blocks of size 1024, log size 1024 blocks
    unlimited inodes, largefiles supported
    258048 data blocks, 256896 free data blocks
    8 allocation units of 32768 blocks, 32768 data blocks
    last allocation unit has 28672 data blocks
+ newfs -F vxfs -o largefiles /dev/vg07/rlvol4
    version 5 layout
    258048 sectors, 258048 blocks of size 1024, log size 1024 blocks
    unlimited inodes, largefiles supported
    258048 data blocks, 256896 free data blocks
    8 allocation units of 32768 blocks, 32768 data blocks
    last allocation unit has 28672 data blocks
+ newfs -F vxfs -o largefiles /dev/vg07/rlvol5
    version 5 layout
    258048 sectors, 258048 blocks of size 1024, log size 1024 blocks
    unlimited inodes, largefiles supported
    258048 data blocks, 256896 free data blocks
    8 allocation units of 32768 blocks, 32768 data blocks
    last allocation unit has 28672 data blocks
+ newfs -F vxfs -o largefiles /dev/vg07/rlvol6
    version 5 layout
    258048 sectors, 258048 blocks of size 1024, log size 1024 blocks
    unlimited inodes, largefiles supported
    258048 data blocks, 256896 free data blocks
    8 allocation units of 32768 blocks, 32768 data blocks
    last allocation unit has 28672 data blocks
```

```
+ newfs -F vxfs -o largefiles /dev/vg07/rlvol7
    version 5 layout
    258048 sectors, 258048 blocks of size 1024, log size 1024 blocks
    unlimited inodes, largefiles supported
    258048 data blocks, 256896 free data blocks
    8 allocation units of 32768 blocks, 32768 data blocks
    last allocation unit has 28672 data blocks
+ newfs -F vxfs -o largefiles /dev/vg07/rlvol8
    version 5 layout
    258048 sectors, 258048 blocks of size 1024, log size 1024 blocks
    unlimited inodes, largefiles supported
    258048 data blocks, 256896 free data blocks
    8 allocation units of 32768 blocks, 32768 data blocks
    last allocation unit has 28672 data blocks
+ mkdir /u01/dev/oracle/lv_fs_indx1_250
+ mkdir /u01/dev/oracle/lv_fs_indx2_250
+ mkdir /u01/dev/oracle/lv_fs_indx3_250
+ mkdir /u01/dev/oracle/lv_fs_indx4_250
+ mkdir /u01/dev/oracle/lv_fs_indx5_250
+ mkdir /u01/dev/oracle/lv_fs_indx6_250
+ mkdir /u01/dev/oracle/lv_fs_indx7_250
+ mkdir /u01/dev/oracle/lv_fs_indx8_250
+ print /dev/vg07/lvol1 /u01/dev/oracle/lv_fs_indx1_250 vxfs delaylog 0 2
+ 1>> /etc/fstab
+ print /dev/vg07/lvol2 /u01/dev/oracle/lv_fs_indx2_250 vxfs delaylog 0 2
+ 1>> /etc/fstab
+ print /dev/vg07/lvol3 /u01/dev/oracle/lv_fs_indx3_250 vxfs delaylog 0 2
+ 1>> /etc/fstab
+ print /dev/vg07/lvol4 /u01/dev/oracle/lv_fs_indx4_250 vxfs delaylog 0 2
+ 1>> /etc/fstab
+ print /dev/vg07/lvol5 /u01/dev/oracle/lv_fs_indx5_250 vxfs delaylog 0 2
+ 1>> /etc/fstab
+ print /dev/vg07/lvol6 /u01/dev/oracle/lv_fs_indx6_250 vxfs delaylog 0 2
+ 1>> /etc/fstab
+ print /dev/vg07/lvol7 /u01/dev/oracle/lv_fs_indx7_250 vxfs delaylog 0 2
+ 1>> /etc/fstab
+ print /dev/vg07/lvol8 /u01/dev/oracle/lv_fs_indx8_250 vxfs delaylog 0 2
+ 1>> /etc/fstab
+ mount -a
```

Although much output is produced for volume group 07 because tracing is on, you get to see all the commands that were executed. As a result of
having executed the commands for all the seven volume groups (one at a
time), I have all of the logical volumes mounted for all seven volume groups,
as shown in the following listing:

```
# bdf
Filesystem          kbytes     used    avail %used Mounted on
/dev/vg00/lvol3     524288   209944   311896   40% /
/dev/vg00/lvol1     311296   100936   208768   33% /stand
/dev/vg00/lvol8    4718592  3758776   952384   80% /var
/dev/vg00/lvol7    2703360  2078816   619680   77% /usr
/dev/vg00/lvol4     212992    10224   201248    5% /tmp
/dev/vg00/lvol6    3194880  2026808  1158976   64% /opt
/dev/vg00/lvol5      32768     8432    24160   26% /home
/dev/vg01/lvol2     102400     1141    94938    1% /u01/dev/oracle/lv_fs_temp_100
/dev/vg01/lvol1     409600     1213   382870    0% /u01/dev/oracle/lv_fs_system_40
0
/dev/vg01/lvol3     114688     1141   106458    1% /u01/dev/oracle/lv_fs_ctl1_110
/dev/vg02/lvol2     114688     1141   106458    1% /u01/dev/oracle/lv_fs_ctl2_110
/dev/vg02/lvol1     512000     1237   478848    0% /u01/dev/oracle/lv_fs_undo_500
/dev/vg03/lvol3     122880     1141   114138    1% /u01/dev/oracle/lv_fs_logA3_120

/dev/vg03/lvol2     122880     1141   114138    1% /u01/dev/oracle/lv_fs_logA2_120

/dev/vg03/lvol1     122880     1141   114138    1% /u01/dev/oracle/lv_fs_logA1_120

/dev/vg04/lvol3     122880     1141   114138    1% /u01/dev/oracle/lv_fs_logB3_120
```

```
/dev/vg04/lvol2      122880    1141   114138     1% /u01/dev/oracle/lv_fs_logB2_120

/dev/vg04/lvol1      122880    1141   114138     1% /u01/dev/oracle/lv_fs_logB1_120

/dev/vg05/lvol8      258048    1173   240828     0% /u01/dev/oracle/lv_fs_users_
                                                    data8_250
/dev/vg05/lvol7      258048    1173   240828     0% /u01/dev/oracle/lv_fs_users_
                                                    data7_250
/dev/vg05/lvol6      258048    1173   240828     0% /u01/dev/oracle/lv_fs_users_
                                                    data6_250
/dev/vg05/lvol5      258048    1173   240828     0% /u01/dev/oracle/lv_fs_users_
                                                    data5_250
/dev/vg05/lvol4      258048    1173   240828     0% /u01/dev/oracle/lv_fs_users_
                                                    data4_250
/dev/vg05/lvol3      258048    1173   240828     0% /u01/dev/oracle/lv_fs_users_
                                                    data3_250
/dev/vg05/lvol2      258048    1173   240828     0% /u01/dev/oracle/lv_fs_users_
                                                    data2_250
/dev/vg05/lvol1      258048    1173   240828     0% /u01/dev/oracle/lv_fs_users_
                                                    data1_250
/dev/vg06/lvol8      258048    1173   240828     0% /u01/dev/oracle/lv_fs_data8_250

/dev/vg06/lvol7      258048    1173   240828     0% /u01/dev/oracle/lv_fs_data7_250

/dev/vg06/lvol6      258048    1173   240828     0% /u01/dev/oracle/lv_fs_data6_250

/dev/vg06/lvol5      258048    1173   240828     0% /u01/dev/oracle/lv_fs_data5_250

/dev/vg06/lvol4      258048    1173   240828     0% /u01/dev/oracle/lv_fs_data4_250

/dev/vg06/lvol3      258048    1173   240828     0% /u01/dev/oracle/lv_fs_data3_250

/dev/vg06/lvol2      258048    1173   240828     0% /u01/dev/oracle/lv_fs_data2_250

/dev/vg06/lvol1      258048    1173   240828     0% /u01/dev/oracle/lv_fs_data1_250

/dev/vg07/lvol8      258048    1173   240828     0% /u01/dev/oracle/lv_fs_indx8_250

/dev/vg07/lvol7      258048    1173   240828     0% /u01/dev/oracle/lv_fs_indx7_250

/dev/vg07/lvol6      258048    1173   240828     0% /u01/dev/oracle/lv_fs_indx6_250

/dev/vg07/lvol5      258048    1173   240828     0% /u01/dev/oracle/lv_fs_indx5_250

/dev/vg07/lvol4      258048    1173   240828     0% /u01/dev/oracle/lv_fs_indx4_250

/dev/vg07/lvol3      258048    1173   240828     0% /u01/dev/oracle/lv_fs_indx3_250

/dev/vg07/lvol2      258048    1173   240828     0% /u01/dev/oracle/lv_fs_indx2_250

/dev/vg07/lvol1      258048    1173   240828     0% /u01/dev/oracle/lv_fs_indx1_250
```

All the entries are in **/etc/fstab** so that the logical volumes will be mounted every time the system is rebooted, as shown in the following listing:

```
# cat /etc/fstab
# System /etc/fstab file.  Static information about the file systems
# See fstab(4) and sam(1M) for further details on configuring devices.
/dev/vg00/lvol3 / vxfs delaylog 0 1
/dev/vg00/lvol1 /stand vxfs tranflush 0 1
/dev/vg00/lvol4 /tmp vxfs delaylog 0 2
/dev/vg00/lvol5 /home vxfs delaylog 0 2
/dev/vg00/lvol6 /opt vxfs delaylog 0 2
/dev/vg00/lvol7 /usr vxfs delaylog 0 2
/dev/vg00/lvol8 /var vxfs delaylog 0 2
/dev/vg01/lvol1 /u01/dev/oracle/lv_fs_system_400 vxfs delaylog 0 2
/dev/vg01/lvol2 /u01/dev/oracle/lv_fs_temp_100 vxfs delaylog 0 2
```

```
/dev/vg01/lvol3 /u01/dev/oracle/lv_fs_ctl1_110 vxfs delaylog 0 2
/dev/vg02/lvol1 /u01/dev/oracle/lv_fs_undo_500 vxfs delaylog 0 2
/dev/vg02/lvol2 /u01/dev/oracle/lv_fs_ctl2_110 vxfs delaylog 0 2
/dev/vg03/lvol1 /u01/dev/oracle/lv_fs_logA1_120 vxfs delaylog 0 2
/dev/vg03/lvol2 /u01/dev/oracle/lv_fs_logA2_120 vxfs delaylog 0 2
/dev/vg03/lvol3 /u01/dev/oracle/lv_fs_logA3_120 vxfs delaylog 0 2
/dev/vg04/lvol1 /u01/dev/oracle/lv_fs_logB1_120 vxfs delaylog 0 2
/dev/vg04/lvol2 /u01/dev/oracle/lv_fs_logB2_120 vxfs delaylog 0 2
/dev/vg04/lvol3 /u01/dev/oracle/lv_fs_logB3_120 vxfs delaylog 0 2
/dev/vg05/lvol1 /u01/dev/oracle/lv_fs_users_data1_250 vxfs delaylog 0 2
/dev/vg05/lvol2 /u01/dev/oracle/lv_fs_users_data2_250 vxfs delaylog 0 2
/dev/vg05/lvol3 /u01/dev/oracle/lv_fs_users_data3_250 vxfs delaylog 0 2
/dev/vg05/lvol4 /u01/dev/oracle/lv_fs_users_data4_250 vxfs delaylog 0 2
/dev/vg05/lvol5 /u01/dev/oracle/lv_fs_users_data5_250 vxfs delaylog 0 2
/dev/vg05/lvol6 /u01/dev/oracle/lv_fs_users_data6_250 vxfs delaylog 0 2
/dev/vg05/lvol7 /u01/dev/oracle/lv_fs_users_data7_250 vxfs delaylog 0 2
/dev/vg05/lvol8 /u01/dev/oracle/lv_fs_users_data8_250 vxfs delaylog 0 2
/dev/vg06/lvol1 /u01/dev/oracle/lv_fs_data1_250 vxfs delaylog 0 2
/dev/vg06/lvol2 /u01/dev/oracle/lv_fs_data2_250 vxfs delaylog 0 2
/dev/vg06/lvol3 /u01/dev/oracle/lv_fs_data3_250 vxfs delaylog 0 2
/dev/vg06/lvol4 /u01/dev/oracle/lv_fs_data4_250 vxfs delaylog 0 2
/dev/vg06/lvol5 /u01/dev/oracle/lv_fs_data5_250 vxfs delaylog 0 2
/dev/vg06/lvol6 /u01/dev/oracle/lv_fs_data6_250 vxfs delaylog 0 2
/dev/vg06/lvol7 /u01/dev/oracle/lv_fs_data7_250 vxfs delaylog 0 2
/dev/vg06/lvol8 /u01/dev/oracle/lv_fs_data8_250 vxfs delaylog 0 2
/dev/vg07/lvol1 /u01/dev/oracle/lv_fs_indx1_250 vxfs delaylog 0 2
/dev/vg07/lvol2 /u01/dev/oracle/lv_fs_indx2_250 vxfs delaylog 0 2
/dev/vg07/lvol3 /u01/dev/oracle/lv_fs_indx3_250 vxfs delaylog 0 2
/dev/vg07/lvol4 /u01/dev/oracle/lv_fs_indx4_250 vxfs delaylog 0 2
/dev/vg07/lvol5 /u01/dev/oracle/lv_fs_indx5_250 vxfs delaylog 0 2
/dev/vg07/lvol6 /u01/dev/oracle/lv_fs_indx6_250 vxfs delaylog 0 2
/dev/vg07/lvol7 /u01/dev/oracle/lv_fs_indx7_250 vxfs delaylog 0 2
/dev/vg07/lvol8 /u01/dev/oracle/lv_fs_indx8_250 vxfs delaylog 0 2
#
```

If you must go back and change the size of a logical volume, you can determine what users and processes are using a directory with the **fuser** command.

An additional command that I like to run after executing the commands for each of the volume groups is a **vgdisplay -v**, as shown for **vg01** in the following listing:

```
# vgdisplay -v /dev/vg01
--- Volume groups ---
VG Name                    /dev/vg01
VG Write Access            read/write
VG Status                  available
Max LV                     255
Cur LV                     8
Open LV                    7
Max PV                     128
Cur PV                     4
Act PV                     4
Max PE per PV              3473
VGDA                       8
PE Size (Mbytes)           4
Total PE                   13884
Alloc PE                   359
Free PE                    13525
Total PVG                  2
Total Spare PVs            0
Total Spare PVs in use     0

   --- Logical volumes ---
   LV Name                 /dev/vg01/lv_fs_temp
   LV Status               available/syncd
   LV Size (Mbytes)        100
   Current LE              25
```

```
Allocated PE              25
Used PV                   4

LV Name                   /dev/vg01/lvol1
LV Status                 available/syncd
LV Size (Mbytes)          400
Current LE                100
Allocated PE              100
Used PV                   4

LV Name                   /dev/vg01/lv_fs_system_400
LV Status                 available/syncd
LV Size (Mbytes)          400
Current LE                100
Allocated PE              100
Used PV                   4

LV Name                   /dev/vg01/lv_fs_temp_100
LV Status                 available/syncd
LV Size (Mbytes)          100
Current LE                25
Allocated PE              25
Used PV                   4

LV Name                   /dev/vg01/lv_fs_ctl1_110
LV Status                 available/syncd
LV Size (Mbytes)          112
Current LE                28
Allocated PE              28
Used PV                   4

LV Name                   /dev/vg01/lvol2
LV Status                 available/syncd
LV Size (Mbytes)          100
Current LE                25
Allocated PE              25
Used PV                   4

LV Name                   /dev/vg01/lvol3
LV Status                 available/syncd
LV Size (Mbytes)          112
Current LE                28
Allocated PE              28
Used PV                   4


--- Physical volumes ---
PV Name                   /dev/dsk/c7t0d0
PV Name                   /dev/dsk/c10t0d0 Alternate Link
PV Status                 available
Total PE                  3471
Free PE                   3379
Autoswitch                On

PV Name                   /dev/dsk/c7t0d1
PV Name                   /dev/dsk/c10t0d1 Alternate Link
PV Status                 available
Total PE                  3471
Free PE                   3382
Autoswitch                On

PV Name                   /dev/dsk/c7t0d2
PV Name                   /dev/dsk/c10t0d2 Alternate Link
PV Status                 available
Total PE                  3471
Free PE                   3382
Autoswitch                On

PV Name                   /dev/dsk/c7t0d3
PV Name                   /dev/dsk/c10t0d3 Alternate Link
PV Status                 available
Total PE                  3471
Free PE                   3382
Autoswitch                On
```

```
--- Physical volume groups ---
PVG Name                           PVG01
PV Name                            /dev/dsk/c7t0d0
PV Name                            /dev/dsk/c7t0d1
PV Name                            /dev/dsk/c7t0d2
PV Name                            /dev/dsk/c7t0d3

PVG Name                           PVG01_ALT
PV Name                            /dev/dsk/c10t0d0
PV Name                            /dev/dsk/c10t0d1
PV Name                            /dev/dsk/c10t0d2
PV Name                            /dev/dsk/c10t0d3
```

At the end of this listing is information on both the primary and alternate disk paths. The very end of the listing shows the *PVG Name* of *PVG01_ALT* that I specified in the "alternate" script run earlier.

Commonly Used LVM Procedures

The best way to learn how to use LVM commands is to evaluate some commonly used procedures. System administrators tend to be careful before running any intrusive. (There is a chance something LVM-related will be changed.) Always back up your system and create a bootable recovery tape with Ignite-UX before you run any intrusive LVM commands. The following are some procedures for tasks I have encountered on a regular basis. Please modify them to suit your needs. Don't run the commands as shown. You need to prepare your system, substitute the names of your volumes, and perform additional steps. These commands, however, serve as good examples for ways in which the tasks shown can be performed.

The first task we perform is to mirror the root disk to a second disk. This is one of the most commonly run procedures. Most HP servers are ordered with a minimum of two internal disks for root and swap. After loading the first disk with HP-UX, selecting logical volume sizes, file system types, and so on, we're ready to mirror the disk. (See Chapter 3 "Installing HP-UX" to see this procedure.)

Figure 4-3 shows some typical steps to mirror root and swap.

```
# pvcreate -B  /dev/rdsk/cxtxdx          ; create physical volume for disk to be used as mirror

# vgextend /dev/vg00 /dev/dsk/cxtxdx     ; extend vg00 to include disk to be used as mirror

# mkboot /dev/rdsk/cxtxdx                ; mkboot places boot utilities in boot area

# mkboot -a "hpux -lq" /dev/rdsk/cxtxdx  ; add the AUTO file and specify low quorum

# mkboot -a "hpux -lq" /dev/rdsk/primary ; update the AUTO file on primary disk low quorum

# lvextend -m 1 /dev/vg00/lvol1 /dev/dsk/cxdxtx ; mirror lvol1 which is /stand
# lvextend -m 1 /dev/vg00/lvol2 /dev/dsk/cxtxdx ; mirror lvol2 which is root
# lvextend -m 1 /dev/vg00/lvol3 /dev/dsk/cxtxdx ; mirror lvol3 which is swap
# lvextend all others on primary

# setboot -a 8/8.6.0         ; have alternate boot path point to H/W path  of new mirror disk
```

Figure 4-3   Mirror root and swap Disk

This is the one of the most common procedures performed in LVM because you like to have the root and swap disk mirrored whenever possible.

Because this is such an important procedure to know, let's go through an example of running this procedure.

Let's first see what volume groups we have on the system by running **strings /etc/lvmtab**. Then, run **ioscan** to see what disks exist on the system:

```
# strings /etc/lvmtab
/dev/vg00
/dev/dsk/c1t15d0
# ioscan -funC disk
Class     I  H/W Path         Driver   S/W State   H/W Type     Description
===========================================================================
disk      0  0/0/1/0.1.0      sdisk    CLAIMED     DEVICE       HP      DVD-ROM 305
                              /dev/dsk/c0t1d0   /dev/rdsk/c0t1d0
disk      1  0/0/1/1.15.0     sdisk    CLAIMED     DEVICE       SEAGATE ST318404LC
                              /dev/dsk/c1t15d0   /dev/rdsk/c1t15d0
disk      2  0/0/2/1.15.0     sdisk    CLAIMED     DEVICE       SEAGATE ST318404LC
                              /dev/dsk/c3t15d0   /dev/rdsk/c3t15d0
disk      3  0/4/0/0/4/0.8.0    sdisk    CLAIMED     DEVICE       HP 18.2GST318406LC
                              /dev/dsk/c4t8d0    /dev/rdsk/c4t8d0
disk      4  0/4/0/0/4/0.10.0 sdisk    CLAIMED     DEVICE       HP 18.2GST318406LC
                              /dev/dsk/c4t10d0   /dev/rdsk/c4t10d0
#
```

The disk at *3* is on a different bus than the internal disk and would therefore be an ideal disk on which to mirror the root disk. We take the disk at *3*, get some information on it with **diskinfo**, and run a **vgdisplay** to ensure that there is now only one disk in the volume group:

```
# diskinfo /dev/rdsk/c4t8d0
SCSI describe of /dev/rdsk/c4t8d0:
            vendor: HP 18.2G
        product id: ST318406LC
              type: direct access
              size: 17783240 Kbytes
   bytes per sector: 512
# vgdisplay -v /dev/vg00
--- Volume groups ---
VG Name                     /dev/vg00
VG Write Access             read/write
VG Status                   available
Max LV                      255
Cur LV                      8
Open LV                     8
Max PV                      16
Cur PV                      1
Act PV                      1
Max PE per PV               4350
VGDA                        2
PE Size (Mbytes)            4
Total PE                    4340
Alloc PE                    1965
Free PE                     2375
Total PVG                   0
Total Spare PVs             0
Total Spare PVs in use      0

   --- Logical volumes ---
   LV Name                  /dev/vg00/lvol1
   LV Status                available/syncd
   LV Size (Mbytes)         300
   Current LE               75
   Allocated PE             75
   Used PV                  1

   LV Name                  /dev/vg00/lvol2
   LV Status                available/syncd
   LV Size (Mbytes)         2048
   Current LE               512
   Allocated PE             512
   Used PV                  1

   LV Name                  /dev/vg00/lvol3
   LV Status                available/syncd
   LV Size (Mbytes)         200
   Current LE               50
   Allocated PE             50
   Used PV                  1

   LV Name                  /dev/vg00/lvol4
   LV Status                available/syncd
   LV Size (Mbytes)         500
   Current LE               125
   Allocated PE             125
   Used PV                  1

   LV Name                  /dev/vg00/lvol5
   LV Status                available/syncd
   LV Size (Mbytes)         200
   Current LE               50
   Allocated PE             50
   Used PV                  1

   LV Name                  /dev/vg00/lvol6
   LV Status                available/syncd
   LV Size (Mbytes)         1032
   Current LE               258
```

```
                Allocated PE             258
                Used PV                  1

                LV Name                  /dev/vg00/lvol7
                LV Status                available/syncd
                LV Size (Mbytes)         1032
                Current LE               258
                Allocated PE             258
                Used PV                  1

                LV Name                  /dev/vg00/lvol8
                LV Status                available/syncd
                LV Size (Mbytes)         2548
                Current LE               637
                Allocated PE             637
                Used PV                  1


                --- Physical volumes ---
                PV Name                  /dev/dsk/c1t15d0
                PV Status                available
                Total PE                 4340
                Free PE                  2375
                Autoswitch               On
```

Now that we're sure of the way in which **vg00** is set up and we have all of the information on the disk, we want to act as a mirror for the root disk. Let's run all the commands necessary to create the mirror:

```
# pvcreate -B /dev/rdsk/c4t8d0
Physical volume "/dev/rdsk/c4t8d0" has been successfully created.
# vgextend /dev/vg00 /dev/dsk/c4t8d0
Volume group "/dev/vg00" has been successfully extended.
Volume Group configuration for /dev/vg00 has been saved in /etc/lvmconf/vg00.conf
# mkboot /dev/rdsk/c4t8d0
# mkboot -a "hpux -lq" /dev/rdsk/c4t8d0
# mkboot -a "hpux -lq" /dev/rdsk/c1t15d0
# lvextend -m 1 /dev/vg00/lvol1 /dev/dsk/c4t8d0
The newly allocated mirrors are now being synchronized. This operation will
take some time. Please wait ....
Logical volume "/dev/vg00/lvol1" has been successfully extended.
Volume Group configuration for /dev/vg00 has been saved in /etc/lvmconf/vg00.conf
#
# lvextend -m 1 /dev/vg00/lvol2 /dev/dsk/c4t8d0
The newly allocated mirrors are now being synchronized. This operation will
take some time. Please wait ....
Logical volume "/dev/vg00/lvol2" has been successfully extended.
Volume Group configuration for /dev/vg00 has been saved in /etc/lvmconf/vg00.conf
# lvextend -m 1 /dev/vg00/lvol3 /dev/dsk/c4t8d0
The newly allocated mirrors are now being synchronized. This operation will
take some time. Please wait ....
Logical volume "/dev/vg00/lvol3" has been successfully extended.
Volume Group configuration for /dev/vg00 has been saved in /etc/lvmconf/vg00.conf
# lvextend -m 1 /dev/vg00/lvol4 /dev/dsk/c4t8d0
The newly allocated mirrors are now being synchronized. This operation will
take some time. Please wait ....
Logical volume "/dev/vg00/lvol4" has been successfully extended.
Volume Group configuration for /dev/vg00 has been saved in /etc/lvmconf/vg00.conf
# lvextend -m 1 /dev/vg00/lvol5 /dev/dsk/c4t8d0
The newly allocated mirrors are now being synchronized. This operation will
take some time. Please wait ....
Logical volume "/dev/vg00/lvol5" has been successfully extended.
Volume Group configuration for /dev/vg00 has been saved in /etc/lvmconf/vg00.conf
# lvextend -m 1 /dev/vg00/lvol6 /dev/dsk/c4t8d0
The newly allocated mirrors are now being synchronized. This operation will
take some time. Please wait ....
Logical volume "/dev/vg00/lvol6" has been successfully extended.
Volume Group configuration for /dev/vg00 has been saved in /etc/lvmconf/vg00.conf
# lvextend -m 1 /dev/vg00/lvol7 /dev/dsk/c4t8d0
```

```
The newly allocated mirrors are now being synchronized. This operation will
take some time. Please wait ....
Logical volume "/dev/vg00/lvol7" has been successfully extended.
Volume Group configuration for /dev/vg00 has been saved in /etc/lvmconf/vg00.conf
# lvextend -m 1 /dev/vg00/lvol8 /dev/dsk/c4t8d0
The newly allocated mirrors are now being synchronized. This operation will
take some time. Please wait ....
Logical volume "/dev/vg00/lvol8" has been successfully extended.
Volume Group configuration for /dev/vg00 has been saved in /etc/lvmconf/vg00.conf
# setboot -a 0/4/0/0/4/0.8.0
```

The setup of the mirrored volume should now be complete. Run
strings /etc/lvmtab and **vgdisplay** again to ensure that your disk has been
added to the volume group:

```
# strings /etc/lvmtab
/dev/vg00
/dev/dsk/c1t15d0
/dev/dsk/c4t8d0
# vgdisplay -v /dev/vg00
--- Volume groups ---
VG Name                     /dev/vg00
VG Write Access             read/write
VG Status                   available
Max LV                      255
Cur LV                      8
Open LV                     8
Max PV                      16
Cur PV                      2
Act PV                      2
Max PE per PV               4350
VGDA                        4
PE Size (Mbytes)            4
Total PE                    8680
Alloc PE                    3930
Free PE                     4750
Total PVG                   0
Total Spare PVs             0
Total Spare PVs in use      0

    --- Logical volumes ---
    LV Name                 /dev/vg00/lvol1
    LV Status               available/syncd
    LV Size (Mbytes)        300
    Current LE              75
    Allocated PE            150
    Used PV                 2

    LV Name                 /dev/vg00/lvol2
    LV Status               available/syncd
    LV Size (Mbytes)        2048
    Current LE              512
    Allocated PE            1024
    Used PV                 2

    LV Name                 /dev/vg00/lvol3
    LV Status               available/syncd
    LV Size (Mbytes)        200
    Current LE              50
    Allocated PE            100
    Used PV                 2

    LV Name                 /dev/vg00/lvol4
    LV Status               available/syncd
    LV Size (Mbytes)        500
    Current LE              125
    Allocated PE            250
    Used PV                 2

    LV Name                 /dev/vg00/lvol5
```

```
LV Status                      available/syncd
LV Size (Mbytes)               200
Current LE                     50
Allocated PE                   100
Used PV                        2

LV Name                        /dev/vg00/lvol6
LV Status                      available/syncd
LV Size (Mbytes)               1032
Current LE                     258
Allocated PE                   516
Used PV                        2

LV Name                        /dev/vg00/lvol7
LV Status                      available/syncd
LV Size (Mbytes)               1032
Current LE                     258
Allocated PE                   516
Used PV                        2

LV Name                        /dev/vg00/lvol8
LV Status                      available/syncd
LV Size (Mbytes)               2548
Current LE                     637
Allocated PE                   1274
Used PV                        2


--- Physical volumes ---
PV Name                        /dev/dsk/c1t15d0
PV Status                      available
Total PE                       4340
Free PE                        2375
Autoswitch                     On

PV Name                        /dev/dsk/c4t8d0
PV Status                      available
Total PE                       4340
Free PE                        2375
Autoswitch                     On
```

These outputs look great in that both disks are in **vg00**. The end of the **vgdisplay** output (*Physical Volumes)* shows both disks with identical *Total PE* and *Free PE*.

Run **lvdisplay** to see that the physical extents are mirrored across the two disks, **lifls** on both disks to see the boot information, and **setboot** to ensure that we have the *primary* and *alternate* paths set up properly:

```
# lvdisplay -v /dev/vg00/lvol1
--- Logical volumes ---
LV Name                        /dev/vg00/lvol1
VG Name                        /dev/vg00
LV Permission                  read/write
LV Status                      available/syncd
Mirror copies                  1
Consistency Recovery           MWC
Schedule                       parallel
LV Size (Mbytes)               300
Current LE                     75
Allocated PE                   150
Stripes                        0
Stripe Size (Kbytes)           0
Bad block                      off
Allocation                     strict/contiguous
IO Timeout (Seconds)           default
```

```
--- Distribution of logical volume ---
PV Name                 LE on PV  PE on PV
/dev/dsk/c1t15d0        75          75
/dev/dsk/c4t8d0         75          75

--- Logical extents ---
LE     PV1                    PE1    Status 1 PV2                    PE2    Status 2
00000 /dev/dsk/c1t15d0       00000 current   /dev/dsk/c4t8d0        00000 current
00001 /dev/dsk/c1t15d0       00001 current   /dev/dsk/c4t8d0        00001 current
00002 /dev/dsk/c1t15d0       00002 current   /dev/dsk/c4t8d0        00002 current
00003 /dev/dsk/c1t15d0       00003 current   /dev/dsk/c4t8d0        00003 current
00004 /dev/dsk/c1t15d0       00004 current   /dev/dsk/c4t8d0        00004 current
00005 /dev/dsk/c1t15d0       00005 current   /dev/dsk/c4t8d0        00005 current
00006 /dev/dsk/c1t15d0       00006 current   /dev/dsk/c4t8d0        00006 current
00007 /dev/dsk/c1t15d0       00007 current   /dev/dsk/c4t8d0        00007 current
00008 /dev/dsk/c1t15d0       00008 current   /dev/dsk/c4t8d0        00008 current
00009 /dev/dsk/c1t15d0       00009 current   /dev/dsk/c4t8d0        00009 current
00010 /dev/dsk/c1t15d0       00010 current   /dev/dsk/c4t8d0        00010 current
00011 /dev/dsk/c1t15d0       00011 current   /dev/dsk/c4t8d0        00011 current

                    •

                    •

                    •

00071 /dev/dsk/c1t15d0       00071 current   /dev/dsk/c4t8d0        00071 current
00072 /dev/dsk/c1t15d0       00072 current   /dev/dsk/c4t8d0        00072 current
00073 /dev/dsk/c1t15d0       00073 current   /dev/dsk/c4t8d0        00073 current
00074 /dev/dsk/c1t15d0       00074 current   /dev/dsk/c4t8d0        00074 current
```

```
# lifls /dev/rdsk/c1t15d0
ODE           MAPFILE       SYSLIB        CONFIGDATA    SLMOD2
SLDEV2        SLDRV2        SLSCSI2       MAPPER2       IOTEST2
PERFVER2      PVCU          SSINFO        ISL           AUTO
HPUX          LABEL
# lifls /dev/rdsk/c4t8d0
ISL           AUTO          HPUX          PAD           LABEL

# setboot
Primary bootpath : 0/0/1/1.15.0
Alternate bootpath : 0/4/0/0/4/0.8.0

Autoboot is ON (enabled)
Autosearch is ON (enabled)

#
```

It looks as though this setup of a mirrored volume is complete in that the data is mirrored across two different disks on two different buses and that the mirrored volume is also bootable.

Another important procedure that is helpful to know is to create a new volume group and add a disk to it. We also put a logical volume on the disk and mount it. Figure 4-4 shows the steps involved in this procedure.

```
# pvcreate  /dev/rdsk/cxtxdx              ; create physical volume for disk to be used in VG

# mkdir /dev/vg01                         ; make directory for new vg01

# mknod /dev/vg01/group c 64 0x010000     ; mknod of vg01 ( minor 01 corresponds to vgnum)

# vgcreate /dev/vg01 /dev/dsk/cxtxdx      ; create vg01

# lvcreate -L 2000 /dev/vg01              ; create default lvol1 in vg01 of 2 GBytes

# newfs -F vxfs -o largefiles /dev/vg01/rlvol1   ; create a new filesystem on lvol1

# mkdir /backup                           ; create a directory on which to mount lvol1

# mount /dev/vg01/lvol1 /backup           ; mount lvol1

# bdf                                     ; to see mounted filesystem
```

Figure 4-4   Create a New Volume Group and Add a Disk to It with a Logical Volume

Because this is such an important procedure to know, let's go through an example of running it.

In the previous example, we performed a **diskinfo** to see all the disks on our system. We'll use the disk at *4* in this example as the basis for creating a new volume group.

Run the steps as they appear in Figure 4-4 to create **vg01** and mount one of its logical volumes on **/backup**:

```
# pvcreate -B -f /dev/rdsk/c3t15d0
Physical volume "/dev/rdsk/c3t15d0" has been successfully created.
# mkdir /dev/vg01
# mknod /dev/vg01/group c 64 0x010000
# vgcreate /dev/vg01 /dev/dsk/c3t15d0
Increased the number of physical extents per physical volume to 4341.
Volume group "/dev/vg01" has been successfully created.
Volume Group configuration for /dev/vg01 has been saved in /etc/lvmconf/
vg01.conf
# lvcreate -L 2000 /dev/vg01
Logical volume "/dev/vg01/lvol1" has been successfully created with
character device "/dev/vg01/rlvol1".
Logical volume "/dev/vg01/lvol1" has been successfully extended.
Volume Group configuration for /dev/vg01 has been saved in /etc/lvmconf/
vg01.conf
# newfs -F vxfs -o largefiles /dev/vg01/rlvol1
    version 4 layout
    2048000 sectors, 2048000 blocks of size 1024, log size 1024 blocks
    unlimited inodes, largefiles supported
    2048000 data blocks, 2046392 free data blocks
```

```
      63 allocation units of 32768 blocks, 32768 data blocks
      last allocation unit has 16384 data blocks
# mkdir /backup
# mount /dev/vg01/lvol1 /backup
# bdf
Filesystem          kbytes     used    avail %used Mounted on
/dev/vg00/lvol3     204800    67065   129166   34% /
/dev/vg00/lvol1     299157    26222   243019   10% /stand
/dev/vg00/lvol8    2609152   138568  2316618    6% /var
/dev/vg00/lvol7    1056768   767077   271632   74% /usr
/dev/vg00/lvol5     204800     1338   190810    1% /tmp
/dev/vg00/lvol6    1056768   691085   342889   67% /opt
/dev/vg00/lvol4     512000     1234   478849    0% /home
/dev/vg01/lvol1    2048000     1606  1918502    0% /backup
# strings /etc/lvmtab
/dev/vg00
/dev/dsk/c1t15d0
/dev/dsk/c4t8d0
/dev/vg01
/dev/dsk/c3t15d0
#
```

We successfully created a new volume group in this example of size 2 GB. We later increase this size of this logical volume without unmounting **/backup**. We did not have to put boot-related files on this physical volume because we don't need to boot off of it.

The next series of figures give tips on performing some additional frequently performed LVM procedures.

---

vgcfgrestore - /dev/vgXX /dev/rdsk/cxtxdx   ; volume group configuration restore

vgchange -a y /dev/vgXX   ; change volume group to available (*-a y*)

newfs -F fstype /dev/vgXX/rlvolx   ; create filesystem for every *lvol* on physical volume

mount /*mountpointname*   ; mount every new filesystem

Notes:

Confirm you have **/etc/lvmconf/vgXX.conf**

vgcfgbackup is run automatically

Defective disk was not mirrored before it failed

Additional steps may be required on your system

Figure 4-5   Replace a Non-Mirrored Disk

In Figure 4-5, we have a non-mirrored and non-root disk that are defective and need to be replaced. After replacing the disk, the volume group information is restored for the specific disk with **vgcfgrestore**. We then change the volume group to available, run a **newfs** on the disk, and mount the file systems that used the disk.

In Figure 4-6, we again replace a defective non-root disk, but this time, the disk will be mirrored.

\# **vgcfgrestore -n /dev/vgXX /dev/rdsk/cxtxdx**   ; volume group configuration restore

\# **vgchange -a y /dev/vgXX**   ; change volume group to available (*-a y*)

\# **vgsync /dev/vgXX**   ; resync logical volumes in volume group

Notes:

Defective disk was mirrored before it failed

Additional steps may be required on your system

Figure 4-6   Replace a Mirrored Disk

In this example, we perform the same first two steps of restoring the volume group configuration and changing the volume group to available. Because the disk is mirrored, we only have to synchronize the data on the new disk with that on its mirror with **vgsync**.

In Figure 4-7, we again replace a mirrored disk, but this time, the disk has a boot area on it.

```
# vgcfgrestore -n /dev/vgXX /dev/rdsk/cxtxdx    ; volume group configuration restore

# vgchange -a y /dev/vgXX                        ; change volume group to available (-a y)

# vgsync /dev/vgXX                               ; resync logical volumes in volume group

# mkboot /dev/rdsk/cxtxdx                         ; create boot area on disk

# mkboot -a "hpux lq" /dev/rdsk/cxtxdx          ; specify low quorum in boot area

# shutdown <desired options>                      ; reboot system to take effect

vgcfgbackup is run automatically

Notes:
Confirm you have /etc/lvmconf/vgXX.conf

Defective disk was mirrored before it failed

Addtional steps may be required on your system
```

Figure 4-7   Replace Mirrored Disk Boot Disk

In this example, we perform the same first three steps as the previous example, but we also have to create a boot area on the disk. The system must be rebooted in order for this to take effect.

In Figure 4-8, we want to move a volume group onto a different system.

On system 1:

vgchange -a n /dev/vg01   ; change volume group to unavailable (*-a n*) on sys 1

vgexport -v -m /tmp/mapfile -s /dev/vg01   ; make volume group unavailable on 1st system
                                                 ; use *-p -s -m* options if you need shared for HA
rcp /tmp/mapfile system2:/tmp/mapfile   ; copy mapfile to *target* or *second* system.

   On system 2:

mkdir /dev/vg01   ; make directory on 2nd system for volume group

mknod /dev/vg01/group c 64 0xyy0000   ; create special file for vol group (*yy*=group number
                                                     such as *00* for *vg00*, *01* for *vg01*, and so on)
vgimport -v -m mapfile -s /dev/vg01   ; import volume group using mapfile copied from
                                                     1st system or specify device filenames
                                                     (use *-s* and *-m* in HA cluster)

vgchange -a y /dev/vg01   ; make volume group available

mkdir /backup

mount /dev/vg01/backup /backup   ; add to **/etc/fstab** if you want this mounted at boot

Notes:
vgcfgbackup must be run.

Addtional steps may be required on your system

The *-s -p -m -v* options are used in HA cluster environments to create sharable mapfile with
vgexport and *-s -m* on **vgmport**

Figure 4-8   Exporting (Removing) and Importing a Volume Group Onto
Another System

In this example, we perform the first three steps on the system from
which we're moving the volume group. We make the volume group
unavailable and then export the volume group. The mapfile from the first
system needs to be copied to the second system. You don't have to specify
the mapfile name if standard names, such as **/dev/vg01**, are used. In any
event, the mapfile has to be copied to the system to which the volume group
is being migrated.

On the second system, we create a directory and device special file for
the new volume group. We then import the mapfile for the volume group
and make the volume group active. We then make the volume group available and perform the appropriate mounts.

There are many comments regarding a High Availability Cluster and the options used. In a ServiceGuard environment you don't have to make the volume group unavailable and you use some different options for sharing. Figure 4-9 shows the ServiceGuard steps.

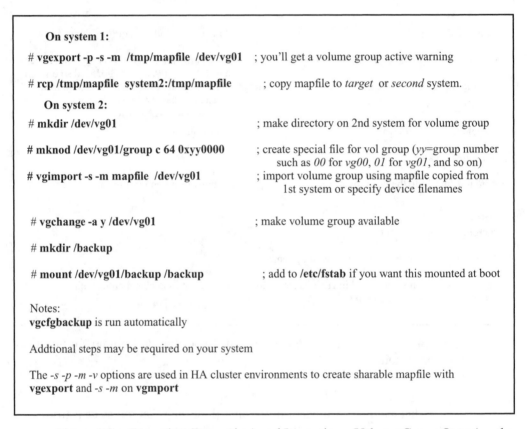

Figure 4-9   Exporting (Removing) and Importing a Volume Group Onto Another System in a ServiceGuard Environment

These steps are similar to those in Figure 4-9. The options to **vgexport** and **vgimport** are different, and you may want to look at those manual pages.

Figure 4-10 shows extending a VxFS filesystem by 800 MB.

---

lvextend -L 800 /dev/vgXX/lvolY   ; extend logical volume *rlvolY* by 800 MBytes
fsadm -F vxfs -b 800M */mountpointname*   ; use **fsadm** to extend or **extendfs** on non-JFS

Notes:

This is a VxFS filesystem and OnlineJFS is installed on system

Additional steps may be required on your system

Figure 4-10   Extend VxFS File System Using OnlineJFS

This procedure is a commonly run because OnLineJFS is used in most high-availability environments. Let's extend the logical volume in **vg01** that we earlier created from 2 GB to 4 GB using the steps in the following example:

```
# bdf
Filesystem            kbytes    used   avail %used Mounted on
/dev/vg00/lvol3       204800   67067  129164   34% /
/dev/vg00/lvol1       299157   26222  243019   10% /stand
/dev/vg00/lvol8      2609152  138519 2316664    6% /var
/dev/vg00/lvol7      1056768  767085  271624   74% /usr
/dev/vg00/lvol5       204800    1338  190810    1% /tmp
/dev/vg00/lvol6      1056768  691085  342889   67% /opt
/dev/vg00/lvol4       512000    1234  478849    0% /home
/dev/vg01/lvol1      2048000    1606 1918502    0% /backup
# lvextend -L 4000 /dev/vg01/lvol1
Logical volume "/dev/vg01/lvol1" has been successfully extended.
Volume Group configuration for /dev/vg01 has been saved in /etc/lvmconf/
vg01.conf
# fsadm -F vxfs -b 4000M /backup
vxfs fsadm: /dev/vg01/rlvol1 is currently 2048000 sectors - size will be in-
creased
# bdf
Filesystem            kbytes    used   avail %used Mounted on
/dev/vg00/lvol3       204800   67067  129164   34% /
/dev/vg00/lvol1       299157   26222  243019   10% /stand
/dev/vg00/lvol8      2609152  138521 2316663    6% /var
/dev/vg00/lvol7      1056768  767085  271624   74% /usr
/dev/vg00/lvol5       204800    1338  190810    1% /tmp
/dev/vg00/lvol6      1056768  691085  342889   67% /opt
/dev/vg00/lvol4       512000    1234  478849    0% /home
/dev/vg01/lvol1      4096000    2104 3838035    0% /backup
#
```

Note that this change from 2 GB to 4 GB took place while **/backup** was mounted. The ability to resize logical volumes while they're mounted is one of the advanced features of OnLineJFS.

If this directory were to be mounted at boot time, we would add an entry to **/etc/fstab**.

Figure 4-11 shows changing a VxFS file system to support large files.

---

fsadm -F vxfs -o largefiles /dev/vgXX/rlvolY   ; use *fsadm* and specify *largefile* option

Notes:

This is VxFS filesystem, you can substitute *hfs* for *vxfs* in above example for an *hfs* filesystem and use
    lvolY in place of *rlvolY*
Unmount filesystem before running

Additional steps may be required on your system

Figure 4-11   Change a Logical Volume to Support Large Files

Using **fsadm**, we specify the raw logical volume on which we want large files supported.

This change would be unnecessary had the logical volume been created to support large files, which is the default in most cases.

Some Additional File System-Related Commands

Viewing File Systems with bdf

You can manually view the file systems you have mounted by using the **bdf** command. **bdf** provides the following output:

File system	Block device file system name. In the following example, several logical volumes are shown.
KB	Number of KB of total disk space on the file system.
used	The number of used KBytes on the file system.
avail	The number of available KB on the file system.
%used	The percentage of total available disk space that is used on the file system.
Mounted on	The directory name on which the file system is mounted.
iused	Number of inodes in use (only if you use the *-i* option with **bdf**).
ifree	Number of free inodes (only if you use the *-i* option with **bdf**).
%iuse	Percentage of inodes in use (only if you use the *-i* option with **bdf**).

Here is an example of **bdf** that is also in the section "Logical Volume Manager Background," covered earlier in this chapter:

$ bdf

File system	kbytes	used	avail	%used	Mounted on
/dev/vg00/lvol3	47829	18428	24618	43%	/
/dev/vg00/lvol1	67733	24736	36223	41%	/stand
/dev/vg00/lvol8	34541	8673	22413	28%	/var
/dev/vg00/lvol7	299157	149449	119792	56%	/usr

File system	kbytes	used	avail	%used	Mounted on
/dev/vg00/lvol4	23013	48	20663	0%	/tmp
/dev/vg00/lvol6	99669	32514	57188	36%	/opt
/dev/vg00/lvol5	19861	9	17865	0%	/home
/dev/dsk/c0t6d0	802212	552120	169870	76%	/mnt/9.x

File System Maintenance with fsck

fsck is a program used for file system maintenance on HP-UX systems. **fsck** checks file system consistency and can make many "life-saving" repairs to a corrupt file system. **fsck** can be run with several options, including the following:

-F	Allows you to specify the file system type (see the explanation of file system types in Chapter 15). Be sure to specify a file system type. On some UNIX variants, **/etc/fstab** determines the file system type: on others, it will not be used. See the **fstab** description later in this section.
-m	A sanity check of the file system. If you run this, you are told whether your file system is okay or not. I did the following to check lvol5, which is mounted as **/home**:

```
$ umount /home
$ fsck -m /dev/vg00/lvol5

vxfs fsck: sanity check: /dev/vg00/lvol5 OK
```

-y	**fsck** asks questions if run in interactive mode, which is the default. Using the *-y* option causes a "yes" response to all questions asked by **fsck**. Don't use this! If you have a serious problem with your file system, data will probably have to be removed, and the *-y* indicates that the response

to every question, including removing data, will
be "yes."

-*n* The response to all questions asked by **fsck** is
"no." Don't use this, either. If your file system is
in bad shape, you may have to respond "yes" to
some questions to repair the file system. All "no"
responses will not do the job.

Because your system runs **fsck** on any file systems that were not
marked as clean at the time you shut down the system, you can rest assured
that when your system boots, any disks that were not properly shut down
will be checked. It is a good idea to run **fsck** interactively on a periodic basis
just so you can see firsthand that all of your file systems are in good working
order.

Should **fsck** find a problem with a directory or file, it places these in
the **lost+found** directory, which is at the top level of each file system. If a
file or directory appears in **lost+found,** you may be able to identify the file
or directory by examining it and move it back to its original location. You
can use the **file**, **what**, and **strings** commands on a file to obtain more information about it to help identify its origin.

How are file system problems created? The most common cause of a
file system problem is improper sytem shutdown. The information written to
file systems is first written to a buffer cache in memory. It is later written to
the disk with the **sync** command by unmounting the disk, or through the
normal use of filling the buffer and writing it to the disk. If you walk up to a
system and shut off the power, you will surely end up with a file system
problem. Data in the buffer that was not synchronized to the disk will be
lost, the file system will not be marked as properly shut down, and **fsck** will
be run when the system boots. A sudden loss of power can also cause an
improper system shutdown.

Proper system shutdown is described with the **shutdown** command.
Although **fsck** is a useful utility that has been known to work miracles on
occasion, you don't want to take any unnecessary risks with your file systems. So, be sure to properly shut down your system.

fsck uses the **/etc/fstab** file mentioned earlier to determine the
sequence of the file system check if it is required at the time of boot. The
sequence of entries in **/etc/fstab** is important if a "pass number" for any of
the entries does not exist. Here is an example of the **/etc/fstab** file:

```
# System /etc/fstab file. Static information about the file
# systems. See fstab(4) and for further details.

/dev/vg00/lvol3     /             vxfs   delaylog    0  1
/dev/vg00/lvol1     /stand        hfs    defaults    0  1
/dev/vg00/lvol4     /tmp          vxfs   delaylog    0  2
/dev/vg00/lvol6     /opt          vxfs   delaylog    0  2
/dev/vg00/lvol5     /home         vxfs   delaylog    0  2
/dev/vg00/lvol7     /usr          vxfs   delaylog    0  2
/dev/vg00/lvol8     /var          vxfs   delaylog    0  2
/dev/dsk/c0tt6d0    /tmp/mnt9.x   hfs    rw, suid    0  2

         |                |             |           |        |  |

         v                v             v           v        v  v
```

device special file	directory	type	options	backup frequency	pass #

device special file

The device block file, such as **/dev/vg00/lvol1** in the example.

directory

The name of the directory under which the device special file is mounted.

type

Can be one of several types, including the following:
cdfs (local CD-ROM file system)
hfs (high performance local file system)
nfs (network file system)
vxfs (journaled file system)
swap or
swapfs

options

Several options are available, including those shown in the example. *rw* is read and write; *ro* is read only.

backup frequency

To be used by backup utilities in the future.

pass #

Used by **fsck** to determine the order in which file system checks (**fsck**) take place.

comment

Anything you want, as long as it's preceded by a #.

Initialize with mediainit

A command you probably won't use, but should be aware of, is **mediainit**. Check the manual page and be careful when using this command.

Here are some of the options of **mediainit**:

-v

This is the verbose option. **mediainit** normally just prints error messages to the screen. You can get continuous feedback on what **mediainit** is doing with the *-v* option.

-i interleave

Allows you to specify the interleave factor, which is the relationship between sequential logical and physical records. **mediainit** provides this if one is not specified.

-f format

The format option allows you to specify format options for devices, such as floppy disks, that support different format options. This is not required for hard disks.

pathname

The character device file to be used for **mediainit**.

newfs, which was used in some of the earlier examples, create a new file system. **newfs** calls the **mkfs** (make file system) command. **newfs** builds a file system of the type you specify. (This is one of the commands that uses the *-F* option, so you can specify the file system type.)

Chapter 5

Configuring an HP-UX Kernel

Introduction

Kernel management in HP-UX 11i Version 2 is done with a set of kernel configuration commands or through the web-based **kcweb** tool. This chapter covers the kernel-related commands, gives some examples of using the commands to modify and build kernels, and gives an overview of **kcweb**.

Most applications require that you to modify your kernel in some way. You may need to create a new HP-UX kernel to add device drivers or subsystems, tune the kernel to get improved performance, alter configurable parameters, or change the dump and swap devices. If you update or modify a dynamic element of your kernel, as shown in an example in this chapter, a reboot is not required. Updating or modifying a static element requires a reboot and may also require some additional steps, which a later example shows.

This chapter covers the following topics:

- Overview, examples, and running kernel-related commands: **kcmodule**, **kctune**, **kconfig**, **kclog**, **kcalarm**, **kcusage**, and **kcmod**
- A flowchart showing a typical kernel rebuild
- Example of using the entries in the flowchart to rebuild a kernel
- Example of booting a saved kernel configuration

167

• The **system** file and making multiple kernel changes using it

• Overview of the Web-based kernel tool **kcweb**

Kernel Commands

A new set of kernel-related commands has been developed that have a common behavior. This section covers all the commands and provides examples of using some of them.

kcmodule

kcmodule queries and changes kernel modules in the currently running kernel configuration or a saved kernel configuration that you are staging for future use. Hundreds of modules are present in an HP-UX kernel that consists of device drivers, kernel subsystems, and other kernel code.

kcmodule with no options provides the modules in your system and both their current state and the state on next boot if any changes are pending, as shown in this abbreviated example:

```
# kcmodule
Module            State    Cause    Notes
DeviceDriver      unused
KeyboardMUX       unused
LCentIf           static   best
MouseMUX          unused
UsbBootKeyboard   unused
UsbBootMouse      unused
UsbHub            unused
UsbMiniBus        unused
UsbOhci           unused
acpi_node         static   best
arp               static   depend
asio0             static   best
audio             static   best
autofsc           static   best
azusa_psm         static   best
beep              static   depend
btlan             static   best
c460gx_psm        static   depend
c8xx              static   best
cachefsc          static   best
ccio              unused
cdfs              auto     best     auto-loadable, unloadable
cec_hp            static   depend
cell              static   best
cifs              static   best
clone             static   best
consp1            unused
```

```
diag2            static  best
dlpi             static  best
dm_sample_fsid   unused
dmapi            unused
dmp              static  depend
dmsample         unused
echo             static  best
ehci             unused
fcd              static  best
fcms             static  depend
fcp              static  depend
fcp_cdio         static  depend
fcparray         static  depend
fcpdev           static  depend
fcpmux           static  depend
fddi4            static  best
ffs              static  best
framebuf         unused
gelan            static  best
graph3           unused
gvid             unused
gvid_core        unused
hcd              unused
hid              unused
hpstreams        static  best
hsx              static  explicit   loadable, unloadable
hub              unused
ia64_psm         static  best
idds             unused
                      .
                      .
                      .
```

This abbreviated output shows some of the modules in the system without much detail. We modify the last module shown, idds, in a later example. To get detailed information on a specific module, use the -v option, as shown for vxfs:

```
# kcmodule -v vxfs
Module               vxfs  [3F559170]
Description          Veritas Journal File System (VxFS)
State               static (best state)
State at Next Boot  static (best state)
Capable             static unused
Depends On          module libvxfs:0.0.0
                    interface HPUX_11_23:1.0

#
```

This verbose output shows more information for the specific module that we specified, or would have shown verbose output for every module if I had not specified the name of a specific module.

For every module in the verbose output, there is a name and description such as a name of vxfs, the version number in square brackets after the name, and a short description of the module in the example. It is possible for multiple versions to be listed if, for instance, the currently running kernel uses a different version than will be used on the next boot.

The state of the module is relative to the currently running kernel (which is shown in the example), the next boot (both the currently running and next boot states are shown), or a saved configuration. The module in the example is for the currently running kernel, so *static* means that the module is statically bound into the kernel and changing this state would require relinking the kernel executable and rebooting. The module could also be in the *unused* state, which means it is installed but not used, the *loaded* state, which means it has been dynamically loaded into the kernel, or the *auto* state, which means it will be dynamically loaded when it is first needed but hasn't been loaded yet.

The following list shows commonly used options to **kcmodule**:

kcmodule command-line flags:

-a	Includes all modules in the output.
-B	Backs up the currently running configuration prior to changing it.
-c config	Specifies the saved configuration to manage. If none is specified, manage the currently running configuration.
-C comment	Includes a comment pertaining to this invocation of the command in the kernel configuration log file.
-d	Adds the description for each item.
-D	Displays elements for which there is a pending change at the next boot.
-h	Holds the specified change(s) for the next boot.
-K	Keeps the currently running configuration, but does not back it up. Keep the existing backup unmodified.
-P	Parses using the specified output format.
-S	Displays the elements that have been set to something other than the default.
-v	Displays items using verbose output.

Some of these options will be used in the upcoming example of updating the kernel.

kctune

kctune queries and changes the value of kernel tunable parameters in the currently running kernel configuration or a saved kernel configuration that you are staging for future use.

kctune with no options provides the parameters in your system, as shown in the following abbreviated example:

```
# kctune
Tunable                     Value  Expression   Changes
NSTREVENT                      50  Default
NSTRPUSH                       16  Default
NSTRSCHED                       0  Default
STRCTLSZ                     1024  Default
STRMSGSZ                        0  Default
acctresume                      4  Default
acctsuspend                     2  Default
aio_listio_max                256  Default       Immed
aio_max_ops                  2048  Default       Immed
aio_monitor_run_sec            30  Default       Immed
aio_physmem_pct                10  Default
aio_prio_delta_max             20  Default       Immed
aio_proc_thread_pct            70  Default       Immed
aio_proc_threads             1024  Default       Immed
aio_req_per_thread              1  Default       Immed
allocate_fs_swapmap             0  Default
alwaysdump                      0  Default       Immed
bufcache_hash_locks           128  Default
chanq_hash_locks              256  Default
core_addshmem_read              1  1             Immed
core_addshmem_write             1  1             Immed
create_fastlinks                0  Default
dbc_max_pct                    50  Default       Immed
dbc_min_pct                     5  Default       Immed
default_disk_ir                 0  Default
disksort_seconds                0  Default
dma32_pool_size         268435456  Default
dmp_rootdev_is_vol              0  Default
dmp_swapdev_is_vol              0  Default
dnlc_hash_locks               512  Default
dontdump                        0  Default       Immed
dst                             1  Default
dump_compress_on                1  Default       Immed
enable_idds                     0  Default       Immed
eqmemsize                      15  Default
executable_stack                0  Default       Immed
fs_async                        0  Default
fs_symlinks                    20  Default       Immed
ftable_hash_locks              64  Default
hp_hfs_mtra_enabled             1  Default
io_ports_hash_locks            64  Default
ksi_alloc_max               33600  Default       Immed
ksi_send_max                   32  Default
max_acct_file_size        2560000  Default       Immed
max_async_ports                50  Default
max_mem_window                  0  Default
max_thread_proc               256  Default       Immed
```

```
maxdsiz                      1073741824  Default      Immed
maxdsiz_64bit                4294967296  Default      Immed
maxfiles                           8192  8192
maxfiles_lim                       8192  8192         Immed
maxrsessiz                      8388608  Default
maxrsessiz_64bit                8388608  Default
maxssiz                         8388608  Default      Immed
maxssiz_64bit                 268435456  Default      Immed
maxtsiz                       100663296  Default      Immed
maxtsiz_64bit                1073741824  Default      Immed
maxuprc                             256  Default      Immed
maxvgs                               10  Default
msgmap                             1026  Default
msgmax                             8192  Default      Immed
msgmnb                            16384  Default      Immed
msgmni                              512  Default
msgseg                             8192  Default
msgssz                               96  Default
msgtql                             1024  Default
ncdnode                             150  Default      Immed
nclist                             8292  Default
ncsize                             8976  Default
nfile                             65536  Default      Auto
nflocks                            4096  Default      Auto
ninode                             4880  Default
                                      .
                                      .
                                      .
```

This output shows the tunable parameter, its current value, the expressions used to compute the value (which is the default in all cases in the example except for maxfiles), and changes to the value if any are pending. In an upcoming example, I modify the nproc tunable.

Using the -d option, which also works with **kcmodule**, adds a description for each parameter, as shown in the following truncated example:

```
# kctune -d
Tunable                    Value  Expression    Changes
    Description
NSTREVENT                     50  Default
    Maximum number of concurrent Streams bufcalls
NSTRPUSH                      16  Default
    Maximum number of Streams modules in a stream
NSTRSCHED                      0  Default
    Number of Streams scheduler daemons to run (0 = automatic)
STRCTLSZ                    1024  Default
    Maximum size of the control portion of a Streams message (bytes)
STRMSGSZ                       0  Default
    Maximum size of the data portion of a Streams message (bytes; 0 = unlimited)
acctresume                     4  Default
    Relative percentage of free disk space required to resume accounting
acctsuspend                    2  Default
    Relative percentage of free disk space below which accounting is suspended
aio_listio_max               256  Default         Immed
    Maximum number of async IO operations that can be specified in lio_list call
aio_max_ops                 2048  Default         Immed
    Maximum number of async IO operations that can be queued at any time
aio_monitor_run_sec           30  Default         Immed
    Frequency of AIO Thread Pool Monitor Execution (in seconds)
aio_physmem_pct               10  Default
                                  .
                                  .
                                  .
```

Each module now has a more detailed description associated with it as a result of using the -d option.

To group parameters based on the kernel module that defines the tunable, use the -g option, as shown in the following abbreviated example:

```
# kctune -g
Module      Tunable               Value  Expression  Changes
cdfs        ncdnode                 150  Default     Immed
dump        alwaysdump                0  Default     Immed
dump        dontdump                  0  Default     Immed
dump        dump_compress_on          1  Default     Immed
fs          bufcache_hash_locks     128  Default
fs          dbc_max_pct              50  Default     Immed
fs          dbc_min_pct               5  Default     Immed
fs          disksort_seconds          0  Default
fs          dnlc_hash_locks         512  Default
fs          fs_async                  0  Default
fs          fs_symlinks              20  Default     Immed
fs          ftable_hash_locks        64  Default
fs          maxfiles               8192  8192
fs          maxfiles_lim           8192  8192        Immed
fs          ncsize                 8976  Default
fs          nfile                 65536  Default     Auto
fs          nflocks                4096  Default     Auto
fs          o_sync_is_o_dsync         0  Default
fs          sendfile_max              0  Default
fs          vnode_cd_hash_locks     128  Default
fs          vnode_hash_locks        128  Default
hpstreams   NSTREVENT                50  Default
hpstreams   NSTRPUSH                 16  Default
hpstreams   NSTRSCHED                 0  Default
hpstreams   STRCTLSZ               1024  Default
hpstreams   STRMSGSZ                  0  Default
hpstreams   streampipes               0  Default
idds        enable_idds               0  Default     Immed
inet        tcphashsz              2048  Default
io          aio_listio_max          256  Default     Immed
io          aio_max_ops            2048  Default     Immed
io          aio_monitor_run_sec      30  Default     Immed
io          aio_physmem_pct          10  Default
io          aio_prio_delta_max       20  Default     Immed
io          aio_proc_thread_pct      70  Default     Immed
io          aio_proc_threads       1024  Default     Immed
io          aio_req_per_thread        1  Default     Immed
io          io_ports_hash_locks      64  Default
io          max_async_ports          50  Default
ite         scroll_lines            100  Default     Immed
lvm         maxvgs                   10  Default
pm          acctresume                4  Default
pm          acctsuspend               2  Default
pm          chanq_hash_locks        256  Default
pm          dst                       1  Default
            .
            .
            .
```

This output shows all the tunables grouped with their kernel modules. You can see that, in the case of the *fs* module, for example, many tunables are associated with some modules.

The -v output, as shown in the following abbreviated example, provides a lot of tunable-related information:

```
# kctune -v
Tunable             NSTREVENT
Description         Maximum number of concurrent Streams bufcalls
Module              hpstreams
Current Value       50 [Default]
Value at Next Boot  50 [Default]
Value at Last Boot  50
Default Value       50
Can Change          At Next Boot Only

Tunable             NSTRPUSH
Description         Maximum number of Streams modules in a stream
Module              hpstreams
Current Value       16 [Default]
Value at Next Boot  16 [Default]
Value at Last Boot  16
Default Value       16
Can Change          At Next Boot Only

Tunable             NSTRSCHED
Description         Number of Streams scheduler daemons to run (0 = automatic)
Module              hpstreams
Current Value       0 [Default]
Value at Next Boot  0 [Default]
Value at Last Boot  0
Default Value       0
Can Change          At Next Boot Only

Tunable             STRCTLSZ
Description         Maximum size of the control portion of a Streams message (by
tes)
Module              hpstreams
Current Value       1024 [Default]
Value at Next Boot  1024 [Default]
Value at Last Boot  1024
Default Value       1024
Can Change          At Next Boot Only

Tunable             STRMSGSZ
Description         Maximum size of the data portion of a Streams message (bytes
; 0 = unlimited)
Module              hpstreams
Current Value       0 [Default]
Value at Next Boot  0 [Default]
Value at Last Boot  0
Default Value       0
Can Change          At Next Boot Only
Standard input
```

.
.
.

This output shows additional information, including the value the parameter will have upon the next boot.

All tunables have manual pages. If, for example, you want to know more about a tunable, just issue the **man** for the tunable, as shown in the following example for *nproc*:

```
# man nproc

nproc(5)                                                                     nproc(5)
                            Tunable Kernel Parameters

NAME
     nproc - limits the number of processes allowed to exist simultaneously

VALUES
   Failsafe
     4200

   Default
     4200

   Allowed values
     100 - 30000

     This may be set higher, but more will not be used.  Setting nproc
     below 110 will interfere with the systems ability to execute in
     multi-user mode.  Some configurations may have a higher minimum.

     nproc must be greater than nkthread + 100.

Standard input
```

Only the beginning of the *nproc* output is shown, but you can see there is a lot of useful information in the man page, such as the default and allowed values. The following list shows commonly used options to **kctune**.

kctune command-line flags:

-a	Includes all information in the output that is normally suppressed.
-B	Backs up the currently running configuration prior to changing it.
-c config	Specifies the saved configuration to manage. If none is specified, manages the currently running configuration.
-C comment	Includes a comment pertaining to this invocation of the command in the kernel configuration log file.
-d	Displays the descriptions of each item.
-D	Displays elements for which there is a pending change at the next boot.
-g	Groups related tunables in the output.
-h	Holds the specified change(s) for the next boot.

-K	Keeps the currently running configuration, but does not back it up. Keeps the existing backup unmodified.
-P	Parses using the specified output format.
-S	Displays the elements that have been set to something other than the default.
-u	Allows the creation of user-defined tunables.
-v	Displays items using verbose output.

Some of these options are used in the upcoming kernel configuration example.

kconfig

kconfig manages kernel configurations.

Running **kconfig** with no options shows you all the saved kernel configurations on your system. You can view the output using -a for all, -v for verbose, and -P for parse.

Changes to the kernel can be delayed until the next boot using the -n option to **kconfig**. (Next boot options are also available with the -h option for **kcmodule** and **kctune**.)

To obtain a list of changes being held for the next boot, you would use the -D option to **kconfig** to show differences between the currently running kernel and what is planned for the next boot. You could also run **kcmodule** and **kctune** with the -D option to get this same list. If you don't want these changes to be applied at the next boot, use the -H option to **kconfig**, which "unholds" the settings.

To obtain a list of non-default kernel values, use the -S option to **kconfig**. This too is a shortcut for running both **kcmodule** and **kctune** with the -S option.

You can specify a saved configuration with no option to **kconfig** by just naming it on the command line or by using the -c option for **kcmodule** and **kctune**.

If you have made changes to the currently running kernel and want to save, use the -s option to **kconfig**.

You can load a saved configuration using the -l option to **kconfig**. If the configuration can be loaded without a reboot, the change takes effect immediately. If not, the change is held for the next reboot. You can specify that the change be applied at the next reboot with the -n option for **kconfig**. You can identify the configuration to be loaded a the next boot using the -w option to **kconfig**.

Several of these options are used in the upcoming kernel reconfiguration example.

The following is a list of commonly used **kconfig** options.

kconfig command-line flags:

-a	Includes all information in the output that is normally suppressed. This provides a lot of information so you may want to pipe this to **more**.
-B	Backs up the currently running configuration prior to changing it.
-C comment	Includes a comment pertaining to this invocation of the command in the kernel configuration log file.
-d config	Deletes the specified kernel configuration.
-D	Displays elements for which there is a pending change at the next boot.
-e	Exports the saved configuration.
-h	Holds the specified change(s) for the next boot.
-H	Discards all changes being held for the next boot.
-i config	Imports the specified configuration.
-K	Keeps the currently running configuration, but does not back it up. Keeps the existing backup unmodified.
-l config	Loads the specified configuration.
-P	Parses using the specified output format.
-S	Displays the elements that have been set to something other than the default.
-v	Displays items using verbose output.

kclog

kclog manages the kernel configuration log file.

All the commands previously covered (**kcmodule**, **kctune**, and **kconfig**) update and maintain the kernel configuration plain text log file called **/var/adm/kc.log**. You can view this file directly to see the kernel-related commands that have been issued, which is the way that I view kernel-related changes, or issue the **kclog** command to view **/var/adm/kc.log**.

kclog has the following commonly used command-line flags:

kclog commonly used command line options:

-a	Prints all entries matching
-c config	Prints log file entries from the specified configuration.
-C comment	Includes the specified comment.

kcusage

kcusage shows the usage level of kernel resources. If you issue the **kcusage** command with no options, you get output for the currently running system, as shown in the following output:

```
# kcusage
Tunable              Usage / Setting
================================================
dbc_max_pct                 5 / 50
maxdsiz              37666816 / 1073741824
maxdsiz_64bit         7258112 / 4294967296
maxfiles_lim               56 / 8192
maxssiz               1179648 / 8388608
maxssiz_64bit           20480 / 268435456
maxtsiz                421888 / 100663296
maxtsiz_64bit          237568 / 1073741824
maxuprc                     0 / 256
max_thread_proc            57 / 256
msgmni                      2 / 512
msgseg                      0 / 8192
msgtql                      0 / 1024
nfile                     586 / 65536
```

```
nflocks                    20 /  4096
ninode                    653 /  4880
nkthread                  484 /  8416
nproc                     150 /  4200
npty                        0 / 60
nstrpty                     0 / 60
nstrtel                     0 / 60
semmni                     23 / 2048
semmns                     25 / 8192
shmmax               17906400 / 68719476736
shmmni                      7 / 400
[rx8620b{root}:/roothome] >
```

This is an idle system so the resources are used minimally.

You can specify the time period over which data should be printed, including 24 hours, 31 days, and 52 weeks. Two interesting options to **kcusage** are -l, which prints a long format, and -t, which prints the top 5 users or processes that have consumed each resource. The following is an obviated listing of these two outputs:

```
# kcusage -l
Parameter:     dbc_max_pct
Usage:         5
Setting:       50
Percentage:    10.0

Parameter:     maxdsiz
Usage:         37666816
Setting:       1073741824
Percentage:    3.5

Parameter:     maxdsiz_64bit
Usage:         7258112
Setting:       4294967296
Percentage:    0.2

Parameter:     maxfiles_lim
Usage:         56
Setting:       8192
Percentage:    0.7

Parameter:     maxssiz
Usage:         1179648
Setting:       8388608
Standard input
                   .
                   .
                   .


# kcusage -t
Tunable              Usage / Setting        Usage      Id Name
============================================================================
dbc_max_pct              5 / 50
maxdsiz           37666816 / 1073741824
                                        37666816    3009 java
                                        28766208    1278 prm3d
                                        26869760    1254 midaemon
                                         4468736    1289 scopeux
                                         2424832    2438 rep_server
maxdsiz_64bit      7258112 / 4294967296
                                         7258112    1125 cimserver
                                         2019328     383 utmpd
                                         1814528    1506 icodd
                                         1134592     501 ipmon
                                           69632    1505 cimserverd
maxfiles_lim            56 / 8192
```

```
                                                     56    3009 java
                                                     30     757 inetd
                                                     22    1156 pwgrd
                                                     20    1289 scopeux
                                                     20    2439 agdbserver
         maxssiz              1179648 / 8388608
                                                   1179648  3009 java
                          .
                          .
                          .
```

kcusage has the following commonly used command-line flags:

-h	Prints kernel usage data over the past hour in 5-minute intervals
-d	Prints kernel usage data over the past 24 hours in hourly intervals
-m	Prints kernel usage data over the past 31 days in daily intervals
-y	Prints kernel usage data for the past 52 weeks in weekly intervals
-l	Prints the listing in long format
-t	Prints a listing that includes the top 5 processes or users of each resource

kcalarm

kcalarm manages alarms of kernel tunable parameters. By using **kcalarm**, you can perform a variety of alarm-related tasks.

kcalarm has the following command-line flags:

-a	Adds a tunable alarm.
-d	Deletes a tunable alarm.
-F	Forces a change in the status of an alarm.

-t threshold	Sets the threshold, which is based on a percentage of the current tunable value, such as 80%, which is the default
-e	Specifies the type of event that will trigger an alarm, such as *initial*, *repeat*, or *return*
-i interval	Specifies the sampling interval of the tunable in minutes. The default is 5 minutes
-c comment	Identifies the alarm request with your comment
-k key	Specifies a key that makes clear the alarm
-n notification	Target to be notified if the alarm is triggered such as the email address to which an email will be sent or a **syslog** entry to be written
-l	Produces a long listing
-s(on/off)	Sets the alarm on or off
-m(on/off/status)	Sets the monitoring of the kernel tunable as on, off, or view its present status

kcmond

The **kcmond** daemon monitors the amount of kernel resources consumed as part of Event Monitoring Service (EMS.) The data that **kcmond** captures can be displayed with **kcusage**. **kcmond** is an important part of managing alarms with **kcalarm** as described earlier. **kcmond** is started as part of EMS and is not designed to be run from the command line.

Building a Kernel

This section shows an example of taking an existing kernel running on an Integrity (Itanium) server and making some changes to it. Figure 5-1 shows some commonly performed kernel-related steps. I perform many of these steps in the following example.

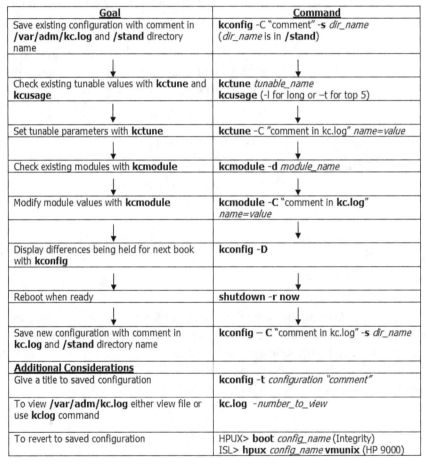

Goal	Command
Save existing configuration with comment in **/var/adm/kc.log** and **/stand** directory name	**kconfig** -C "comment" -s *dir_name* (*dir_name* is in **/stand**)
Check existing tunable values with **kctune** and **kcusage**	**kctune** *tunable_name* **kcusage** (-l for long or –t for top 5)
Set tunable parameters with **kctune**	**kctune** -C "comment in kc.log" *name=value*
Check existing modules with **kcmodule**	**kcmodule** -d *module_name*
Modify module values with **kcmodule**	**kcmodule** -C "comment in **kc.log**" *name=value*
Display differences being held for next book with **kconfig**	**kconfig** -D
Reboot when ready	**shutdown -r now**
Save new configuration with comment in **kc.log** and **/stand** directory name	**kconfig** – C "comment in kc.log" -s *dir_name*
Additional Considerations	
Give a title to saved configuration	**kconfig** -t *configuration* "comment"
To view **/var/adm/kc.log** either view file or use **kclog** command	**kc.log** -*number_to_view*
To revert to saved configuration	HPUX> **boot** *config_name* (Integrity) ISL> **hpux** *config_name* **vmunix** (HP 9000)

Figure 5-1   Commonly Performed Kernel Configuration Steps

Normally, you should change the kernel configuration before making any changes to it. To save the configuration, use -s and place a comment with -C as shown in the following command:

```
# kconfig -C "Initial configuration of vPars/Oracle/Peoplesoft system" -s
            Initial_vPars_Oracle_Peoplesoft
     * The current configuration has been saved to
       'Initial_vPars_Oracle_Peoplesoft'.
#
```

This command results in the following entry being made in **/var/adm/ kc.log**:

```
========================================================================

Change to configuration 'Initial_vPars_Oracle_Peoplesoft'
at 09:38:45 EDT on 21 September 2004 by root:
Configuration saved from currently running configuration.

Initial configuration of vPars/Oracle/Peoplesoft system
```

This is the last entry in **/var/adm/kc.log** immediately after the **kconfig** command was issued. The -s option results in this kernel having been saved in the directory **/stand/Initial_vPars_Oracle_Peoplesoft**, as shown in the following long listing of **/stand**:

```
Initial configuration of vPars/Oracle/Peoplesoft system

# ll /stand
total 96976
drwxr-xr-x    5 root      sys      8192 Sep 21 09:38 Initial_vPars_Oracle_Peoplesoft
drwxr-xr-x    5 root      sys      8192 Sep 21 09:11 backup
dr-xr-xr-x    3 bin       bin        96 May  5 15:46 boot.sys
-rw-r--r--    1 root      sys        21 May  5 15:44 bootconf
lrwxr-xr-x    1 root      root       14 Sep 21 09:17 bootfs -> current/bootfs
drwxr-xr-x    5 root      root     8192 May 25 12:03 crashconfig
drwxr-xr-x    5 root      sys      8192 Sep 21 09:11 current
drwxr-xr-x    5 root      sys      8192 Sep 19 15:38 initial_11iv2
drwxr-xr-x    5 root      sys      8192 Sep 12 20:28 installed
-rw-r--r--    1 root      sys     16024 Sep 21 09:17 ioconfig
-r--r--r--    1 root      sys        82 May  5 16:11 kernrel
drwxr-xr-x    2 root      sys        96 Sep 21 09:21 krs
drwxr-xr-x    5 root      sys      8192 May  5 16:12 last_install
drwxr-xr-x    2 root      root       96 May  5 15:43 lost+found
lrwxr-xr-x    1 root      root        7 Sep 21 09:17 nextboot -> current
-rw-------    1 root      root       12 Sep 21 09:17 rootconf
lrwxr-xr-x    1 root      root       15 Sep 21 09:17 system -> nextboot/system
-r--r--r--    1 root      sys      1996 May  5 16:01 system.import
-rw-r--r--    1 root      sys      2537 May  5 16:51 system.prev
-rwxr-xr-x    5 root      other    4656 Jun 15 15:49 vmunix
#
```

This directory contains all files associated with the currently running kernel, as shown in the following long listing which are in the directory **Initial_vPars_Oracle_Peoplesoft**:

```
# ll
total 96784
-rw-r--r--    1 root     sys               0 Sep 21 09:38 .config
-rw-r--r--    1 root     sys             147 Sep 21 09:38 README
drwxr-xr-x    3 root     sys              96 Sep 21 09:38 bootfs
drwxr-xr-x    2 root     sys              96 Sep 21 09:38 krs
drwxr-xr-x    2 root     sys              96 Sep 21 09:38 mod
-rw-r--r--    1 root     sys            2877 Sep 21 09:38 system
-rwxr-xr-x    5 root     other    49534656 Jun 15 15:49 vmunix
#
```

This directory contains the currently running kernel **vmunix**, the current **system** file, and other files associated with the currently running kernel. You may also want to give each configuration a title using the -t option to **kconfig**.

At this point I am protected in that if I had to revert to the saved kernel configuration after making changes I can do so. Now that the current configuration has been saved I will view an existing tunable parameter and module that I plan to change with the following commands:

```
# kctune -d nproc
Tunable  Value  Expression  Changes
    Description
nproc    4200   Default     Immed
    Maximum number of processes on the system
```

```
# kcmodule -d idds
Module   State    Cause
    Description
idds     unused
    Intrusion Detection Data Source
#
```

I also issue **kcusage** on a system before making a change to see the level of usage. If the system is not in use, however, and you're preparing it for use, the usage will be low so the output is not meaningful.

In this example, I change *nproc* from 4200 to 8020 and change *idds* to best. Immediately before making these changes I add a comment to **/var/adm/kc.log** so that a record exists of why these changes were made:

```
# kctune -C "first of many tunable changes for vPars/Oracle/Peoplesoft config"
  nproc=8020

WARNING: The automatic 'backup' configuration currently contains the
         configuration that was in use before the last reboot of this
         system.
    ==> Do you wish to update it to contain the current configuration
        before making the requested change? y
      * The automatic 'backup' configuration has been updated.
      * The requested changes have been applied to the currently
        running system.
Tunable           Value  Expression  Changes
nproc   (before)   4200   Default     Immed
        (now)      8020   8020
#
```

```
# kcmodule -C "first of many module changes for vPars/Oracle/Peoplesoft
             config" idds=best

NOTE:    The configuration being loaded contains the following change(s)
         that cannot be applied immediately and which will be held for
         the next boot:
    -- The configuration is supposed to include a module 'idds' which
       is not available without a kernel rebuild.
     * The automatic 'backup' configuration has been updated.
     * Building a new kernel for configuration 'nextboot'...
     * Adding version information to new kernel...
     * The requested changes have been saved, and will take effect at
       next boot.
Module           State    Cause
idds   (now)     unused
       (next boot) static  explicit
#
```

This tunable is dynamic, so the change was made immediately as you can see at the bottom of the listing with *now*. The **kcmodule** command changed *idds*; however, this will be applied at *next boot*, as shown in the following **kconfig** command:

```
# kconfig -D
Module           State    Cause
idds   (now)     unused
       (next boot) static  explicit
NOTE:    There are no tunable changes being held until next boot.
#
```

In both the **kctune** and **kcmodule** commands, I preceded the change with a comment (-C) that appears on the **/var/adm/kc.log** file.

For the module change to take place, a reboot is required. After the reboot takes place, I again issue the **kcmodule** command to show that the *idds* change has been incorporated into the new current kernel:

```
# kcmodule -d idds
Module State    Cause
    Description
idds    static  explicit
    Intrusion Detection Data Source
#
```

You would probably make more changes to the kernel than the two used in this example. After the changes are made, you would save the update configuration with the **kconfig** command:

```
# kconfig -C "Rev1 of vPars/Oracle/Peoplesoft kernel configuration"
 -s rev1_vPars_oracle_peoplesoft

    * The current configuration has been saved to
      'rev1_vPars_oracle_peoplesoft'.

# ll /stand
total 96992
drwxr-xr-x   5 root    sys       8192 Sep 21 09:38 Initial_vPars_Oracle_Peoplesoft
drwxr-xr-x   5 root    sys       8192 Sep 21 10:34 backup
dr-xr-xr-x   3 bin     bin         96 May  5 15:46 boot.sys
-rw-r--r--   1 root    sys         21 May  5 15:44 bootconf
lrwxr-xr-x   1 root    root        14 Sep 21 10:51 bootfs -> current/bootfs
drwxr-xr-x   5 root    root      8192 May 25 12:03 crashconfig
drwxr-xr-x   5 root    sys       8192 Sep 21 10:34 current
drwxr-xr-x   5 root    sys       8192 Sep 19 15:38 initial_11iv2
drwxr-xr-x   5 root    sys       8192 Sep 12 20:28 installed
-rw-r--r--   1 root    sys      16024 Sep 21 10:52 ioconfig
-r--r--r--   1 root    sys         82 May  5 16:11 kernrel
drwxr-xr-x   2 root    sys         96 Sep 21 10:56 krs
drwxr-xr-x   5 root    sys       8192 May  5 16:12 last_install
drwxr-xr-x   2 root    root        96 May  5 15:43 lost+found
lrwxr-xr-x   1 root    root         7 Sep 21 10:51 nextboot -> current
drwxr-xr-x   5 root    sys       8192 Sep 21 11:06 rev1_vPars_oracle_peoplesoft
-rw-------   1 root    root        12 Sep 21 10:51 rootconf
lrwxr-xr-x   1 root    root        15 Sep 21 10:51 system -> nextboot/system
-r--r--r--   1 root    sys       1996 May  5 16:01 system.import
-rw-r--r--   1 root    sys       2537 May  5 16:51 system.prev
-rwxr-xr-x   3 root    sys   49536344 Sep 21 10:34 vmunix
#
```

The long listing of **/stand** shows the **kconfig** command did indeed save the current kernel configuration under the name specified, beginning with *rev1*. In addition, a new comment in **/var/adm/kc.log** identifies that this step was taken. Now both the original configuration that was saved earlier and the current configuration exist in **/stand**.

I don't think you can save your kernel configuration too often. I sometimes make hundreds of kernel configuration parameter changes when I prepare a new system to run a specific application, so I'm careful to save my kernel before making these many changes. The only problem with saving many kernel configurations is the space consumed in **/stand**. If you run out of space in **/stand** it can be difficult to increase it, so you must keep an eye on the available space in **/stand**.

You may find yourself in a situation where you have to boot a saved kernel configuration, which is covered in the next section.

Reverting to a Saved Kernel Configuration

Although the two configuration changes made in the previous section were trivial if, for any reason, you need to revert to a saved kernel configuration you can do so. The easiest way to do this is to run **kconfig -n** *oldconfig*. An alternative is to load the saved configuration at the time of boot. In the following example, I could revert back to *Initial_vPars_Oracle_Peoplesoft* or *initial_11iv2* which were saved in **/stand**. To revert to this kernel configuration issue the following command at the HP-UX prompt on an Itanium system running EFI:

```
Please select a boot option

    HP-UX Primary Boot: 0/0/0/2/0.6.0
    Acpi(000222F0,0)/Pci(1|0)/Mac(00306E4B9AD9)
    Acpi(000222F0,100)/Pci(1|0)/Mac(00306E4BAA28)
    EFI Shell [Built-in]
    Boot option maintenance menu


    Use ^ and v to change option(s). Use Enter to select an option
Loading.: HP-UX Primary Boot: 0/0/0/2/0.6.0
Starting: HP-UX Primary Boot: 0/0/0/2/0.6.0

(c) Copyright 1990-2003, Hewlett Packard Company.
All rights reserved

HP-UX Boot Loader for IPF  --  Revision 1.73

Press Any Key to interrupt Autoboot
\EFI\HPUX\AUTO ==> boot vmunix
Seconds left till autoboot -   9
   Type 'help' for help

HPUX> boot initial_11iv2
```

From EFI, I select the *HP-UX Primary Boot* and then interrupt the boot. At this point, I enter *initial_11iv2* as the configuration to load.

On a PA-RISC system, this old configuration would have been entered at the ISL prompt with ISL> **hpux** *config_name* **vmunix**.

System File

Although the kernel commands covered support modifying your configuration and building a new kernel, you can still use **/stand/system** or the **system** file for any kernel configuration. There is a **system** file in the directory for all the kernel configurations that you've built on your system. These can be exported from one system and imported to another system in order to replicate a kernel configuration that you like onto another system. You can, for example, export a configuration with **kconfig -e** *name* on one system, import a configuration on another system with **kconfig -i** *name,* and thereby replicate a configuration on another system.

Device bindings are also managed in the system files. Device bindings are configuration settings that have to do with specific hardware devices such as primary swap (*swap* lines in the system file), dump devices (*dump* in the system file). and device driver (*device* in the system file) specifications.

Another common use of system files is to make multiple changes in the system file and have all the changes take effect on the next reboot.

The following is an abbreviated **system** file showing some of the lines in the currently running **system** file:

```
# example system file

* Module entries
*
module prm best [3F56E2F0]
module ipf loaded 0.1.0
module mpt best [40075F90]
module vols best [3F41B706]
                .
                .
                .

* Swap entries
*
*
* Dump entries
*
dump lvol
*
* Driver binding entries
*
*
* Tunables entries
*
tunable nproc 4200
tunable shmmax 68719476736
tunable semume 512
tunable semmnu 4092
tunable semmns 8192
tunable maxfiles 8192
tunable maxfiles_lim 8192
                .
                .
                .
```

This listing shows module, swap (none present), dump, and tunable entries.

You could update numerous entries in the **system** file. Issue **kconfig -i** *system_file_name* and reboot this system to incorporate the changes incorporated into the running kernel, as shown in the following listing:

```
# kconfig -i /stand/Initial_vPars_Oracle_Peoplesoft/system
WARNING: The automatic 'backup' configuration currently contains the
         configuration that was in use before the last reboot of this
         system.
     ==> Do you wish to update it to contain the current configuration
         before making the requested change? y
       * The automatic 'backup' configuration has been updated.
NOTE:    The configuration being loaded contains changes that cannot be
         applied immediately:
NOTE:    The changes will be held for next boot.
       * /stand/Initial_vPars_Oracle_Peoplesoft/system has been
         imported.  The changes will take effect at next boot.
[rx8620b{root}:/]>
```

The **kconfig** command updates the currently running kernel. The changes can not be applied immediately, so a reboot is required. The file **/stand/current/system** reflects the changes that you made to the configuration. You can also give a name to the updated configuration so that a new configuration is produced, as shown in the next example.

You can also make changes to **/stand/current/system** and save the configuration to a specific name, as shown the following example:

```
# kconfig -i test2 /stand/current/system
WARNING: The system file was created from the configuration 'nextboot'.
         The import operation is targeted at 'test2'.
     ==> Do you wish to continue? y
       * /stand/current/system has been imported to 'test2'.
    #
```

Prior to running this **kconfig** command, I update **/stand/current/system** with numerous changes. The changes were made immediately and no reboot was required for these dynamic changes to take effect. This **kconfig** command imports the **system** file and saves it to configuration called *test2*. This results in a **test2** directory in **/stand**, as shown in the following listing:

```
# ll /stand/test2
total 96784
-rw-r--r--   1 root      sys              0 Sep 25 11:24 .config
-rw-r--r--   1 root      sys            147 Sep 25 11:24 README
drwxr-xr-x   3 root      sys             96 Sep 25 11:24 bootfs
drwxr-xr-x   2 root      sys             96 Sep 25 11:24 krs
drwxr-xr-x   2 root      sys             96 Sep 25 11:24 mod
-rw-r--r--   1 root      sys           2902 Sep 25 11:24 system
-rwxr-xr-x   5 root      other     49534656 Jun 15 15:49 vmunix
#
```

This results in a saved configuration reflecting the changes that have been made. This configuration has been saved and can be loaded anytime.

The **mk_kernel -s** *system_file_name* command can also build the new kernel. **mk_kernel** is fully supported and is great for those of us who have used this command in past releases of HP-UX.

kcweb

kcweb is one of many Web-based system-administration tools. It can be invoked from SAM or directly in a browser window. In this section you perform a variety of functions through the Web-based interface. In this section we'll perform the following in **kcweb**:

- View kernel parameters
- Get details on a specific kernel parameter in the bottom of the **kcweb** page and the man page
- Modify a dynamic kernel parameter and apply the new value
- Set an alarm to inform you when a kernel parameter exceeds the specified value

At the time of this writing, **kcweb** is invoked from a browser with the URL https://*ip_address*:1188/casey/login.cgi, where *ip_address* is the IP address of the system on which you want to run **kcweb**. Figure 5-2 shows the main screen you see after invoking **kcweb**.

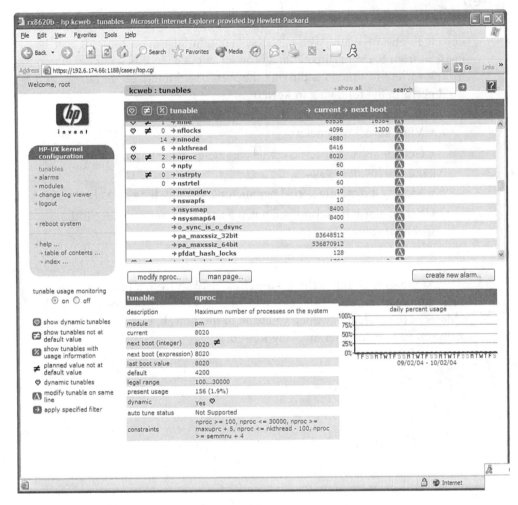

Figure 5-2   **kcweb** Showing *tunables*

The upper left of Figure 5-2 shows that **kcweb** has *tunables, alarms, modules*, and other functions.

Notice that in the bottom left of the figure, there is a legend that includes descriptions of the symbols used in **kcweb**. Those tunables with a heart next to them are dynamically tunable parameters. If you select the heart on the bar across the top of the tunables, only dynamically tunable parameters will be shown. The "not equal to" sign indicates parameters that are not set to their default value. Several other entries exist in the legend as

well. This makes for viewing groups of icons easy and the legend helps identify the status of icons.

The bottom of the screen provides information about the kernel parameter selected: in this case, *nproc*. A graph in the bottom right shows the
usage of this parameter over time. For system-wide parameters, the graph
shows usage on a system basis. For user-specific or process-specific parameters, the graph includes the top five consumers of the parameter.

The *constraints* at the very bottom of the page give an excellent overview of the tunable. If you need to get detailed information about a kernel
parameter, select the *man page...* button, as shown in Figure 5-3.

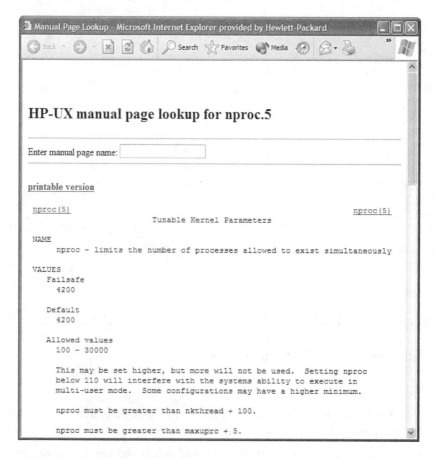

Figure 5-3   **kcweb** Man Page of *nproc*

You can also modify one of the parameters by highlighting the parameter and then selecting *modify <parameter name>* as is done for the *nproc* parameter, as shown in Figure 5-4.

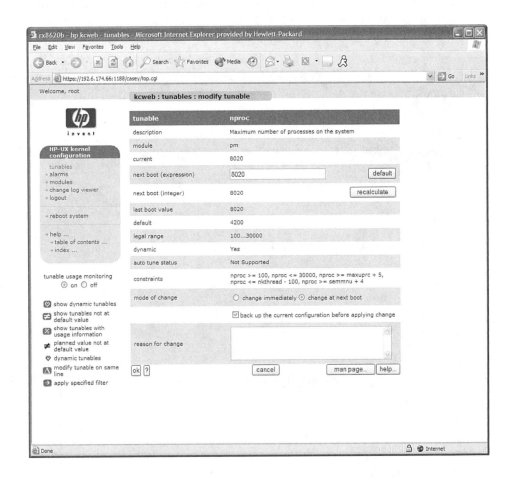

Figure 5-4   **kcweb** Showing *modify nproc*

You can change the value of *nproc* and then select whether you want a change immediately or at the next boot.

You can set an alarm to be informed when the parameter reaches a specified threshold. Figure 5-5 shows the process of setting up this alarm.

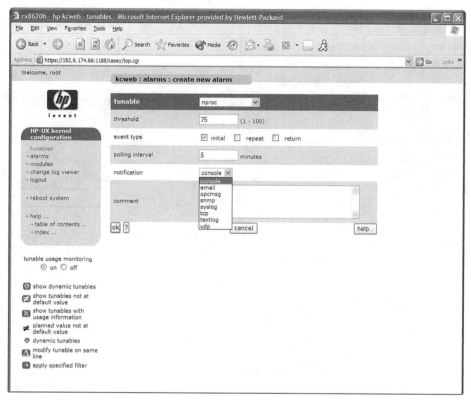

Figure 5-5   **kcweb** Showing *nproc* Alarm

We get to the *kcweb:alarms* page by selecting *create new alarm...* in Figure 5-5. All the parameters related to the alarm are shown in Figure 5-5. The setup of the alarm allows you to specify a *threshold*. All of the options for notification are shown such as sending an email

You can also work with kernel modules in the same way that you work with kernel tunables. Those that are dynamic can be loaded on-the-fly, and those that are not dynamic can be built into the kernel with a rebuild.

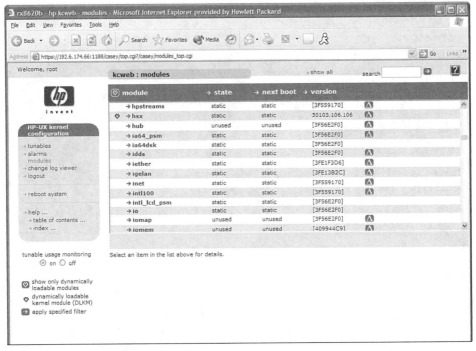

Figure 5-6   **kcweb** Showing *modules*

As with tunables, modules can be dynamic. In Figure 5-6, the idds module that we worked with earlier in the chapter is shown, which is static, as well as hsx, which has a heart next to it to indicate that it is a Dynamically Loadable Kernel Module (DLKM.)

You can also view **/var/adm/kc.log** with *change log viewer,* as shown in Figure 5-7.

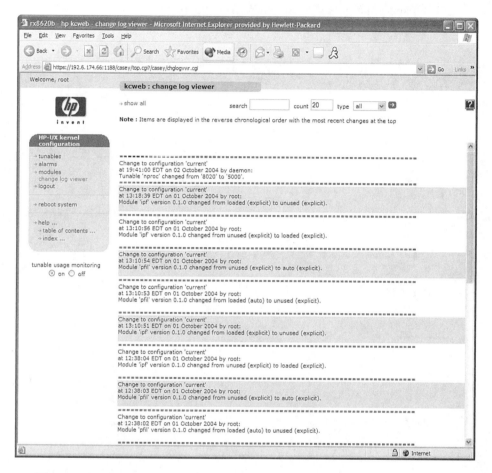

Figure 5-7   **kcweb** Showing Log File

There is also a table of contents and index that you can refer to if you need help with any kernel-related task.

Using **kcweb**, you can accomplish the tasks as you can at the command line. It's a matter of preference whether you take the graphical **kcweb** interface or the command line approach covered earlier in the chapter.

This chapter gave a quick overview of **kcweb**, which included some of the most commonly performed tasks. Because this is a Web-based interface, it is easy to use and most of the screens and information are self-explanatory.

Other Web-based management tools can be invoked through SAM including **pdweb** and **parmgr**; those are covered in other chapters.

Chapter 6

Devices

Introduction

With the proliferation of cell-based partitionable HP-UX systems, there is a lot to know about devices. Cell-based systems greatly increase the complexity of working with devices, such as determining in what partition devices are located, mapping card and slot numbers in I/O chassis, and other topics. Whether you use cell-based systems or not, you need to understand many important device-related commands, such as **ioscan**. Keep in mind that most device-related work on cell-based systems is relative to the partition in which you're working and not on a global systems basis. The tear-out card provided with this book also contains a lot of useful information related to devices. This chapter covers a variety of topics, including the following:

- Overview of device file.
- The **ioscan** command on an Integrity Superdome to show the components of an nPartition.
- The **info io** command run at the EFI shell prompt on HP Integrity (Itanium) servers provides information about all the components contained in a Node partition or nPartition.
- Identify card and slot numbers on and Integrity (Itanium) Superdome and rx system.

• Overview of OnLine Addition and Replacement (OLA/R) on an
rx8620. This is done using the Web-based Peripheral Devices Tool (pd)
that is invoked through the System Administration Manager (SAM).

• Overview of device-related commands **lsdev** and **lssf**.

The following section is a general overview of device files.

Device File Background

A device file is an interface to a physical device in the file system, and configuration information associated with each device file tells the kernel which
device you're accessing and some details on how you want to access it. The
HP-UX kernel needs to know a lot about a device before Input/Output (I/O)
operations can be performed. Device files are in the **/dev** directory. There
may also be a subdirectory under **/dev** used to further categorize the device
files. Examples of a subdirectories are **/dev/dsk**, where disk device files are
usually located, and **/dev/rmt**, where tape drive device files are located. Figure 6-1 shows the device filenaming convention.

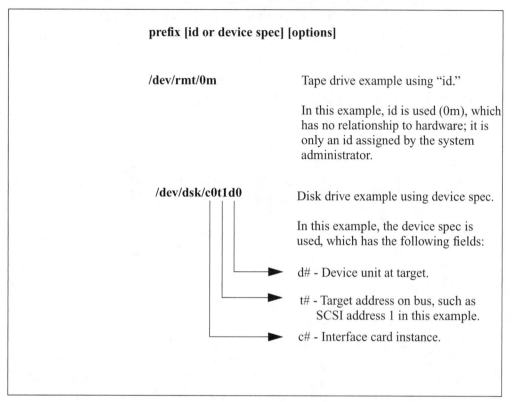

Figure 6-1   HP-UX 11i Device Filenaming Convention

If you list the contents of **/dev**, you see many device files. These are for a variety of different devices that are created for you by HP-UX.

Most of the balance of this chapter discusses performing various tasks with devices, such as listing them with **ioscan**, mapping cards to physical slots, and so on.

The next section covers the **ioscan** command.

The ioscan Command

This section starts by issuing some **ioscan** commands so you can see the various components in an nPartition on a 16-cell board system. The first command shows the processors. Coming shortly is an overview of the **olrad -q** command in which processors are not shown because, at the time of this writing, they are not OLA/R. The following **ioscan** output uses options to produce information about the processors in nPartition 0 that are configured into the kernel:

```
[rx8620b{root}:/roothome]>ioscan -fnkCprocessor
Class      I  H/W Path  Driver     S/W State H/W Type  Description
==================================================================
processor  0  0/120     processor CLAIMED    PROCESSOR Processor
processor  1  0/121     processor CLAIMED    PROCESSOR Processor
processor  2  0/122     processor CLAIMED    PROCESSOR Processor
processor  3  0/123     processor CLAIMED    PROCESSOR Processor
processor  4  2/120     processor CLAIMED    PROCESSOR Processor
processor  5  2/121     processor CLAIMED    PROCESSOR Processor
processor  6  2/122     processor CLAIMED    PROCESSOR Processor
processor  7  2/123     processor CLAIMED    PROCESSOR Processor
processor  8  3/120     processor CLAIMED    PROCESSOR Processor
processor  9  3/121     processor CLAIMED    PROCESSOR Processor
processor 10  3/122     processor CLAIMED    PROCESSOR Processor
processor 11  3/123     processor CLAIMED    PROCESSOR Processor
[rx8620b{root}:/roothome]>
```

This output shows 12 processors in the nPartition that are on cell boards 0, 2, and 3 as indicated by the leading number in the hardware path. The second number in the hardware path is that of the processor.

This **ioscan** output produced information about the cell boards that are configured into nPartition *0,* but 4 cell boards exist in this system. To see information about a specific cell board in the system, issue **parstatus -c***cellboardnumber,* such as **parstatus -c3**, for information about cell board 3, as shown in the following listing:

```
[rx8620b{root}:/roothome]>parstatus -c3

[Cell]
                           CPU     Memory                          Use
                           OK/     (GB)                    Core    On
Hardware    Actual         Deconf/ OK/                     Cell    Next  Par
Location    Usage          Max     Deconf   Connected To   Capable Boot  Num
========== ============= ======= ========= ================== ======= ==== ===
cab0,cell3 Active Base    4/0/8   16.0/0.0  -                  no      yes  0

Notes: * = Cell has no interleaved memory.
```

nPartition commands are covered extensively in Chapter 17, "Node Partitions (nPartitions) and Management Processor Overview." This command shows that cell board 3 is part of *Par Num* 0 which is the partition to which we're connected. Cell board 1 is missing from the list of 12 processors that are part of nPartition 0, as we saw in the earlier **ioscan -fnkCprocessor** output. I now run **parstatus -c1** to see if cell board 1 is devoted to an nPartition:

```
[rx8620b{root}:/roothome]>parstatus -c1


[Cell]
                        CPU     Memory                          Use
                        OK/     (GB)                    Core    On
        Hardware  Actual  Deconf/ OK/                   Cell    Next Par
        Location  Usage   Max     Deconf   Connected To Capable Boot Num
        ========= ============ ======= ========= =================== ======= ==== ===
        cab0,cell1 Active Core  4/0/8   16.0/0.0 cab0,bay0,chassis1  yes     yes  1


Notes: * = Cell has no interleaved memory.
          [rx8620b{root}:/roothome]>
```

Although Chapter 17 covers partition-related commands in detail, it is important to know the basics of working with cell boards and partition commands in order to work with devices. The **info io** command, which is run at the EFI shell prompt, is also an important command related to devices that is covered in an upcoming section.

To see all the components in your nPartition, issue the **ioscan -f** command as shown in the following listing.

```
[rx8620b{root}:/roothome]>ioscan -f
Class     I  H/W Path      Driver   S/W State  H/W Type   Description
===================================================================================
root      0                root     CLAIMED    BUS_NEXUS
cell      0  0             cell     CLAIMED    BUS_NEXUS
ioa       0  0/0           sba      CLAIMED    BUS_NEXUS  System Bus
                                                         Adapter (127b)
ba        1  0/0/0         lba      CLAIMED    BUS_NEXUS  Local PCI Bus
                                                         Adapter (1054)
tty       0  0/0/0/0/0     asio0    CLAIMED    INTERFACE  PCI SimpleComm
                                                         (103c1290)
tty       1  0/0/0/0/1     asio0    CLAIMED    INTERFACE  PCI Serial (103c1048)
lan       0  0/0/0/1/0     igelan   CLAIMED    INTERFACE  HP A7109-60001 PCI
                                                         1000Base-T Core
ext_bus   0  0/0/0/2/0     c8xx     CLAIMED    INTERFACE  SCSI C1010 Ultra Wide
                                                         Single-Ended
target    1  0/0/0/2/0.6   tgt      CLAIMED    DEVICE
disk      0  0/0/0/2/0.6.0 sdisk    CLAIMED    DEVICE     HP 146 GST3146807LC
target    2  0/0/0/2/0.7   tgt      CLAIMED    DEVICE
ctl       0  0/0/0/2/0.7.0 sctl     CLAIMED    DEVICE     Initiator
ext_bus   1  0/0/0/2/1     c8xx     CLAIMED    INTERFACE  SCSI C1010 Ultra Wide
                                                         Single-Ended
target    0  0/0/0/2/1.2   tgt      CLAIMED    DEVICE
disk      1  0/0/0/2/1.2.0 sdisk    CLAIMED    DEVICE     HP       DVD-ROM 305
target    3  0/0/0/2/1.7   tgt      CLAIMED    DEVICE
ctl       1  0/0/0/2/1.7.0 sctl     CLAIMED    DEVICE     Initiator
ext_bus   2  0/0/0/3/0     c8xx     CLAIMED    INTERFACE  SCSI C1010 Ultra Wide
```

```
                                                              Single-Ended
target       4    0/0/0/3/0.6      tgt      CLAIMED    DEVICE
disk         2    0/0/0/3/0.6.0    sdisk    CLAIMED    DEVICE       HP 146 GST3146807LC
target       5    0/0/0/3/0.7      tgt      CLAIMED    DEVICE
ctl          2    0/0/0/3/0.7.0    sctl     CLAIMED    DEVICE       Initiator
ext_bus      3    0/0/0/3/1        c8xx     CLAIMED    INTERFACE    SCSI C1010 Ultra160
                                                                    Wide LVD
target       6    0/0/0/3/1.7      tgt      CLAIMED    DEVICE
ctl          3    0/0/0/3/1.7.0    sctl     CLAIMED    DEVICE       Initiator
ba           2    0/0/1           lba      CLAIMED    BUS_NEXUS    Local PCI-X Bus
                                                                    Adapter (122e)
ba           3    0/0/2           lba      CLAIMED    BUS_NEXUS    Local PCI-X Bus
                                                                    Adapter (122e)
ba           4    0/0/4           lba      CLAIMED    BUS_NEXUS    Local PCI-X Bus
                                                                    Adapter (122e)
ba           5    0/0/6           lba      CLAIMED    BUS_NEXUS    Local PCI-X Bus
                                                                    Adapter (122e)
ext_bus      4    0/0/6/1/0        c8xx     CLAIMED    INTERFACE    SCSI C1010 Ultra160
                                                                    Wide LVD A6829-60101
target       7    0/0/6/1/0.7      tgt      CLAIMED    DEVICE
ctl          4    0/0/6/1/0.7.0    sctl     CLAIMED    DEVICE       Initiator
ext_bus      5    0/0/6/1/1        c8xx     CLAIMED    INTERFACE    SCSI C1010 Ultra160
                                                                    Wide LVD A6829-60101
target       8    0/0/6/1/1.7      tgt      CLAIMED    DEVICE
ctl          5    0/0/6/1/1.7.0    sctl     CLAIMED    DEVICE       Initiator
ba           6    0/0/8           lba      CLAIMED    BUS_NEXUS    Local PCI-X Bus
                                                                    Adapter (122e)
fc           0    0/0/8/1/0        td       CLAIMED    INTERFACE    HP Tachyon XL2 Fibre
                                                         Channel Mass Storage Adapter
ba           7    0/0/10          lba      CLAIMED    BUS_NEXUS    Local PCI-X Bus
                                                                    Adapter (122e)
fc           1    0/0/10/1/0       td       CLAIMED    INTERFACE    HP Tachyon XL2 Fibre
                                                         Channel Mass Storage Adapter
ba           8    0/0/12          lba      CLAIMED    BUS_NEXUS    Local PCI-X Bus
                                                                    Adapter (122e)
lan          1    0/0/12/1/0       igelan   CLAIMED    INTERFACE    HP A6825-60101 PCI
                                                                    1000Base-T Adapter
ba           9    0/0/14          lba      CLAIMED    BUS_NEXUS    Local PCI-X Bus
                                                                    Adapter (122e)
lan          2    0/0/14/1/0       igelan   CLAIMED    INTERFACE    HP A6825-60101 PCI
                                                                    1000Base-T Adapter
processor    0    0/120        processor   CLAIMED    PROCESSOR    Processor
processor    1    0/121        processor   CLAIMED    PROCESSOR    Processor
processor    2    0/122        processor   CLAIMED    PROCESSOR    Processor
processor    3    0/123        processor   CLAIMED    PROCESSOR    Processor
ba          10    0/250        pdh          CLAIMED    BUS_NEXUS    Core I/O Adapter
ipmi         0    0/250/0      ipmi         CLAIMED    INTERFACE    IPMI Controller
acpi_node    0    0/250/1      acpi_node   CLAIMED    INTERFACE    Acpi Hardware
cell         1    2            cell         CLAIMED    BUS_NEXUS
processor    4    2/120        processor   CLAIMED    PROCESSOR    Processor
processor    5    2/121        processor   CLAIMED    PROCESSOR    Processor
processor    6    2/122        processor   CLAIMED    PROCESSOR    Processor
processor    7    2/123        processor   CLAIMED    PROCESSOR    Processor
ba          11    2/250        pdh          CLAIMED    BUS_NEXUS    Core I/O Adapter
acpi_node    1    2/250/0      acpi_node   CLAIMED    INTERFACE    Acpi Hardware
cell         2    3            cell         CLAIMED    BUS_NEXUS
processor    8    3/120        processor   CLAIMED    PROCESSOR    Processor
processor    9    3/121        processor   CLAIMED    PROCESSOR    Processor
processor   10    3/122        processor   CLAIMED    PROCESSOR    Processor
processor   11    3/123        processor   CLAIMED    PROCESSOR    Processor
ba          12    3/250        pdh          CLAIMED    BUS_NEXUS    Core I/O Adapter
acpi_node    2    3/250/0      acpi_node   CLAIMED    INTERFACE    Acpi Hardware
ba           0    255/255      swspBus     CLAIMED    VIRTBUS
[rx8620b{root}:/roothome] >
```

The **ioscan** output has the following fields in it:

• The device class

• The instance number of the device

• The hardware path of the device

• The kernel driver used for the device

• The software state of the device which is *CLAIMED* for all the devices in the output

• The hardware type of the device

• A description field

All components in nPartition 0 are shown in this output. Because I did not use the *-k* option, all components are listed, not just those built into the kernel. This **ioscan** output includes all components in nPartition *0*. The form of the **ioscan** output for an nPartition looks like the following for the hardware path:

```
Field 1          Field 2        Field3        Field 4    Field 5   Field 6

Global cell no./proc, mem, or SBA/LBA/Card address/Function/dev addr
```

Because the cell number is the first field, you know immediately what cells are in the partition you're viewing. The I/O chassis connected to a cell board is automatically part of the partition. The global cell number is related to multiple cabinets.

This output is ideal for viewing the hierarchy of the system, in this case, an rx8620, which is a four-cell-board HP Integrity (Itanium) system. The second line of the listing shows a cell board at 0. The next line shows a system bus adapter (SBA) at 0/0. The next line shows a local bus adapter (LBA) at 0/0/0. These three lines provide an overview of the hierarchy of the system with a cell board, SBA, and LBA as you work your way down the tree.

Chapter 17 also covers **ioscan** and the components in partitions.

This output shows cell boards 0, 2, and 3 in this nPartition, as you saw in the **ioscan -fnkCprocessor** output.

Many LBAs are shown in the **ioscan** output, which means that there are many slots in the I/O chassis of this system. This hierarchy is further evident if you use the *-e* option in **ioscan**, which shows the EFI device paths:

```
[rx8620b{root}:/dev/dsk]>ioscan -e
H/W Path        Class                      Description
========================================================
                root
0               cell
0/0                    ioa               System Bus Adapter (127b)
0/0/0                      ba            Local PCI Bus Adapter (1054)
0/0/0/0/0                       tty      PCI SimpleComm (103c1290)
0/0/0/0/1                       tty      PCI Serial (103c1048)
0/0/0/1/0                       lan      HP A7109-60001 PCI 1000Base-T Core
0/0/0/2/0                   ext_bus      SCSI C1010 Ultra Wide Single-Ended
0/0/0/2/0.6                     target
0/0/0/2/0.6.0                     disk   HP 146 GST3146807LC
        Acpi(000222F0,0)/Pci(2|0)/Scsi(Pun6,Lun0)/HD(Part1,Sig75AD9336-9ECC-11D8-8002-
D6217B60E588)/\EFI\HPUX\HPUX.EFI
0/0/0/2/0.7                     target
0/0/0/2/0.7.0                     ctl    Initiator
0/0/0/2/1                   ext_bus      SCSI C1010 Ultra Wide Single-Ended
0/0/0/2/1.2                     target
0/0/0/2/1.2.0                     disk   HP       DVD-ROM 305
        Acpi(000222F0,0)/Pci(2|1)/Scsi(Pun2,Lun0)/\EFI\HPUX\HPUX.EFI
0/0/0/2/1.7                     target
0/0/0/2/1.7.0                     ctl    Initiator
0/0/0/3/0                   ext_bus      SCSI C1010 Ultra Wide Single-Ended
0/0/0/3/0.6                     target
0/0/0/3/0.6.0                     disk   HP 146 GST3146807LC
        Acpi(000222F0,0)/Pci(3|0)/Scsi(Pun6,Lun0)/\EFI\HPUX\HPUX.EFI
0/0/0/3/0.7                     target
0/0/0/3/0.7.0                     ctl    Initiator
0/0/0/3/1                   ext_bus      SCSI C1010 Ultra160 Wide LVD
0/0/0/3/1.7                     target
0/0/0/3/1.7.0                     ctl    Initiator
0/0/1                      ba            Local PCI-X Bus Adapter (122e)
0/0/2                      ba            Local PCI-X Bus Adapter (122e)
0/0/4                      ba            Local PCI-X Bus Adapter (122e)
0/0/6                      ba            Local PCI-X Bus Adapter (122e)
0/0/6/1/0                   ext_bus      SCSI C1010 Ultra160 Wide LVD A6829-60101
0/0/6/1/0.7                     target
0/0/6/1/0.7.0                     ctl    Initiator
0/0/6/1/1                   ext_bus      SCSI C1010 Ultra160 Wide LVD A6829-60101
0/0/6/1/1.7                     target
0/0/6/1/1.7.0                     ctl    Initiator
0/0/8                      ba            Local PCI-X Bus Adapter (122e)
0/0/8/1/0                       fc       HP Tachyon XL2 Fibre Channel Mass Storage Adapter
0/0/10                     ba            Local PCI-X Bus Adapter (122e)
0/0/10/1/0                      fc       HP Tachyon XL2 Fibre Channel Mass Storage Adapter
0/0/12                     ba            Local PCI-X Bus Adapter (122e)
0/0/12/1/0                      lan      HP A6825-60101 PCI 1000Base-T Adapter
0/0/14                     ba            Local PCI-X Bus Adapter (122e)
0/0/14/1/0                      lan      HP A6825-60101 PCI 1000Base-T Adapter
0/120               processor            Processor
0/121               processor            Processor
0/122               processor            Processor
0/123               processor            Processor
0/250               ba                   Core I/O Adapter
0/250/0                  ipmi            IPMI Controller
0/250/1                  acpi_node       Acpi Hardware
2               cell
2/120               processor            Processor
2/121               processor            Processor
2/122               processor            Processor
2/123               processor            Processor
2/250               ba                   Core I/O Adapter
2/250/0                  acpi_node       Acpi Hardware
3               cell
3/120               processor            Processor
3/121               processor            Processor
3/122               processor            Processor
3/123               processor            Processor
3/250               ba                   Core I/O Adapter
3/250/0                  acpi_node       Acpi Hardware
255/255             ba
[rx8620b{root}:/dev/dsk]>
```

I like the output of this command because the hierarchy of the devices is easy to visualize. This output is relative to the nPartition in which you're working. The components of the other nPartitions are not shown for **ioscan** outputs.

The next section covers determining what slot numbers correspond to what LBAs.

Mapping LBA to Slot Number

It is not immediately apparent from an I/O listing in what slot a card is located. This mapping can be important should you have to replace or add a card and need to know slot versus LBA information.

You know the LBA from the **ioscan** output, but you don't know the slot number. (Remember that the **ioscan** output is in the form of *Cell/SBA/LBA/ Device.*) The I/O cardcage itself has on it the mapping of slot and LBA. Table 6-1 shows this mapping for an Integrity Superdome.

Table 6-1   *SLOT* Versus *LBA* Information Shown on Integrity Superdome

SLOT	11	10	9	8	7	6	5	4	3	2	1	0
LBA	8	9	10	11	12	14	6	4	3	2	1	0

This information is for a 12-slot I/O cardcage on an Integrity Superdome.

The LBA numbers and slot numbers do not correspond in the table. The LBA number is the same as the "rope." The rope is an internal connection to the slot. In the case of some LBA slots, such as 4 through 7, two ropes are connected to the slot, thereby doubling its speed. The LBA number for those slots is the first of the two ropes of the slot.

Identify the Cards and Slot Numbers—Integrity Superdome Example

Vital to the operation of an enterprise system is documenting the I/O of a system. A variety of commands gives you insight into the makeup of your system. It's useful to get an understanding of the hierarchy of I/O on your system.

A good place to start documenting your system is with the System Bus Adapter (SBAs) and Local Bus Adapters (LBAs). These can both be displayed with **ioscan**. These are internal components. There are typically several LBAs per SBA. In the following example I check the partition number with **parstatus -w**, and run **ioscan** looking for *sba* and *lba*. The following output displays the SBAs and LBAs on a 16-cell board Integrity Superdome:

```
# parstatus -w
The local partition number is 1.
# ioscan -f | grep sba
ioa        0  4/0         sba      CLAIMED    BUS_NEXUS    System Bus Adapter (127b)
# ioscan -f | grep lba
ba         0  4/0/0       lba      CLAIMED    BUS_NEXUS    Local PCI-X Bus Adapter (122e)
ba         1  4/0/1       lba      CLAIMED    BUS_NEXUS    Local PCI-X Bus Adapter (122e)
ba         2  4/0/2       lba      CLAIMED    BUS_NEXUS    Local PCI-X Bus Adapter (122e)
ba         3  4/0/3       lba      CLAIMED    BUS_NEXUS    Local PCI-X Bus Adapter (122e)
ba         4  4/0/4       lba      CLAIMED    BUS_NEXUS    Local PCI-X Bus Adapter (122e)
ba         5  4/0/6       lba      CLAIMED    BUS_NEXUS    Local PCI-X Bus Adapter (122e)
ba         6  4/0/8       lba      CLAIMED    BUS_NEXUS    Local PCI-X Bus Adapter (122e)
ba         7  4/0/9       lba      CLAIMED    BUS_NEXUS    Local PCI-X Bus Adapter (122e)
ba         9  4/0/10      lba      CLAIMED    BUS_NEXUS    Local PCI-X Bus Adapter (122e)
ba        10  4/0/11      lba      CLAIMED    BUS_NEXUS    Local PCI-X Bus Adapter (122e)
ba        11  4/0/12      lba      CLAIMED    BUS_NEXUS    Local PCI-X Bus Adapter (122e)
ba        12  4/0/14      lba      CLAIMED    BUS_NEXUS    Local PCI-X Bus Adapter (122e)
```

The SBA is in the form *Global cell number/SBA*. The SBA number on an HP Integrity Superdome is always 0. The LBAs are in the form *Global cell number/SBA/LBA/device/function.target.LUN*.

A specific LBA can be displayed in **ioscan** and then mapped to a slot. Table 6-2 shows the mapping of slot to LBA.

Table 6-2 *SLOT, LBA,* and *Rope* on Integrity Superdome for PCI/X

SLOT	11	10	9	8	7	6	5	4	3	2	1	0
LBA	8	9	10	11	12	14	6	4	3	2	1	0
Rope(s)	8	9	10	11	12 and 13	14 and 15	6 and 7	4 and 5	3	2	1	0

From an operational perspective, you're now able to relate an LBA to a slot number. A PCI-X slot with one rope runs at 66MHz and one with two ropes runs at 133 MHz. Slots 4, 5, 6, and 7 have two ropes. You can see in Table 6-2 that the LBAs get their number assignments from the ropes. In the case of a slot with two ropes, the LBA number comes from the first of the two ropes.

You still need more information to make this useful, however. Let's get the details on the card in LBA 6, as shown in the following listing:

```
# ioscan -fneC disk                          <- LBA 6 only display
          Acpi(000222F0,469)/Pci(1|0)/Fibre(WWN39DC812,Lun0)/\EFI\HPUX\HPUX.EFI
disk       18 4/0/6/1/0.3.1.0.0.0.1    sdisk   CLAIMED     DEVICE       HP      OPEN-E*2
                               /dev/dsk/c4t0d1     /dev/dsk/c4t0d1s1     /dev/dsk/c4t0d1s2
/dev/dsk/c4t0d1s3     /dev/rdsk/c4t0d1     /dev/rdsk/c4t0d1s1    /dev/rdsk/c4t0d1s2   /dev/
rdsk/c4t0d1s3
          Acpi(000222F0,469)/Pci(1|0)/Fibre(WWN39DC812,Lun0)/HD(Part1,SigD5A6EB12-30EE-
11D8-8002-D6217B60E588)/\EFI\HPUX\HPUX.EFI
disk       38 4/0/6/1/0.3.1.0.0.0.2    sdisk   CLAIMED     DEVICE       HP      OPEN-E
                               /dev/dsk/c4t0d2     /dev/rdsk/c4t0d2
          Acpi(000222F0,469)/Pci(1|0)/Fibre(WWN39DC812,Lun0)/\EFI\HPUX\HPUX.EFI
disk       40 4/0/6/1/0.3.1.0.0.0.3    sdisk   CLAIMED     DEVICE       HP      OPEN-E
                               /dev/dsk/c4t0d3     /dev/rdsk/c4t0d3
          Acpi(000222F0,469)/Pci(1|0)/Fibre(WWN39DC812,Lun0)/\EFI\HPUX\HPUX.EFI
disk       42 4/0/6/1/0.3.1.0.0.0.4    sdisk   CLAIMED     DEVICE       HP      OPEN-E
                               /dev/dsk/c4t0d4     /dev/rdsk/c4t0d4
          Acpi(000222F0,469)/Pci(1|0)/Fibre(WWN39DC812,Lun0)/\EFI\HPUX\HPUX.EFI
disk       44 4/0/6/1/0.3.1.0.0.0.5    sdisk   CLAIMED     DEVICE       HP      OPEN-E
                               /dev/dsk/c4t0d5     /dev/rdsk/c4t0d5
          Acpi(000222F0,469)/Pci(1|0)/Fibre(WWN39DC812,Lun0)/\EFI\HPUX\HPUX.EFI
disk       45 4/0/6/1/0.3.1.0.0.0.6    sdisk   CLAIMED     DEVICE       HP      OPEN-E
                               /dev/dsk/c4t0d6     /dev/rdsk/c4t0d6
          Acpi(000222F0,469)/Pci(1|0)/Fibre(WWN39DC812,Lun0)/\EFI\HPUX\HPUX.EFI
disk       46 4/0/6/1/0.3.1.0.0.0.7    sdisk   CLAIMED     DEVICE       HP      OPEN-E
                               /dev/dsk/c4t0d7     /dev/rdsk/c4t0d7
          Acpi(000222F0,469)/Pci(1|0)/Fibre(WWN39DC812,Lun0)/\EFI\HPUX\HPUX.EFI
disk       19 4/0/6/1/0.3.1.0.0.1.0    sdisk   CLAIMED     DEVICE       HP      OPEN-E
                               /dev/dsk/c4t1d0     /dev/rdsk/c4t1d0
          Acpi(000222F0,469)/Pci(1|0)/Fibre(WWN39DC812,Lun0)/\EFI\HPUX\HPUX.EFI
disk       49 4/0/6/1/0.3.1.0.0.1.1    sdisk   CLAIMED     DEVICE       HP      OPEN-E
                               /dev/dsk/c4t1d1     /dev/rdsk/c4t1d1
          Acpi(000222F0,469)/Pci(1|0)/Fibre(WWN39DC812,Lun0)/\EFI\HPUX\HPUX.EFI
disk       50 4/0/6/1/0.3.1.0.0.1.2    sdisk   CLAIMED     DEVICE       HP      OPEN-E
                               /dev/dsk/c4t1d2     /dev/rdsk/c4t1d2
          Acpi(000222F0,469)/Pci(1|0)/Fibre(WWN39DC812,Lun0)/\EFI\HPUX\HPUX.EFI
disk       52 4/0/6/1/0.3.1.0.0.1.3    sdisk   CLAIMED     DEVICE       HP      OPEN-E
                               /dev/dsk/c4t1d3     /dev/rdsk/c4t1d3
```

For now, just ignore the lines beginning with *Acpi,* which was produced in the **ioscan** output with the **-e** option. The **-e** in this output displays EFI device paths when available. These outputs are in the form *Global cell number/SBA/LBA/device/function.target.LUN.* There is clearly a fibre card in LBA 6 that corresponds to slot 5 as shown in Table 6-2. If there were to be a problem with this card, you would know the type of card and that it is in slot 5. On-line addition and replacement (OLAR) may be possible for this card. (OLAR is covered later in this chapter.) For now let's further investigate this card and slot.

Let's now evaluate the Acpi portion of the **ioscan** output. The ACPI varies from system to system, but this is a useful analysis even though it's unique to a particular system. ACPI stands for Advanced Configuration and Power Interface. This is an open industry specification developed by several companies, including HP. This standard defines power and configuration management interfaces between the operating system and the firmware. On HP Integrity Servers you see ACPI output in EFI, such as when you run the **map** command or **info io** at the EFI shell prompt, and in the **ioscan** output. The Acpi lines are in the form:

Acpi(..., XYY)/Pci(A|B)/Scsi(PunC, LunD)/...

The following bullets describe some of these fields:

- X is the cell number in hex. To determine the cell number you would convert X to decimal. Hex A = decimal 10, Hex B = decimal 11, Hex C = decimal 12, and so on. In an earlier example, the fibre card is connected to cell number 4. The cell is not shown for devices connected to cell 0.

- YY is the PCI bus number in hex. This number can be converted to its corresponding rope number, LBA number, and slot number. The best way to get this number is with the **info io** command at the EFI shell (see the next section to get the **info io** output on an rx8620.)

- A is the PCI device in hex which is usually a 1 or 0. In an earlier example, the device number is a 1, indicating PCI-X, in the Acpi output and a 1 in the "disk" output line as well. A 0 would be a PCI device.

- B is the PCI function in hex which is usually a 1 or 0. In the earlier example, the function number is a 0 in the Acpi output and a 0 in the "disk" output line as well.

- C is the target or Physical Unit Number (PUN) in hex. In the earlier example, the worldwide name is the physical unit number in the Acpi output and a 3 in the "disk" output. It is useful to have both of these PUN assignments.

- D is the logical unit number in hex, which is usually 0. This is a 0 in both outputs in an earlier example.

An ideal output to have is from the **info io** command, which you issue at the EFI shell prompt on an HP Integrity Server when the complex is down and you can get access to the EFI shell prompt. There is an example of this output for the rx8620 in that section.

Much device-related information was produced in this section. The following bullet list summarizes some of the steps that I recommend you run on your server:

- Run **ioscan | grep sba** and **ioscan | grep LBA** to get a list of SBAs and LBAs. These outputs are in the form shown here:

  cell/SBA/LBA

- From the previous **ioscan** output you can select an LBA about which you want to get details with **ioscan -f | grep 0/0/6** or substitute whatever LBA number about which you want to know more information. This output is in the following form:

  cell/SBA/LBA/device/function.target.LUN.

- Produce a table that maps slot to LBA, and include the ropes and frequency if you like, so that when you run **ioscan** and get the LBA of a card, you immediately know in what slot it is located.

- Include the Acpi lines with the **-e** option to **ioscan** if you're working on an HP Integrity Server.

- Run **info io** at the EFI shell prompt to produce a list of I/O chassis and the cell to which they are connected, the slot and rope information, and the slot number and description of the card in the slot. Among the information that you don't know at this point is the LBA that corresponds to the slot number produced by **info io**. There may be a mapping of slot to LBA printed on the card cage itself which is usually the case on a Superdome. This command is run at the EFI shell prompt, which means that the complex hasn't been booted.

Identify the Cards and Slot Numbers—rx Example

Vital to the operation of an enterprise system is documenting the I/O of a system. One of the easiest ways to determine the cards in specific slots is with EFI. By using the EFI command **info io** at the EFI shell prompt you can see information related to slots as shown in the following example:

```
Shell> info io

I/O INFORMATION

    I/O CHASSIS INFORMATION    cell to which I/O chassis is connected


         Cell Info              I/O Chassis Info
        Cell  Cab/Slot      Cabinet  Bay  Chassis  Type
        ----  --------      -------  ---  -------  -----
          0    0/0             0       0      0     PCI-X
          1    0/1             0       0      1     PCI-X
          2    0/2           -----     -    -----    ---
          3    0/3           -----     -    -----    ---


    IO MODULE INFORMATION for Root CELL 0

                          Slot    Rope
        Type               #       #
        ----              ----    -----
        System Bus Adapter
        Local Bus Adapter   0       0          slot and rope information
        Local Bus Adapter   1      8/9
        Local Bus Adapter   2     10/11
        Local Bus Adapter   3     12/13
        Local Bus Adapter   4     14/15
        Local Bus Adapter   5      6/7
        Local Bus Adapter   6      4/5
        Local Bus Adapter   7      2/3
        Local Bus Adapter   8       1


    PCI DEVICE INFORMATION

    Seg Bus Dev Fnc Vendor Device Slot            slot number and card
     #   #   #   #    ID     ID    #   Description
    --- --- --- --- ------ ------ ---- -----------
     00  00  00  00 0x103C 0x1290  00  Simple Communications Controllers - Other
     00  00  00  01 0x103C 0x1048  00  Simple Communications Controllers - Serial
     00  00  00  02 0x0000 0x0000  00  Serial Bus Controllers - UNDEFINED
     00  00  01  00 0x14E4 0x1645  00  Network Controller - Ethernet controller
     00  00  02  00 0x1000 0x0021  00  Mass Storage Controller - SCSI controller
     00  00  02  01 0x1000 0x0021  00  Mass Storage Controller - SCSI controller
     00  00  03  00 0x1000 0x0021  00  Mass Storage Controller - SCSI controller
     00  00  03  01 0x1000 0x0021  00  Mass Storage Controller - SCSI controller
     00  30  01  00 0x1000 0x0021  05  Mass Storage Controller - SCSI controller
     00  30  01  00 0x1000 0x0021  05  Mass Storage Controller - SCSI controller
     00  40  01  00 0x103C 0x1029  01  Serial Bus Controllers - Fibre Channel
     00  50  01  00 0x103C 0x1029  02  Serial Bus Controllers - Fibre Channel
     00  60  01  00 0x14E4 0x1645  03  Network Controller - Ethernet controller
     00  70  01  00 0x14E4 0x1645  04  Network Controller - Ethernet controller
     01  00  00  00 0x103C 0x1290  00  Simple Communications Controllers - Other
     01  00  00  01 0x103C 0x1048  00  Simple Communications Controllers - Serial
     01  00  00  02 0x0000 0x0000  00  Serial Bus Controllers - UNDEFINED
     01  00  01  00 0x14E4 0x1645  00  Network Controller - Ethernet controller
     01  00  02  00 0x1000 0x0021  00  Mass Storage Controller - SCSI controller
     01  00  02  01 0x1000 0x0021  00  Mass Storage Controller - SCSI controller
```

```
01  00  03  00 0x1000 0x0021  00  Mass Storage Controller - SCSI controller
01  00  03  01 0x1000 0x0021  00  Mass Storage Controller - SCSI controller
01  30  01  00 0x1000 0x0021  05  Mass Storage Controller - SCSI controller
01  30  01  01 0x1000 0x0021  05  Mass Storage Controller - SCSI controller
01  40  01  00 0x103C 0x1029  01  Serial Bus Controllers - Fibre Channel
01  50  01  00 0x103C 0x1029  02  Serial Bus Controllers - Fibre Channel
01  60  01  00 0x14E4 0x1645  03  Network Controller - Ethernet controller
01  70  01  00 0x14E4 0x1645  04  Network Controller - Ethernet controller

Shell>
```

This output clarifies a lot of important operational information, but keep in mind that you have to run this command at the EFI shell prompt, which implies that the complex is not yet booted.

The first part of the output shows the cell to which each I/O chassis is connected. An I/O chassis is connected directly to a cell board. The rx8620, without an expansion I/O cabinet, has a maximum of two I/O chassis in the enclosure.

The slot and ropes are shown in the next part of the output. A PCI-X slot with one rope runs at 66MHz and one with two ropes runs at 133 MHz.

The end of the output shows, among other information, the slot number and the description of the card in the slot. This is important information to record. If you encounter a problem with a card and the system is in a remote facility, you can direct the technician to the proper slot.

The previous information is obtained with the EFI command **info io**. The System Bus Adapter (SBAs) and Local Bus Adapters (LBAs) can both be displayed with **ioscan**. These are internal components. There are typically several LBAs per SBA. The following output displays the SBAs and LBAs on an rx8620:

```
[rx8620b{root}:/roothome]>ioscan -f | grep sba
ioa       0  0/0          sba      CLAIMED    BUS_NEXUS    System Bus Adapter (127b)
ioa       1  1/0          sba      CLAIMED    BUS_NEXUS    System Bus Adapter (127b)

[rx8620b{root}:/roothome]>ioscan -f | grep lba
ba    1   0/0/0 lba      CLAIMED    BUS_NEXUS    Local PCI Bus Adapter (1054)
ba    2   0/0/1  lba      CLAIMED    BUS_NEXUS    Local PCI-X Bus Adapter (122e)
ba    3   0/0/2  lba      CLAIMED    BUS_NEXUS    Local PCI-X Bus Adapter (122e)
ba    4   0/0/4  lba      CLAIMED    BUS_NEXUS    Local PCI-X Bus Adapter (122e)
ba    5   0/0/6  lba      CLAIMED    BUS_NEXUS    Local PCI-X Bus Adapter (122e)
ba    6   0/0/8  lba      CLAIMED    BUS_NEXUS    Local PCI-X Bus Adapter (122e)
ba    7   0/0/10 lba      CLAIMED    BUS_NEXUS    Local PCI-X Bus Adapter (122e)
ba    8   0/0/12 lba      CLAIMED    BUS_NEXUS    Local PCI-X Bus Adapter (122e)
ba    9   0/0/14 lba      CLAIMED    BUS_NEXUS    Local PCI-X Bus Adapter (122e)
ba   11   1/0/0  lba      CLAIMED    BUS_NEXUS    Local PCI Bus Adapter (1054)
ba   12   1/0/1  lba      CLAIMED    BUS_NEXUS    Local PCI-X Bus Adapter (122e)
ba   13   1/0/2  lba      CLAIMED    BUS_NEXUS    Local PCI-X Bus Adapter (122e)
ba   14   1/0/4  lba      CLAIMED    BUS_NEXUS    Local PCI-X Bus Adapter (122e)
ba   15   1/0/6  lba      CLAIMED    BUS_NEXUS    Local PCI-X Bus Adapter (122e)
ba   16   1/0/8  lba      CLAIMED    BUS_NEXUS    Local PCI-X Bus Adapter (122e)
ba   17   1/0/10 lba      CLAIMED    BUS_NEXUS    Local PCI-X Bus Adapter (122e)
ba   18   1/0/12 lba      CLAIMED    BUS_NEXUS    Local PCI-X Bus Adapter (122e)
ba   19   1/0/14 lba      CLAIMED    BUS_NEXUS    Local PCI-X Bus Adapter (122e)
[rx8620b{root}:/roothome] >
```

Two SBAs are shown in the form *Global cell number/SBA*. The LBAs are in the form *Global cell number/SBA/LBA/device/function.target.LUN*.

A specific LBA can be displayed in **ioscan** and then mapped to a slot number using Table 17-3 (in Chapter 17). The following **ioscan** output was produced on an rx8620 and shows LBA *0/0/10*:

```
[rx8620b{root}:/roothome]> ioscan -f | grep 0/0/10
ba       7  0/0/10          lba      CLAIMED    BUS_NEXUS   Local PCI-X Bus
                                                            Adapter (122e)
fc       1  0/0/10/1/0      td       CLAIMED    INTERFACE   HP Tachyon XL2
                                              Fibre Channel Mass Storage Adapter
fcp      1  0/0/10/1/0.1    fcp      CLAIMED    INTERFACE   FCP Domain
ext_bus 12  0/0/10/1/0.1.2.0.0       fcparray  CLAIMED     INTERFACE   FCP
                                                            Array Interface
target   1  0/0/10/1/0.1.2.0.0.0    tgt       CLAIMED     DEVICE
ctl     13  0/0/10/1/0.1.2.0.0.0.0  sctl      CLAIMED     DEVICE      COMPAQ
                                                            HSV110 (C)COMPAQ
hsx      0  0/0/10/1/0.1.2.0.0.0.1  hsx       CLAIMED     DEVICE      COMPAQ
                                                            HSV110 (C)COMPAQ
hsx      8  0/0/10/1/0.1.2.0.0.0.2  hsx       CLAIMED     DEVICE      COMPAQ
                                                            HSV110 (C)COMPAQ
hsx     10  0/0/10/1/0.1.2.0.0.0.3  hsx       CLAIMED     DEVICE      COMPAQ
                                                            HSV110 (C)COMPAQ
hsx     12  0/0/10/1/0.1.2.0.0.0.4  hsx       CLAIMED     DEVICE      COMPAQ
                                                            HSV110 (C)COMPAQ
hsx     33  0/0/10/1/0.1.2.0.0.0.5  hsx       CLAIMED     DEVICE      COMPAQ
                                                            HSV110 (C)COMPAQ
ext_bus 15  0/0/10/1/0.1.2.255.0     fcpdev   CLAIMED     INTERFACE   FCP
                                                            Device Interface
target   4  0/0/10/1/0.1.2.255.0.0  tgt       CLAIMED     DEVICE
ctl     45  0/0/10/1/0.1.2.255.0.0.0 sctl     CLAIMED     DEVICE      COMPAQ
                                                            HSV110 (C)COMPAQ
ext_bus 17  0/0/10/1/0.1.3.0.0       fcparray  CLAIMED     INTERFACE   FCP Array
                                                            Interface
target   6  0/0/10/1/0.1.3.0.0.0    tgt       CLAIMED     DEVICE
ctl     47  0/0/10/1/0.1.3.0.0.0.0  sctl      CLAIMED     DEVICE      COMPAQ
                                                            HSV110 (C)COMPAQ
hsx      2  0/0/10/1/0.1.3.0.0.0.1  hsx       CLAIMED     DEVICE      COMPAQ
                                                            HSV110 (C)COMPAQ
hsx     14  0/0/10/1/0.1.3.0.0.0.2  hsx       CLAIMED     DEVICE      COMPAQ
                                                            HSV110 (C)COMPAQ
hsx     16  0/0/10/1/0.1.3.0.0.0.3  hsx       CLAIMED     DEVICE      COMPAQ
                                                            HSV110 (C)COMPAQ
hsx     18  0/0/10/1/0.1.3.0.0.0.4  hsx       CLAIMED     DEVICE      COMPAQ
                                                            HSV110 (C)COMPAQ
hsx     35  0/0/10/1/0.1.3.0.0.0.5  hsx       CLAIMED     DEVICE      COMPAQ
                                                            HSV110 (C)COMPAQ
ext_bus 19  0/0/10/1/0.1.3.255.0     fcpdev   CLAIMED     INTERFACE   FCP
                                                            Device Interface
target   8  0/0/10/1/0.1.3.255.0.0  tgt       CLAIMED     DEVICE
ctl     79  0/0/10/1/0.1.3.255.0.0.0 sctl     CLAIMED     DEVICE      COMPAQ
                                                            HSV110 (C)COMPAQ
[rx8620b{root}:/roothome]>
```

All the devices in this output are a 1, which indicates that they are PCI-X. A 0 in this field would be PCI. This output shows an LBA at 0/0/10 and the SAN-related devices connected to it. The LBA of 0/0/10 corresponds to card slot 2. Table 6-3 shows this information for an rx8620 Integrity Cardcage.

Table 6-3   *SLOT* versus *LBA* Information Shown on Integrity rx8620

SLOT	4	3	2	1	5	6	7	8	Core I/O
LBA	14	12	10	8	6	4	2	1	0
Rope(s)	14 and 15	12 and 13	10 and 11	8 and 9	6 and 7	4 and 5	2 and 3	8 and 9	0

This jives with the **info io** command output (produced earlier) that showed the fibre card at LBA 10 in card slot 2.

The combination of **ioscan** and the mapping of LBA to slot number gives you the physical location of the card.

From physical inspection, I know that there are Gigabit LAN cards in slots 3 and 4 in both I/O chassis in this system. The following **ioscan** output searches for these cards:

```
[rx8620b{root}:/roothome]>ioscan -f | grep 1000
lan       0  0/0/0/1/0      igelan   CLAIMED     INTERFACE    HP A7109-60001 PCI
                                                              1000Base-T Core
lan       1  0/0/12/1/0     igelan   CLAIMED     INTERFACE    HP A6825-60101 PCI
                                                              1000Base-T Adapter
lan       2  0/0/14/1/0     igelan   CLAIMED     INTERFACE    HP A6825-60101 PCI
                                                              1000Base-T Adapter
lan       3  1/0/0/1/0      igelan   CLAIMED     INTERFACE    HP A7109-60001 PCI
                                                              1000Base-T Core
lan       4  1/0/12/1/0     igelan   CLAIMED     INTERFACE    HP A6825-60101 PCI
                                                              1000Base-T Adapter
lan       5  1/0/14/1/0     igelan   CLAIMED     INTERFACE    HP A6825-60101 PCI
                                                              1000Base-T Adapter
[rx8620b{root}:/roothome] >
```

This output produced what I expected. There are LAN cards at LBAs 12 and 14, which correspond to slots 3 and 4, in both I/O chassis. In addition, the Core I/O card in slot 0 and LBA 0 also has built-in LAN interface.

Still more information can be produced for I/O, including the disk output as shown in the following listing:

```
[rx8620b{root}:/roothome]>ioscan -fneC disk
Class     I  H/W Path       Driver   S/W State   H/W Type     Description
=========================================================================
disk      0  0/0/0/2/0.6.0  sdisk    CLAIMED     DEVICE       HP 146 GST3146807LC
                            /dev/dsk/c0t6d0      /dev/rdsk/c0t6d0
                            /dev/dsk/c0t6d0s1    /dev/rdsk/c0t6d0s1
                            /dev/dsk/c0t6d0s2    /dev/rdsk/c0t6d0s2
                            /dev/dsk/c0t6d0s3    /dev/rdsk/c0t6d0s3
        Acpi(000222F0,0)/Pci(2|0)/Scsi(Pun6,Lun0)/HD(Part1,Sig75AD9336-9ECC-11D8-8002-
D6217B60E588)/\EFI\HPUX\HPUX.EFI
```

```
disk      1   0/0/0/2/1.2.0   sdisk    CLAIMED      DEVICE         HP       DVD-ROM 305
                            /dev/dsk/c1t2d0    /dev/rdsk/c1t2d0
          Acpi(000222F0,0)/Pci(2|1)/Scsi(Pun2,Lun0)/\EFI\HPUX\HPUX.EFI
disk      2   0/0/0/3/0.6.0   sdisk    CLAIMED      DEVICE         HP 146 GST3146807LC
                            /dev/dsk/c2t6d0    /dev/rdsk/c2t6d0
          Acpi(000222F0,0)/Pci(3|0)/Scsi(Pun6,Lun0)/\EFI\HPUX\HPUX.EFI
disk      3   1/0/0/2/0.6.0   sdisk    CLAIMED      DEVICE         HP 146 GMAP3147NC
                            /dev/dsk/c6t6d0    /dev/rdsk/c6t6d0
          Acpi(000222F0,100)/Pci(2|0)/Scsi(Pun6,Lun0)/\EFI\HPUX\HPUX.EFI
disk      4   1/0/0/3/0.6.0   sdisk    CLAIMED      DEVICE         HP 73.4GMAS3735NC
                            /dev/dsk/c8t6d0    /dev/rdsk/c8t6d0
          Acpi(000222F0,100)/Pci(3|0)/Scsi(Pun6,Lun0)/\EFI\HPUX\HPUX.EFI
disk      9   255/255/1/0.0   sdisk    CLAIMED      DEVICE         HSV110 (C)COMPAQ
                            /dev/dsk/c29t0d0   /dev/rdsk/c29t0d0
disk     10   255/255/1/0.1   sdisk    CLAIMED      DEVICE         HSV110 (C)COMPAQ
                            /dev/dsk/c29t0d1   /dev/rdsk/c29t0d1
disk     11   255/255/1/0.2   sdisk    CLAIMED      DEVICE         HSV110 (C)COMPAQ
                            /dev/dsk/c29t0d2   /dev/rdsk/c29t0d2
disk     12   255/255/1/0.3   sdisk    CLAIMED      DEVICE         HSV110 (C)COMPAQ
                            /dev/dsk/c29t0d3   /dev/rdsk/c29t0d3
disk     13   255/255/1/0.4   sdisk    CLAIMED      DEVICE         HSV110 (C)COMPAQ
                            /dev/dsk/c29t0d4   /dev/rdsk/c29t0d4
[rx8620b{root}:/roothome]>
```

The lines beginning with *Acpi* were produced in this output in the **ioscan** output with the **-e** option. The **-e** in this output displays EFI device paths when available. The lines beginning with disk are in the form *Global cell number/SBA/LBA/device/function.target.LUN*. On-line addition and replacement (OLAR) may be possible for this card. (OLAR is covered in another section.) I proceed here with further investigating this card and slot.

Let's now evaluate the Acpi portion of the **ioscan** output. This standard defines power and configuration management interfaces between the operating system and the firmware. On HP Integrity Servers, you see ACPI output in EFI, such as when you run the **map** command or **info io** at the EFI shell prompt, and in the **ioscan** output. The Acpi lines are in the form:

Acpi(..., XYY)/Pci(A|B)/Scsi(PunC, LunD)/...

The following bullets describe some of these fields:

- X is the cell number in hex. To determine the cell number, convert X to decimal. Hex Z = decimal 10, Hex B = decimal 11, Hex C = decimal 12, and so on. The cell is not shown for devices connected to cell 0.

- YY is the PCI bus number in hex. This number can be converted to its corresponding rope number, LBA number, and slot number.

- A is the PCI device in hex, which is usually a 1 or 0.

- B is the PCI function in hex, which is usually a 1 or 0.

• C is the target or Physical Unit Number (PUN) in hex, of these PUN assignments.

• D is the logical unit number in hex, which is usually a 0.

Much device-related information was produced in this section. The following bullet list summarizes some of the steps that I recommend you run on your server:

• Run **info io** at the EFI shell prompt to produce a list of I/O chassis and the cell to which they are connected, the slot and rope information, and the slot number and description of the card in the slot. Among the information that you don't know at this point is the LBA that corresponds to the slot number produced by **info io**. There may be a mapping of slot to LBA printed on the card cage itself, which is usually the case on a Superdome. This command is run at the EFI shell prompt, which means that the complex hasn't been booted.

• Run **ioscan | grep sba** and **ioscan | grep LBA** to get a list of SBAs and LBAs. These outputs are in the form shown here:

cell/SBA/LBA

• From the previous **ioscan** output, you can select an LBA about which you want to get details with **ioscan -f | grep 0/0/6** or substitute whatever LBA number about which you want to know more information. This output is in the form:

cell/SBA/LBA/device/function.target.LUN.

• Produce a table that maps slot to LBA, and include the ropes and frequency if you like, so that when you run **ioscan** and get the LBA of a card, you'll immediately know in what slot it is located.

• Include the Acpi lines with the **-e** option to **ioscan** if you're working on an HP Integrity Server.

OLA/R

Important to the operation of your system is to determine the cards that can be replaced and added on-line, which is referred to as On Line Addition and Replacement OLA/R slots. The following listing shows the PCI detail with the **olrad -q** command on an rx8620 system:

```
[rx8620b{root}:/roothome]>parstatus -w
The local partition number is 0.

[rx8620b{root}:/roothome]>olrad -q
                                                  Driver(s)
                                                  Capable
Slot       Path        Bus  Max  Spd  Pwr  Occu  Susp  OLAR  OLD  Max    Mode
                       Num  Spd                                        Mode
0-0-0-1    0/0/8/1     64   133  N/A  On   Yes   No    Yes   N/A  PCI-X  N/A
0-0-0-2    0/0/10/1    80   133  N/A  On   Yes   No    Yes   N/A  PCI-X  N/A
0-0-0-3    0/0/12/1    96   133  N/A  On   Yes   No    Yes   N/A  PCI-X  N/A
0-0-0-4    0/0/14/1    112  133  N/A  On   Yes   No    Yes   N/A  PCI-X  N/A
0-0-0-5    0/0/6/1     48   133  N/A  On   Yes   No    Yes   N/A  PCI-X  N/A
0-0-0-6    0/0/4/1     32   133  N/A  Off  No    N/A   N/A   N/A  PCI-X  N/A
0-0-0-7    0/0/2/1     16   133  N/A  Off  No    N/A   N/A   N/A  PCI-X  N/A
0-0-0-8    0/0/1/1     8    133  N/A  Off  No    N/A   N/A   N/A  PCI-X  N/A
0-0-1-1    1/0/8/1     64   133  N/A  On   Yes   No    Yes   N/A  PCI-X  N/A
0-0-1-2    1/0/10/1    80   133  N/A  On   Yes   No    Yes   N/A  PCI-X  N/A
0-0-1-3    1/0/12/1    96   133  N/A  On   Yes   No    Yes   N/A  PCI-X  N/A
0-0-1-4    1/0/14/1    112  133  N/A  On   Yes   No    Yes   N/A  PCI-X  N/A
0-0-1-5    1/0/6/1     48   133  N/A  On   Yes   No    Yes   N/A  PCI-X  N/A
0-0-1-6    1/0/4/1     32   133  N/A  Off  No    N/A   N/A   N/A  PCI-X  N/A
0-0-1-7    1/0/2/1     16   133  N/A  Off  No    N/A   N/A   N/A  PCI-X  N/A
0-0-1-8    1/0/1/1     8    133  N/A  Off  No    N/A   N/A   N/A  PCI-X  N/A
[rx8620b{root}:/roothome] >
```

A lot of detail in this output is not as easy to understand as the **parstatus** output, so let's look at a couple of these fields.

The first field of the **olrad** output is the slot information, which is in the following form:

```
Cabinet-Bay-Chassis-Slot     such as 0-0-0-1 for the first entry
```

This example shows the that the first card is in cabinet 0, bay 0, chassis 0, and slot 1. The hierarchy is such that the cabinet is the overall enclosure, the bay holds two I/O chassis, and there are slots within each I/O chassis.

The second field, which is the *Path*, contains the following:

```
Cell/SBA/LBA/Device     such as 0/0/8/0 for the first entry
```

For this entry, the cell board is 0, the System Bus Adapter (SBA) is 0, the Local Bus Adapter (LBA) is 8, and the device is 0. All the cards in this nPartition are connected to cell 0 because the **parstatus** output showed that I/O chassis is connected to cell 0. If you refer to Table 5-3 (in Chapter 5) you can see that LBA 8 is in slot 1 of the I/O chassis.

The **olrad -q** output shows that all five slots (1-5) that are occupied in both I/O chassis are OLAR cards. Slots 1 and 2 are fibre cards, slots 3 and 4 are LAN cards, and slot 5 is a SCSI card. All of these are shown in the output as *Yes* in the *OLAR* heading.

As with Virtual Partitions (vPars) covered in Chapter 16, you need to know something about the structure of your system in order to work with nPartitions. The System Bus Adapter (SBA) and Local Bus Adapters (LBA) are not components that you would typically worry about if you were not working with partitions. For the purpose of working through the information in this chapter, it is sufficient to know that there is a hierarchical I/O structure on servers in which the SBA exists at a higher level than the LBA and there are typically several LBAs per SBA. That is why for the second field, SBA of *0,* for example, you see several third fields, which are many LBAs per SBA.

The way to replace and add components online is through System Administration Manager (SAM). This can be done at the command line but it is much easier to do with SAM. After invoking SAM and selecting *Peripheral Devices* and *Cards and Devcies,* SAM brings up the Peripheral Devices tool (pd) in your browser. Figure 6-2 shows the pd browser screen.

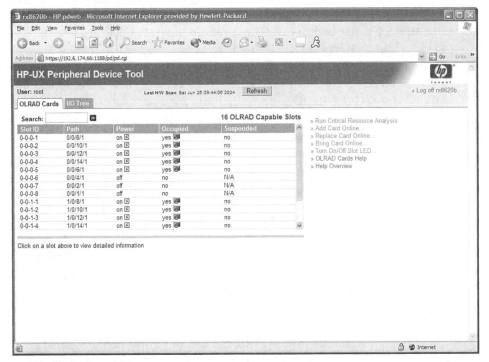

Figure 6-2   Peripheral Devices Tool (pd) Screen Showing *Cards*

Figure 6-2 shows all the slots and paths for the rx8620. To replace one of the cards online or add a card online, use the menus on the right. This technique is easy to perform with the system running and is safe as well.

The combination of **olrad**, **ioscan**, and **SAM** can be used to get all information about paths, descriptions, and OLAR for components.

lsdev and lssf

lsdev lists the drivers configured into your system. When adding a device file, you need to have the driver for the device configured into the system. You can use the manual kernel configuration process, which was covered earlier, to add a driver to the kernel. There are columns for the major number for a character device and block device, the driver name, and the class of the driver. The major number, character device, and other parameters are defined later. Here is an example of running **lsdev** on an rx8620:

```
[rx8620b{root}:/roothome]>lsdev
    Character      Block        Driver          Class
          0          -1         cn              pseudo
          1          -1         asio0           tty
          2          -1         dev_olar        olar
          3          -1         mm              pseudo
          4          -1         LCentIf         ext_bus
          5          -1         dev_acpi        pseudo
          6          -1         acpi_node       acpi_node
          7          -1         udp6            pseudo
          8          -1         udp             pseudo
          9           9         ramdisc         pseudo
         10          -1         tcp6            pseudo
         11          -1         tcp             pseudo
         12          -1         rawip6          pseudo
         13          -1         rawip           pseudo
         14          -1         nuls            pseudo
         15          -1         ip6             pseudo
         16          -1         ptym            ptym
         17          -1         ptys            ptys
         18          -1         ip              pseudo
         19          -1         arp             pseudo
         20          -1         keybd_ps2       ps2
         21          -1         gvid            unknown
         22          -1         olar_psm_if     olar
         23          -1         ciss            unknown
         25          -1         tlcotsod        pseudo
         26          -1         tlcots          pseudo
         27          -1         dmem            pseudo
         31          -1         tlclts          pseudo
         32          -1         devkrs          pseudo
         33           0         dmp             vxvm
         36          -1         usbd            unknown
         37          -1         hub             unknown
         44          -1         hid             unknown
         45          -1         hcd             unknown
         46          -1         netdiag1        unknown
         48          -1         evp             pseudo
         49          -1         fcd             fc
         50          -1         fcp             fcp
         51          -1         ipmi            ipmi
         54          -1         ipsecpol        pseudo
         57          -1         ipseckey        pseudo
         58          -1         mpt             ext_bus
         61          -1         stcpmap         pseudo
         62          -1         td              fc
         63          -1         tels            strtels
         64          64         lv              lvm
         66          -1         audio           audio
         67          -1         telm            strtelm
         68          -1         tun             pseudo
         69          -1         dev_config      pseudo
         72          -1         clone           pseudo
         73          -1         strlog          pseudo
         74          -1         sad             pseudo
         75           2         vol             vxvm
         76          -1         vols            vxvm
         77          -1         fake            pseudo
```

```
           78              -1          cifs           pseudo
           79              -1          fddi4          lan
           95              -1          ipf            pseudo
           96              -1          rng            pseudo
           97              -1          vxportal       pseudo
           98               3          hsx            hsx
          101              -1          asyncdsk       pseudo
          116              -1          echo           pseudo
          119              -1          dlpi           pseudo
          156              -1          ptm            strptym
          157              -1          pts            strptys
          164              -1          pipedev        unknown
          168              -1          beep           graf_pseudo
          188              31          sdisk          disk
          189              -1          klog           pseudo
          203              -1          sctl           ctl
          205              -1          stape          tape
          207              -1          sy             pseudo
          227              -1          kepd           pseudo
          232              -1          diag2          diag
           -1               1          swapdev        pseudo
[rx8620b{root}:/roothome] >
```

This output shows the major device numbers and driver names of device drivers configured into the system.

To get more information about a specific device, such as the boot disk in this system, you can use a few different commands. The following output shows a long listing of **/dev/dsk**, an **lssf** on the boot disk, and an **ioscan** on the boot disk:

```
[rx8620b{root}:/dev/dsk]>ll
total 0
brw-r-----   1 bin      sys          31 0x006000 May  5 15:44 c0t6d0
brw-r-----   1 bin      sys          31 0x006001 May  5 15:47 c0t6d0s1
brw-r-----   1 bin      sys          31 0x006002 May  5 15:44 c0t6d0s2
brw-r-----   1 bin      sys          31 0x006003 May  5 15:44 c0t6d0s3
brw-r-----   1 bin      sys          31 0x012000 May  5 15:44 c1t2d0
brw-r-----   1 bin      sys          31 0x1c0000 May 18 09:39 c28t0d0
brw-r-----   1 bin      sys          31 0x1c0100 May 18 09:58 c28t0d1
brw-r-----   1 bin      sys          31 0x1c0200 May 18 09:58 c28t0d2
brw-r-----   1 bin      sys          31 0x1c0300 May 18 09:58 c28t0d3
brw-r-----   1 bin      sys          31 0x1d0000 May 25 11:20 c29t0d0
brw-r-----   1 bin      sys          31 0x1d0100 May 25 11:20 c29t0d1
brw-r-----   1 bin      sys          31 0x1d0200 May 25 11:20 c29t0d2
brw-r-----   1 bin      sys          31 0x1d0300 May 25 11:20 c29t0d3
brw-r-----   1 bin      sys          31 0x1d0400 May 25 11:20 c29t0d4
brw-r-----   1 bin      sys          31 0x026000 May  5 15:44 c2t6d0
brw-r-----   1 bin      sys          31 0x066000 May 12 15:08 c6t6d0
brw-r-----   1 bin      sys          31 0x086000 May 12 15:08 c8t6d0

[rx8620b{root}:/dev/dsk]>lssf /dev/dsk/c0t6d0
sdisk card instance 0 SCSI target 6 SCSI LUN 0 section 0 at address 0/0/0/
2/0.6.0 /dev/dsk/c0t6d0
```

```
[rx8620b{root}:/dev/dsk]>lssf /dev/dsk/c0t6d0s1
sdisk card instance 0 SCSI target 6 SCSI LUN 0 section 1 at address 0/0/0/
2/0.6.0 /dev/dsk/c0t6d0s1

[rx8620b{root}:/dev/dsk]>ioscan -f /dev/dsk/c0t6d0
Class     I  H/W Path        Driver S/W State    H/W Type     Description
=========================================================================
disk      0  0/0/0/2/0.6.0  sdisk CLAIMED      DEVICE       HP 146 GST3146807LC
[rx8620b{root}:/dev/dsk]>
```

This output produces plenty of useful information about the boot device. I listed both sections 0 and 1 of the boot device with the **lssf** command.

SAM also provides useful information about the disks in the system. Figure 6-3 shows a SAM screen shot for the disks in the system:

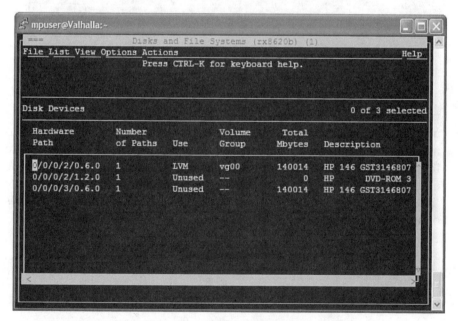

Figure 6-3   SAM Screen Shot Showing Disks

This output shows the three disk devices in the system, the first one of which is the boot device for which we earlier ran several commands. Figure 6-4 shows the logical volumes on the disk device.

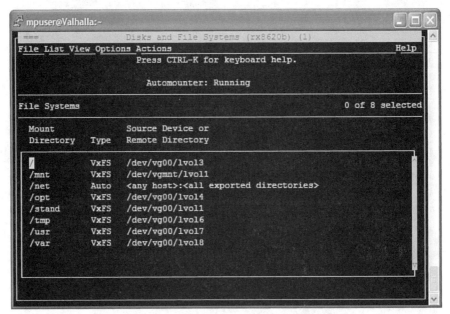

Figure 6-4   SAM Logical Volumes on Disk Device

Figure 6-4 shows the logical volumes on this disk.

Chapter 4 has an example of configuring external storage on a system included a detailed shell program and command file to semi-automate the process of adding many disks in volume groups to a system. The first commands to run on a server when new external disks are configured are **ioscan** and **insf** for the disks to be recognized and special files to be installed, respectively. Chapter 4 also covers **fcmutil** to report the worldwide fibre port names. See Chapter 4 and this procedure to understand the details of adding disks to a system.

Chapter 7

Backup

Built-In Backup Programs

Most HP-UX system administrators employ a dual backup strategy. The first is to use the **make_tape_recovery** command of Ignite-UX to create a bootable backup tape of the root volume (**make_tape_recovery** is covered in Chapter 10, "Ignite-UX"). You can create a bootable recovery archive across a network with **make_net_recovery**. Secondly, a backup program is used to back up the balance of data on the system. In this chapter I'll give an overview of several backup commands. It doesn't cover any advanced backup programs, such as HP's OmniBack. Advanced backup tools, however, can make tasks such as centralized backup and overall management of backup much easier. The last section in this chapter covers backup of Virtual Partitions (vPars) and can be applied to node partitions (nPartitions) as well.

Here is a brief overview of the backup programs that this chapter covers:

> tar   **tar** is widely considered the most *portable* of the backup and restore programs. **tar** is the most popular generic backup utility. You will find that many applications are

shipped on **tar** tapes. This is the most widely used format for exchanging data with other UNIX systems. **tar** is the oldest UNIX backup method and, therefore, runs on all UNIX systems. You can append files to the end of a **tar** tape, which you can't do with **fbackup**. When sending files to another UNIX user, I would strongly recommend **tar**, but **tar** is as slow as molasses, so you won't want to use it for your full or incremental backups. One highly desirable aspect of **tar** is that when you load files onto a tape with **tar** and then restore them onto another system, the original users and groups are retained.

fbackup   **fbackup** has a lot of functionality associated with it, such as specifying whether the backup is full or incremental; different *levels* of backup; files and directories to be included or excluded; support for a *graph* file, which specifies files to be included and excluded; and other advanced features. **fbackup** is an HP-UX-only utility, and tapes can be read using **frecover** on HP-UX systems only.

cpio   **cpio** is also portable and easy to use, like **tar**. In addition, **cpio** is much faster than **tar**, not as fast as **fbackup**, but much faster than **tar**. **cpio** is good for replicating directory trees.

dd   This is a bit-for-bit copy. It is not smart in the sense that it does not copy files and ownerships; it just copies bits. You could not, therefore, select an individual file from a **dd** tape as you could with **frecover**, **tar**, **restore**, or **cpio**. **dd** is used primarily to convert data, such as EBCDIC, to ASCII.

dump   **dump** is similar to **fbackup**. If you use **fbackup** on HP-UX, you will see much similarity when you use **dump**. **dump** provides the same level backup scheme as **fbackup** and creates **/var/adm/dumpdates**, which lists the last time a file system was backed up. **restore** reads information backed up with **dump**. **dump**, however, works only with HFS file systems and not VxFS, and it assumes that you are using a reel tape. **vxdump** is used for VxFS.

pax
This command performs a variety of functions. It extracts and writes member files of archive files, writes lists of the member files of archive,; and copies directory hierarchies. The -r and -w flags specify the archive operation performed by the **pax** command. I don't supply examples of **pax** in this chapter but you can view the man page for it if you want to know more.

tar

tar is widely considered the most *portable* of the backup and restore programs. You will find that many applications are shipped on **tar** tapes and
many UNIX files downloaded from the Internet are in **tar** format. This is the
most widely used format for exchanging data with other UNIX systems. **tar**
is the oldest UNIX backup method and therefore runs on all UNIX systems.
You can append files to the end of a **tar** tape, which you can't do with many
other programs. When sending files to another UNIX user, I would strongly
recommend **tar**. **tar** is as slow as molasses, so you won't want to use it for
your full or incremental backups if you have a lot of data to back up. One
highly desirable aspect of **tar** is that when you load files onto a tape with **tar**
and then restore them onto another system, the original users and groups are
retained.

We use several **tar** commands in the upcoming examples, including the
following:

```
# tar cf /dev/rmt/0m /var          ;use tar to create (c) an archive of
                                    the directory /var and put it on
                                    tape /dev/rmt/0m.


# tar tvf /dev/rmt/0m              ;obtain table of contents (t) from
                                    tape /dev/rmt/0m and produce
                                    produce verbose (v) output.


# tar xvf /dev/rmt/0m              ;extract (x) the entire contents
                                     of the archive on tape /dev/rmt/0m
                                    to default destination.


# tar xvf /dev/rmt/0m file1        ;extract (x) only file1
                                     from the archive on tape /dev/rmt/0m
                                    to default destination.
```

Notice that when you view the man pages for **tar**, the options are preceded by a hyphen. The command works without the hyphen so most **tar**
examples, including those in this chapter, omit the hyphen.

Let's look at some examples using **tar**. Let's begin by performing a **tar**
backup (usually called *creating an archive*) of the directory **/var** to tape
device **/dev/rmt/0m**. Use the *c* option to create a backup and the *f* option to
specify the file of the tape drive **/dev/rmt/0m**:

```
# tar cf /dev/rmt/0m /var
tar: /var/opt/dce/rpc/local/01060/reaper is not a file. Not dumped
tar: /var/opt/dce/rpc/local/00997/reaper is not a file. Not dumped
tar: /var/opt/dce/rpc/local/00997/c-3/7000 is not a file. Not dumped
tar: /var/opt/dce/rpc/local/00997/c-3/shared is not a file. Not dumped
tar: /var/opt/dce/rpc/local/00997/c-3/7002 is not a file. Not dumped
tar: /var/opt/dce/rpc/local/s-0/135 is not a file. Not dumped
tar: /var/opt/dce/rpc/local/s-0/2121 is not a file. Not dumped
tar: /var/opt/dce/rpc/local/s-3/135 is not a file. Not dumped
tar: /var/opt/dce/rpc/local/s-3/2121 is not a file. Not dumped
tar: /var/spool/sockets/pwgr/client933 is not a file. Not dumped
tar: /var/spool/sockets/pwgr/client1028 is not a file. Not dumped
tar: /var/spool/sockets/pwgr/client1152 is not a file. Not dumped
tar: /var/spool/sockets/pwgr/client1172 is not a file. Not dumped
tar: /var/spool/sockets/pwgr/client1173 is not a file. Not dumped
tar: /var/spool/sockets/pwgr/client1139 is not a file. Not dumped
tar: /var/spool/sockets/pwgr/client2500 is not a file. Not dumped
tar: /var/spool/sockets/pwgr/client2592 is not a file. Not dumped
tar: /var/spool/sockets/pwgr/client2490 is not a file. Not dumped
tar: /var/spool/sockets/pwgr/client2593 is not a file. Not dumped
tar: /var/spool/pwgr/daemon is not a file. Not dumped
#
```

The result of this command printed only problem-related messages to *standard output*. You will often see the *v* option used with **tar** to produce verbose output, which would have listed both the messages just shown and those related to files that were successfully written to the tape archive.

Next, let's look at only the files on the tape with the string *eaaa* in them. To produce a table of contents, use the *t* option.

The following example also uses *v* for verbose output:

```
# tar tvf /dev/rmt/0m | grep eaaa
rw-rw-rw-   0/3      28 Jul 11 15:37 2000 /var/tmp/eaaa01299
rw-rw-rw-   0/3      28 Jul 11 15:37 2000 /var/tmp/eaaa01333
rw-rw-rw-   0/3      28 Jul 11 15:38 2000 /var/tmp/eaaa01354
rw-rw-rw-   0/3      28 Jul 11 15:40 2000 /var/tmp/eaaa01380
rw-rw-rw-   0/3      28 Jul 11 15:40 2000 /var/tmp/eaaa01405
rw-rw-rw-   0/3      28 Jul 11 15:45 2000 /var/tmp/eaaa01487

#
```

This output shows several files that begin with *eaaa* on the tape. We delete the last of these files from the computer and restore it from tape using the *x* option to extract the file from the **tar** archive. We then list the directory on the system to confirm that the file we deleted has been restored to the directory from tape.

```
# rm /var/tmp/eaaa01487
#
# tar xvf /dev/rmt/0m /var/tmp/eaaa01487

x /var/tmp/eaaa01487, 28 bytes, 1 tape blocks

#
# ls -l /var/tmp/eaaa*
-rw-rw-rw-  1 root      sys            28 Jul 11 15:37 /var/tmp/eaaa01299
-rw-rw-rw-  1 root      sys            28 Jul 11 15:37 /var/tmp/eaaa01333
-rw-rw-rw-  1 root      sys            28 Jul 11 15:38 /var/tmp/eaaa01354
-rw-rw-rw-  1 root      sys            28 Jul 11 15:40 /var/tmp/eaaa01380
-rw-rw-rw-  1 root      sys            28 Jul 11 15:40 /var/tmp/eaaa01405
-rw-rw-rw-  1 root      sys            28 Jul 11 15:45 /var/tmp/eaaa01487

#
```

This backup and restore using **tar** is simple and gets the job done.

A common use for **tar** is to back up files from one directory and restore them to another directory. We back up the contents of **/var/tmp** and restore them to the directory **/tmp/puttarfileshere**. In the following example, we create a **tar** backup archive to a file rather than to tape. The file is called **tartest**. We then move this file to the destination directory and extract it there. We don't use a tape at all in this example:

```
# cd /var/tmp
# ls -l
total 72
-rw-------   1 root      sys             0 Jul 11 15:57 OBAMFEAa01630
-rw-------   1 root      sys             0 Jul 11 15:20 OBAMHBAa01020
-rw-------   1 root      sys             0 Jul 11 15:50 OBAMHBAa01540
-rw-rw-rw-   1 root      sys           102 Jul 11 15:20 aaaa01112
-rw-rw-rw-   1 root      sys           102 Jul 11 15:37 aaaa01299
-rw-rw-rw-   1 root      sys           102 Jul 11 15:37 aaaa01333
-rw-rw-rw-   1 root      sys           102 Jul 11 15:38 aaaa01354
-rw-rw-rw-   1 root      sys           102 Jul 11 15:40 aaaa01380
-rw-rw-rw-   1 root      sys            99 Jul 11 15:40 aaaa01405

                .
                .
                .
     1 root      sys            28 Jul 11 15:37 eaaa01333
-rw-rw-rw-   1 root      sys            28 Jul 11 15:38 eaaa01354
-rw-rw-rw-   1 root      sys            28 Jul 11 15:40 eaaa01380
-rw-rw-rw-   1 root      sys            28 Jul 11 15:40 eaaa01405
-rw-rw-rw-   1 root      sys            28 Jul 11 15:45 eaaa01487
-rwxr--r--   1 root      root           28 Jul 11 16:04 envd.action2
-rwxr--r--   1 root      root           28 Jul 11 16:04 envd.action5
dr-xr-xr-x   2 bin       bin            96 Jul 11 13:50 ntp
-rw-r--r--   1 root      sys           600 Jul 11 15:27 swagent.log
#
# tar cvf /tmp/tartest `ls`
a OBAMFEAa01630 0 blocks
a OBAMHBAa01020 0 blocks
a OBAMHBAa01540 0 blocks
```

```
a aaaa01112 1 blocks
a aaaa01299 1 blocks
a aaaa01333 1 blocks
a aaaa01354 1 blocks
a aaaa01380 1 blocks
a aaaa01405 1 blocks


                      .
                      .
                      .

a eaaa01354 1 blocks
a eaaa01380 1 blocks
a eaaa01405 1 blocks
a eaaa01487 1 blocks
a envd.action2 1 blocks
a envd.action5 1 blocks
a swagent.log 2 blocks
#
# cd /tmp
# mkdir puttarfileshere
# cp tartest puttarfileshere
# cd puttarfileshere
# ls -l
total 80
-rw-rw-rw-  1 root        sys          40960 Jul 11 17:09 tartest
#
# tar xvf tartest
x OBAMFEAa01630, 0 bytes, 0 tape blocks
x OBAMHBAa01020, 0 bytes, 0 tape blocks
x OBAMHBAa01540, 0 bytes, 0 tape blocks
x aaaa01112, 102 bytes, 1 tape blocks
x aaaa01299, 102 bytes, 1 tape blocks
x aaaa01333, 102 bytes, 1 tape blocks
x aaaa01354, 102 bytes, 1 tape blocks
x aaaa01380, 102 bytes, 1 tape blocks
x aaaa01405, 99 bytes, 1 tape blocks


                      .
                      .
                      .

x daaa01405, 28 bytes, 1 tape blocks
x daaa01487, 28 bytes, 1 tape blocks
x eaaa01299, 28 bytes, 1 tape blocks
x eaaa01333, 28 bytes, 1 tape blocks
x eaaa01354, 28 bytes, 1 tape blocks
x eaaa01380, 28 bytes, 1 tape blocks
x eaaa01405, 28 bytes, 1 tape blocks
x eaaa01487, 28 bytes, 1 tape blocks
x envd.action2, 28 bytes, 1 tape blocks
x envd.action5, 28 bytes, 1 tape blocks
x swagent.log, 600 bytes, 2 tape blocks
#
```

When creating the **tar** backup, I first change to the **/var/tmp** directory and then use the **ls** command (a *grav* or *accent*, which is near the upper left of most keyboards on the same key as a *tilde*; appears before and after the **ls**). This produce relative path names that I can easily restore to the **/tmp/puttarfileshere** directory. Alternatively, I could simply change the directory to **/var** and issue the command **tar cf /dev/rmt/0m tmp** to back up the entire contents of the **/var/tmp** directory.

This entire process could have been done on a single command line. The following line is from the **tar** file man page and shows the procedure for producing an archive in the *fromdir* and restoring it to the *todir*:

cd *fromdir* ; **tar cf - .** | (**cd** *todir* ; **tar xf -i**)

The "-" in the **tar cf** command tells **tar** to send its data to *standard output*. The "-" in the **tar xf** command tells **tar** to look to *standard input* for data, which is the data produced by **tar cf -** issued earlier on the command line.

cpio

cpio is a powerful utility that is used in conjunction with **find** to perform full and incremental backups. **cpio** is an established UNIX utility that works similarly on most UNIX variants.

We use several commands in the upcoming examples, including the following:

```
# find . -print | cpio -oBv > /dev/rmt/0m   ;find the contents of
                                             the current dir and
                                             write them to tape.

# cpio -it < /dev/rmt/0m        ;read table of contents (t) of tape.

# cpio -icvBdum < /dev/rmt/0m ;restore (i) the contents of tape,
                               this is the most widely used
                               cpio command.

# find . -print | cpio -oBv | (remsh tapesys dd of=/dev/rmt/0m)
            ;find the contents of the current dir and
          write (o) them to tape on remote machine tapesys.

# remsh tapesys "dd if=/dev/rmt/0m bs=8k" | cpio -icvBdum
                ;restore the contents (i) of a tape on remote system
                tapesys to the local system.
```

You could use **ssh** in place of **remsh** for security reasons in these examples. The first command we issue is to **find** the contents in **/var/tmp** and write them to our tape device **/dev/rmt/0m**. The options to **cpio** used in the following example are *o* for output mode, *B* for block output, and *v* for verbose reporting:

```
# cd /var/tmp
# find . -print | cpio -oBv > /dev/rmt/0m
(Using tape drive with immediate report mode enabled (reel #1).)
.
envd.action2
envd.action5
swagent.log
ntp
```

```
OBAMHBAa01020
aaaa01558
aaaa01426
aaaa01112
OBAMHBAa01540
aaaa01299

             .
             .
             .

eaaa01487
OBAMFEAa01630
cmd_res8215
tmp_cfg_file
cmd_res8708
exclude.temp
arch.include.1
3570 blocks
#
```

In the example, we first change directory to **/var/tmp**, then issue the **find** command and pipe its output to **cpio**. **cpio** is almost always used in conjunction with **find** in the manner shown in the example. This produced a backup with relative path names because we changed to the directory **/var/ tmp** before issuing the backup commands.

Next, we view the contents of the tape to see the files we wrote to it with **cpio**. The *i* option is used for input, and the *t* option gets a table of contents in the following listing:

```
# cpio -it < /dev/rmt/0m
.
envd.action2
envd.action5
swagent.log
ntp
OBAMHBAa01020
aaaa01558
aaaa01426
aaaa01112
OBAMHBAa01540
aaaa01299

             .
             .
             .

eaaa01487
OBAMFEAa01630
cmd_res8215
tmp_cfg_file
cmd_res8708
exclude.temp
arch.include.1
3570 blocks
#
```

Now that we have written to the tape and viewed its table of contents, we restore the contents of **/var/tmp**. In the following example, we use several options to **cpio**, including *i* for input mode, *c* for ASCII header format, *v* for verbose, *B* for block output, *d* for directories, *u* for unconditional write over existing files, and *m* to restore the original modification times:

```
# cpio -icvBdum < /dev/rmt/0m
.
envd.action2
envd.action5
swagent.log
ntp
OBAMHBAa01020
aaaa01558
aaaa01426
aaaa01112
OBAMHBAa01540
aaaa01299

                    .
                    .
                    .
eaaa01487
OBAMFEAa01630
cmd_res8215
tmp_cfg_file
cmd_res8708
exclude.temp
arch.include.1
3570 blocks
#
```

The **cpio** command produces a list of files that is read from the tape and restored to the system. Because we include the verbose option, we see all the information related to the restore.

Now that we've seen how to write a tape, produce a table of contents, and read the contents of a tape on a local system, let's work with a tape drive on a remote system. We perform a backup to a remote tape drive, view the table of contents on the tape, and then restore using the remote tape drive.

First let's perform a backup to a remote tape drive. The local system, which does not have a tape drive attached to it, is *or1*. The remote system, which has a tape drive attached to it, is *tapesys*. We run **cpio** (using the same three options earlier described) on *or1* and run a remote shell and **dd** on *tapesys,* which stores the contents of the backup. We run these commands from **/var/tmp** on *or1* in the following example:

```
# find . -print | cpio -oBv | (remsh tapesys dd of=/dev/rmt/0m)
.
envd.action2
envd.action5
swagent.log
ntp
OBAMHBAa01020
aaaa01558
aaaa01426
aaaa01112
OBAMHBAa01540
aaaa01299

                    .
                    .
                    .
eaaa01487
OBAMFEAa01630
cmd_res8215
tmp_cfg_file
cmd_res8708
exclude.temp
arch.include.1
3570 blocks
#
```

Now, let's come back to our local system without the tape drive and
restore the contents of the **cpio** tape we just produced, but let's restore them
to a different directory. The directory to which we restore the contents of the
tape (originally in **/var/tmp**) is **/tmp/remotecpiofiles**. This is similar to the
process we performed in the **tar** section earlier in this chapter in which we
restored **tar** files to a different location.

In the following example, we issue a series of commands while on *or1*.
The last of these commands is to issue a **remsh** to system *tapesys*, which has
on it a tape drive with the **cpio** tape we just created. We **dd** the information
and pipe it through **cpio** to restore the contents of the tape. In this example,
we use the same restore options to **cpio**, including *i* for input mode, *c* for
ASCII header format, *v* for verbose, *B* for block output, *d* for directories, *u*
for unconditional write over existing files, and *m* to restore original modification times:

```
# hostname
or1
# cd /tmp
# mkdir remotecpiofiles
# cd remotecpiofiles
# pwd
/tmp/remotecpiofiles
# remsh tapesys "dd if=/dev/rmt/0m bs=8k" | cpio -icvBdum

envd.action2
envd.action5
```

```
swagent.log
ntp
OBAMHBAa01020
aaaa01558
aaaa01426
aaaa01112
OBAMHBAa01540
aaaa01299

                 .
                 .
                 .

eaaa01487
OBAMFEAa01630
cmd_res8215
tmp_cfg_file
cmd_res8708
exclude.temp
arch.include.1
3570 blocks
#
# pwd
/tmp/remotecpiofiles
# ls
envd.action2
envd.action5
swagent.log
ntp
OBAMHBAa01020
aaaa01558
aaaa01426
aaaa01112
OBAMHBAa01540
aaaa01299

                 .
                 .
                 .

eaaa01487
OBAMFEAa01630
cmd_res8215
tmp_cfg_file
cmd_res8708
exclude.temp
arch.include.1
#
```

The **ls** we issued at the end of this example confirmed that we did write the contents of the tape on the remote system to the new directory **/tmp/ remotecpiofiles**. You may want to add the *-a* command to the **ls** option to ensure that the files have contents.

You can build from the simple examples in this **cpio** section to develop backup and restore commands to meet your needs in a modest environment.

fbackup and frecover

fbackup and **frecover** are the preferred backup and restore programs on HP-UX. Backups produced with **fbackup** are not portable to other UNIX variants. If you work in a heterogeneous environment, you won't be able to take **fbackup** tapes produced on an HP-UX system and recover them to a system running a different UNIX variant.

This section covers issuing **fbackup** and **frecover** at the command line. Although **fbackup** and **frecover** are the most advanced programs bundled with your HP-UX system for backup and restore, your needs may go beyond these programs. There are also advanced backup programs you can procure from both HP and third parties. In general, I find that the capabilities of **fbackup** and **frecover** are sufficient for new HP-UX installations. If, however, you have a highly distributed environment or need to back up large amounts of data, perform backups on systems with a variety of operating systems, or need to use several backup devices simultaneously, you may want to consider a more advanced product.

fbackup has the capability of performing backups at different *levels*. The levels define the amount of information to be included in the backup. A full backup, which is covered in this section, is backup level 0. The other levels define various degrees of incremental backups. I am a strong advocate of performing a full backup, and then performing incremental backups of every file that has changed since the *last full backup*. This means that to recover from a completely "hosed" (a technical term meaning *destroyed*) system, you need your full backup tape and only one incremental tape. (You would restore your root volume with a bootable Ignite-UX tape produced with **make_tape_recovery**, which is covered in Chapter 10.) If, for example, you perform a full backup on Sunday and an incremental backups on Monday through Friday, you need to load only Sunday's full backup tape and Friday's incremental backup tape to completely restore your system. **fbackup** supports this scheme.

Here is an explanation of the **fbackup** command and *some* of its options:

```
/usr/sbin/fbackup -f device [-0-9] [-u] [-i path] [-e path] [-g graph]
```

        -f device   The tape drive for the backup, such as **/dev/rmt/ 0m** for your local tape drive.

[-0-9]	The level of the backup. If you run a full backup on Sunday at level 0, you would run an incremental backup at level 1 the other days of the week. An incremental backup will back up all information changed since a backup was made at a lower level. You could back up at 0 on Sunday, 1 on Monday, 2 on Tuesday, and so on. However, to recover your system, you need to load Sunday's tape, then Monday's tape, then Tuesday's tape, and so on, to fully recover.
[-u]	Updates the database of past backups so that it contains such information as the backup level, time of the beginning and end of the backup session, and the graph file (described later) used for the backup session. This is valid only with the -g (graph) option.
[-i path]	The specified path is to be included in the backup. This can be issued any number of times.
[-e path]	The specified path is to be excluded from the backup. This can also be specified any number of times.
[-g graph]	Contains the list of files and directories to be included or excluded from the backup.

Although **fbackup** is thorough and easy to use, it does not have embedded in it the day and time at which full and incremental backups will be run. You have to make a **cron** entry to run **fbackup** automatically.

In its simplest form, we could run **fbackup** and specify only the tape drive with the *f* option and the directory to back up with the *i* option, as shown in the following example:

```
# fbackup -f /dev/rmt/0m -i /var/tmp
fbackup(1004): session begins on Wed Jul 12 14:26:30 2000
fbackup(3205): WARNING: unable to read a volume header
fbackup(3024): writing volume 1 to the output file /dev/rmt/0m
fbackup(3055): total file blocks read for backup: 3606
fbackup(3056): total blocks written to output file /dev/rmt/0m: 3857
fbackup(1030): warnings encountered during backup
#
```

fbackup did not produce a list of files included in the backup becuase we did not include the *v* option for verbose.

To view the contents of the tape, we run **frecover** with the options *r* for read, *N* to prevent the contents of the tape from being restored to the system, and *v* for verbose, as shown in the following example:

```
# frecover -rNv -f /dev/rmt/0m
drwxr-xr-x        root      root      /
dr-xr-xr-x        bin       bin       /var
drwxrwxrwx        bin       bin       /var/tmp
-rw-------        root      sys       /var/tmp/OBAMFEAa01630
-rw-------        root      sys       /var/tmp/OBAMHBAa01020
-rw-------        root      sys       /var/tmp/OBAMHBAa01540
-rw-------        root      sys       /var/tmp/OBAMHBAa07762
-rw-rw-rw-        root      sys       /var/tmp/aaaa01112
                                 .
                                 .
                                 .
-rw-rw-rw-        root      sys       /var/tmp/eaaa01487
-rwxr--r--        root      root      /var/tmp/envd.action2
-rwxr--r--        root      root      /var/tmp/envd.action5
-rw-rw-rw-        root      sys       /var/tmp/exclude.temp
dr-xr-xr-x        bin       bin       /var/tmp/ntp
-rw-r--r--        root      sys       /var/tmp/swagent.log
-rw-rw-rw-        root      sys       /var/tmp/tmp_cfg_file
#
```

Let's now delete a file from the system that was included as part of the **fbackup**. We'll then restore only the file we deleted. We use the *x* option for extract and the *i* option to specify the file to include with **frecover**, as shown in the following example:

```
# cd /var/tmp
# ls -l aa*
-rw-rw-rw-   1 root        sys              102 Jul 11 15:20 aaaa01112
-rw-rw-rw-   1 root        sys              102 Jul 11 15:37 aaaa01299
-rw-rw-rw-   1 root        sys              102 Jul 11 15:37 aaaa01333
-rw-rw-rw-   1 root        sys              102 Jul 11 15:38 aaaa01354
-rw-rw-rw-   1 root        sys              102 Jul 11 15:40 aaaa01380
-rw-rw-rw-   1 root        sys               99 Jul 11 15:40 aaaa01405
-rw-rw-rw-   1 root        sys              102 Jul 11 14:57 aaaa01426
-rw-rw-rw-   1 root        sys               99 Jul 11 15:45 aaaa01487
-rw-rw-rw-   1 root        sys              102 Jul 11 14:24 aaaa01558
# rm aaaa01487
# cd /
# frecover -x -i /var/tmp/aaaa01487 -f /dev/rmt/0m
# cd /var/tmp
# ls -l aaa*
-rw-rw-rw-   1 root        sys              102 Jul 11 15:20 aaaa01112
-rw-rw-rw-   1 root        sys              102 Jul 11 15:37 aaaa01299
-rw-rw-rw-   1 root        sys              102 Jul 11 15:37 aaaa01333
-rw-rw-rw-   1 root        sys              102 Jul 11 15:38 aaaa01354
```

```
-rw-rw-rw-   1 root        sys            102 Jul 11 15:40 aaaa01380
-rw-rw-rw-   1 root        sys             99 Jul 11 15:40 aaaa01405
-rw-rw-rw-   1 root        sys            102 Jul 11 14:57 aaaa01426
-rw-rw-rw-   1 root        sys             99 Jul 11 15:45 aaaa01487
-rw-rw-rw-   1 root        sys            102 Jul 11 14:24 aaaa01558
#
```

In the previous example, we successfully restored the file **/var/tmp/aaa01487** from the tape using **frestore**.

In the example, we did not employ some powerful aspects to **fbackup**. These include *backup levels, graph files*, and *index files*.

fbackup supports backup levels 0-9. 0 is used for full backups and the other digits indicate various incremental backup levels. (See the **fbackup** man page at the end of this chapter for additional information.)

Graph files specify the files to be included in the backup.

Index files contain a list of files produced as part of the backup.

Let's look at an example that employs all of these functions. First, we create a graph file that contains the files we want to include (*i*) or exclude (*e*) as part of the backup. In this case, the file contains only the following line:

```
i /var/tmp
```

Let's now run **fbackup** with *u* to update the backup database, *0* for a full backup, *f* to specify the file to which we want to write the backup (we use a file rather than tape in this example), *g* to specify our graph file, *I* to specify the name of the index file, and finally, we redirect messages to a file that will contain the backup log. We add the date and time to the end of the index and backup log files:

```
# fbackup -0u -f /tmp/testbackup -g /tmp/backupgraph
          -I /tmp/backupindex.`date '+%y%m%d.%H:%M'` 2>
          /tmp/backuplog.`date '+%y%m%d.%H:%M'`
#
```

Let's now see what files were produced as a result of having issued this command. First, let's look at the backup index and backup log files:

```
# ls /tmp/backup*
backupgraph
backupgraph000712.15.04
backupindex.000712.15:04
backuplog.000712.15:04
#
# cat /tmp/backupindex000712.15:04
```

```
1024                    1 /
1024                    1 /var
2048                    1 /var/tmp
0                       1 /var/tmp/OBAMFEAa01630
0                       1 /var/tmp/OBAMHBAa01020
0                       1 /var/tmp/OBAMHBAa01540
336                     1 /var/tmp/OBAMHBAa07762
102                     1 /var/tmp/aaaa01112
                .
                .
                .
28                      1 /var/tmp/eaaa01487
28                      1 /var/tmp/envd.action2
28                      1 /var/tmp/envd.action5
4608                    1 /var/tmp/exclude.temp
96                      1 /var/tmp/ntp
1595                    1 /var/tmp/swagent.log
205                     1 /var/tmp/tmp_cfg_file
#
# cat /tmp/backupgraph000712.15:04
i/var/tmp
#
# cat /tmp/backuplog000712.15:04

fbackup(1004): session begins on Wed Jul 12 14:56:19 2000
fbackup(3024): writing volume 1 to the output file /tmp/testbackup
fbackup(1030): warnings encountered during backup
fbackup(3055): total file blocks read for backup: 3614
fbackup(3056): total blocks written to output file /tmp/testbackup:3876
#
```

The three files with the date appended (*7/12/00 time 15:04*) to the end of the filename were produced by the **fbackup** command issued earlier. The date appended to the end of the file can help in the organization of backup files. We could restore any or all of these files with **frestore** from the file that contains the backup information (**/tmp/testbackup**), as demonstrated earlier.

We are not restricted to performing backups to a tape drive attached to the local system. We can back up to a remote tape with **fbackup** by specifying the system name and tape drive, or file, to which we want to store the files. The following example uses **fbackup** options covered earlier and includes the name of the system with the tape drive:

```
# fbackup -f tapesys:/dev/rmt/0m -i /var/tmp -v
fbackup(1004): session begins on Wed Jul 12 15:56:22 2000
fbackup(3307): volume 1 has been used -1 time(s) (maximum: 100)
fbackup(3024): writing vol 1 to output file tapesys:/dev/rmt/0m
    1: / 2
    2: /var 2
    3: /var/tmp 4
    4: /var/tmp/AAAa11812 0
    5: /var/tmp/AAAa11992 0
    6: /var/tmp/BEQ19522 19
```

```
    7: /var/tmp/DCE19522 0
    8: /var/tmp/DEC19522 0
    9: /var/tmp/ISPX19522 0
         .
         .
         .
   73: /var/tmp/eaaa13306 1
   74: /var/tmp/ems_inittab.old 2
   75: /var/tmp/envd.action2 1
   76: /var/tmp/envd.action5 1
   77: /var/tmp/inetd.conf.old 9
   78: /var/tmp/net19522 1799
   79: /var/tmp/swagent.log 16
fbackup(1005): run time: 43 seconds
fbackup(3055): total file blocks read for backup: 1974
fbackup(3056): total blocks written to output file or1:/dev/rmt/0m: 0
#
```

This command performs the backup of **/var/tmp** on system *or1* by sending the files to the tape drive on system *tapesys*. We could have used many additional options to **fbackup**, as demonstrated in earlier examples, but I want to keep the example simple so it would be easy to see the remote tape drive specification.

dd

dd is a utility for writing the contents of a device, such as a disk, to tape. You can also use **dd** to copy an image of a tape to a file on your system, and then you can look at the file.

First, let's write the contents of a directory to tape using **tar**, then we use **dd** to copy the tape contents as a file. The only option to **dd** required in this example is *if,* which specifies the input file as the tape drive:

```
# cd /var/tmp
# tar cf /dev/rmt/0m `ls`
# cd /tmp
# dd if=/dev/rmt/0m > /tmp/tapecontents
183+0 records in
183+0 records out
# tar tv /tmp/tapecontents
rw-------    0/3        0 Jul 11 15:57 2000 OBAMFEAa01630
rw-------    0/3        0 Jul 11 15:20 2000 OBAMHBAa01020
rw-------    0/3        0 Jul 11 15:50 2000 OBAMHBAa01540
rw-------    0/3      336 Jul 12 13:18 2000 OBAMHBAa07762
rw-------    0/3        0 Jul 12 13:44 2000 OBAMHBAa08333
rw-rw-rw-    0/3      102 Jul 11 15:20 2000 aaaa01112
                      .
                      .
                      .
rw-rw-rw-    0/3       28 Jul 11 15:45 2000 eaaa01487
rwxr--r--    0/0       28 Jul 11 21:53 2000 envd.action2
rwxr--r--    0/0       28 Jul 11 21:53 2000 envd.action5
rw-rw-rw-    0/3     2304 Jul 12 12:42 2000 exclude.temp
r-xr-xr-x    2/2        0 Jul 11 13:50 2000 ntp/
rw-r--r--    0/3     1595 Jul 12 12:23 2000 swagent.log
rw-rw-rw-    0/3      205 Jul 12 12:39 2000 tmp_cfg_file
#
```

Now we can look at the contents of the file with **tar** as shown in an earlier section, with the following command:

```
# tar tv /tmp/tapecontents
```

Another common use of **dd** is to extract a **cpio** archive from a tape drive on a remote system to a local system. In the following example, the local system without a tape drive is *or1,* and the remote system with a tape drive is *tapesys*. We read the tape to a directory on *or1* using **dd** and **cpio** (see the earlier **cpio** section for an explanation of the options) in the following example:

```
# hostname
or1
# pwd
/tmp/remotecpiofiles
# remsh tapesys "dd if=/dev/rmt/0m bs=8k" | cpio -icvBdum
.
envd.action2
envd.action5
swagent.log
ntp
OBAMHBAa01020
aaaa01558


                        .
                        .
                        .

eaaa01487
OBAMFEAa01630
cmd_res8215
tmp_cfg_file
cmd_res8708
OBAMHBAa07762
exclude.temp
arch.include.1
3580 blocks
0+358 records in
0+358 records out
#
```

This command runs a remote shell (**remsh**) to run the **dd** command on *tapesys*. The output of this command is piped to **cpio** on the local system to extract the archive. In this example, only the *if* option specifies the input file. The *of* option, which specifies the output file is not needed. If you were to perform a **dd** of a disk device to a tape drive, the *of* would be the tape drive on your system, such as **/dev/rmt/0m**.

dump and restore

dump is similar to **fbackup**. If you use **fbackup** on HP-UX, you will see much similarity when you use **dump**. **dump** provides levels as part of the backup scheme and creates **/var/adm/dumpdates**, which lists the last time a file system was backed up. **restore** is used to read information backed up with **dump**. **dump**, however, works only with HFS file systems, not with VxFS, and it assumes that you are using a reel tape. **vxdump** and **vxrestore** are used for VxFS. Generally speaking, you will not find **dump** (and **vxdump**) and **restore** (and **vxrestore**) recommended as backup and restore programs on HP-UX. **fbackup** and **cpio** are the preferred backup programs on HP-UX. There is, however, no reason why you can't use **dump** and **restore** as long as you keep in mind the file system type limitation.

Let's look at some examples using **dump** and **restore**. The examples actually use **vxdump** and **vxrestore**, however. Nearly the same usage applies to both the HFS and VxFS programs. We use several commands in the upcoming examples, including the following:

```
# vxdump 0fu /dev/rmt/0m /var        ;dump vxfs file system /var to tape
                                      /dev/rmt/0m using level 0 and
                                      update /var/adm/dumpdates.


# vxrestore tf /dev/rmt/0m | grep eaaa   ;obtain table of contents from
                                         tape /dev/rmt/0m and look for
                                         file name containing "eaaa"

# vxrestore -x -f /dev/rmt/0m ./tmp/eaaa01487      ;restore file to
                                                   current directory
```

Let's look at some of these commands in more detail and I provide more explanation for what is taking place.

The first example runs **vxdump** to back up the directory **/var** with a backup level of *0* for full backup, the *f* option to specify the output file **/dev/rmt/0m**, and *u* for a write to **/var/adm/dumpdates**:

```
# vxdump 0fu /dev/rmt/0m /var
  vxdump: Date of this level 0 dump: Tue Jul 11 16:41:27 2000
  vxdump: Date of last level 0 dump: the epoch
  vxdump: Dumping /dev/vg00/rlvol10 to /dev/rmt/0m
```

```
vxdump: mapping (Pass I) [regular files]
vxdump: mapping (Pass II) [directories]
vxdump: estimated 428058 blocks (209.01MB).
vxdump: dumping (Pass III) [directories]
vxdump: dumping (Pass IV) [regular files]
vxdump: vxdump: 214146 tape blocks on 1 volumes(s)
vxdump: level 0 dump on Tue Jul 11 16:41:27 2000
vxdump: Closing /dev/rmt/0m
vxdump: vxdump is done
#
```

vxdump provides information related to the backup to *standard output*.

Next, let's view the table of contents on the tape using **vxrestore**, looking for files that begin with *eaaa*. We'll then delete one of these files from the system and use **vxrestore** to restore it from tape. To produce the table of contents, we use the *t* option, and to extract the file from tape, we use the *x* option to **vxrestore**, as shown in the following listing:

```
# vxrestore tf /dev/rmt/0m | grep eaaa
        404        ./tmp/eaaa01299
        678        ./tmp/eaaa01333
        700        ./tmp/eaaa01354
        736        ./tmp/eaaa01380
        741        ./tmp/eaaa01405
        717        ./tmp/eaaa01487
#
#
# rm /var/tmp/eaaa01487
#
# vxrestore -x -f /dev/rmt/0m ./tmp/eaaa01487
You have not read any tapes yet.
Unless you know which volume your file(s) are on you should start
with the last volume and work towards the first.
Specify next volume #: 1
set owner/mode for '.'? [yn] y

# cd /var/tmp
# ls -l eaaa01487
total 2
-rw-rw-rw-   1 root         sys                28 Jul 11 15:45 eaaa01487
#
```

Notice that as part of restoring the file, we must specify a volume number of *1* and whether or not we want to set the mode for the file.

The examples in this section showed creating a backup tape with **vxdump**, producing a table of contents, and restoring with **vxrestore**. Although **fbackup** and **cpio** are the recommended backup solutions on HP-UX, you can use **dump** and **restore** if you are familiar with these programs and want to use them. Because of the portability of **tar**, it is often used for backup and restore.

Back Up of Virtual Partitions

There are some unique challenges in backing up Virtual Partitions, which I cover in this section. Backup of Virtual Partitions takes place in almost the same manner as in non-vPars systems. The primary difference is that rather than run one backup on a physical system, you have to run a backup of every Virtual Partition that exists on your physical system. You also want to run a **make_net_recovery** on every Virtual Partition as well. This creates a bootable recovery archive for the Virtual Partition. This is covered in the Ignite/UX Chapter 10.

We perform a backup of the first vPar on a system that has the tape drive configured as one of its components (this is a backup to a local tape drive). We'll then perform a backup of a second vPar on the same computer to the tape drive that is configured on the first vPar (this is a backup to a remote tape drive). The tape drive is remote to the second vPar because it does not have the tape drive configured as one of its I/O components. Since the two vPars are distinct and independent systems, the tape drive on the first vPar is remote to the second vPar.

Back Up to a Tape Drive on the Local Virtual Partition

Let's now backup a vPar called *cable1* to the local DDS drive at path *0.0.1.0.3.0*. This is a backup of a vPar to a local tape drive, meaning that the tape drive resource is tied to the vPar for which the backup will be performed. The following **vparstatus** shows that the Local Bus Adapter (LBA) at *0.0* is dedicated to *cable1*:

```
# vparstatus -p cable1 -v

[Virtual Partition Details]
Name:          cable1
State:         Up
Attributes:    Dynamic,Manual
Kernel Path:   /stand/vmunix
Boot Opts:

[CPU Details]
Min/Max:   1/3
Bound by User [Path]:
```

```
Bound by Monitor [Path]:   33
Unbound [Path]:   97

[IO Details]
   0.0                              <-- path of Core I/O card
   0.0.0.0
   0.0.1.1.2.0  BOOT
   0.0.4.0  CONSOLE

[Memory Details]
Specified [Base   /Range]:
          (bytes) (MB)
Total Memory (MB):   1024

#
```

Although the tape drive at *0.0.1.0.3.0* does not appear in this **vparstatus -v** output, the tape drive is connected to the Core I/O card at *0.0* and is therefore accessible to *cable1* to use as a backup device.

As a side note, if the tape interface were not on the Core I/O card, which is devoted to *cable1*, we could move the interface from *cable1* to a second vPar on the same computer called *cable2*, confirm that the driver is in **/stand/system**, and then backup *cable2*.

Because there are many devices that you may want to move among the vPars running on your system, you want to make sure that you have all the device drivers required to support these devices in your kernel.

Let's now run **fbackup** with *u* to update the backup database, *0* for a full backup, *f* to specify the file to which we want to write the backup, *g* to specify our graph file, *I* to specify the name of the index file, and finally, we redirect messages to a file that contains the backup log. We'll add the date and time to the end of the index and backup log files.

The following example shows the **fbackup** command issued:

```
fbackup -0u -f /dev/rmt/0m -g /tmp/backupgraph -I
        /tmp/backupindex.`date '+%y%m%d.%H:M'` 2>
        /tmp/backuplog.`date '+%y%m%d.%H:%M'`
```

Graph files specify the files to be included in the backup. Index files contain a list of files produced as part of the backup. The graph file contains the files we want to include (*i*) or exclude (*e*) as part of the backup. In this case, the file contains only the following line:

```
i /var/tmp
```

Let's now see what files are produced as a result of having issued this command. First, let's look at the backup index and backup log files:

```
# ls -l /tmp/backup*
-rw-rw-rw-  1 root    sys      11 Aug 29 14:45 backupgraph
-rw-------  1 root    sys     778 Aug 29 15:08 backupindex.010829.15:08
-rw-rw-rw-  1 root    sys     521 Aug 29 15:08 backuplog.010829.15:08
#
```

```
# cat /tmp/backupindex.010829.15:08
1024              1 /
1024              1 /var
1024              1 /var/tmp
108               1 /var/tmp/aaaa04686
1241              1 /var/tmp/ems_inittab.old
28                1 /var/tmp/envd.action2
28                1 /var/tmp/envd.action5
4106              1 /var/tmp/inetd.conf.old
96                1 /var/tmp/ntp
0                 1 /var/tmp/rdskUBAa02185
0                 1 /var/tmp/rdskWAAa01840
310               1 /var/tmp/sh1649.1
343               1 /var/tmp/sh1649.2
166               1 /var/tmp/sh1649.3
440               1 /var/tmp/sh1649.4
611               1 /var/tmp/swagent.log
0                 1 /var/tmp/sysstat_em.fmt
22734848          1 /var/tmp/vmunix.noreloc
#
```

```
# cat /tmp/backupgraph
i/var/tmp
#
```

```
# cat /tmp/backuplog.010829.15:08
fbackup(1417): cannot open the dates file /var/adm/fbackupfiles/dates for reading
fbackup(1004): session begins on Wed Aug 29 15:08:10 2001
fbackup(3203): volume 1 has been used 1 time(s)
fbackup(3024): writing volume 1 to the output file /dev/rmt/0m
fbackup(1423): WARNING: could not open the dates file /var/adm/fbackupfiles/dates
for writing
fbackup(1030): warnings encountered during backup
fbackup(3055): total file blocks read for backup: 44432
#
```

The two files with the date appended (*8/29/01 time 15:08*) to the end of the filename were produced by the **fbackup** command issued earlier. The date appended to the end of the file can help in the organization of backup files. We could restore any or all of these files with **frestore**.

The backup of vPar *cable1* to the local tape drive is a backup of the system with a hostname of *cvhdcon3*. The other vPar running on this system, *cable2*, was not included in the backup because its host, *cvhdcon4,* is viewed as a separate system. The next section shows how we would backup *cable2* to the tape drive dedicated to *cable1*.

Back Up to a Tape Drive on a Different Local Virtual Partition

The tape drive in the preceding section was connected to *cable1* and used to back up *cable1*. Let's now back up *cable2* with the tape drive as part of the *cable1* Virtual Partition. Keep in mind that vPar *cable2* with its hostname *cvhdcon4* is a separate system from *cable1* and its hostname *cvhdcon3*. We will, therefore, have to backup vPar *cable2* to a remote tape drive on *cable1*.

We will back up to a remote tape that's connected to *cable1*, with **fbackup** by specifying the system name and tape drive, or file, to which we want to store the files. The following example uses **fbackup** options. We are connected to *cable2* and specify that it is to be backed up to the tape drive on *cable1* (hostname *cvhdcon3*.) The following **fbackup** command performs the backup to the remote tape drive:

```
# fbackup -f cvhdcon3:/dev/rmt/0m -i /var/tmp -v


fbackup(1004): session begins on Wed Aug 29 16:09:28 2001
fbackup(3307): volume 1 has been used 6 time(s) (maximum: 100)
fbackup(3024): writing volume 1 to the output file cvhdcon3:/dev/rmt/0m
     1: /
     2: /tmp
     3: /tmp/.AgentSockets
     4: /tmp/.AgentSockets/A
     5: /tmp/X11_newfonts.log
     6: /tmp/install.vars
     7: /tmp/llbdbase.dat
     8: /tmp/lost+found
     9: /tmp/portmap.file
    10: /tmp/rpcbind.file
    11: /tmp/sd_ipd_acl.1417
    12: /tmp/services
    13: /tmp/swlist
    14: /tmp/typescript
fbackup(1005): run time: 17 seconds
fbackup(3055): total file blocks read for backup: 141
fbackup(3056): total blocks written to output file
cvhdcon3:/dev/rmt/0m: 0
#
```

It takes a little getting used to running **fbackup** to a remote device, even when the device is physically connected to the computer on which you're working. Because the two vPars are different hosts, however, it makes sense that a tape drive used by a different vPar would indeed be remote.

The **fbackup** runs over the network from *cable2* to *cable1*. This is one of the many reasons that you want to have a network card for every vPar on your system.

We can also issue other remote backup commands. The following example shows running **cpio** on *cable2* to the tape drive on *cable1* (hostname *cvhdcon3*):

```
# find . -print | cpio -oBv | (remsh cvhdcon3 dd of=/dev/rmt/0m)
.
lost+found
.AgentSockets
Socket <.AgentSockets/A> not backed up
typescript
install.vars
swlist
X11_newfonts.log
sd_ipd_acl.1417
services
rpcbind.file
portmap.file
llbdbase.dat
140 blocks

140+0 records in
140+0 records out
#
```

This command performs the backup of **/tmp** on vPar *cable2* by sending the files to the tape drive on system *cvhdcon3* (vPar *cable1*).

Chapter 8

System Startup and Shutdown

Introduction

This chapter covers a variety of topics related to startup and shutdown scripts including the following:

- The overall organization of the startup and shutdown mechanism in HP-UX
- Example of a startup file
- **/etc/inittab** file
- **shutdown** command
- Virtual Partitions (vPars) and startup

System Startup and Shutdown Mechanism

Startup and shutdown scripts for HP-UX 11i are based on a mechanism that separates the actual startup and shutdown scripts from configuration information. To modify the way your system starts or stops, you don't have to modify scripts, which in general is considered somewhat risky; you can instead modify configuration variables. The startup and shutdown sequence is based on an industry standard that is similar to many other UNIX-based systems, so your knowledge of HP-UX applies to many other systems.

Startup and shutdown are going to become increasingly more important to you as your system administration work becomes more sophisticated. As you load and customize more applications, you will need more startup and shutdown knowledge. This section overviews startup and shutdown and the commands you can use to control your system.

The following components are in the startup and shutdown model:

Execution Scripts

> Execution scripts read variables from configuration variable files and run through the startup or shutdown sequence. These scripts are located in **/sbin/init.d**.

Configuration Variable Scripts

> These are the files you would modify to set variables that enable or disable a subsystem or to perform some other function at the time of system startup or shutdown. These are located in /**etc/rc.config.d**.

Link Files

> These files control the order in which scripts execute. These are actually links to execution scripts to be executed when moving from one run level to another. These files are located in the directory for the appropriate run level, such as **/sbin/rc0.d** for run level 0, **/sbin/rc1.d** for run level 1, and so on.

Sequencer Script

> This script invokes execution scripts based on run-level transition. This script is located in **/sbin/rc**.

Figure 8-1 shows the directory structure for startup and shutdown scripts.

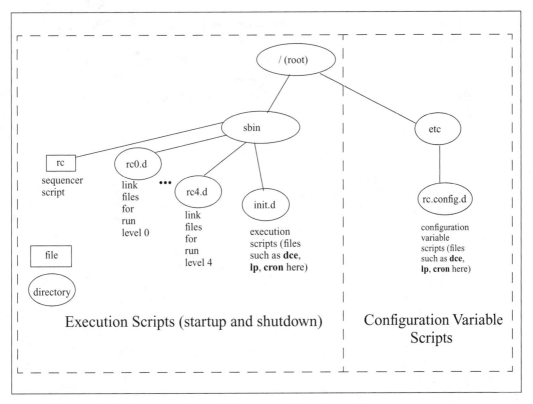

Figure 8-1   Organization of Startup and Shutdown Files

Execution scripts perform startup and shutdown tasks. **/sbin/rc** invokes the execution script with the appropriate start or stop arguments, and you can view the appropriate start or stop messages on the console. The messages you see will have one of the three following values:

OK   Indicates that the execution script started or shut down properly.

FAIL   A problem occurred at startup or shutdown.

N/A   The script was not configured to start.

To start up a subsystem, simply edit the appropriate configuration file in **/etc/rc.config.d**.

Let's look at an example startup and shutdown file for an application loaded onto an HP-UX system that is widely used for Internet applications called Cold Fusion. Like many applications loaded on HP-UX systems, Cold Fusion installs startup and shutdown scripts as a standard part of the installation of the product.

As previously mentioned, the script used as part of the startup and shutdown process is in **/etc/init.d**. In this case, the name of the program is **/etc/init.d/coldfusion** and is shown in the following listing:

```
# cat /sbin/init.d/coldfusion
#!/bin/sh
#
# Start the Cold Fusion servers
#

# set at install
CFHOME=/apps/coldfusion
CFBIN=$CFHOME/bin

export CFHOME

#
# Start/stop processes for Cold Fusion
#

rval=0

case "$1" in

    start_msg)
        print "Starting ColdFusion Application Server"
        ;;

    stop_msg)
        print "Stopping ColdFusion Application Server"
        ;;

    'start')
        #First, check "on/off switch", to set CF_AUTOSTART, in config.d file.
        RCFILE=/etc/rc.config.d/coldfusion
        if [ -f $RCFILE ] ; then
                . $RCFILE
        else
                print "Warning: $RCFILE defaults file missing."
                print "         Starting ColdFusion by default."
                CF_AUTOSTART=1
        fi

        # Start CF if switch is on.
        if [ "$CF_AUTOSTART" -eq 1 ]; then
            if [ -x $CFBIN/start ]; then
                $CFBIN/start
                rval=$?
            else
                print "Error: ColdFusion startup script $CFBIN/start missing."
                print "         ColdFusion not started."
                rval=1
```

```
            fi
        else
            print "Notice: ColdFusion startup disabled in $RCFILE"
            rval=2
        fi
        ;;

    'stop')
        if [ -x $CFBIN/stop ]; then
                $CFBIN/stop -force
        fi
        ;;

    *)
        echo "Usage: $0 { start | stop }"
        rval=1
        ;;
esac

exit $rval

#
```

The startup and shutdown scripts in **/etc/init.d** generally perform both startup and shutdown functions. The startup and shutdown scripts, including the one in our example, recognize the following four arguments:

- *start_msg* - This is an argument passed to scripts so that the script can report a message indicating what the "start" action will do.
- *stop_msg* - This is an argument passed to scripts so that the script can report a message indicating what the "stop" action will do.
- *start* - The script will start the application.
- *stop* - The script will shut down the application.

You may encounter problems during boot with one of the startup programs being hung. If this is the case, *Ctrl* / (*control* and *pipe*) keys normally break out of the script and continue to the next script.

All startup and shutdown scripts, including the one in the previous listing, obtain configuration data from variables in **/etc/rc.config.d**. Our example script checks the value of the "on/off" switch in **/etc/rc.confi.d/coldfusion**, which is shown in the following listing, to determine if Cold Fusion should be started:

```
# cat /etc/rc.config.d/coldfusion
# ColdFusion Application Server configuration file
#
CF_AUTOSTART=1  #Set to 1 to restart at boot time
#
```

The variable in this file is set to *1,* so the application starts at the time of system boot.

Startup and shutdown scripts are run based on the directory in which a link to the script appears. Our example script should be started at run level *3.* Therefore, a link to the script appears in the directory **/sbin/rc3.d**, shown as the third link in the following listing:

```
# ls -l /sbin/rc3.d
total 0
lrwxr-xr-x  1 root sys  23 Apr 26 14:32 S100nfs.server -> /sbin/init.d/nfs.server
lrwxr-xr-x  1 root sys  19 Apr 26 14:52 S200tps.rc -> /sbin/init.d/tps.rc
lrwxrwxrwx  1 root sys  20 May 16 20:57 S790coldfusion -> ../init.d/coldfusion
lrwxr-xr-x  1 root sys  23 Apr 26 14:44 S990dtlogin.rc -> /sbin/init.d/dtlogin.rc
#
```

The significance of the naming of the link is discussed shortly. For the time being, it is sufficient to know that a link called **/sbin/rc3.d/S790coldfusion** points to our script **/init.d/coldfusion**.

Applications are shut down in the opposite order from which they are started. This means that a link to the startup and shutdown script appears in a lower-level directory for shutdown. In this example, the startup link appears in **/sbin/rc3.d**, but the shutdown link appears in **/etc/rc1.d**, as shown in the following listing:

```
# ls -l /sbin/rc1.d

lrwxr-xr-x  1 root    sys  17 Apr 26 14:52 K220slsd -> /sbin/init.d/slsd
lrwxr-xr-x  1 root    sys  18 Apr 26 14:45 K230audio -> /sbin/init.d/audio
lrwxr-xr-x  1 root    sys  21 Apr 26 14:46 K240auditing -> /sbin/init.d/auditing
lrwxr-xr-x  1 root    sys  17 Apr 26 14:43 K250envd -> /sbin/init.d/envd
lrwxr-xr-x  1 root    sys  17 Apr 26 14:43 K270cron -> /sbin/init.d/cron
lrwxr-xr-x  1 root    sys  15 Apr 26 14:45 K278pd -> /sbin/init.d/pd
lrwxr-xr-x  1 root    sys  15 Apr 26 14:45 K280lp -> /sbin/init.d/lp
lrwxr-xr-x  1 root    sys  21 Apr 26 14:49 K290hparamgr -> /sbin/init.d/hparamgr
lrwxr-xr-x  1 root    sys  20 Apr 26 14:43 K290hparray -> /sbin/init.d/hparray
lrwxrwxrwx  1 root    sys  20 May 16 20:57 K300coldfusion -> ../init.d/coldfusion
                        .
                        .
                        .
```

The link called **/sbin/rc3.d/K300coldfusion** points to the script **/init.d/coldfusion**. Startup for this application takes place at run level 3 and shutdown takes place at run level 1.

There is significance associated with the names of the links shown in the previous two listings. The following example is the startup link in the example:

```
/sbin/rc3.d/S790coldfusion
    |    |  | |       |
    |    |  | |       v
    |    |  | |      script name - coldfusion in ex
    |    |  | v
    |    |  | sequence number - 790 in example
    |    |  v
    |    |  "S" for startup, "K" for shutdown
    |    v
    v  run level number - 3 in example
```

This example is for the Cold Fusion startup script. Startup links begin with an "S" for *startup*. The shutdown script has a similar entry in **/sbin/rc1.d**, it but has a "K" as the first character of the link name to indicate *kill*.

Scripts are executed in lexicographical order. Gaps are left between startup scripts at a given run level and between shutdown scripts at a given run level, so when additional scripts are added, you don't have to renumber any existing scripts within a run level.

Because applications are shut down in the opposite order in which they are started, shutdown scripts do not usually have the same numbers as their startup counterparts. Two applications that start in a given order because of dependencies will usually be shut down in the opposite order in which they were started. In this example, the startup number is *S790coldfusion* and the shutdown number is *K300coldfusion*.

Scripts are run when there is a change in run level. **/sbin/rc** is a program that is run whenever a change in run level occurs. The following listing shows **/etc/inittab**:

```
init:3:initdefault:
ioin::sysinit:/sbin/ioinitrc >/dev/console 2>&1
tape::sysinit:/sbin/mtinit > /dev/console 2>&1
muxi::sysinit:/sbin/dasetup    </dev/console >/dev/console 2>&1 # mux init
stty::sysinit:/sbin/stty 9600 clocal icanon echo opost onlcr ixon icrnl ignpar </dev/
systty
brc1::bootwait:/sbin/bcheckrc </dev/console >/dev/console 2>&1 # fsck, etc.
link::wait:/sbin/sh -c "/sbin/rm -f /dev/syscon; \
                /sbin/ln /dev/systty /dev/syscon" >/dev/console 2>&1
cprt::bootwait:/sbin/cat /etc/copyright >/dev/syscon        # legal req
sqnc::wait:/sbin/rc </dev/console >/dev/console 2>&1        # system init
#powf::powerwait:/sbin/powerfail >/dev/console 2>&1         # powerfail
cons:123456:respawn:/usr/sbin/getty console console         # system console
#ttp1:234:respawn:/usr/sbin/getty -h tty0p1 9600
#ttp2:234:respawn:/usr/sbin/getty -h tty0p2 9600
```

```
#ttp3:234:respawn:/usr/sbin/getty -h tty0p3 9600
#ttp4:234:respawn:/usr/sbin/getty -h tty0p4 9600
#ttp5:234:respawn:/usr/sbin/getty -h tty0p5 9600
#ups::respawn:rtprio 0 /usr/lbin/ups_mond -f /etc/ups_conf
```

The **/sbin/rc** line is always present in the **/etc/inittab** file. There is more information about **/etc/inittab** coming shortly.

If you are booting your system to run level 3, **/sbin/rc** will run the startup scripts present in **/sbin/rc1.d**, **/sbin/rc2.d**, and **/sbin/rc3.d**.

I have mentioned run levels several times in this discussion. Both the startup and shutdown scripts described here, as well as the **/etc/inittab** file, depend on run levels. In HP-UX 11i, the following run levels exist:

0	Halted run level.
s	Run level s, also known as single-user mode, ensures that no one else is on the system so that you can proceed with system administration tasks.
1	Run level 1 starts various basic processes.
2	Run level 2 allows users to access the system. This is also known as multi-user mode.
3	Run level 3 is for exporting NFS file systems.
4	Run level 3 or 4 starts the graphical manager, including HP Common Desktop Environment (HP CDE).
5 and 6	Not currently used.

/etc/inittab also defines a variety of processes that will be run, and it is used by **/sbin/init**. The **/sbin/init** process ID is 1. It is the first process started on your system, and it has no parent. The **init** process looks at   **/etc/inittab** to determine the run level of the system.

Entries in the **/etc/inittab** file have the following format:

id:run state:action:process

id	The name of the entry. The id is up to four characters long and must be unique in the file. If the line in **/etc/inittab** is preceded by a "#," the entry is treated as a comment.
run state	Specifies the run level at which the command is executed. More than one run level can be specified. The command is executed for every run level specified.
action	Defines which of 11 actions will be taken with this process. The 11 choices for action are *initdefault, sysinit, boot, bootwait, wait, respawn, once, powerfail, powerwait, ondemand,* and *off.*
process	The shell command to be executed *if* the run level and/or action field so indicates.

Here is an example of an **/etc/inittab** entry:

cons:123456:respawn:/usr/sbin/getty   console console

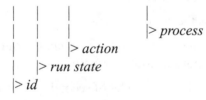

This is in the **/etc/inittab** file, as opposed to being defined as a startup script, because the console may be killed and have to be restarted whenever it dies, even if no change has occurred in run level. **respawn** starts a process if it does not exist and restarts the process after it dies. This entry shows all run states, because you want the console to be activated at all times.

Another example is the first line from **/etc/inittab**:

init:3:initdefault:

The default run level of the system is defined as *3*.

The basics of system startup and shutdown described here are important to understand. You will be starting up and shutting down your system and possibly even modifying some of the files described here. Please take a close look at the startup and shutdown files before you begin to modify them.

Now, I cover the commands you can issue to shut down your system.

System Shutdown

What does it mean to shut down the system? In its simplest form, a shutdown of the system simply means issuing the **/sbin/shutdown** command. The **shutdown** command terminates all processing. It has many options, including the following:

-r	Automatically reboots the system; that is, brings it down and brings it up.
-h	Halts the system completely.
-y	Completes the shutdown without asking you any questions it would normally ask.
grace	Specifies the number of seconds you want to wait before the system is shut down to give your users time to save files, quit applications, and log out.

Here are some of the things your system does when you issue the **shutdown** command:

- Checks to see whether the user who executed **shutdown** does indeed have permission to execute the command.
- Changes the working directory to root (/).
- Sets *PATH* to **/usr/bin/:/usr/sbin:/sbin**.

- Updates all superblocks.
- Informs users that a **shutdown** has been issued and asks them to log out.
- Executes **/sbin/rc**, which does such things as shut down subsystems via shutdown scripts such as the spooler and CDE, unmount file systems and other such tasks.
- Runs **/sbin/reboot** if the -r option is used.

To shut down and automatically reboot the system, you would type

```
$ shutdown -r
```

To halt the system type

```
$ shutdown -h
```

You are asked whether you want to type a message to users informing them of the impending system shutdown. After you type the message, it is immediately sent to all users. After the specified time elapses (60 seconds is the default), the system begins the shutdown process. After you receive a message that the system is halted, you can power off all of your system components.

To shut down the system in two minutes without being asked any questions or sending any message, type

```
$ shutdown -h -y 120
```

At times, you need to go into single-user mode with **shutdown** to perform some task such as a backup or to expand a logical volume, and then reboot the system to return it to its original state.

To shut down the system into single-user mode, you type

```
$ shutdown
```

The **shutdown** command with no options puts you into single-user mode. On older versions of the operating system, you could go to single-user mode by using the **init** command with the s option (**init s**). However, this is highly discouraged because this command does not terminate other system activity nor does it log users off; therefore, it does not result in a true single-user state.

If the system is already in single-user mode or you like to live dangerously, you can execute **/usr/sbin/reboot**. I strongly suggest that you issue **shutdown**, which calls **reboot**. The **reboot** command abruptly terminates all processes and then halts or reboots the system. Also, with dynamically loadable kernel modules, **reboot** does not load these modules; only **shutdown** does.

Again, I recommend using the **shutdown** command, not **reboot**.

System Startup and Shutdown Scripts in Virtual Partitions

Every Virtual Partition has separate startup and shutdown scripts just as you would have separate scripts on individual systems. There isn't any unique activity that takes place from a startup and shutdown standpoint due to Virtual Partitions; however, because each vPar runs its own HP-UX, you can customize the startup and shutdown to meet the needs of the applications you're running in each vPar. In addition, a *heartbeat* deamon synchronizes the Virtual Partition database every few seconds.

I cover an application running in a vPar and the startup and shutdown procedures employed to support this application. In addition, I discus the means by which the *heartbeat* deamon is started and stopped to synchronize the Virtual Partition database.

Application Startup in Virtual Partitions

Each Virtual Partition is like a separate server. The applications running in a vPar run independently of applications and activity running in other vPars. All applications in a vPar require startup scripts to be run as they would on any system.

In the vPar used in this example, I have a variety of applications running, including Broadvision. Look at **/etc/rc.config.d**, where the configuration variable scripts are located, to see what *bv* files (those that relate to Broadvision) exist:

```
# ll | grep bv
-rwxr-xr-x   1 root      sys            9 Sep 26 09:31 bv
# cat bv
BV_CTL=1
#
```

This listing shows the **bv** file and its contents. The *BV_CTL=1* variable indicates that Broadvision is to be started when the system boots.

Starting the *bv* application processes results in several Broadvision-related daemons being started, including those in the following listing:

```
# ps -ef | grep bv1
pbcombv  3111  3096  0  Sep 26  ?  0:04 bvconf_srv p_1221_3 -f -install_name bv1to1/bvconf_srv_a
pbcombv  3404  3096  0  Sep 26  ?  1:19 cntdb p_1221_5 -install_name bv1to1/cntdb_1
pbcombv  3707  3096  0  Sep 26  ?  0:20 genericdb p_1221_8 -install_name bv1to1/genericdb_1
pbcombv  3479 3096 0 Sep 26 ? 0:05 cntdb p_1221_7 -install_name bv1to1/
                                        DiscussionForum_cntdb_1
root  7572  7232  0 13:17:33 pts/0      0:00 grep bv1
#
```

You can see that many processes are related to the *bv1to1* application running on this system. These start automatically as part of the startup structure of HP-UX. The following listing shows the link in **/sbin/rc1.d**, for run level 1, and **/sbin/rc2.d**, for run level 2, for *bv*:

```
# ll /sbin/rc1.d | grep bv
lrwxr-xr-x   1 root       sys        15 Sep 26 10:42 K105bv -> /sbin/init.d/bv
# ll /sbin/rc2.d | grep bv
lrwxr-xr-x   1 root       sys        15 Sep 26 10:41 S930bv -> /sbin/init.d/bv
#
```

The *bv kill* script, as indicated by the "K" preceding the link, is shown in **/sbin/rc1.d**, and the *start* script, as indicated by the "S" preceding the link, is shown in **/sbin/rc2.d**.

The script **/sbin/init.d/bv,** which is shown in the links, runs a variety of commands at both startup and shutdown of the Virtual Partition. The following listing shows the **/sbin/init.d/bv** script:

```
#
# <Insert comment about your script here>
#

# Allowed exit values:
#       0 = success; causes "OK" to show up in checklist.
#       1 = failure; causes "FAIL" to show up in checklist.
#       2 = skip; causes "N/A" to show up in the checklist.
#           Use this value if execution of this script is overridden
#           by the use of a control variable, or if this script is not
#           appropriate to execute for some other reason.
#       3 = reboot; causes the system to be rebooted after execution.
#       4 = background; causes "BG" to show up in the checklist.
#           Use this value if this script starts a process in background mode.

# Input and output:
#       stdin is redirected from /dev/null
#
#       stdout and stderr are redirected to the /etc/rc.log file
#       during checklist mode, or to the console in raw mode.

PATH=/usr/sbin:/usr/bin:/sbin
export PATH

# NOTE: If your script executes in run state 0 or state 1, then /usr might
#       not be available.  Do not attempt to access commands or files in
```

```
#            /usr unless your script executes in run state 2 or greater.  Other
#            file systems typically not mounted until run state 2 include /var
#            and /opt.

rval=0

# Check the exit value of a command run by this script.  If non-zero, the
# exit code is echoed to the log file and the return value of this script
# is set to indicate failure.

set_return() {
        x=$?
        if [ $x -ne 0 ]; then
                echo "EXIT CODE: $x"
                rval=1  # script FAILed
        fi
}

# Kill the named process(es).
# $1=<search pattern for your process>

killproc() {
        pid=`ps -el | awk '( ($NF ~ /'"$1"'/) && ($4 != mypid) && ($5 != mypid)  ){
print $4 }' mypid=$$ `
        if [ "X$pid" != "X" ]; then
                if kill "$pid"; then
                        echo "$1 stopped"
                else
                        rval=1
                        echo "Unable to stop $1"
                fi
        fi
}


case $1 in
'start_msg')
        # Emit a _short_ message relating to running this script with
        # the "start" argument; this message appears as part of the checklist.
        echo "Starting the BroadVision subsystem"
        ;;

'stop_msg')
        # Emit a _short_ message relating to running this script with
        # the "stop" argument; this message appears as part of the checklist.
        echo "Stopping the BroadVision subsystem"
        ;;

'start')

        # source the system configuration variables
        if [ -f /etc/rc.config.d/bv ] ; then
                . /etc/rc.config.d/bv
        else
                echo "ERROR: /etc/rc.config.d/bv defaults file MISSING"
        fi

        # Check to see if this script is allowed to run...
        if [ "$BV_CTL" != 1 ]; then
                rval=2
        else

        # Execute the commands to start your subsystem
        su - pbcombv -c "/opt/bv1to1/bin/bvconf execute"
        :
        fi
        ;;

'stop')
        # source the system configuration variables
        if [ -f /etc/rc.config.d/bv ] ; then
                . /etc/rc.config.d/bv
        else
                echo "ERROR: /etc/rc.config.d/bv defaults file MISSING"
        fi
```

```
     # Check to see if this script is allowed to run...
     if [ "$BV_CTL" != 1 ]; then
               rval=2
     else
     :
     # Execute the commands to stop your subsystem
     su - pbcombv -c "/opt/bv1to1/bin/bvconf shutdown"
     fi
     ;;

*)
     echo "usage: $0 {start|stop|start_msg|stop_msg}"
     rval=1
     ;;
esac

exit $rval
```

All the *start* and *stop* information related to Broadvision is present in this file because this script is run for both *kill* (*K*) and *start* (*S*).

```
     if [ "$BV_CTL" != 1 ]; then
```

which checks to see if the variable we viewed earlier in **/etc/rc.con-fig.d/bv** is equal to one as it was when we checked the file.

The installation and startup of Broadvision is required in all Virtual Partitions in which you want to run this application. What is taking place in vPar used in this example is what you would see in every vPar running Broadvision.

Virtual Partition Startup

Now, I cover **/etc/rc.config.d**, where the configuration variable scripts are located to see what vPar-related scripts exist. I perform a long listing of this directory and search for *vpar*:

```
# ll /etc/rc.config.d | grep vpar
-r--r--r--    1 bin          bin            291 Aug 21 14:38 vpard
-r--r--r--    1 bin          bin            399 Aug 13 14:31 vparhb
-r--r--r--    1 bin          bin            702 Aug 13 14:30 vparinit
#
```

This listing shows three vPar-related configuration variable scripts. **vparhb** is the *heartbeat* daemon that is started with **/sbin/init.d/vparhb**. The *heartbeat* deamon provides consistent heartbeat status.

vpard synchronizes the database between memory and all vPars. The default synchronization interval is five seconds. **vpard** is started with **/sbin/init.d/vpard**. The following listing shows the contents of **/stand** in a Virtual Partition:

```
# ll /stand
total 143232
-rw-r--r--   1 root     sys           19 Jul 13 15:04 bootconf
drwxr-xr-x   4 root     sys         2048 Sep 17 15:47 build
drwxrwxrwx   5 root     root        1024 Sep 17 15:52 dlkm
drwxrwxrwx   5 root     sys         1024 Sep 17 14:10 dlkm.vmunix.prev
-rw-r--r--   1 root     sys         3388 Sep 26 13:01 ioconfig
-r--r--r--   1 root     sys           82 Jul 13 15:34 kernrel
drwxr-xr-x   2 root     sys         1024 Sep 26 13:04 krs
drwxr-xr-x   2 root     root        1024 Sep 26 13:01 krs_lkg
drwxr-xr-x   2 root     root        1024 Sep 26 13:04 krs_tmp
drwxr-xr-x   2 root     root        8192 Jul 13 15:04 lost+found
-rw-------   1 root     root          12 Sep 26 13:01 rootconf
-r--r--r--   1 root     sys         2035 Sep 17 14:09 system
-r--r--r--   1 root     sys          994 Jul 13 15:28 system.01
-r--r--r--   1 root     sys          999 Jul 13 15:56 system.02
-r--r--r--   1 root     sys          994 Jul 13 15:28 system.base
drwxr-xr-x   2 root     sys         1024 Jul 13 15:37 system.d
-r--r--r--   1 root     sys         2030 Sep 17 14:07 system.prev
-rwxr-xr-x   1 root     root    22682568 Sep 17 15:52 vmunix
-rwxr-xr-x   1 root     sys     21916712 Sep 17 14:10 vmunix.prev
-rw-------   1 root     root        8232 Sep 26 13:01 vpdb
-rw-------   1 root     root        8232 Jul 17 14:11 vpdb.OLD
-r-xr-xr-x   1 bin      bin       837616 Aug 31 18:59 vpmon
-rw-------   1 root     root     5078504 Jul 18 11:36 vpmon.dmp
#
#
```

The daemon **vphb** is shown in the following **ps -ef** listing:

```
# ps -ef | grep vphb
    root   352      1  0 13:01:53 ?         0:00 vphbd -d 10 -p /var/run/vphbd.pid
    root  7289   7232  1 12:18:28 pts/0     0:00 grep vphb
#
```

vphb starts automatically as part of the startup structure of HP-UX. The following listing shows all the links in **/sbin/rc0.d**, for run level *0*, including the two vPar-related links at the beginning of this listing:

```
# ll /sbin/rc0.d
total 0
lrwxr-xr-x 1 bin    bin     18 Sep 17 14:11 K425vpard -> /sbin/init.d/vpard
lrwxr-xr-x 1 bin    bin     19 Sep 17 14:11 K431vparhb -> /sbin/init.d/vparhb
lrwxr-xr-x 1 root   root    19 Jul 13 15:08 K480syncer -> /sbin/init.d/syncer
lrwxr-xr-x 1 root   root    15 Jul 13 15:08 K650kl -> /sbin/init.d/kl
lrwxr-xr-x 1 root   root    20 Jul 13 15:08 K800killall -> /sbin/init.d/killall
lrwxr-xr-x 1 root   root    19 Jul 13 15:08 K888kminit -> /sbin/init.d/kminit
lrwxr-xr-x 1 root   root    20 Jul 13 15:08 K890kmbuild -> /sbin/init.d/kmbuild
lrwxr-xr-x 1 root   root    23 Jul 13 15:08 K900localmount -> /sbin/init.d/localmount
#
```

These are *kill* scripts, as indicated by the "K" preceding each link. The links to the *start* scripts are found in **/sbin/rc1.d**.

Look at the file **/sbin/init.d/vparhb**, which is shown in the *heartbeat* link and is run at startup in the following listing:

```
# cat /sbin/init.d/vparhb
#!/sbin/sh

#
# NOTE: This script is not configurable!  Any changes made to this
#       script will be overwritten when you upgrade to the next
#       release of HP-UX.
#

#
# vphbd startup: Startup and kill script for the virtual partition
#                heartbeat daemon
#

PATH=/sbin:/usr/sbin:/usr/bin
export PATH

if [ -r /etc/rc.config.d/vparhb ]
then . /etc/rc.config.d/vparhb
fi

case "$1" in

    'start_msg') echo "Starting Virtual Partition Heartbeat Daemon" ;;

    'start')
        vphbd -d "${VPHBD_DELAY-10}" -p "${VPHBD_PID_FILE-/var/run/vphbd.pid}"
        exit $?
        ;;

    'stop_msg') echo "Stopping Virtual Partition Heartbeat Daemon" ;;

    'stop')
        [ ! -r "${VPHBD_PID_FILE=/var/run/vphbd.pid}" ] && exit 2
        pid=`cat "$VPHBD_PID_FILE"`
        [ "$pid" -le "0" ] && exit 1
        kill "$pid"
        rm -f "$VPHBD_PID_FILE"
        exit 0
        ;;

    *)
        echo "Usage: $0 { start | start_msg | stop | stop_msg }"
        ;;

esac

exit 0
#
```

All the *start* and *stop* information related to the *heartbeat* daemon is present in this file because this script is run for both *kill* (*K*) and *start* (*S*) .

The vPar-specific startup and shutdown setup, such as the *heartbeat* daemon just covered, are automatically performed for you when vPars software is installed. Your application-related startup configuration must be performed on each vPar just as it would on separate servers.

Chapter 9

Users and Groups

Set Up Users and Groups

This chapter covers the basics of users on HP-UX systems. Topics such as users, groups, permissions, Virtual Partitions (vPars) and users, and NIS are covered.

This chapter does not cover Common Desktop Environment (CDE) and GNU Network Object Model Environment (GNOME) as the previous edition of this book did. Both of these user interfaces are available for HP-UX, however, this book is clearly server-centric, and these user interfaces aren't used much on servers. A wealth of information on these user interfaces exists at *docs.hp.com;* visit this site if you're interested in knowing more about using them.

You need to make a few basic decisions about users. Where should users' data be located? Who needs to access data from whom, thereby defining "groups" of users? What kind of particular startup is required by users and applications? Is there a shell that your users prefer?

Put some thought into these important user-related questions. I spend a lot of time working with my customers rearranging user data for several reasons. It doesn't fit on a whole disk (and for this reason, I strongly recommend using Logical Volume Manager or Veritas Volume Manager); users can't freely access one another's data, or even worse, users *can* access one another's data too freely.

We consider these questions, but first, let's look at the basic steps to adding a user. Here is a list of activities:

- Select a user name to add.
- Select a user ID number.
- Select a group for the user.
- Create an **/etc/passwd** entry.
- Assign a user password (including expiration options).
- Select and create a home directory for user in **/home**.
- Select the shell the user will run (I strongly recommend the default POSIX shell).
- Place startup files in the user's home directory.
- Test the user account.

Most of what you do is entered in the **/etc/passwd** file, where information about all users is stored. You can make these entries to the **/etc/passwd** file with the **/usr/sbin/vipw** command. Figure 9-1 is a sample **/etc/passwd** entry.

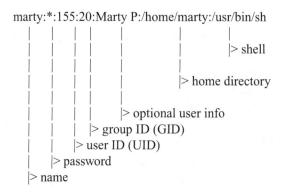

Figure 9-1   Sample **/etc/passwd** Entry

Here is a description of each of these fields:

name. The user name you assign. This name should be easy for the user and other users on the system to remember. When sending electronic mail or copying files from one user to another, the easier it is to remember the user name, the better. If a user has a user name on another system, you may want to assign the same user name on your HP-UX system. Some systems don't permit nice, easy user names, so you may want to break the tie with the old system and start using sensible, easy-to-remember user names on your HP-UX system. Remember, no security is tied to the user name; security is handled through the user's password and the file permissions.

password. The user's password in encrypted form. If an asterisk appears in this field, the account can't be used. If it is empty, the user has no password assigned and can log in by typing only his or her user name. I strongly recommend that each user have a password that he or she changes periodically. Every system has different security needs, but at a minimum, every user on every system should have a password. When setting up a new user, you can force the user to create a password at first login by putting ,.. in the password field.

Here are some features of a good password:

• Use a minimum of six characters, which should include special characters such as a slash (/), a dot (.), or an asterisk (*).

• No words should be used for a password.

• Don't make the password personal, such as using your name, address, favorite sports team, etc.

• Don't use something easy to type, such as 123456, or qwerty.

• Some people say that misspelled words are acceptable, but I don't recommend using them. Spell-check programs that match misspelled words to correctly spelled words can be used to guess at words that might be misspelled for a password.

•A password generator that produces an intelligible passwords works the best.

user ID (UID).   The identification number of the user. Every user on your system should have a unique UID. I would recommend that you reserve UIDs less than 100 for system-level users.

group ID (GID).   The identification number of the group. The members of the group and their GIDs are in the **/etc/group** file. You can change the GID assigned if you don't like it, but you may also have to change the GID of many files. As a user creates a file, his or her UID is assigned to the file as well as the GID. This means that if you change the GID well after users of the same group have created many files and directories, you may have to change the GID of all these elements. I usually save GIDs of less than 10 for system groups.

optional user info.   In this space, you can make entries, such as the user's phone number or full name. You can leave this blank, but if you manage a system or network with many users, you may want to add the user's full name and extension so that if you need to get in touch with him or her, you have the information at your fingertips. (This field is sometimes referred to as the GECOs field.)

home directory.   The home directory defines the default location for all the users' files and directories. This is the present working directory at the time of login.

shell.   The startup program the user runs at the time of login. The shell is really a command interpreter for the commands the user issues from the command line. I recommend using the default POSIX shell (**/usr/bin/sh**), but there are also three traditional, popular shells in the HP-UX environment: the C shell (**/usr/bin/csh**); Bourne shell, which is seldom used (**/usr/old/bin/sh**); and Korn shell (**/usr/bin/ksh**).

The location of the user's home directory is another important entry in the **/etc/passwd** file. You must select a location for the user's "home" directory in the file system where the user's files will be stored. With NFS, Samba or some similar remote file-access technology, the user's home directory does not even have to be on a disk that is physically connected to the computer that he or she is using! The traditional place to locate a user's home directory on an HP-UX system is the **/home** directory in HP-UX 11.x.

The **/home** directory is typically the most dynamic area in terms of growth. Users create and delete files in their home directory on a regular basis. This means that you have to do more planning related to your user area than in more static areas, such as the root file system and application areas. You would typically load HP-UX and your applications and then perform relatively few accesses to these in terms of adding and deleting files and directories. The user area is continuously updated, which makes it more difficult to maintain.

Assigning Users to Groups

After defining all user-related information, you need to consider groups. Groups are often overlooked in the HP-UX environment until the system administrator finds that all his or her users are in the same group, even though from an organizational or project standpoint, they are in different groups. Before I cover the groups in general, let's look at a file belonging to a user and the way access is defined for a file:

```
$ 11
-rwxr-x--x   1 marty      users      120 Jul 26 10:20 sort
```

For every file on the system, HP-UX supports three classes of access:

- User access (u). Access is granted to the owner of the file.
- Group access (g). Access is granted to members of the same group as the owner of the file.
- Other access (o). Access is granted to everyone else.

These access rights are defined by the position of r (read), write (w), and execute (x) when the long listing command is issued. For the long listing (**ll**), you see the permissions in Table 9-1.

Table 9-1 Long Listing Permissions

Access	User Access	Group Access	Other
Read	r	r	—
Write	w	—	—
Execute	x	x	x

You can see that access rights are arranged in groups of three. Three groups of permissions exist with three access levels each. The owner, in this case, marty, is allowed read, write, and execute permissions on the file. Anyone in the group is permitted to read and execute access to the file. Others are permitted only execute access to the file.

These permissions are important to consider as you arrange your users into groups. If several users require access to the same files, you want to put those users in the same group. The trade-off here is that you can give all users within a group rwx access to files, but then you run the risk of several users editing a file without other users knowing it, thereby causing confusion. On the other hand, you can make several copies of a file so that each user has his or her personal copy, but then you have multiple versions of a file. If possible, assign users to groups based on their work.

The **/etc/group** file contains the group name, an encrypted password (which is rarely used), a group ID, and a list of users in the group. Here is an example of an **/etc/group** file:

```
root::0:root
other::1:root, hpdb
bin::2:root,bin
sys::3:root,uucp
adm::4:root,adm
daemon::5:root,daemon
mail::6:root
lp::7:root,lp
tty::10:
nuucp::11:nuucp
military::25:jhunt,tdolan,vdallesandro
commercial::30:ccascone,jperwinc,devers
nogroup:*:-2:
```

This **/etc/group** file shows two different groups of users. Although all users run the same application, which is a desktop publishing tool, some work on documents of "commercial" products while others work on only "military" documents. It made sense for the system administrator to create two groups, one for commercial document preparation and the other for military document preparation. All members of a group know what documents are current and respect one another's work and its importance. You will have few problems among group members who know what the other members are doing and you will find that these members don't delete files that shouldn't be deleted. If you put all users into one group, however, you may find that you spend more time restoring files, because users in this broader group don't find files that are owned by other members of their group to be important. Users can change group with the **newgrp** command.

You could issue commands on the command line such as **useradd**, **groupadd**, **userdel**, and **groupdel** to create and delete users and groups or use SAM. I prefer to use SAM for this because all the details are taken care of for you, but these commands work great.

You may be using nPartitions or vPars on your system and have to manage users in these partitions. The next section covers working with users specifically in vPars, but the same principles appy to nPartitions.

Partitions and Users: vPars Examples

Each partition, either nPartition or Virtual Partition, is like a separate server. This means that you have separate users in your respective nPartition or Virtual Partition. This section covers Virtual Partitions and users.

Any user-related information that needs to be shared between Virtual Partitions is done in the same manner as sharing between physically separate servers. For example, you may want to have users have the capability to remotely log in from one Virtual Partition to another. You would accomplish this by setting up the appropriate network files in each Virtual Partition just as you would with separate servers.

The vPars are isolated from a software perspective, so it is just as if the users exist on different servers. To share information among users, such as a database of users, implement technology such as Network Information System (NIS, NIS+, or LDAP). With NIS, you could create a database of user information that is shared among different systems, and in this case, different vPars because they are the same as different servers from a software standpoint.

Let's now create a new user on each of the two vPars. On *cable1,* we create the user *cable1us* and verify that this user does not exist on *cable2*. On *cable2,* we create the user *cable2us* and verify that this user does not exist on *cable1*.

I create the user *cable1us* in vPar *cable1* and it exists only in *cable1*. I'll verify this shortly. I also create a user *cable2us* in vPar *cable2*.

There should now be one user in *cable1* that is not viewable in *cable2,* and vice versa. The following shows connecting to *cable1* and listing the contents of **/etc/passwd**:

```
cvhdcon3:/ # cat /etc/passwd
root:hiIXKsAzUIFy6:0:3::/:/sbin/sh                    cable1 listing
daemon:*:1:5::/:/sbin/sh
bin:*:2:2::/usr/bin:/sbin/sh
sys:*:3:3::/:
adm:*:4:4::/var/adm:/sbin/sh
uucp:*:5:3::/var/spool/uucppublic:/usr/lbin/uucp/uucico
lp:*:9:7::/var/spool/lp:/sbin/sh
nuucp:*:11:11::/var/spool/uucppublic:/usr/lbin/uucp/uucico
hpdb:*:27:1:ALLBASE:/:/sbin/sh
nobody:*:-2:-2::/:
www:*:30:1::/:
webadmin:*:40:1::/usr/obam/server/nologindir:/usr/bin/false
smbnull:*:101:101:DO NOT USE OR DELETE - needed by Samba:
                            /home/smbnull:/sbin/sh
```

```
opc_op:*:777:77:OpC default operator:/home/opc_op:/usr/bin/ksh
cable1us::102:20:,,,:/home/cable1us:/usr/bin/sh      <-- cable1us
cvhdcon3:/ #
```

This listing for *cable1* shows that *cable1us* exists in the **/etc/passwd** file on *cable1*; however, there is no *cable2us* present in this file.

The following shows connecting to *cable2* and listing the contents of **/etc/passwd**:

```
# cat /etc/passwd                        cable2 listing
root:Jx66ARmhj.aBs:0:3::/:/sbin/sh
daemon:*:1:5::/:/sbin/sh
bin:*:2:2::/usr/bin:/sbin/sh
sys:*:3:3::/:
adm:*:4:4::/var/adm:/sbin/sh
uucp:*:5:3::/var/spool/uucppublic:/usr/lbin/uucp/uucico
lp:*:9:7::/var/spool/lp:/sbin/sh
nuucp:*:11:11::/var/spool/uucppublic:/usr/lbin/uucp/uucico
hpdb:*:27:1:ALLBASE:/:/sbin/sh
nobody:*:-2:-2::/:
www:*:30:1::/:
webadmin:*:40:1::/usr/obam/server/nologindir:/usr/bin/false
sam_exec:xxx:0:1::/home/sam_exec:/usr/bin/sh
cable2us::101:20:,,,:/home/cable2us:/usr/bin/sh      <-- cable2us
#
```

This listing for *cable2* shows that *cable2us* exists in the **/etc/passwd** file on *cable2*; however, there is no *cable1us* present in this file

This listing shows that the unique users for the respective vPars exist only on the vPar on which they were created. In addition, each vPar has its own *root* and other system-level users.

Next, let's look at setup information of individual users in vPars.

Individual User Setup

As far as setup for users is concerned, you perform setup in a vPars environment just as you would in a non-vPars environment. The prompt, for example, might include the host name of your system. On a system where the host name and vPar name are different, you still probably want your prompt to include the hostname. You can, however; also include the vPar name at the prompt if you want. The following is the section of **/.profile** that includes some minor customization for the user *root*:

```
# Added for prompt, history etc.

        HISTFILE=~/.sh_history;                    export HISTFILE
        EDITOR=vi;                                 export EDITOR
        PS1="`whoami`@`hostname`"'[${PWD}] > '; export PS1
```

This is the information I typically add for *root* to provide history file information and the prompt. I included the host name here, which results in a prompt that includes the user's name, host name, and present working directory:

```
root@actappd1[/.root] >
```

If your users need to see the vPar name, this can be added to or substituted for the hostname in **.profile**. This is another example of the advantage of having your hostname and vPar name be identical. It may be; however, that your hostname is confusing, and substituting a simple vPar name in the prompt may be advantageous to users. In either case, your user setup does not change with vPars, because vPars are the same as separate systems from a user perspective.

Application Users

Users that are required for specific applications need to be set up on all vPars on which an application is going to run. Because vPars are like individual systems, put the users, including application users, on the vPars where you need them and not on others. On a system running Broadvision and Oracle, for example, set up the users required for those applications. The following shows an **/etc/passwd** output on a system running these two applications:

```
# cat /etc/passwd
root:9Obj3Cya98pFo:0:3::/.root:/sbin/sh
daemon:*:1:5::/:/sbin/sh
bin:*:2:2::/usr/bin:/sbin/sh
sys:*:3:3::/:
adm:*:4:4::/var/adm:/sbin/sh
uucp:*:5:3::/var/spool/uucppublic:/usr/lbin/uucp/uucico
lp:*:9:7::/var/spool/lp:/sbin/sh
nuucp:*:11:11::/var/spool/uucppublic:/usr/lbin/uucp/uucico
hpdb:*:27:1:ALLBASE:/:/sbin/sh
```

```
nobody:*:-2:-2::/:
www:*:30:1::/:
webadmin:*:40:1::/usr/obam/server/nologindir:/usr/bin/false
smbnull:*:101:101:DO NOT USE OR DELETE - needed by Samba:/home/smbnull:/sbin/sh
opc_op:*:777:77:OpC default operator:/home/opc_op:/usr/bin/ksh
stssmrp:HFQrTOZx920Fg:1108:20:Martin Paul:/home/stssmrp:/bin/ksh
stssmrpr:pugxhblYiahZI:0:3:Martin Paul:/home/stssmrp:/bin/ksh
stssjtf:VammVKnIwD/T.:1185:20:John Fontanilla:/home/stssjtf:/usr/bin/ksh
pbcombv:UzGN5gDTNfgQM:102:20:PB.COM User:/home/pbcombv:/usr/bin/ksh      <-- BV user
oracle:11Z/oQQfEHzOo:1012:111:Oracle User:/home/oracle:/bin/ksh    <-- Oracle user
#
```

Note the last two users in the file for Broadvision (*pvcombv*) and Oracle (*oracle*) with their respective home directories. With these two applications running on the Virtual Partition, the appropriate users had to be set up.

The remainder of this chapter covers background information related to users.

NIS for Managing Users

One of the most popular ways to manage user-related information in a distributed environment is the Network Information System (NIS). NIS provides a method for multiple systems to share a centralized database of password, group, and other optional databases such as services and/or hosts. By doing so, the administration of user accounts is simplified for both end-users and system administrators. You often hear NIS referred to as "Yellow Pages" or "YP"; in fact, most of the NIS commands begin with the letters "yp."

NIS and other such technologies are required only in a distributed environment where users have to be managed on many systems. This is because changes in information, such as adding and removing users, must be disseminated to many systems. This is normally not required in a centralized environment, where only a small number of copies of such information must be maintained.

NIS on HP-UX is interoperable with Solaris and Sun-licensed NIS implementations, including Linux. Like most of these implementations, HP's NIS is not implemented in C2 or Trusted System mode. Additionally, Microsoft-based operating systems, such as Windows, do not use or interoperate with NIS.

What Does NIS Manage?

NIS can manage many different databases. We focus on the user password and group information. Table 9-2 lists of some of the databases that NIS can manage.

Table 9-2   Some NIS Databases That NIS Can Manage

Filename	Information Contained in file.
/etc/passwd	Usernames, user IDs primary groups, and encrypted passwords.
/etc/group	User group memberships.
/etc/hosts	Hostnames and IP addresses.
/etc/services	Network port numbers and service names.
/etc/aliases	Aliases and mailing lists for the mail system.
/etc/netgroup	Netgroup definitions.
/etc/rpc	Remote procedure call program numbers.
/etc/protocols	Network protocol names and numbers.
	The following are optional for HP, but not used by HP-UX NIS clients.
/etc/bootparms	Information about diskless nodes.
/etc/ethers	Ethernet numbers (MAC addresses).
/etc/netmasks	Network masks.

NIS also calls each of these databases a *map*. They are called maps because NIS allows you to map a key, such as a user name, to a value field, such as the user's **passwd** entry from the **passwd** map on the NIS Master Server.

How Do I Plan for NIS?

NIS requires one NIS Master Server and typically at least one NIS Slave Server per IP subnet. A NIS Master or Slave Server answers requests from NIS clients typically seeking user password information when a user login occurs. NIS is designed in a *top-down* or *hierarchical* manner, with all changes being made through the NIS Master Server. When a change is made to the NIS Master, the changes can be made visible to the NIS Slaves by "pushing" the updated database to the Slaves. Generally, an NIS server should satisfy the demands of 25 to 50 NIS clients. NIS Masters and Slaves are typically also NIS clients.

On the NIS Master server, you need to decide where you want to keep the NIS database "source" files. Typically, the **/etc** files are used on the NIS Master for all databases except passwords, which are generally put into an "alternate" or "private" password file such as **/etc/passwd.nis**. Put only the user password database there and not the "system" users, such as root, sys, bin, and so on. The "system" users should always be put in **/etc/passwd** on any NIS server or client.

NIS provides a small additional network and system load on an NIS Slave and Master server. Most typically, this extra load is encountered when updating a map or database and pushing the changes to the Slave servers.

The design of NIS requires that you first configure the NIS Master Server, then the NIS Slave Servers, and finally, the NIS clients.

How Do I Configure an NIS Master or Slave Server?

You can configure an NIS Master and Slave Server either by using the management GUI or by performing the process manually. If you use the GUI to perform this process, most of the work takes place for you in the background. You enter the pertinent information and the GUI performs the configuration. You perform the steps in the manual procedure. Many good documents that can help you in this configuration, including HP's *Installing and Administering NFS Services* manual. This manual covers configuring Master and Slave Servers and can be obtained from *www.docs.hp.com*. HP support likes you to follow these step-by-step procedures so that if you encounter a problem, your execution of the steps can be reviewed.

To configure with SAM, select *Networking/Communications*, then *NIS*. You are first prompted to specify the NIS domain name. After that, you can proceed to the *Enable NIS Master Server* or *Enable NIS Slave Server* menus.

How Do I Configure an NIS Client?

You can also configure an NIS client by either using SAM or by performing the process manually. Again, the *Installing and Administering NFS Services* manual provides an excellent step-by-step procedure for configuring the client.

To configure with SAM, select *Networking/Communications*, then *NIS*. You are first prompted to specify the NIS domain name. After that, you can proceed to the *Enable NIS Client* menu.

In either case, I have two additional tips. First, HP supplies the following **/etc/nsswitch.compat** file as a template to copy into **/etc/nsswitch.conf**. This allows you to use the "+" and "-" syntax in **/etc/passwd** and **/etc/group**:

```
# /etc/nsswitch.compat:
#
# An example file that could be copied over to
# /etc/nsswitch.conf; it
# uses NIS (YP) in conjunction with files. #

passwd:       compat
group:        compat
hosts:        nis [NOTFOUND=return] files
networks:     nis [NOTFOUND=return] files
protocols:    nis [NOTFOUND=return] files
rpc:          nis [NOTFOUND=return] files
publickey:    nis [NOTFOUND=return] files
netgroup:     nis [NOTFOUND=return] files
automount:        files nis
aliases:      files nis
services:     files nis
```

Second, you may prefer DNS over NIS to manage the hosts database and use the following "hosts" entry in **/etc/nsswitch.conf**:

```
hosts:        files [NOTFOUND=continue] dns ...
```

or

```
hosts:          dns [NOTFOUND=continue,UNAVAILABLE=continue]  files  [NOT-
FOUND=continue,UNAVAILABLE=continue] nis
```

How Do I Maintain My NIS Environment?

The most common user activity is changing a user password. A user can use either the **passwd -r nis** (not supported on all systems) or **yppasswd** command to do this. This prompts for the old NIS password and the new password; make the change on the NIS server and, by default, re-make the NIS map and push it out to all the Slave Servers.

A system administrator can change user passwords either with SAM or with shell scripts or commands such as **passwd -r nis** *<username>* or **yppasswd** *<username>*. You can also use SAM to add new users or you can do this with shell scripts or commands.

Often, when a user changes a database file by editing with **vi**, the changes need to be compiled into the NIS maps (called "making" a map) and pushing the maps out to the Slave Servers if the "make" does not do this. For example, after modifying some users' home directories in **/etc/passwd.nis**, the system administrator needs to

```
1. cd /var/yp   # Change to directory of NIS Makefile
2. make passwd  # "make" or compile the passwd map
3. yppush passwd (if step #2 did not push to the NIS slaves)
```

Here is a tip that applies to HP-UX and to any NIS vendor's implementation with group files: There are times when users are members of multiple groups, producing lines in **/etc/group** that are longer than the NIS limitation of 1,024 characters per line. To work around this, use different group names for the same GIDs, for example:

```
102 support:brian,sam,charlie
102 support1:bill,julie,maria
```

You don't need to specify a user's primary group membership in **/etc/group** because that is already specified by the GID in **/etc/passwd**. If users are members of multiple groups, you only need to put their user name in **/etc/group** entries for their secondary groups.

NIS provides a centralized database scheme for managing user password and group information. Administration techniques used for NIS setup and administration are well documented, integrated into SAM, and are generally interoperable with other NIS implementations.

Although this chapter did not cover Lightweight Directory Access Protocol (LDAP), you may want to investigate it on the HP Web site. LDAP provides authentication for directories using a variety of techniques, including password based, Secure Socket Layer (SSL), and Kerberos.

Chapter 10

Ignite-UX

Ignite-UX Overview

Ignite-UX is a versatile product. It has a great deal of functionality associated with it that would take an entire book to cover. This chapter covers what I believe to be the two major functional areas of Ignite-UX:

- Network installation of client, or target, systems from a server that has on it software depots. These depots are usually created by copying software from media and other sources into depots on the Ignite-UX server. This is somewhat the same as the software installation covered in Chapter 3, "Installing HP-UX," except that the software is on a server rather than media. There is also a User Interface, both graphical and character (I use character in the examples), that allows you to control this process from the server. This technique would allow you to select the specific software that you want to load on each individual client. You can either "push" software from the server to the client or "pull" software to the client from the server. I show booting a client and pulling the software from a server.

- Creating a network recovery archive using **make_net_recovery**. This allows you to have a centralized system on which all of your recovery archives are stored. You could later boot off of this network archive and restore your system. You can also run **make_tape_recovery**, which produces a bootable archive on tape which is very similar to the **make_net_recovery** process that I cover in this chapter. In addition to creating software depots from media, you can create an operating system archive from a "golden image." The "golden image" is a perfectly running system that you want to replicate to many systems. The **make_sys_image** command produces a compressed image of the "golden system."

This chapter covers setting up the Ignite-UX server, booting a client from the server and loading HP-UX onto the client. It then covers **make_net_recovery**. Be sure to check *www.docs.hp.com* to obtain some good documents available on Ignite-UX and *www.software.hp.com* to obtain the latest Ignite-UX software. Some of these documents have much more detail than what I include in the upcoming "how to" sections, but I've used Ignite-UX a lot, so I cover the basics that I use in every client installation.

I assume that you already have the Ignite-UX product loaded on your server system. This software comes bundled with HP-UX 11i, so it is just a matter of loading it on your server system from media. You can be sure you're getting the latest version of Ignite-UX if you download it from the *software.hp.com* Web site.

Set Up the Ignite/UX Server and Boot From It

You can use most any system as your Ignite-UX server. You can have depots on your server for HP-UX 11i and 11.0. This chapter's examples use an HP-UX 11i version 2 update 2 system as the Ignite/UX server. All the setup is done using a Character Line Interface (CLI) rather than the Graphical User Interface (GUI) because there is no guarantee that all readers will have GUI access. Some people call this the Terminal User Interface (TUI), which is fine, but I call it the CLI in this chapter.

I walk through setting up the Ignite/UX server, loading a depot on the server, and booting clients from the depots.

The software depots you create on your Ignite-UX server consume much disk space. A core operating system with many applications will consume several Gigabytes of disk space. I devote several GB of disk space to

Ignite servers so I don't have to increase the size of **/var** (the default location for software depots) when additional depots are loaded on a system.

You must perform a few basic steps on your Ignite-UX server (network install boot server.) I install Ignite-UX on the server and run the server setup process, which is shown in the next section, and then go through the following steps. The **instl_adm** command manages the Ignite-UX server. The following listing shows using **instl_adm** with -d to display the current settings, sending the output to **/tmp/file** where you can edit the settings, and then using the -f option to write the changes:

```
[rx8620b{root}:/var/opt/ignite/depots]>instl_adm -d
# instl_adm defaults:
# NOTE: Manual additions between the lines containing "instl_adm defaults"
#       and "end instl_adm defaults" will not be preserved.
server="192.6.174.66"
netmask[]="255.255.255.240"
route_gateway[0]="192.6.174.65"
route_destination[0]="default"
# end instl_adm defaults.

[rx8620b{root}:/var/opt/ignite/depots]>instl_adm > /tmp/file
[rx8620b{root}:/var/opt/ignite/depots]>cat /tmp/file
# instl_adm defaults:
# NOTE: Manual additions between the lines containing "instl_adm defaults"
#       and "end instl_adm defaults" will not be preserved.
server="192.6.174.66"
netmask[]="255.255.255.240"
route_gateway[0]="192.6.174.65"
route_destination[0]="default"
# end instl_adm defaults.
```

Make changes to **/tmp/file** and then implement them with the following command:

```
[rx8620b{root}:/var/opt/ignite/depots]>instl_adm -f /tmp/file
```

After the Ignite-UX server network information is set up, modify the file **/etc/inetd.conf** to include the following bootps line and run **inetd -c** for the change to take effect:

```
[rx8620b{root}:/var/opt/ignite/depots]>cat /etc/inetd.conf | grep bootps
#bootps      dgram  udp wait   root /usr/lbin/bootpd     bootpd
bootps       dgram  udp wait   root /opt/ignite/lbin/instl_bootd instl_bootd -d 3

[rx8620b{root}:/var/opt/ignite/depots]>inetd -c
```

The old bootps line is commented and the new line is shown beneath it. Be sure that **rbootd** is not running.

These simple steps are all that is required to set up the Ignite/UX server.

Some additional steps you can perform are to set up boot addresses in the file **/etc/opt/ignite/instl_boottab** which can also be done during the server setup procedure, which is covered in the next section. The contents of this file on my system showing only the IP addresses for clients is shown in the following output:

```
192.6.174.67:0x00306E4BAA28:20041104125110:
192.6.174.68:::
192.6.174.69:::
192.6.174.70:::
192.6.174.71:::
192.6.174.72:::
192.6.174.73:::
192.6.174.74:::
192.6.174.75:::
192.6.174.76:::
192.6.174.77:::
192.6.174.78:::
```

These addresses were automatically filled in when the Ignite-UX CLI was run, as shown in an upcoming section, but you can make or modify these entries manually in **/etc/opt/ignite/instl_boottab**. The first entry also has a MAC address next to it because it was used to boot a partition.

The significant files and commands involved in this setup are as follows:

- **/etc/inetd.conf** - Contains information such as the bootps command.

- **/etc/opt/ignite/instl_boottab** - Has in it client information

- **instl_adm** - Used to maintain Ignite/UX configuration files.

Here are steps I perform to set up the Ignite-UX server:

1. Using the Ignite-UX CLI set up the Ignite-UX server with such information as a IP address range of clients, and load HP-UX 11i Core OS software on to a server. This is covered in detail in the next section.

2. Set up **/etc/inetd.conf** and **/etc/opt/ignite/instl_boottab** as previously described. Use **instl_adm** to check and modify Ignite-UX server setup.

3. Load additional software, such as applications for HP-UX 11i version 2 update 2 (11.23), on the Ignite-UX server with the following command:

```
swcopy -x enforce_dependencies=false -s /cdrom \* @
                               /var/opt/ignite/depots/Rel_B.11.23_apps
```

```
(/cdrom is mounted on /dev/dsk/c9t2d0)
```

4. Run **make_config**, which builds Ignite-UX configuration files, as shown in the following example for the application's software:

```
make_config -s /var/opt/ignite/depots/Rel_B.11.23_apps -c /var/opt/ignite/depots
```

5. Run **manage_index**, which manages the **INDEX** fie, as shown in the following example for the application's software:

```
manage_index -a -r B.11.23 -f /var/opt/ignite/depots/Rel_B.11.23_apps/apps.11.23
```

This updates the **INDEX** file so that it looks like the following:

```
# /var/opt/ignite/INDEX
# This file is used to define the Ignite-UX configurations
# and to define which config files are associated with each
# configuration.  See the ignite(5), instl_adm(4), and
# manage_index(1M) man pages for details.
#
# NOTE: The manage_index command is used to maintain this file.
#       Comments, logic expressions and formatting changes are not
#       preserved by manage_index.
#
# WARNING: User comments (lines beginning with '#' ), and any user
#          formatting in the body of this file are _not_ preserved
#          when the version of Ignite-UX is updated.
#
cfg "HP-UX B.11.23 Default" {
        description "This selection supplies the default system configuration th
at HP supplies for the B.11.23 release."
        "/opt/ignite/data/Rel_B.11.23/config"
        "/opt/ignite/data/Rel_B.11.23/hw_patches_cfg"
        "/var/opt/ignite/depots/Rel_B.11.23_apps/apps.11.23_cfg"   <- new entry
        "/var/opt/ignite/config.local"
}
```

This file has a section for 11.23, which is HP-UX 11i version 2 update 2. It does not, however, have an 11.11 section, which is added in the next step. I have older PA-RISC systems for which I want to have the Ignite-UX server set up.

6. Load the application *Ignite-UX-11-11*, 11.11 or HP-UX 11i version 1 (for PA-RISC only), so that HP-UX 11i version 1 Core OS, applications, and other version 1 software can be loaded. I loaded this file from the software from the Core OS DVD. Loading this application updates the **INDEX** file, as shown in the following listing:

```
# /var/opt/ignite/INDEX
# This file is used to define the Ignite-UX configurations
# and to define which config files are associated with each
```

```
# configuration.  See the ignite(5), instl_adm(4), and
# manage_index(1M) man pages for details.
#
# NOTE: The manage_index command is used to maintain this file.
#       Comments, logic expressions and formatting changes are not
#       preserved by manage_index.
#
# WARNING: User comments (lines beginning with '#' ), and any user
#          formatting in the body of this file are _not_ preserved
#          when the version of Ignite-UX is updated.
#
cfg "HP-UX B.11.23 Default" {
        description "This selection supplies the default system configuration
that HP supplies for the B.11.23 release."
        "/opt/ignite/data/Rel_B.11.23/config"
        "/opt/ignite/data/Rel_B.11.23/hw_patches_cfg"
        "/var/opt/ignite/depots/Rel_B.11.23_apps/apps.11.23_cfg"
        "/var/opt/ignite/config.local"
}
cfg "HP-UX B.11.11 Default" {                              <- new section
        description "This selection supplies the default system configuration
that HP supplies for the B.11.11 release."
        "/opt/ignite/data/Rel_B.11.11/config"
        "/opt/ignite/data/Rel_B.11.11/hw_patches_cfg"
        "/var/opt/ignite/config.local"
}
```

Now the **INDEX** file has an entry for 11.11, as well as others which I removed, such as 10.20, which will be updated for Core OS and applications in the next two steps.

7. Load 11.11 Core OS software, configure it, and manage it:

```
swcopy  -x  enforce_dependencies=false  -s  /cdrom  \*  @  /var/opt/ignite/depots/
Rel.11.11_coreos

make_config -s /var/opt/ignite/depots/Rel.11.11_coreos -c /var/opt/ignite/depots
/Rel.11.11_coreos/coreos.11.11_cfg

manage_index -a -r B.11.11 -f /var/opt/ignite/depots/Rel.11.11_coreos/coreos.11.
11_cfg
```

This updates the end of the **INDEX** file to have an entry for 11.11_coreos, as shown in the following listing:

```
}
cfg "HP-UX B.11.11 Default" {
        description "This selection supplies the default system configuration
that HP supplies for the B.11.11 release."
        "/opt/ignite/data/Rel_B.11.11/config"
        "/opt/ignite/data/Rel_B.11.11/hw_patches_cfg"
        "/var/opt/ignite/depots/Rel.11.11_coreos/coreos.11.11_cfg"   <- new entry
        "/var/opt/ignite/config.local"
}
```

8. Load 11.11 applications software, configure it, and manage it with the following commands:

```
swcopy -x enforce_dependencies=false -s /cdrom \* @ /var/opt/ignite/depots/
Rel.11.11.apps
```

```
make_config -s /var/opt/ignite/depots/Rel.11.11.apps -c /var/opt/ignite/depots/
Rel.11.11.apps/apps.11.11_cfg

manage_index -a -r B.11.11 -f /var/opt/ignite/depots/Rel.11.11.apps/apps.11.11_c
fg
swcopy -x enforce_dependencies=false -s /cdrom \* @ /var/opt/ignite/depots/Rel.1
1.11.apps
```

This updates the end of the **INDEX** file to have an entry for
11.11_apps, as shown in the following listing:

```
cfg "HP-UX B.11.11 Default" {
      description "This selection supplies the default system configuration
that HP supplies for the B.11.11 release."
      "/opt/ignite/data/Rel_B.11.11/config"
      "/opt/ignite/data/Rel_B.11.11/hw_patches_cfg"
      "/var/opt/ignite/depots/Rel.11.11_coreos/coreos.11.11_cfg"
      "/var/opt/ignite/depots/Rel.11.11.apps/apps.11.11_cfg"    <- new entry
      "/var/opt/ignite/config.local"
}
```

After these steps are performed, the Ignite-UX server has been set up,
the Core OS and application software has been loaded for 11.23, the
INDEX file has been updated, and 11.11 software has been loaded on the
Ignite-UX server as well.

You could also load software, such as vPars software or other applications.

Run Ignite-UX CLI to Set Up and Load Software on the Server

Before running the Ignite-UX tool, you can confirm that you have Ignite
loaded with the following command:

```
# swlist | grep Ignite
  B5725AA               B.6.0.57       HP-UX Installation Utilities (Ignite-UX)
```

The version shown is the latest at the time of this writing. I'm running
11i version 2 update 2 on an Integrity server that acts as the Ignite-UX
server.

You can type **ignite** if you have set up your path for **/opt/ignite/bin**, or you can type the full path **/opt/ignite/bin/ignite** to bring up the CLI or GUI for Ignite-UX, as shown in Figure 10-1.

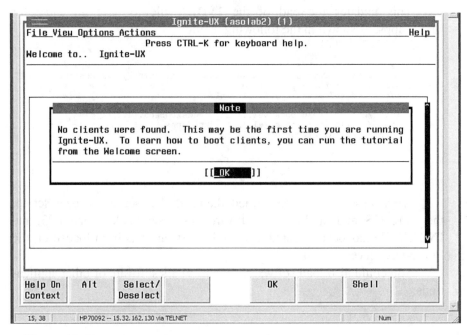

Figure 10-1   Ignite-UX CLI

This initial Ignite-UX screen supplies a message indicating that no clients are set up. After you select OK, the screen in Figure 10-2 is shown.

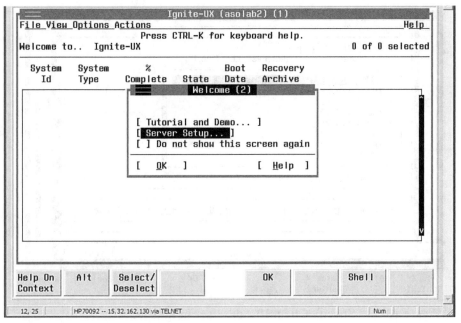

Figure 10-2   Ignite-UX Server Setup

I select Server Setup, which brings up several screens. You can select DHCP or specify IP addresses for clients. I choose to specify IP addresses for clients, which brings up the screen shown in Figure 10-3.

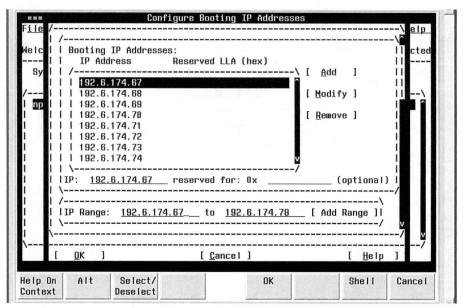

Figure 10-3   Specify Client IP Addresses in Ignite-UX

I specify a bank of IP addresses for the clients that will boot off this Ignite-UX server.

The next step is to load the HP-UX operating system software on to the server that will be loaded on the clients, as shown in Figure 10-4.

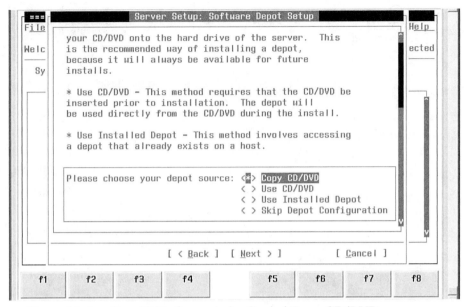

Figure 10-4   Specify Software to be Copied From CD/DVD

Figure 10-4 shows that I select to copy software from the CD/DVD, as well as the other options available.

Figure 10-5 shows the information related to this copy, including the target directory.

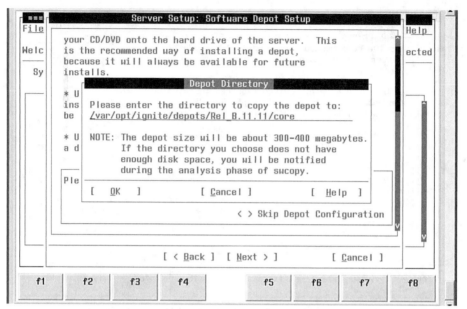

Figure 10-5   Select the Destination to Which Software Will Be Copied

Figure 10-5 shows selecting the directory to which the depot will be copied. The software copied is HP-UX 11i version 2 update 2 (11.23) for Integrity servers.

Figure 10-6 shows the command used to copy the software to the depot.

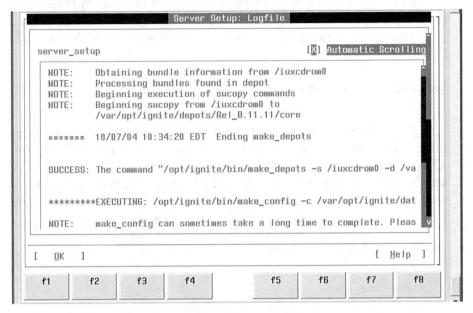

Figure 10-6   **make_depots** Copy Command

Figure 10-6 shows the **make_depots** copy command that is run. This command could have been issued at the command line without invoking the CLI. The destination is truncated, but you see the full directory in the next screen.

You would load as many depots as you need for booting servers. If, for example, you have older servers and need old releases of HP-UX 11i version 1 or HP-UX 11.0, you can create depots for these as well.

Loading these depots can be done from the CLI, as I have done in this example, from the GUI, or from the command line with the **make_depots** command.

Booting systems from these depots is done differently on HP Integrity and HP 9000 servers, which the upcoming sections cover.

Booting a Client From an Ignite-UX Server

With an Ignite-UX server in place, you can boot off the Ignite-UX server and load software from the server depots. The process of doing this on Integrity and HP 9000 servers is different because of the firmware differences on the two platforms.

The format to boot from the server on an HP 9000 (PA-RISC) server is as follows:

```
boot lan.server_ip_address install
```

On an Integrity (Itanium) server, the boot process is done with selections in EFI. On partitioned systems, it is common to have no DVD from which to load software; in this case, you'd load HP-UX from an Ignite-UX server. The following listing shows two LAN cards. One is the built-in LAN on the Core I/O board, and the other is an independent LAN card (the Core I/O LAN card is shown in EFI in the following listing):

```
EFI Boot Manager ver 1.10 [14.60]

Please select a boot option

    HP-UX Primary Boot: 1/0/0/2/0.6.0
    Acpi(000222F0,0)/Pci(1|0)/Mac(00306E4B9AD9)
    Acpi(000222F0,100)/Pci(1|0)/Mac(00306E4BAA28)        <- Core I/O LAN
    EFI Shell [Built-in]
    LAN1boot
    Boot option maintenance menu


    Use ^ and v to change option(s). Use Enter to select an option
```

You can also create a custom boot option, as I had done for LAN1boot in the previous listing, using the Boot option maintenance menu. However, this is not required because you can just select the LAN interface.

After the boot process begins, information is downloaded from the Ignite-UX server to the client, as shown in the following listing:

```
Booting from Lan
Downloading file AUTO   (26 bytes)
Press Any Key to interrupt Autoboot
AUTO ==> boot Rel_B.11.23/IINSTALL
Seconds left till autoboot -    0
AUTOBOOTING...
AUTO BOOT> boot Rel_B.11.23/IINSTALL
Downloading file Rel_B.11.23/IINSTALL   (52628816 bytes)
> System Memory = 16351 MB
loading section 0
............................................... (complete)
loading section 1
............ (complete)
loading symbol table
Downloading file Rel_B.11.23/IINSTALLFS   (29753344 bytes)
loading ram disk file (Rel_B.11.23/IINSTALLFS).
.................................................................
 (complete)
Launching Rel_B.11.23/IINSTALL
```

```
SIZE: Text:24913K + Data:5919K + BSS:5356K = Total:36189K

Console is on a Serial Device
Booting kernel...
```

The installation file is downloaded from the Ignite-UX server to this client.

After the installation file is downloaded and invoked, the standard HP-UX installation screen appears, as shown in the following listing:

```
                        Welcome to Ignite-UX!

Use the <tab> key to navigate between fields, and the arrow keys
within fields.  Use the <return/enter> key to select an item.
Use the <return/enter> or <space-bar> to pop-up a choices list.  If the
menus are not clear, select the "Help" item for more information.


Hardware Summary:       System Model: ia64 hp server rx8620
+--------------------+-----------------+-------------------+ [ Scan Again  ]
| Disks: 2  (205.1GB) | Floppies: 0   | LAN cards:   3   |
| CD/DVDs:          0 | Tapes:    1   | Memory:  16351Mb |
| Graphics Ports: 0   | IO Buses: 6   | CPUs:        4   | [ H/W Details ]
+--------------------+-----------------+-------------------+

                [       Install HP-UX        ]

                [    Run a Recovery Shell    ]

                [      Advanced Options      ]

       [  Reboot  ]                          [  Help  ]
```

From this point on, a standard HP-UX installation takes place if you select *Install HP-UX*.

After the operating system is loaded, you can go back to any depot, including the Core OS depot, and load additional software after invoking **swinstall**, as shown in Figure 10-7.

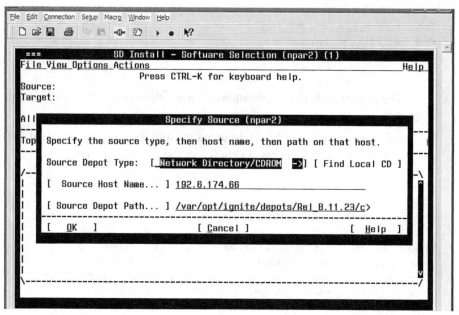

Figure 10-7   **swinstall** Core OS Load from Ignite-UX Server Depot

Figure 10-7 shows the **swinstall** screen contents you would enter after HP-UX is running to load additional software. The Ignite-UX server IP address is specified as well as the full path of the depot **/var/opt/ignite/depots/Rel_B.11.23/core** (which can't be fully seen in the figure). Figure 10-8 shows the contents of the Core OS components.

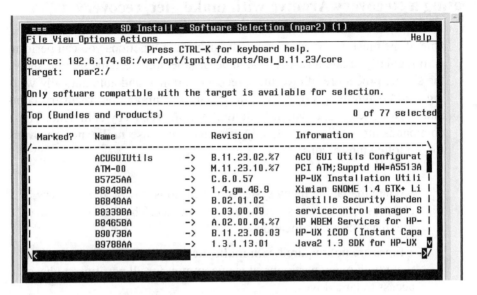

Figure 10-8   **swinstall** Core OS Components

Figure 10-8 shows the contents of **/var/opt/ignite/depots/ Rel_B.11.23/core**. From this depot, you can load any of its components.

Among the advantages of booting and installing software from an Ignite-UX server are 1) media is not required when software is loaded on the clients, and 2) multiple clients can boot from a single Ignite-UX server simultaneously. I install many systems, so this is a big advantage for me.

An Ignite-UX server can also be used to load a virtual partition (vPar) from a running vPar. This is done with the **vparboot** command, which is executed from running vPar. You point to the existing Ignite-UX server from **vparboot**. The mini-kernel called WINSTALL is loaded into memory. The mini-kernel boots the target vPar.

The next section covers the important process of creating recovery archives and storing them on the Ignite-UX server.

Creating a Recovery Archive with make_net_recovery

One of the most important system administration functions you can perform is to regularly create a recovery archive or tape archive. This section shows the simple procedure of creating a recovery archive and automatically writing it to an Ignite server. This is done with the **make_net_recovery** command. To write to tape, you use the **make_tape_recovery** command. These commands are similar and equally effective, but I use **make_net_recovery** for the following reasons:

• When managing many systems or partitions, saving the recovery archives on a central server is a good practice. The recovery archives are in a centralized location.

• Tapes are not required with **make_net_recovery** and, in an environment with many partitions, it is uncommon for all partitions to have access to tape drives.

• The archives can be produced in an unattended manner with no tape handling.

To run **make_net_recovery** on a client and write the file to a server, you must have the same version of Ignite-UX running on both systems.

The following steps are executed to create and restore a recovery archive:

On Server:

• Include path of client recovery directory in **/etc/exports**. The path entry for a recovery archive is **/var/opt/ignite/recovery/archives/***client*. (The path entry for a golden image is **/var/opt/ignite/clients - anon=2**.) You may have to create the directory with **mkdir**.

• Run **exportfs -a** for changes to take effect and **exportfs -v** to see its contents.

On Client:

• Load *HP-UX Installation Utilities (Ignite-UX)* from **swinstall** to ensure you have **make_net_recovery** and the same release of Ignite on both the client and server or you'll get an error when you run **make_net_recovery** on the client.

• Run a **make_net_recovery** command, such as **make_net_recovery -A -s** *server_IP_address*, to create a recovery archive with all (-A) volume groups part of the archive, and save the archive to the server specified by the IP address or hostname. The full path is **/var/opt/ignite/bin/make_net_recovery**.

On Server:

• View **/var/opt/ignite/recovery/archives/***client_name* and **/var/opt/ignite/clients** for recovery-related files.

On Client:

• To use recovery files from the server to recover a client, boot off the network interface and select the recovery archive from the list of installation options.

The next section covers setting up the server for creating the recovery archive.

Recovery Archive with Ignite-UX: Server Setup

The server setup for recovery archives with Ignite-UX is simple. The first step is to export the directory with read and write permissions; that will be used to store the client recovery archives. This is by default **/var/opt/ignite/recovery/archives/***client*, as shown in the third line of the following listing of **/etc/exports**:

On Server:

```
[rx8620b{root}:/var/opt/ignite/depots/Rel_B.11.23]>cat /etc/exports
/var/opt/ignite/clients -anon=2                          #golden image
/var/opt/ignite/depots/npar2 -ro,anon=2
/var/opt/ignite/recovery/archives/npar2 -anon=2,access=npar2 #recovery archive
[rx8620b{root}:/var/opt/ignite/depots/Rel_B.11.23]>
```

The configuration files need to boot and install the client are in **/var/opt/ignite/client/***macaddress*. To get any changes to **/etc/exports** to take effect, issue **exportfs -a**.

Recovery Archive with Ignite-UX: Client Setup

In this section, I set up and initiate the recovery archive from the client. The **make_net_recovery** command must be present on the client. In addition, the revision of tools must be the same on both the server and client or you get an error message on the client when you run **make_net_recovery**. Load the same release of *HP-UX Installation Utilities (Ignite-UX)* from swinstall on both the server and client to ensure you have the same release loaded. Next, on the client (hostname npar2 in the example) the following command is issued to create a recovery archive of all volume groups (-A) and write the recovery archive to Ignite-UX server (-s) at the IP address shown:

On Client:

```
# make_net_recovery -A -s 192.6.174.66
       * Creating NFS mount directories for configuration files.

=======  11/06/04 11:28:34 EST  Started make_net_recovery. (Sat Nov 06 11:28:34
         EST 2004)
         @(#) Ignite-UX Revision C.6.0.57
         @(#) net_recovery (opt) $Revision: 10.645 $

       * Testing pax for needed patch
       * Passed pax tests.
       * Checking Versions of Recovery Tools
       * Creating System Configuration.
       * /opt/ignite/bin/save_config -f /var/opt/ignite/recovery/client_mnt/0x0
         0306E4BAA28/recovery/2004-11-06,11:28/system_cfg vg00
       * Backing Up Volume Group /dev/vg00
       * /usr/sbin/vgcfgbackup /dev/vg00
       * Creating Map Files for Volume Group /dev/vg00
       * /usr/sbin/vgexport -p -m /etc/lvmconf/vg00.mapfile /dev/vg00

       * Creating Control Configuration.
       * Creating Archive File List
       * Creating Archive Configuration

       * /opt/ignite/bin/make_arch_config -c /var/opt/ignite/recovery/client_
         mnt/0x00306E4BAA28/recovery/2004-11-06,11:28/archive_cfg -g /var/opt/
         ignite/recovery/client_mnt/0x00306E4BAA28/recovery/2004-11-06,11:28/flist
         -n 2004-11-06,11:28 -r 64 -d Recovery\ Archive -L
         /var/opt/ignite/recovery/arch_mnt -l
         192.6.174.66:/var/opt/ignite/recovery/archives/npar2 -i 1 -m t
       * Saving the information about archive to
         /var/opt/ignite/recovery/previews
       * Creating The Networking Archive

       * /opt/ignite/data/scripts/make_sys_image -d
         /var/opt/ignite/recovery/arch_mnt -t n -s local -n 2004-11-06,11:28 -m
         t -w /var/opt/ignite/recovery/client_mnt/0x00306E4BAA28/recovery/2004-
         11-06,11:28/recovery.log -u -R -g /var/opt/ignite/recovery/client_mnt/
         0x00306E4BAA28/recovery/2004-11-06,11:28/flist -a 6586930

       * Preparing to create a system archive
       * The archive is estimated to reach 3293465 kbytes.
       * Free space on /var/opt/ignite/recovery/arch_mnt
         after archive should be about 26554207 kbytes.

       * Archiving contents of npar2 via tar to
         /var/opt/ignite/recovery/arch_mnt/2004-11-06,11:28.
       * Creation of system archive complete
```

```
NOTE:  The following files are in the list of files that were on the
       system, but they are no longer present.  These files are not
       included in the back-up:
       /var/tmp/ign_configure/make_sys_image.log

NOTE:  Could not read the /etc/resolv.conf file.
       * Creating CINDEX Configuration File

       * /opt/ignite/bin/manage_index -q -c 2004-11-06,11:28\ Recovery\ Archive
         -i /var/opt/ignite/recovery/client_mnt/0x00306E4BAA28/CINDEX -u
         Recovery\ Archive

======= 11/06/04 11:46:00 EST  make_net_recovery completed successfully!
#
```

Although I used the -A option, there are several ways to include or exclude specific files and directories with **make_net_recovery**:

- -x include=<*file*/*directory*>

- -x inc_cross=<*file*/*directory*> (This can contain any number of *include*, *exclude*, *inc_entire*, and *inc_cross* options.)

- -x exclude=<*file*/*directory*>

- -x inc_entire=<*vgname*>//*dev*/*dsk*/<*name*>

- -f <*contents_file*>

- -A (archive all volume groups that contain essential files)

The recovery file for system npar2 is shown in the **/var/opt/ignite/clients** directory on the Ignite-UX server, as shown in the following listing:

On Server:

```
[rx8620b{root}:/var/opt/ignite/recovery/archives/npar2]>ll
total 4347856
-rw-------   1 bin          sys         2226091645 Nov  6 11:52 2004-11-06,11:28
[rx8620b{root}:/var/opt/ignite/recovery/archives/npar2]>
```

The recovery file with date and time is present on the Ignite-UX server in the default directory **/var/opt/ignite/recovery/archives/npar2**. Once this file is present, you are protected with a full recovery archive for the client.

In addition, the files needed to boot and install the client are in **/var/opt/ignite/client/***macaddress:*:

On Server:

```
[rx8620b{root}:/var/opt/ignite/clients]>pwd
/var/opt/ignite/clients
```

```
[rx8620b{root}:/var/opt/ignite/clients]>ll
total 16
drwxr-xr-x   4 bin        bin              8192 Nov  6 11:33 0x00306E4BAA28
lrwxr-xr-x   1 bin        bin                14 Nov  6 11:34 npar2 -> 0x00306E4BAA28
[rx8620b{root}:/var/opt/ignite/clients]>cd 0*
[rx8620b{root}:/var/opt/ignite/clients/0x00306E4BAA28]>ll
total 864
-rw-r--r--   1 bin        sys               987 Nov  6 11:52 CINDEX
-rw-r--r--   1 bin        sys                 6 Nov  3 16:07 client_name
-rw-r--r--   1 bin        sys                65 Nov  5 10:34 client_status
-rw-r--r--   1 bin        bin              4275 Nov  5 10:34 config.bak
-rw-r--r--   1 bin        bin             33804 Nov  3 16:36 config.full
-rw-r--r--   1 bin        bin               570 Nov  5 10:34 config.sys
-rw-r--r--   1 bin        sys               223 Nov  5 10:34 env.vars
-rw-r--r--   1 bin        bin               597 Nov  5 10:34 host.info
-rw-r--r--   1 bin        bin              1097 Nov  5 10:34 hw.info
-rw-r--r--   1 bin        bin              5576 Nov  5 10:34 install.log
-rw-r--r--   1 bin        bin            299258 Nov  3 16:53 install.log.prev
-rw-r--r--   1 bin        bin                 0 Nov  5 10:41 lockfile
drwxr-xr-x   2 bin        bin              8192 Nov  3 16:53 manifest
drwxr-xr-x   5 bin        bin              8192 Nov  6 11:34 recovery
-rw-rw-rw-   1 bin        bin               108 Nov  5 10:44 server.state
[rx8620b{root}:/var/opt/ignite/clients/0x00306E4BAA28]>
```

All the recovery archive files from the client are now present on the server. In the next section, I restore the recovery archive to a client.

Recovery Archive with Ignite-UX: Client Recovery

Now that the recovery archive has been created with **make_net_recovery** and saved on the server, you can boot the client and recover it. At the time of boot, select the LAN interface off which to boot—just as I did in the earlier example loading software to the client initially with Ignite-UX—but now, there are also recovery archives from which to select, as shown in the following listing:

```
-------++----------+--------------------------------++                        ≠
≠ ≠ Basic ≠# Software ≠ HP-UX B.11.22 Default            ##                    ≠
≠ ≠        \----------≠ HP-UX B.11.23 Default            ≠-------------------+≠
≠ ≠                    ≠ 2004-11-06,11:22 Recovery Archive ≠                  ##
≠ ≠ Configurations:  [≠ 2004-11-06,11:28 Recovery Archive ≠iption...  ]        ##
≠ ≠                    ≠ 2004-11-07,08:05 Recovery Archive ≠                   ##
≠ ≠ Environments:    [+--------------------------------+X B.11.23)             ##
≠ ≠                                                                            ##
≠ ≠ [ Root Disk... ] HP_146_GMAP3147NC, 1/0/0/2/0.6.0, 140014                 ##
≠ ≠                                                                            ##
≠ ≠ File System:     [ HP-UX save_config layout              ->]              ##
≠ ≠                                                                            ##
≠ ≠ [ Root Swap (MB)... ] 4096      Physical Memory (RAM) = 16351 MB          ##
≠ ≠                                                                            ##
≠ ≠ [ Languages... ] English          [ Keyboards... ] [ Additional... ]##
≠ ≠                                                                            ##
≠ +--------------------------------------------------------------------------+≠
≠       [ Show Summary... ]                         [ Reset Configuration ]  ≠
≠--------------------------------------------------------------------------≠
≠ [  Go!  ]                         [ Cancel ]                   [ Help ] ≠
+--------------------------------------------------------------------------+
```

You can select any of the recovery archives shown in the previous listing. Several selections are shown in the window. Every time you create a recovery archive, another selection appears in the window if indeed they're on the INDEX file on the server. The following listing shows the directory where the recovery INDEX is located and the contents of the file:

```
[rx8620b{root}:/var/opt/ignite/clients/npar2]>pwd
/var/opt/ignite/clients/npar2
[rx8620b{root}:/var/opt/ignite/clients/npar2]>ll
total 320
-rw-r--r--  1 bin     sys        1185 Nov  7 08:29 CINDEX
-rw-r--r--  1 bin     sys           6 Nov  3 16:07 client_name
-rw-r--r--  1 bin     sys         462 Nov  7 07:56 client_status
-rw-r--r--  1 bin     bin        1257 Nov  7 07:52 config
-rw-r--r--  1 bin     bin        8980 Nov  7 07:52 config.full
-rw-r--r--  1 bin     bin         570 Nov  7 07:34 config.sys
-rw-r--r--  1 bin     sys         223 Nov  7 07:34 env.vars
-rw-r--r--  1 bin     bin         669 Nov  7 07:34 host.info
-rw-r--r--  1 bin     bin        1097 Nov  7 07:51 hw.info
-rw-r--r--  1 bin     bin       36244 Nov  7 07:56 install.log
-rw-r--r--  1 bin     bin        5576 Nov  5 10:34 install.log.prev
-rw-r--r--  1 bin     bin           0 Nov  5 10:41 lockfile
drwxr-xr-x  2 bin     bin        8192 Nov  7 07:56 manifest
drwxr-xr-x  6 bin     bin        8192 Nov  7 08:12 recovery
-rw-rw-rw-  1 bin     bin         162 Nov  8 15:32 server.state
-rw-r--r--  1 bin     bin         634 Nov  7 07:35 tmp.cfg
[rx8620b{root}:/var/opt/ignite/clients/npar2]>cat CINDEX
# CINDEX
# This file is used to define the Ignite-UX configurations
# and to define which config files are associated with each
# configuration.  See the ignite(5), instl_adm(4), and
# manage_index(1M) man pages for details.
#
# NOTE: The manage_index command is used to maintain this file.
#       Comments, logic expressions and formatting changes are not
#       preserved by manage_index.
#
# WARNING: User comments (lines beginning with '#' ), and any user
#          formatting in the body of this file are _not_ preserved
#          when the version of Ignite-UX is updated.
#
cfg "2004-11-06,11:22 Recovery Archive" {
        description "Recovery Archive"
        "recovery/2004-11-06,11:22/system_cfg"
        "recovery/2004-11-06,11:22/control_cfg"
        "recovery/2004-11-06,11:22/archive_cfg"
}
cfg "2004-11-06,11:28 Recovery Archive" {
        description "Recovery Archive"
        "recovery/2004-11-06,11:28/system_cfg"
        "recovery/2004-11-06,11:28/control_cfg"
        "recovery/2004-11-06,11:28/archive_cfg"
}
cfg "2004-11-07,08:05 Recovery Archive" {
        description "Recovery Archive"
        "recovery/2004-11-07,08:05/system_cfg"
        "recovery/2004-11-07,08:05/control_cfg"
        "recovery/2004-11-07,08:05/archive_cfg"
}=TRUE
[rx8620b{root}:/var/opt/ignite/clients/npar2]>
```

This is different than the INDEX file where the operating system distributions are recorded as shown in the following listing:

```
[rx8620b{root}:/var/opt/ignite]>pwd
/var/opt/ignite
[rx8620b{root}:/var/opt/ignite]>ll
total 80
-rw-r--r--   1 bin      bin         1707 Nov  6 11:26 INDEX
-rw-r--r--   1 bin      bin         1971 Oct 30 15:05 INDEX_B.10.20
drwxr-xr-x   3 bin      bin           96 Nov  7 08:12 clients
-rw-r--r--   1 bin      bin           81 May  6  2004 config.local
drwxr-xr-x   7 bin      bin         8192 May  6  2004 data
drwxr-xr-x   5 root     sys           96 Nov  6 11:26 depots
drwxr-xr-x   3 bin      bin         8192 May  5  2004 local
drwxr-xr-x   2 bin      bin           96 Oct 30 13:35 logs
drwxr-xr-x   3 bin      bin           96 Nov  5 10:45 recovery
drwxr-xr-x   2 bin      bin           96 May  6  2004 saved_cfgs
drwxr-xr-x   2 bin      bin           96 May  6  2004 scripts
drwxr-xr-x   3 bin      bin           96 Nov  6 11:26 server
[rx8620b{root}:/var/opt/ignite]>cat INDEX
# /var/opt/ignite/INDEX
# This file is used to define the Ignite-UX configurations
# and to define which config files are associated with each
# configuration.  See the ignite(5), instl_adm(4), and
# manage_index(1M) man pages for details.
#
# NOTE: The manage_index command is used to maintain this file.
#       Comments, logic expressions and formatting changes are not
#       preserved by manage_index.
#
# WARNING: User comments (lines beginning with '#' ), and any user
#          formatting in the body of this file are _not_ preserved
#          when the version of Ignite-UX is updated.
#
cfg "HP-UX B.11.22 Default" {
        description "This selection supplies the default system configuration that HP
supplies for the B.11.22 release."
        "/opt/ignite/data/Rel_B.11.22/config"
        "/opt/ignite/data/Rel_B.11.22/hw_patches_cfg"
        "/var/opt/ignite/config.local"
}
cfg "HP-UX B.11.23 Default" {
        description "This selection supplies the default system configuration that HP
supplies for the B.11.23 release."
        "/opt/ignite/data/Rel_B.11.23/config"
        "/opt/ignite/data/Rel_B.11.23/hw_patches_cfg"
        "/var/opt/ignite/data/Rel_B.11.23/core_cfg"
        "/var/opt/ignite/config.local"
}=TRUE
cfg "HP-UX B.11.00 Default" {
        description "This selection supplies the default system configuration that HP
supplies for the B.11.00 release."
        "/opt/ignite/data/Rel_B.11.00/config"
        "/opt/ignite/data/Rel_B.11.00/hw_patches_cfg"
        "/var/opt/ignite/config.local"
}
cfg "HP-UX B.11.11 Default" {
        description "This selection supplies the default system configuration that HP
supplies for the B.11.11 release."
        "/opt/ignite/data/Rel_B.11.11/config"
        "/opt/ignite/data/Rel_B.11.11/hw_patches_cfg"
        "/var/opt/ignite/config.local"
}
[rx8620b{root}:/var/opt/ignite]>
```

When you restore the recovery archive, you are asked the standard questions from **set_parms initial**, such as hostname, IP address, and so on. The recovery archive can be restored to other systems with this information customized.

The process of setting up and creating recovery archives is easy and runs quickly. I recommend creating recovery archives often so that, should you encounter a problem, you can quickly recover from the archive saved on your Ignite-UX server.

You can also produce a "golden image" of HP-UX, which is an operating system you want to replicate to other systems. This is done with the **make_system_image** command as shown in the following listing:

On Client:

```
# make_sys_image -d /var/opt/ignite/archives/ -s local

# pwd
/var/opt/ignite/archives
# ll
total 579632
-rw-rw-rw-   1 root        sys              737 Nov  4 22:49 make_sys_image.log
-rw-rw-rw-   1 root        sys        296763392 Nov  4 22:49 npar2.gz
#
```

With the golden image saved on the client, you can use **ftp** to send it to the server, as shown in the following listing:

ftp from npar2 (Ignite client) to rx8620b (Ignite server)

```
# ftp 192.6.174.66
Connected to 192.6.174.66.
220 rx8620b FTP server (Revision 1.1 Version wuftpd-2.6.1 Tue Jul 15 07:42:07 GMT 2003)
ready.
Name (192.6.174.66:root):
331 Password required for root.
Password:
230 User root logged in.
Remote system type is UNIX.
Using binary mode to transfer files.
ftp> cd /tmp
250 CWD command successful.
ftp> put npar2.gz
200 PORT command successful.
150 Opening BINARY mode data connection for npar2.gz.
226 Transfer complete.
296763392 bytes sent in 3.50 seconds (82906.87 Kbytes/s)
ftp> put make_sys_image.log
200 PORT command successful.
150 Opening BINARY mode data connection for make_sys_image.log.
226 Transfer complete.
737 bytes sent in 0.00 seconds (3911.56 Kbytes/s)
ftp> bye
221-You have transferred 296764129 bytes in 2 files.
221-Total traffic for this session was 296764882 bytes in 2 transfers.
221-Thank you for using the FTP service on rx8620b.
221 Goodbye.
#
```

There is then some additional server setup as shown in the following
steps:

On ignite server setup Configuration file

```
[rx8620b{root}:/var/opt/ignite/depots/npar2]>ll
total 579632
-rw-r--r--   1 root        sys          737 Nov  5 09:12 make_sys_image.log
-rw-r--r--   1 root        sys     296763392 Nov  5 09:12 npar2.gz
[rx8620b{root}:cp /depots/npar2/npar2_golden.cfg
[rx8620b{root}:/var/opt/ignite/depots/npar2]>cat npar2_golden.cfg

    nfs_source = "192.6.174.66:/var/opt/ignite/depots/npar2"
    description = "npar2 golden image"
    archive_path = "npar2.gz"
```

Export on server:

```
[rx8620b{root}:/var/opt/ignite/depots/npar2]>exportfs -a
[rx8620b{root}:/var/opt/ignite/depots/npar2]>exportfs -v
/var/opt/ignite/clients       -anon=2
/var/opt/ignite/depots/npar2 -ro,anon=2
[rx8620b{root}:/var/opt/ignite/depots/npar2]>
```

This quick summary of the golden image process is useful if you have
to install several similar systems.

What is more important, and what I encourage all of my clients to create as often as they can, is the recovery archive to ensure that they are protected should they have to replace a system.

Chapter 11

HP System Insight Manager (HP SIM)

HP SIM

HP System Insight Manager (HP SIM) is a hardware-management environment for all HP systems. With HP SIM, you can manage various systems including HP Integrity and HP 9000 servers running HP-UX; HP Integrity Servers running Windows and Linux; ProLiant servers running Windows, Linux, and NetWare; and monitor Alpha servers running Tru64 UNIX and OpenVMS. Although this chapter focuses on HP-UX system management with HP SIM, you can manage many more systems with HP SIM.

The *Central Management Server (CMS)* for HP SIM can run on HP-UX, Linux, or Windows. To manage HP-UX systems, you don't need a separate Windows or Linux system. You can run CMS right on one of your HP-UX systems, which I cover in this chapter.

There is one CMS per management domain. The CMS executes HP SIM software and initiates all HP SIM-related operations within the management domain. The CMS also maintains a database for storage of persistent objects. An HP-UX and Linux CMS uses PostgreSQL. A Windows CMS uses Microsoft SQL Server Desktop Engine (MSDE), which ships with HP SIM or Microsoft SQL 2000. The CMS also manages itself as part of the management domain or makes it a managed system within another management domain.

Systems in the management domain are *managed systems*. Managed systems are any device on the network that communicates with HP SIM. These can be devices such as servers (which will be part of the example in this chapter) desktops, workstations, hubs, routers, printers, laptops, and so on. Most of these devices have one or more IP addresses associated with them.

Every managed system must run one or more management agents. In the case of our HP-UX systems, Event Management System (EMS) is running.

HP SIM uses *system lists*, which provide a way to search the database for systems that share common attributes, such as running HP-UX. Standard system lists are provided in an upcoming example.

System groups are a way of organizing managed systems in terms of authorizations. Authorizations can be assigned to multiple systems at the same time using system groups.

Network clients access HP SIM using either a browser, to access the HP SIM Graphical User Interface (GUI), or Secure Shell (SSH), to access the HP SIM Command Line Interface (CLI).

HP CLI uses the operating system login to identify HP SIM users. This book doesn't cover the CLI. To access the HP SIM CMS from a browser, log in using the secure HTML login page. The user name and password are the same as those on the CMS operating system. The user name and password are transmitted using Secure Socket Layer (SSL) which provides data encryption and server authentication using public and private key technology.

SSH plays a large role in HP SIM for outbound connections such as running **dir** or **ls** on managed nodes.

Figure 11-1 shows some of the components in an HP SIM environment.

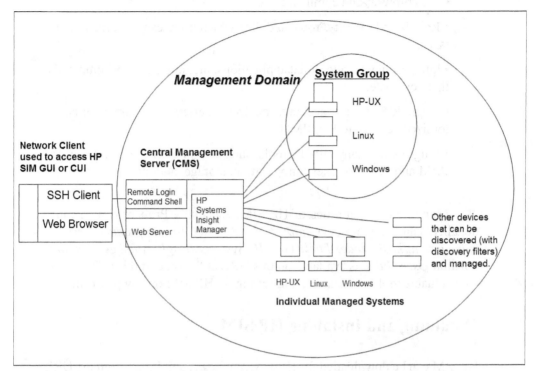

Figure 11-1   HP SIM Environment

Figure 11-1 is a simplified HP SIM environment, but it contains many of the components that you would typically manage in an HP SIM environment.

HP SIM grew out of several existing HP tools. It contains features from Insight Manager, HP Servicecontrol Manager (SCM) on HP-UX, and HP Toptools. This chapter covers a subset of HP SIM capabilities. Some HP-UX functionality of HP SIM is provided in the following list:

- Run the CMS on HP-UX, Linux, or Windows.

- Manage many systems running many operating systems, including HP-UX on HP Integrity and HP 9000 Servers, and Windows and Linux on HP Integrity Servers.

- Automatic discovery and identification of managed devices.

- Event management and notification services.

- Web browser and command line interface.

- Role-based security. You can define which users can perform which tasks.

- Integration with additional applications, including custom commands that you write.

- Upgrade SCM user accounts, devices, queries, tasks, and other customized settings to HP SIM.

- Plug-ins for many HP-UX tools, such as Ignite-UX, ServiceGuard, PRM and WLM, kernel configuration, storage, and others.

Many other capabilities of HP SIM, especially Proliant-related functionality, can be viewed at *http://h18013.www1.hp.com/products/servers/ management/hpsim/index.html*. The *HP Systems Insight Manager Installation and User Guide* is available on this URL at the time of this writing; it is an invaluable tool for installing and setting up HP SIM on any platform.

Obtaining and Installing HP SIM

HP SIM can be downloaded for HP-UX, Windows, and Linux from the URL listed at the end of the previous section. The plug-ins, documentation, and other tools can be downloaded from the URL as well. When you download HP SIM for a given platform, it is a self-contained exercise in which all the tools you need are included in the download. In the case of HP-UX, for example, a depot was produced that was roughly 264 MB in size and contained all the programs need to run HP SIM on an HP-UX system.

HP SIM will be installed in a Virtual Partition on a Superdome in the upcoming example. It can be installed in any type of partition or independent server provided the requirements are met as described in *HP Systems Insight Manager Installation and User Guide.*

Prior to installing HP SIM, you must perform a number of steps. The *HP Systems Insight Manager Installation and User Guide* contains many kernel parameter setting recommendations. These can be set using **kcweb**, described in the Chapter 5, "Configuring an HP-UX Kernel," which covers the kernel, which is a Web-based kernel tool. At the time of this writing, the parameter settings specified in the manual are as follows:

```
max_thread_proc=3000
maxdsize=2063835136
maxfiles=2048
maxfiles_lim=2048
maxusers=512
ncallout=6000
nfile=4097
nkthread=6000
nproc=2048
tcp_conn_request_max=2048
```

You also have to check to see if Servicecontrol Manager (SCM) is installed. If so, it has to be removed, which you'd do if you haven't used SCM, or upgrade it to HP SIM, which is described in *HP Systems Insight Manager Installation and User Guide.*

The following listing shows the contents of **/tmp/swlist_for_SCM**, which contains an **swlist** command with the *-l product* option to list the product level, to search for SCM-related products, and then the results of having run the search:

```
[/.root] > chmod 775 /tmp/swlist_for_SCM
[/.root] > cat /tmp/swlist_for_SCM
swlist -l product ServControlMgr AgentConfig SysMgmtServer SysMgmtAgent

[/.root] > /tmp/swlist_for_SCM
# Initializing...
# Contacting target "extraq1"...
ERROR:   Software "AgentConfig" was not found on host "extraq1:/".
ERROR:   Software "SysMgmtServer" was not found on host "extraq1:/".
ERROR:   Software "SysMgmtAgent" was not found on host "extraq1:/".
#
# Target:  extraq1:/
#

  ServControlMgr     A.02.03        HP-UX ServiceControl Manager
```

Alternatively, I could use product numbers rather than names as arguments to the **swlist** command. The **swlist** command reports that the first three products were not found on the system, but SCM does indeed exist so I run the following **swremove** command:

```
[/.root] > swremove ServControlMgr

======= 08/09/04 10:55:09 EDT  BEGIN swremove SESSION
        (non-interactive) (jobid=extraq1-0143)

    * Session started for user "root@extraq1".

    * Beginning Selection
    * Target connection succeeded for "extraq1:/".
    * Software selections:
          ServControlMgr.MX-AGENT,l=/,r=A.02.03,a=HP-UX_B.11.11_32/
              64,v=HP,fr=A.02.03,fa=HP-UX_B.11.11_32/64
          ServControlMgr.MX-CMS,l=/,r=A.02.03,a=HP-UX_B.11.11_32/
              64,v=HP,fr=A.02.03,fa=HP-UX_B.11.11_32/64
          ServControlMgr.MX-ENG-MAN,l=/,r=A.02.03,a=HP-UX_B.11.11_32/
              64,v=HP,fr=A.02.03,fa=HP-UX_B.11.11_32/64
          ServControlMgr.MX-TOOLS,l=/,r=A.02.03,a=HP-UX_B.11.11_32/
              64,v=HP,fr=A.02.03,fa=HP-UX_B.11.11_32/64
    * Selection succeeded.


    * Beginning Analysis
    * Session selections have been saved in the file
      "/.root/.sw/sessions/swremove.last".
    * The analysis phase succeeded for "extraq1:/".
    * Analysis succeeded.


    * Beginning Execution
    * The execution phase succeeded for "extraq1:/".
    * Execution succeeded.


NOTE:   More information may be found in the agent logfile using the
        command "swjob -a log extraq1-0143 @ extraq1:/".

======= 08/09/04 10:55:38 EDT  END swremove SESSION (non-interactive)
        (jobid=extraq1-0143)
```

The **swremove** succeeds as evidenced by the output of the **swlist** command:

```
root[/tmp] > /tmp/swlist_for_SCM
# Initializing...
# Contacting target "extraq1"...
ERROR:  Software "ServControlMgr" was not found on host "extraq1:/".
ERROR:  Software "AgentConfig" was not found on host "extraq1:/".
ERROR:  Software "SysMgmtServer" was not found on host "extraq1:/".
ERROR:  Software "SysMgmtAgent" was not found on host "extraq1:/".
```

This is the same **swlist** command that was run earlier, which shows that *ServControlMgr* was installed on the system.

Having removed SCM and set the kernel parameters I now proceed to load HP SIM.

A depot was previously downloaded to install HP SIM. Using Software Distributor, I installed the depot by selecting *Local Directory* and the name of the file to which I saved the depot. Figure 11-2 shows the installation window for HP SIM.

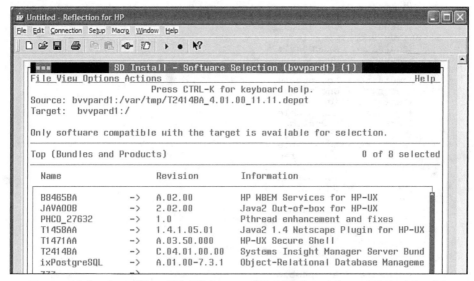

Figure 11-2   Installing HP SIM on an HP-UX Superdome Virtual Partition

Figure 11-2 shows the source is the host name *bvvpard1*, which is a Virtual Partition and the full path of the depot. The target is the host name of the virtual partition. In this **swinstall** window, select the HP SIM components you want to install. In this case, I select all the components. Several products in the depot make up all the components required for HP SIM.

After installation, the HP SIM setup required in *HP Systems Insight Manager Installation and User Guide* includes the following steps:

• Run the prerequisite tool with **/opt/mx/bin/mxinitconfig -l**, which produces the following output:

```
[/.root] > /opt/mx/bin/mxinitconfig -l
Listing current status of server components (15):
  1. Check Kernel Parameters
    - Requisite : Warning
    - Status    : Unconfigured
```

```
  2. Node Security File
     - Requisite : Acceptable
     - Status    : Unconfigured
  3. Server Property File
     - Requisite : Acceptable
     - Status    : Unconfigured
  4. Server Authentication Keys
     - Requisite : Acceptable
     - Status    : Unconfigured
  5. SSH Keys
     - Requisite : Acceptable
     - Status    : Unconfigured
  6. Status Property File
     - Requisite : Acceptable
     - Status    : Unconfigured
  7. Task Results Output Cleanup
     - Requisite : Acceptable
     - Status    : Unconfigured
  8. Database Configuration
     - Requisite : Acceptable
     - Status    : Unconfigured
  9. Database Content
     - Requisite : Acceptable
     - Status    : Configured
 10. Setup Property File
     - Requisite : Acceptable
     - Status    : Unconfigured
 11. Web Server
     - Requisite : Acceptable
     - Status    : Unconfigured
 12. Setup Property File
     - Requisite : Acceptable
     - Status    : Unconfigured
 13. Management Services
     - Requisite : Acceptable
     - Status    : Unconfigured
 14. Agent Configuration
     - Requisite : Acceptable
     - Status    : Unconfigured
 15. Database Population
     - Requisite : Acceptable
     - Status    : Unconfigured
Completed all tasks successfully.
Details can be found in the log file at /var/opt/mx/logs/initconfig.log
```

This tool caught the fact that I got lazy and didn't update the kernel parameters to the value specified by issuing a warning in step 1 for the kernel parameters. All other checks produced an acceptable output.

- Initialize HP SIM with **/opt/mx/bin/mxinitconfig -a**. This command can take a long time to execute. In the case of this example, it took more than one hour to populate the database:

```
[/.root] > /opt/mx/bin/mxinitconfig -a
Checking Prerequisites (15):
  1. Check Kernel Parameters
     - Requisite : Warning
  2. Node Security File
```

```
           - Requisite : Acceptable
      3. Server Property File
           - Requisite : Acceptable
      4. Server Authentication Keys
           - Requisite : Acceptable
      5. SSH Keys
           - Requisite : Acceptable
      6. Status Property File
           - Requisite : Acceptable
      7. Task Results Output Cleanup
           - Requisite : Acceptable
      8. Database Configuration
           - Requisite : Acceptable
      9. Database Content
           - Requisite : Acceptable
      10. Setup Property File
           - Requisite : Acceptable
      11. Web Server
           - Requisite : Acceptable
      12. Setup Property File
           - Requisite : Acceptable
      13. Management Services
           - Requisite : Acceptable
      14. Agent Configuration
           - Requisite : Acceptable
      15. Database Population
           - Requisite : Acceptable
Prerequisite scan completed successfully.
Configuring Server Components (15):
      1. Check Kernel Parameters
           - Successful
      2. Node Security File
           - Successful
      3. Server Property File
           - Successful
      4. Server Authentication Keys
           - Successful
      5. SSH Keys
           - Successful
      6. Status Property File
           - Successful
      7. Task Results Output Cleanup
           - Successful
      8. Database Configuration
           - Current Status : 65% Completed
           - Current Status : 100% Completed
           - Successful
Completed all tasks successfully.
Details can be found in the log file at /var/opt/mx/logs/initconfig.log
[/.root] >
```

The *Database Configuration* in step 8 of this listing took about an hour to complete. This was the configuration of PostgreSQL, which is the default database for HP SIM on HP-UX PostreSQL that was loaded as part of the depot. Continual status was provided during this configuration in the form of percentage complete. All the steps completed successfully, although the kernel parameter warning still exists, so I move to the next step.

• Verify the daemons for HP SIM are running: **mxagent**, **mxdomain-mgr**, and **mxdtf** . You can run **ps -ef |grep mx**. If the agents are not running, you can start them with **/opt/mx/bin/mxstart**. You can also stop the agents using the command **/opt/mx/bin/mxstop**. The following listing shows the output of looking for processes with *mx* in them after all the steps in this bullet list were run:

```
root@bvvpard1[/.root] > ps -ef | grep mx
    root  1682     1  0 14:49:01 ?         0:27 /opt/mx/lbin/mxagent
    root  1681     1  0 14:49:01 ?         0:03 /opt/mx/lbin/mxdtf
postgres  3688  1289  0 15:06:47 ?         0:15 postgres: mxadmin insight_v1_0 1
27.0.0.1 idle
postgres  3702  1289  0 15:07:44 ?         0:00 postgres: mxadmin insight_v1_0 1
27.0.0.1 idle
    root  3692     1  0 15:06:49 ?         0:12 /opt/mx/lbin/mxinventory -DMI 10
93547209857
    root  3681     1  0 15:06:24 ?         1:48 /opt/mx/lbin/mxdomainmgr
postgres  3701  1289  7 15:07:44 ?         0:01 postgres: mxadmin insight_v1_0 1
27.0.0.1 idle
    root  3690     1  0 15:06:49 ?         0:24 /opt/mx/lbin/mxinventory -WBEM 1
093547209749
postgres  3700  1289  0 15:07:17 ?         0:06 postgres: mxadmin insight_v1_0 1
27.0.0.1 idle
```

• Stop the SNMP agent on the CMS with **/sbin/init.d/SnmpMaster stop**.

• Edit **/etc/SnmpAgent.d/snmpd.conf** and add the CMS address with **trap-dest** *CMS_address*.

• Start the SNMP daemon with **/sbin/init.d/SnmpMaster start**.

• Use the GUI to add the default WBEM user name and password to the *Options-Protocol Settings-Global Protocol Settings* page. To initiate an HP SIM session using a browser, use *http:/hostname:280/*. (The next section covers using the GUI.) You may notice that this switches to port 50000, which runs over HTTP/S using SSL.

• In the *Default WBEM settings* section, check the *Enable WBEM* box.

• Install and configure agents on managed systems. This can be a time consuming process and requires work on all the systems that you want to manage with HP SIM.

• Perform additional HP SIM setup, such as adding managed systems and users, specifying user authorizations, configuring event handling, and other setup.

HP Systems Insight Manager Installation and User Guide does a great job of walking you through installation, configuration, and upgrading from Insight Manager and SCM to HP SIM.

Now that HP SIM is installed on an HP-UX system, the next section covers working with the regions of the GUI.

Working with the HP SIM GUI

Now that HP SIM is installed and configured, I begin working with the GUI. There is also a Character User Interface (CUI) for HP SIM, which I won't cover other than to say that it exists. There are some commands that were run in the setup, including **mxstart** and **mxstop**, that are part of the CUI, but I cover only the GUI in this book.

Immediately after completing the installation, I invoke the GUI with *http://hostname:280/*. Figure 11-3 appears when you first invoke the GUI.

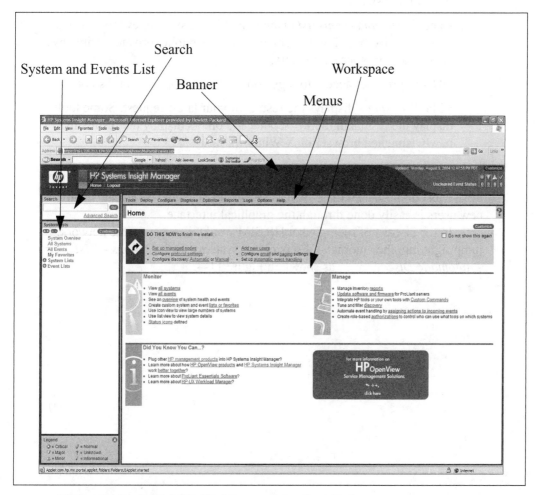

Figure 11-3   Initial HP SIM Screen After Installation

Figure 11-3 lists the five major areas of the HP SIM GUI. A lot of initial customization can be performed in the workspace immediately after it is first invoked, as described in *HP Systems Insight Manager Installation and User Guide.*

Here is a brief description of the five major areas of the HP SIM GUI:

• The top region is a *Banner* with summary views. It provides information such as status and an alarm for specified events. The banner can be customized.

• The *Search* region allows you to specify a name or attribute to use to search for systems.

• The *System and events list* displays all known systems events. You can specify the list based on information such as public, private, visible by creator, all, or other parameters.

• *Menus* provides access to logs, tools, software options, and so on.

• The *Workspace* displays the results of your latest request. Some tools display the results in the *Workspace* and others display the results in a newly launched browser or X Windows.

You could spend a lot of time in customization after first invoking HP SIM. Most of these activities, such as setting up managed nodes and creating new users is easily done through the graphical interface.

In the interest of seeing what HP SIM would discover on the network, I jump right into the automatic discovery of systems, with *Options - Discover - Automatic Discovery ...,* as shown in Figure 11-4.

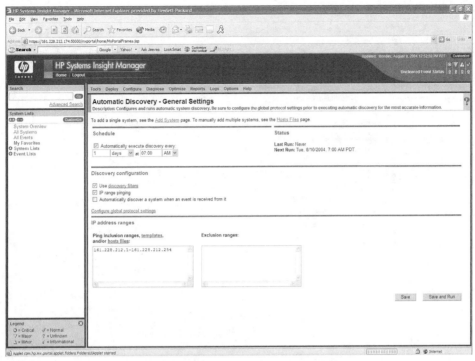

Figure 11-4   HP SIM Configuration of Automatic Discovery

I decide to just run the automatic discovery searching for systems on my subnet, as described in the *IP address ranges*. I could select manual discovery under the *Options* menu. You can select a *Schedule* of automatic discovery as I've done in the example. Network administrators aren't always happy when many pings take place during automatic discovery, so keep this in mind. All the entries shown in Figure 11-4 are the defaults, so I hit *Save and Run* to see what would be discovered. Status is provided as the discovery takes place, showing the number of pings attempted, the number of pings processed, and the percentage complete.

You can select the type of devices to be discovered by selecting *Discovery Filters,* as shown on Figure 11-5.

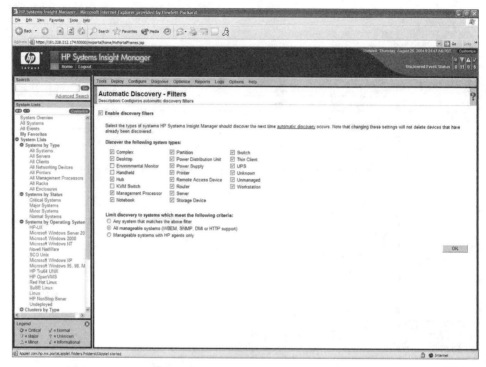

Figure 11-5   HP SIM Discovery Filters

The discovery completed on this small subnet in about one minute. On large networks, this discovery could take several hours and is best run over a weekend or in the evening, if possible.

The discovery takes place with the CMS pinging devices to see if the address is alive, it then issues appropriate SNMP GETS and DMI commands to collect the details of each devices. This is the process that feeds the reports. Also, periodic System Identification tasks are run to keep the inventory up to date so that if you replace a disk drive, the replacement disk drive's serial number is updated; the same goes for disk space and other hardware configuration things.

After the discovery completes I select *System Lists - All Systems* from the System and Events List on the left side of the screen, and the systems on the subnet are displayed, as shown in Figure 11-6.

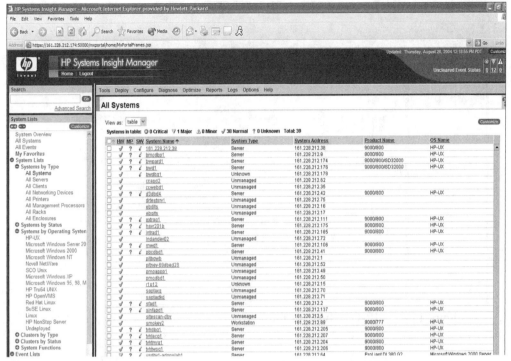

Figure 11-6   *System List - All Systems* After Automatic Discovery

The automatic discovery tool takes only about one minute for this subnet and produces a list of additional Superdome hard and virtual partitions, non-partitionable HP-UX systems, and some Proliants running Windows. At this level, there is no distinction made between vPars, nPartitions, and other HP-UX systems. Note the many ways that systems can be listed based on the options available under system lists. There are many unmanaged components in the list which are a variety of types of devices. To list only HP-UX, or another type of operating system, select by operating system which is shown for HP-UX in Figure 11-7.

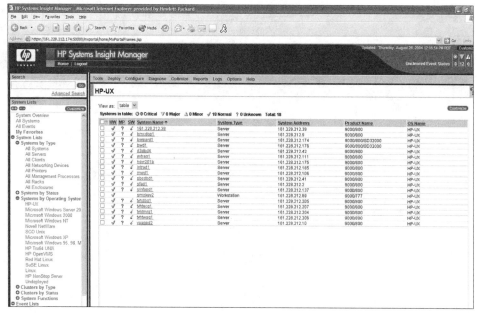

Figure 11-7   HP-UX Systems Only

A minimal amount of information is provided for the HP-UX systems because these have not yet been setup as managed nodes. The next section provides an example of setting up a managed node and the type of information that is provided to the CMS.

Set Up an HP-UX Managed System

Setting up a managed HP-UX system requires you to perform the following steps:

- Install the SSH software on the managed system.
- Copy the SSH public key from the CMS to the managed node.
- Configure DMI on the managed system.
- Configure the managed system to send SNMP traps to the CMS.
- Install and configure WEBM.
- Add a default WBEM user name and password to the managed node.

The following example shows configuring one of the systems, which is really a Superdome partition, as a managed node. The first step is to install the software components shown in Figure 11-8 onto the managed node.

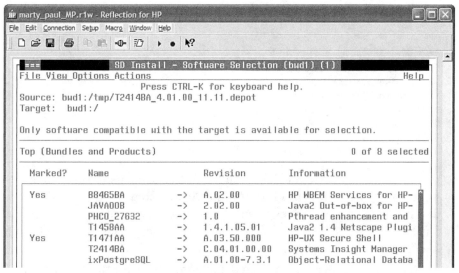

Figure 11-8   Using Software Distributor to Load Software on Managed Node

Both WBEM and SSH were installed from the software depot. All the components for HP SIM were downloaded from *www.hp.com*.

The next step is to run the command **mxagentconfig -g** to invoke the X Windows-based interface through which SSH keys are managed. The only information that you have to enter is the managed node hostname, user, and password. There is then a connect button that you select. This process can also be done at the command line:

```
root > mxagentconfig -a -n bwd1 -u root -p password
Successfully registered as an agent to bwd1
```

This command performs the agent registration.

Next, configure DMI (Desktop Management Interface) on the managed node. DMI is used by the CMS to support discovery and identification of DMI devices.

This is done by stopping DMI with **/sbin/init.d/Dmisp stop**, adding the name of the CMS to the end of **/var/dmi/dmiMachines**, and then restarting DMI with **/sbin/init.d/Dmisp start**. The **dmiMachines** file has nothing in it but the names of systems, such as the CMS. A variety of daemons are stopped and started. The following listing shows only stopping DMI so that you can see the daemons affected:

```
root > /sbin/init.d/Dmisp stop
hpuxci daemon stopped
sdci daemon stopped
swci daemon stopped
DMI SP daemon dmisp stopped
root >
```

Next is the SNMP configuration on the managed node. This is done by stopping SNMP with **/sbin/init.d/SnmpMaster stop**, modifying the trap-dest line in the file **/etc/SnmpAgent.d/snmpd.conf** to read trap-dest *address* (such as `trap-dest: 161.228.212.174`), and then restarting SNMP with **/etc/SnmpAgent.d/snmpd.conf start**.

The last managed node-related configuration step is to set up WEBM in the HP SIM GUI. Figure 11-9 shows selecting *Options - Protocol Settings - Global Protocol Settings* to add a WBEM account.

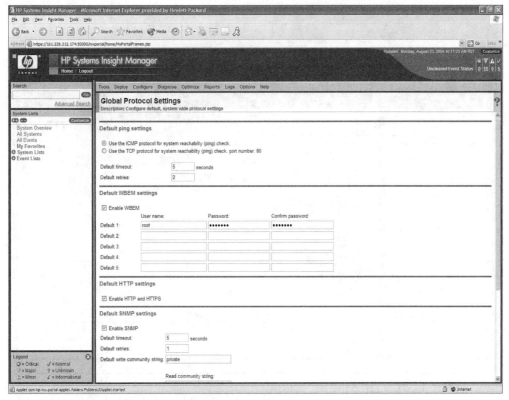

Figure 11-9   Adding a WBEM Account

With the DMI, SNMP, and WBEM managed node setup now complete, a substantial amount of information can be reported in the HP SIM GUI for the managed node. Figure 11-10 shows the type of information that can be reported for managed HP-UX nodes. If a node hasn't been set up as a managed node, only minimal information is reported for these selections.

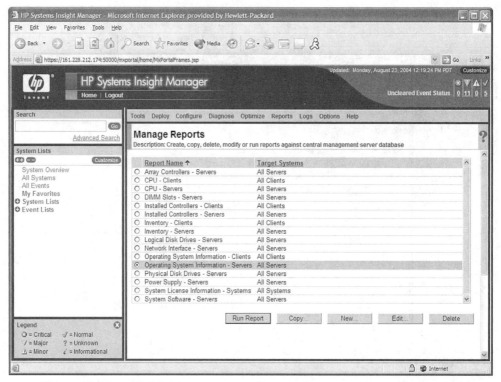

Figure 11-10   HP SIM Reports

You can also issue specific commands on managed nodes. Figure 11-11 shows command-line tasks that you can run on managed nodes.

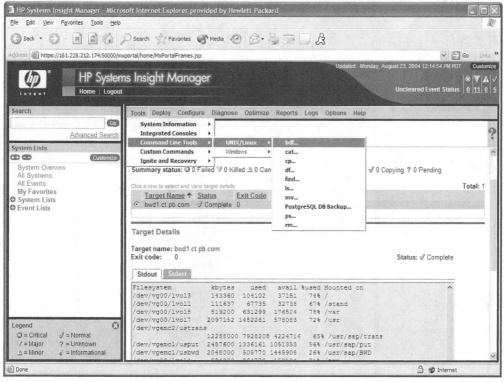

Figure 11-11   **bdf** on a Managed Node

With login information having been setup, you can run such tasks as the **bdf** that I've run on the managed node that we just set up or one of the many other commands.

You can also keep track of events taking place on systems. Figure 11-12 shows viewing the events that have taken place on the systems earlier discovered on this subnet.

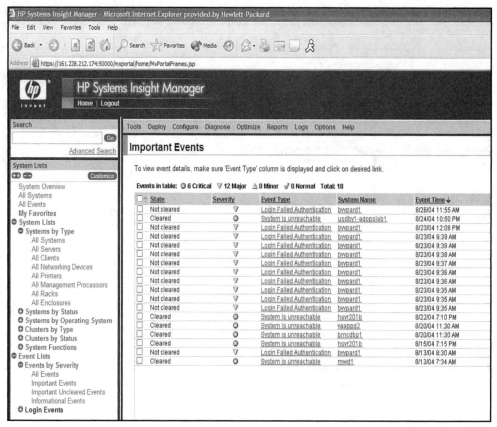

Figure 11-12   Viewing Events

You can select from severity of events in the System Lists area on the left. In this case, I selected *Important Events*, which include events such as failed login attempts, which are good to know about.

This quick HP SIM overview shows the power of this hardware management tool. It can also be used to manage Windows and Linux systems as well as report to enterprise-management systems such as HP OpenView.

HP SIM CLI Commands

Although the graphical interface supplied with HP SIM is highly functional, you may need to issue HP SIM CLI commands. In the previous section, for example, there were some commands issued during the installation such as **mxagentconfig**. There are many commands associated with the CLI that are summarized in Table 11-1.

Table 11-1   Summary of HP SIM CLI Commands

Command	Description
mcompile	Compiles an SNMP MIB file into an intermediate CFG format file for importing into HP SIM using the **mxmib** command
mxagentconfig	Configures an agent to work with a CMS
mxauth	Adds, removes, or lists a toolbox-based authorization
mxdtf	Contains the DTF used to execute commands on managed systems running SSH
mxexec	Executes tools, verifies the status of running tools, and enables a fully privileged user to kill or cancel a task
mxinitconfig	Performs the initial CMS configuration as shown in the earlier example
mxmib	Adds, deletes, and processes a list of MIBS for HP SIM
mxngroup	Works with HP SIM groups
mxnode	Works with HP SIM nodes
mxnodesecurity	Manipulates SNMP and WBEM security credentials
mxpassword	Works with HP SIM passwords
mxquery	Works with HP SIM lists
mxrepositoryrestore	Restores the HP SIM database from a backup
mxrepositorysave	Backsup the HP SIM database
mxserver	Works with the HP SIM SSL port number in the embedded CMS Web server
mxstart	Starts daemons and processes used by the CMS
mxstm	Works with HP SIM System Type Manager rules

Command	Description
mxstop	Stops daemons and processes used by the CMS
mxtask	Works with HP SIM scheduled tasks
mxtool	Works with HP SIM tools
mxtoolbox	Works with HP SIM system
mxuser	Works with HP SIM users
mxwbemsub	Works with WBEM subscriptions

Some of these commands were issued earlier when HP SIM was initially set up. **mxagentconfig** was issued when the managed system was set up. **mxstart** and **mxstop** were issued as part of the CMS setup.

You can perform most HP SIM functions at the command line and don't have to use the GUI; however, the GUI provides an easy-to-read interface.

Chapter 12

System Administration Manager (SAM)

SAM Overview

You can use System Administration Manager (SAM) to automate and perform various system-administration tasks. SAM has been refined over many releases of HP-UX and is a highly functional and reliable tool for performing most system-administration tasks, even advanced tasks such as managing partitions.

As you see in the upcoming sections, SAM has many *functional areas* in which you can perform system-administration tasks. There is a lot of "coverage" with SAM, meaning that most system-administration tasks can be performed with SAM, so you can use it for the vast majority of your system-administration tasks.

Although several Web-based functional areas of SAM are covered in other chapters, I focus on the Terminal User Interface (TUI) or what I call the Character Line Interface (CLI) of SAM in this chapter. Many organizations don't like Web servers running on systems for the purpose of system-administration interfaces, so there is a CLI for all functional areas of SAM. In other chapters, you find the Web-based tools covered for peripheral devices (**pd**, which is automatically invoked in SAM under peripheral devices - cards and devices), partitions (**parmgr**), and kernel (**kcweb**). In the kernel area, **kcweb** is automatically invoked, in the partitions area **parmgr** is automatically invoked, and under peripheral devices - cards and devices, **pd** is automatically invoked.

You can also run SAM in an X Windows environment by specifying the *DISPLAY* environment variable.

Four features of SAM that make it particularly useful are

1. It provides a central point from which system administration tasks can be performed. This includes both the built-in tasks that come with SAM and those you can add into the SAM menu hierarchy. You can run SAM on a remote system and display it locally so that you truly have a central point of control.

2. It provides an easy way to perform tasks that are difficult, in that you have to perform many steps. SAM performs these steps for you.

3. It provides a summary of what your system currently looks like for any of the categories of administration tasks you want to perform. If you want to do something with the disks on your system, SAM first lists the disks you currently have connected. If you want to play with a printer, SAM first lists all of your printers and plotters for you. This capability cuts down on mistakes by putting your current configuration right in front of you.

4. You can assign non-root users to perform some of the system-administration functions in SAM. If, for example, you feel comfortable assigning one of your associates to manage users, you can give them permission to perform user-related tasks and give another user permission to perform backups, and so on.

There aren't any tasks performed by SAM that you could not perform in another user interface, such as the Web-based tools previously mentioned, or at the command line.

This chapter covers the basics of each functional area in SAM but you'll see and work with the specifics of your systems when you work with SAM, so I strongly suggest you do so.

Running and Using SAM as Superuser

To run SAM, log in as root and type the following:

```
# sam          (or sam &)
```

This invokes SAM. If you have a graphics display, SAM runs in X Windows. If you have a character-based display, SAM runs in character mode. You have nearly all the same functionality in both modes.

If you have a graphics display and SAM does not come up in X Windows, you probably don't have your *DISPLAY* variable set for root.

Type the following to set the *DISPLAY* variable for default POSIX, Korn, and Bourne shells:

```
# DISPLAY=system_name:0.0
# export DISPLAY
```

Substitute the name of your computer for *system_name*. This can be set in your local **.profile** file. If you're running HP CDE, you may want to put these lines in your **.dtprofile** file.

Type the following to set the *DISPLAY* variable for C shell:

```
# setenv DISPLAY system_name:0.0
```

Again, substitute the name of your computer for *system_name*. This typically is done in your **.login** file, but if you're running HP CDE, you may want to put this in your **.dtprofile** file. Most CDE users, however, have **.dtprofile** as the source for **.profile** or **.login**.

Figure 12-1 is the SAM CLI with some of the bottom selections not shown.

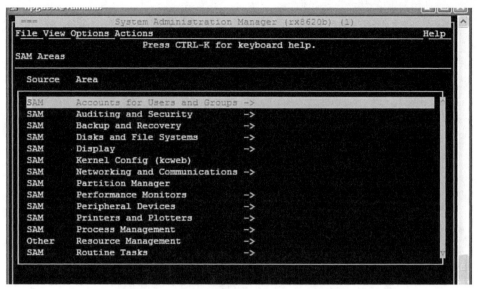

Figure 12-1   SAM Startup Window in Character Mode

     The *View* menu can be used in character mode to tailor the information desired, filter out some entries, or search for particular entries.

     Because you don't have a mouse on a text terminal, you use the keyboard to make selections. The point-and-click method of using SAM when in graphics mode is highly preferable to using the keyboard; however, the same structure to the functional areas exists in both environments. When you see an item in reverse video on the text terminal (such as *Accounts for Users and Groups* in Figure 12-1), you know that you have that item selected. After having selected *Accounts for Users and Groups* as shown in Figure 12-1, you would then use the *tab* key (or *F4*) to get to the menu bar, use the <- -> *(arrow)* keys to select the desired menu, and use the *space bar* to display the menu. This situation is where having a mouse to make your selections is highly desirable. Figure 12-2 shows a menu bar selection in the CLI with the *Actions* menu selected.

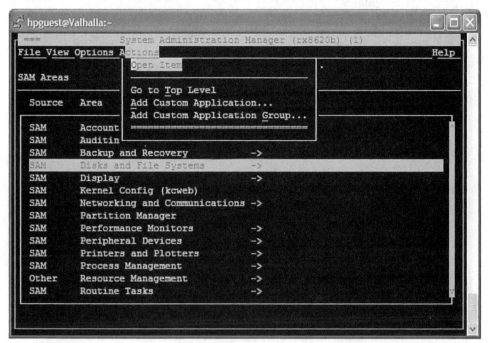

Figure 12-2   SAM Menu Selection for Text and Graphics Displays

Of particular interest on the pull-down menu are *Add Custom Application* and *Add Custom Application Group*. When you use *Add Custom Application Group,* you are prompted for a *Label* and optional *Help File* for the group. After you enter this information, a new icon appears, if you have a graphics display, with the name of your application group. You can then go into this application group and *Add Custom Applications*. This means that you can customize SAM to meet your specific administration needs by adding functionality to SAM. After you familiarize yourself with the aspects of system administration SAM can help you with, you want to test adding your own application to SAM. Adding a simple application such as opening a log file or issuing the **/usr/bin/find** command, takes only seconds to create.

You can also create users who have restricted access to SAM. You can specify areas within SAM to which specific users can have access. You may have users to whom you would like to give access to backup and restore, or managing users, or handling the print spooler. Invoking SAM with the *-r* option allows you to select a user to whom you want to give access to a SAM area and then select the specific area(s) to which you want to enable that user to have access. You can also give a user partial access to some areas, such as providing access to backup and recovery, but not providing access to handling automated backups. As you progress through the detailed descriptions of SAM areas in this chapter, you want to think about which of these areas may be appropriate for some of your users to access.

Author's Disclaimer: SAM Is a Moving Target

SAM is improving all the time. One example are the Web-based interfaces that are included in some SAM areas. Because SAM is being improved continuously, you may see some minor differences between your SAM and the exmaples in this book.

I now cover each of the functional areas of SAM.

Accounts for Users and Groups

An earlier chapter covers users and groups in general. In this chapter I cover users and groups in SAM only.

Every user has information associated with them. There is an entry in the **/etc/passwd** file for each user and an entry in **/etc/group** for each group. Figure 12-3 is an example of a user entry from **/etc/passwd** and an example of a group entry from **/etc/group**.

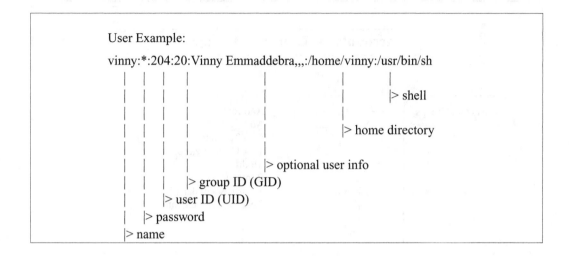

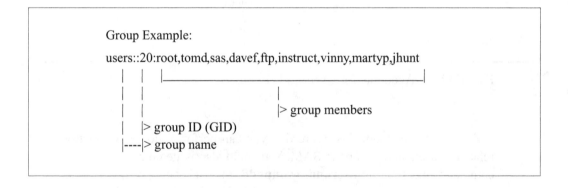

Figure 12-3   Sample **/etc/passwd** and **/etc/group** Entry

The *Accounts for Users and Groups* top-level SAM category, or area, has beneath it only two picks: *Groups* and *Users*. The menu hierarchy for "Users and Groups" is shown in Figure 12-4.

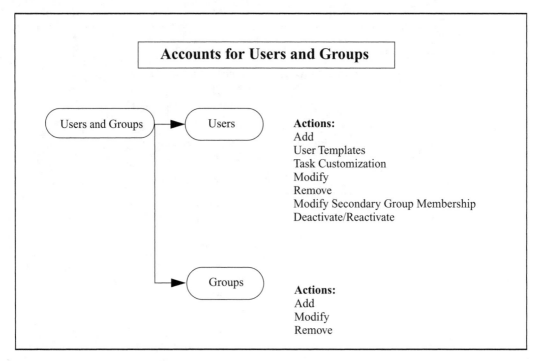

Figure 12-4   Accounts for Users and Groups

You can see from this figure that you can perform most any function related to users and groups in SAM. You could also issue commands on the command line such as **useradd**, **groupadd**, **userdel**, and **groupdel** rather than use SAM for user- and group-related functions. SAM provides a great interface for working with users and groups, so you may want to consider using it rather than the command line.

When you select *Accounts for Users and Groups* and then *Users* from the SAM menu, you are provided a list of all the users on your system. Figure 12-5 shows a list of users provided by SAM.

```
 ===              Accounts for Users and Groups (rx8620b) (1)
File List View Options Actions                                         Help
                   Press CTRL-K for keyboard help.
Template In Use: None
Filtering:  Displaying all users

Users                                              0 of 15 selected

  Login      User ID                              Primary   O
  Name       (UID)    Real Name                   Group     P

  adm          4                                    adm
  bin          2                                    bin
  daemon       1                                    daemon
  hpdb        27       ALLBASE                       other
  lp           9                                    lp
  mysql      102                                    mysql
  nobody      -2                                    nogroup
  nuucp       11                                    nuucp
  root         0                                    sys
  smbnull    101       DO NOT USE OR DELETE - needed by Samba  smbnull
```

Figure 12-5   List of Users

Adding a User

SAM is ideal for performing administration tasks related to users and groups. These routine tasks are not complex but require you to edit the **/etc/passwd** and **/etc/group** files, make directories, and copy default files, all of which SAM performs for you. Finally, take a minute to check what SAM has done for you, especially if you modify an existing user or group.

To add an additional user, you would select *Add* from the *Actions* menu under *Users* and then fill in the information as shown in Figure 12-6.

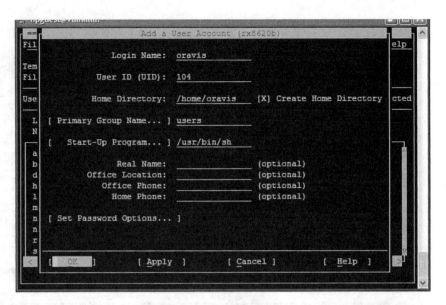

Figure 12-6   Example of Adding a New User

To see the **/etc/passwd** entry that was made, I issued the following **cat** and **grep** commands that showed oravis:

```
[rx8620b{root}:/roothome]>cat /etc/passwd | grep oravis
oravis::104:20:,,,:/home/oravis:/usr/bin/sh
[rx8620b{root}:/roothome]>
```

This output shows the user oravis.

You can view the log file that SAM produces with the menu selection *Options - View SAM Log.* Figure 12-7 show the end of the log file, which indicates that our user was successfully added.

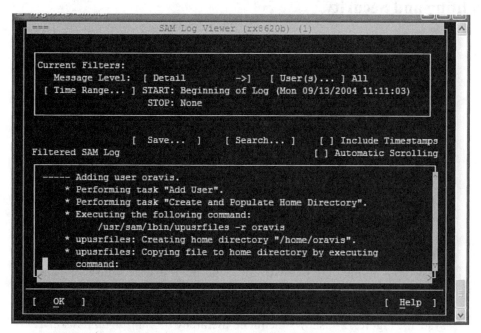

Figure 12-7   SAM Log Viewer for Adding a User

The scroll bar on the right-hand side of the SAM Log Viewer allows you to scroll to any point in the log file. We are viewing only the part of the log file that pertains to adding the user oravis. You can select the level of detail you want to view with the log file. The four levels are *Summary, Detail, Verbose,* and *Commands Only.* The level shown in Figure 12-7 is *Detail.* I like this level because you can see what has taken place without getting mired down in too much detail. When you view the log file, you typically see the calls to SAM scripts that SAM has made and other commands that SAM is issuing.

Adding an additional group is similar to adding a new user. To add an additional group, you would select *Add* from the *Actions* menu under *Groups*.

Auditing and Security

Under *Auditing and Security,* you manage the security of your system. This is becoming an increasingly important aspect of system management. Some installations care very little about security because of well-known, limited groups of users who will access a system. Other installations, such as those connected to the Internet, may go to great pains to make their systems into fortresses, with firewalls checking each and every user who attempts to access a system.

Although SAM makes creating and maintaining a trusted system easy, a lot of files are created for security management, which takes place under the umbrella of Auditing and Security. Among the modifications that will be made to your system, should you choose to convert to a trusted system, is the **/etc/rc.config.d/auditing** file, which will be updated by SAM. In addition, passwords in the **/etc/passwd** file will be replaced with "*," and the encrypted passwords are moved to a password database. All users are also given audit ID numbers. Not all applications are compatible with trusted systems. Figure 12-8 shows the menu hierarchy of *Auditing and Security.*

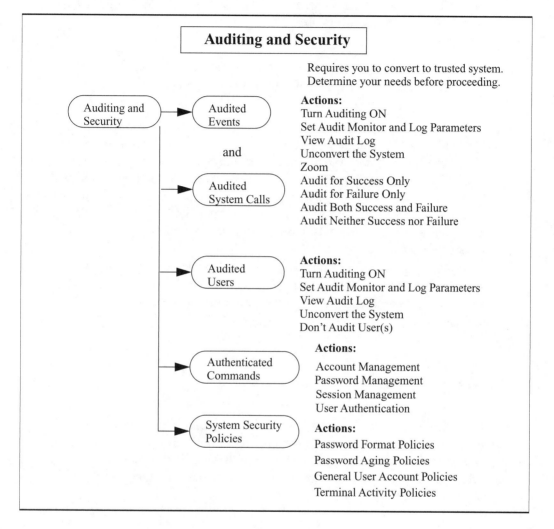

Figure 12-8   *Auditing and Security* Menu Structure

In order to traverse this hierarchy for yourself, you must first convert to a trusted system. Before you do, please read this section to get an idea of the functionality this will provide and then convert to a trusted system if you think there is adequate benefit.

One choice to observe in Figure 12-8 is an *Actions* menu choice to *Unconvert the System*. This means to reverse the trusted system environment. I have tried this on various systems and it seems to work fine, but you should have a good idea of what a trusted system can do for and to you before you make the conversion.

Audited Events and Audited System Calls

Under *Audited Events,* you can select the particular events you want to analyze and detect, which may cause security breaches. Under *Audited System Calls,* you can monitor system calls. This option is a function of the trusted system to which you must convert in order to perform auditing. You may have in mind particular events and system calls that are most vital to your system's security that you want to audit, and not bother with the balance. There are a number of events and system calls that you may want to keep track of for security reasons.

Auditing these events gives you a detailed report of each event. The same is true of system calls. SAM uses the auditing commands of HP-UX such as **audsys**, **audusr**, **audevent**, **audomon**, and **audisp**, to perform auditing.

Audited Users

Under *Audited Users,* you can use the *Actions* menu to turn auditing on and off for specific users. Because the audit log files, which you can also control and view through the *Actions* menu, grow large quickly, you may want to select specific users to monitor to better understand the type of user audit information that is created.

Authenticated Commands

This security feature is the ability to perform authentication based on user, password, session, or account. This industry-standard authentication framework is known as the Pluggable Authentication Module, or PAM. The PAM framework allows for authentication modules to be implemented without modifying any applications. Authentication is currently provided for CDE components, HP-UX standard commands, trusted systems, and DCE (the Distributed Computing Environment), as well as third-party modules.

System Security Policies

The most important part of HP-UX security is the policies you put in place. If, for example, you choose to audit each and every system call, but don't impose any restrictions on user passwords, you are potentially opening up your system to any user. You would be much better off restricting users and not worrying so much about what they're doing. Being proactive is more important in security than being reactive.

Password Aging Policies, when enabled, allows you to set

• Time between Password Changes

• Password Expiration Time

• Password Expiration Warning Time

• Password Life Time

• Expire All User Passwords Immediately

General User Account Policies, when enabled, allows you to specify the time at which an account will become inactive and lock it. In addition, you can specify the number of unsuccessful login tries that are permitted.

Terminal Security Policies allows you to set

• Number of unsuccessful Login Tries Allowed

• Delay between Login Tries

• Login Timeout Value in Seconds

• Required Login upon Boot to Single-User State

Backup and Recovery

The most important activities you perform as a system administrator are system backup and recovery. The SAM team put a lot of thought into giving you all the options you need to ensure the integrity of your system through backup and recovery. You may also want to review Chapter 7, "Backup," which covers various backup commands available on HP-UX. Figure 12-9 shows the hierarchy of the *Backup and Recovery* SAM menu.

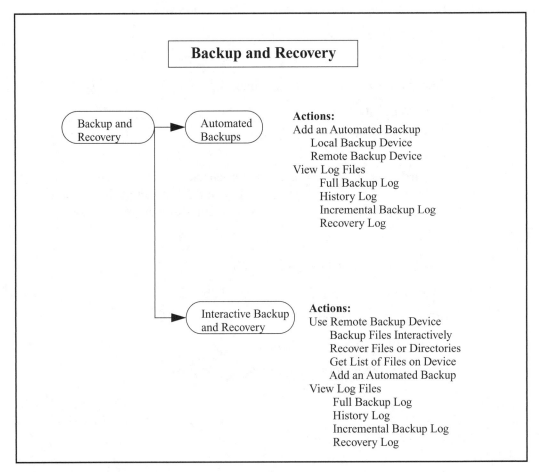

Figure 12-9   *Backup and Recovery* Menu Structure

From this menu hierarchy, you can schedule backup and recovery. After a backup is performed, you can perform recovery as well.

For an automated backup, you select the scope of the backup, the backup device, the backup time, and the additional parameters, such as whether or not you want to create an index log.

After specifying backup information, you can view the **crontab** entry that SAM has made for root for your backups. The **crontab** file is used to schedule jobs that are automatically executed by **cron**. **crontab** files are in the **/var/spool/cron/crontabs** directory. **cron** is a program that runs other programs at the specified time. **cron** reads files that specify the operation to be performed and the date and time it is to be performed. Because we want to perform backups on a regular basis, SAM activates **cron**.

The format of entries in the **crontab** file is as follows:

minute   hour   monthday   month   weekday   user name   command

> *minute* - the minute of the hour, from 0-59
> *hour* - the hour of the day, from 0-23
> *monthday* - the day of the month, from 1-31
> *month* - the month of the year, from 1-12
> *weekday* - the day of the week, from 0 (Sunday) - 6 (Saturday)
> *user name* - the user who will run the command if necessary
>   (not used in the example)
> *command* - specifies the command line or script file to run

You have many options in the **crontab** for specifying the *minute, hour, monthday, month,* and *weekday* to perform a task. You could list one entry in a field and then a space, several entries in any field separated by a comma, two entries separated by a dash indicating a range, or an asterisk, which corresponds to all possible entries for the field.

To list the contents of the **crontab** file, you would issue the command **crontab -l**. SAM creates a **crontab** entry for any backups you specify.

You see various *crontab* **commands** when you use the *SAM Log Viewer* to see what SAM has done for you to create the **crontab** files. For instance, if you change your backup plan, SAM removes the old **crontab** file with this command:

```
$ crontab -r
```

This removes the **crontab** file for the user from the **/var/spool/cron/ crontabs** directory.

To place a file in the **crontab** directory, simply issue the **crontab** command and the name of the **crontab** file:

```
$ crontab crontabfile
```

You can schedule cron jobs using SAM. The section in this chapter covering *Process Management* has a section called *Scheduling Cron Jobs*.

For an interactive backup, you select a backup device and the files to be backed up interactively.

To perform a restore of either a full or incremental backup, you specify the restore device and options such as *Select Recovery Scope; Specify Tape Device Options*; and *Set Additional Parameters*. The device options you specify will depend on the tape device you are using. You can enter the name of a file that has in it the files to be recovered or you can just manually list the files. There are many parameters you can set for the restore including:

• Overwrite Newer Files

• Preserve Original File Ownership

• Recover Files Using Full Path Name

• Place Files in Non-Root Directory

After you begin the recovery, you are given the status of the recovery as it takes place and may also View Recovery Log from the *Actions* menu after the recovery has completed. If you View Recovery Log, you receive a window that provides the name of the index log and the names of the files recovered.

Disks and File Systems

Disks and File Systems helps you manage disk devices, file systems, logical volumes, swap, and volume groups (you may also manage other HP disk devices, such as XP and disk arrays, through SAM if you have these installed on your system). I normally perform disk-related functions at the command line, but SAM does a good job of this. See Chapter 4, "Logical Volume Manager," for some advanced work with external disks and the scripts and command file I use to configure them in the example. Figures 12-10 and 12-11 show the hierarchy of *Disks and File Systems*.

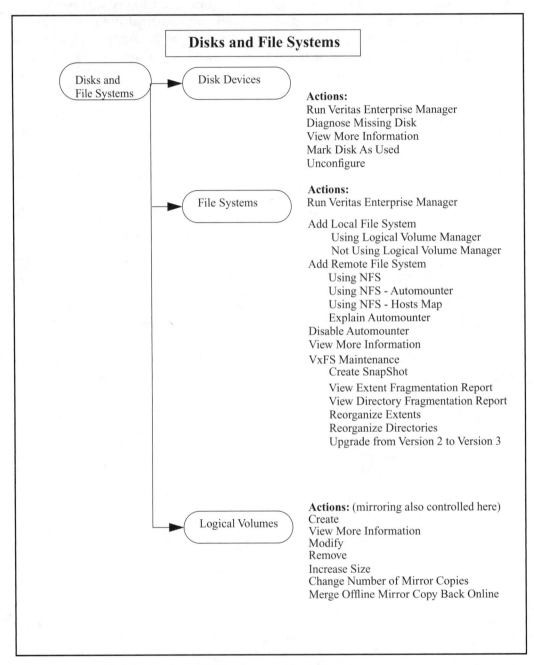

Figure 12-10   *Disks and File Systems* Menu Structure

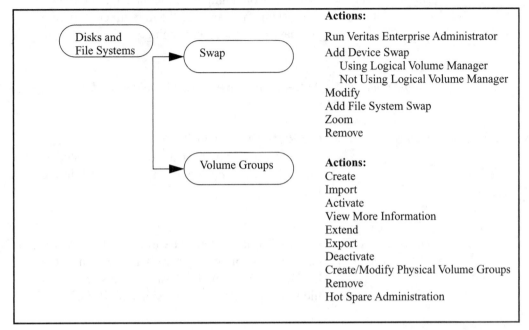

Figure 12-11   *Disks and File Systems* Menu Structure (continued)

Disk Devices

When you enter the Disk Devices area, SAM shows you the disk devices connected to your system in a format similar to **ioscan** output.

File Systems

File Systems shows the *Mount Directory, Type* of file system, and *Source Device or Remote Directory.*

At this level, you can perform such tasks as *Add Local File System* and *Add Remote File System,* and you can perform *VxFS Maintenance* from the *Actions* menu.

Several types of file systems may be listed under the Type column. The most common are

Auto-Indirect	Directory containing auto-mountable remote NFS file systems. You may see the **/net** directory here if you have auto-mounter running.
Auto-Mount	Auto-mountable remote NFS file system.
CDFS	CD-ROM file system if it is currently mounted. If, for example, you have a CD-ROM mounted as /SD_CDROM, you see this as type CDFS in the list.
HFS	Local HFS file system. These local HFS file systems are part of your system. HP's version of the UNIX File System. This was the most common file system under earlier versions of HP-UX.
NFS	Remote NFS file system that is currently mounted.
LOFS	Loopback file system that allows you to have the same file system in multiple places.
VxFS	Local Journaled File System (JFS). This is the HP-UX implementation of the Veritas Journaled File System (VxFS), which supports fast file system recovery. JFS is the default HP-UX file system.

Logical Volumes

You can perform several functions related to logical volume manipulation in SAM. Such tasks as *Create, Modify, Remove,* and *Increase Size* can be performed in SAM.

SAM will increase the size of the logical volume only if it can be unmounted. Viewing the log file after this task is complete shows that SAM ran such commands as **/sbin/lvextend** and **/sbin/extendfs** to extend the size of the logical volume and file system, and **/usr/sbin/umount** and **/usr/sbin/ mount** to unmount and mount the file system.

See the Logical Volume Manager detail in Chapter 4 for definitions of Logical Volume Manager terms. This chapter also contains a description of Logical Volume Manager commands.

Swap

Both device swap and file system swap are listed when you enter *Swap*. Listed for you are the *Device File/Mount Directory, Type, Mbytes Available*, and *Enabled*. You can get more information about an item by highlighting it and selecting *Zoom* from the *Actions* menu.

Volume Groups

Listed for you when you enter volume groups are *Name, Mbytes Available, Physical Volumes*, and *Logical Volumes*. If you have an unused disk on your system, you can extend an existing volume group or create a new volume group. This window is useful to see how much disk space within a volume group has not been allocated yet. Another function here is the ability to import volume groups from other systems or ready a volume group for export to a remote system. You would use this when moving a volume group contained on an entire disk drive (or set of disk drives) from one system to another.

Display

In the Display area in SAM, you can perform work related to the graphics display(s) on your system. You can perform *Monitor Configuration* and X Server Configuration.

Kernel Configuration

Chapter 5, "Configuring an HP-UX Kernel," is devoted to kernel configuration at the command line and through **kcweb**. SAM immediately invokes **kcweb** to perform kernel-related work. Be sure to look at **kcweb** in Chapter 5. **kcweb** is a Web-based tool for working wtih the kernel.

Between the command line and **kcweb** examples in Chapter 5, you can determine what tasks you prefer to perform manually versus with **kcweb**.

Networking and Communications

The menu hierarchy for *Networking and Communications* is shown in Figures 12-12 through 12-14. This area contains many advanced networking features. Virtually any networking-related function can be performed through SAM.

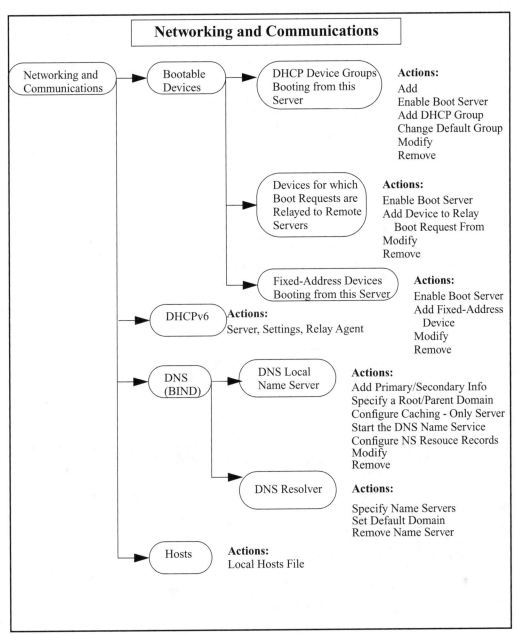

Figure 12-12 *Networking and Communications* Menu Structure

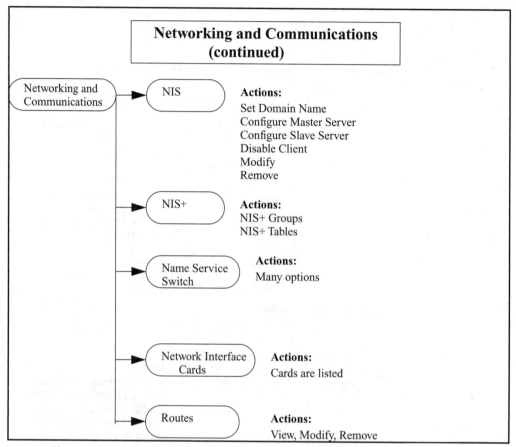

Networking and Communications (continued)

Networking and Communications

NIS

Actions:
Set Domain Name
Configure Master Server
Configure Slave Server
Disable Client
Modify
Remove

NIS+

Actions:
NIS+ Groups
NIS+ Tables

Name Service Switch

Actions:
Many options

Network Interface Cards

Actions:
Cards are listed

Routes

Actions:
View, Modify, Remove

Figure 12-13　*Networking and Communications* Menu Structure (cont.)

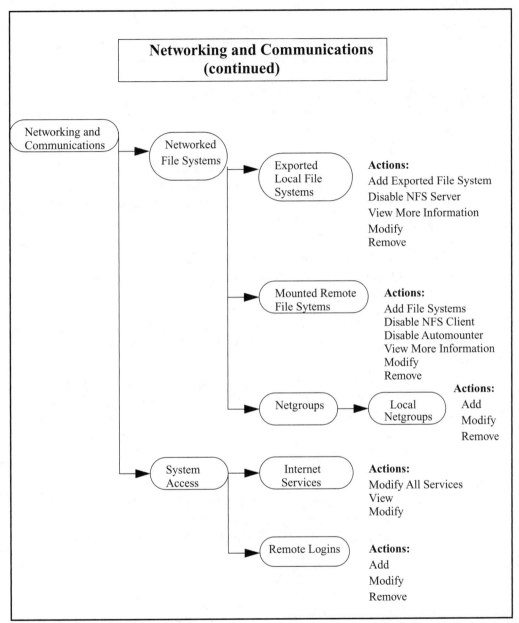

Figure 12-14 *Networking and Communications* Menu Structure (cont.)

Bootable Devices

The *Bootable Devices* area is further subdivided into three subareas: *DHCP Device Groups Booting From This Server, Devices for Which Boot Requests Are Relayed to Remote Servers*, and *Fixed-Address Devices Booting From This Server*. I briefly describe each subarea and its use. DHCP (Dynamic Host Configuration Protocol) is now available on HP-UX and is used by many services.

The *DHCP Device Groups Booting From This Server* subarea is where the device groups can be configured. Each group would contain a set of IP addresses for use by that device group. Devices could be such things as specific types of printers or specific types of terminals.

In the *Devices for Which Boot Requests Are Relayed to Remote Servers* subarea, you can view information about Bootstrap Protocol (Bootp) client devices that get their booting information from remote Bootp or DHCP servers. Information is displayed on the client or client groups, including the IP addresses of the remote servers and the maximum number of hops a boot request from a client or client group can be relayed.

In the *Fixed-Address Devices Booting From This Server* subarea, you can specify systems that boot from your system using Bootstrap Protocol (Bootp) or DHCP. Bootp is a means by which a system can discover network information and boot automatically. The Bootp software must be loaded on your system in order for other devices to use it as a boot source. (See the **swlist** command in Chapter 2 regarding how to list software installed on your system.) In this subarea, you can add, modify, or remove a Bootp device. In addition, you can enable or disable the Bootp Server. Similarly, DHCP allows the client to use one of a pool of IP addresses to boot automatically. Applications such as Ignite-UX can be configured to use this protocol.

DNS (BIND)

Domain Name Service (DNS) is a name server used to resolve host-name-to-IP addressing. HP-UX uses BIND, which is one of the name services that can be used to implement DNS. A DNS server is responsible for the resolution of all host names on a network or subnet. Each DNS client relies on the server to resolve all IP address-to-host name issues on the client's behalf. A boot file is used by the server to locate database files. The database files map host names to IP addresses and IP addresses to host names. Through SAM, a DNS server can be easily set up.

Hosts

The Hosts subarea is used to maintain the default gateway and remote hosts on your system. When you enter this subarea, you receive a list of hosts specified on your system. This information is retrieved from the **/etc/hosts** file on your system.

You can then *Add* a new host, *Specify Default Gateway*, *Modify* one of the hosts, or *Remove* one of the hosts, all from the *Actions* menu. When adding a host, you are asked for information pertaining to the host, including its Internet Address, system name, aliases for the system, and comments.

NIS

Network Information Service (NIS) is a database system used to propagate common configuration files across a network of systems. Managed on a master server are such files as **/etc/passwd**, **/etc/hosts**, and **/etc/auto***, files used by automounter. Formerly called "yellow pages," NIS converts these files to its own database files, called *maps*, for use by clients in the NIS domain. When a client requests information, such as when a user logs in and enters their password, the information is retrieved from the server rather than from the client's system. Thus, this information needs to be maintained only on the server.

Through SAM, the NIS master server, slave servers, and clients can be configured, enabled, disabled, and removed. Once the master, slaves, and clients are established, you can easily build, modify, and push the various maps to the slaves.

NIS is not available on trusted systems.

NIS+

HP-UX 11i supports NIS+, which is not an enhancement of NIS, but rather a new service that includes standard and trusted systems and non-HP-UX systems. If you already use NIS, a compatibility mode version of NIS+ allows servers to answer requests from both NIS and NIS+ clients. When NIS+ is configured on a trusted system, in the *Auditing and Security* area of SAM, a new subarea, *Audited NIS+ Users*, is displayed.

Name Service Switch

The Name Service Switch file, **/etc/nsswitch.conf**, can now be configured through SAM. This service allows you to prioritize which name service (FILES, NIS, NIS+, DNS, or COMPAT) to use to look up information. Unless you specifically use one of these services, the default of FILES should be used. The FILES designation supports the use of the local **/etc** directory for such administrative files as **/etc/passwd**, **/etc/hosts**, and **/etc/ services**. (COMPAT is used with the compatibility mode of NIS+.)

    More information about the Name Service Switch file and its setup is described in the HP-UX manual *Installing and Administering NFS Services*.

Network Interface Cards

The Network Interface Cards subarea is used to configure any networking cards in your system. You can *Enable, Disable*, and *Modify* networking cards, as well as *Modify System Name,* all from the *Actions* menu. Under *Add IP Logical Interface,* you can add additional logical IP addresses to an existing network card. The *Network Interface Cards* screen lists the network cards installed on your system.

Network Services

The Network Services subarea enables or disables *some* of the network services on your system. This screen has three columns, which are the Name, Status, and Description of the network services.

Network File Systems

The Network File Systems subarea is broken down into *Exported Local File Systems, Mounted Remote File Systems,* and *Netgroups.* NFS is broken down into these first two areas because you can export a local file system without mounting a remote file system, and vice versa. This means that you can manage these independently of one another. You may have an NFS server in your environment that won't mount remote file systems, and you may have an NFS client that mounts only remote file systems and never exports its local file system.

Under *Exported Local File Systems,* you can select the file systems you want to export. The first time you enter this screen, you have no exported file systems listed. When you select *Add Exported File System* from the *Actions* menu, you enter such information as:

- Local directory name

- User ID

- Whether or not to allow asynchronous writes

- Permissions

After this exported file system is added, you can select it and choose from a number of *Actions,* including *Modify* and *Remove.*

Under *Mounted Remote File Systems,* you have listed for you all the directories and files that are mounted using NFS. These can be either mounted or unmounted on demand with the automounter. After selecting one of the mounted file systems, you can perform various *Actions.* For every remote file system mounted, you have the following columns:

- *Mount Directory,* which displays the name of the local directory name used to mount the remote directory

- *Type*, which is either *NFS* for standard NFS or *Auto* for automounter (see the following paragraph)

- *Remote Server*, which displays the name of the remote system where the file or directory is mounted

- *Remote Directory*, which is the name of the directory under which the directory is remotely mounted

Think about whether you want to use the NFS automounter. With automounter, you mount a remote file or directory on demand, that is, when you need it. Using a master map, you can specify which files and directories will be mounted when needed. The files and directories are not continuously mounted with automounter, resulting in more efficiency as far as how system resources are used. There is, however, some overhead time associated with mounting a file or directory on-demand, as opposed to having it continuously mounted. From a user standpoint, this may be slightly more undesirable, but from an administration standpoint, using the automounter offers advantages. Because SAM manages the automounter, there is little additional work you must perform to enable it.

System Access

The System Acess subarea is broken down into *Internet Services* and *Remote Logins*.

When you select *Internet Services,* the screen lists the networking services that are started by the Internet daemon **/usr/sbin/inetd**. I previously covered **/etc/inetd.conf**, which is a configuration file that lists all the network services supported by a system that is read by **inetd**. There is also a security file, **/var/adm/inetd.sec**, which serves as a security check for **inetd**. Although many other components are involved, you can view **inetd**, **/etc/ inetd.conf**, and **/var/adm/inetd.sec** as working together to determine what network services are supported and the security level of each.

Listed for you in the *System Access* subarea are *Service Name, Description, Type*, and *System Permission*. Figure 12-15 shows the defaults for my system.

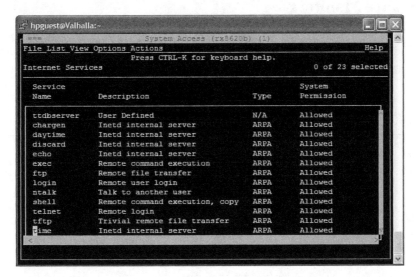

Figure 12-15   *System Access* - Internet Services Window

You could change the permission for any of these entries by selecting them, using the *Modify* command from the *Actions* menu, and selecting the desired permissions.

Remote Logins manages security restrictions for remote users who access the local system. Two HP-UX files are used to manage users. The file **/etc/hosts.equiv** handles users, and **/.rhosts** handles superusers (root). When you enter this subarea, you get a list of users and the restrictions on each user. You can then *Add, Remove*, or *Modify* login security. Keep in mind that **ssh** might be a better solution than **hosts.equiv** and **/.rhosts**.

Partition Manager

parmgr manages node partitions (nPartitions) and can be invoked through SAM or at the command line. **parmgr** is covered in Chapter 17, "Node Partitions (nPartitions) and Management Processor Overview," along with many other techniques for managing nPartitions.

Performance Monitors

Under *Performance Monitors,* you can view the performance of your system in several different areas, such as disk and virtual memory. Figure 12-16 shows the menu hierarchy of *Performance Monitors*.

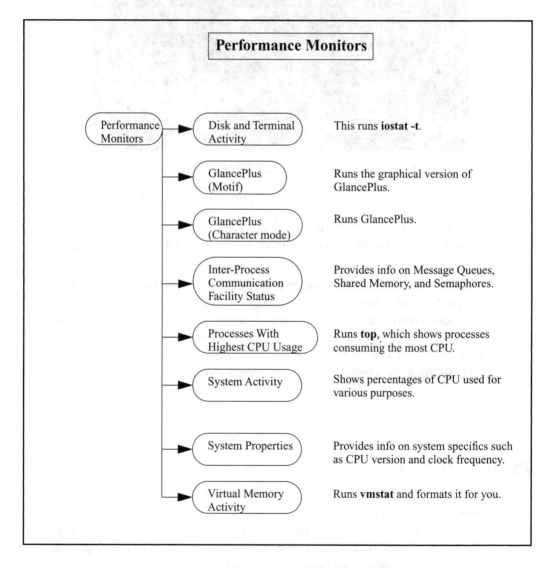

Figure 12-16   *Performance Monitors* Menu Structure

Performance Monitors provides you with a window into several areas of your system. An introduction to some HP-UX performance tools appears in Chapter 13, "Introduction to HP-UX Performance Tools." This chapter is devoted to getting a handle on how your system resources are being used, including many of the selections in SAM. If you are serious about becoming familiar with the tools available on your system to help you understand how your system resources are being used, you should read the text *HP-UX 11i Tuning and Performance (2nd Edition)* by Robert F. Sauers.

Disk and Terminal Activity

Selecting *Disk and Terminal Activity* opens a window that shows the output of **iostat -t**. I include the description of **iostat** from Chapter 15, "Configuring and Using Networking," to save you the trouble of flipping ahead. When the *Disks and Terminal Activity* window with the output of **iostat** is open, it shows a single **iostat** output. When you press *Return,* the window is automatically closed for you. (**iostat** is covered in Chapter 15).

GlancePlus

GlancePlus is available here if it is installed on your system. The character interface to GlancePlus is covered in Chapter 13.

Inter-Process Communication Facility Status

Inter-Process Communication Facility Status shows categories of information related to communication between processes. You receive status on Message Queues, Shared Memory, and Semaphores. This is a status window only, so again, when you press *Return,* and the window closes.

Processes with Highest CPU Usage

Processes with Highest CPU Usage is a useful window that lists the processes consuming the most CPU on your system. Such useful information as the *Process ID*, its *Resident Set Size*, and the *Percentage of CPU* it is consuming are listed.

System Activity

System Activity provides a report of CPU utilization. You receive the following list:

%usr	Percentage of CPU spent in user mode
%sys	Percentage of CPU spent in system mode
%wio	Percentage of CPU idle with some processes waiting for I/O, such as virtual memory pages moving in or moving out
%idle	Percentage of CPU completely idle

System Properties

System Properties gives you a great overview of system specifics. Included here are those hard-to-find items, such as processor information, CPU version, clock frequency, kernel support (32-bit or 64-bit), memory information, operating system version, and network IP and MAC addresses.

Virtual Memory Activity

Virtual Memory Activity runs the **vmstat** command, which is covered in Chapter 13. Some of the columns of **vmstat** are moved around a little when the *Virtual Memory Activity* window is open for you.

Peripheral Devices

With *Peripheral Devices,* you can view any I/O cards installed in your system and peripherals connected to your system. These include both used and unused devices. You can also quickly configure any peripheral, including printers, plotters, tape drives, terminals, modems, and disks. This is a particularly useful area in SAM, because configuring peripherals in HP-UX is tricky. You perform one procedure to connect a printer, a different procedure to connect a disk, and so on, when you use the command line. In SAM, these procedures are menu-driven and therefore much easier.

Two of the six subareas, *Disks and File Systems* and *Printers and Plotters,* have their own dedicated hierarchy within SAM and are covered in this chapter. I don't cover these again in this section. The other four subareas, *Cards, Device List, Tape Drives*, and *Terminals and Modems,* are covered in this section.

It's impossible to cover every possible device that can be viewed and configured in SAM. What I do is give examples of what you would see reported as devices on a server so that you can get a feel for what you can do under *Peripheral Devices* with SAM. From what I show here, you should be comfortable with letting SAM help you configure peripherals.

Figure 12-17 shows the hierarchy of *Peripheral Devices.*

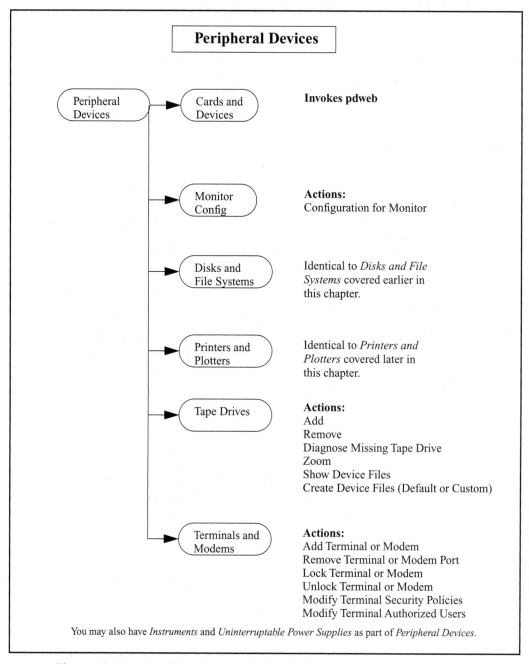

Figure 12-17   *Peripheral Devices* Menu Structure

Cards and Devices

When you select *Cards and Devices,* SAM brings up the Peripheral Devices
tool (pd) in your browser. Figure 12-18 shows the pd browser screen.

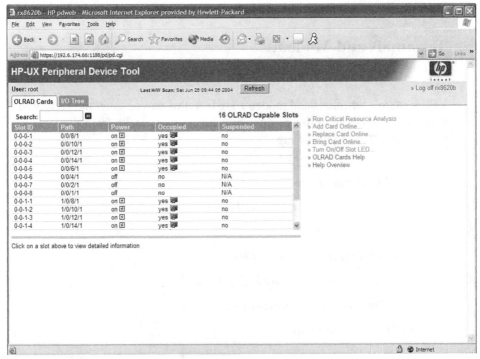

Figure 12-18   Peripheral Devices Tool (pd) Screen Showing *Cards*

Figure 12-18 shows all the slots and paths for the rx8620. To replace
one of the cards online or add a card online, use the menus on the right. This
technique is easy to perform with the system running and is safe.

Tape Drives

Tape Drives lists the tape drives connected to your system. You are shown the *Hardware Path*, *Driver*, and *Description* for each tape drive. You can add, remove, and diagnose tape drives, list tape drive device files, and add new tape drive device files.

Terminals and Modems

Your system's terminals and modems are listed when you enter the Terminals and Modems subarea. You can perform a variety of tasks from the *Actions* menu, including the following:

- *Add Terminal or Modem*
- *Remove Terminal or Modem Port*
- *Lock Terminal or Modem Port*
- *Unlock Terminal or Modem Port*
- *Modify Terminal Security Policies*
- *Modify Terminal Authorized Users*
- *Additional Information*

Uninterruptable Power Supplies

Your system's uninterruptable power supplies are listed when you enter the Uninterruptable Power Supplies area, including the UPS type, device file of the UPS, hardware path, port number, and whether shutdown is enabled. The *Actions* you can select are *Modify Global Configuration, Add, Zoom, Remove,* and *Modify.*

Printers and Plotters

Printers and Plotters is divided into two subareas: *Print Server Configuration* and *LP Spooler*. Figure 12-19 shows the hierarchy of *Printers and Plotters*.

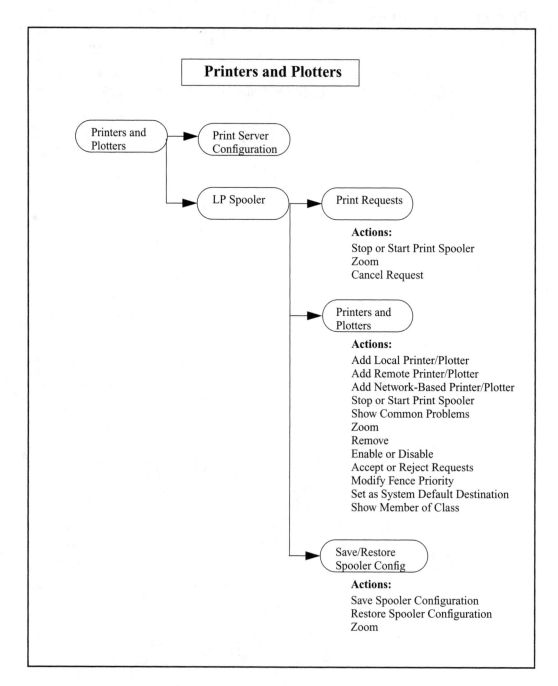

Figure 12-19   *Printers and Plotters* Menu Structure

Print Requests

Under *Print Requests,* you can manage the print spooler and specific print jobs. You can start or stop the print spooler and cancel print jobs. The following information on print requests is listed:

Request ID   An ID is associated with each print job. This is the Printer Name followed by a number.

Owner   The name of the user who requested the print job.

Priority   The priority of a print job is assigned when the job is submitted. The **-p** option of **lp** can be used to assign a priority to a job. Each print destination has a default priority, which is assigned to jobs when **-p** is not used on the **lp** command.

File   The name of the file sent to the print queue.

Size   The size of the print job in bytes.

The *Actions* menu allows you to act on print jobs by cancelling them. In addition, the print spooler can be stopped and started.

Printers and Plotters

You can configure both local and remote printers in *Printers and Plotters.* You may also want to investigate JetDirect configuration for HP-UX, which uses TCP/IP. When you select *Add Local Printer/Plotter* from the *Actions* menu and then the appropriate type of printer, a window opens where you can supply the specifics about the printer. Before this window opens, however, you must specify whether the *type* of printer to be added is parallel serial; HP-IB; non-standard device file; or a printer connected to a TSM terminal, as well as to which I/O card to add the printer. One huge advantage to adding the printer using SAM is that this process is entirely menu-driven, so you only have to select from among the information that is supplied.

A window appears to ask you for the following information:

Printer Name You can pick any name for the printer. I usually like to use a name that is somewhat descriptive, such as *ljet5* for a LaserJet 5. The name is limited to 14 alphanumeric characters and underscores.

Printer Model/Interface

SAM supplies a list of all interface models for you when this window is opened. These models are located in the **/usr/lib/lp/model** directory. Each printer has an interface program that is used by the spooler to send a print job to the printer. When an interface model is selected, the model is copied to **/etc/lp/interface/**<*printer-name*>, where it becomes the printer's interface program. Models can be used without modification, or you can create customized interface programs.

Printer Class You can define a group of printers to be in a class, which means that print requests won't go to a specific printer; instead, they will go to the first available printer within the class. (This is optional.)

Default Request Priority

This request defines the default priority level of all requests sent to this printer.

Default Destination

Users who do not specify a printer when requesting a print job have the print request sent to the default printer.

You can use SAM to view printers or you can use the **lpstat** command to show the printers configured on a system, as shown in the following example:

```
$ /usr/bin/lpstat -t
scheduler is running
system default destination: ljet5
members of class laser:
        ljet5
device for ljet5: /dev/c1t0d0_lp
ljet5 accepting requests since Nov 21 22:45
printer ljet5 is idle. enabled since Nov 21 22:45
        fence priority : 0
no entries
```

As with all the other tasks that SAM helps you with, you can manage printers and plotters manually or you can use SAM. Not only does SAM make this easier for you, but I have also had nothing but good results having SAM do this for me. As you go through the SAM Log file, you see a variety of **lp** commands that were issued. Some of the more common commands, including the **lpstat** command issued earlier, are listed in Table 12-1.

Table 12-1   lp Commands

Command	Description
/usr/sbin/accept	Start accepting jobs to be queued
/usr/bin/cancel	Cancel a print job that is queued
/usr/bin/disable	Disable a device for printing
/usr/bin/enable	Enable a device for printing
/usr/sbin/lpfence	Set minimum priority for spooled file to be printed
/usr/bin/lp	Queue a job or jobs for printing
/usr/sbin/lpadmin	Configure the printing system with the options provided
/usr/sbin/lpmove	Move printing jobs from one device to another

Table 12-1   lp Commands (Continued)

Command	Description
/usr/sbin/lpsched	Start the **lp** scheduling daemon
/usr/sbin/lpshut	Stop the **lp** scheduling daemon
/usr/bin/lpstat	Show the status of printing based on the options provided
/usr/sbin/reject	Stop accepting jobs to be queued

Save/Restore Spooler Configuration

Occasionally, the spooler can get into an inconsistent state (usually, something else has to go wrong with your system that ends up somehow changing or renaming some of the spooler configuration files). SAM keeps a saved version of the spooler's configuration each time it is used to make a change (only the most recent one is saved). This saved configuration can be restored by SAM to recover from the spooler having gotten into an inconsistent state. Your latest configuration is automatically saved by SAM, provided that you used SAM to create the configuration as opposed to issuing **lp** commands at the command line, and it can be restored with *Restore Spooler Configuration* from *Save/Restore Spooler Config*. This screen allows you to save your current spooler configuration or restore a previously saved spooler configuration.

Process Management

Process Management is broken down into two areas that allow you to control and schedule processes. *Process Control* allows you to control an individual process by performing such tasks as viewing it, changing its *nice* priority, killing it, stopping it, or continuing it. You can also view and schedule **cron** jobs under *Scheduled Cron Jobs*. Figure 12-20 shows the menu hierarchy of *Process Management*.

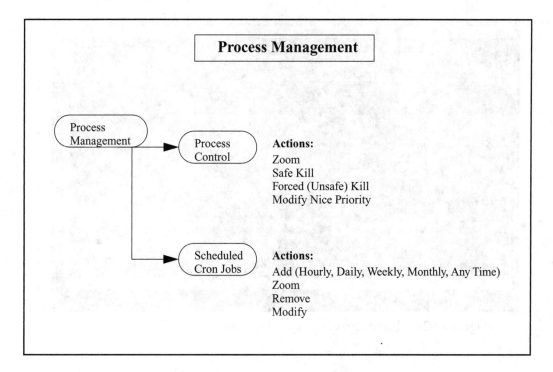

Figure 12-20   *Process Management* Menu Structure

Process Control

When you pick *Process Control,* SAM lists the processes on your system
and allows you to perform various actions. Using *Process Control* is a much
easier way to control the processes on your system than is executing commands such as **ps**, **nice**, etc. Figure 12-21 shows a partial listing of the
processes.

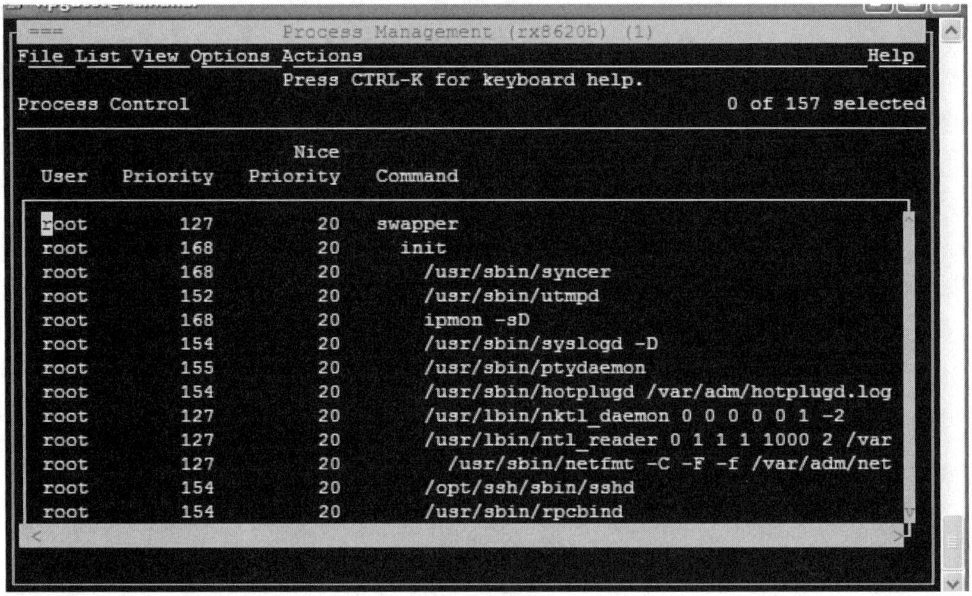

Figure 12-21   Partial *Process Control* Listing.

There are the four columns of information listed for.

• *User* - The name of the user who owns the process.

• *Priority* - The priority of the process determines its scheduling by the CPU. The lower the number, the higher the priority. Unless you modify these priorities, they will be the default priorities. Changing the priority is done with the **nice** command.

• *Nice Priority* - If you have a process that you want to run at a lower or higher priority, you could change this value. The lower the value, the higher the CPU scheduling priority.

• *Command* - Lists the names of all the commands currently being run or executed on the system.

In addition to these four columns, there are several others you can specify to be included in the list by selecting *Columns* from the *View* menu. You can include such information as the *Process ID, Parent Process ID, Processor Utilization, Core Image Size*, and so on. Adding *Processor Utilization* as a column, for example, shows me how much of the processor all processes are consuming, including SAM.

You can now select one of the processes and an *Action* to perform.

When you select a process to kill and pick *Safe Kill* from the *Actions* menu, you see a message that indicates the process number killed and that it may take a few minutes to kill it in order to terminate cleanly. If you select a process to kill and pick *Forced Kill* from the *Actions* menu, you don't get any feedback; SAM just kills the process and you move on.

Chapter 11 "HP System Insight Manager (HP SIM)," covered the **kill** command. To save you the trouble of flipping I include some of the information related to **kill** here. The **kill** command can be either **/usr/bin/kill** or **kill**, which is part of the POSIX shell. The POSIX shell is the default shell for HP-UX 11i. The other shells provide their own **kill** commands as well. We use the phrase "kill a process" in the UNIX world all the time, I think, because it has a powerful connotation associated with it. What we are really saying is that we want to terminate a process. This termination is done with a signal. The most common signal to send is "SIGKILL," which terminates the process. There are other signals you can send to the process, but SIGKILL is the most common. As an alternative to sending the signal, you could send the corresponding signal number. Here is a list of signal numbers and their corresponding signals:

Signal Number	Signal
0	SIGNULL
1	SIGHUP
2	SIGINT
3	SIGQUIT
9	SIGKILL
15	SIGTERM
24	SIGSTOP
25	SIGTSTP
26	SIGCONT

I obtained this list of processes from the **kill** manual page.

To **kill** a process with a process ID of *234*, you would issue the following command:

```
$ kill -9 234
  |    |   |
  |    |   |> process id (PID)
  |    |> signal number
  |> kill command to terminate the process
```

The final selection from the *Actions* menu is to *Modify Nice Priority* of the process you have selected. If you were to read the manual page on **nice**, you would be happy to see that you can modify this with SAM. Modifying the **nice** value in SAM simply requires you to select a process and specify its new **nice** value within the acceptable range.

Scheduling Cron Jobs

The *Scheduled Cron Jobs* menu selection lists all the **cron** jobs you have scheduled and allows you to *Add, Zoom, Remove*, and *Modify* **cron** jobs through the *Actions* menu. **cron** was described earlier in this chapter in the section, "Backup and Recovery." I previously included some of the **cron** background covered earlier to save you the trouble of flipping.

The **crontab** file schedules jobs that are automatically executed by **cron**. **crontab** files are in the **/var/spool/cron/crontabs** directory. **cron** is a program that runs other programs at the specified time. **cron** reads files that specify the operation to be performed and the date and time it is to be performed.

The format of entries in the **crontab** file is as follows:

minute   hourmonth   day   month   weekday   user name   command

   minute - the minute of the hour, from 0-59
   hour - the hour of the day, from 0-23
   monthday - the day of the month, from 1-31
   month - the month of the year, from 1-12
   weekday - the day of the week, from 0 (Sunday) - 6 (Saturday)
   user name - the user who runs the command if necessary
   command - specifies the command line or script file to run

You have many options in the **crontab** file to specify the *minute, hour, monthday, month,* and *weekday* to perform a task. You could list one entry in a field and then a space, several entries in any field separated by a comma, two entries separated by a dash indicating a range, or an asterisk, which corresponds to all possible entries for the field.

To list the contents of a **crontab** file, issue the **crontab -l** command.

Resource Management

Event Monitoring Service (EMS) is under Resource Management. You can perform a variety of EMS-related functions, such as changing the polling interval and specifying notification to such places as the console or an email address.

With EMS, you can add monitoring requests, such as the number of users and be notified when the user count exceeds a value. You specify the polling interval, such as 30 seconds and the means by which you'd like to be notified, such as email. You can create many other requests in EMS, and I encourage you to experiment with it through SAM.

Routine Tasks

The following subareas exist under *Routine Tasks* in SAM:

• Backup and Recovery

• Selective File Removal

• System Log Files

• System Shutdown

Figure 12-22 shows the hierarchy of *Routine Tasks*. Note that *Backup and Recovery* is identical to the SAM top-level *Backup and Recovery* area discussed earlier in this chapter.

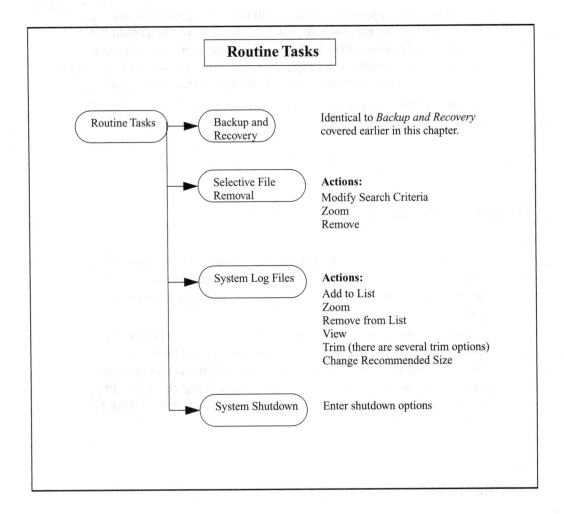

Figure 12-22   *Routine Tasks* Menu Structure

Backup and Recovery

This is identical to the *Backup and Recovery* area covered earlier in this chapter.

Selective File Removal

Selective File Removal allows you to search for files to remove. You can specify a variety of criteria for selecting files to remove, including the following:

Type of file	There are three different file types you can search for: *Large Files, Unowned Files*, and *Core Files*. A pop-up menu allows you to select which of these to search for. With *Large Files,* you search for files of a minimum size that haven't been modified in the specified time. *Unowned Files* are owned by someone other than a valid system user. *Core Files* contain a core image of a terminated process when the process was terminated under certain conditions. Core files are usually related to a problem with a process and contain such information as data, stack, and so on.
Mount Points	Specify whether you want to search across non-NFS mount points. If you select *Yes,* this means that the search includes mount points on your system, but does not extend to NFS mount points. I choose not to include other mount points in the example.
Beginning Path	Your search can begin at any point in the system hierarchy. You can specify the start point of the search in this field. If you want to search only the **/home** directory for files, change this entry to **/home** and you search only that directory, as I did in the example.
Minimum Size	Specify the smallest size file (in bytes) that you want to search for. Files smaller than this size will not be reported as part of the search. The minimum size in the example is 500,000 bytes.

Last Modification

> If you select *Large Files*, you can make an entry in this field. You enter the minimum number of days since the file was last modified, and files that have been modified within that time period are excluded from the search. This is *30* days in the example.

The way to approach removing files is to start with an exceptionally large file size and work your way down in size. It may be that you have a few "unexpected" large files on your system that you can remove and ignore the smaller files.

System Log Files

System Log Files manages the size of your system log files. Log files are generated by HP-UX for a variety of reasons, including backup, shutdown, **cron**, and so on. Your applications may very well generate log files as well. Some of these log files can grow in size indefinitely, creating a potential catastrophe on your system by growing and crashing your system. You can be proactive and manage these log files in this subarea.

SAM is aware of many of the log files generated by HP-UX. When you enter the *System Log Files* subarea, information related to these log files is listed. You can add to the list of log files SAM knows about and have a complete list of log files presented to you each time you enter this subarea. SAM lists the following information related to log files each time you enter this subarea. You may have to increase the size of the window to see all this information:

File Name　　　The full path name of the log file.

Percent Full　　SAM has what it thinks should be the maximum size of a log file. You can change this size by selecting *Change Recommended Size* from the

Actions menu. The *Percent Full* is the percentage of the recommended size that the log file consumes.

Current Size

The size of the file in bytes is listed. You may want to take a look at this. The current size of a log file may be much bigger than you would like. You could then change the recommended size and quickly see which files are greater than 100 percent. The converse may also be true. You may think that the recommended size for a log file is far too small and change the recommended size to a larger value. In either case, you would like to quickly see which files are much bigger than recommended.

Recommended Size

What you define as the recommended size for the file. Check to make sure that you agree with this value.

Present on System

Yes if this file is indeed present on your system; *No* if it is not present on your system. If a file is not present on your system and it simply does not apply to you, you can select *Remove from List* from the *Actions* menu. For example, you may not be running UUCP and therefore want to remove all the UUCP-related log files.

File Type

The only file types listed are *ASCII* and *Non-ASCII*. I found it interesting that **/var/sam/log/samlog** was not one of the log files listed. This is not an ASCII file and must be viewed through *View SAM Log* from the *Actions* menu, but it is indeed a log file that I thought would appear on the list.

You can trim a log file using the *Trim* command from the *Actions* menu. You then have several options for trimming the file which have to do with the size of the file when the trim is complete and so on.

System Shutdown

SAM offers you the following three ways to shut down your system:

• Halt the System

• Reboot (Restart) the System

• Go to Single-User State

In addition, you can specify the number of minutes before shutdown occurs.

Run SAM on Remote Systems

I think SAM is great. If it works well on one system, then you, as the system administrator, might as well use it on other systems from a central point of control. *Run SAM on Remote Systems* allows you to set up the system on which you will run SAM remotely from a central point of control.

You can specify any number of remote systems to be controlled by a central system. With the *Actions* menu, you can

Add System   A window opens up in which you can specify the name of the remote system that you want to administer locally.

Run SAM   You can select the remote system on which you want to run SAM.

Remove System(s)

Remote systems can be removed from the list of systems on which you will run SAM remotely.

Software Management

Software Management under SAM uses Software Distributor-HP-UX (I call this Software Distributor), which was covered in Chapter 2. SAM gives you an interface to Software Distributor that allows you to perform software management by selecting the task you want to perform. In the end, all the same Software Distributor commands are run, so I won't cover those again in this section. The following subareas exist under *Software Management* in SAM:

- Copy Software to Depot

- Install Software to Local Host

- Remove Depot Software

- Remove Local Host Software

- View Depot Software

- View Installed Software

Chapter 3 covers Software Distributor, which is invoked when SAM tasks are selected.

Time

The *Time* area of SAM allows you to configure Network Time Protocol or NTP, and set the system clock. NTP is a service that allows you to synchronize the time on all of your systems using NTP server. I won't cover this area of SAM other than to say that NTP can be a little tricky to configure, so using SAM for this greatly simplifies NTPP.

SAM Log Viewer

The SAM Log Viewer, selected from the Options menu with View SAM Log..., keeps a full log of commands that were run. You can run the same commands shown in the log file at the command line. I show the log file for mounting a DVD-ROM in this example.

To load software from DVD-ROM, you must first mount the DVD-ROM. This can be done at the command line or in SAM. Figure12-23 shows the SAM log file after the DVD-ROM was mounted and the directory **dvdrom** was searched for in the SAM log file.

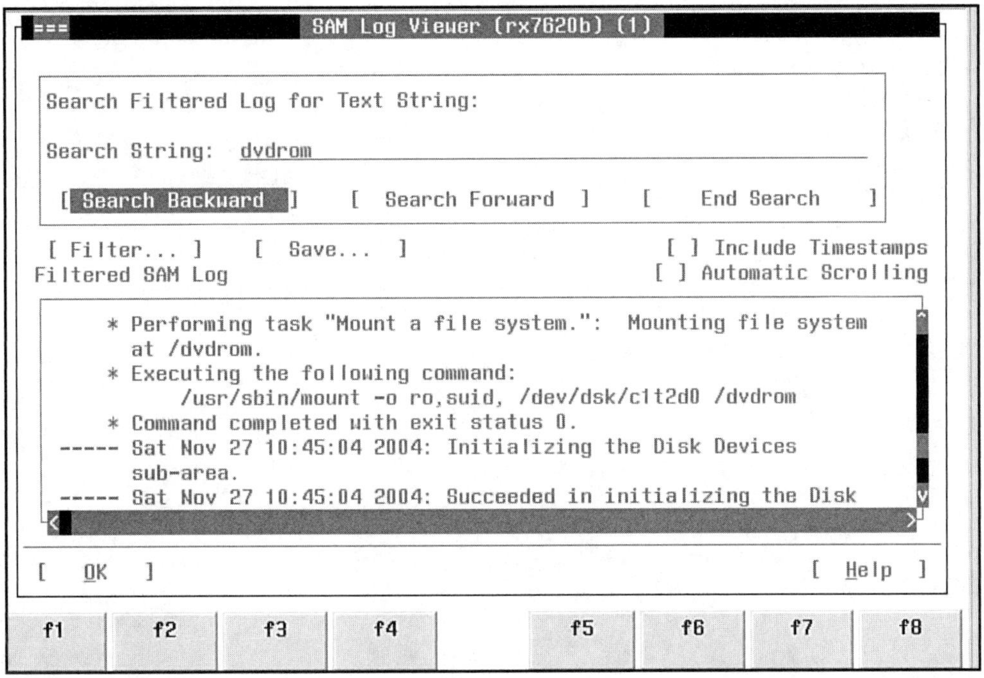

```
┌─┌───────────────────────────────────────────────────────────────────┐
│ ===          SAM Log Viewer (rx7620b) (1)                             │
│ ┌───────────────────────────────────────────────────────────────┐   │
│ │ Search Filtered Log for Text String:                          │   │
│ │                                                                │   │
│ │ Search String:  dvdrom_____│   │
│ │ [ Search Backward ]    [  Search Forward  ]    [   End Search  ]│   │
│ │                                                                │   │
│ │ [ Filter... ]   [  Save...  ]             [ ] Include Timestamps│   │
│ │ Filtered SAM Log                          [ ] Automatic Scrolling│  │
│ │ ┌──────────────────────────────────────────────────────────┐▲ │   │
│ │ │   * Performing task "Mount a file system.":  Mounting file system│ │
│ │ │     at /dvdrom.                                             │  │   │
│ │ │   * Executing the following command:                       │  │   │
│ │ │        /usr/sbin/mount -o ro,suid, /dev/dsk/c1t2d0 /dvdrom  │  │   │
│ │ │   * Command completed with exit status 0.                  │  │   │
│ │ │ ----- Sat Nov 27 10:45:04 2004: Initializing the Disk Devices │ │   │
│ │ │     sub-area.                                               │  │   │
│ │ │ ----- Sat Nov 27 10:45:04 2004: Succeeded in initializing the Disk│▼│ │
│ │ │◄                                                          ►│  │   │
│ │ └──────────────────────────────────────────────────────────┘  │   │
│ │ [   OK   ]                                        [  Help  ]   │   │
│ └───────────────────────────────────────────────────────────────┘   │
│ ┌────┐┌──────┐┌──────┐┌──────┐   ┌──────┐┌──────┐┌──────┐┌──────┐    │
│ │ f1 ││  f2  ││  f3  ││  f4  │   │  f5  ││  f6  ││  f7  ││  f8  │    │
│ └────┘└──────┘└──────┘└──────┘   └──────┘└──────┘└──────┘└──────┘    │
└───────────────────────────────────────────────────────────────────────┘
```

Figure 12-23   SAM Log Viewer Showing mount of **dvdrom**

Figure 12-23 shows the **mount** command of the DVD-ROM that could have been issued at the command line. If you're unsure of the device file of the DVD-ROM, issue **ioscan -funC disk** and all the disk devices, including the DVD-ROM, are listed.

You can search for a string, as I did in this example, or scroll through the log file to see all commands that were issued.

Chapter 13

Introduction to HP-UX Performance Tools

Introduction

This chapter is an introduction to performance analysis. Don't think of using this as a guide to perform detailed performance analysis. For that, you need: *HP-UX 11i Tuning and Performance (2nd Edition)* by Robert F. Sauers. Mr. Sauers' book provides both the background in performance analysis as well as the tools required to perform detailed performance analysis.

This chapter provides an overview of many commonly used commands for analyzing performance as well as an introduction to GlancePlus/UX (GlancePlus). Although I don't perform detailed performance analysis, I always check the basics on a system using these commands and Glance to look for glaring problems and see if additional analysis is required. Knowledge of these commands and Glance is important to have in your HP-UX system administration bag-of-tricks.

Although I focus on quick snapshots that take but a few seconds to create, you may want to run long-range capacity planning programs for weeks or months before you even begin to analyze the data they produce. For this long-range work, you can use HP OpenView Performance manager, agents, and monitor.

The first section covers standard HP-UX and, in most cases, UNIX commands.

Standard UNIX Commands

To begin, I cover some commands you can issue from the HP-UX prompt to
give you some information about your system. These commands vary somewhat among different UNIX variants, but most of these commands exist on
most UNIX variants. The commands I cover are

- **iostat**
- **vmstat**
- **netstat**
- **ps**
- **kill**
- **showmount**
- **swapinfo and swap**
- **sar**
- **timex**

I first look at each of these commands so that you get an understanding
of the output produced by them and how this output may be used. There are
manual pages on your system for these commands, so be sure to look at the
man page for a command if you decide to use it extensively.

I/O and CPU Statistics with iostat (complete)

The **iostat** command gives you an indication of the level of effort the CPU is
putting into I/O and the amount of I/O taking place among your disks and
terminals. The following examples show issuing **iostat** on an HP-UX system. The following HP-UX example includes the -*t* option executed five
times at five-second intervals:

```
# iostat -t 5 5
                    tty              cpu
                  tin tout        us  ni  sy  id
                   1    58         5   1  10  84

    device    bps     sps     msps

    c1t2d0     0      0.0     1.0
```

```
                    tty                 cpu
                tin tout            us  ni  sy  id
                 0    30             0   2  26  72

    device     bps      sps     msps

    c1t2d0     484     249.6     1.0

                    tty                 cpu
                tin tout            us  ni  sy  id
                 0    31             1   3  23  73

    device     bps      sps     msps

    c1t2d0     517     256.1     1.0

                    tty                 cpu
                tin tout            us  ni  sy  id
                 0    35             0   2  23  75

    device     bps      sps     msps

    c1t2d0     456     254.4     1.0

                    tty                 cpu
                tin tout            us  ni  sy  id
                 0   744             1   6  38  55

    device     bps      sps     msps

    c1t2d0     155      83.1     1.0

    #
```

For every terminal you have connected (*tty*), you see a "tin" and "tout," which represent the number of characters read from your terminal and the number of characters written to your terminal, respectively.

For your CPU, you see the percentage of time spent in user mode ("us"), the percentage of time spent running user processes at a low priority called nice ("ni"), the percentage of time spent in system mode ("sy"), and the percentage of time the CPU is idle ("id").

For every locally mounted file system, you receive information on the blocks per second ("bps"), number of seeks per second ("sps"), and number of milliseconds per average seek ("msps"). For disks that are NFS-mounted or disks on client nodes of your server, you do not receive a report; **iostat** reports only on locally mounted file systems.

When viewing the output of **iostat**, there are some parameters to take note of.

First, note the time that your CPU is spending in the four categories shown. The CPU report is produced with the *-t* option. I have worked on systems with poor performance that the administrator assumed to be a result of a slow CPU because the "id" number was very high, indicating that the CPU was actually idle most of the time. If the CPU is mostly idle, the chances are that the bottleneck is not the CPU, but may be I/O, memory, or networking. If the CPU is indeed busy most of the time ("id" is very low), see whether any processes are running "nice" (check the "ni" number). It may be that there are some background processes consuming a lot of CPU time that can be changed to run "nice."

Second, compare the number of transfers taking place. These are usually indicated by something like blocks per second (bps), transfers per second (*tps*), or seeks per second (*sps*). These numbers indicate the amount of activity taking place on a disk. If one volume is consistently much higher than other volumes, it may be performing an inordinate amout of the workload. Notice that the milliseconds per average seek (*msps*) for all disks is always equal to one.

Virtual Memory Statistics with vmstat

vmstat provides virtual memory statistics. It provides information on the status of processes, virtual memory, paging activity, faults, and a breakdown of the percentage of CPU time. In the following examples, the output was produced nine times at five-second intervals. The first argument to the **vmstat** command is the interval; the second is the number of times you would like the output produced:

```
# vmstat 5 9
```

procs			memory				page					faults			cpu		
r	b	w	avm	free	re	at	pi	po	fr	de	sr	in	sy	cs	us	sy	id
5	240	0	17646	3979	2	0	0	0	0	0	0	0	778	193	17	3	80
4	242	0	16722	4106	0	0	0	0	0	0	0	814	20649	258	89	10	2
4	240	0	16649	4106	0	0	0	0	0	0	0	83	18384	218	91	9	0
4	240	0	16468	4106	0	0	0	0	0	0	0	792	19552	273	89	11	1
5	239	0	15630	4012	9	0	0	0	0	0	0	804	18295	270	93	8	-1
5	241	0	16087	3934	6	0	0	0	0	0	0	920	21044	392	89	10	0
5	241	0	15313	3952	11	0	0	0	0	0	0	968	20239	431	90	10	0
4	242	0	16577	4043	3	0	0	0	0	0	0	926	19230	409	89	10	0
6	238	0	17453	4122	0	0	0	0	0	0	0	837	19269	299	89	9	2

You certainly get a lot for your money out of the **vmstat** command. Here is a brief description of the categories of information produced by **vmstat**.

Processes are classified into one of three categories: runnable ("r"), blocked on I/O or short-term resources ("b"), or swapped ("w").

Next, you see information about memory. "avm" is the number of virtual memory pages owned by processes that have run within the last 20 seconds. If this number is roughly the size of physical memory minus your kernel, you are near forced paging. The "free" column indicates the number of pages on the system's free list. It doesn't mean that the process is finished running and these pages won't be accessed again; it just means that they have not been accessed recently. I suggest that you ignore this column.

Next, is paging activity. The first field ("re") shows the pages that were reclaimed. These pages made it to the free list but were later referenced and had to be salvaged.

Next you see the number of faults in three categories: interrupts per second, which usually come from hardware ("in"), system calls per second ("sy"), and context switches per second ("cs").

The final output is CPU usage percentage for user ("us"), system ("sy"), and idle ("id"). The *nice* processes are lumped together with user processes in this output.

If you run an I/O-intensive workload, you may indeed see a much activity in runnable processes ("r"), blocked processes ("b"), and the runnable but swapped ("w") processes. If you have many runnable but swapped processes, you probably have insufficient memory. If you see a lot of waiting on I/O, you probably have an I/O bottleneck.

Network Statistics with netstat

netstat provides information related to network statistics. Because network bandwidth has as much to do with performance as the CPU and memory in some networks, you want to get an idea of the level of network traffic you have.

I use two forms of **netstat** to obtain network statistics. The first is **netstat -i**, which shows the state of interfaces that are autoconfigured. Although **netstat -i** gives a good rundown of the primary LAN interface, such as the network it is on, its name, and so on, it does not show useful statistical information.

The following shows the output of **netstat -i**:

```
[ root : / ]> netstat -i

Name    Mtu   Network      Address      Ipkts      Ierrs Opkts      Oerrs Coll
lan0    1500  10.14.16.0   otcapdv2     70555096   0     69629027   0     0
lo0     4136  loopback     localhost    20205721   0     20205724   0     0
```

netstat provides a concise output. Put another way, most of what you get from **netstat** is useful. Here is a description of the nine fields in the **netstat** example:

Name	The name of your network interface (Name), in this case, "lan0."
Mtu	The "maximum transmission unit," which is the maximum packet size sent by the interface card.
Network	The network address of the LAN to which the interface card is connected (10.14.16.0).
Address	The host name of your system. This is the symbolic name of your system as it appears in the **/etc/hosts** file if your networking is configured to use **/etc/hosts**.

Here is the statistical information:

Ipkts	The number of packets received by the interface card, in this case, "lan0."
Ierrs	The number of errors detected on incoming packets by the interface card.
Opkts	The number of packets transmitted by the interface card.
Oerrs	The number of errors detected during the transmission of packets by the interface card.
Col	The number of collisions that resulted from packet traffic.

netstat provides cumulative data since the node was last powered up; therefore, you might have a long elapsed time over which data was accumulated. If you are interested in seeing useful statistical information, you can use **netstat** with different options. You can also specify an interval to report statistics. I usually ignore the first entry, because it shows all data since the system was last powered up. This means that the data includes non-prime hours when the system was idle. I prefer to view data at the time the system works its hardest. The following examples show running **netstat -I** and specifying the *lan* interface. The **netstat** command is run at an interval of five seconds:

```
[ root : / ]> netstat -I lan0 5
(lan0)-> input      output      (Total)-> input       output
      packets      packets              packets      packets
    70565365     69639133             90773686     89847457
         227          222                  227          222
         377          374                 1243         1240
         266          261                  291          286
         248          241                  255          248
         313          308                  425          420
         335          329                  367          361
         258          254                  258          254
         298          299                  310          311
         278          276                  285          283
         255          249                  289          283
         336          334                  484          482
         268          265                  300          297
         308          297                  308          297
         265          261                  277          273
         329          320                  354          345
         299          295                  306          302
```

With this example, you get multiple outputs of what takes place on the LAN interface, including the totals on the right side of the output. As previously mentioned, you may want to ignore the first output, because it includes information over a long time period. This may include a time when your network was idle, and therefore, the data may not be important to you.

You can specify the network interface on which you want statistics reported by using **-I interface**; in the case of this example, it was **-I** and *lan0*. An interval of five seconds was also used in this example.

You can also obtain information related to routing with **netstat** (see Chapter 15, "Configuring and Using Networking"). The *-r* option to **netstat** shows the routing tables, which you usually want to know about, and the *-n* option can be used to print network addresses as numbers rather than as names. In the following examples, **netstat** is issued with the *-r* option (this will be used when describing the **netstat** output) and the *-rn* options so that you can compare the two outputs:

```
[ root : / ]> netstat -r
Routing tables
Destination        Gateway           Flags   Refs Interface  Pmtu
localhost          localhost         UH         0 lo0        4136
otcapdv2           otcapdv2          UH         0 lan0       4136
10.14.16.0         otcapdv2          U          2 lan0       1500
loopback           localhost         U          0 lo0           0
default            NJSEC6506RTR_VL51
                                     UG         0 lan0          0
```

```
[ root : / ]> netstat -rn
Routing tables
Destination          Gateway           Flags   Refs Interface  Pmtu
127.0.0.1            127.0.0.1         UH         0 lo0         4136
10.14.16.19          10.14.16.19       UH         0 lan0        4136
10.14.16.0           10.14.16.19       U          2 lan0        1500
127.0.0.0            127.0.0.1         U          0 lo0            0
default              10.14.16.1        UG         0 lan0           0
```

With **netstat**, some information is provided about the router, which is the last entry called *default*. The *-r* option shows information about routing, but many other useful options to this command are available. Of particular interest in this output is "Flags," which defines the type of routing that takes place. The following are descriptions of the most common flags:

1=*U*   Route to a *network* via a gateway that is the local host itself.

3=*UG*   Route to a *network* via a gateway that is the remote host.

5=*UH*   Route to a *host* via a gateway that is the local host itself.

7=*UGH*   Route to a *host* via a remote gateway that is a host.

The first line is for the local host, or loopback interface called *lo0* at address 127.0.0.1. (You can see this address in the **netstat -rn** example.) The *UH* flags indicate that the destination address is the local host itself. This Class A address allows a client and server on the same host to communicate with one another via TCP/IP. A datagram sent to the loopback interface won't go out onto the network; it simply goes through the loopback.

The last line is for the default route. This entry says to send packets to 10.14.16.1, as shown in the **netstat -rn** example, if a more specific route can't be found. In this case, the default has a *UG* under *Flags*.

The second line is for the system's network interface, *lan0*. This means to use this network interface for packets to be sent to otcapdv2.

Check Processes with ps

Knowing about the processes running on your system and knowing how to stop them are important to both system administration and performance.

To find the answer to, "What is my system doing?," use **ps -ef**, which provides information about every running process on your system. If, for example, you want to know whether NFS is running, simply type **ps -ef** and look for NFS daemons. Although **ps** tells you every process that is running on your system, it doesn't provide a good summary of the level of system resources being consumed. I would guess that **ps** is the most often issued system administration command. There are a number of options you can use with **ps**. I normally use *e* and *f*, which provide information about every ("*e*") running process and lists this information in full ("*f*"). The following is a greatly abbreviated **ps -ef** output:

```
[ root : / ]> ps -ef
     UID   PID  PPID  C    STIME TTY       TIME COMMAND
    root     0     0  0  Dec  1  ?         0:28 swapper
    root     8     0  0  Dec  1  ?         0:00 supsched
    root     9     0  0  Dec  1  ?         0:00 strmem
    root    10     0  0  Dec  1  ?         0:00 strweld
    root    11     0  0  Dec  1  ?         0:00 strfreebd
    root     2     0  0  Dec  1  ?         0:02 vhand
    root     3     0  0  Dec  1  ?         3:55 statdaemon
    root     4     0  0  Dec  1  ?         0:19 unhashdaemon
    root    12     0  0  Dec  1  ?         0:00 ttisr
    root    13     0  0  Dec  1  ?         0:00 ioconfigd
    root     1     0  0  Dec  1  ?         0:01 init
    root    19     0  0  Dec  1  ?         0:00 lvmkd
    root    20     0  0  Dec  1  ?         0:00 lvmkd
    root    21     0  0  Dec  1  ?         0:00 lvmkd
    root    22     0  0  Dec  1  ?         0:00 lvmkd
    root    23     0  0  Dec  1  ?         0:00 lvmkd
    root    24     0  0  Dec  1  ?         0:00 lvmkd
    root    25     0  0  Dec  1  ?         0:00 lvmschedd
    root    26     0  0  Dec  1  ?         0:00 smpsched
    root    27     0  0  Dec  1  ?         0:00 smpsched
    root    28     0  0  Dec  1  ?         0:00 sblksched
    root    29     0  0  Dec  1  ?         0:00 sblksched
                    .
                    .
                    .
  applvis  4980  4908  0  Dec  1  ?         0:13 RCVOLTM APPS/9393A6A200000000000
000000000000000000000000000000000
  applvis  4981  4908  0  Dec  1  ?         0:42 FNDLIBR FND Concurrent_Processor
MANAGE OLOGIN="APPS/9994A0B200
   oravis  1200     1  0 10:09:03 ?         0:00 oraclevis (LOCAL=NO)
   oravis 29434     1  0 09:16:31 ?         0:00 oraclevis (LOCAL=NO)
     root  2064  3010  0 10:33:27 ?         0:00 <defunct>
   oravis 29108     1  0 09:06:01 ?         0:00 oraclevis (LOCAL=NO)
  applvis 24943  4531  0 06:53:20 ?         0:06 f60webmx webfile=5,89,otcapdv2_9
000_vis
   oravis  4999     1  0  Dec  1  ?         0:55 oraclevis (LOCAL=NO)
   oravis  5001     1  0  Dec  1  ?         3:37 oraclevis (LOCAL=NO)
   oravis  5003     1  0  Dec  1  ?         0:19 oraclevis (LOCAL=NO)
   oravis  5005     1  0  Dec  1  ?         0:39 oraclevis (LOCAL=NO)
   oravis  5007     1  0  Dec  1  ?         0:34 oraclevis (LOCAL=NO)
   oravis  5009     1  0  Dec  1  ?         0:34 oraclevis (LOCAL=NO)
```

```
    oravis  5011    1   0  Dec  1  ?        0:34 oraclevis (LOCAL=NO)
    oravis  5013    1   0  Dec  1  ?        0:34 oraclevis (LOCAL=NO)
    oravis  5015    1   0  Dec  1  ?        0:36 oraclevis (LOCAL=NO)
    oravis  5017    1   0  Dec  1  ?        0:35 oraclevis (LOCAL=NO)
    oravis  5019    1   0  Dec  1  ?        0:34 oraclevis (LOCAL=NO)
    oravis  5021    1   0  Dec  1  ?        0:34 oraclevis (LOCAL=NO)
    oravis  5168    1   0  Dec  1  ?        6:22 oraclevis (LOCAL=NO)
    oravis  1954    1   0 10:30:04 ?        0:00 oraclevis (LOCAL=NO)
  applvis   480  4531   0 09:47:07 ?        0:00 f60webmx webfile=5,94,otcapdv2_9
000_vis
    oravis 23507    1   0 06:07:27 ?        0:00 oraclevis (LOCAL=NO)
    oravis 24264    1   0 06:31:29 ?        0:00 oraclevis (LOCAL=NO)
    oravis 25326    1   0 07:05:17 ?        0:01 oraclevis (LOCAL=NO)
    oravis   516    1   0 09:48:02 ?        0:00 oraclevis (LOCAL=NO)
    oravis  1438    1   0 10:16:02 ?        0:00 oraclevis (LOCAL=NO)
    oravis  1104    1   0 10:06:02 ?        0:00 oraclevis (LOCAL=NO)
      root  1289 1062   0 10:11:53 pts/ta   0:00 telnetd
  applvis   1951 1949   0 10:30:03 ?        0:00 /u02/oracle/visora/8.0.6/discwb4
/bin/dis4ws -session otcapdv2.s
    oravis   773    1   0 09:56:01 ?        0:00 oraclevis (LOCAL=NO)
  applvis   1949 4756   0 10:30:03 ?        0:00 /bin/ksh /u02/oracle/visora/8.0.
6/discwb4/util/runses.sh -sessi
    oravis 24953    1   0 06:53:31 ?        0:00 oraclevis (LOCAL=NO)
      root  1290 1289   0 10:11:54 pts/ta   0:00 -sh
```

This an Oracle development system, so you can see the *oravis* processes. There are many other Oracle-related processes that are also running
but are not shown in the abbreviated output.

The following is a brief description of the headings:

UID	The user ID of the process owner.
PID	The process ID (you can use this number to kill the process).
PPID	The process ID of the parent process.
C	Processor utilization. On a multi-processor system, you may see this number go beyond 100%. It could potentially go to 100% per processor, so a two-processor system may show 200% utilization. This varies among UNIX variants.
STIME	The start time of the process.
TTY	The controlling terminal for the process.
TIME	The cumulative execution time for the process.
COMMAND	The command name and arguments.

ps gives a quick profile of the processes running on your system. To
get more detailed information, you can include the "*l*" option, which
includes a lot of useful additional information, as shown in the following
example:

```
[ root : / ]> ps -efl
  F S        UID   PID  PPID  C PRI NI        ADDR    SZ  WCHAN     STIME TTY TIME COMD

1003 S      root     0     0  0 127 20     c52e18     0 a73064    Dec  1  ?   0:28 swapper

1003 S      root     8     0  0 100 20   4a635040     0 ee0fb0    Dec  1  ?   0:00 supsched

1003 S      root     9     0  0 100 20   4a635180     0 c526c8    Dec  1  ?   0:00 strmem

1003 S      root    10     0  0 100 20   4a6352c0     0 d32f80    Dec  1  ?   0:00 strweld

1003 S      root    11     0  0 100 20   4a635400     0 cacac0    Dec  1  ?   0:00 strfreebd

1003 S      root     2     0  0 128 20   4a635540     0 10a6e50   Dec  1  ?   0:02 vhand

1003 S      root     3     0  0 128 20   4a635680     0 a73064    Dec  1  ?   3:56 statdaemon

1003 S      root     4     0  0 128 20   4a6357c0     0 d238b8    Dec  1  ?   0:19 unhashdaem

1003 S      root    12     0  0 -32 20   4a635900     0 c4ad50    Dec  1  ?   0:00 ttisr


                          .
                          .
                          .

   1 S  applvis  4977  4908  0 154 20   4dd9f440  1439 4de8e528 Dec  1  ?   0:15
RCVOLTM APPS/9393A6A2000000000000000000000000000000000000000000

   1 R     root  2978  1290  2 178 20   505e31c0    61     -  11:00:43 pts/ta  0:00 ps -efl

   1 R  applvis  2657  2655  0 152 20             4d53cec0  - 10:51:04 ?      0:00
/u02/oracle/visora/8.0.6/discwb4/bin/dis4ws -session otcapdv2.s
1001 S   oravis 24953     1  0 154 20   4b3d3480 17264 50c098a8 06:53:31 ?0:00
oraclevis (LOCAL=NO)

   1 S     root  1290  1289  0 158 20   4df50e80   108 50640040 10:11:54 pts/ta  0:00 -sh
[ root : / ]>
```

Each line contains a lot of information so that some of the fields wrap to the next line. In this example, the first column is *F* for flags. *F* provides octal information about whether the process is swapped, in core, a system process, and so on. The octal value sometimes varies from system to system, so check the manual pages for your system to see the octal value of the flags.

S is for state. The state can be sleeping, as indicated by *S* for most of the processes shown in this example, waiting, running, intermediate, terminated, and so on. Again, some of these values may vary from system to system, so check your manual pages.

Some additional useful information in this output are *NI* for the nice value, *ADDR* for the memory address of the process, *SZ* for the size of the process in physical pages, and *WCHAN*, which is the event for which the process is waiting.

Killing a Process

If you issue the **ps** command and find that one of your processes is hung, or if you started a large job that you want to stop, you can do so with the **kill** command. **kill** is a utility that sends a signal to the process you identify. You can **kill** any process that you own. In addition, the superuser can kill almost any process on the system.

To kill a process that you own, simply issue the **kill** command and the Process ID (PID). The following example shows issuing the **ps** command to find all processes owned by *martyp*, killing a process, and checking to see that it has disappeared:

```
martyp $ ps -ef | grep martyp
  martyp 19336 19334 0 05:24:32 pts/4   0:01 -ksh
  martyp 19426 19336 0 06:01:01 pts/4   0:00 grep martyp
  martyp 19424 19336 5 06:00:48 pts/4   0:01 find / -name .login
martyp $ kill 19424
martyp $ ps -ef | grep martyp
  martyp 19336 19334 0 05:24:32 pts/4   0:01 -ksh
  martyp 19428 19336 1 06:01:17 pts/4   0:00 grep martyp
[1] + Terminated              find / -name .login &
martyp $
```

The example shows killing process *19424,* which is owned by *martyp*. We confirm that the process has indeed been killed by reissuing the **ps** command. You can also use the *-u* option to **ps** to list processes with the login name you specify.

You can kill several processes on the command line by issuing **kill** followed by a space-separated list of all the process numbers you want to kill.

Take special care when killing processes if you are logged in as superuser. You may adversely affect the way the system runs and have to manually restart processes or reboot the system.

Signals

When you issue the **kill** command and process number, you are also sending a *signal* associated with the **kill**. We did not specify a *signal* in the **kill** example; however, the default *signal* of 15, or *SIGTERM*, was used. These *signals* are used by the system to communicate with processes. The *signal* of 15 we used to terminate our process is a software termination *signal* that is usually enough to terminate a user process, such as the **find** we had started. A process that is difficult to kill may require the *SIGKILL*, or 9 *signal*. This *signal* causes an immediate termination of the process. I use this only as a last resort because processes killed with *SIGKILL* do not always terminate smoothly. To kill such processes as the shell, you sometimes have to use *SIGKILL*.

You can use either the *signal* name or number. These signal numbers sometimes vary from system to system, so view the manual page for *signal*, usually in section 5, to see the list of *signals* on your system. Here is a list of some of the most frequently used *signal* numbers and corresponding *signals*:

Signal Number	Signal
1	SIGHUP
2	SIGINT
3	SIGQUIT
9	SIGKILL
15	SIGTERM
24	SIGSTOP

To kill a process with id *234* with *SIGKILL*, issue the following command:

```
$ kill -9 234
        |    |  |
        |    |  |> process id (PID)
        |    |> signal number
        |> kill command to terminate the process
```

Show Remote Mounts with showmount

showmount is used to show all remote systems (clients) that have mounted a local file system. **showmount** is useful for determining the file systems that are most often mounted by clients with NFS. The output of **showmount** is particularly easy to read because it lists the host name and directory that was mounted by the client.

NFS servers often end up serving many NFS clients that were not originally intended to be served. This situation ends up consuming additional UNIX system resources on the NFS server, as well as additional network bandwidth. Keep in mind that any data transferred from an NFS server to an NFS client consumes network bandwidth and, in some cases, it may be a substantial amount of bandwith if large files or applications are being transferred from the NFS server to the client. The three following options are available for the **showmount** command:

-**a** prints output in the format "name:directory," as previously shown.
-**d** lists all the local directories that have been remotely
mounted by clients.
-**e** prints a list of exported file systems.

The following are examples of **showmount -d** and **showmount -e**:

```
[ root ]> showmount -d
/crp
/stage
/u01b

[ root ]> showmount -e
export list for otcapdv1:
/stage (everyone)
/u01b  (everyone)
/crp   (everyone)
```

Show System Swap

If your system has insufficient main memory for all the information it needs to work with, it moves pages of information to your swap area or swaps entire processes to your swap area. Pages that were most recently used are kept in main memory, and those not recently used are the first moved out of main memory.

System administrators spend a lot of time determining the right amount of swap space for their systems. Insufficient swap may prevent a system from starting additional processes, hang applications, or not permit additional users to get access to the system. Having sufficient swap prevents these problems from occurring. System administrators usually go about determining the right amount of swap by considering many important factors:

1. How much swap is recommended by the application(s) you run? Use the swap size recommended by your applications. Application vendors tend to be realistic when recommending swap space. There is sometimes competition among application vendors to claim the lowest memory and CPU requirements in order to keep the overall cost of solutions as low as possible, but swap space recommendations are usually realistic.

2. How many applications will you run simultaneously? If you run several applications, sum the swap space recommended for each application you plan to run simultaneously. If you have a database application that recommends 200 MB of swap and a development tool that recommends 100 MB of swap, then configure your system with 300 MB of swap, minimum.

3. Will you use substantial system resources on peripheral functionality such as NFS? The nature of NFS is to provide access to file systems, some of which may be very large, so this use may have an impact on your swap space requirements.

You can view the amount of swap being consumed with **swapinfo**:

```
# swapinfo

            Kb       Kb      Kb   PCT START/     Kb
TYPE     AVAIL     USED    FREE  USED LIMIT RESERVE  PRI  NAME
dev      49152    10532   38620   21%     0       -    1  /dev/vg00/lvol2
dev     868352    10888  759160    1%     0       -    1  /dev/vg00/lvol8
reserve      -   532360 -532360
memory  816360   469784  346576   58%
```

The following is a brief overview of what **swapinfo** gives you.

In the previous example, the "TYPE" field indicates whether the swap was "dev" for device, "reserve" for paging space on reserve, or "memory." Memory is a way to allow programs to reserve more virtual memory than you have hard disk paging space setup for on your system.

"Kb AVAIL" is the total swap space available in 1,024-byte blocks. This includes both used and unused swap.

"Kb USED" is the current number of 1024-byte blocks in use.

"Kb FREE" is the difference between "Kb AVAIL" and "Kb USED."

"PCT USED" is "Kb USED" divided by "Kb AVAIL."

"START/LIMIT" is the block address of the start of the swap area.

"Kb RESERVE" is "-" for device swap or the number of 1024-byte blocks for file system swap.

"PRI" is the priority given to this swap area.

"NAME" is the device name of the swap device.

You can also issue the **swapinfo** command with a series of options. Here are some of the options that you can include:

-*m* displays output of **swapinfo** in MB rather than in 1,024-byte blocks.

-*d* prints information related to device swap areas only.

-*f* prints information about file system swap areas only.

sar: The System Activity Reporter

sar is another UNIX command for gathering information about activities on your system. You can gather data over an extended time period with **sar** and later produce reports based on the data. The following are some useful options to **sar**, along with examples of reports produced with these options where applicable:

sar -o *\<file>*	Saves data in a file specified by "o." After the file name, you would usually also enter the time interval for samples and the number of samples. The following example shows saving the binary data in file /tmp/sar.data at an interval of 5 seconds 200 times:

sar -o /tmp/sar.data 5 200

The data in **/tmp/sar.data** can later be extracted from the file.

sar -f *<file>*   Specifies a file from which you will extract data.

sar -u   Reports CPU utilization with the headings %usr, %sys, %wio, %idle with some processes waiting for block I/O, %idle. This report is similar to the **iostat** and **vmstat** CPU reports. You extract the binary data saved in a file to get CPU information, as shown in the following example. The following is a **sar -u** example:

```
[ root : / ]> sar -u -f /tmp/sar.data

HP-UX otcapdvl B.11.11 U 9000/800     01/27/05

13:57:25    %usr    %sys    %wio    %idle
13:57:55     51      1       0       48
13:58:25     51      1       0       48
13:58:55     51      1       0       48
13:59:25     54      1       0       44
13:59:55     51      1       0       48
14:00:25     54      1       1       43
14:00:55     51      1       0       47
14:01:25     53      2       0       45
14:01:55     52      1       0       46
14:02:25     51      1       0       48
14:02:55     52      1       0       47
14:03:25     50      1       0       48
14:03:55     57      1       0       41
14:04:25     55      1       1       43
14:04:55     51      1       0       48
14:05:25     51      1       1       47
14:05:55     51      1       0       48
14:06:25     52      2       0       46
14:06:55     51      1       0       47
14:07:25     51      1       0       48
14:07:55     51      1       0       48
14:08:25     53      1       2       44
14:08:55     52      1       0       47
14:09:25     51      1       0       48
14:09:55     52      1       0       47

Average      52      1       0       47
```

sar -b   Reports buffer cache activity. A database application, such as Oracle, recommends that you use this option to see the effectiveness of buffer cache use. You extract the binary data saved in a file to get CPU information, as shown in the following example:

```
[ root : / ]>      sar -b -f /tmp/sar.data

HP-UX otcapdv1 B.11.11 U 9000/800     01/27/05

13:57:25 bread/s lread/s %rcache bwrit/s lwrit/s %wcache pread/s pwrit/s
13:57:55       0     127     100       7      12      43       0       0
13:58:25       0     148     100       7      12      45       0       0
13:58:55       0     149     100       7      12      44       0       0
13:59:25       0     141     100       6      11      46       0       0
13:59:55       0     125     100       6      11      38       0       0
14:00:25       0     163     100       6      17      63       0       0
14:00:55       0     158     100       8      14      42       0       0
14:01:25       0    5228     100      14      23      40       0       0
14:01:55       0     203     100       8      15      48       0       0
14:02:25       0     136     100       7      12      44       0       0
14:02:55       0     141     100       6      10      39       0       0
14:03:25       0     148     100       7      13      48       0       0
14:03:55       0     189     100       8      14      44       0       0
14:04:25      17     175      90      12      17      31       0       0
14:04:55       2     156      99      12      17      29       0       0
14:05:25       0     141     100      12      17      27       0       0
14:05:55       0     178     100      10      21      53       0       0
14:06:25       1    4912     100      11      22      51       0       0
14:06:55       0     170     100       9      16      44       0       0
14:07:25       0     131     100       8      13      42       0       0
14:07:55       0     149     100       7      12      39       0       0
14:08:25      15     182      92      10      17      43       0       0
14:08:55       1     216      99       9      13      32       0       0
14:09:25       0     153     100       9      14      38       0       0
14:09:55       2     139      99       6      11      51       0       0

Average        2     550     100       8      15      43       0       0
```

sar -d

Reports disk activity. You get the device name, percent that the device was busy, average number of requests outstanding for the device, number of data transfers per second for the device, and other information. You extract the binary data saved in a file to get CPU information, as shown in the following example:

```
[ root : / ]> sar -d -f /tmp/sar.data

HP-UX otcapdv1 B.11.11 U 9000/800     01/27/05

13:57:25  device   %busy   avque   r+w/s  blks/s  avwait  avserv
13:57:55  c4t6d0    0.90    0.50       3      24    3.15    6.20
          c7t6d0    0.57    0.50       2      20    3.30    4.49
          c10t0d0   0.03    0.50       0       7    2.11    1.37
```

```
            c10t0d1    0.07   0.50    0       6     3.21    1.90
            c10t1d0    0.17   0.50    3      54     5.24    0.64
13:58:25    c4t6d0     0.90   0.50    3      22     3.73    5.21
            c7t6d0     0.57   0.50    2      18     3.88    4.40
            c10t1d0    0.30   0.50    4      70     5.12    0.62
13:58:55    c4t6d0     0.77   0.50    2      20     3.28    5.39
            c7t6d0     0.50   0.50    2      17     3.32    4.47
            c10t1d0    0.03   0.50    1      16     5.19    0.64
            c10t1d1    0.17   0.50    3      47     5.06    0.64
13:59:25    c4t6d0     2.43   1.64    8     331     8.47   11.18
            c7t6d0     1.87   1.46    6     323     8.31   11.34
            c10t0d5    0.03   0.50    1      24     5.00    0.72
            c10t1d1    0.20   0.50    3      61     4.98    0.60
13:59:55    c4t6d0     0.73   0.50    2      18     3.51    7.14
            c7t6d0     0.63   0.50    2      16     3.78    5.33
            c10t1d1    0.17   0.50    3      58     4.91    0.64
14:00:25    c4t6d0     2.33   0.50    7      30     4.59    3.71
            c7t6d0     2.17   0.50    6      24     4.65    3.84
            c10t0d4    0.03   0.50    0      16     5.53    0.74
            c10t1d1    0.20   0.50    3      66     4.99    0.67

                        .
                        .
                        .

14:09:25    c4t6d0     0.80   0.50    3      24     3.19    5.45
            c7t6d0     0.57   0.50    2      19     3.24    4.96
            c10t0d0    0.07   0.50    1      13     3.38    0.68
            c10t1d0    0.17   0.50    3      58     4.98    0.60
14:09:55    c4t6d0     0.63   0.50    2      18     3.05    6.52
            c7t6d0     0.50   0.50    2      15     3.39    5.77
            c10t0d1    0.03   0.50    0       6     3.05    1.10
            c10t0d2    0.07   0.62    1      23     2.65    2.28
            c10t0d5    0.10   0.50    0       2     6.94    4.71
            c10t0d6    0.03   0.50    0       1     8.32    9.46
            c10t1d0    0.13   0.50    3      55     5.13    0.64
            c10t1d1    0.03   0.50    0       2     5.09    4.49
Average     c4t6d0     1.01   0.68    4      38     4.39    5.98
Average     c7t6d0     0.72   0.65    3      32     4.36    5.57
Average     c10t0d0    0.05   0.50    0       7     3.41    1.66
Average     c10t0d1    0.04   0.50    0       8     4.21    1.69
Average     c10t1d0    0.12   0.50    2      29     5.02    0.86
Average     c10t1d1    0.16   0.51    2      44     5.05    0.94
Average     c10t0d5    0.05   0.52    0       4     5.04    3.73
Average     c10t0d4    0.06   0.51    0       6     5.17    4.18
Average     c10t0d2    0.02   0.53    0       3     2.59    1.93
Average     c10t0d6    0.04   0.50    0       4     5.01    3.02
Average     c10t0d3    0.03   0.50    0       4     3.48    1.60
Average     c10t0d7    0.05   0.54    0       4     4.95    4.07
Average     c10t3d2    0.00   0.50    0       0     7.68    0.80
```

sar -q   Reports average queue length. You may have a problem any time the run queue length is greater than the number of processors on the system:

```
[ root : / ]> sar -q -f /tmp/sar.data

HP-UX otcapdv1 B.11.11 U 9000/800    01/27/05

13:57:25 runq-sz %runocc swpq-sz %swpocc
13:57:55    2.1       70    0.0        0
13:58:25    1.9       60    0.0        0
```

```
13:58:55      1.5      70      0.0        0
13:59:25      1.7      72      0.0        0
13:59:55      1.4      75      0.0        0
14:00:25      2.3      58      0.0        0
14:00:55      2.2      65      0.0        0
14:01:25      2.4      75      0.0        0
14:01:55      1.9      73      0.0        0
14:02:25      1.6      80      0.0        0
14:02:55      2.2      73      0.0        0
14:03:25      3.0      73      0.0        0
14:03:55      3.7      62      0.0        0
14:04:25      1.5      60      0.0        0
14:04:55      1.9      63      0.0        0
14:05:25      4.5      43      0.0        0
14:05:55      2.4      60      0.0        0
14:06:25      1.4      75      0.0        0
14:06:55      1.3      73      0.0        0
14:07:25      1.4      68      0.0        0
14:07:55      1.4      77      0.0        0
14:08:25      1.9      78      0.0        0
14:08:55      2.4      85      0.0        0
14:09:25      2.8      65      0.0        0
14:09:55      2.0      72      0.0        0

Average       2.1      69      0.0        0
```

sar -w   Reports system swapping activity:

```
[ root : / ]> sar -w -f /tmp/sar.data

HP-UX otcapdv1 B.11.11 U 9000/800      01/27/05

13:57:25 swpin/s bswin/s swpot/s bswot/s pswch/s
13:57:55   2.00    0.0    2.00     0.0     626
13:58:25   2.03    0.0    2.07     0.0     660
13:58:55   1.97    0.0    1.93     0.0     630
13:59:25   1.70    0.0    1.77     0.0     646
13:59:55   1.60    0.0    1.57     0.0     598
14:00:25   2.03    0.0    2.00     0.0     669
14:00:55   2.00    0.0    2.00     0.0     654
14:01:25   2.00    0.0    2.00     0.0     655
14:01:55   1.97    0.0    2.00     0.0     689
14:02:25   2.00    0.0    2.00     0.0     645
14:02:55   2.03    0.0    2.00     0.0     639
14:03:25   1.97    0.0    2.00     0.0     623
14:03:55   2.07    0.0    2.07     0.0     780
14:04:25   2.00    0.0    2.00     0.0     727
14:04:55   2.00    0.0    2.00     0.0     670
14:05:25   2.00    0.0    2.00     0.0     639
14:05:55   1.93    0.0    1.93     0.0     675
14:06:25   2.00    0.0    2.00     0.0     695
14:06:55   2.07    0.0    2.07     0.0     647
14:07:25   1.93    0.0    1.93     0.0     619
14:07:55   2.07    0.0    2.07     0.0     626
14:08:25   2.00    0.0    2.00     0.0     696
14:08:55   1.97    0.0    1.93     0.0     646
14:09:25   2.03    0.0    2.07     0.0     623
14:09:55   1.97    0.0    1.93     0.0     612

Average    1.97    0.0    1.97     0.0     656
```

top

The command line is a way of life when working with UNIX. UNIX grew out of the command line and is still primarily command line-based. Although you need to know a lot when issuing commands, especially when it comes to system performance, you can dig deeply quickly with many of the commands just covered.

top is found on many UNIX variants and supplies a lot of useful system information. Many system administrators coming to HP-UX from a different UNIX variant invoke **top** so I cover it breifly in this section. Figure 13-1 shows top running on an HP-UX system.

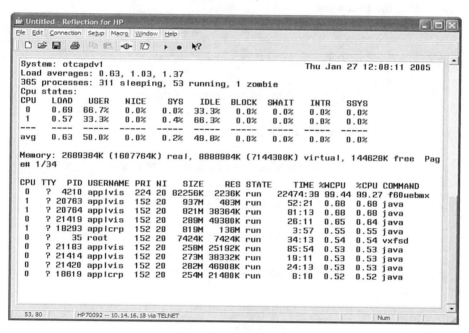

Figure 13-1   **top** Output Showing Two CPUs

Among the useful **top** system data displayed is the following:

- Load averages in the last 1, 5, and 15 minutes

- Number of existing processes and the number of
  processes in each state

- Percentage of time spent in each of the processor
  states per processor on the system

Next in the **top** window is memory data, including real, virtual, and free.

Data is also provided for individual processes in a format similar to **ps**, including the following:

PID - Process ID number.

USER - Name of the owner of the process.

PRI - Current priority of the process.

NI - Nice value, ranging from -20 to +20.

SIZE - Total size of the process in kilobytes.

RSS - Resident size of the process in kilobytes.

STATE - Current state of the process.

TIME - Number of system and CPU seconds the
        process has consumed.

%CPU - CPU percentage.

%MEM - Memory percentage.

COMMAND - Name of the command the process is
        currently running.

You can see in the **top** window that the program **cc1**, used to compile the kernel, was consuming a substantial amount of the CPU resources on the system.

HP GlancePlus/UX

Using HP-UX commands to get a better understanding of what your system is doing requires that you to do a lot of work. In the first case, issuing HP-UX commands gives you the advantage of obtaining data about what is taking place on your system that very second. Unfortunately, you can't always issue additional commands to probe more deeply into an area, such as a process, about which you want to know more.

Now I describe another technique, a tool that can help get useful data in real time, allow you to investigate a specific process, and not bury you in reports. This tool is HP GlancePlus/UX (GlancePlus). This tool runs on several UNIX variants, including Solaris, HP-UX, and AIX, however, because this is an HP-UX system administration book, I provide only HP-UX screen shots.

GlancePlus can be run in character mode or graphic mode. I choose to use the character-based version of GlancePlus, because it runs on any display, either graphics- or character-based, and the many colors used by the X Windows version of GlancePlus do not show up well in a book. My examples are displayed more clearly in this book when using the character mode. I recommend that you try both versions of GlancePlus to see which you prefer.

The system used in the examples has 8 processors, 4 GB of RAM, and a substantial amount of EMC Symmetrix disk connected to it.

Figure 13-2 shows one of several interactive screens of GlancePlus. This one is the *Process List* screen, also referred to as the *Global* screen. This is the default screen when bringing up GlancePlus.

Two features of the screen shown in Figure 13-2 are worth noticing immediately:

1. Four histograms at the top of the screen give you a graphical representation of your CPU, Disk, Memory, and Swap Utilization in a format much easier to assimilate than a column of numbers.

2. The "Process Summary" has columns similar to **ps -ef**, with which many system administrators are familiar and comfortable. Glance-Plus, however, gives you the additional capability of filtering out processes that are using few resources by specifying thresholds.

Using GlancePlus, you can take a close look at your system in many areas, including the following:

- Process List
- CPU Report
- Memory Report
- Swap Space
- Disk Report
- LAN Detail
- NFS by System
- PRM Summary (Process Resource Manager)
- I/O by File System
- I/O by Disk
- I/O by Logical Volume
- System Tables

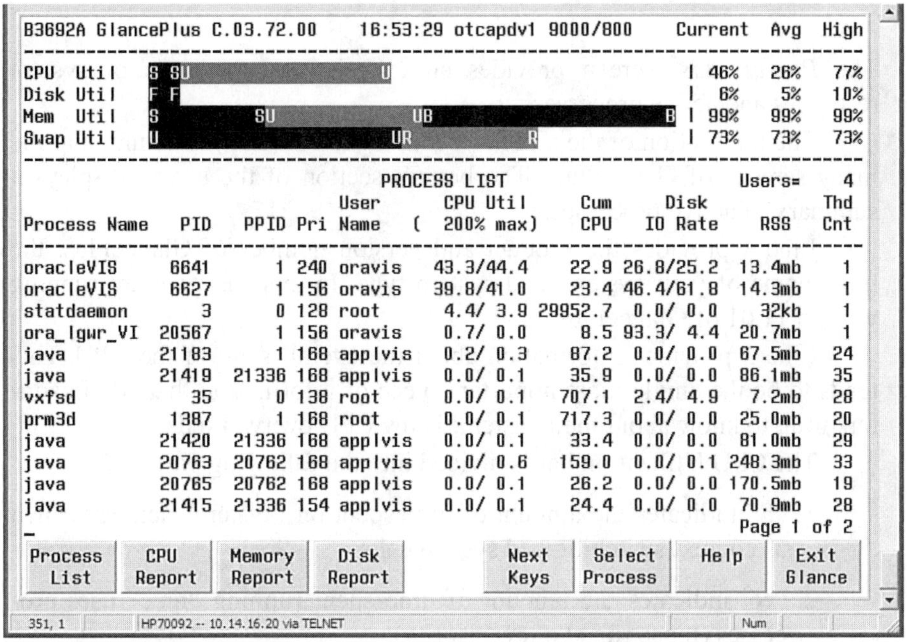

```
B3692A GlancePlus C.03.72.00    16:53:29 otcapdv1 9000/800    Current  Avg  High

CPU  Util  S SU                        U                    |  46%   26%   77%
Disk Util  F F                                             |   6%    5%   10%
Mem  Util  S        SU              UB                    B |  99%   99%   99%
Swap Util  U                    UR              R          |  73%   73%   73%

                          PROCESS LIST                     Users=    4
                      User      CPU Util     Cum      Disk         Thd
Process Name   PID   PPID Pri Name  ( 200% max)   CPU    IO Rate     RSS  Cnt

oracleVIS     6641      1 240 oravis   43.3/44.4   22.9 26.8/25.2  13.4mb    1
oracleVIS     6627      1 156 oravis   39.8/41.0   23.4 46.4/61.8  14.3mb    1
statdaemon       3      0 128 root      4.4/ 3.9 29952.7  0.0/ 0.0   32kb    1
ora_lgwr_VI  20567      1 156 oravis    0.7/ 0.0    8.5 93.3/ 4.4  20.7mb    1
java         21183      1 168 applvis   0.2/ 0.3   87.2  0.0/ 0.0  67.5mb   24
java         21419  21336 168 applvis   0.0/ 0.1   35.9  0.0/ 0.0  86.1mb   35
vxfsd           35      0 138 root      0.0/ 0.1  707.1  2.4/ 4.9   7.2mb   28
prm3d         1387      1 168 root      0.0/ 0.1  717.3  0.0/ 0.0  25.0mb   20
java         21420  21336 168 applvis   0.0/ 0.1   33.4  0.0/ 0.0  81.0mb   29
java         20763  20762 168 applvis   0.0/ 0.6  159.0  0.0/ 0.1 248.3mb   33
java         20765  20762 168 applvis   0.0/ 0.1   26.2  0.0/ 0.0 170.5mb   19
java         21415  21336 154 applvis   0.0/ 0.1   24.4  0.0/ 0.0  70.9mb   28
_                                                            Page 1 of 2

 Process    CPU     Memory   Disk          Next    Select    Help   Exit
 List      Report   Report   Report        Keys    Process          Glance

 351, 1      HP70092 -- 10.14.16.20 via TELNET                    Num
```

Figure 13-2   HP GlancePlus/UX *Process List* Screen Shot

Because the *Process List* shown in Figure 13-2 tells you where your system resources are going at the highest level, I start my description here. I use a terminal emulator on my portable computer to display GlancePlus. I find that many system administrators use a PC and a terminal emulator to perform UNIX management functions. Keep in mind that the information shown on this screen can be updated at any interval you choose. If your system is running in a steady-state mode, you may want to have a long interval because you don't expect things to much change. On the other hand, you may have a dynamic environment and want to see the histograms and other information updated every few seconds. In either case, you can change the update interval to suit your needs. You can use the function keys at the bottom of the screen to go into other functional areas.

Process List **Description**

The *Process List* screen provides an overview of the state of system resources and active processes.

The top section of the screen (the histogram section) is common to the many screens of GlancePlus. The bottom section of the screen displays a summary of active processes.

Line 1 provides the product and version number of GlancePlus, the time, name of your system, and system type. In this case, we are running version 11.01 of GlancePlus.

Line 3 provides information about the overall state of the CPU. This tends to be the single most important piece of information that administrators want to know about their system: Is my CPU overworked?

The CPU Utilization bar is divided into the following parts:

1. "S" indicates the amount of time spent on "system" activities such as context switching and system calls.

2. "N" indicates the amount of time spent running "nice" user processes (those run at a low priority).

3. "U" indicates the amount of time spent running user processes.

4. "R" indicates real-time processes.

5. "A" indicates the amount of time spent running processes at a negative "nice" priority.

The far right of line 3 shows the percentage of CPU utilization. If your system is "CPU-bound," you consistently see this number near 100 percent. You get statistics for Current, Average (since analysis was begun), and High.

Line 4 shows Disk Utilization for the busiest mounted disk. This bar indicates the percentage of File System and Virtual Memory disk I/O over the update interval. This bar is divided into two parts:

1. "F" indicates the amount of file system activity of user reads and writes and other non-paging activities.

2. "V" indicates the percentage of disk I/O devoted to paging virtual memory.

The Current, Avg, and High statistics have the same meaning as in the CPU Utilization description.

Line 5 shows the system memory utilization. This bar is divided into three parts:

1. "S" indicates the amount of memory devoted to system use.

2. "U" indicates the amount of memory devoted to user programs and data.

3. "B" indicates the amount of memory devoted to buffer cache.

The Current, Avg, and High statistics have the same meaning as in the CPU Utilization description.

Line 6 shows Swap Utilization information, which is divided into two parts:

1. "R" indicates reserved, but not in use.

2. "U" indicates swap space in use.

All three of these areas (CPU, Memory, and Disk) may be further analyzed by using the F2, F3, and F4 function keys, respectively. Again, you may see different function keys, depending on the version of GlancePlus you run. When you select one of these keys, you move from the *Process List* screen to a screen that provides more in-depth functions in the selected area. In addition, more detailed screens are available for many other system areas. Because most investigation beyond the *Process List* screen takes place on the CPU, Memory, and Disk screens, I describe these in more detail shortly.

The bottom of the *Process List* screen shows the active processes running on your system. Because there are typically many processes running on a UNIX system, you may want to consider using the **o** command to set a threshold for CPU utilization. If you set a threshold of five percent, for example, then only processes that exceed the average CPU utilization of five percent over the interval will be displayed. There are other types of thresholds that can be specified such as the amount of RAM used (Resident Size). If you specify thresholds, you see only the processes you're most interested in, that is, those consuming the greatest system resources.

There is a line for each active process that meets the threshold requirements you define. There may be more than one page of processes to display. The message in the bottom-right corner of the screen indicates which page you are on. You can scroll forward to view the next page with **f** and backwards with **b**. Usually, only a few processes consume most of your system resources, so I recommend setting the thresholds so that only one page of processes is displayed. There are a whole series of commands you can issue in GlancePlus. Figure 13-7 toward the end of this section shows the commands recognized by GlancePlus.

Here is a brief summary of the process headings:

Process Name	The name or abbreviation used to load the executable program.
PID	The process identification number.
PPID	The PID of the parent process.
Pri	The priority of the process. The lower the number, the higher the priority. System-level processes usually run between 0 and 127. Other processes usually run between 128 and 255. "Nice" processes are those with the lowest priority, and they have the largest number.
User Name	Name of the user who started the process.
CPU Util	The first number is the percentage of CPU utilization that this process consumed over the update interval. Note that this is 800% maximum for our eight-processor system. The second number is the percentage of CPU utilization that this process consumed since GlancePlus was invoked. Most system administrators leave GlancePlus running continuously on their systems with a low update interval. Because GlancePlus uses very little system overhead, there is virtually no penalty for this.
Cum CPU	The total CPU time used by the process. GlancePlus uses the "midaemon" to gather information. If the **midaemon** started before the process, you get an accurate measure of cumulative CPU time used by the process.
Disk IO Rate	The first number is the average disk I/O rate per second over the last update interval. The second number is the average disk I/O rate since GlancePlus was started or since the process was started. Disk I/O can mean a lot of different things. Disk I/O could mean taking blocks of data off the disk for the first time and putting them in RAM, or it could be entirely paging and swapping. Some processes will simply require a lot more Disk I/O than others. When this number is very high, however, take a close look at whether or not you have

enough RAM. Keep in mind that pageout activity, such as deactivation and swapping, are attributed to the *vhand* process.

RSS Size The amount of RAM in KB that is consumed by the process. This is called the Resident Size. Everything related to the process that is in RAM is included in this column, such as the process's data, stack, text, and shared memory segments. This is a good column to inspect. Because slow systems are often erroneously assumed to be CPU-bound, I always make a point of looking at this column to identify the amount of RAM that the primary applications are using. This is often revealing. Some applications use a small amount of RAM but use large data sets, a point often overlooked when RAM calculations are made. This column shows all the RAM your process is currently using.

Block On The reason the process was blocked (unable to run). If the process is currently blocked, you see why. If the process is running, you see why it was last blocked. There are many reasons a process can be blocked. After *Thd Cnt* is a list of the most common reasons for the process being blocked.

Thd Cnt The total number of threads for this current process.

Abbreviation Reason for the Blocked Process.

CACHE Waiting for a cache buffer to become available.

DISK Waiting for a disk operation to complete.

INODE Waiting for an inode operation to complete.

IO Waiting for a non-disk I/O to complete.

IPC Waiting for a shared memory operation to complete.

LAN	Waiting for a LAN operation to complete.
MESG	Waiting for a message queue operation to complete.
NFS	Waiting for an NFS request to complete.
PIPE	Waiting for data to or from a pipe.
PRI	Waiting because a higher-priority process is running.
RFA	Waiting for a Remote File Access to complete.
SEM	Waiting for a semaphore to become available.
SLEEP	Waiting because the process called **sleep** or **wait**.
SOCKT	Waiting for a socket operation to complete.
SYS	Waiting for system resources.
TERM	Waiting for a terminal transfer.
VM	Waiting for a virtual memory operation to complete.
OTHER	Waiting for a reason GlancePlus can't determine.

CPU Report **Screen Description**

If the *Process List* screen indicates that the CPU is overworked, you want to refer to the *CPU Report* screen shown in Figure 13-3. It provides useful information about the seven types of states on which GlancePlus reports.

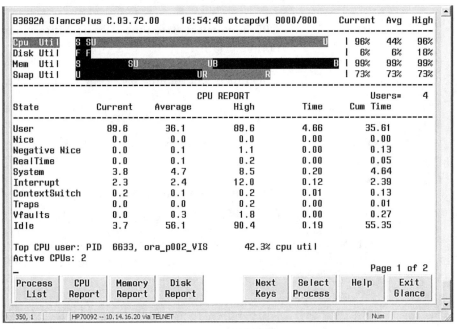

```
B3692A GlancePlus C.03.72.00    16:54:46 otcapdv1 9000/800    Current  Avg  High

Cpu  Util  S SU                                           U  | 96%   44%   96%
Disk Util  F F                                               |  6%    6%   18%
Mem  Util  S         SU              UB                    B  | 99%   99%   99%
Swap Util  U                    UR              R            | 73%   73%   73%
------------------------------------------------------------------------------
                                    CPU REPORT                   Users=    4
State           Current    Average      High        Time     Cum Time
------------------------------------------------------------------------------
User              89.6       36.1        89.6        4.66       35.61
Nice               0.0        0.0         0.0        0.00        0.00
Negative Nice      0.0        0.1         1.1        0.00        0.13
RealTime           0.0        0.1         0.2        0.00        0.05
System             3.8        4.7         8.5        0.20        4.64
Interrupt          2.3        2.4        12.0        0.12        2.39
ContextSwitch      0.2        0.1         0.2        0.01        0.13
Traps              0.0        0.0         0.2        0.00        0.01
Vfaults            0.0        0.3         1.8        0.00        0.27
Idle               3.7       56.1        90.4        0.19       55.35

Top CPU user: PID  6633, ora_p002_VIS       42.3% cpu util
Active CPUs: 2
_                                                          Page 1 of 2

 Process    CPU     Memory    Disk        Next    Select   Help    Exit
  List     Report   Report   Report       Keys    Process          Glance

350, 1       HP70092 -- 10.14.16.20 via TELNET                    Num
```

Figure 13-3   HP GlancePlus/UX *CPU Report*

For each of the seven types of states, there are columns that provide additional information. The following is a description of the columns:

Current	Displays the percentage of CPU time devoted to this state over the last time interval
Average	Displays the average percentage of CPU time spent in this state since GlancePlus was started
High	Displays the highest percentage of CPU time devoted to this state since GlancePlus was started
Time	Displays the CPU time spent in this state over the last interval
Cum Time	Displays the total amount of CPU time spent in this state since GlancePlus was started

A description of the seven states follows:

User	CPU time spent executing user activities under normal priority.
Nice	CPU time spent running user code in nice mode.
Negative Nice	CPU time spent running code at a high priority.
Realtime	CPU time spent executing real-time processes that run at a high priority.
System	CPU time spent executing system calls and programs.
Interrupt	CPU time spent executing system interrupts. A high value here may indicate of a lot of I/O, such as paging and swapping.
ContSwitch	CPU time spent context switching between processes.
Traps	CPU time spent handling traps.
Vfaults	CPU time spent handling page faults.
Idle	CPU time spent idle.

The *CPU Report* screen also shows your system's run queue length or load average. This is displayed on the second page of the *CPU Report* screen. The Current, Average, and High values for the number of runnable processes waiting for the CPU are shown. You may want to get a gauge of your system's run queue length when the system is mostly idle and compare these numbers with those you see when your system is in normal use.

The final area reported on the *CPU Report* screen is load average, system calls, interrupts, and context switches. I don't inspect these too closely, because if one of these is high, it is normally the symptom of a problem and not the cause of a problem. If you correct a problem, you see these numbers decrease.

You can use GlancePlus to view all the CPUs in your system, as shown in Figure 13-4. This is an eight-processor system.

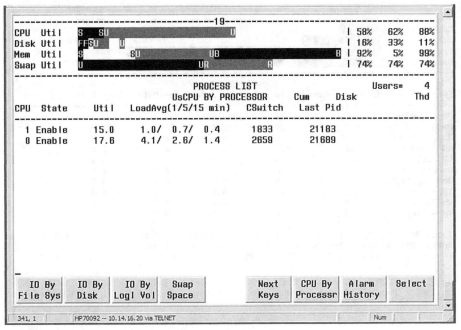

Figure 13-4 *All CPUs* Screen in GlancePlus

Memory Report Screen Description

The *Memory Report* screen, shown in Figure 13-5, provides information on several types of memory-management events. The statistics shown are in the form of counts, not percentages. You may want to look at these counts for a mostly idle system and then observe what takes place as the load on the system is incrementally increased. My experience has been that many more memory bottlenecks occur than CPU bottlenecks, so you may find this screen revealing.

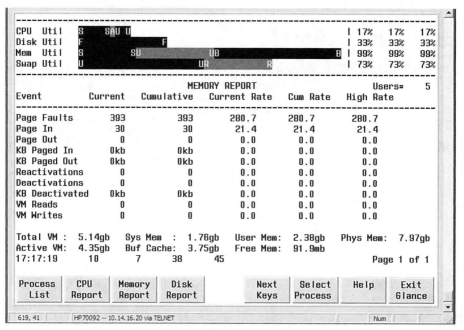

Figure 13-5   HP GlancePlus/UX *Memory Report* Screen Shot

The following five statistics are shown for each memory management event:

Current	The number of times an event occurred in the last interval. The count changes if you update the interval, so you may want to select an interval you are comfortable with and stick with it.
Cumulative	The sum of all counts for this event since Glance-Plus was started.
Current Rate	The number of events per second.
Cum Rate	Average of the rate over the cummulative collection interval.
High Rate	The highest rate recorded.

The following are brief descriptions of the memory-management events for which statistics are provided:

Page Faults   Any address translation fault, such as reclaims, pid faults, and so on.

Page In/Page Out   Pages of data moved from virtual memory (disk) to physical memory (page in), or vice versa.

KB Paged In   The amount of data paged in because of page faults.

KB Paged Out   The amount of data paged out to disk.

Reactivations/Deactivations

The number of processes swapped in and out of memory. A system low on RAM spends a lot of time swapping processes in and out of RAM. If a lot of this type of swapping is taking place, you may have high CPU utilization and see some other statistics may increase as well. These may only be symptoms that a lot of swapping is taking place.

KB Reactivated   The amount of information swapped into RAM as a result of processes having been swapped out earlier due to insufficient RAM.

KB Deactivated   The amount of information swapped out when processes are moved to disk.

VM Reads   The total count of the number of vitual memory reads to disk. The higher this number, the more often your system is going to disk.

VM Writes   The total count of memory management I/O.

The following values are also on the Memory screen:

Total VM   The amount of total virtual memory used by all processes

Active VM   The amount of virtual memory used by all active processes

Sys Mem	The amount of memory devoted to system use
Buf Cache Size	The current size of buffer cache
User Mem	The amount of memory devoted to user use
Free Memory	The amount of RAM not currently allocated for use
Phys Memory	The total RAM in your system

This screen gives you a lot of information about how your memory subsystem is being used. You may want to view some statistics when your system is mostly idle and when it is heavily used and compare the two. Some good numbers to record are "Free Memory" (to see whether you have any free RAM under either condition) and "Total VM" (to see how much virtual memory has been allocated for all your processes). A system that is RAM-rich has available memory; a system that is RAM-poor allocates a lot of virtual memory.

Disk Report Screen Description

The *Disk Report* screen appears in Figure 13-6. You may see groupings of "local" and "remote" information.

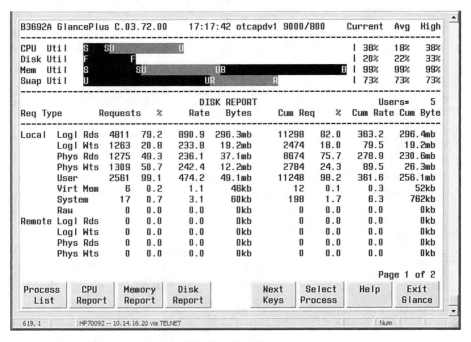

Figure 13-6   HP GlancePlus/UX *Disk Report* Screen Shot

There are eight disk statistics provided for eight events related to logical and physical accesses to all the disks mounted on the local system. These events represent all the disk activity taking place on the system.

Here are descriptions of the eight disk statistics provided:

Requests	The total number of requests of that type over the last interval
%	The percentage of this type of disk event relative to other types
Rate	The average number of requests of this type per second
Bytes	The total number of bytes transferred for this event over the last interval

Cum Req	The cumulative number of requests since GlancePlus started
%	The relative percentage of this type of disk event since GlancePlus started
Cum Rate	Average of the rate over the cumulative collection interval
Cum Bytes	The total number of bytes transferred for this type of event since GlancePlus started

The following are descriptions of the disk events for which these statistics are provided, which may be listed under "Local" on your system:

Logl Rds and Logl Wts	
	The number of logical reads and writes to a disk. Because disks normally use memory buffer cache, a logical read may not require physical access to the disk.
Phys Rds	The number of physical reads to the disk. These physical reads may be due to either file system logical reads or to virtual memory management.
Phys Wts	The number of physical writes to the disk. This may be due to file system activity or virtual memory management.
User	The amount of physical disk I/O as a result of user file I/O operations.
Virtual Mem	The amount of physical disk I/O as a result of virtual memory management activity.
System	Housekeeping I/O, such as inode updates.
Raw	The amount of raw mode disk I/O.

A lot of disk activity may also take place as a result of NFS mounted disks. Statistics are provided for "Remote" disks as well.

Disk access is required on all systems. The question to ask is: What disk activity is unnecessary and slowing down my system? A good place to start is to compare the amount of "User" disk I/O with "Virtual Mem" disk I/O. If your system is performing much more virtual memory I/O than user I/O, you may want to investigate your memory needs.

GlancePlus Summary

In addition to the Process List, or Global, screen and the CPU, Memory, and Disk screens previously described, there are many other useful screens, including the following:

Swap Space | Shows details of all swap areas. May be called by another name in other releases.

Netwk By Intrface | Gives details about each LAN card configured on your system. This screen may have another name in other releases.

NFS Global | Provides details on inbound and outbound NFS-mounted file systems. May be called by another name in other releases.

Select Process | Allows you to select a single process to investigate. May be called by another name in other releases.

I/O By File Sys | Shows details of I/O for each mounted disk partition.

I/O By Disk | Shows details of I/O for each mounted disk.

I/O By Logl Vol | Shows details of I/O for each mounted logical volume.

System Tables | Shows details of internal system tables.

Process Threshold | Defines which processes will be displayed on the Process List screen. May be called by another name, such as the Global screen, in other releases.

As you can see, although I describe the four most commonly used screens in detail, you can use many others to investigate your system further.

There are also many commands that you can issue within GlancePlus. Figures 13-7 and 13-8 show the *Command List* screens in GlancePlus.

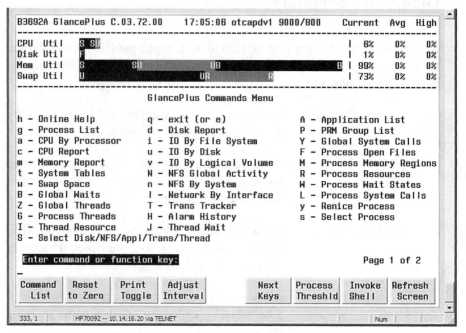

Figure 13-7   HP GlancePlus/UX *Command List* Screen

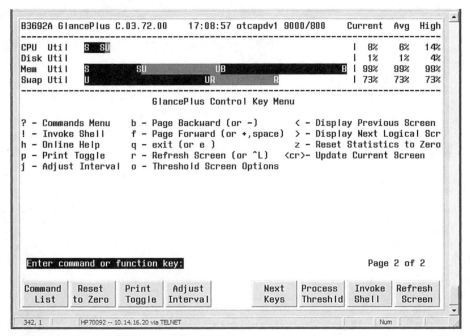

Figure 13-8   HP GlancePlus/UX *Command List* Screen 2

Advanced Tools: Performance Manager

To perform advanced performance-related work, HP has some OpenView tools. HP Performance manager is a graphical analysis and planning tool. Performance manager uses extensive historical data that allows you to examine resource utilization. HP Performance agent logs and collects data. Alarms are sent based on this data if necessary. HP Performance monitor performs real-time monitoring, which can be used to configure custom actions, such as sending emails or paging technical experts.

More information is available for these tools on *www.hp.com* and evaluation copies of these tools are also available.

Chapter 14

Networking Background

This chapter covers the background of UNIX networking and Chapter 15 "Configuring and Using Networking," covers networking configuration and using networking commands. If you don't have any UNIX background then you want to review this chapter before moving on to the next one. If you have networking background and want to know how to configure UNIX networking and use networking commands then you can jump directly to the Chapter 15.

The following is a list of topics covered in this chapter:

- TCP/IP and IEEE802.3 (Ethernet) background
- Internet Protocol (IP) addressing (classes A, B, and C)
- Subnet Mask

An Overview of IEEE802.3, TCP/IP

In order to understand how the networking on your UNIX system works, you first need to understand the components of your network that exist on your UNIX system. Seven layers of network functionality exist on your UNIX system, as shown in Figure 14-1. I cover the bottom four layers at a cursory level so that you can see how each plays a part in the operation of your network and, therefore, be more informed when you configure and troubleshoot networking on your UNIX system. The top layers are the ones that most UNIX system administrators spend time working with because those layers are closest to the functionality to which you can relate. The bottom layers are, however, also important to understand at some level, so that you can perform any configuration necessary to improve the network performance of your system, which has a major impact on the overall performance of your system.

Layer Number	Layer Name	Data Form	Comments
7	Application		User applications here.
6	Presentation		Applications prepared.
5	Session		Applications prepared.
4	Transport	Packet	Port-to-port transportation handled by TCP.
3	Network	Datagram	Internet Protocol (IP) handles routing by going directly to either the destination or default router. There can be multiple routers per subnet and multiple subnets to which an IP node is attached.
2	Link	Frame	Data encapsulated in Ethernet or IEEE 802.3 with source and destination addresses.
1	Physical		Physical connection between systems.

Figure 14-1   ISO/OSI Network Layer Functions

I start reviewing Figure 14-1 at the bottom with layer 1 and then describe each of the four bottom layers. These layers are known as the International Standards Organization Open Systems Interconnection (ISO/OSI) model. It is helpful to visualize the way in which networking layers interact.

Physical Layer

The beginning is the physical interconnection between the systems on your network. Without the **physical layer**, you can't communicate between systems, and all the great functionality that you would like to implement is not possible. The physical layer converts the data you would like to transmit to the analog signals that travel along the wire (I assume for now that whatever physical layer you have in place uses wires). The information traveling into a network interface is taken off the wire and prepared for use by the next layer.

Link Layer

In order to connect to other systems local to your system, you use the link layer that is able to establish a connection to all the other systems on your local segment. This is the layer where you have either IEEE 802.3 or Ethernet. 802.3 is the officially sanctioned version of Ethernet, so it is almost univerally used. I include Ethernet encapsulation for completness purposes. Your UNIX system supports both of these "encapsulation" methods. This is called encapsulation because your data is put in one of these two forms (either IEEE 802.3 or Ethernet). Data is transferred at the link layer in frames (just another name for data), with the source and destination addresses and some other information attached. You might think that because two different encapsulation methods exist, they must be very different. This assumption, however, is not the case. IEEE 802.3 and Ethernet are nearly identical. For this reason, many UNIX systems can handle both types of encapsulation. So with the bottom two layers, you have a physical connection between your systems and data that is encapsulated into one of two formats with a source and destination address attached. Figure 14-2 lists the components of an **Ethernet** encapsulation and makes comments about IEEE802.3 encapsulation where appropriate.

destination address	6 bytes	address data is sent to
source address	6 bytes	address data is sent from
type	2 bytes	this is the "length count" in 802.3

data	46-1500 bytes	38-1492 bytes for 802.3; the difference in these two data sizes (MTU) can be seen with the **ifconfig** command
crc	4 bytes	checksum to detect errors

Figure 14-2   Ethernet Encapsulation

One interesting item to note is the difference in the maximum data size between IEEE 802.3 and Ethernet of 1,492 and 1,500 bytes, respectively. This is the Maximum Transfer Unit (MTU). The **ifconfig** command covered shortly displays the MTU for your interface. The data in Ethernet is called a *frame* (the re-encapsulation of data at the next layer up is called a *datagram* in IP, and encapsulation at two levels up is called a *packet* for TCP).

Keep in mind that Ethernet and IEEE 802.3 run on the same physical connection, but there are indeed differences between the two encapsulation methods. With your UNIX systems, you don't have to spend much, if any, time setting up your network interface for encapsulation.

Network Layer

Next, we work up to the third layer, which is the network layer. This layer on UNIX systems is synonymous with Internet Protocol (IP). Data at this layer is transported as *datagrams*. This is the layer that handles the routing of data around the network. Data that gets routed with IP sometimes encounters an error of some type, which is reported back to the source system with an Internet Control Message Protocol (ICMP) message. We see some ICMP messages shortly. **ifconfig** and **netstat** are two UNIX commands that are commonly used to configure this routing.

Most IP packets fit inside a single Ethernet frame. If the information that IP uses does not conveniently fit inside an Ethernet frame, you end up with fragmented data. This is really re-encapsulation of the data, so you end up with a lot of inefficiency as you work your way up the layers.

In the very simplist environment, with one router, IP handles routing in a simple fashion. If data is sent to a destination connected directly to your system, then the data is sent directly to that system. If, on the other hand, the destination is not connected directly to your system, the data is sent to the default router. The default router then has the responsibility of getting the data to its destination. This routing can be a little tricky to understand, so I cover it in detail shortly. This is oversimplified in that most networks are much more complex, but my description gives you an idea of how a router works.

Transport Layer

The *trasport level* is the next level up from the network layer. It communicates with *ports*. TCP is the most common protocol found at this level, and it forms packets that are sent from port to port. The port used by a program is usually defined in **/etc/services**, along with the protocol (such as TCP). These ports are used by network programs, such as **telnet**, **rlogin**, **ftp**, and so on. You can see that these programs, associated with ports, are the highest level we have covered while analyzing the OSI model.

Internet Protocol (IP) Addressing and Subnet Mask

Many changes have taken place with address classes based on Classless Inter-Domain Routing (CIDR.) As part of CIDR address blocks are allocated based on CIDR and not as cell-based blocks. Having said that I still present Internet Protocol addresses (IP address) because this technique is still widely used and is good to understand.

An IP address is either a class "A," "B," or "C" address (there are also class "D" and "E" addresses I not cover). A class "A" network supports many more nodes per network than either a class "B" or "C" network. IP addresses consist of four fields. The purpose of breaking down the IP address into four fields is to define a node (or host) address and a network address. Figure 14-3 summarizes the relationships between the classes and addresses.

Address Class	Networks	Nodes per Network	Bits Defining Network	Bits Defining Nodes per Network
A	a few	the most	8 bits	24 bits
B	many	many	16 bits	16 bits
C	the most	a few	24 bits	8 bits

Address Class	Networks	Nodes per Network	Bits Defining Network	Bits Defining Nodes per Network
Reserved	-	-	-	-

Figure 14-3   Comparison of Internet Protocol (IP) Addresses

These bit patterns are significant in that the number of bits defines the ranges of networks and nodes in each class. For instance, a class A address uses 8 bits to define networks, and a class C address uses 24 bits to define networks. A class A address therefore supports fewer networks than a class C address. A class A address, however, supports many more nodes per network than a class C address. Taking these relationships one step further, we can now view the specific parameters associated with these address classes in Figure 14-4.

Address Class	Networks Supported	Nodes per Network	Address Range	
A	127	16777215	0.0.0.1	-	127.255.255.254
B	16383	65535	128.0.0.1	-	191.255.255.254
C	2097157	255	192.0.0.1	-	223.255.254.254
Reserved	-	-	224.0.0.0	-	255.255.255.255

Looking at the 32-bit address in binary form, you can see how to determine the class of an address:

Figure 14-4   Address Change

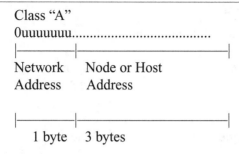

Class "A"
0uuuuuuu......................................

| | |
Network   Node or Host
Address   Address

| | |
   1 byte   3 bytes

net.host.host.host

A class "A" address has the first bit set to 0. You can see how so many nodes per network can be supported with all the bits devoted to the node or host address. The first bit of a class A address is 0, and the remaining 7 bits of the network portion are used to define the network. Then a total of 3 bytes are devoted to defining the nodes with a network.

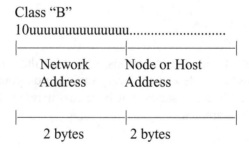

Class "B"
10uuuuuuuuuuuuuu...........................

| | |
  Network   Node or Host
  Address   Address

| | |
   2 bytes   2 bytes

net.net.host.host

A class "B" address has the first bit set to a 1 and the second bit to a 0. More networks are supported here than with a class A address, but fewer nodes per network. With a class B address, 2 bytes are devoted to the network portion of the address and 2 bytes devoted to the node portion of the address.

Figure 14-4   Address Change

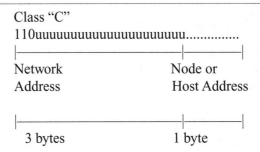

Class "C"
110uuuuuuuuuuuuuuuuuuuuuu...............

|————————————————|————————|
Network   Node or
Address   Host Address

|————————————————|————————|
   3 bytes   1 byte

net.net.net.host

A class "C" address has the first bit and second bit set to 1, and the third bit is 0. The greatest number of networks and fewest number of nodes per network are associated with a class C address. With a class C address, 3 bytes are devoted to the network and 1 byte is devoted to the nodes within a network.

Figure 14-4   Address Change

These addresses are used in various setup files that are covered later when the **/etc/hosts** file is described. Every interface on your network must have a unique IP address. Systems that have two network interfaces must have two unique IP addresses.

Subnet Mask

Your UNIX system uses the subnet mask to determine whether an IP datagram is for a host on its own subnet, a host on a different subnet but the same network, or a host on a different network. Using subnets, you can have some hosts on one subnet and other hosts on a different subnet. The subnets can be separated by routers or other networking electronics that connect the subnets.

To perform routing, the only aspects of an address that your router uses are the net and subnet. The subnet mask is used to mask the host part of the address. Because you can set up network addresses in such a way that you are the only one who knows which part of the address is the host, subnet, and network, use the subnet mask to make your system aware of the bits of your IP address that are for the host and which are for the subnet.

In its simplest form, what you are really doing with subnet masking is specifying which portion of your IP address defines the host, and which part defines the network. One of the most confusing aspects of working with subnet masks is that most books show the subnet masks in Figure 14-5 as the most common.

Address Class	Decimal	Hex
A	255.0.0.0	0xff000000
B	255.255.0.0	0xffff0000
C	255.255.255.0	0xffffff00

Figure 14-5   Subnet Masks

This way of thinking, however, assumes that you are devoting as many bits as possible to the network and as many bits as possible to the host, and that no subnets are used. Figure 14-6 shows an example of using subnetting with a class B address.

Address Class	Class B		
host IP address	152.128.	12.	1
breakdown	network	subnet	hostid
number of bits	16 bits	8 bits	8 bits
subnet mask in decimal	255.255.	255.	0
subnet mask in hexadecimal	0xffffff00		
Example of different host on same subnet	152.128.	12.	2
Example of host on different subnet	152.128.	13.	1

Figure 14-6   Class B IP Address and Subnet Mask Example

In Figure 14-6, the first two bytes of the subnet mask (255.255) define the network, the third byte (255) defines the subnet, and the fourth byte (0) is devoted to the host ID. Although this subnet mask for a class B address did not appear in the earlier default subnet mask figure, the subnet mask of 255.255.255.0 is widely used in class B networks to support subnetting.

How does your UNIX system perform the comparison using the subnet mask of 255.255.255.0 to determine that 152.128.12.1 and 152.128.13.1 are on different subnets? Figure 14-7 shows this comparison.

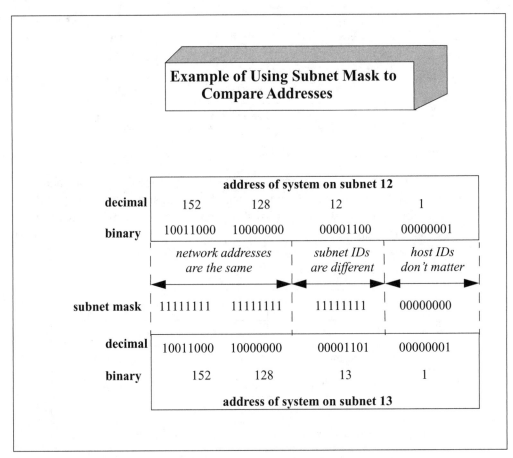

Figure 14-7   Example of Using Subnet Mask to Compare Addresses

Figure 14-8 shows these two systems on the different subnets.

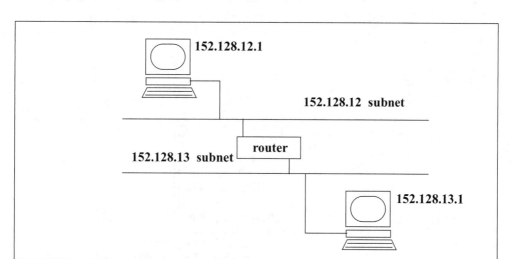

Figure 14-8   Class B Systems on Different Subnets

You don't have to use the 8-bit boundaries to delineate the network, subnet, and host ID fields. If, for example, you want to use part of the subnet field for the host ID, you can do so. A good reason for this approach would be to accommodate future expandability. You might want subnets 12, 13, 14, and 15 to be part of the same subnet today and make these into separate subnets in the future. Figure 14-9 shows this setup.

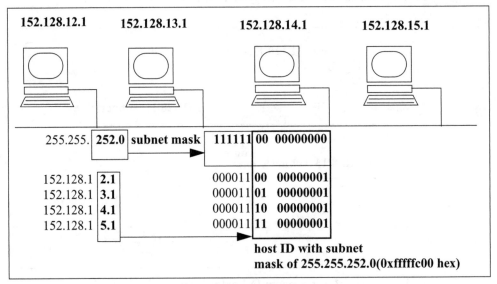

Figure 14-9   Future Expandability Using Subnet Mask

These systems are connected to the same subnet, even though part of the third byte, normally associated with the subnet, is used for the host ID. In the future, the subnet mask could be changed to 255.255.252.0 and have four separate subnets of 12, 13, 14, and 15. This arrangement would require putting routers in place to route to these separate subnets.

Chapter 15 covers configuring and using UNIX networking.

Chapter 15

Configuring and Using Networking

Introduction

In this chapter I configure LAN cards and use various networking commands. If you don't know the basics of UNIX networking please see the previous chapter, which covers UNIX networking background. In this chapter I focus on identifying and configuring LAN cards and use of many networking commands. The following is a bullet list of the topics I cover in this chapter:

- Configuring LAN Adapters (Identify LAN adapters, use **set_parms** to configure, and manually configure)
- Commonly Used Networking Commands, such as **ping**, **netstat**, **route**, **ifconfig** and others
- ARPA Services
- Berkeley commands
- Host name mapping
- DNS Setup
- Network File System (NFS) background

I use abbreviated host names in most cases instead of the fully qualified domain name to make reading easier.

Please keep in mind that in this chapter, I present many commands and techniques that are considered insecure such as FTP, telnet, **rcp**, **rlogin**, and **remsh**. You can substitute FTP/SSL, SFTP, Telent/SSL, SCP, SSH, and others. The concepts and techniques for these more secure tools are the same as those I cover.

At the time of this writing, the latest HP-UX Secure Shell is version A.03.71.000 which is based on OpenSSH 3.7.1p2. This version offers transparent encrypted security for HP-UX 11.0, 11i v1, 11i v1.6, and 11i v2. The client/server architecture supports the SSH-1 and SSH-2 protocols and provides secured remote login, file transfer, and remote command execution. A lot of information on SSH is available on *www.hp.com*, so I encourage you to look at this material.

In the next section I cover LAN card configuration.

Configuring Networking and LAN Adapters

This section covers several topics in this section. First, I identify the LAN cards in the system. Next, I use **set_parms** to configure the first LAN card and view all of the configuration files that were updated. Then, I manually configure the second LAN card.

Identify LAN Cards in System

The first step to take when configuring networking is to identify the networking cards in your HP server. You can have multiple LAN cards in a system and configure multiple IP addresses on the same LAN card if you wish. The following **ioscan** listing shows three LAN cards in a server:

```
[ root : / ]> ioscan -funC lan
Class     I  H/W Path        Driver   S/W State   H/W Type     Description
========================================================================
lan       0  0/0/8/1/0/4/0   igelan   CLAIMED     INTERFACE    HP A6794-60001 PC
I 1000Base-T
lan       1  0/0/10/1/0/6/0  igelan   CLAIMED     INTERFACE    HP A9784-60001 PC
I/PCI-X 1000Base-T FC/GigE Combo Adapter
lan       2  0/0/12/1/0/6/0  igelan   CLAIMED     INTERFACE    HP A9784-60001 PC
```

```
I/PCI-X 1000Base-T FC/GigE Combo Adapter
[ root : / ]>
```

This output shows three 1000 Base-T LAN interfaces in this nPartition. in three different PCI slots at *0/0/8, 10,* and *12.* Two of these are combination cards that have both a LAN adapter and fibre interface on them. These three interfaces are *lan0, lan1,* and *lan2.* All these cards use the *igelan* driver that can be viewed with the **lsdev -C lan** command.

Use set_parms to Configure First LAN Interface

In this section, I configure the first LAN card, *lan0,* with **set_parms initial**. I'll skip over some of the dialogue asking me to confirm settings that I have specified. The information for this system was entered when it was booted after installation, but you can see in the following output that you could add or modify any of the parameters related to *lan0* when prompted. I have a comment before each screen indicating the information, such as hostname or IP address, that will be specified.

Initial Screen:

```
                        Welcome to HP-UX!
Before using your system, you will need to answer a few questions.

The first question is whether you plan to use this system on a network.

Answer "yes" if you have connected the system to a network and are ready
to link with a network.

Answer "no" if you:

    * Plan to set up this system as a standalone (no networking).

    * Want to use the system now as a standalone and connect to a
      network later.
```

```
Are you ready to link this system to a network?

Press [y] for yes or [n] for no, then press [Enter]
```

Hostname:

```
For the system to operate correctly, you must assign it a unique
system name or "hostname".  The hostname can be a simple name
(example: widget) or an Internet fully-qualified domain name
(example: widget.redrock-cvl.hp.com).

A simple name, or each dot (.) separated component of a domain name, must:

    * Start and end with a letter or number.

    * Contain no more than 63 characters.

    * Contain only letters, numbers, underscore (_), or dash (-).
      The underscore (_) is not recommended.

NOTE: The first or only component of a hostname should contain 8
      characters or less for compatibility with HP-UX `uname'.

The current hostname is otcapdv2.
```

```
Enter the system name, then press [Enter] or simply press [Enter]
```

Time Zone:

```
The following procedure enables you to set the time zone.

Select your location from the following list:

   1) North America or Hawaii

   2) Central America

   3) South America

   4) Europe

   5) Africa

   6) Asia

   7) Australia, New Zealand
```

Time Zone:

```
Select your time zone from the following list:

   1) Newfoundland Standard/Daylight        8) Pacific Standard/Daylight

   2) Atlantic Standard/Daylight            9) Yukon Standard/Daylight

   3) Eastern Standard/Daylight            10) Aleutian Standard/Daylight

   4) Eastern Standard Only                11) Hawaii Standard
        (US: Most of Indiana)
                                           12) Unlisted time zone
   5) Central Standard/Daylight
                                           13) Previous menu
   6) Mountain Standard/Daylight

   7) Mountain Standard Only (Arizona)
```

System time:

```
The current system time is Wed Dec 15 11:30:01 EST 2004

Is this correct?
```

IP address:

```
If you wish networking to operate correctly, you must assign the
system a unique Internet Protocol (IP) address.  The IP address must:

  * Contain 4 numeric components.

  * Have a period (.) separating each numeric component.

  * Contain numbers between 0 and 255.

  For example:  134.32.3.10

Warning: Leading zeros within a component signify an octal number!

Your current address is 10.14.16.19.  To retain this address,
just press [Enter].
```

```
Enter your IP address, then press [Enter] or press [Enter] to select
the current address (10.14.16.19):
```

Subnet Mask:

```
Additional Network Parameters: Subnetwork Mask and Default Gateway

Enter the subnetwork mask and default gateway information.

Example:

    Subnetwork mask:    255.255.255.0
    Gateway IP address: 10.14.16.1

Current Settings:

 -> Subnetwork mask:    255.255.255.0
    Gateway IP address: 10.14.16.1
```

```
Enter the subnetwork mask, then press [Enter] or just press [Enter]
```

Default Gateway:

```
Additional Network Parameters: Subnetwork Mask and Default Gateway

Enter the subnetwork mask and default gateway information.

Example:

    Subnetwork mask:    255.255.255.0
```

```
        Gateway IP address: 10.14.16.1

   Current Settings:

     Subnetwork mask:    255.255.255.0
   -> Gateway IP address: 10.14.16.1
```

```
Enter the gateway address, then press [Enter] or just press [Enter]
to select the current gateway address (10.14.16.1):
```

I entered a lot of information using **set_parms initial**. I did not use
DHCP; instead I entered *hostname*, *IP address*, *subnet mask*, *default gateway*, and others.

Let's look at some of the files that were updated and run some commands to see that networking-related updates were made. The first file I view
is **/etc/rc.config.d/netconf**:

```
[ root : / ]> cat /etc/rc.config.d/netconf
# netconf:  configuration values for core networking subsystems
#
# @(#)B.11.11_LR $Revision: 1.6.119.6 $ $Date: 97/09/10 15:56:01 $
#
# HOSTNAME:          Name of your system for uname -S and hostname
#
# OPERATING_SYSTEM:  Name of operating system returned by uname -s
#                    ---- DO NOT CHANGE THIS VALUE ----
#
# LOOPBACK_ADDRESS:  Loopback address
#                    ---- DO NOT CHANGE THIS VALUE ----
#
# IMPORTANT:  for 9.x-to-10.0 transition, do not put blank lines between
# the next set of statements

HOSTNAME="otcapdv2"
OPERATING_SYSTEM=HP-UX
LOOPBACK_ADDRESS=127.0.0.1

# Internet configuration parameters.  See ifconfig(1m), autopush(1m)
#
# INTERFACE_NAME:    Network interface name (see lanscan(1m))
#
# IP_ADDRESS:        Hostname (in /etc/hosts) or IP address in decimal-dot
#                    notation (e.g., 192.1.2.3)
#
# SUBNET_MASK:       Subnetwork mask in decimal-dot notation, if different
#                    from default
#
# BROADCAST_ADDRESS: Broadcast address in decimal-dot notation, if
#                    different from default
#
# INTERFACE_STATE:   Desired interface state at boot time.
#                    either up or down, default is up.
#
# DHCP_ENABLE        Determines whether or not DHCP client functionality
#                    will be enabled on the network interface (see
#                    auto_parms(1M), dhcpclient(1M)). DHCP clients get
#                    their IP address assignments from DHCP servers.
#                    1 enables DHCP client functionality; 0 disables it.
#
# For each additional network interfaces, add a set of variable assignments
# like the ones below, changing the index to "[1]", "[2]" et cetera.
#
# IMPORTANT:  for 9.x-to-10.0 transition, do not put blank lines between
# the next set of statements

INTERFACE_NAME[0]=lan0
```

```
IP_ADDRESS[0]=10.14.16.19
SUBNET_MASK[0]=255.255.255.0
BROADCAST_ADDRESS[0]=""
INTERFACE_STATE[0]=up
DHCP_ENABLE[0]=0

# Internet routing configuration.  See route(1m), routing(7)
#
# ROUTE_DESTINATION:  Destination hostname (in /etc/hosts) or host or network
#                     IP address in decimal-dot notation, preceded by the word
#                     "host" or "net"; or simply the word "default".
#
# ROUTE_MASK:         Subnetwork mask in decimal-dot notation, or C language
#                     hexadecimal notation.  This is an optional field.
#                     A IP address, subnet mask pair uniquely identifies
#                     a subnet to be reached. If a subnet mask is not given,
#                     then the system will assign the longest subnet mask
#                     of the configured network interfaces to this route.
#                     If there is no matching subnet mask, then the system
#                     will assign the default network mask as the route's
#                     subnet mask.
#
# ROUTE_GATEWAY:      Gateway hostname (in /etc/hosts) or IP address in
#                     decimal-dot notation.  If local interface, must use the
#                     same form as used for IP_ADDRESS above (hostname or
#                     decimal-dot notation). If loopback interface, i.e.,
#                     127.0.0.1, the ROUTE_COUNT must be set to zero.
#
# ROUTE_COUNT:        An integer that indicates whether the gateway is a
#                     remote interface (one) or the local interface (zero)
#                     or loopback interface (e.g., 127.*).
#
# ROUTE_ARGS:         Route command arguments and options.  This variable
#                     may contain a combination of the following arguments:
#                     "-f", "-n" and "-p pmtu".
#
# For each additional route, add a set of variable assignments like the ones
# below, changing the index to "[1]", "[2]" et cetera.
#
# IMPORTANT:  for 9.x-to-10.0 transition, do not put blank lines between
# the next set of statements

# ROUTE_DESTINATION[0]=default
# ROUTE_MASK[0]=""
# ROUTE_GATEWAY[0]=""
# ROUTE_COUNT[0]=""
# ROUTE_ARGS[0]=""

# Dynamic routing daemon configuration.  See gated(1m)
#
# GATED:       Set to 1 to start gated daemon.
# GATED_ARGS:  Arguments to the gated daemon.

GATED=0
GATED_ARGS=""

#
# Router Discover Protocol daemon configuration.  See rdpd(1m)
#
# RDPD:        Set to 1 to start rdpd daemon
#

RDPD=0

#
# Reverse ARP daemon configuration.  See rarpd(1m)
#
# RARP:        Set to 1 to start rarpd daemon
#

RARP=0

ROUTE_GATEWAY[0]=10.14.16.1
ROUTE_COUNT[0]=1
ROUTE_DESTINATION[0]=default
```

All information related to *lan0* that was entered as part of **set_parms intitial** is present in this file. Note that variables related to *lan0* use a *[0]*, which is significant in the next section I manually add to this file information related to *lan1* and use *[1]*.

The **/etc/hosts** file (see the **/etc/hosts** overview later in this chapter) was also automatically updated to include the hostname and address I entered earlier. This file should be updated to include systems to which you'll connect as you see in the next section. The following is the **/etc/hosts** file for the system:

```
[ root : / ]> cat /etc/hosts
## Configured using SAM by root on Wed Oct 27 11:36:55 2004
# @(#)B.11.11_LRhosts $Revision: 1.9.214.1 $ $Date: 96/10/08 13:20:01 $
#
# The form for each entry is:
# <internet address>    <official hostname> <aliases>
#
# For example:
# 192.1.2.34    hpfcrm loghost
#
# See the hosts(4) manual page for more information.
# Note: The entries cannot be preceded by a space.
#        The format described in this file is the correct format.
#        The original Berkeley manual page contains an error in
#        the format description.
#

10.14.16.19     otcapdv2
10.14.16.12     corpnjdc1.corp.scholasticinc.local   corpnjdc1
127.0.0.1       localhost        loopback
192.151.53.128  isee.americas.hp.com
```

The *hostname* of *otcapdv2* appears in **/etc/hosts**.

I now run form 2 of the **ifconfig** command to view parameters related to *lan0*:

```
[ root : / ]>    ifconfig lan0
lan0: flags=1843<UP,BROADCAST,RUNNING,MULTICAST,CKO>
      inet 10.14.16.19 netmask ffffff00 broadcast 10.14.16.255
```

This **ifconfig** output shows the IP address I entered for *lan0* of *10.14.16.19*, and the subnet mask I entered, in hex form, of *255.255.255.0*. The interface is *UP* so it is operational.

I have not confirmed that the *default gateway* that was specified. The following **netstat -rn** command is used to show *routing* in *number* format for *lan0*:

```
[ root : / ]> netstat -rn
Routing tables
Destination            Gateway            Flags    Refs Interface    Pmtu
127.0.0.1              127.0.0.1          UH         0  lo0          4136
10.14.16.19            10.14.16.19        UH         0  lan0         4136
10.14.16.0             10.14.16.19        U          2  lan0         1500
127.0.0.0              127.0.0.1          U          0  lo0             0
default                10.14.16.1         UG         0  lan0            0
```

The *default* route I specified of *10.14.16.1* is shown in the last line of this output. Any IP addresses to which I connect that are not on the subnet will use this *default* route.

The gateway I specified as the default route in the **netconf** file of *10.14.16.1* is shown as the default gateway in this **netstat** output. Routes can be added and deleted with the **route** command (see the **route** overview later in this chapter).

Using **set_parms**, I set up a lot of host and networking-related information. In the next section I manually expand these files to include information related to the second networking interface.

Manually Configure Second LAN Interface

In the previous section, I used **set_parms** to set up the first LAN card in the system, as well has hostname and other parameters, and in this section, I perform the same work manually for the second LAN card.

The information I added to **netconf** includes the IP address, subnet mask, broadcast address, gateway, and all information related to *lan0*. *[0]* identifies entries made in the file for *lan0*.

The first step is to expand **/etc/rc.config.d/netconf** to include variable information for the second LAN card. I add the following second block of information for lan1 to **netconf**:

```
INTERFACE_NAME[0]=lan0
IP_ADDRESS[0]=10.14.16.19
SUBNET_MASK[0]=255.255.255.0
BROADCAST_ADDRESS[0]=""
INTERFACE_STATE[0]=up
DHCP_ENABLE[0]=0

INTERFACE_NAME[1]=lan1
IP_ADDRESS[1]=10.14.16.25
SUBNET_MASK[1]=255.255.255.0
BROADCAST_ADDRESS[1]=""
INTERFACE_STATE[1]=up
DHCP_ENABLE[0]=0
```

With this block of information in **netconf** the file has now been expanded to include information for *lan1* with *[1]*.

Similarly, the **/etc/hosts** file was expanded to include the host name and IP address of the second LAN card as the last entry, as shown in the following listing:

```
# The form for each entry is:
# <internet address>    <official hostname> <aliases>
#
# For example:
# 192.1.2.34    hpfcrm  loghost
#
# See the hosts(4) manual page for more information.
# Note: The entries cannot be preceded by a space.
#       The format described in this file is the correct format.
#       The original Berkeley manual page contains an error in
#       the format description.
#
127.0.0.1       localhost       loopback
10.14.16.18     otcapdv1        otcapdv1
10.14.16.19     otcapdv2        otcapdv2
10.14.16.21     otcdbdv1        otcdbdv1
10.14.16.22     otcdbdv2        otcdbdv2
10.14.16.25     otcapdvtest2 otcapdvtest2
```

The second LAN card and its IP address were added to the file as well as other systems.

I can make these entries take effect by running **/sbin/init.d/net stop** and then **/sbin/init.d/net start** to reread the networking files, and then run **ifconfig** and **netstat -rn** to see if the additions were made for *lan1*, as shown in the following output:

```
# /sbin/init.d/net stop
# /sbin/init.d/net start
# ifconfig lan0
lan0: flags=1843<UP,BROADCAST,RUNNING,MULTICAST,CKO>
        inet 10.14.16.19 netmask ffffff00 broadcast 10.14.16.255
# ifconfig lan1
lan1: flags=1843<UP,BROADCAST,RUNNING,MULTICAST,CKO>
        inet 10.14.16.25 netmask ffffff00 broadcast 10.14.16.255
# netstat -rn
Routing tables
Destination          Gateway          Flags  Refs Interface  Pmtu
127.0.0.1            127.0.0.1        UH        0  lo0        4136
10.14.16.25          10.14.16.25      UH        0  lan1       4136
10.14.16.19          10.14.16.19      UH        0  lan0       4136
10.14.16.0           10.14.16.25      U         2  lan1       1500
10.14.16.0           10.14.16.19      U         2  lan0       1500
127.0.0.0            127.0.0.1        U         0  lo0           0
default              10.14.16.1       UG        0  lan0          0
```

The output of the two **ifconfig** commands shows that the two LAN cards have been configured. The gateway I had specified as the default route in the **netconf** file is shown as the default gateway in this **netstat** output.

Routes can be added and deleted with the **route** command (see the **route** overview later in this chapter). I use these interfaces for more advanced work in other chapters. As a test to ensure that these interfaces work I was able to **ping** another system.

I could also have configured *lan1* at the command line with **ifconfig** (see the **ifconfig** overview later in this chapter). **ifconfig** can be used to configure a LAN interface or display information related to a LAN interface configuration. The following example shows running **ifconfig** to configure *lan1*:

```
# /etc/ifconfig lan1 inet 10.14.16.25 netmask 255.255.255.0
```

This is the first form of the **ifconfig** command in which LAN card parameters are specified.

As an added piece of information, make sure that you do not have duplicate files in **/etc/rc.config.d** such as **netconf** and **netconf.old**. The system isn't smart enough and read all files and get confused. The work around is to reverse naming convention. For example, **netconf.old** needs to be **old.netconf**. If you do have duplicate files in this directory, you need to reboot after changing the naming convention.

I have covered manually configuring a LAN card and the files related to doing so in this section. I have a third LAN card in this system that I could configure with **set_parms** or manually by performing the steps in this section.

The next section covers some frequently used networking commands, including many of those I used in this section.

Commonly Used Networking Commands

Setting up a network is an intensive planning exercise for both network and system administrators. No two networking environments are alike. There is typically a lot of networking electronics to which your system is connected. There are many useful commands related to testing connectivity to other systems and networking configuration. Should you encounter a problem, you want to have an understanding of some networking commands that can be lifesavers. In addition, you can encounter some tricky aspects to networking setup if you have some networking hardware that your UNIX systems must interface to, such as routers, gateways, bridges, and so on. I give an example of one such case: connecting a UNIX system to a router. At the same time, I cover some of the most handy networking commands as part of this description. I also give examples of some commands on a variety of UNIX variants because many installations run more than one variant of UNIX.

Consider Figure 15-1, in which a UNIX system is connected directly to a router.

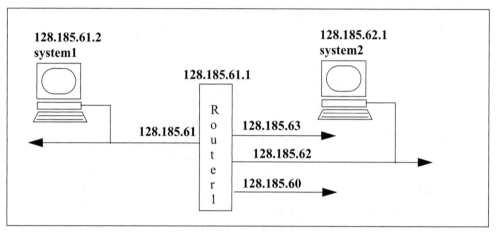

Figure 15-1   UNIX System and Router Example

Here, I have a UNIX system connected to segment 128.185.61. This is a class "B" Internet address with subnetting enabled. Keep in mind the reference in the previous chapter on Classless Inter-Domain Routing (CIDR.) As part of CIDR address blocks are allocated based on CIDR and not as cell-based blocks.

The **/etc/hosts** file needs to have in it the UNIX system with node ID 2, the router, and any other systems on this segment or segments on the other side of the router.

If the router is properly configured, I should be able to seamlessly connect from 61 to systems on segments 60, 62, and 63. The router should be configured to allow the system to connect to systems on other segments (60, 62, and 63) by going through the router. Some unforeseen configuration was required to make this simple network operate seamlessly. In this case, a problem occurred getting system1 to connect to systems on the other side of the router on 60, 62, and 63. Before discussing the additional configuration that needs to be done, I first show the **/etc/hosts** file and then use some very useful UNIX commands that show the state of the network. Here is the **/etc/hosts** file showing just the UNIX system and router:

```
$ cat /etc/hosts
127.0.0.1      localhosts loopback
128.185.61.1   router1# router
128.185.61.2   system1# UNIX system on 61
128.185.62.1   system2# UNIX system on 62
```

This host file is simple and allows system1 to connect to router1 and system2. The connection from system1 to system2 is accomplished by going through the router.

ping

Let's look at one of the most commonly used networking commands - **ping**. This command is used to determine whether or not a connection exists between two networking components. **ping** is a simple command that sends an ICMP echo packet to the host you specify once per second. You may recall that ICMP was covered earlier under the network, or third layer. **ping** stands for Packet InterNet Groper. **ping** differs somewhat among UNIX variants, mostly in the reporting that **ping** produces when no options are provided.

Some systems provide performance information when **ping** is issued with no options; others report that the system "is alive." The following is an example shows checking the connection between the local system and another system on the network called *austin*:

```
martyp $ ping austin
austin is alive
martyp $
```

You can adjust the packet size and number of iterations on most UNIX variants as in the following HP-UX example, specifying a packet size of *4096* and interval of *5*:

```
# ping 12 4096 5
PING 12: 4096 byte packets
4096 bytes from 10.1.1.12: icmp_seq=0. time=2. ms
4096 bytes from 10.1.1.12: icmp_seq=1. time=2. ms
```

```
4096 bytes from 10.1.1.12: icmp_seq=2. time=2. ms
4096 bytes from 10.1.1.12: icmp_seq=3. time=2. ms
4096 bytes from 10.1.1.12: icmp_seq=4. time=2. ms

----12 PING Statistics----
5 packets transmitted, 5 packets received, 0% packet loss
round-trip (ms)  min/avg/max = 2/2/2
#
```

How do I know that I have a connection between system1 and the router and the other systems on the other side of the router? I use the **ping** command. Here is how I know that system1 is connected to router1:

```
$ ping router1
PING router1: 64 byte packets
64 bytes from 128.185.61.2: icmp_seq=0. time=0. ms
64 bytes from 128.185.61.2: icmp_seq=1. time=0. ms
64 bytes from 128.185.61.2: icmp_seq=2. time=0. ms
```

Each line of output here represents a response that was returned from the device that was pinged. This means that the device responded. You continue to get this response indefinitely and have to type ^c (control c) to terminate the **ping**. If no output is produced, as shown in the following example, then no response occurred and you may have a problem between your system and the device to which you are checking the connection:

```
$ ping system2
PING router1: 64 byte packets
```

In this scenario, you see this message and that is as far as you would get. A ^c kills the **ping**, and you see that some number of packets were sent and none were received. I did get this response when issuing the **ping** command, so I know that a problem exists with the connection between system1 and router1.

ping should be used only for testing purposes, such as manual fault isolation, because it can generate a substantial amount of network traffic if you sweep a lot of addresses often.

A nice variation of **ping** that I use is to specify a packet size of 4,096 bytes, rather than the default of 64 bytes shown in the previous examples, and count the number of times **ping** transmits before terminating, rather than having to type ^c to terminate **ping**. The following example shows this:

```
$ ping router1 4096 5

PING router1: 64 byte packets
4096 bytes from 128.185.51.2: icmp_seq=0. time=8. ms
4096 bytes from 128.185.51.2: icmp_seq=1. time=8. ms
4096 bytes from 128.185.51.2: icmp_seq=2. time=9. ms
4096 bytes from 128.185.51.2: icmp_seq=3. time=8. ms
4096 bytes from 128.185.51.2: icmp_seq=4. time=8. ms
```

Notice that the time required to transmit and receive a response, the round-trip time, is substantially longer than with only 64 bytes transmitted. I usually find that the round-trip time for 64 bytes is 0 ms, although this depends on a number of factors, including network topology and network traffic.

netstat

From the previous description of the subnet mask, you can see that routing from one host to another can be configured in a variety of ways. The path that information takes in getting from one host to another depends on routing.

You can obtain information related to routing with the **netstat** command. The *-r* option to **netstat** shows the routing tables, which you usually want to know, and the *-n* option can be used to print network addresses as numbers rather than as names. With the *-v* option, you get additional information related to routing, such as the subnet mask. In the following examples, **netstat** is issued with the *-r* option (this is used when describing the **netstat** output), the *-rn* options, and the *-rnv* options, so you can compare the outputs:

```
# netstat -r
Routing tables
Dest/Netmask      Gateway        Flags  Refs      Use  Interface  Pmtu
o2                o2             UH      0    1890905  lo0        4136
o2                o2             UH      0        343  lan1       4136
o2                o2             UH      0          0  lan0       4136
10.1.1.0          o2             U       2          0  lan0       1500
10.1.1.0          o2             U       2          0  lan1       1500
127.0.0.0         o2             U       0          0  lo0        4136
default           10.1.1.1       UG      0          0  lan1       1500
#
```

```
# netstat -rn
Routing tables
Dest/Netmask          Gateway          Flags Refs       Use  Interface  Pmtu
127.0.0.1             127.0.0.1        UH      0     1891016  lo0        4136
10.1.1.10             10.1.1.10        UH      0         343  lan1       4136
10.1.1.110            10.1.1.110       UH      0           0  lan0       4136
10.1.1.0              10.1.1.110       U       2           0  lan0       1500
10.1.1.0              10.1.1.10        U       2           0  lan1       1500
127.0.0.0             127.0.0.1        U       0           0  lo0        4136
default               10.1.1.1         UG      0           0  lan1       1500
#


# netstat -rnv
Routing tables
Dest/Netmask                  Gateway       Flags Refs     Use  Interface  Pmtu
127.0.0.1/255.255.255.255     127.0.0.1     UH      0  1891036  lo0        4136
10.1.1.10/255.255.255.255     10.1.1.10     UH      0      343  lan1       4136
10.1.1.110/255.255.255.255    10.1.1.110    UH      0        0  lan0       4136
10.1.1.0/255.255.255.0        10.1.1.110    U       2        0  lan0       1500
10.1.1.0/255.255.255.0        10.1.1.10     U       2        0  lan1       1500
127.0.0.0/255.0.0.0           127.0.0.1     U       0        0  lo0        4136
default/0.0.0.0               10.1.1.1      UG      0        0  lan1       1500
#
```

The first and second outputs show that the system, *o2*, has three interfaces: The first is the loopback interface called *lo0*. The second is at *.10*, and the third is at *.110* (which you can see from the *-rn* output). The next two lines show that the destination of *10.1.1.0*, which is a network, can be accessed through either the card at *.10* or *.110*. The third output provides verbose information. The last line is for the default route. This entry says to send packets to *10.1.1.1* if a more direct route can't be found.

With **netstat**, some information is provided about the router. The *-r* option shows information about routing, but many other useful options to this command are also available. Of particular interest in this output is "Flags," which defines the type of routing that takes place. Here are descriptions of the most common flags from the UNIX manual pages:

1=U   Route to a *network* via a gateway that is the local host itself.

3=U   Route to a *network* via a gateway that is the remote host.

5=UH   Route to a *host* via a gateway that is the local host itself.

7=UG   Route to a *host* via a remote gateway that is a host.

Also, I use two forms of **netstat** to obtain network statistics, as opposed to routing information. The first is **netstat -i**, which shows the state of interfaces that are autoconfigured. Because I am most interested in getting a summary of **lan0**, I issue this command. **netstat -i** gives a good rundown of *lan0*, such as the network it is on, its name, and so on.

The following example shows the output of **netstat -i** on an HP-UX system:

```
# netstat -i

Name  Mtu    Network       Address         Ipkts Ierrs   Opkts Oerrs  Coll
ni0*  0      none          none                0     0       0     0     0
ni1*  0      none          none                0     0       0     0     0
lo0   4608   loopback      127.0.0.1         232     0     232     0     0
lan0  1500   169.200.112   169.200.112.2 3589746     2   45630     0   104


# netstat -i
Name        Mtu Network       Address            Ipkts       Opkts
lan1        1500 10.1.1.0      o2              59935480   163641547
lan0        1500 10.1.1.0      o2                139173    12839358
lo0         4136 127.0.0.0     o2               1892333     1892345
#
```

Here is a description of the fields in the **netstat** example:

Name	The name of your network interface (Name), in this case, *lan0*.
MTU	The "maximum transmission unit," which is the maximum packet size sent by the interface card.
Network	The network address of the LAN to which the interface card is connected (169.200).
Address	The host name of your system. This is the symbolic name of your system as it appears in the file **/etc/hosts**.

The statistical information includes:

Ipkts	The number of packets received by the interface card, in this case **lan0**.
Ierrs	The number of errors detected on incoming packets by the interface card (on some UNIX variants).
Opkts	The number of packets transmitted by the interface card.
Oerrs	The number of errors detected during the transmission of packets by the interface card (on some UNIX variants).
Collis	The number of collisions that resulted from packet traffic (on some UNIX variants).

netstat provides cumulative data since the node was last powered up; you might have a long elapsed time over which data was accumulated. If you are interested in seeing useful statistical information, you can use **netstat** with different options. You can also specify an interval over which to report statistics. I usually ignore the first entry, because it shows all data since the system was last powered up. Therefore, the data includes non-prime hours when the system was idle. I prefer to view data at the time the system is working its hardest. The following **netstat** example provides network interface information every five seconds:

```
# netstat -I lan0 5
```

(lan0)-> input		output			(Total)-> input		output		
packets	errs	packets	errs	colls	packets	errs	packets	errs	colls
3590505	2	45714	0	104	3590737	2	45946	0	104
134	0	5	0	0	134	0	5	0	0
174	0	0	0	0	174	0	0	0	0
210	0	13	0	0	210	0	13	0	0
165	0	0	0	0	165	0	0	0	0
169	0	0	0	0	169	0	0	0	0
193	0	0	0	0	193	0	0	0	0
261	0	7	0	0	261	0	7	0	0
142	0	8	0	0	142	0	8	0	0
118	0	0	0	0	118	0	0	0	0
143	0	0	0	0	143	0	0	0	0
149	0	0	0	0	149	0	0	0	0

With this example, you get multiple outputs of what is taking place on the LAN interface. As previously mentioned, you may want to ignore the first output, because it includes information over a long time period. This may include a time when your network was idle and therefore, the data is not important to you.

The following **netstat** example provides network interface information every five seconds on an HP-UX 11i system:

```
# netstat -I lan0 5
(lan0)-> input      output       (Total)-> input     output
        packets     packets                packets    packets
        2500745     2236834                3781914    3518003
             13          14                   1190       1191
              6           4                   1140       1138
            282         278                    282        278
             32          28                     32         28
              2           2                      2          2
             52          52                     52         52
```

Notice that delta values are shown and not the totals, as was the case in older releases of HP-UX.

You can specify the network interface on which you want statistics reported by using **-I interface**; in the case of the example, it was *-I lan0*. An interval of five seconds was also used in this example.

Yet another use of **netstat** is to show the state of network sockets. **netstat -a** produces a list of protocols, queues, local and remote addresses, and protocol states. All this information is useful for showing active communications, as shown in the following abbreviated example:

```
[ root : /]> netstat -a
Active Internet connections (including servers)
Proto Recv-Q Send-Q  Local Address            Foreign Address          (state)
tcp        0      0  otcapdv2.54599           otcapdv2.54597           CLOSE_WAIT
tcp        0      0  otcapdv2.60949           otcapdv2.60947           FIN_WAIT_2
tcp        0      0  otcapdv2.55306           otcapdv2.55308           FIN_WAIT_2
tcp        0      0  otcapdv2.55220           otcapdv2.55218           CLOSE_WAIT
tcp        0      0  otcapdv2.52118           otcapdv2.52121           FIN_WAIT_2
tcp        0      0  otcapdv2.49968           otcapdv2.49966           CLOSE_WAIT
tcp        0      0  otcapdv2.57592           otcapdv2.57590           CLOSE_WAIT
tcp        0      0  localhost.1521           localhost.50212          ESTABLISHED
tcp        0      0  otcapdv2.65063           otcapdv2.65061           CLOSE_WAIT
tcp        0      0  otcapdv2.56173           otcapdv2.56176           FIN_WAIT_2
tcp        0      0  otcapdv2.65171           otcapdv2.65169           CLOSE_WAIT
tcp        0      0  otcapdv2.1521            otcapdv2.50178           ESTABLISHED
tcp        0      0  localhost.50147          localhost.63798          ESTABLISHED
tcp        0      0  otcapdv2.56191           otcapdv2.56193           FIN_WAIT_2
tcp        0      0  otcapdv2.50409           otcapdv2.50406           CLOSE_WAIT
tcp        0      0  otcapdv2.61438           otcapdv2.61436           CLOSE_WAIT
tcp        0      0  otcapdv2.51072           otcapdv2.51070           CLOSE_WAIT
tcp        0      0  otcapdv2.54653           otcapdv2.54655           FIN_WAIT_2
tcp        0      0  otcapdv2.60357           otcapdv2.60359           FIN_WAIT_2
tcp        0      0  otcapdv2.54353           otcapdv2.54351           CLOSE_WAIT
tcp        0      0  otcapdv2.62806           otcapdv2.62808           FIN_WAIT_2
                        .
                        .
                        .
tcp        0      0  *.64304                  *.*                      LISTEN
tcp        0      0  *.50157                  *.*                      LISTEN
```

```
tcp       0       0   *.console            *.*                    LISTEN
tcp       0       0   *.1521               *.*                    LISTEN
tcp       0       0   *.49298              *.*                    LISTEN
tcp       0       0   *.1626               *.*                    LISTEN
tcp       0       0   *.49360              *.*                    LISTEN
tcp       0       0   *.49152              *.*                    LISTEN
tcp       0       0   *.portmap            *.*                    LISTEN
tcp       0       0   *.hacl-probe         *.*                    LISTEN
tcp       0       0   *.hacl-cfg           *.*                    LISTEN
tcp       0       0   *.dtspc              *.*                    LISTEN
tcp       0       0   *.recserv            *.*                    LISTEN
tcp       0       0   *.7000               *.*                    LISTEN
tcp       0       0   *.49362              *.*                    LISTEN
tcp       0       0   *.7161               *.*                    LISTEN
tcp       0       0   *.swat               *.*                    LISTEN
tcp       0       0   *.49157              *.*                    LISTEN
tcp       0       0   *.49366              *.*                    LISTEN
tcp       0       0   *.samd               *.*                    LISTEN
tcp       0       0   *.nfsd               *.*                    LISTEN

              .
              .
              .
```

A lot of information is given in this output. You can refer to the manual page if you want a detailed explanation of the fields.

There are some lines that show the *Proto tcp* to the *Local Address system1.telnet* as having a *(state)* of *ESTABLISHED*. These are connections that have been established to this system.

I added the *tcp* protocol entries that are listening at the end of the listing. This means that they are listening for incoming connections, as indicated by the *LISTEN*. They have a wild card in the *Foreign Address* field, which will contain the address when a connection is established.

All the send and receive queues, shown as *Recv-Q* and *Send-Q*, are empty as indicated by *0*.

This output gives you an appreciation of the immense amount of activity taking place from a networking perspective on your UNIX system.

route

The information displayed with **netstat** comprises the routing tables for your system. Some are automatically created with the **ifconfig** command when your system is booted or when the network interface is initialized. Routes to networks and hosts that are not directly connected to your system are entered with the **route** command.

Routing changes can be made on the fly, as I did to change the *Flags* from *U* to *UG*:

```
$ /usr/sbin/route add default 128.185.61.1 3
```

First is the **route** command. Second, I specify that I want to add a route; the other option is to delete a route. Third, I specify the destination, in this case, the default. This could be a specific host name, a network name, an IP address, or default that signifies the wild card gateway route that is shown in the example. Fourth is the gateway through which the destination is reached. In the previous example, the IP address was used, but this could also be a host name. The 3 corresponds to the count that is used to specify whether the gateway is the local host or a remote gateway. If the gateway is the local host, then a count of 0 is used. If the gateway is a remote host, which is the case in the example, a count of >0 is used. This corresponds to *UG* for *Flags*. This manually changed the network routing table by adding a default route with the appropriate *Flags*. Issuing this command fixed the problem I encountered trying to get system1 to talk to the systems on the other side of the router (remember Figure 12-10 in Chapter 12?).

Before issuing **/usr/sbin/route** with the **add** option, you can first use the **delete** option to remove the existing default route, which is not working.

route commands usually appear in one of the system's startup files so that every time the system boots, **route** commands are issued. This ensures that the right connectivity information is in place every time the system starts.

ifconfig

The **ifconfig** command provides additional information on a LAN interface. The following example provides the configuration of a network interface:

```
$ /etc/ifconfig lan0
lan0:   flags=863<UP,BROADCAST,NOTRAILERS,RUNNING>
        inet 128.185.61.2 netmask ffff0000 broadcast 128.185.61.255
```

From this example, I can quickly see that the interface is up, it has an address of 128.185.61.2, and it has a netmask of *ffff0000*. Again, keep in mind that your network interface may have a different name, such as *le0*.

You can use **ifconfig** to get the status of a network interface, as I have done here to assign an address to a network interface, or to configure network interface parameters. The network address you have falls into classes such as "A," "B," or "C," as mentioned earlier. You want to be sure that you know the class of your network before you start configuring your LAN interface. This example is a class "B" network, so the netmask is defined as ffff0000 (typical for a class "B" address), as opposed to ffffff00, which is typical for a class "C" network. The netmask is used to determine how much of the address to reserve for subdividing the network into smaller networks. The netmask can be represented in hex, as just shown or in decimal format, as in the **/etc/hosts** file. Here is the **ifconfig** command I issued to configure the interface:

```
$ /etc/ifconfig lan0 inet 128.185.61.2 netmask 255.255.0.0
```

- The *255.255.0.0* corresponds to the hex *ffff000* previously shown for the class "B" subnet mask.

- *lan0* is the interface being configured.

- *inet* is the address family, which is currently the only one supported for this system.

- *128.185.61.2* is the address of the LAN interface for system1.

- **netmask** shows how to subdivide the network.

- *255.255.0.0* is the same as *ffff0000*, which is the netmask for a class "B" address.

I have made good use of **netstat**, **ping**, and **ifconfig** to help get the status of the network. **ifconfig**, **route**, and **/etc/hosts** are used to configure the network, should you identify any changes you need to make. The subnet examples show how flexible you can be when configuring your network for both your current and future needs. In simple networks, you may not need to use many of these commands or complex subnetting. In complex networks, or at times when you encounter configuration difficulties, you may have to make extensive use of these commands. In either case, network planning is an important part of setting up UNIX systems.

Most of the commands used throughout this chapter are a part of every system administrator's tool box. Networking is so vital to the use of UNIX systems, however, that having background in this area can help with your overall understanding of the system and how to use it more effectively.

rpcinfo

As a user, you may have a need to NFS mount a directory on another system or perform some other function that you haven't before used on your system. You can determine whether various pieces of functionality have been enabled by evaluating the daemons running on your system. **rpcinfo** allows you to query the Remote Procedure Call (RPC) port wrapper, called *rpcbind* on a system, including your local system, by issuing the command **rpc -p** *system_name*.

The following example shows issuing **rpcinfo -p** on the local system:

```
[ root : / ]> rpcinfo -p
   program vers proto   port  service
    100000    4   tcp    111  rpcbind
    100000    3   tcp    111  rpcbind
    100000    2   tcp    111  rpcbind
    100000    4   udp    111  rpcbind
    100000    3   udp    111  rpcbind
    100000    2   udp    111  rpcbind
    100024    1   tcp  49152  status
    100024    1   udp  49153  status
    100021    1   tcp  49153  nlockmgr
    100021    1   udp  49156  nlockmgr
    100021    3   tcp  49154  nlockmgr
    100021    3   udp  49157  nlockmgr
    100021    4   tcp  49155  nlockmgr
    100021    4   udp  49158  nlockmgr
    100020    1   udp   4045  llockmgr
    100020    1   tcp   4045  llockmgr
    100021    2   tcp  49156  nlockmgr
    100068    2   udp  49163  cmsd
    100068    3   udp  49163  cmsd
    100068    4   udp  49163  cmsd
    100068    5   udp  49163  cmsd
    100083    1   tcp  49157  ttdbserver
 805306352    1   tcp    811
    100005    1   udp  49416  mountd
    100005    3   udp  49416  mountd
    100005    1   tcp  49226  mountd
    100005    3   tcp  49226  mountd
    100003    2   udp   2049  nfs
    100003    3   udp   2049  nfs
    100003    2   tcp   2049  nfs
    100003    3   tcp   2049  nfs
```

Many daemons are running on the system that are important to the functionality I like to use. **mountd** and **nfs** are running, which indicates that another system or PC could NFS mount file systems on this computer. There is other setup required for the mount to take place, but at least the daemon is running to support this functionality.

arp

The mechanism used to maintain a list of IP addresses and their corresponding MAC addresses is the Address Resolution Protocolr (*ARP*) *cache*. The mapped addresses are only held in the cache for minutes, so if you want to see what addresses have been mapped recently, you can use the **arp** command, as shown in the following example:

```
[ root : / ]> /usr/sbin/arp -a
corpnjdc1 (10.14.16.12) at 0:6:5b:3e:3b:ed ether
NJSEC6506RTR_VL51 (10.14.16.1) at 0:3:6b:6c:58:82 ether

10.14.16.43 (10.14.16.43) at 0:b0:d0:20:c4:5b ether
schnjftpqa.scholastic.com (10.14.16.25) at 0:b0:d0:fe:a2:14 ether
10.14.16.61 (10.14.16.61) at 0:b0:d0:e1:9d:50 ether
10.14.16.56 (10.14.16.56) at 0:b0:d0:ab:74:8c ether
schnjhrqaweb1.corp.scholasticinc.local (10.14.16.82) at 0:b0:d0:fc:f5:60 ether
10.14.16.73 (10.14.16.73) at 0:b0:d0:fc:e6:cf ether
```

Current *arp* entries are displayed with the *-a* command. You can create an entry with the *-s* option if pinging the host does not do it for you. This will rarely needs to be done; however, some system administrators need to delete **arp** table entries to flush the **arp** cache. Use **arp -d** *hostname* or *IP address* to do this.

lanadmin

lanadmin is used to view and perform administration on network cards. Issuing **lanadmin** with no options brings you into the interactive interface as shown in the following example:

```
[ root : / ]> /usr/sbin/lanadmin

              LOCAL AREA NETWORK ONLINE ADMINISTRATION, Version 1.0
                         Thu, Jan 27,2005  08:46:44

                   Copyright 1994 Hewlett Packard Company.
                         All rights are reserved.
```

```
Test Selection mode.

        lan       = LAN Interface Administration
        menu      = Display this menu
        quit      = Terminate the Administration
        terse     = Do not display command menu
        verbose   = Display command menu

Enter command: lan

LAN Interface test mode. LAN Interface PPA Number = 0

        clear     = Clear statistics registers
        display   = Display LAN Interface status and statistics registers
        end       = End LAN Interface Administration, return to Test Selection
        menu      = Display this menu
        ppa       = PPA Number of the LAN Interface
        quit      = Terminate the Administration, return to shell
        reset     = Reset LAN Interface to execute its selftest
        specific  = Go to Driver specific menu

Enter command: d
                        LAN INTERFACE STATUS DISPLAY
                        Thu, Jan 27,2005  08:47:01

PPA Number                          = 0
Description                         = lan0 HP PCI Core I/O 1000Base-T Release B.11.1
1.15
Type (value)                        = ethernet-csmacd(6)
MTU Size                            = 1500
Speed                               = 100000000
Station Address                     = 0xf202b335c
Administration Status (value)       = up(1)
Operation Status (value)            = up(1)
Last Change                         = 1856
Inbound Octets                      = 2087734645
Inbound Unicast Packets             = 4406242
Inbound Non-Unicast Packets         = 12007525
Inbound Discards                    = 0
Inbound Errors                      = 0
Inbound Unknown Protocols           = 3913814
Outbound Octets                     = 1003945398
Outbound Unicast Packets            = 4399588
Outbound Non-Unicast Packets        = 556227
Outbound Discards                   = 0
Outbound Errors                     = 0
Outbound Queue Length               = 0
Specific                            = 655367
```

In this example, I issue **lanadmin** and specify that I wanted to go into the *lan* interface administration and that I want to display information about the interface.

To switch to a different LAN interface or *PPA,* just enter the *PPA* number for it. This is usually the same as the LAN number and can be found in the **lanscan** output.

lanadmin can also be used to perform such tasks as to change the MTU or speed of a LAN interface with the *-M* and *-s* options, respectively. To see the speed at which your LAN interface is set you can issue the following command:

```
[ root: / ]> /usr/sbin/lanadmin -x 0
Speed = 100 Full-Duplex.
Autonegotiation = On.
```

The **lanadmin** command was issued for LAN interface *0* which is shown to be at 100 MB per second and Full-Duplex.

nslookup and nsquery

nslookup resolves a host name into an IP address. You issue **nslookup** *host-name* and **nslookup** will access either the **/etc/resolv.conf** file or **/etc/hosts** to resolve the host name. **resolv.conf** is used to determine how DNS servers are accessed. The following example shows a system using **/etc/hosts** to produce the IP address of system *12*:


```
[ root : /]> nslookup otcapdv1
Name Server:  corpnjdc1
Address:  10.14.16.12

Trying DNS
Name:    otcapdv1
Address:  10.14.16.18
```


You can also run **nslookup** in interactive mode by issuing the command with no command-line arguments. The following example shows issuing the command with no command line arguments to get into interactive mode and then typing **help** to get information on commands you can issue:


```
[ root : / ]> nslookup
Default Name Server:  corpnjdc1
Address:  10.14.16.12

> help
Commands:      (identifiers are shown in uppercase, [] means optional)
NAME           - print info about the host/domain NAME using default server
NAME1 NAME2    - as above, but use NAME2 as server
exit           - exit the program, ^D also exits
finger [USER]  - finger the optional NAME at the current default host
help or ?      - print info on common commands; see nslookup(1) for details
ls [opt] DOMAIN [> FILE] - list addresses in DOMAIN (optional: output to FILE)
   -a          - list canonical names and aliases
   -h          - list HINFO (CPU type and operating system)
   -s          - list well-known services
   -d          - list all records
   -t TYPE     - list records of the given type (e.g., A,CNAME,MX, etc.)
```

```
policy            - print switch policy information
root              - set current default server to the root
server NAME       - set default server to NAME, using current default server
lserver NAME      - set default server to NAME, using initial server
reset             - lookups use the switch policy; resets DNS servers
set OPTION        - set an option
   all            -  print options, current server and host
   [no]debug      -  print debugging information
   [no]d2         -  print exhaustive debugging information
   [no]defname    -  append domain name to each query
   [no]swtrace    -  print source lookup and source switch messages
   [no]recurse    -  ask for recursive answer to query
   [no]vc         -  always use a virtual circuit
   domain=NAME    -  set default domain name to NAME
   srchlist=N1[/N2/.../N6]  -  set domain to N1 and search list to N1,N2, etc.
   root=NAME      -  set root server to NAME
   retry=X        -  set number of retries to X
   timeout=X      -  set time-out interval to X
   querytype=X    -  set query type, e.g., A,ANY,CNAME,HINFO,MX,NS,PTR,SOA,WKS
   type=X         -  synonym for querytype
   class=X        -  set query class to one of IN (Internet), CHAOS, HESIOD or ANY

view FILE         - sort an 'ls' output file and view it with more
```

Used in conjunction with **nslookup** is the **nsquery** command. **nsquery** is used to verify a hostname or IP lookup as well as verify lookups of usernames and groups based on the policies of **/etc/nsswitch.conf**. It is a more trustworthy tool than **nslookup** because it implements resolver timeouts and policies for DNS, NIS, NIS+, and local files. It can perform lookup of a name, user ID, group ID, or IP address.

To query information about the user *hackley* in the **passwd** file, you would issue **nsquery passwd hackley**.

To query the **group** file for users, you would issue **nsquery group users**.

To search the **hosts** file for *www.hp.com*, you would issue **nsquery hosts www.hp.com**. Depending on the configuration of **nsswitch.conf** the **hosts** file and then **dns** would be queried if *www.hp.com* were not found in **hosts**.

To search **hosts** for *192.16.16.204,* you would issue **nsquery hosts 192.16.16.204**.

ndd

ndd is used to perform network tuning and view information about network parameters. To view information about all supported tunable parameters with **ndd**, you would issue **ndd -h supported**. You can get the value of a parameter using the *-get* option; you can set the value of a parameter with the *-set* option.

Changes made with the **ndd** command are not permanent meaning that they will not be in place after a reboot of the system. To make permanent changes you would edit the **/etc/rc.config.d/nddconf** file.

An example of using **ndd** would be to work with the ICMP source quench. This is often disabled for security purposes. To check the current value you would use **ndd -get /dev/ip_send_source_quench**. To disable this with **ndd** you would use **ndd -set /dev/ip ip_send_source_quench 0**.

To make this a permanent change, you would create the following **/etc/rc.config.d/nddconf** entries:

```
TRANSPORT_NAME[0]=ip
NDD_NAME[0]=ip_send_source_quench
NDD_VALUE[0]=0
```

In general, using files in **/etc/rc.confg.d** is a good practice because these changes are normally permanent.

Using Networking

The ISO/OSI model is helpful for visualizing the way in which the networking layers interact. The model does not, however, tell you how to use networking. Two widely used networking services that may be running on your system(s) and are worth taking a look at are ARPA and NFS. Many other services are widely used, such as HTTP, Samba, ONC-RCP, and others.

The products I cover in the upcoming sections fall under the umbrella of "Internet Services." The first networking product to try on your system is what is sometimes called ARPA Services - what I have been calling ARPA. ARPA is a combination of "ARPA Services" and "Berkeley Services." ARPA Services supports communications among systems running different operating systems, and Berkeley Services supports UNIX systems. The terms *ARPA* and *Berkeley* aren't used as often as they once were; however, since the roots of these command are in ARPA and Berkeley I use these terms in the following sections, which list of the most common ARPA and Berkeley commands. Although many programs can be run under each of these services, the following are the most commonly used services in the UNIX world. In some cases, there are examples that show how these commands are used. For most examples, the local host is **system1** and the remote host is **system2**.

The next section covers serveral commands that are considered insecure, such as FTP, **telnet**, **rcp**, **rlogin**, and **remsh**. You can substitute FTP/SSL, SFTP, Telent/SSL, SCP, SSH, and others.

Internet Services ARPA (Communication Among Systems with Different OS)

File Transfer Protocol (ftp)

Transfer a file, or multiple files, from one system to another. This is often used when transferring files between a UNIX workstation and a Windows PC, VAX, etc. The following example shows copying the file **/tmp/krsort.c** from system2 (remote host) to the local directory on system1 (local host):

	Comments
$ ftp system2	Issue ftp command
Connected to system2.	
system2 FTP server (Version 4.1) ready.	
Name (system2:root): root	Log in to system2
Password required for root.	
Password:	Enter password
User root logged in.	
Remote system type is UNIX.	
Using binary mode to transfer files.	
ftp> **cd /tmp**	**cd** to **/tmp** on system2
CWD command successful	
ftp> **get krsort.c**	Get krsort.c file
PORT command successful	
Opening BINARY mode data connection for **krsort.c**	
Transfer complete.	
2896 bytes received in 0.08 seconds	
ftp> **bye**	Exit ftp
Goodbye.	
$	

In this example, both systems are running UNIX; however, the commands you issue through **ftp** are operating system-independent. The **cd** for change directory and **get** commands used above work for any operating system on which **ftp** is running. If you become familiar with just a few **ftp** commands, you may find that transferring information in a heterogeneous networking environment is not difficult.

Chances are that you are using your UNIX system(s) in a heterogeneous environment and may therefore use **ftp** to copy files and directories from one system to another. Because **ftp** is so widely used, I describe some of the more commonly used **ftp** commands:

ascii	Sets the type of file transferred to ASCII. This means that you are transferring an ASCII file from one system to another. **binary** is usually the default.
	Example: **ascii**
binary	Sets the type of file transferred to binary. This means that you are transferring a binary file from one system to another. If, for example, you want to have a directory on your UNIX system that holds applications that you copy to non-UNIX systems, then you want to use binary transfer.
	Example: **binary**
cd	Changes to the specified directory on the remote host.
	Example: **cd /tmp**
dir	Lists the contents of a directory on the remote system to the screen or to a file on the local system, if you specify a local file name.
get	Copies the specified remote file to the specified local file. If you don't specify a local file name, then the remote file name is used.
lcd	Changes to the specified directory on the local host.
	Example: **lcd /tmp**

ls	Lists the contents of a directory on the remote system to the screen or to a file on the local system, if you specify a local file name.
mget	Copies multiple files from the remote host to the local host. Example: **mget *.c**
put	Copies the specified local file to the specified remote file. If you don't specify a remote file name, then the local file name is used. Example: **put test.c**
mput	Copies multiple files from the local host to the remote host. Example: **mput *.c**
bye/quit	Closes the connection to the remote host. Example: **bye**

Other **ftp** commands are available in addition to those I cover here. If you need more information on these commands or want to review additional **ftp** commands, the UNIX manual pages for **ftp** are helpful.

telnet	Used to communicate with another host using the telnet protocol. Telnet is an alternative to using **rlogin**, described later. The following example shows how to establish a telnet connection with the remote host, system2:

	Comments
$ telnet system2	
Connected to system2.	Telnet to system2
HP-UX	
login: **root**	Log in as root on system2
password:	Enter password
Welcome to system2.	
$	HP-UX prompt on system2

Internet Services Berkeley (Communication Between UNIX Systems)

Remote Copy (rcp)

This program copies files and directories from one UNIX system to another. To copy **/tmp/ krsort.c** from system1 to system2, do the following:

```
$ rcp    system2:/tmp/krsort.c  /tmp/krsort.c
```

Some networking configuration needs to be made to files to get this level of functionality. In this example, the user who issues the command is considered "equivalent" on both systems and has permission to copy files from one system to the other with **rcp**. (These terms are described shortly).

Remote login (rlogin)

Supports login to a remote UNIX system. To remotely log in to system2 from system1, do the following:

```
$ rlogin system2
password:
Welcome to system2
$
```

If a password is requested when the user issues the **rlogin** command, the users are not equivalent on the two systems. If no password is requested, the users are indeed equivalent. You can also issue **rlogin** *system* **-l** *user* to specify the *system* and *user* as part of the command.

Remote shell (remsh)

With the **remsh** command, you can sit on one UNIX system and issue a command to be run remotely on a different UNIX system and have the results displayed locally. This command is called **rsh** on Linux and some other UNIX variants. In this case, a **remsh** is issued to show a long listing of **/tmp/krsort.c**. The command is run on system2, but the result is displayed on system1, where the command was typed:

```
$ remsh system2 ll /tmp/krsort.c
-rwxrwxrwx 1 root sys 2896 Sept 1 10:54 /tmp/krsort.c
$
```

In this case, the users on system1 and system2 must be equivalent, or else permission is denied to issue this command.

Remote who (rwho)

Find out who is logged in on a remote UNIX system. Here is the output of issuing **rwho**:

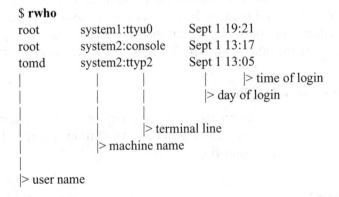

```
$ rwho
root          system1:ttyu0        Sept 1 19:21
root          system2:console      Sept 1 13:17
tomd          system2:ttyp2        Sept 1 13:05
  |             |      |             |      |> time of login
  |             |      |             |> day of login
  |             |      |
  |             |      |> terminal line
  |             |> machine name
  |
  |> user name
```

For **rwho** to work, the **rwho** daemon (**rwhod**) must be running.

Other "r" commands, in addition to those covered, are available. Also, variations of these commands occur going from one UNIX variant to another, so you may not run exactly the same "r" command on your UNIX system.

Host Name Mapping

The most important decision related to networking is how host name mapping is implemented on your system in Internet Services ARPA. Three techniques are available for host name mapping:

- BIND
- Network Information Service (NIS)
- UNIX file **/etc/hosts**

The simplest way to implement host name mapping is with **/etc/hosts**, so I cover this technique in the next section. DNS is also widely used for host name mapping as well. Keep in mind that there are probably networking manuals for your UNIX variant devoted to many networking topics including NFS, ARPA, and others. These manuals serve as a good reference material if you need to know more about networking than is covered here.

Using the **/etc/hosts** file, as you are about to see, becomes difficult for environments where there are many systems deployed. With this solution there is one **/etc/hosts** file that must be kept up-to-date and propagated to all other systems.

The Domain Name System (DNS) is widely used in large environments. DNS uses Berkeley Internet Name Domain Service (BIND) to resolve names to addresses. There are name servers that fill a request for name data. This is the server side to BIND. There is a client side to BIND, called the resolver, that accesses the name server(s) to resolve names. Using this client/server model, it is much easier to maintain naming information, because it only needs to be kept in a few places as opposed to one for each system.

Clients use a file called **/etc/resolv.conf** to configure the resolver. The name server and its corresponding address are the keys to resolving information.

This solution makes it much easier to maintain system names and addresses in large environments. DNS and BIND are primarily a system administration exercise to set up. From a user standpoint, you don't need to know much about them. What I instead focus on in the upcoming sections are some of the programs in which users are more interested. I supply some background so that the way in which the programs are used has more meaning. In general, however, I concentrate on the user aspect of these networking topics, as opposed to the system administration aspect of them.

/etc/hosts

The **/etc/hosts** file contains information about the other systems to which you are connected. It contains the Internet address of each system, the system name, and any aliases for the system name. If the **/etc/hosts** file is modified to contain the names of the systems on your network, they have provided the basis for **rlogin** to another system. Although you can now **rlogin** to other UNIX systems, you cannot yet **rcp** or **remsh** to another system. Although adding **remsh** and **rcp** functionality is easy, it does indeed compromise security, so it is not always set up on all systems. Here is an example **/etc/hosts** file:

```
127.0.0.1        localhost loopback
15.32.199.42     a4410827
15.32.199.28     a4410tu8
15.32.199.7      a4410922
15.32.199.21     a4410tu1
15.32.199.22     a4410tu2
15.32.199.62     a4410730
15.32.199.63     hpxterm1
15.32.199.64     a4410rd1
15.32.199.62     a4410750hp1
```

This file is in the following format:

<internet_address>   *<official_hostname>*   *<alias>*

The Internet Protocol address (IP address) is a class "A," "B," or "C" address. A class "A" network supports many more nodes per network than either a class "B" or "C" network. The purpose of breaking down the IP address into four fields is to define a node (or host) address and a network address. These were described in detail in Figures 14-3 through 14-6.

Assuming that this **/etc/hosts** file contains class "C" addresses, the right-most field is the host or node address, and the other three fields comprise the network address.

You could use either the official_hostname or the alias from the **/etc/ hosts** file when issuing one of the ARPA or Berkeley Internet Services commands previously described. For example, either of the following ARPA commands works:

```
$ telnet a4410750
```

    or

```
$ telnet hp1
```

Similarly, either of the following Berkeley commands works:

```
$ rlogin a4410750
```

    or

```
$ rlogin hp1
```

/etc/hosts.equiv

Your system may be set up so that user's don't have to issue a password when they **rlogin** to a remote system, they can set up equivalent hosts by editing this file. As previously mentioned, this technique is sometimes considered a security risk, so it is not always employed. The login names must be the same on both the local and remote systems for **/etc/hosts.equiv** to allow the user to bypass entering a password. You can either list all the equivalent hosts in **/etc/hosts.equiv** or list the host and user name you want to be equivalent. Users can now use **rcp** and **remsh**, because they are equivalent users on these systems. I usually just enter all the host names on the network. Here is an example of **/etc/hosts.equiv**:

```
a4410730
a4410tu1
a4410tu2
hpxterm1
a4410827
a4410750
```

Keep in mind the potential security risks of using **/etc/hosts.equiv**. If a user can log in to a remote system without a password, you have reduced the overall level of security on your network. Even though users may find it convenient to not have to enter a password when logging in to a remote system, you have given every user in **/etc/hosts.equiv** access to the entire network. If you could ensure that all the permissions on all the files and directories on all systems are properly set up, you wouldn't care who had access to what system. In the real UNIX world, however, permissions are sometimes not what they are supposed to be. Users have a strong tendency to "browse around," invariably stumbling upon a file they want to copy to which they really shouldn't have access.

/.rhosts

The **/.rhosts** file is the **/etc/hosts.equiv** for a superuser. If you log in as root, you want to have this file configured with exactly the same information as **/etc/hosts.equiv**. If you do, however, you have compounded your network security risk by allowing the superuser on any system to log in to a remote system without a root password. If you are the undisputed ruler of your network and you're 100 percent certain that no security holes exist, then you may want to set up **/.rhosts** so that you don't have to issue a password when you log in remotely to a system as superuser. From a security standpoint, however, you should know that this setup is frowned upon.

I have described the process of setting up the appropriate files to get the most commonly used ARPA Services up and running. There is sometimes even more advanced functionality, such as DNS/BIND, required. Your system may have DNS/BIND or similar functionality set up that gives you access to some or all of the commands covered throughout this section.

Set Up DNS Servers Using BIND 8.1.2 and 9.2 on HP-UX 11i

This procedure documents how to set up a Master (primary), a Slave (secondary), and a Caching-only DNS server on HP-UX 11.0/11i platforms with the latest supported BIND version 8.1.2 and 9.2.0 releases for HP-UX. BIND 8.1.2 is loaded on 11.0 via a patch from *http://software.hp.com* and is provided on the 11i v1 (11.11) release media. BIND 9.2.0 is available for download on *software.hp.com.* For a more detailed discussion on BIND 8.1.2 and 9.2, please refer to the O'Reilly and Associates 3rd Edition book, *DNS and BIND*, by Albitz and Liu. BIND 8.1.2 and 9.2 are only available on the 11.0/11i platforms. 10.20 uses the older 4.9.7 version. It is important to be aware that the older 4.9.X versions of BIND have a different configuration file (boot file) format. There are also some terminology differences. The "boot" file is now called a "config" or "conf" file. HP Primary name servers are now called Master nameservers; Secondary name servers are now called Slaves.

In most cases, DNS implementation is fairly straightforward, i.e., resource records and database files, etc. The real test comes in planning. Considerations such as whether the DNS system will be protected behind a firewall, whether or not you want your resolvers to "peer" out on the Internet, and nslookup remote domains and addresses must be considered. Some administrators choose to turn off looking out on the Internet to reduce the network traffic it creates. If you are directly attached to the Internet, you need to register at least two name servers with an authorized Internet Domain Name provider. You can find a list of these providers can be found at http://*www.icann.org/registrars/accredited-list.html*. If you are not directly attached, i.e., sitting behind a firewall, an ISP is a good choice for DNS services and will do most of the work for you.

When you have completed your planning, you need to configure your DNS server. What names should you use? Some people use planets, locational references, and sometimes people use names for their network computers and printers. The decision is up to you, but do not use underscores in your hostnames (see "check-names" boot file options), and make the names easy to remember. Here are the steps to creating a Master (Primary) DNS server for your network:

1. Populate **/etc/hosts** with all the hosts that you want to administer (separated by network segment and domains), and keep everything in an orderly

fashion so that a tool, such as hosts_to_named, can safely and efficiently administer database files for you, as in the following example:

```
/etc/hosts
15.17.186.159 wtec712-rtr

127.0.0.1 localhost loopback
# 812 Bogus Domain BASEBALL.HP.COM

# NL - EAST DIVISION
10.1.1.1 atlantabraves atlantabraves.baseball.hp.com

10.1.1.2 newyork newyorkmets.baseball.hp.com
# NL - CENTRAL DIVISION

10.1.2.1 houstonastros houstonastros.baseball.hp.com

10.1.2.2 chicagocubs chicagocubs.baseball.hp.com

10.1.2.3 stlouiscardinals stlouscardinals.baseball.hp.com
```

2. Create a *param* file with the parameters for your domain, as shown in the following example for **/tmp/param**:

```
/tmp/param

-d baseball.hp.com   <--------- Your domain.
-n 10.1.1            <--------- Your subnet(s).
-n 10.1.2
-n 10.1.3
-n 15.17.186
-H /etc/hosts.dnstest <--------- hosts file you will use.
-r                    <--------- If this nameserver is a
                                 root NS. Our examples
                                 below are NOT for root NS.
```

3. Run **hosts_to_named** with your newly created **param** file from the directory in which you want to place the database. Note that the **param** file is not necessary, but it is a good idea; the options can be run from the command line instead of including a file. Another common error with **hosts_to_named** is not running it in a "clean" directory. If you need to preserve results before you run it, **mkdir /etc/named.data.old**; **mv /etc/named.data/* /etc/named.data.old** to preserve the prior configuration:

```
# cd /etc/named.data

# hosts_to_named -f /tmp/param

Translating /tmp/hosts.dns to lower case ...

Collecting network data ...

10.1.1
10.1.2
```

```
10.1.3
15.17.186

Creating list of multi-homed hosts ...
Creating "A" data (name to address mapping) for net 10.1.1 ...
Creating "PTR" data (address to name mapping) for net 10.1.1 ...
Creating "A" data (name to address mapping) for net 10.1.2 ...
Creating "PTR" data (address to name mapping) for net 10.1.2 ...
Creating "A" data (name to address mapping) for net 10.1.3 ...
Creating "PTR" data (address to name mapping) for net 10.1.3 ...
Creating "A" data (name to address mapping) for net 15.17.186 ...
Creating "PTR" data (address to name mapping) for net 15.17.168 ...
Creating "MX" (mail exchanger) data ...
Building default named.boot file …

Building default db.cache file ...
WARNING: db.cache must be filled in withthe name(s) and address(es) of the
rootserver(s)
Building default boot.cacheonly for caching only servers ...
done
```

4. **hosts_to_named** produces both a BIND 4.X **named.boot** file and a BIND 8.X and 9.X **named.conf** file. Match the db files created in **/etc/named.data** with those found in **/etc/named.data/named.conf.** Here is an example for a non-root name server from 8.1.2:

```
// generated by named-bootconf.pl

options {
check-names response fail;    // do not change this
check-names slave warn;
directory "/etc/named.data"; // running directory for named
/*
* If there is a firewall between you and nameservers you want
* to talk to, you might need to uncomment the query-source
* directive below. Previous versions of BIND always asked
* questions using port 53, but BIND 8.1 uses an unprivileged
* port by default.
*/
// query-source address * port 53;
};

//
// type domain source file
//

zone "0.0.127.IN-ADDR.ARPA" {
type master;
file "db.127.0.0";
};

zone "baseball.hp.com" {
type master;
file "db.baseball";
};

zone "1.1.10.IN-ADDR.ARPA" {
type master;
file "db.10.1.1";
};
```

```
zone "2.1.10.IN-ADDR.ARPA" {
type master;
file "db.10.1.2";
};

zone "3.1.10.IN-ADDR.ARPA" {
type master;
file "db.10.1.3";
};

zone "186.17.15.IN-ADDR.ARPA" {
type master;
file "db.15.17.186";
};

zone "." {
type hint;
file "db.cache";
};

(wtec712-rtr)named.data- ls

boot.cacheonly db.10.1.2 db.15.17.186 named.boot
conf.cacheonly db.10.1.3 db.baseball named.conf
db.10.1.1 db.127.0.0 db.cache params-file
```

As you can see, **hosts_to_named** creates reverse lookup (IP addresses to names) db files with one parent domain, **baseball.hp.com**. Each of the nodes in the network has the fully qualified name **shortname.baseball.hp.com**.

5. Because many installations still use underscores in hostnames, I highly recommend that you allow for this by modifying the *check-names* options lists in the **named.conf** file that **hosts_to_named** generates. For example, you may want to change these lines:

```
options {
check-names response fail           // do not change this
check-names slave warn
.
.
.

to:

options {
check-names response ignore    //change "fail" to "ignore"
check-names slave ignore       //change "warn" to "ignore"
check-names master ignore      //add this whole new line
.
.
.
```

Note that BIND 9.X does not support the *check-names* option and notifies **syslog** about it.

6. Fill in **db.cache** with the addresses of the root name servers. If you are directly connected to the Internet and will be querying the root name servers at the NIC, obtain an updated list from the site *ftp://internic.net/domain/named.cache.*

Next, copy the file to **db.cache** after you have downloaded it. If you are not directly connected to the Internet and have to go through a firewall to query the root name servers, make the firewall your root name server and point your **db.cache** entry at the firewall in the same fashion that you would specify the root name servers. It is very important to configure **db.cache** correctly or services such as mail and name resolution will be affected. Here is an example of this:

```
; FILL IN THE NAMES AND ADDRESSES OF THE ROOT SERVERS
;
; . 99999999 IN NS root.server.
; root.server. 99999999 IN A ??.??.??.??
;
. 99999999 IN NS firewall.baseball.hp.com.
firewall.baseball.hp.com. 99999999 IN A 15.17.186.99
```

In this case, **firewall.baseball.hp.com.** is my firewall and because my name server cannot directly query the root nameservers, **db.cache** is directed to my firewall.

7. If you are going to have a Master (primary) name server that will not talk to the internet in any way, shape, or form, then you need to set up your name server as a root name server by doing a few things. Either use the *-r* option in your **params** file to **hosts_to_named** or make the following changes:

In your **named.conf** file, change

```
zone "." {
type hint;
file "db.cache";
```

to:

```
zone "." {

type master;

file "db.root";
```

The root name server database file **db.root** would contain:

```
.   IN   SOA   m3107ced.baseball.hp.com.   root.m3107ced.base-
ball.hp.com.

(

                1          ; Serial
                10800      ; Refresh every 3 hours
                3600       ; Retry every hour
                604800     ; Expire after a week
                86400 )    ; Minimum ttl of 1 day

     IN NS m3107ced.baseball.hp.com.
m3107ced.baseball.hp.com. IN A 15.50.73.92
```

What I have done is set up an internal root name server, **db.root**, with one record, **m3107ced.baseball.hp.com.**

8. The next consideration is where to send queries for domains for which you are not authoritative. If your domain is **baseball.hp.com** and someone asks for **jughead.ibm.com**, what happens to the request? Well, if you've configured a root name server with no forwarder statements, the answer is nothing. The query fails with host not found. This might be a good thing if you do not want your internal systems querying Internet domains. Security and network congestion are usually the reason. What if you want to resolve Internet names and addresses, however? Easy, configure a forwarders statement in your **/etc/named.conf** to point to the firewall or whichever system is talking directly to the root name servers, as shown in the following BIND 9.2.0 example:

```
Example 9.2.0 forwarders config file options

# type domain source file

options {
        forwarders { 15.227.128.51 ; } ;
```

```
                    forward only;
                    directory "/etc/named.data";
                    query-source address * port 53;
};
```

What is happening here is that queries for domains that I am not authoritative for, basically anything outside **baseball.hp.com**, I send to the forwarders to let them handle it. As you can see, there are two forwarders, each listed twice. The reason for this is that forwarders tend to be quite busy and by specifying two of them, you prevent the query from timing out. Be sure to copy **/etc/named.data/named.conf** to **/etc/named.conf**. All versions of BIND look for the boot file in **/etc/** by default, so don't forget to copy it to **/etc** when you are ready.

9. Configure **/etc/resolv.conf** and **/etc/nsswitch.conf** on your name server and all clients that will be pointed at the name server:

/etc/resolv.conf

```
domain baseball.hp.com
search baseball.hp.com atl.hp.com hp.com rose.hp.com cup.hp.com
external.hp.com

nameserver 15.50.73.92 # authoritative name server 4 atl.hp.com
nameserver 15.51.240.8 # non-authoritative cache only servers
```

/etc/resolv.conf is pretty simple: The domain statement identifies which domain the system is part of; the search statements are used to simplify typing when more than one domain exists. When you issue a query for, say, *jughead*, it searches for *jughead* first in **baseball.hp.com**, then **atl.hp.com**, **rose.hp.com**, and finally, **cup.hp.com**. **/etc/nsswitch.conf** modifies the switch order you will use to look up hosts and IP addresses. There are four possible sources for this information: 1) **/etc/hosts**, 2) **nis**, 3) **nisplus**, 4) and **dns**. By default, the hard coded order is **dns nis** files. To modify the switch order, you need to copy in a fresh **/etc/nsswitch.conf** file from **/usr/newconfig/etc/nsswitch.hp_defaults** and modify the *hosts* entry:

```
# /etc/nsswitch.hp_defaults:

#

# An example file that could be copied over to /etc/nsswitch.conf; it

# uses NIS (YP) in conjunction with files.

#
```

```
passwd: compat

group: compat

hosts: files [NOTFOUND=return] dns

networks: nis [NOTFOUND=return] files

protocols: nis [NOTFOUND=return] files

rpc: nis [NOTFOUND=return] files

publickey: nis [NOTFOUND=return] files

netgroup: nis [NOTFOUND=return] files

automount: files nis

aliases: files nis

services: nis [NOTFOUND=return] files
```

As you can see, the *hosts* line has been modified so that I consult the **/etc/ hosts** file first then continue to *dns* if the query is unsuccessful. There are many ways to modify the switch order and many ways to mess things up. Use discretion when changing the switch order and consult the man pages on *switch* for more information.

10. Start up the DNS name server process as follows:

```
# /usr/sbin/named.
# ps -eaf|grep named
root 8074 1 0 08:42:08 ? 0:00 /usr/sbin/named <--- check to make
                                            sure it is running..
root 8077 8072 2 08:42:13 ttyp7 0:00 grep named
```

After the name server is started, you use can **sig_named** to perform various functions. After you modify any of the *db* files or **/etc/named.boot**, tell **named** to refresh its databases. You can accomplish this using either of the two following commands:

```
 # sig_named restart
 # kill -HUP `/var/run/named.pid`
```

This reloads the databases, which you can verify by viewing the end of file **/ var/adm/syslog/syslog.log**:

```
Oct 12 08:49:13 m3107ced named[8074]: primary zone "0.0.127.IN-ADDR.ARPA"
loaded (serial 1)

Oct 12 08:49:13 m3107ced named[8074]: primary zone "baseball.hp.com" loaded
(serial 1)

Oct 12 08:49:13 m3107ced named[8074]: primary zone "1.1.10.IN-ADDR.ARPA"
loaded(serial 1)

Oct 12 08:49:13 m3107ced named[8074]: primary zone "2.1.10.IN-ADDR.ARPA"
loaded(serial 1)

Oct 12 08:49:13 m3107ced named[8074]: primary zone "3.1.10.IN-ADDR.ARPA"
loaded(serial 1)

Oct 12 08:49:13 m3107ced named[8074]: primary zone "1.168.192.IN-ADDR.ARPA"
loaded (serial 1)

Oct 12 08:49:13 m3107ced named[8074]: primary zone "2.168.192.IN-ADDR.ARPA"
loaded (serial 1)

Oct 12 08:49:13 m3107ced named[8074]: primary zone "3.168.192.IN-ADDR.ARPA"
loaded (serial 1)

Oct 12 08:49:13 m3107ced named[8074]: Ready to answer queries.
```

As you can see, **named** loaded each of the databases, or zones, and is ready
to answer queries.

11. Test queries both by name and IP address:

```
# nslookup atlantabraves
Using /etc/hosts on: wtec712-rtr
looking up FILES
Trying DNS

Name: atlantabraves.baseball.hp.com

Address: 10.1.1.1

# nslookup 10.1.1.1

Using /etc/hosts on: wtec712-rtr
looking up FILES
Trying DNS
Trying DNS
Name: atlantabraves.baseball.hp.com
Address: 10.1.1.1
```

Looking up *atlantabraves* by name and IP address worked, and generally we
are done.
I always check **/var/adm/syslog/syslog.log** for messages from **named**,
which logs a lot of seemingly unimportant chatter, but it always deserves at
least a short look.

A Word on Slave (Secondary) Name Servers

After you create a Master (primary) DNS server, you have completed all the hard work. Creating Slaves and cache-only servers is simple. Let's walk through this process step-by-step:

1. Use **ftp** to copy the **named.conf** file and **db.cache** from the Master (primary).

2. Edit the **named.conf** file as follows:

- Change each instance of "master" to "slave," except for the loopback domain db.127.0.0 and the cache entry.
- Add a "masters" entry for each zone with the IP address of the Master DNS server.
Using the previous BIND 8.1.2 example:

```
# cat /etc/named.conf

// generated by named-bootconf.pl

options {

check-names response fail; // do not change this
check-names slave warn;
directory "/etc/named.data"; // running directory for named

/*
 * If there is a firewall between you and nameservers you want
 * to talk to, you might need to uncomment the query-source
 * directive below. Previous versions of BIND always asked
 * questions using port 53, but BIND 8.1 uses an unprivileged
 * port by default.
 */
// query-source address * port 53;
};

//
// type domain source file
//
zone "0.0.127.IN-ADDR.ARPA" {
type master;
file "db.127.0.0";
};

zone "baseball.hp.com" {
type slave;
file "db.baseball";
masters ( 15.17.186.159);
};
```

```
zone "1.1.10.IN-ADDR.ARPA" {
type slave;
file "db.10.1.1";
masters ( 15.17.186.159);
};

zone "2.1.10.IN-ADDR.ARPA" {
type slave;
file "db.10.1.2";
masters ( 15.17.186.159);
};

zone "3.1.10.IN-ADDR.ARPA" {
type slave;
file "db.10.1.3";
masters ( 15.17.186.159);
};

zone "186.17.15.IN-ADDR.ARPA" {
type slave;
file "db.15.17.186";
masters ( 15.17.186.159);
};

zone "." {
type hint;
file "db.cache";
};
```

3. Now, all you need to do, after your **named.boot** is copied to **/etc/ named.boot** and your **/etc/named.data** directory is created, is kick off a zone transfer.

To kick off a zone transfer, all you need to do is **kill named** with

```
# sig_named restart
```

or

```
# kill -HUP `/var/run/named.pid`
```

to start the transfer.

Look at **/etc/named.data**. You see all the database files there now. Also, check **/var/adm/syslog/sylog.log** to make sure that the zones were loaded properly, as shown in the following example:

```
Oct 12 09:21:34 stimpy named[1893]: secondary zone "1.1.10.IN-ADDR.ARPA"
loaded (serial 1)

Oct 12 09:21:35 stimpy named[1893]: secondary zone "baseball.hp.com" loaded
(ser ial 1)
```

```
Oct 12 09:21:35 stimpy named[1893]: secondary zone "2.1.10.IN-ADDR.ARPA"
loaded (serial 1)

Oct 12 09:21:35 stimpy named[1893]: secondary zone "1.168.192.IN-ADDR.ARPA"
loaded (serial 1)

Oct 12 09:21:35 stimpy named[1893]: secondary zone "3.1.10.IN-ADDR.ARPA"
loaded (serial 1)

Oct 12 09:21:36 stimpy named[1893]: secondary zone "2.168.192.IN-ADDR.ARPA"
loaded (serial 1)

Oct 12 09:21:36 stimpy named[1893]: secondary zone "3.168.192.IN-ADDR.ARPA"
loaded (serial 1)
```

Notice the serial number entries. They should match on the Master (primary) and Slaves (secondaries).

A Word On Cache-Only Name Servers

Why in the world would you want a cache-only name server? In a word, performance. If you want to maintain a local cache but do not want to manage database files, this is the way to go. It acts as any other name server, responding to queries in the same fashion, except queries that are built in the cache will be non-authoritative. Any query that comes back with a non-authoritative reply is a query received from cache. Is that a bad thing? No, but be aware that the data may have changed on the Master (primary) and the cache replies may be outdated. The Time To Live (TTL) flag for each query is a way to manipulate the time, in seconds, that a name server may cache the answer to a query, versus having to contact an authoritative name server. The default TTL for records is usually 86,400 seconds, or 24 hours. You may want to play with this value, depending on how frequently the records are updated. A good rule of thumb is to have at least one name server per subnet, and cache-only name servers are an excellent choice.

To configure a cache-only name server, copy the **conf.cacheonly** file and db.cache from the Master (primary) name server, as shown in the following BIND 8.1.2 example:

```
// generated by named-bootconf.pl

options {
check-names response fail; // do not change this
```

```
check-names slave warn;
directory "/tmp/testhack"; // running directory for named
/*
* If there is a firewall between you and nameservers you want
* to talk to, you might need to uncomment the query-source
* directive below. Previous versions of BIND always asked
* questions using port 53, but BIND 8.1 uses an unprivileged
* port by default.
*/
// query-source address * port 53;
};

//
// type domain source file
//
zone "0.0.127.IN-ADDR.ARPA" {
type master;
file "db.127.0.0";
};

zone "." {
type hint;
file "db.cache";
};
```

Please don't forget to fill in **db.cache** with the name server(s) for which you cache data for.

A Final Word on Name Server Setup

This section in no way offers a comprehensive discussion on setting up DNS. It is only intended to act as a cookbook after all of your planning is complete. Please refer to the book *HP-UX IP Address and Client Management Administrator's Guide* at *http://docs.hp.com*. DNS is relatively straightforward, but any syntax errors or problems with **/etc/named.boot** can have dramatic consequences. The **syslog** can be your best friend when zones are not transferring or problems occur with the data.

Network File System (NFS)

NFS allows you to mount disks on remote systems so that they appear as though they are local to your system. Similarly, NFS allows remote systems to mount your local disk so that it looks as though it is local to the remote system. I go through a simple NFS server and client setup in this section after NFS background is supplied. You can use standard-mounted directories or automounted directories with NFS. The upcoming example uses standard-mounted directories, but you can find out more about automounted directories and all NFS-related topics in *NFS Services Administrator's Guide* from *docs.hp.com*. Configuring NFS to achieve this functionality is simple. Here are the steps to go through in order to configure NFS:

1. Configure NFS startup files to specify whether your system will be an NFS Client, NFS Server, or both.

2. Start NFS server processes.

3. Specify which of your local file systems can be mounted by remote systems.

4. Specify the remote disks you want to mount and view as if they were local to your system.

As with Internet Services, you could enable other aspects to NFS, but again, I cover what I know to be the NFS functionality that nearly every UNIX installation uses.

Because NFS may be set up on your system to meet the needs of many users, you may want to understand the terminology associated with NFS. The following are commonly used NFS terms:

Node	A computer system that is attached to or is part of a computer network
Client	A node that requests data or services from other nodes (servers)
Server	A node that provides data or services to other nodes (clients) on the network
File System	A disk partition or logical volume

Export	Makes a file system available for mounting on remote nodes using NFS
Mount	Accesses a remote file system using NFS
Mount Point	The name of a directory on which the NFS file system is mounted
Import	Mounts a remote file system

Some of the specific configuration tasks and related files are different among UNIX variants. The following are some general tasks and examples related to configuring NFS. Your system administrator, of course, has to deal with the specifics of configuration on the UNIX variants.

Your system must be an NFS client, NFS server, or both. There are also daemons that must be running to support NFS. Both of these tasks are performed somewhat differently among the UNIX variants.

Your system then imports remote file systems to which you have local access and exports local file systems that are accessed by other systems.

A remote file system that you are mounting locally has an entry similar to the one that follows in **/etc/fstab**, **/etc/filesystems**, or whatever file is used to mount file systems:

```
system2:/opt/app3   /opt/app3   nfs rw,suid  0 0
```

In this case, I mount **/opt/app3** on *system2* locally as **/opt/app3**. This is an NFS mount with the permissions shown.

You can use the **showmount** command to show all remote systems (clients) that have mounted a local file system. This command is supported on most UNIX variants. **showmount** is useful for determining the file systems that are most often mounted by clients with NFS. The output of **showmount** is particularly easy to read, because it lists the host name and the directory that was mounted by the client. You have the three following options to the **showmount** command:

-a prints output in the format "name:directory."

-d lists all the local directories that have been remotely mounted by clients.

-e prints a list of exported file systems.

Example NFS Configuration

Let's take a look at the steps to set up an NFS server and client. I perform the following steps on the NFS server, with hostname *asodevlab1*, to export the directory **/home/frame**:

1. Configure NFS startup files by setting the following variables to *1* in **/etc/rc.config.d/nfsconf**:

```
NFS_CLIENT=1
NFS_SERVER=1
NUM_NFSD=16
NUM_NFSIOD=16
PCNFS_SERVER=1
```

All the startup variables have been set to *1* thereby enabling all NFS-related functionality at startup. I left the number of daemons (*NUM_NFSD* and *NUM_NFSIOD*) with default values.

2. Next I start the NFS server and check to see what NFS-related processes are running, as shown in the following output:

```
# /sbin/init.d/nfs.server start
    starting NFS SERVER networking

    starting up the rpcbind daemon
        rpcbind already started, using pid: 837
    Reading in /etc/exports
    starting up the mount daemon
        rpc.mountd already started, using pid: 1938
    starting up the NFS daemons
        nfsd(s) already started, using pid(s): 1970 1971 1973 1974 1975 1958 1959 1960 196
1 1962 1963 1964 1965 1966 1967 1968 1976
    starting up the Status Monitor daemon
        rpc.statd already started, using pid: 884
    starting up the Lock Manager daemon
        rpc.lockd already started, using pid: 890
# ps -ef | grep nfs
    root    842     0  0  Apr 29  ?         0:00 nfskd
    root   1970  1959  0  Apr 29  ?         0:00 /usr/sbin/nfsd 16
    root   1971  1959  0  Apr 29  ?         0:00 /usr/sbin/nfsd 16
    root   1973  1959  0  Apr 29  ?         0:00 /usr/sbin/nfsd 16
    root   1974  1959  0  Apr 29  ?         0:00 /usr/sbin/nfsd 16
```

```
root  1975  1959  0  Apr 29  ?           0:00 /usr/sbin/nfsd 16
root  1958     1  0  Apr 29  ?           0:00 /usr/sbin/nfsd 16
root  1959     1  0  Apr 29  ?           0:00 /usr/sbin/nfsd 16
root  1960  1959  0  Apr 29  ?           0:00 /usr/sbin/nfsd 16
root  1961  1960  0  Apr 29  ?           0:00 /usr/sbin/nfsd 16
root  1962  1960  0  Apr 29  ?           0:00 /usr/sbin/nfsd 16
root  1963  1959  0  Apr 29  ?           0:00 /usr/sbin/nfsd 16
root  1964  1960  0  Apr 29  ?           0:00 /usr/sbin/nfsd 16
root  1965  1960  0  Apr 29  ?           0:00 /usr/sbin/nfsd 16
root  1966  1960  0  Apr 29  ?           0:00 /usr/sbin/nfsd 16
root  1967  1960  0  Apr 29  ?           0:00 /usr/sbin/nfsd 16
root  1968  1960  0  Apr 29  ?           0:00 /usr/sbin/nfsd 16
root  1976  1959  0  Apr 29  ?           0:00 /usr/sbin/nfsd 16
root 23825     0  0 12:00:10  ?          0:00 nfsktcpd
root 24527 23078  0 12:44:29 pts/ta      0:00 grep nfs
#
```

Now that I have the server started, I can proceed to export file systems in step 3.

3. I'll update the **/etc/exports** file to include a directory that will be available to all systems, as shown below:

```
# cat /etc/exports
/home/frame      #exported read/write to all systems
#
```

I export **/home/frame** to all systems with read/write access.

4. Run the **exportfs** command in order to make **/home/frame** available to other systems:

```
# exportfs -av //home/frame
```

You can also run **showmount -e** to see the mounted file system. I have performed all the setup required on the server to export this file system. Next, I proceed to the client part of the setup.

The first step is to update the **/etc/rc.config.d/nfsconf** conf file to enable the NFS client. On the client, with hostname of *m4415mxp*, I enable both the NFS server and client as I did on the server.

1. Configure NFS startup files by setting the following variables to *1* in **/etc/rc.config.d/nfsconf**:

```
NFS_CLIENT=1
```

```
NFS_SERVER=1
NUM_NFSD=16
NUM_NFSIOD=16
PCNFS_SERVER=1
```

All the startup variables have been set to *1* thereby enabling all NFS-related functionality at startup. I left the number of daemons (*NUM_NFSD* and *NUM_NFSIOD*) with default values. I also ran the **server start** command on the client in the example as well so that all the NFS daemons are running. The NFS client is enabled by default in the **nfsconf** file.

2. Next I update the **/etc/fstab** file to include the mount:

```
# cat /etc/fstab
# System /etc/fstab file.  Static information about the file systems
# See fstab(4) and for further details on configuring devices
/dev/vg00/lvol3 / vxfs delaylog 0 1
/dev/vg00/lvol1 /stand hfs defaults 0 1
/dev/vg00/lvol4 /home vxfs delaylog 0 2
/dev/vg00/lvol5 /tmp vxfs delaylog 0 2
/dev/vg00/lvol6 /opt vxfs delaylog 0 2
/dev/vg00/lvol7 /usr vxfs delaylog 0 2
/dev/vg00/lvol8 /var vxfs delaylog 0 2
asodevlab1:/home/frame /home/frame nfs rw,suid 0 0
#
```

The **/home/frame** directory is automatically mounted at the next boot. I have to run the **mount** command as shown below to manually mount the file system at this time:

```
# mount /home/frame
# bdf
Filesystem          kbytes      used    avail %used Mounted on
/dev/vg00/lvol3     409600     69466   318923   18% /
/dev/vg00/lvol1     299157     26357   242884   10% /stand
/dev/vg00/lvol8    4706304    146362  4275401    3% /var
/dev/vg00/lvol7    1036288    748400   269946   73% /usr
/dev/vg00/lvol5     409600      1388   382763    0% /tmp
/dev/vg00/lvol6    3047424    749463  2154357   26% /opt
/dev/vg00/lvol4     409600      1210   382871    0% /home
asodevlab1:/home/frame
                     20480      1128    18144    6% /home/frame
# ls -l /home/frame
total 20
-r--r--r--   1 root       sys        959 May  6 12:14 copy.l.pm.Z
-r--r--r--   1 root       sys       2570 May  6 12:14 copy1.xwd
-r--r--r--   1 root       sys       2574 May  6 12:14 copy_done.xwd
-r--r--r--   1 root       sys       2575 May  6 12:14 copy_sched.xwd
#
```

I manually mount **/home/frame**, ran **bdf** to get information on all mounted file systems, and then ran **ls -l** to see its contents. Keep in mind that the client is accessing data on a server. I can write to this directory and the data will be written on the server.

The **nfsstat -m** command can also be used to verify active NFS client mounts and options. Useful data on the NFS server is also provided by this command.

There are many NFS mount options and trade-offs related to standard-mounting vs. automounting that are not covered in this book. These options are covered in *Installing and Administering NFS Services*. This example, however, shows how simple it is to get NFS mounts up-and-running quickly on two systems. With *PCNFSD* running, the PC NFS daemon, you can also mount this directory from a PC.

Chapter 16

Virtual Partitions (vPars)

Introduction

With Virtual Partitions (vPars) you can take almost any HP Integrity or HP 9000 server and turn it into many "virtual" computers. These virtual computers each run their own instance of HP-UX and associated applications. The virtual computers are isolated from one another at the software level. Software running on one Virtual Partition does not affect software running in any other Virtual Partition. In the Virtual Partitions you can run different patch levels of HP-UX, different applications, or any software you want and not affect other partitions.

Virtual Partitions (vPars) work nearly identically on HP Integrity and HP 9000 servers. At the time of this writing, vPars are not available on HP-UX 11i Version 2, but they are available on Version 1. vPars are nearly identical on Version 2 and Version 1 so most of the material in this chapter applies to Version 2. Since Version 1 is a PA-only release of HP-UX 11i, all the examples in this chapter are performed on PA-based HP 9000 Servers. HP-UX 11i Version 2 and vPars for both HP Integrity and HP 9000 Servers will be available by the time you read this book.

There are be differences between vPars running on HP 9000 and HP Integrity servers in that EFI, used on Integrity and described in Chapter 1,

"Booting HP Integrity Servers," and ISL on HP 9000 are different. The other aspects of using vPars on the two platforms are very similar.

The version of vPars that runs on Integrity and HP 9000 has additional enhancements as well, such as specifying a System Bus Adapter (SBA) as part of a vPar which is not available on the version of vPars used in this chapter. The **vparstatus** output changes in the new release as well. The vast majority of the material in this chapter applies to vPars on Integrity when it is released even though there are many enhancements that I can't cover in this chapter.

About Virtual Partitions

There are some base requirements that must be met in order to run vPars on your system. At the time of this writing, the following minimum requirements must be met for each vPar on your system:

- Minimum of one CPU.

- Sufficient memory to run HP-UX and any other software that will be present in the vPar.

- A boot disk off which HP-UX can be booted. The example in this chapter uses a cell-based system. If you use the *internal* disks on cell-based systems for different vPars, the internal disks must be connected to different cell boards. If you boot off of a SAN, you must use separate Local Bus Adapters (LBAs). On low-end systems that do not employ cell boards you only have to ensure that the boot devices are on separate LBAs.

- A console for managing the system. The console can be either physical or virtual. We cover the console later in this chapter.

- An HP Integrity server supported by HP-UX 11i Version 2 Update 2 or an HP 9000 system supported by HP-UX 11i Version 2 Update 2 or Version 1. Again, the example in this chapter will be an HP 9000 running Version 1 because Version 2 vPars are not available at the time of this writing.

The system we use in most of the examples throughout this chapter is an rp8420 that meets all the requirements in the previous list. You may also want to have additional disks and a separate LAN card in your vPars. I strongly recommend the LAN card so that you can establish Telnet or other sessions to your vPars rather than connecting to them only from the console. The LAN card is also required to perform backup and Ignite-UX-related work.

If you have Instant Capacity on Demand (iCOD) employed on your server, all CPUs must be activitated in order for vPars to work. When employing Processor Sets (psets) in a vPar, use only bound CPUs.

The vPars product is mature so you can confidently use it in production environments, keeping in mind that full software isolation is employed in vPars but not hardware isolation. If you need the additional confidence of hardware isolation, then you want to use nPartitions, which are covered in Chapter 17, "Node Partitions (nPartitions) and Management Processor Overview."

Virtual Partitions Background

HP-UX Virtual Partitions (vPars) allow you to run multiple instances of HP-UX on the same HP Integrity or 9000 Server. From a hardware perspective, a vPar consists of CPU, memory, and I/O that is a subset of the overall hardware on the computer. From a software perspective, a vPar consists of the HP-UX 11i Operating Environment and all application-related software to successfully run your workload. Figure 16-1 shows a conceptual diagram of the way in which HP 9000 computer-system resources can be allocated to support multiple vPars.

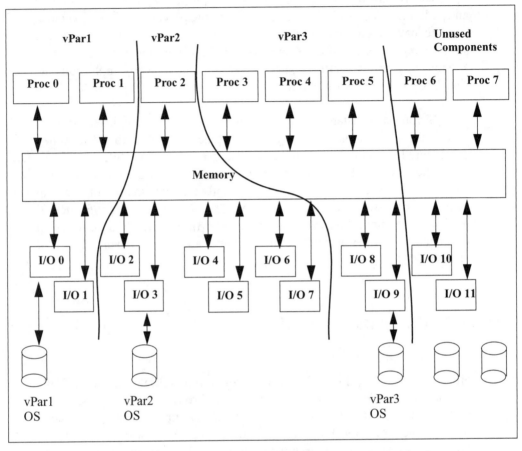

Figure 16-1   Example of HP System Resource Allocation with vPars

The components of which your HP server is comprised can be allocated in a variety of ways. You can see that the eight-way system shown in Figure 16-1 has a different number of processors, different amount of memory, and different number of I/O cards allocated to each vPar. The unused components can be added to any of the vPars or be the basis for yet another vPar. In addition, components can be moved from one vPar to another (with some restrictions described later in this chapter). Cell boards are not depicted in Figure 16-1. There are some nuances related to working with vPars on cell-based systems that are described in an example in this chapter.

Uses of Virtual Partitions

I have worked on many vPars installations that have a variety of uses for vPars. The following is a sampling of the reasons to use vPars:

Increased System Utilization

> Many servers are underutilized. With vPars, you can devote a subset of system resources to each vPar. With each vPar running its own instance of HP-UX 11i and associated applications, you get higher overall system utilization.

Quick Deployment

> You can deploy a new environment quickly without procuring an entire new system.

Flexibility

> Many applications have resource needs that change. With vPars, you can devote fewer system components when application needs are low and additional resources when an application needs them. An increased end-of-the-month workload, for example, can be given more system resources to complete faster.

Server Consolidation

> Running multiple instances of HP-UX 11i and their assoicated applications on one HP server reduces the overall number of servers required. Web servers that had run on different servers can now run in different vPars on the same computer.

Application Isolation

> HP vPars are fully software-isolated from one another. A software failure in one vPar does not affect other vPars.

Mixed Production, Test, and Development

> Production and testing can take place on the same server with vPars. When testing is complete, the test vPar can become the production

vPar. Similarly, development usually takes place on a separate system. With the software isolation of vPars, however; development can take place on the same system with other applications.

These are just a sampling of the uses I've seen for vPars. Many others will emerge as vPars become widely used and systems experts implement them in more computing environments.

Loading the Software

Chapter 3, "Installing HP-UX," covers loading HP-UX 11i in detail. If you haven't before loaded HP-UX 11i, Chapter 3 helps you complete the task of loading 11i on all of the disks that you will use for your vPars. Based on the previous discussion of disks, we might load HP-UX 11i on the internal disk at path *0/0/1/1.2.0* and the device at path *0/8/0/0.8.0.5.0.0.0*. Chapter 3 walks you through the process of selecting a target device on which to load HP-UX 11i as well as the process of loading 11i. The following is a list of steps you need to perform on every disk that acts as a vPar boot device:

1. Install the HP-UX 11i *Operating Environment*.
2. Set system parameters at the time of first boot after loading HP-UX 11i with **set_parms**.
3. Download and install select patches on your system (at the time of this writing there are many patches required to support vPars).
4. Install vPars software.
5. Configure vPars.
6. Install additional software.

You would typically load software in the order just shown: Install the *Operating Environment*; boot your system and use **set_parms**; load patches;

install vPars software; configure vPars; and then install and configure all other software.

I cover installing Virtual Partitions software in this section. I assume that you already have HP-UX 11i installed on your system or know how to do so. If you have not yet installed HP-UX 11i, see Chapter 3, which covers installing HP-UX 11i.

Keep in mind that HP-UX must be loaded for each Virtual Partition you want to run. If, for example, you want to run two Virtual Partitions, as we do in our examples in this book, HP-UX 11i needs to be loaded for both Virtual Partitions. The procedure covered for loading HP-UX 11i needs to be performed for every Virtual Partition you want to run. HP-UX 11i can be loaded from media, such as your HP-UX 11i distribution on a CD-ROM or from an Ignite/UX server. You can use any method to load HP-UX 11i and the Virtual Partitions software for every Virtual Partition you want to run.

Figure 16-2 shows an example of the software components that appear for vPars software.

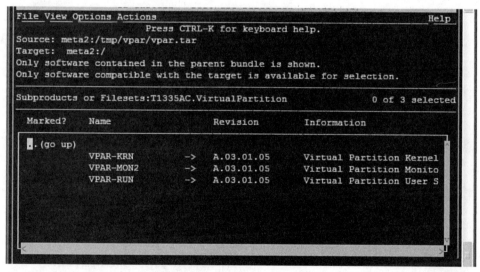

Figure 16-2   Example of Loading vPars Software

Figure 16-2 shows the components of which vPars software is comprised.

All the vPars software must be loaded on every HP-UX 11i volume that will be used on your vPars server. The loading of this software takes place for every HP-UX 11i instance that you want to run simultaneously on

your vPars server. After loading this software, you can run the following
swlist command to see the filesets:

```
[metal] / # swlist -l fileset | grep Vir
# VirtualPartition              A.03.01.05   HP-UX Virtual Partitions Functionality
  VirtualPartition.VPAR-KRN     A.03.01.05   Virtual Partition Kernel Files
  VirtualPartition.VPAR-MON     A.03.01.05   Virtual Partition Monitor
  VirtualPartition.VPAR-RUN     A.03.01.05   Virtual Partition User Space Commands
[metal] / #
```

Your revision number of vPars software will be newer than mine, which
was just released at the time of this writing.

There are two ways to load the HP-UX 11i operating system and vPars
software on all the volumes used for vPars. The first, which is the method
used throughout this book, is to load HP-UX 11i and vPars software on all
vPars volumes prior to creating Virtual Partitions. The second is to load only
the volume of the first vPar with all software, create as many vPars as you
want, and then use **vparboot -p** *vp_name* **-I** *ignite_kernel* to boot and load
HP-UX 11i on the other disks. Using Ignite/UX you have to specify the full
path of the kernel, as shown in this command:

```
vaprboot -p <name> -I /opt/ignite/boot/Rel_B.11.11/WINSTALL
```

In this chapter, I first load HP-UX 11i and vPars software on all disks
before creating vPars.

A lot of software has been loaded as a result of loading the vPars software. The **/sbin** directory has in it the *vpar* commands we'll use in upcoming
sections. The following is a long listing of the *vpar* commands in **/sbin**:

```
[metal] / # ll /sbin/vpar*
-r-xr-xr-x   1 bin        bin          120624 Apr  8 15:49 /sbin/vparboot
-r-xr-xr-x   1 bin        bin          148224 Apr  8 15:49 /sbin/vparcreate
-r-xr-xr-x   1 bin        bin           87800 Apr  8 16:06 /sbin/vpard
-r-xr-xr-x   1 bin        bin           54976 Apr  8 16:06 /sbin/vpardump
-r-xr-xr-x   1 bin        bin           30240 Apr  8 16:06 /sbin/vparextract
-r-xr-xr-x   1 bin        bin          132000 Apr  8 15:49 /sbin/vparmodify
-r-xr-xr-x   1 bin        bin           47712 Apr  8 16:06 /sbin/vparreloc
-r-xr-xr-x   1 bin        bin          114488 Apr  8 15:49 /sbin/vparremove
-r-xr-xr-x   1 bin        bin          119288 Apr  8 15:49 /sbin/vparreset
-r-xr-xr-x   1 bin        bin          147880 Apr  8 15:49 /sbin/vparstatus
-r-xr-xr-x   1 bin        bin           25728 Apr  8 16:06 /sbin/vparutil
[metal] / #
```

These are the commands that you use to create, view, modify, and work
with vPars in general.

There are several files in **/stand** related to the vPars kernel. The following listing shows some of them:

```
[meta1] / # ll /stand/vp*
-rw-------   1 root      root        20520 Sep 17 11:56 /stand/vpdb
-r-xr-xr-x   1 bin       bin       1168728 Apr  8 15:44 /stand/vpmon
-rw-------   1 root      root     18350080 Sep 17 10:47 /stand/vpmon.dmp
[meta1] / #
```

vpmon is loaded at the time of system startup and is the basis for running vPars. **vpdb** is the vPars database that contains all information related to all the vPars running on your system. This file is automatically synchronized by the vPars monitor to ensure that all vPars have the same information about all vPars on your system. **vpmon.dmp** is the vPars dump file.

There are several startup-related files, including those shown below, which are covered in more detail in Chapter 8, "System Startup and Shutdown."

```
[meta1] / # ll /etc/rc.config.d/vpar*
-r--r--r--   1 bin       bin          291 Oct 27  2001 /etc/rc.config.d/vpard
-r--r--r--   1 bin       bin          553 Oct 29  2003 /etc/rc.config.d/vparhb
-r--r--r--   1 bin       bin         1246 Oct 27  2001 /etc/rc.config.d/vparinit

[meta1] / # ll /sbin/init.d/vpar*
-r-xr-xr-x   1 bin       bin          793 Oct 27  2001 /sbin/init.d/vpard
-r-xr-xr-x   1 bin       bin          922 Oct 27  2001 /sbin/init.d/vparhb
-r-xr-xr-x   1 bin       bin         7808 Aug 13  2003 /sbin/init.d/vparinit
[meta1] / #
```

Of particular interest is **vparhp**, which is the *heartbeat* daemon related to keeping **vpdb** synchronized on all of your vPars.

Very important to your work related to vPars are the online man pages. The following listing shows the man pages loaded on my system at the time of this writing:

```
[meta1] / # man -k vpar
vparboot(1M)        - boot a virtual partition
vparcreate(1M)      - create a virtual partition
vpardump(1M)        - manage monitor dump files
vparextract(1M)     - extract memory images from a running virtual partition system
vparmodify(1M)      - rename a virtual partition or modify the attributes of a
                      virtual partition
vparreloc(1M)       - relocate the load address of a vmunix file, determine if a vmunix
                      file is relocatable, or promote the scope of symbols in a
                      relocatable vmunix file
vparremove(1M)      - remove a virtual partition
vparreset(1M)       - reset a virtual partition
vparresources(5)    - description of virtual partition resources and their
requirements
vparstatus(1M)      - display information about one or more virtual partitions
vpartition(5)       - display information about the Virtual Partition Command
```

```
                         Line Interface
vparutil(1M)          - get and set SCSI parameters for SCSI controllers from a
                         virtual partition
[metal] / #
```

You may have to run the **catman** command to create cat files for these manaual pages.

At this point, we have HP-UX 11i and the Virtual Partitions software loaded on the system.

The remainder of this chapter covers numerous vPars topics, including creating, booting, and modifying vPars.

With both HP-UX 11i and the Virtual Partitions software on our disk, we can begin the process of creating partitions. Our goal is to have a system that looks like what's shown in Figure 16-3.

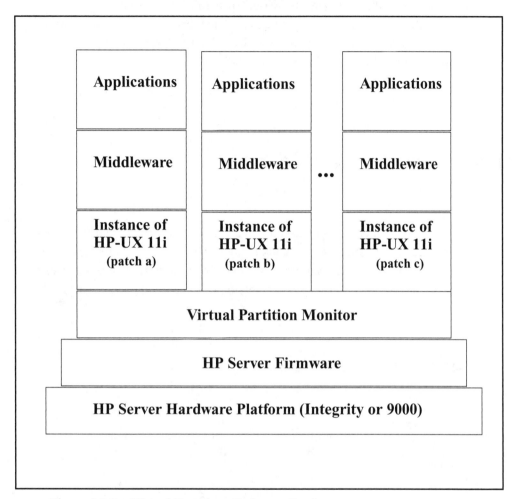

Figure 16-3   Virtual Partitions Software Stack

There are many components in Figure 16-3. We already have many of the components in this diagram on our system. Starting from the bottom, we have the hardware, firmware, Virtual Partition Monitor, and HP-UX 11i installed on two different disks. There are two HP-UX 11i instances shown in the left-most two stacks of Figure 16-3. These are the operating systems that we have already loaded.

The two HP-UX 11i instances can't run simultaneously on a system because we have not yet created our Virtual Partitions. Without Virtual Partitions created, we can boot HP-UX off of one *or* the other of these disks, but

we can't run both. Let's now create our Virtual Partitions so that we can have
two instances of HP-UX 11i running simultaneously. After Virtual Partitions
have been created, you can proceed to load the middleware and applications
shown on top of HP-UX 11i in Figure 16-3.

Virtual Partitions Command Summary

There are several commands used to create and work with Virtual Partitions.
A table and a tear-out card in my vPars book, *HP-UX Virtual Partitions*, provide an overview of many commonly used Virtual Partitions related commands. Table 16-1 is an abbreviated version of the command summary:

Table 16-1   Virtual Partition Commands

Command	Description

ISL>
 	
Initial System Load prompt.
	Virtual Partitions Monitor is loaded from *ISL>* with:
	`ISL> hpux /stand/vpmon`
	`MON>`
	To load Virtual Partitions directly from *ISL>*, use:
	`ISL> hpux /stand/vpmon vparload -p ` *vPar_name*

MON>
 	
Virtual Partitions Monitor prompt. (Also see **vparload** command.)
	This is loaded from *ISL* with:
	`ISL> hpux /stand/vpmon`
	`MON>`
	To load an alternate database from *ISL*, use:
	`ISL> hpux /stand/vpmon -D ` *db_file*
	To load one vPar from *MON* , use:
	`MON> vparload ` *vPar_name*
	
	Many other commands can be issued from *MON*. Type **help** or **?** to list. (Commands include: **scan, vparinfo, ls, log, getauto, lifls, cbuf, cat**.)

vparload Load Virtual Partitions from *MON>* prompt only.	To boot a Virtual Partition from *MON>*: `MON> vparload -p ` *vPar_name*

Command	Description
vparboot Boot a Virtual Partition from the command line only.	To boot a Virtual Partition from the command line: `# vparboot -p ` *`vPar_name`*

vparcreate
 	
Create a Virtual Partition.
	To create a Virtual Partition with three processors (*num*) total, two bound (*min*), 2048MB RAM, all components on 0/0, boot disk at 0/0/1/1.2.0, with a kernel of **/stand/vmunix**, autoboot on, and console at 0/0/4/0:
	
	`# vparcreate -p ` *`vPar_name`* ` -a cpu::3 -a cpu:::2:4`
	`-a mem::2048 -a io:0/0 -a io:0/0/1/1.2.0:boot`
	`-b /stand/vmunix -B auto`

vparmodify Modify the attributes of a Virtual Partition.	To add processor at path *109* (adds this proc to those already assigned): `# vparmodify -p ` *`vPar_name`* ` -a cpu:109`
vparremove Delete a Virtual Partition.	To delete a Virtual Partition in the currently running database: `# vparremove -p ` *`vPar_name`*
vparreset Reset a Virtual Partition.	To reset a Virtual Partition without TOC (t), hard (h), bypassing display of PIM data (q), or forcing (f): `# vparreset -p ` *`vPar_name`*
vparresources(5) man page Provides description of Virtual Partitions and their resources.	This is a manual page that describes Virtual Partition resources in general and how resources are specified in other commands, such as **vparmodify**.
vparstatus Display the status of Virtual Partitions.	To display the status of a Virtual Partition in verbose mode: `# vparstatus -v -p ` *`vPar_name`*

Command	Description
vpartition man page Display information about the Virtual Partition Command Line Interface.	Provides the following brief description of Virtual Partitions commands: **vparboot** Boot (start) a virtual partition. **vparcreate** Create a new virtual partition. **vparmodify** Modify an existing virtual partition. **vparremove** Remove (delete) an existing virtual partition. **vparreset** Simulate a TOC or hard reset to a virtual partition. **vparstatus** Display virtual partition and available resources information.
Specify CPU Resources by:	Number of bound and unbound CPUs: *cpu::num* CPU hardware path(s): *cpu:path* Minimum and maximum number: *cpu:::[min][:[max]]*
Specify Memory by:	Size *mem::size* Base and range: *mem:::base:range* combination of both above.
Specify I/O:	Use path: *io:path[:attr1[,attr2[...]]]* (see man page **vparresources** for details).
To add resources use: (This adds component relative to what already exists if running **vparmodify**.)	*-a cpu:path* *-a cpu::num* (can be done with vPar running) *[-a cpu::num] [-a cpu:::[min]:[max]] -[a cpu:path]* (*:::* is **vparcreate** only) *-a io:path[:attr1[,attr2[...]]* *-a mem::size* *-a mem:::base:range*
To delete resources use (This deletes component relative to what already exists if running **vparmodify**.)	*-d cpu:path* *-d cpu::num* (can be done with vPar running) *-d io:path[:attr1[,attr2[...]]* *-d mem::size* *-d mem:::base:range*
To modify resources use: (This modifies to absolute number rather than relative.)	*-m cpu::num* (can be done with vPar running) *-m cpu:::[min][:[max]]* *-m io:path[:attr1[,attr2[...]]* *-m mem::size*
vPars **setboot** Options: *-a* *-b* *-p* *-s* no options	Changes the alternate boot path of the Virtual Partition. Sets the autoboot attribute of the Virtual Partition. Changes the primary boot path of the Virtual Partition. No affect. Displays information about boot attributes. To set Autoboot *on*: `# setboot -b on`

Command	Description
vPars States:	
load	The kernel image of a Virtual Partition is being loaded into memory. This is done by the Virtual Partition monitor.
boot	The Virtual Partition is in the process of booting. The kernel image has been successfully loaded by the Virtual Partition monitor.
up	The Virtual Partition has been successfully booted and is running.
shut	The Virtual Partition is in the process of shutting down.
down	The Virtual Partition is not running and is down.
crash	The Virtual Partition has experienced a panic and is crashing.
hung	The Virtual Partition is not responding and is hung.

We use some of the commands shown in Table 16-1 in the upcoming section on creating virtual partitions.

Let's now move on to creating virtual partitions.

Steps to Create Virtual Partitions

This section covers the steps to create Virtual Partitions. I performed these steps while working with some of my clients on their vPars environments. This list should serve as a framework for working with vPars. You may chose not to perform some of the steps and to add others. It is only a framework for getting vPars working on your system.

In our upcoming examples to create our Virtual Partitions, we execute the steps shown in Figure 16-4.

1) Load HP-UX 11i onto the disks on which you want to run a Virtual Partition* (media or Ignite/UX server.)

2) Load Virtual Partitions software onto the disk(s) on which you want to run a Virtual Partition.

3) Gather information on system components and hardware paths using **ioscan**, **dmesg**, and other commands.

4) List components of which Virtual Partitions will be comprised such as:
- name
- CPUs
- memory
- others
5) Create first Virtual Partition with **vparcreate**.

6) Boot first Virtual Partition with **vparload** at *MON>* prompt. Use **vparstatus -v** to see running vPar and **vparstatus -A** to see available components.

7) Create second Virtual Partition with **vparcreate** (can also be done before booting any vPars.)

8) Boot second Virtual Partition with **vparboot** from the first vPar and monitor it booting with **vparstatus**. After it has booted, view remaining available components with **vparstatus -A**.

9) Modify Virtual Partition(s) as required with **vparmodify** and view modifications with **vparstatus -v** and **vparstatus -A**. Modifications can be any type, such as adding CPUs, changing attributes, and so on.

Other tasks and comments:

- Many other tasks can be performed. Commands **vparremove** and **vparreset** were not used in steps above.

- A typical list of components of which a vPar would be comprised looks like the following:

```
name          vpar1
processors    min of 1 (bound) max of 3 (1 bound 2 unbound) with num equal to 1
memory        1024 MB
LAN           0/0/0/0 (not specified explicity)
boot disk     0/0/1/1.2.0
kernel        /stand/vmunix
autoboot      off (manual)
```

* HP-UX 11i must be loaded on volume before or after Virtual Partition is created. If HP-UX 11i is loaded after vPar is created, then `vparboot -p vp_name -I ignite_kernel` is used to load 11i.

Figure 16-4   Steps to Create Virtual Partitions

1) Load HP-UX 11i

HP-UX 11i must be loaded on the volumes that will be used to host all vPars. The method you use to install 11i, whether media, Ignite-UX, or some other technique, are all acceptable provided that HP-UX 11i is present on all the disks. HP-UX 11i must be present on the first disk before you begin the vPar creation. You can create vPars on other disks before HP-UX 11i is loaded on them and then use **vparboot -p** *vp_name* **-I** *ignite_kernel* to boot and load HP-UX 11i on the other disks. In this chapter, I first load HP-UX 11i on all disks before creating vPars. Loading HP-UX and vPars software was previously covered in this chapter. In the upcoming example, two virtual partitions are created on two different internal disks on an rp8420.

HP-UX and vPars software can be loaded on internal disks, which will be covered in the upcoming example, or on a Storage Area Network (SAN.) The following listing shows the internal disk as the boot path for vPar *meta1* and a boot disk on the SAN for vPar *meta2*:

```
[meta1] / # vparstatus -v -p meta1
vparstatus: Warning: Virtual partition monitor not running, Requested resources shown.
[Virtual Partition Details]
Name:        meta1
State:       N/A
Attributes:  Dynamic,Autoboot
Kernel Path: /stand/vmunix
Boot Opts:

[CPU Details]
Min/Max:  1/<default>
Bound by User [Path]:
Bound by Monitor [Path]:  <no path>
Unbound [Path]:  <no path>
                 <no path>
                 <no path>
                 <no path>
                 <no path>
                 <no path>
                 <no path>
                 <no path>
                 <no path>
                 <no path>

[IO Details]
   0.0.0.2.0.6.0.0.0.0.0  BOOT                    <- internal SCSI boot disk

[Memory Details]
Specified [Base  /Range]:
        (bytes) (MB)
Total Memory (MB):  24576
```

```
[meta1] / # vparstatus -v -p meta2
vparstatus: Warning: Virtual partition monitor not running, Requested resources shown.
[Virtual Partition Details]
Name:        meta2
State:       N/A
Attributes:  Dynamic,Autoboot
Kernel Path: /stand/vmunix
Boot Opts:

[CPU Details]
Min/Max:  1/<default>
Bound by User [Path]:
Bound by Monitor [Path]:  <no path>
Unbound [Path]:  <no path>
                 <no path>
                 <no path>

[IO Details]
   0.0.8.1.0.20.4.0.0.0.1  BOOT                         <- SAN boot disk
   0.0.12.1.0

[Memory Details]
Specified [Base  /Range]:
          (bytes) (MB)
Total Memory (MB):  8192
[meta1] / #
```

The **vparstatus** command is covered later in this chapter but, at this time, it is sufficient to know that the vPars boot device can be on the SAN and **vparstatus** displays this.

An interesting nuance to working with vPars is the naming of hosts and vPars. In a nutshell, you supply hostnames when installing 11i and Virtual Partition names when creating vPars. It reduces confusion if both the hostname and vPar name are the same for an instance of HP-UX 11i. In some cases, however, organizations require hostnames to conform to conventions that result in names that are difficult to remember. In this case, some system administrators pick easy-to-remember vPar names.

You may also have many more vPars defined than instances of HP-UX. You can shut down and load different vPars as often as you like. In this case the hostname and vPars name are not always the same.

The upcoming examples have hostnames of *vPar1* and *vPar2* and the vPar names used are *vPar1* and *vPar2*.

2) Load the Virtual Partitions Application Software

The Virtual Partitions software must also be loaded on the volumes that will be used to host all vPars. The vPars release changes regularly to include new functionality and fix problems with vPars software. (I use vPars A.03.01 in the examples in this chapter.) After loading the vPars software on one of the root volumes, I run **swlist**, which results in the following output:

```
# swlist | grep Vir
  T1335AC                   A.03.01.05    HP-UX Virtual Partitions
  VPARMGR                   B.11.11.01.02 Virtual Partition Manager - HP-UX
#
```

The *HP-UX Virtual Partitions* software and the *Virtual Partitions Manager* software have been loaded on this system. I now proceed to gather the information required to create virtual partitions.

3) Gather the System Component and Hardware Paths

You get to know your hardware at an intimate level when working with vPars. You not only need to know the components of which your system is comprised, you also need to know the paths of much of the hardware. Some system components, such as *System Bus Adapters* and the *memory controller*, are shared among vPars, so you don't specify those components as part of individual Virtual Partitions. Most other components in your system, such as processors, I/O cards, disks, and others, are fixed to specific vPars.

In the example in this chapter, I create one nPartition that contains all four cell boards in the system. Because all the cell boards are in one nPartition, all the Core I/O boards and I/O chassis connected to the cell boards will be in one nPartition. I run **ioscan -f** in the following listing to show the hardware in the nPartition:

```
# ioscan -f
Class      I  H/W Path      Driver     S/W State   H/W Type    Description
==========================================================================
root       0                root       CLAIMED     BUS_NEXUS
cell       0  0             cell       CLAIMED     BUS_NEXUS
ioa        0  0/0           sba        CLAIMED     BUS_NEXUS   System Bus
                                                               Adapter (805)
ba         0  0/0/0         lba        CLAIMED     BUS_NEXUS   Local PCI
                                                               Bus Adapter (782)
tty        0  0/0/0/0/0     asio0      CLAIMED     INTERFACE   PCI SimpleComm
                                                               (103c1290)
tty        1  0/0/0/0/1     asio0      CLAIMED     INTERFACE   PCI Serial
                                                               (103c1048)
lan        0  0/0/0/1/0     igelan     CLAIMED     INTERFACE   HP A7109-60001
                                                               PCI 1000Base-T Core
ext_bus    0  0/0/0/2/0     c8xx       CLAIMED     INTERFACE   SCSI C1010 Ultra
                                                               Wide Single-Ended
target     0  0/0/0/2/0.6   tgt        CLAIMED     DEVICE
disk       0  0/0/0/2/0.6.0 sdisk      CLAIMED     DEVICE      HP 73.4GMAS3735NC
target     1  0/0/0/2/0.7   tgt        CLAIMED     DEVICE
ctl        0  0/0/0/2/0.7.0 sctl       CLAIMED     DEVICE      Initiator
```

ext_bus	1	0/0/0/2/1	c8xx	CLAIMED	INTERFACE	SCSI C1010 Ultra Wide Single-Ended
target	2	0/0/0/2/1.2	tgt	CLAIMED	DEVICE	
disk	1	0/0/0/2/1.2.0	sdisk	CLAIMED	DEVICE	HP DVD-ROM
target	3	0/0/0/2/1.7	tgt	CLAIMED	DEVICE	
ctl	1	0/0/0/2/1.7.0	sctl	CLAIMED	DEVICE	Initiator
ext_bus	2	0/0/0/3/0	c8xx	CLAIMED	INTERFACE	SCSI C1010 Ultra Wide Single-Ended
target	4	0/0/0/3/0.7	tgt	CLAIMED	DEVICE	
ctl	2	0/0/0/3/0.7.0	sctl	CLAIMED	DEVICE	Initiator
ext_bus	3	0/0/0/3/1	c8xx	CLAIMED	INTERFACE	SCSI C1010 Ultra160 Wide LVD
target	5	0/0/0/3/1.7	tgt	CLAIMED	DEVICE	
ctl	3	0/0/0/3/1.7.0	sctl	CLAIMED	DEVICE	Initiator
ba	1	0/0/1	lba	CLAIMED	BUS_NEXUS	Local PCI-X Bus Adapter (783)
ba	2	0/0/2	lba	CLAIMED	BUS_NEXUS	Local PCI-X Bus Adapter (783)
ba	3	0/0/4	lba	CLAIMED	BUS_NEXUS	Local PCI-X Bus Adapter (783)
ba	4	0/0/6	lba	CLAIMED	BUS_NEXUS	Local PCI-X Bus Adapter (783)
ba	5	0/0/8	lba	CLAIMED	BUS_NEXUS	Local PCI-X Bus Adapter (783)
fc	0	0/0/8/1/0	fcd	CLAIMED	INTERFACE	HP 2Gb Dual Port PCI/PCI-X Fibre Channel Adapter (Port 1)
fc	1	0/0/8/1/1	fcd	CLAIMED	INTERFACE	HP 2Gb Dual Port PCI/PCI-X Fibre Channel Adapter (Port 2)
ba	6	0/0/10	lba	CLAIMED	BUS_NEXUS	Local PCI-X Bus Adapter (783)
fc	2	0/0/10/1/0	fcd	CLAIMED	INTERFACE	HP 2Gb Dual Port PCI/PCI-X Fibre Channel Adapter (Port 1)
fc	3	0/0/10/1/1	fcd	CLAIMED	INTERFACE	HP 2Gb Dual Port PCI/PCI-X Fibre Channel Adapter (Port 2)
ba	7	0/0/12	lba	CLAIMED	BUS_NEXUS	Local PCI-X Bus Adapter (783)
lan	1	0/0/12/1/0	igelan	CLAIMED	INTERFACE	HP A6825-60101 PCI 1000Base-T Adapter
ba	8	0/0/14	lba	CLAIMED	BUS_NEXUS	Local PCI-X Bus Adapter (783)
lan	2	0/0/14/1/0	igelan	CLAIMED	INTERFACE	HP A6825-60101 PCI 1000Base-T Adapter
memory	0	0/5	memory	CLAIMED	MEMORY	Memory
ipmi	0	0/6	ipmi	CLAIMED	INTERFACE	IPMI Controller
processor	0	0/10	processor	CLAIMED	PROCESSOR	Processor
processor	1	0/11	processor	CLAIMED	PROCESSOR	Processor
processor	2	0/12	processor	CLAIMED	PROCESSOR	Processor
processor	3	0/13	processor	CLAIMED	PROCESSOR	Processor
processor	4	0/14	processor	CLAIMED	PROCESSOR	Processor
processor	5	0/15	processor	CLAIMED	PROCESSOR	Processor
processor	6	0/16	processor	CLAIMED	PROCESSOR	Processor
processor	7	0/17	processor	CLAIMED	PROCESSOR	Processor
cell	1	1	cell	CLAIMED	BUS_NEXUS	
ioa	1	1/0	sba	CLAIMED	BUS_NEXUS	System Bus Adapter (805)
ba	9	1/0/0	lba	CLAIMED	BUS_NEXUS	Local PCI Bus Adapter (782)
tty	2	1/0/0/0/0	asio0	CLAIMED	INTERFACE	PCI SimpleComm (103c1290)
tty	3	1/0/0/0/1	asio0	CLAIMED	INTERFACE	PCI Serial (103c1048)
lan	3	1/0/0/1/0	igelan	CLAIMED	INTERFACE	HP A7109-60001 PCI 1000Base-T Core
ext_bus	4	1/0/0/2/0	c8xx	CLAIMED	INTERFACE	SCSI C1010 Ultra Wide Single-Ended
target	6	1/0/0/2/0.6	tgt	CLAIMED	DEVICE	
disk	2	1/0/0/2/0.6.0	sdisk	CLAIMED	DEVICE	HP 73.4GST373453LC
target	7	1/0/0/2/0.7	tgt	CLAIMED	DEVICE	
ctl	4	1/0/0/2/0.7.0	sctl	CLAIMED	DEVICE	Initiator
ext_bus	5	1/0/0/2/1	c8xx	CLAIMED	INTERFACE	SCSI C1010 Ultra Wide Single-Ended
target	8	1/0/0/2/1.2	tgt	CLAIMED	DEVICE	
disk	3	1/0/0/2/1.2.0	sdisk	CLAIMED	DEVICE	HP DVD-ROM

```
target     9  1/0/0/2/1.7    tgt     CLAIMED    DEVICE
ctl        5  1/0/0/2/1.7.0  sctl    CLAIMED    DEVICE       Initiator
ext_bus    6  1/0/0/3/0      c8xx    CLAIMED    INTERFACE    SCSI C1010 Ultra
                                     Wide Single-Ended
target    10  1/0/0/3/0.7    tgt     CLAIMED    DEVICE
ctl        6  1/0/0/3/0.7.0  sctl    CLAIMED    DEVICE       Initiator
ext_bus    7  1/0/0/3/1      c8xx    CLAIMED    INTERFACE    SCSI C1010
                                                            Ultra160
                                     Wide LVD
target    11  1/0/0/3/1.7    tgt     CLAIMED    DEVICE
ctl        7  1/0/0/3/1.7.0  sctl    CLAIMED    DEVICE       Initiator
ba        10  1/0/1          lba     CLAIMED    BUS_NEXUS    Local PCI-X Bus
                                                            Adapter (783)
ba        11  1/0/2          lba     CLAIMED    BUS_NEXUS    Local PCI-X Bus
                                                            Adapter (783)
ba        12  1/0/4          lba     CLAIMED    BUS_NEXUS    Local PCI-X Bus
                                                            Adapter (783)
ba        13  1/0/6          lba     CLAIMED    BUS_NEXUS    Local PCI-X Bus
                                                            Adapter (783)
ba        14  1/0/8          lba     CLAIMED    BUS_NEXUS    Local PCI-X Bus
                                                            Adapter (783)
fc         4  1/0/8/1/0      fcd     CLAIMED    INTERFACE    HP 2Gb Dual Port
                             PCI/PCI-X Fibre Channel Adapter (Port 1)
fc         5  1/0/8/1/1      fcd     CLAIMED    INTERFACE    HP 2Gb Dual Port
                             PCI/PCI-X Fibre Channel Adapter (Port 2)
ba        15  1/0/10         lba     CLAIMED    BUS_NEXUS    Local
                             PCI-X Bus Adapter (783)
fc         6  1/0/10/1/0     fcd     CLAIMED    INTERFACE    HP 2Gb Dual Port
                             PCI/PCI-X Fibre Channel Adapter (Port 1)
fc         7  1/0/10/1/1     fcd     CLAIMED    INTERFACE    HP 2Gb Dual Port
                             PCI/PCI-X Fibre Channel
                                                            Adapter (Port 2)
ba        16  1/0/12         lba     CLAIMED    BUS_NEXUS    Local PCI-X Bus
                                                            Adapter (783)
lan        4  1/0/12/1/0     igelan  CLAIMED    INTERFACE    HP A6825-60101
                             PCI 1000Base-T Adapter
ba        17  1/0/14         lba     CLAIMED    BUS_NEXUS    Local PCI-X Bus
                                                            Adapter (783)
lan        5  1/0/14/1/0     igelan  CLAIMED    INTERFACE    HP A6825-60101
                             PCI 1000Base-T Adapter
memory     1  1/5            memory    CLAIMED    MEMORY       Memory
processor  8  1/10           processor CLAIMED    PROCESSOR    Processor
processor  9  1/11           processor CLAIMED    PROCESSOR    Processor
processor 10  1/12           processor CLAIMED    PROCESSOR    Processor
processor 11  1/13           processor CLAIMED    PROCESSOR    Processor
processor 12  1/14           processor CLAIMED    PROCESSOR    Processor
processor 13  1/15           processor CLAIMED    PROCESSOR    Processor
processor 14  1/16           processor CLAIMED    PROCESSOR    Processor
processor 15  1/17           processor CLAIMED    PROCESSOR    Processor
cell       2  2              cell      CLAIMED    BUS_NEXUS
memory     2  2/5            memory    CLAIMED    MEMORY       Memory
processor 16  2/10           processor CLAIMED    PROCESSOR    Processor
processor 17  2/11           processor CLAIMED    PROCESSOR    Processor
processor 18  2/12           processor CLAIMED    PROCESSOR    Processor
processor 19  2/13           processor CLAIMED    PROCESSOR    Processor
processor 20  2/14           processor CLAIMED    PROCESSOR    Processor
processor 21  2/15           processor CLAIMED    PROCESSOR    Processor
processor 22  2/16           processor CLAIMED    PROCESSOR    Processor
processor 23  2/17           processor CLAIMED    PROCESSOR    Processor
cell       3  3              cell      CLAIMED    BUS_NEXUS
memory     3  3/5            memory    CLAIMED    MEMORY       Memory
processor 24  3/10           processor CLAIMED    PROCESSOR    Processor
processor 25  3/11           processor CLAIMED    PROCESSOR    Processor
processor 26  3/12           processor CLAIMED    PROCESSOR    Processor
processor 27  3/13           processor CLAIMED    PROCESSOR    Processor
processor 28  3/14           processor CLAIMED    PROCESSOR    Processor
processor 29  3/15           processor CLAIMED    PROCESSOR    Processor
processor 30  3/16           processor CLAIMED    PROCESSOR    Processor
processor 31  3/17           processor CLAIMED    PROCESSOR    Processor
#
```

```
# ioscan -f |grep 73
disk       0  0/0/0/2/0.6.0  sdisk     CLAIMED     DEVICE  HP 73.4GMAS3735NC
disk       2  1/0/0/2/0.6.0  sdisk     CLAIMED     DEVICE  HP 73.4GST373453LC
#
```

This **ioscan -f** output shows that 32 processors exist, labeled 1-21, on four different cell boards, labeled 0-3. I use two 73 GB disk drives for the two different vPars. There are also several fibre cards present that could be used for Logical Units (LUNs) on a SAN to support additional vPars.

I list the disk drives separately because I need the paths for the drives later in the chapter when the two vPars are created. Notice that the first disk is connected to cell board 0, as indicated by the leading 0, and the second disk is connected to cell board 1, as indicated by the leading 1. There are four disk slots internal to the rp8420. Two are connected to cell 0 and two are connected to cell 1. Using internal disks on the rp8420, the maximum number of vPars supported is two. The two disks connected to cell 0 are in one vPar and the two connected to cell 1 are on one vPar.

When working with vPars, I like to get a **dmesg** output, which nicely summarizes the paths of components in the system, as shown in the following output:

```
# dmesg

Jul 25 02:00
...
tofs_link(): File system was registered at index 6.
NOTICE: cachefs_link(): File system was registered at index 7.
0 cell
0/0 sba
0/0/0 lba
0/0/0/0/0 asio0
0/0/0/0/1 asio0
0/0/0/1/0 igelan
c8xx BUS: 0 SCSI C1010 Ultra Wide Single-Ended  assigned CPU: 1
0/0/0/2/0 c8xx
0/0/0/2/0.6 tgt
0/0/0/2/0.6.0 sdisk
0/0/0/2/0.7 tgt
0/0/0/2/0.7.0 sctl
c8xx BUS: 1 SCSI C1010 Ultra Wide Single-Ended  assigned CPU: 2
0/0/0/2/1 c8xx
0/0/0/2/1.2 tgt
0/0/0/2/1.2.0 sdisk
0/0/0/2/1.7 tgt
0/0/0/2/1.7.0 sctl
c8xx BUS: 2 SCSI C1010 Ultra Wide Single-Ended  assigned CPU: 3
0/0/0/3/0 c8xx
0/0/0/3/0.7 tgt
0/0/0/3/0.7.0 sctl
c8xx BUS: 3 SCSI C1010 Ultra160 Wide LVD  assigned CPU: 4
0/0/0/3/1 c8xx
0/0/0/3/1.7 tgt
0/0/0/3/1.7.0 sctl
0/0/1 lba
0/0/2 lba
0/0/4 lba
0/0/6 lba
0/0/8 lba
```

```
fcd: Claimed Dual Port 2Gb HBA Port 0 at 0/0/8/1/0
0/0/8/1/0 fcd
fcd: Claimed Dual Port 2Gb HBA Port 1 at 0/0/8/1/1
0/0/8/1/1 fcd
0/0/10 lba
fcd: Claimed Dual Port 2Gb HBA Port 0 at 0/0/10/1/0
0/0/10/1/0 fcd
fcd: Claimed Dual Port 2Gb HBA Port 1 at 0/0/10/1/1
0/0/10/1/1 fcd
0/0/12 lba
0/0/12/1/0 igelan
0/0/14 lba
0/0/14/1/0 igelan
0/5 memory
0/6 ipmi
0/10 processor
0/11 processor
0/12 processor
0/13 processor
0/14 processor
0/15 processor
0/16 processor
0/17 processor
1 cell
1/0 sba
1/0/0 lba
1/0/0/0/0 asio0
1/0/0/0/1 asio0
1/0/0/1/0 igelan
c8xx BUS: 4 SCSI C1010 Ultra Wide Single-Ended  assigned CPU: 9
1/0/0/2/0 c8xx
1/0/0/2/0.6 tgt
1/0/0/2/0.6.0 sdisk
1/0/0/2/0.7 tgt
1/0/0/2/0.7.0 sctl
c8xx BUS: 5 SCSI C1010 Ultra Wide Single-Ended  assigned CPU: 10
1/0/0/2/1 c8xx
1/0/0/2/1.2 tgt
1/0/0/2/1.2.0 sdisk
1/0/0/2/1.7 tgt
1/0/0/2/1.7.0 sctl
c8xx BUS: 6 SCSI C1010 Ultra Wide Single-Ended  assigned CPU: 11
1/0/0/3/0 c8xx
1/0/0/3/0.7 tgt
1/0/0/3/0.7.0 sctl
c8xx BUS: 7 SCSI C1010 Ultra160 Wide LVD  assigned CPU: 12
1/0/0/3/1 c8xx
1/0/0/3/1.7 tgt
1/0/0/3/1.7.0 sctl
1/0/1 lba
1/0/2 lba
1/0/4 lba
1/0/6 lba
1/0/8 lba
fcd: Claimed Dual Port 2Gb HBA Port 0 at 1/0/8/1/0
1/0/8/1/0 fcd
fcd: Claimed Dual Port 2Gb HBA Port 1 at 1/0/8/1/1
1/0/8/1/1 fcd
1/0/10 lba
fcd: Claimed Dual Port 2Gb HBA Port 0 at 1/0/10/1/0
1/0/10/1/0 fcd
fcd: Claimed Dual Port 2Gb HBA Port 1 at 1/0/10/1/1
1/0/10/1/1 fcd
1/0/12 lba
1/0/12/1/0 igelan
1/0/14 lba
1/0/14/1/0 igelan
1/5 memory
1/10 processor
1/11 processor
1/12 processor
1/13 processor
1/14 processor
1/15 processor
1/16 processor
```

```
1/17 processor
2 cell
2/5 memory
2/10 processor
2/11 processor
2/12 processor
2/13 processor
2/14 processor
2/15 processor
2/16 processor
2/17 processor
3 cell
3/5 memory
3/10 processor
3/11 processor
3/12 processor
3/13 processor
3/14 processor
3/15 processor
3/16 processor
3/17 processor

    System Console is on the Built-In Serial Interface
igelan0: INITIALIZING HP A7109-60001 PCI 1000Base-T Core at hardware path 0/0/0/1/0
igelan3: INITIALIZING HP A7109-60001 PCI 1000Base-T Core at hardware path 1/0/0/1/0
igelan4: INITIALIZING HP A6825-60101 PCI 1000Base-T Adapter at hardware path 1/0/12/1/0
igelan5: INITIALIZING HP A6825-60101 PCI 1000Base-T Adapter at hardware path 1/0/14/1/0
igelan1: INITIALIZING HP A6825-60101 PCI 1000Base-T Adapter at hardware path 0/0/12/1/0
igelan2: INITIALIZING HP A6825-60101 PCI 1000Base-T Adapter at hardware path 0/0/14/1/0
Logical volume 64, 0x3 configured as ROOT
Logical volume 64, 0x2 configured as SWAP
Logical volume 64, 0x2 configured as DUMP
    Swap device table:  (start & size given in 512-byte blocks)
        entry 0 - major is 64, minor is 0x2; start = 0, size = 8388608
    Dump device table:  (start & size given in 1-Kbyte blocks)
        entry 0000000000000000 - major is 31, minor is 0x46000; start = 314208, size =
4194304
Starting the STREAMS daemons-phase 1
Create STCP device files
Starting the STREAMS daemons-phase 2
      $Revision: vmunix:    vw: -proj    selectors: CUPI80_BL2000_1108 -c 'Vw for
CUPI80_BL2000_1108 build' -- cupi80_bl2000_1108 'CUPI80_BL2000_1108'   Wed Nov   8
19:24:56 PST 2000 $
Memory Information:
    physical page size = 4096 bytes, logical page size = 4096 bytes
    Physical: 67056640 Kbytes, lockable: 52307120 Kbytes, available: 60012304 Kbytes

#
```

The output of **ioscan -f** and **dmesg** provides plenty of useful information about the system. I use the components and paths in **ioscan** output and the memory information in **dmesg** to create a list of components for the respective vPars in the upcoming step. Many resources in this system can be used for the vPars, such as 32 processors, 64 GB of RAM, and the paths of the two internal disks.

From these two outputs, I have the information we need to create the Virtual Partitions in the next step.

4) List the Components of the Virtual Partitions

I create two modest vPars using a small subset of the components available in the rp8420. From the **ioscan** and **dmesg** messages, I select the components of the first Virtual Partition. The following is a list of the components we'll include in this partition:

First vPar *vPar1*

```
name           vPar1
processors     num=3, min of two (bound) max of four (two
               unbound)
memory         2048 MB
LBA Core I/O   0/0 (all components on 0/0 are implied)
LAN            0/0/0/0 (not specified explicitly, on 0/0)
boot disk      0/0/0/2/0.6
kernel         /stand/vmunix (this is default)
autoboot       on
```

Some components require some explanation concerning the way in which they are implemented with vPars. The following is a more detailed discussion of some of these components, including CPU, memory, LAN, bootdisk, setboot, and kernel. You may want to refer to Table 16-1 throughout this discussion.

CPU

The CPUs used in both this partition (*vPar1*) and the one we will define shortly (*vPar2*) are specified with *min*, *max*, and *num*. We have *min bound* CPUs that have I/O interrupts assigned to them and are, therefore, ideal for I/O-intensive applications. The additional CPUs assigned to the vPars are *unbound* and do not process I/O interrupts. Therefore, *unbound* CPUs are ideal for processor-intensive applications as opposed to I/O-intensive applications. *Unbound* CPUs can be freely moved from one vPar to another while vPars are running, so having *min* bound CPUs gives us freedom to move around the *unbound* CPUs. *Bound* CPUs can also be added to and deleted from Virtual Partitions only when the partition is down.

The new release of vPars that supports Itanium does not have bound and unbound (floating) CPUs. All CPUs handle interrupts and only the boot processor can't be reallocated without a reboot.

In my work with vPars, in general the most common desire is to have a *min* number of *bound* CPUs in all vPars and then move around *unbound* CPUs as the applications in vPars need them. For example, when **vparcreate** is run, we specify the following:

vparcreate -p vpar1 -a cpu::3 -a cpu:::2:4

-a cpu::num -a cpu:::min:max

At the time of creation, *vPar1* has two *bound* CPUs because we specified a *min* of two and a *num* of three. *num* is the total *bound* + *unbound* CPUs, and because we specified three for *num*, we get two *bound* CPUs. Because *max* is four, we leave the door open to add as many as one additional *unbound* CPU.

If we have two *unbound* CPUs on our system, we can move them among the vPars as required using **vparmodify**. To remove the two *unbound* CPUs from *vPar2* and add them to *vPar1*, issue the two following **vparmodify** commands:

vparmodify -p vPar2 -m cpu::1   <-- reduces vPar2 from 3 to 1

vparmodify -p vPar1 -m cpu::3   <-- increases vPar1 from 1 to 3

-m cpu::num

We first remove the two *unbound* CPUs from *vPar2* and then add them to *vPar1*. If the two *unbound* CPUs were not assigned to a vPar, we would not have to remove them from *vPar2* prior to adding them to *vPar1*.

There are many ways to work with CPUs, so by characterizing your applications and understanding the options for using *bound* and *unbound* CPUs, you can use the processor mix that best meets your needs.

Memory

We have identified 2 GB of memory for *vPar1*. Memory can be specified by *range* or *size*.

To add 2 GB of memory to *vPar1* using *size,* use the following **vparcreate** command:

```
vparcreate -p vPar1 -a mem::2048
```

This **vparcreate** command specifies only the memory for use in *vpar1*. The full **vparcreate** command for creating *vPar1* is shown in an upcoming section.

The memory is specified in MB (1,024 MB = 1 GB) in multiples of 64 MB. At the time of this writing, the Virtual Partition Monitor consumes only 20-25 MB of RAM, so this will not be available to allocate to a Virtual Partition. Modifying memory allocation requires that the Virtual Partition be down, at the time of this writing.

LAN

The LAN interface used for this first Virtual Partition is on the Core I/O card connected to cell 0. This means that any other components on this Core I/O card would have to be in this Virtual Partition. This is true for any LBA: that is, an LBA with a card in it assigned to a virtual partition is fully devoted to the virtual partition.

As previously mentioned, it is desirable to use the same name for the hostname and vPar, which is the case with the vPars in this example. But, you can have many vPars defined and load and unload their definitions any time, so you may very well end up with different hostname and vPar names. When HP-UX 11i is loaded on a system, you select the hostnames. (You can also run **set_parms** after loading 11i to set the system name and other parameters.)

Boot Disk

The **ioscan** command (issued earlier in this chapter) showed the disk devices on the rp8420. The boot device for our first Virtual Partition is the internal disk with the hardware path *0/0/0/2/0.6*. The leading 0 indicates that this disk is connected to cell board 0.

Kernel

I use the default HP-UX kernel of **/stand/vmunix** for the kernel in this Virtual Partition. Because we use the default kernel, we don't have to specify this as part of the **vparcreate** command; however, we include it in the **vparcreate** command for completeness.

setboot Command

In our example, we have *autoboot* set to *on* for the Virtual Partition. The **setboot** command on a non-vPars system reads from and writes to stable storage. On a vPars system, the **setboot** command interacts with the Virtual Partition database. In an upcoming example, I set the *autoboot* to *on* when we create *vPar1* with **vparcreate**. Running **setboot** on a vPars system has the effects shown in Table 16-2.

Table 16-2   setboot and Virtual Partitions

vPars setboot Option	Description
-a	Changes the alternate boot path of the Virtual Partition. To set the alternate boot path: `# setboot -a 0/8/0/0.8.0.5.0.0.0`
-b	Sets the autoboot attribute of the Virtual Partition. To set Autoboot *on*: `# setboot -b on`
-p	Changes the primary boot path of the Virtual Partition. To set the primary boot path: `# setboot -p 0/0/1/1.2.0`
-s	Has no effect.
no options	Displays information about boot attributes.

The **setboot** command is one of the aspects of working with vPars that is different from a non-vPars system.

Console

On a cell-based system, such as the one used in the example in this chapter, connection to the console is achieved by connecting to the Management Processor (MP). The MP described in detail in Chapter 17 covers MP and nPartitions. The MP is assigned an IP address and when you connect to this IP address, you have access to a variety of MP prompts, including the console for nPartitions. The rp8420 in the example is set up with one nPartition so when I connect to the console I am given only the option to connect to nPartition 0. Once logged into nPartition 0, however, I can interact with vPars by switching between them, bringing them up and down, and so on. Issuing *Ctrl-A* cycles between virtual console displays.

Database

The Virtual Partition database that contains all vPar-related information is **/stand/vpdb**. This database is managed and synchronized for you, so you don't need to pay too much attention to it if you don't want to. You can, however; create an alternate database if you want. You may want to do this in order to create a completely different Virtual Partition configuration for your system without affecting your currently running database.

When creating Virtual Partitions with **vparcreate** you can use the *-D* option and specify an alternate database name that is a file in the **/stand** directory, such as **/stand/vpdb.app2**. When you boot vPars from this database (with ISL> `hpux /stand/vpmon -D db_file`) it is the default, so all modifications made to vPars defined in this database are made to it rather than the default.

Second vPar *vPar2*

I list the same categories of components for *vPar2* as we did for *vPar1* in the following list:

```
name          vPar2
```

```
processors          min of two (bound) max of four (two unbound)
                    with num (bound + umnbound) equal to one
memory              4096 MB
LAN                 on Core 1/0 connected to cell 1
boot disk           1/0/0/2/0.6
kernel              /stand/vmunix (this is the default)
autoboot            on
console             Management Processor
```

We now have a list of components for two vPars.

5) Virtual Partition Kernel-Related Work

Each Virtual Partition has its own instance of HP-UX 11i, which has its own HP-UX kernel. It is likely that you'll customize these kernels in a variety of ways to suit the applications you are running in the respective vPars. In addition, the patching of the vPars kernels and other work must be done for each vPar. Going from 11i version 1 to 11i version 2 includes changes to the way the kernel is managed. Because vPars isn't available on 11i version 2 at the time of this writing, this section includes 11i version 1 material. Chapter 5 covers the details of working with the HP-UX 11i version 2 kernel.

When you install the vPars software, it automatically reconfigures the kernel to include the vPar drivers and make the kernel relocatable. To accomplish this, the file **/stand/system** has been updated to include the *vpar* driver, as shown in the following listing:

```
# more /stand/system | grep vp
vpar
#
```

The *vpar* driver is a master driver described in **/usr/conf/master.d**, as shown in the following output:

```
# pwd
/usr/conf/master.d
# cat vpar
$CDIO
vpar        0
$$$

$DRIVER_INSTALL
vcn               -1                  209
vcs               -1                  -1
vpar_driver       -1                  -1
$$$

$DRIVER_DEPENDENCY
vcn             vpar asio0
vcs             vpar asio0
vpar            vcs vcn vpar_driver
vpar_driver     vpar
$$$

$DRIVER_LIBRARY
*
* The driver/library table.  This table defines which libraries a given
* driver depends on.  If the driver is included in the dfile, then the
* libraries that driver depends on will be included on the ld(1) command
* line.  Only optional libraries *need* to be specified in this table,
* (but required ones can be included, as well).
*
* Driver handle     <libraries>
*
* subsystems first
vcn             libvpar-pdk.a
vcs             libvpar-pdk.a
vpar            libvpar-pdk.a
vpar_driver     libvpar-pdk.a
$$$

$LIBRARY
*
* The library table.  Each element in the library table describes
* one unique library.  The flag member is a boolean value, it is
* initialized to 1 if the library should *always* be included on
* the ld(1) command line, or 0 if the library is optional (i.e. it
* is only included when one or more drivers require it).  The order
* of the library table determines the order of the libraries on the
* ld(1) command line, (i.e. defines an implicit load order).  New
* libraries must be added to this table.
* Note: libhp-ux.a must be the last entry, do not place anything after it.
*
* Library     <required>
*
libvpar-pdk.a       0
$$$
#
```

You can see in that this file there are multiple drivers present. The *vcn* and *vcs* drivers are used to support the console in a vPars environment. Because you probably only have one physical console for multiple partitions, you need a way to share the physical device. I cover switching the console between vPars later in this chapter.

These files are used after vPars software is loaded and the kernel is rebuilt.

Be sure to read Chapter 6, "Devices," covering the latest kernel commands.

6) Create the First Virtual Partition

The **vparcreate** command creates a vPar. The summary of this command is shown in Table 16-1. The general form of the command is as follows:

```
vparcreate -p vp_name [-B boot_attr] [-D db_file] [-S static_attr]
[-b kernel_path] [-o boot_opts] [-a rsrc] [-a...]
```

When creating this vPar, I place the **vparcreate** command in a file so that I can modify it for the second vPar and execute it. The **vparcreate** command is shown here:

```
# cat /tmp/vpar1
vparcreate -p vpar1 -a cpu::3 -a cpu:::2:4 -a mem::2048
-a io:0/0/0/2/0.6:boot -b /stand/vmunix -B auto
```

After changing the permissions on this file and running it, the vPar *vpar1* was successfully created. We work with this vPar in the upcoming sections.

On systems on which you want to create multiple vPars, I like this technique of creating files for which the vPars definitions will exist. The following shows the output of five files used for creating five vPars on an rp8420:

```
[meta1] /tmp/vpar # cat meta*
vparcreate -p meta1 -a cpu::12 -a mem::24576 -a io:0/0/0/2/0.6.0.0.0.0.0:boot -b /stand/
vmunix -B auto
vparcreate -p meta2 -a cpu::4 -a mem::8192 -a io:0/0/8/1/0.20.4.0.0.0.1:boot -b /stand/
vmunix -B auto -a io:0/0/12/1/0
vparcreate -p meta3 -a cpu::4 -a mem::8192 -a io:0/0/10/1/0.20.5.0.0.0.1:boot -b /stand/
vmunix -B auto -a io:0/0/14/1/0
vparcreate -p meta4 -a cpu::4 -a mem::8192 -a io:1/0/8/1/0.10.9.0.0.0.1:boot -b /stand/
vmunix -B auto -a io:1/0/0/1/0
vparcreate -p meta5 -a cpu::4 -a mem::8192 -a io:1/0/10/1/0.10.8.0.0.0.1:boot -b /stand/
vmunix -B auto -a io:1/0/12/1/0
[meta1] /tmp/vpar #
```

Only vPar *meta1* has a boot device of an internal disk. The four other vPars have SAN boot devices.

Next, we boot the vPar we just created.

7) Boot the First Virtual Partition

Now that the first vPar is created and the kernel automatically rebuilt to support vPars, we can boot the first vPar, which we named *vpar1*.

I boot off the first vPar and check its status. We need to load the Virtual Partition Monitor (**vpmon**) at the *ISL>* prompt. **vpmon** is a *ramdisk* kernel, similar to *vmunix*, that needs to be loaded at the time of boot. From the *ISL>* prompt we run **vpmon** to get the *MON>* prompt. From the *MON>* prompt, we boot our Virtual Partition with **vparload**. Because this is a cell-based system, I have to interface with the MP to reset the system and get to the reboot point. Chapter 17 details this process. The following example shows booting *vpar1*:

```
Firmware Version  20.8

Duplex Console IO Dependent Code (IODC) revision 2
-------------------------------------------------------------------------
    (c) Copyright 1995-2002, Hewlett-Packard Company, All rights reserved
-------------------------------------------------------------------------


          Cab/    Cell     ------- Processor --------    Cache Size
   Cell   Slot    State     #    Speed        State      Inst   Data
   ----   ----   --------   ---  --------   -----------   ------  ------
     0    0/0    Active      0A  1000 MHz   Active        32 MB   32 MB
                             0B  1000 MHz   Idle          32 MB   32 MB
                             1A  1000 MHz   Idle          32 MB   32 MB
```

```
                                1B  1000 MHz  Idle        32 MB    32 MB
                                2A  1000 MHz  Idle        32 MB    32 MB
                                2B  1000 MHz  Idle        32 MB    32 MB
                                3A  1000 MHz  Idle        32 MB    32 MB
                                3B  1000 MHz  Idle        32 MB    32 MB
         1   0/1   Idle         0A  1000 MHz  Idle        32 MB    32 MB
                                0B  1000 MHz  Idle        32 MB    32 MB
                                1A  1000 MHz  Idle        32 MB    32 MB
                                1B  1000 MHz  Idle        32 MB    32 MB
                                2A  1000 MHz  Idle        32 MB    32 MB
                                2B  1000 MHz  Idle        32 MB    32 MB
                                3A  1000 MHz  Idle        32 MB    32 MB
                                3B  1000 MHz  Idle        32 MB    32 MB
         2   0/2   Idle         0A  1000 MHz  Idle        32 MB    32 MB
                                0B  1000 MHz  Idle        32 MB    32 MB
                                1A  1000 MHz  Idle        32 MB    32 MB
                                1B  1000 MHz  Idle        32 MB    32 MB
                                2A  1000 MHz  Idle        32 MB    32 MB
                                2B  1000 MHz  Idle        32 MB    32 MB
                                3A  1000 MHz  Idle        32 MB    32 MB
                                3B  1000 MHz  Idle        32 MB    32 MB
         3   0/3   Idle         0A  1000 MHz  Idle        32 MB    32 MB
                                0B  1000 MHz  Idle        32 MB    32 MB
                                1A  1000 MHz  Idle        32 MB    32 MB
                                1B  1000 MHz  Idle        32 MB    32 MB
                                2A  1000 MHz  Idle        32 MB    32 MB
                                2B  1000 MHz  Idle        32 MB    32 MB
                                3A  1000 MHz  Idle        32 MB    32 MB
                                3B  1000 MHz  Idle        32 MB    32 MB


        Primary Boot Path:  1/0/0/2/0.6
             Boot Actions:  Boot from this path.
                            If unsuccessful, go to BCH.

  HA Alternate Boot Path:  0/0/0/2/0.6
             Boot Actions:  Go to BCH.

     Alternate Boot Path:  0/0/0/2/0.5
             Boot Actions:  Go to BCH.

             Console Path:  0/0/0/0/1.0


Attempting to boot using the primary path.
------------------------------------------------------------


To discontinue, press any key within 10 seconds.


Boot terminated.


---- Main Menu -----------------------------------------------------

     Command                        Description
     -------                        -----------
     BOot [PRI|HAA|ALT|<path>]      Boot from specified path
     PAth [PRI|HAA|ALT] [<path>]    Display or modify a path
     SEArch [ALL|<cell>|<path>]     Search for boot devices
     ScRoll [ON|OFF]                Display or change scrolling capability

     COnfiguration menu             Displays or sets boot values
     INformation menu               Displays hardware information
     SERvice menu                   Displays service commands
```

```
        DIsplay                           Redisplay the current menu
        HElp [<menu>|<command>]           Display help for menu or command
        REBOOT                            Restart Partition
        RECONFIGRESET                 Reset to allow Reconfig Complex Profile
    ----
Main Menu: Enter command or menu > bo

    Primary Boot Path:  1/0/0/2/0.6


 Do you wish to stop at the ISL prompt prior to booting? (y/n) >> y

Initializing boot Device.


Boot IO Dependent Code (IODC) Revision 3


Boot Path Initialized.


HARD Booted.

ISL Revision A.00.43  Apr 12, 2000

ISL> hpux /stand/vpmon

Boot
: disk(1/0/0/2/0.6.0.0.0.0.0;0)/stand/vpmon
679936 + 190216 + 17306888 start 0x23000

Welcome to VPMON (type '?' for a list of commands)

MON>

ISL> hpux /stand/vpmon

Boot
: disk(1/0/0/2/0.6.0.0.0.0.0;0)/stand/vpmon
679936 + 190216 + 17306888 start 0x23000

Welcome to VPMON (type '?' for a list of commands)

MON> vparload -p vpar1                            <- specify load of vpar1
[MON] Booting vpar1...
[MON] Console client set to vpar1
[MON] Console server set to vpar1

[vpar1]

[MON] vpar1 loaded
gate64: sysvec_vaddr = 0xc0002000 for 2 pages
NOTICE: nfs3_link(): File system was registered at index 3.
NOTICE: autofs_link(): File system was registered at index 6.
NOTICE: cachefs_link(): File system was registered at index 7.
igelan0: INITIALIZING HP A7109-60001 PCI 1000Base-T Core at hardware path 0/
0/0/1/0

    Host is virtual System Console slave
Logical volume 64, 0x3 configured as ROOT
Logical volume 64, 0x2 configured as SWAP
Logical volume 64, 0x2 configured as DUMP
    Swap device table:  (start & size given in 512-byte blocks)
        entry 0 - major is 64, minor is 0x2; start = 0, size = 8388608
read_ss_nvm: Cannot validate NVM - -2
```

```
Starting the STREAMS daemons-phase 1

    System Console is virtual
Checking root file system.
file system is clean - log replay is not required
Root check done.
Create STCP device files
Starting the STREAMS daemons-phase 2
         $Revision: vmunix:    vw: -proj    selectors: CUPI80_BL2000_1108 -
c   'Vw    for   CUPI80_BL2000_1108    build'    --   cupi80_bl2000_1108
'CUPI80_BL2000_1108'  Wed Nov  8 19:24:56 PST 2000 $
Memory Information:
    physical page size = 4096 bytes, logical page size = 4096 bytes
     Physical: 2060288 Kbytes, lockable: 1536024 Kbytes, available: 1772252
Kbytes

/sbin/ioinitrc:
                      .
                      .
                      .
```

In this partial output, you see that at the ISL prompt, I load *vpmon* with
the command **hpux /stand/vpmon** and then boot vpar1 with **vparload -p
vpar1**. The **vparload** command has the following three forms:

```
form1: vparload -all

form2: vparload -auto

form3: vparload -p vp_name [-b kernelpath] [-o boot_options]
[-B hardware_path]
```

I issued the third form shown above to boot vpar1.
Now that the partition has booted, I obtain its status:

```
# vparstatus -v -p vpar1
[Virtual Partition Details]
Name:         vpar1
State:        Up
Attributes:   Dynamic,Autoboot
Kernel Path:  /stand/vmunix
Boot Opts:

[CPU Details]
Min/Max:  2/4
Bound by User [Path]:
Bound by Monitor [Path]:  0.10
                          0.11
Unbound [Path]:  0.14

[IO Details]
    0.0.0.2.0.6.0.0.0.0.0   BOOT
```

```
[Memory Details]
Specified [Base   /Range]:
           (bytes) (MB)
Total Memory (MB):  2048
#
```

This is exactly what I expected to see based on the **vparcreate** command previously run:

```
vparcreate -p vpar1 -a cpu::3 -a cpu:::2:4 -a mem::2048
-a io:0/0/0/2/0.6:boot -b /stand/vmunix -B auto
```

The output of **vparstatus** shows that *vpar1* is *up*. The *-v* option obtains a verbose output. You can see from this listing that the bound CPUs at hardware paths *0.10* and *0.11* (the *bound* CPUs are specified with *min*) and the unbound CPU at *0.14* are present. The bound and unbound CPUS are on cell 0, as indicated by the leading 0, and they are hardware paths 10,11, and 14. There are 2 GB of memory in the partition, and the boot device is the path that I specified.

There is no entry for a console because the MP is used for vPars console access on cell-based systems.

You may want to run **vparstatus -A** before you create additional vPars to see the available components. I run this command later.

The following is a **vparstatus** output for a system with five vPars:

```
[meta1] /roothome # vparstatus
[Virtual Partition]
                                                                    Boot
Virtual Partition Name        State Attributes Kernel Path          Opts
============================= ===== ========== ======================= =====
meta1                         Up    Dyn,Auto   /stand/vmunix
meta2                         Up    Dyn,Auto   /stand/vmunix
meta3                         Up    Dyn,Auto   /stand/vmunix
meta4                         Up    Dyn,Auto   /stand/vmunix
meta5                         Up    Dyn,Auto   /stand/vmunix

[Virtual Partition Resource Summary]
                                      CPU    Num      Memory (MB)
                              CPU    Bound/  IO   # Ranges/
Virtual Partition Name        Min/Max Unbound devs  Total MB    Total MB
============================= ======= ======= ==== =============== =========
meta1                         1/ 32   1   11   6    0/  0          24576
meta2                         1/ 32   1    3   4    0/  0           8192
meta3                         1/ 32   1    3   4    0/  0           8192
meta4                         1/ 32   1    3   4    0/  0           8192
meta5                         1/ 32   1    3   4    0/  0           8192
[meta1] /roothome #
```

This system has 5 vPars. The first has 12 CPUs, 1 bound and 11 unbound, and the other has 4 vPars have 1 bound and 3 unbound CPUs.

8) Create the Second Virtual Partition

We already listed all the components of which our second partition is to be comprised and confirmed that these components are still available with the **vparstatus -A** command. HP-UX 11i and the vPars software have already been loaded on a second disk on the same system used to create our first Virtual Partition *vpar1*. I can create the second Virtual Partition, which I call *vpar2*. I create the second one while the first runs and boot the second vPar from the first.

Again, here are the components for the second vPar:

```
name            vPar2
processors      min of two (bound) max of four (two unbound)
                with num (bound + umnbound) equal to one
memory          4096 MB
LAN             on Core 1/O connected to cell 1
boot disk       1/0/0/2/0.6
kernel          /stand/vmunix (this is the default)
autoboot        on
console         Management Processor
```

I now create the second partition with the command shown in the following file:

```
# more /tmp/vpar2
vparcreate -p vpar2 -a cpu::3 -a cpu:::2:4 -a mem::4096
-a io:1/0/0/2/0.6:boot -b /stand/vmunix -B auto
#
```

It is important to obtain the path of the boot device exactly as it appears in the *search* at boot time. When you issue **vparcreate**, you use the path as it appears in the *search*; however, when you issue **vparstatus -v**, you may see a path with additional *0*s added to the boot device.

After executing this file, we can determine if the second vPar has been created and the components of which it is comprised by running **vparstatus**:

```
# vparstatus -v
[Virtual Partition Details]
Name:          vpar1                          <-- vpar1
State:         Up
Attributes:    Dynamic,Autoboot
Kernel Path:   /stand/vmunix
Boot Opts:

[CPU Details]
Min/Max:  2/4
Bound by User [Path]:
Bound by Monitor [Path]:   0.10
                           0.11
Unbound [Path]:  0.14

[IO Details]
   0.0.0.2.0.6.0.0.0.0.0  BOOT

[Memory Details]
Specified [Base  /Range]:
         (bytes) (MB)
Total Memory (MB): 2048
[Virtual Partition Details]

Name:          vpar2                          <-- vpar2
State:         Down
Attributes:    Dynamic,Autoboot
Kernel Path:   /stand/vmunix
Boot Opts:

[CPU Details]
Min/Max:  2/4
Bound by User [Path]:
Bound by Monitor [Path]:   0.12
                           0.13
Unbound [Path]:  <no path>

[IO Details]
   1.0.0.2.0.6.0.0.0.0.0, BOOT

[Memory Details]
Specified [Base  /Range]:
         (bytes) (MB)
Total Memory (MB): 4096
#
```

This output shows that the first vPar is intact and that the second has been successfully created with the name, kernel file, CPU, boot device, and memory components I specified.

With the second vPar created, proceed to the next step and boot it.

9) Boot the Second Virtual Partition

Because we already have the first vPar running, *vpar1*, and the second vPar created, *vpar2*, we can boot the second vPar from the first. There are many options to boot vPars. Because we already have the first vPar running, we simply boot the second vPar from the first with **vparboot** and then run **vparstatus -v**, as shown in the following example. If we type subsequent **vparstatus** commands, we can see the status of vPar *vpar2* progress from *Load*, to *Boot* in the next output, and finally, *Up* when the vPar is running, as shown in the following listing:

```
#
# vparboot -p vpar2
vparboot: Booting vpar2.  Please wait...

# vparstatus
[Virtual Partition]
                                                                    Boot
Virtual Partition Name          State Attributes Kernel Path        Opts
==============================  ===== ========== ========================  =====
vpar1                           Up    Dyn,Auto   /stand/vmunix
vpar2                           Load  Dyn,Auto   /stand/vmunix

[Virtual Partition Resource Summary]
                                             CPU    Num       Memory (MB)
                                CPU       Bound/   IO   # Ranges/
Virtual Partition Name          Min/Max   Unbound  devs Total MB    Total MB
==============================  ===============  ====  ==================
vpar1                             2/  4      2    1      2    0/  0        2048
vpar2                             2/  4      2    1      2    0/  0        4096
[MON] vpar2 loaded


# vparstatus
[Virtual Partition]
                                                                    Boot
Virtual Partition Name          State Attributes Kernel Path        Opts
==============================  ===== ========== ========================  =====
vpar1                           Up    Dyn,Auto   /stand/vmunix
vpar2                           Boot  Dyn,Auto   /stand/vmunix

[Virtual Partition Resource Summary]
                                             CPU    Num       Memory (MB)
                                CPU       Bound/   IO   # Ranges/
Virtual Partition Name          Min/Max   Unbound  devs Total MB    Total MB
==============================  ===============  ====  ==================
vpar1                             2/  4      2    1      2    0/  0        2048
vpar2                             2/  4      2    1      2    0/  0        4096

# vparstatus
[Virtual Partition]
                                                                    Boot
Virtual Partition Name          State Attributes Kernel Path        Opts
==============================  ===== ========== ========================  =====
vpar1                           Up    Dyn,Auto   /stand/vmunix
vpar2                           Up    Dyn,Auto   /stand/vmunix

[Virtual Partition Resource Summary]
                                             CPU    Num       Memory (MB)
                                CPU       Bound/   IO   # Ranges/
Virtual Partition Name          Min/Max   Unbound  devs Total MB    Total MB
==============================  ===============  ====  ==================
vpar1                             2/  4      2    1      2    0/  0        2048
vpar2                             2/  4      2    1      2    0/  0        4096
#
```

This progression of states of *vpar2* reflects the time it takes to boot the operating system from the second volume on which this vPar runs.

In addition to *load*, *boot*, and *up*, there are other states in which you may find a Virtual Partition as well. Table 16-3 summarizes the states of Virtual Partitions at the time of this writing.

Table 16-3   Virtual Partitions States

vPars State	Description
load	The kernel image of a Virtual Partition is being loaded into memory. This is done by the Virtual Partition monitor.
boot	The Virtual Partition is in the process of booting. The kernel image has been successfully loaded by the Virtual Partition monitor.
up	The Virtual Partition has been successfully booted and is running.
shut	The Virtual Partition is in the process of shutting down.
down	The Virtual Partition is not running and is down.
crash	The Virtual Partition has experienced a panic and is crashing.
hung	The Virtual Partition is not responding and is hung.

An Ignite-UX server can also be used to load a vPar from a running vPar. This is done with the **vparboot** command, which is executed from running vPar. You point to the existing Ignite-UX server from **vparboot**. The mini-kernel called WINSTALL is loaded into memory. The mini-kernel boots the target vPar.

With more than one vPar running, you would use the built-in vPars drivers to toggle the console between any number of Virtual Partitions using *Ctrl-A*. Figure 16-5 shows using the console to view *vpar1*. Issuing *Ctrl-A* connects to vPar *vpar2*. When you issue *Ctrl-A* to switch to the next vPar in the console, you are supplied with the name of the vPar to which you have connected in brackets, such as *[vpar1]*.

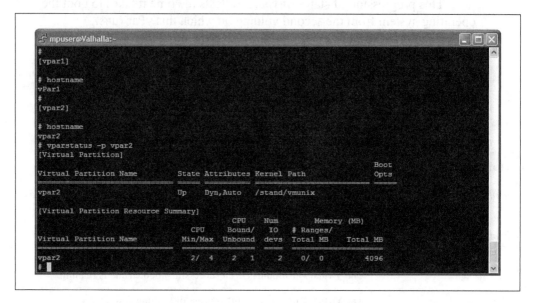

Figure 16-5   Console Shown Using *Ctrl-A* to Toggle Between vPars

You can see in Figure 16-5 that as you toggle between vPars, you are given the name of the vPar to which you're connected in square brackets.

In addition to using the console to switch between vPars, you can also use the LAN cards configured into the respective vPars to open a *TELNET* or another type of session to the vPars. This is the same technique that you would use to connect to any system over the network; it is one of the primary reasons you always want to have a LAN card configured as part of every vPar.

This chapter did not cover the configuration of the two LAN cards, one in each vPar. The LAN configuration has to be complete for both vPars in order to use the networking cards for such operations as a *Telnet* session. Chapter 15 of this book covers many networking topics, including the **/etc/hosts** file; **/etc/rc.config.d/netconf** file, which must be configured on each vPar; and many others.

10) Modify the Virtual Partition

It is likely that you'll want to modify your Virtual Partitions in a variety of ways. You may want to add or remove a CPU, for example. Let's look at an example of adding a CPU to a Virtual Partition.

In the previous section, two vPars were created. The following **vparstatus** command shows the configuration of the two vPars:

```
# vparstatus -p vpar1
[Virtual Partition]
                                                              Boot
Virtual Partition Name      State Attributes Kernel Path      Opts
========================== ===== ========== ====================== =====
vpar1                        Up   Dyn,Auto   /stand/vmunix

[Virtual Partition Resource Summary]
                                      CPU   Num       Memory (MB)
                              CPU    Bound/  IO   # Ranges/
Virtual Partition Name      Min/Max Unbound devs Total MB   Total MB
============================ =============== ==== ====================
vpar1                        2/  4    2   1    2   0/ 0         2048
# vparstatus -v -p vpar1
[Virtual Partition Details]
Name:          vpar1
State:         Up
Attributes:    Dynamic,Autoboot
Kernel Path:   /stand/vmunix
Boot Opts:

[CPU Details]
Min/Max:  2/4
Bound by User [Path]:
Bound by Monitor [Path]:   0.10      <-- two bound CPU on cell 0
                           0.11
Unbound [Path]:  0.14               <-- one unbound CPU on cell 0

[IO Details]
   0.0.0.2.0.6.0.0.0.0.0   BOOT

[Memory Details]
Specified [Base  /Range]:
       (bytes) (MB)
Total Memory (MB):  2048


# vparstatus -p vpar2
[Virtual Partition]
                                                              Boot
Virtual Partition Name      State Attributes Kernel Path      Opts
============================ ===== ========== ==================== =====
vpar2                        Up   Dyn,Auto   /stand/vmunix

[Virtual Partition Resource Summary]
                                      CPU   Num       Memory (MB)
                              CPU    Bound/  IO   # Ranges/
Virtual Partition Name      Min/Max Unbound devs Total MB   Total MB
============================ =============== ==== ====================
vpar2                        2/  4    2   1    2   0/ 0         4096
```

```
#
# vparstatus -v -p vpar2
[Virtual Partition Details]
Name:          vpar2
State:         Up
Attributes:    Dynamic,Autoboot
Kernel Path:   /stand/vmunix
Boot Opts:

[CPU Details]
Min/Max:  2/4
Bound by User [Path]:
Bound by Monitor [Path]:  0.12        <-- two bound CPU on cell 0
                          0.13
Unbound [Path]:  0.15                 <-- one unbound CPU on cell 0

[IO Details]
   1.0.0.2.0.6.0.0.0.0.0   BOOT

[Memory Details]
Specified [Base  /Range]:
          (bytes) (MB)
Total Memory (MB):  4096
#
```

The output of these two **vparstatus** commands shows that both vPars currently have two bound and one unbound CPU. There are many available components on this system, as shown in the earlier **vparstatus -A** output. A total of 26 CPUs are available as shown in the output:

```
# vparstatus -A
[Unbound CPUs (path)]:  0.15
                        0.16
                        0.17
                        1.10
                        1.11
                        1.12
                        1.13
                        1.14
                        1.15
                        1.16
                        1.17
                        2.10
                        2.11
                        2.12
                        2.13
                        2.14
                        2.15
                        2.16
                        2.17
                        3.10
                        3.11
                        3.12
                        3.13
                        3.14
                        3.15
                        3.16
```

```
                                  3.17
[Available CPUs]:  26

[Available I/O devices (path)]:  0.0.1
                                 0.0.2
                                 0.0.4
                                 0.0.6
                                 0.0.8
                                 0.0.10
                                 0.0.12
                                 0.0.14
                                 1.0.1
                                 1.0.2
                                 1.0.4
                                 1.0.6
                                 1.0.8
                                 1.0.10
                                 1.0.12
                                 1.0.14

[Unbound memory (Base  /Range)]:  0x0/64
              (bytes) (MB)        0x8000000/63424
[Available memory (MB)]:  59392
#
```

We can do a lot with these 26 CPUs. I use the **vparmodify** command to change the *num* of CPUs in *vpar1* to 8 CPUs. I do this by *adding* 6 to the current number of CPUs with *-a*. Before doing this, however, I must first change the *max* CPU to 8. This **vparmodify** command must be run with the vPar down or you get the following message if you issue the command while vpar1 is running:

```
# vparmodify -p vpar1 -m cpu:::2:8
vparmodify: Error: Virtual partition vpar1 must be in the Down state.
#
```

After shutting down vpar1, I issue the same command and it works. After bringing up vpar1, the max had been changed based on the following **vparstatus** output:

```
# vparmodify -p vpar1 -m cpu:::2:8       <-- change max to 8 in vpar2
# vparboot -p vpar1                  <-- boot vpar1
vparboot: Booting vpar1.  Please wait...
# [MON] Console server set to vpar1

[MON] vpar1 loaded

# vparstatus -v -p vpar1                 <-- two bound CPU on cell 0
[Virtual Partition Details]
Name:        vpar1
State:       Up
```

```
Attributes:    Dynamic,Autoboot
Kernel Path:   /stand/vmunix
Boot Opts:

[CPU Details]
Min/Max:  2/8                        <-- confirm max CPU in vpar1 is 8
Bound by User [Path]:
Bound by Monitor [Path]:   0.10
                           0.11
Unbound [Path]:   0.14

[IO Details]
   0.0.0.2.0.6.0.0.0.0.0   BOOT

[Memory Details]
Specified [Base  /Range]:
        (bytes) (MB)
Total Memory (MB):  2048
#

# vparmodify -p vpar1 -a cpu::5       <-- add 5 CPUs to vpar1

# vparstatus -v -p vpar1
[Virtual Partition Details]
Name:        vpar1
State:       Up
Attributes:  Dynamic,Autoboot
Kernel Path: /stand/vmunix
Boot Opts:

[CPU Details]
Min/Max:  2/8
Bound by User [Path]:
Bound by Monitor [Path]:   0.10       <-- confirm two unbound CPUs
                           0.11
Unbound [Path]:   0.14                <-- plus six unbound CPUs
                  0.16
                  0.17
                  1.10                <-- note that these are on cell 1
                  1.11
                  1.12

[IO Details]
   0.0.0.2.0.6.0.0.0.0.0   BOOT

[Memory Details]
Specified [Base  /Range]:
        (bytes) (MB)
Total Memory (MB):  2048
#
```

This operation is easily performed. Note that to change the max number of CPUs from 4 to 8, vpar1 has to be down. Then from vpar1, I add the five additional unbound CPUs to vpar1 while it was running. This could have been done from either vpar1 or vpar2, but I want to demonstrate that this addition can take place while vpar1 is running.

This is a relative operation in that five CPUs were added to the current number of three CPUs. You can use **vparmodify -m** if you want to specify the absolute number of CPUs for the vPar rather than the relative number.

Because vpar2 was using three of the eight CPUs on cell board 0, there are now five CPUs on cell board 0 in vpar1 and three CPUs in vpar1 that are part of cell board 1.

In addition, we can run GlancePlus or **top** to confirm that two CPUs are in use on *vpar2*. The following is a **top** output run on *vpar2*:

```
# top

System: vPar1                                    Mon Jul 26 17:28:53 2004
Load averages: 0.02, 0.01, 0.00
105 processes: 94 sleeping, 10 running, 1 zombie
Cpu states:
CPU   LOAD   USER   NICE    SYS    IDLE  BLOCK  SWAIT   INTR   SSYS
 0    0.04   0.0%   0.0%    0.2%   99.8%  0.0%   0.0%   0.0%   0.0%
 1    0.05   0.0%   0.0%    0.0%  100.0%  0.0%   0.0%   0.0%   0.0%
 2    0.00   0.0%   0.0%    0.0%  100.0%  0.0%   0.0%   0.0%   0.0%
 4    0.00   0.0%   0.0%    0.0%  100.0%  0.0%   0.0%   0.0%   0.0%
 5    0.00   0.2%   0.0%    0.0%   99.8%  0.0%   0.0%   0.0%   0.0%
 6    0.04   0.0%   0.0%    0.2%   99.8%  0.0%   0.0%   0.0%   0.0%
 7    0.00   0.2%   0.0%    0.0%   99.8%  0.0%   0.0%   0.0%   0.0%
 8    0.00   0.0%   0.0%    0.0%  100.0%  0.0%   0.0%   0.0%   0.0%
---   ----  -----  -----   -----  -----  -----  -----  -----  -----
avg   0.02   0.2%   0.0%    0.2%   99.6%  0.0%   0.0%   0.0%   0.0%

Memory: 160288K (136432K) real, 387292K (352480K) virtual, 1288100K free  Page#
1/21

CPU TTY    PID USERNAME PRI NI    SIZE     RES STATE   TIME %WCPU   %CPU COMMAND
 4   ?      64 root     152 20    896K    896K run     0:20  0.66   0.66 vxfsd
 0   ?    1234 root     152 20    243M  24076K run     0:26  0.33   0.33 prm3d
 8   ?      13 root     152 20     64K     64K run     0:00  0.32   0.31 vconsd
 8   ?    1882 root     154 20   5092K    812K sleep   0:04  0.18   0.18 lpmc_em
```

This output shows the CPUs in *vpar1*.

Although this is a simple example showing how a Virtual Partition can be modified, it also demonstrates the power of vPars. While both vPars on the system are running, a processor can be added to one or both without interrupting the programs running in the vPars.

The *-a* option to **vparmodify** changes the number of CPUs *relative* to the current number. In this case, the current number of CPUs was one and using *-a cpu::1* added one CPU to the current number of one, resulting in two CPUs. This is true also when we use the *-d* option to **vparmodify** to remove processors. The following example shows running **vparstatus** to see the eight CPUs, using **vparmodify** to change the number of CPUs to four (this is also relative to the current number of CPUs, which is eight) and a **vparstatus** to confirm that this change has taken place:

```
# vparstatus -p vpar1 -v
[Virtual Partition Details]
Name:          vpar1
State:         Up
Attributes:    Dynamic,Autoboot
Kernel Path:   /stand/vmunix
Boot Opts:

[CPU Details]
Min/Max:  2/8
Bound by User [Path]:
Bound by Monitor [Path]:   0.10          <-- two bound CPUs
                           0.11
Unbound [Path]:   0.14                   <-- six unbound CPUs
                  0.16
                  0.17
                  1.10
                  1.11
                  1.12

[IO Details]
   0.0.0.2.0.6.0.0.0.0.0   BOOT

[Memory Details]
Specified [Base  /Range]:
         (bytes) (MB)
Total Memory (MB): 2048
# vparmodify -p vpar1 -d cpu::4          <-- delete four CPUs from vpar1
# vparstatus -p vpar1 -v
[Virtual Partition Details]
Name:          vpar1
State:         Up
Attributes:    Dynamic,Autoboot
Kernel Path:   /stand/vmunix
Boot Opts:

[CPU Details]
Min/Max:  2/8
Bound by User [Path]:
Bound by Monitor [Path]:   0.10          <-- two bound CPUs
                           0.11
Unbound [Path]:   0.14                   <-- two unbound CPUs
                  1.10

[IO Details]
   0.0.0.2.0.6.0.0.0.0.0   BOOT

[Memory Details]
Specified [Base  /Range]:
         (bytes) (MB)
Total Memory (MB): 2048
#
```

Please keep in mind the relative nature of components when using **vparmodify** and that some changes, such as modifying memory or adding I/O components, require the vPar to be down (at the time of this writing).

Virtual Partition Dump Files

When a Virtual Partition crashes, a dump file is created in
/stand/vpmon.dmp. When the Virtual Partition boots, files are created in
/var/adm/crash/vpar. The files have an extension with a number that indicates the number of the dump that occurred. For example, **vpmon.1**,
vpmon.dmp.1, and **summary.1** indicate the first set of files that are saved in
/var/adm/crash/vpar.

An example of what you might see in **/stand** and **/var/adm/crash/
vpar** related to dumps are shown in the following listing:

```
# ll /var/adm/crash/vpar                        <-- vPar dump directory
total 46464
-rw-r--r--   1 root      root              2 Oct 10 10:43 count
-rw-r--r--   1 root      root          16794 Jul 17 13:26 summary.0
-rw-r--r--   1 root      root          17953 Jul 18 10:35 summary.1
-rw-r--r--   1 root      root          19538 Jul 18 11:36 summary.2
-rw-r--r--   1 root      root          10012 Oct 10 10:43 summary.3
-r-xr-xr-x   1 root      root         855928 Jul 17 13:26 vpmon.0
-r-xr-xr-x   1 root      root         855928 Jul 18 10:35 vpmon.1
-r-xr-xr-x   1 root      root         855928 Jul 18 11:36 vpmon.2
-r-xr-xr-x   1 root      root         837616 Oct 10 10:43 vpmon.3
-rw-------   1 root      root        5078504 Jul 17 13:26 vpmon.dmp.0
-rw-------   1 root      root        5078504 Jul 18 10:35 vpmon.dmp.1
-rw-------   1 root      root        5078504 Jul 18 11:36 vpmon.dmp.2
-rw-------   1 root      root        5078504 Oct 10 10:43 vpmon.dmp.3

# ll /stand
total 152304
-rw-r--r--   1 root      sys              19 Jul 21 08:32 bootconf
drwxr-xr-x   4 root      sys            2048 Jul 21 10:05 build
drwxrwxrwx   5 root      root           1024 Jul 21 10:14 dlkm
drwxrwxrwx   6 root      sys            1024 Jul 21 09:23 dlkm.vmunix.prev
-rw-r--r--   1 root      sys            4532 Jul 26 15:59 ioconfig
-r--r--r--   1 root      sys              82 Jul 21 09:08 kernrel
drwxr-xr-x   2 root      sys            1024 Jul 26 16:00 krs
drwxr-xr-x   2 root      root           1024 Jul 26 15:59 krs_lkg
drwxr-xr-x   2 root      root           1024 Jul 26 16:00 krs_tmp
drwxr-xr-x   2 root      root          65536 Jul 21 08:32 lost+found
-rw-------   1 root      root             12 Jul 26 15:59 rootconf
-r--r--r--   1 root      sys            1071 Jul 21 09:32 system
drwxr-xr-x   2 root      sys            1024 Jul 21 09:09 system.d
-r--r--r--   1 root      sys            1066 Jul 21 08:57 system.prev
-rwxr-xr-x   1 root      root       29600328 Jul 23 08:47 vmunix
-rwxr-xr-x   1 root      sys        28364416 Jul 21 08:57 vmunix.prev
-rw-------   1 root      root           8232 Jul 26 15:59 vpdb
-r-xr-xr-x   1 bin       bin         1168728 Apr  8 13:44 vpmon
-rw-------   1 root      root       18350080 Jul 26 15:59 vpmon.dmp <-- vPar dump
#
```

The **/var/adm/crash/vpar** directory has in it the vPar dump-related
files for four (*0-3*) crashes.

The dump file created in **/stand** is saved in **/var/adm/crash/vpar** and
extended with the crash number. The dump file in **/stand** is overwritten with

each crash, but you have a history with all the dump files and related information in **/var/adm/crash/vpar**. Please leave the **/stand/vpmon.dmp** file in place.

Summary

Not all the vPars-related commands were issued in this chapter. The **vparreset** and **vparremove** commands summarized in Table 16-1 were not issued at all for instance. The **vparremove** command can be run on any vPar provided that it is in the *down* state. The general steps to get vPars up and running and to perform some modification were covered to give you a simple framework from which to work.

There are also some considerations related to server technology that I did not cover. If you have Instant Capacity on Demand (iCOD) employed on your server, all CPUs must be activitated in order for vPars to work. When employing Processor Sets (psets) in a vPar, use only bound CPUs.

All the work in this chapter has taken place at the command line. You can use the GUI for working with vPars called **vparmgr**. This is an excellent tool for viewing and modifying vPars.

Chapter 17

Node Partitions (nPartitions) and Management Processor Overview

Introduction to nPartitions

Node Partitions (nPartitions) have dedicated hardware within an HP Integrity Server (Itanium-based) or HP 9000 Server (PA-RISC-based) that work independently from other nPartitions within the same server. This independence includes both hardware and software isolation from other nPartitions. Virtual Partitions (vPars), covered in Chapter 16, "Virtual Partitions," have full software isolation from one another but not hardware isolation. nPartitions have both software *and* hardware isolation from one another. An nPartition can be divided into multiple vPars.

Integral to working on a cell-based system and performing nPartition-related work is the Management Processor (MP). The MP is covered throughout this chapter. I intentionally avoid treating the MP as a separate topic in a separate chapter because it is such an important means of accessing system resources for the system administrator. In addition, the tear-out card supplied with this book acts as a good quick reference for many MP commands that you issue on a regular basis.

The basic building block of an nPartition is the *cell*. Each cell has processors and memory that are assigned exclusively to that nPartition. I/O chassis are also exclusively assigned to nPartitions. Multiple cells can be combined to produce large nPartitions.

nPartitions are supported on all cell-based systems and operate in a similar manner on all models. I use a few different models in this chapter's examples; however, the operation of nPartitions varies very little going from model to model, so most of the commands and principles apply regardless of the model on which you're using nPartitions. There are, however, differences in the hardware going from model to model and this information is important to know. Chapter 6, "Devices," covers devices and some of the hardware differences, including the mapping of I/O slots. The nPartition commands are similar going from model to model because the modular nature of the nPartition components is nearly identical on cell-based systems.

Although the operation of nPartitions is nearly identical going from model to model, the number of supported nPartitions does indeed vary based on the cell capacity of a given model. Some models support only two nPartitions and others support many more. I focus on working with nPartitions in this chapter so you can use the topics covered on any cell-based system that supports nPartitions. In addition, the boot process is different on HP 9000 and HP Integrity Servers.

Because nPartitions are similar to independent servers on a network, with a unique hostname, IP address, and instance of HP-UX, you also need to know about topics such as boot options for nPartitions and other topics. The **setboot** command, covered in Chapter 8 "System Startup and Shutdown," for example, specifies the boot path(s) for an nPartition and whether the nPartition will boot automatically. There are many chapters and topics related to system-level administration in this book that apply to nPartitions as well because they act in much the same way as separate systems.

This chapter introduces working with nPartitions. Much is involved in managing nPartitions, so this chapter covers some of the more common nPartition-related work you might perform. For a complete guide to managing nPartitions, print the document *HP System Partitions Guide: Administration for nPartitions,* which is available on *docs.hp.com.*

Cells and nPartitions

Because the cell is the basic building block of nPartitions, let's spend some time covering some of the basics of cells and nPartitions. An HP 9000 or Integrity server that is capable of supporting nPartitions is sometimes called a *server complex* or just *complex*. In this chapter, I sometimes use *complex* and other times use *system* when referring to the overall system. The following list covers some important background that you need to know to manage nPartitions:

Base Cells	All cells within an nPartition are base cells. When you create an nPartition, the cells to which you assign it are base cells.
Assigned Cells	Assigned cells are included in an nPartition and unassigned cells are not included. Similarly, an I/O chassis that is attached to a cell takes on the assigned or unassigned attribute of the cell.
Unassigned Cells	Cells that are unassigned are available resources that can be used to create new nPartitions or assigned to existing nPartitions.
Core Cells	Every nPartition must have a cell that is attached to an I/O chassis that has a core I/O card in it. You can have multiple core cells, meaning cells to which an I/O chassis is attached with a core I/O card in it, but only one of these is the *active* core cell. If you have multiple core cells in an nPartition and the primary core cell fails, then you have a backup core cell. Not all HP 9000s allow you to have multiple core cells.
Active Cells	Cells that are both assigned to an nPartition and have booted are active cells. There is the concept of *rendezvous* on HP servers. During the boot process an nPartition rendezvous takes place when all the available cells in an nPartition *join* together. Those that rendezvous are active cells.
Inactive Cells	These are cells that are not assigned to an nPartition or have not yet rendezvoused to form a parti-

tion. Some cells are in a boot-is-blocked (BIB) state, which means that they will not rendezvous and are inactive. There are a variety of reasons that a cell is in a BIB state including: it is in an *n* state for the next boot; it boots too late to rendezvous; the cell fails a self-test; and the partition in which the cell exists is ready for reconfiguration.

Genesis nPartition

The Genesis nPartition is a one-cell nPartition used to create all other nPartitions. It can be expanded to include any number of cells but is initially only one cell. This is done for you by HP when your nPartition-capable system is delivered, if you have requested it. You may create the genesis partition at any time and reconfigure your server with a new nPartition structure. The genesis nPartition is number *0*. All cells in an nPartition must have the same clock speed and revision level. This partition is created only at the time of initial installation. Partition information in the Management Processor is destroyed when the genesis partition is created.

Partition Numbers

Every nPartition has a unique number used by the commands and utilities to specify the nPartition.

Local Partition

When working with one of the commands or utilities, the nPartition you are accessing is local and all others are remote.

Now that I've covered some of the basics of nPartitions and cells, let's a look at some of the tools and utilities used to manage them.

Many supported nPartition configurations on all HP 9000 and Integrity servers support nPartitions. To see a complete list of the supported nPartition configurations, see the aforementioned *HP System Partitions Guide: Administration for nPartitions* on *docs.hp.com*.

Ways of Managing nPartitions

nPartitions can be managed across a wide range of system operation. You can work with nPartitions at a very low level of the system, such as the Management Processor (MP), or after HP-UX has booted with nPartitions commands, or the menu-driven Partition Manager (**/opt/parmgr/bin/parmgr**). The following list summarizes the many available options for managing nPartitions, beginning with the lowest level tools and progressing to the highest level tools:

Management Processor

> The Management Processor (MP) is a low level means to access the system. The Management Processor has its own unique set of commands, some of which I cover later. You gain access to the MP by using **telnet**, because it has two network connections on it, one called a *Customer* LAN and the other called a *Private* LAN. You would typically use the *Customer* LAN to access the Management Processor. The Management Processor is also known as the Guardian Service Processor (GSP) and Service Processor (SP) so you may see these names used for the Management Processor, all of which represent the same method of accessing the system.

Virtual Front Panel

> The Virtual Front Panel (VFP) shows activity of one or more nPartitions and is invoked through the Management Processor. Although this is a subset of the overall Management Processor functionality, it is widely used and is therefore considered its own tool.

HP-UX Commands

> There are a variety of commands which you can issue that allow you to get useful information, and to configure and modify nPartitions from HP-UX. I provide examples of some of these commands and list all of them in an upcoming section.

Partition Manager

> Partition Manager provides an interface (**parmgr**) through which you can interact with nPartitions. This interface can also be invoked from System Administration Manager (SAM).

Boot-Related Commands

> There are several ways of interacting with nPartitions at the time of boot, including Extensible Firmware Interface (EFI) on HP Integrity Servers, Boot Control Handler (BCH), Initial System Loader (ISL), and other boot-related interfaces. I cover booting nPartitions in an upcoming section and describe these.

Working with nPartitions is all about navigation. You can easily forget at what level you're working when you start dealing with nPartitions. Are you at the console for the instance of HP-UX running in the nPartition? Are you at the nPartition level to see its status? What if you want to boot the nPartition? At what prompt should you be working? The navigation is especially confusing to new nPartition users, so let's look at working through the Management Processor menus before we work on any examples. Depending on the platform, HP uses the term Management Processor (MP), Guardian Service Processor (GSP), or Service Processor (SP). I use the term MP. Figures 17-1 through 17-3 show the *Consoles, Virtual Front Panel (VFP),* and *Command Menu* selected from the *Main Menu* of the MP.

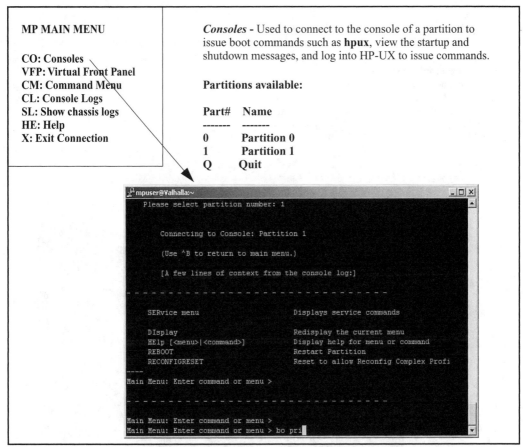

MP MAIN MENU

CO: Consoles
VFP: Virtual Front Panel
CM: Command Menu
CL: Console Logs
SL: Show chassis logs
HE: Help
X: Exit Connection

Consoles - Used to connect to the console of a partition to issue boot commands such as **hpux**, view the startup and shutdown messages, and log into HP-UX to issue commands.

Partitions available:

Part#	Name
0	Partition 0
1	Partition 1
Q	Quit

```
mpuser@Valhalla:~                                                    _ □ ×
    Please select partition number: 1


    Connecting to Console: Partition 1

    (Use ^B to return to main menu.)

    [A few lines of context from the console log:]

- - - - - - - - - - - - - - - - - - - - - - - - - - - - - -

    SERvice menu                        Displays service commands

    DIsplay                             Redisplay the current menu
    HElp [<menu>|<command>]             Display help for menu or command
    REBOOT                              Restart Partition
    RECONFIGRESET                       Reset to allow Reconfig Complex Profi
----
Main Menu: Enter command or menu >

- - - - - - - - - - - - - - - - - - - - - - - - - - - - - -

Main Menu: Enter command or menu >
Main Menu: Enter command or menu > bo pri
```

Figure 17-1   MP *Consoles* with Partition *1* Selected

MP MAIN MENU

CO: Consoles
VFP: Virtual Front Panel
CM: Command Menu
CL: Console Logs
SL: Show chassis logs
HE: Help
X: Exit Connection

Virtual Front Panel - Used to connect to the VFP which provides information about the state of partition at any time. Information such as the state of boot and state of cells.

Partitions available:

Part#	Name
0	**Partition 0**
1	**Partition 1**
S	**System Summary**
Q	**Quit**

Please select partition number:

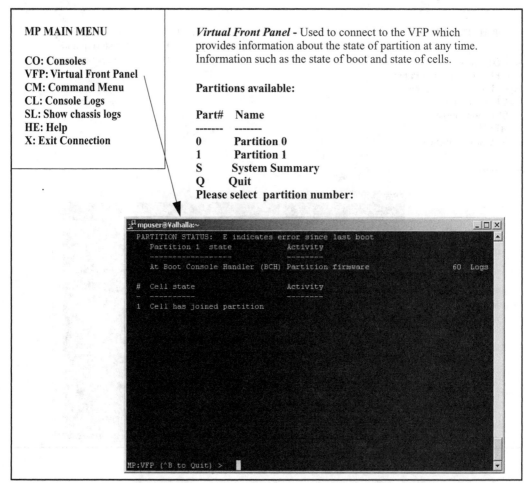

Figure 17-2   MP *Virtual Front Panel (VFP)* with Partition *1* Selected

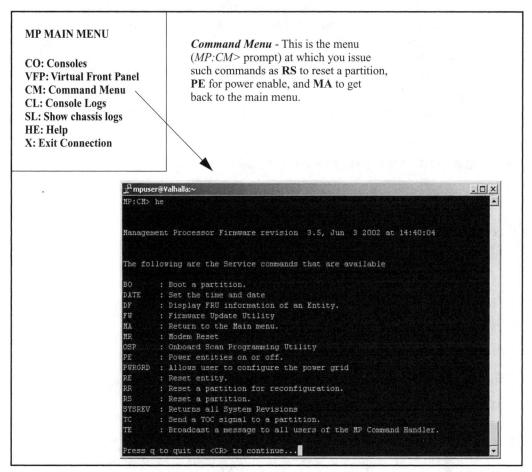

Figure 17-3   MP *Command Menu*

The *Command Menu* (*CM*) issues many commonly used commands, such as **rs** to reset a partition, **ps** to power on and off components including cell boards, cabinet, and I/O chassis, and **cp** to see to what partitions the cell boards are assigned. **he** summarizes the commands available to you. **ma** returns you to the main menu. The tear-out card in this book has a summary of MP commands.

The *Virtual Front Panel* (*VFP*) shows the status of the selected partition. At the time of boot, you can view stages that the partition goes through as it boots. These are not HP-UX boot stages; rather, they're stages related to system boot, such as firmware checks and other information that you'd view on the front panel of a system.

The *Consoles* menu allows you to get access to HP-UX consoles of all the hard partitions on your system. You select the partition to which you want to get access and you can log in to the instance of HP-UX running in the partition and issue HP-UX commands.

You can also see *Console logs* and *Chassis logs* through the *MP Main Menu* as well.

The Management Processor has the menus shown in Table 17-1:

Table 17-1   Management Processor Menus

Menu	Description

CO: Consoles	Lists the available nPartitions, such as
	
	`0) Partition 0`
	`1) Partition 1`

VFP: Virtual Front Panel	Access to all partitions, including *System*
CM: Command Menu	Access to many Management Processor commands.
CL: Console Log Menu	Provides a way to view nPartition logs
SL: Chassis Log Menu	Provides a way to view chassis logs
HE: Help	Help for using Management Processor
X: Exit Connection	Exits Management Processor

As usual, the best way to learn about a topic is to work through some examples. The upcoming section covers some commonly issued commands for working with nPartitions, starting with the *Command Menu*, then using HP-UX commands at the *Console* interface.

Command Menu (CM) From the MP Main Menu

The *Command Menu* (MP: *CM>* prompt) is used for many nPartition-related functions, such as creating the first partition in a system, called the genesis partition, with the **cc** command. You can also view the status of existing partitions and components in the system with a variety of commands. In the following examples, I show a list of available *CM* commands and then issue some of them on a running system. These commands were issued on a 16-cell board HP Integrity Server, but the commands are similar on all systems. At the end of the section, I provide the steps for creating a genesis partition with the **cc** command. To get to the *Main Menu* with the *MP* prompt, you issue ^*B* (*Cntrl B*). From the *Main Menu,* you select **cm**, then issue **he** to produce a list of Command Menu commands, and then issue **ma** to return to the *MP* prompt as shown in the following listing:

```
    MP MAIN MENU:

            CO: Consoles
           VFP: Virtual Front Panel
            CM: Command Menu
            CL: Console Logs
            SL: Show Event Logs
            FW: Firmware Update
            HE: Help
             X: Exit Connection

     MP> cm                             <-- Select Command Menu

                   Enter HE to get a list of available commands

                   (Use ^B to return to main menu.)



     MP:CM> he                          <-- Issue help


    Management Processor (MP) - FW Revision 14.12, Aug 17 2003 at 11:07:31

    Utility Subsystem FW Revision Level: 14.12


    The following are the service commands that are available

    BO       : Boot a partition.
    DF       : Display FRU information of an Entity.
    MA       : Return to the Main menu.
    MR       : Modem Reset
    PCIOLAD  : Activate/Deactivate a PCI card.
    PE       : Power entities on or off.
    RE       : Reset entity.
    RR       : Reset a partition for reconfiguration.
```

```
RS       : Reset a partition.
TC       : Send a TOC signal to a partition.
TE       : Broadcast a message to all users of the MP Command Handler.
VM       : Margin the voltage in a cabinet
WHO      : Display a list of MP connected users



The following are the status commands that are available

CP       : Display partition cell assignments
HE       : Display the list of available commands
IO       : Display IO chassis/cell connectivity
LS       : Display LAN connected console status
MS       : Display the status of the Modem
PS       : Display detailed power and hardware configuration status.
SYSREV   : Display revisions of all firmware entities in the complex.



The following are the system and access config commands that are available

AR       : Configure the Automatic System Restart
CA       : Configure Asynchronous and Modem parameters
CC       : Initiate a Complex Configuration
CP       : Display partition cell assignments
DATE     : Set the time and date
DC       : Reset parameters to default configuration
DI       : Disconnect Remote or LAN Console
ID       : Change certain stable complex configuration profile fields
IO       : Display IO chassis/cell connectivity
IT       : Modify command interface inactivity timeout
LC       : Configure LAN connections
LS       : Display LAN connected console status



The following are the system and access config commands that are available

PARPERM  : Enable/Disable Partition Reconfiguration
PD       : Modify default Partition for this login session.
RL       : Rekey Complex Profile Lock
SA       : Display and Set MP Remote Access
SO       : Configure Security Options and Access Control
XD       : MP Diagnostics and Reset


MP:CM> ma                              <-- Return to the Main Menu

    MP MAIN MENU:

          CO: Consoles
         VFP: Virtual Front Panel
          CM: Command Menu
          CL: Console Logs
          SL: Show Event Logs
          FW: Firmware Update
          HE: Help
           X: Exit Connection

[hp2-hp1-hp5-n067] MP>
```

As you can see from this list, you can issue many categories of Command Menu commands.

Two of the first commands that you would typically issue are **ls** (to see the configuration of the MP LAN) and **lc** (to configure the MP LAN) as shown in the following example:

```
MP:CM> ls                              <-- View MP LAN configuration with ls

Current configuration of MP LAN interface
  MAC address    : 00:30:6e:05:c9:6a
  IP address     : 192.168.0.22    (0xc0a80016)
  Hostname       : rp8400b
  Subnet mask    : 255.255.255.0   (0xffffff00)
  Gateway        : 192.168.0.1     (0xc0a80001)
  Status         : UP and RUNNING
  AutoNegotiate  : Enabled
  Data Rate      : 100 Mb/s
  Duplex         : Half
  Error Count    : 0
  Last Error     : none

MP:CM> lc                              <-- Change MP LAN configuration with lc


This command modifies the LAN parameters.

Current configuration of MP LAN interface
  MAC address    : 00:30:6e:05:c9:6a
  IP address     : 192.168.0.22    (0xc0a80016)
  Hostname       : rp8400b
  Subnet mask    : 255.255.255.0   (0xffffff00)
  Gateway        : 192.168.0.1     (0xc0a80001)
  Status         : UP and RUNNING
  AutoNegotiate  : Enabled
  Data Rate      : 100 Mb/s
  Duplex         : Half
  Error Count    : 0
  Last Error     : none


    Do you want to modify the configuration for the customer LAN? (Y/[N]) n
MP:CM>
```

ls displays the status of the MP LAN and, although I choose not to do so, **lc** allows you to modify the parameters related to the MP LAN. (As a side note, the default IP address of the MP is 127.0.0.1.) I had earlier configured the MP LAN interface to have an address on my local network. At the time that you first issue this command to configure the MP LAN, you probably have a console connected directly to the console port on the MP on your system. After the MP LAN is configured, you can connect over the LAN using *telnet* to access your MP LAN.

Because the MP is accessible from a network, it is possible that multiple users may be accessing a "window," such as a console, at the same time.

You are instructed to gain control with *^Ecf*, that is, *Ctrl E c f*. The *Ctrl* key is pressed along with a capital E and then lowercase c and f are pressed without the *Ctrl* key.

Next, I display partition cell assignments with **cp**:

```
MP:CM> cp                              <-- Display cell assignments with cp

-------------------------------+
Cabinet         |   0    |   1    |
-------------+--------+--------+
  Slot        |01234567|01234567|
-------------+--------+--------+
Partition  0 |XXXX....|........|
Partition  1 |....XXXX|........|
Partition  2 |........|XXXX....|
Partition  3 |........|....XXXX|
```

This example shows that there are 16 cell boards in this system, evenly distributed among the 4 nPartitions.

To get detailed information on the hardware of the system, you issue the **ps** command and select **b** for the cabinet as shown in the following example:

```
MP:CM> ps                     <-- Display power and hardware with ps

This command displays detailed power and hardware configuration status.

The following MP bus devices were found:
+----+-----+-----------+----------------+------------------------------------
--+
|    |     |           |                |           Core IOs                 |
|    |     |           |                | IO Bay | IO Bay | IO Bay | IO Bay |
|    |     |   UGUY    |     Cells      |   0    |   1    |   2    |   3    |
|Cab.|     |           |                |IO Chas.|IO Chas.|IO Chas.|IO Chas.|
| #  | MP  | CLU | PM  |0 1 2 3 4 5 6 7 |0 1 2 3 |0 1 2 3 |0 1 2 3 |0 1 2 3 |
+----+-----+-----+-----+----------------+--------+--------+--------+------
--+
| 0  |  *  |  *  |  *  |* * * * * * * * |   *    |        |   *    |        |
| 1  |     |  *  |  *  |* * * * * * * * |   *    |        |   *    |        |
You may display detailed power and hardware status for the following items:

     B - Cabinet (UGUY)
     C - Cell
     G - MP
     I - Core IO
        Select Device: b          <-- Display cabinet information

     Enter cabinet number: 0      <-- For cabinet 0

HW status for SD64A compute cabinet #0: NO FAILURE DETECTED
Power switch: on;  Power: enabled, good;  Door: closed
Fan speed: normal;  Temperature state: normal
Redundancy state: fans and blowers redundant, BPSs redundant
```

```
                    | Main BP|                   |    IO Backplanes      |
                    | Power  |                   | IO Bay 0 | IO Bay 1   |
            | Main  | Boards |      Cells         | Chassis  | Chassis    |
            | BP    | 0 1 2  | 0 1 2 3 4 5 6 7    | 0 1 2 3  | 0 1 2 3    |
+---------------+------+--------+-----------------+----------+----------+
Populated      |  *   | * * *  | * * * * * * * *  |    *     |       *    |
Power Enabled  |  *   | * * *  | * * * * * * * *  |    *     |       *    |
Powered On     |  *   | * * *  | * * * * * * * *  |    *     |       *    |
Power Fault    |      |        |                 |          |            |
Attention LED  |      |        |                 |          |            |

                        | Cabinet |    IO     |
              |   BPS    | Blowers |   Fans    |
              | 0 1 2 3 4 5 | 0 1 2 3 | 0 1 2 3 4 |
+-----------+-------------+---------+-----------+
Populated  | * * * * * * | * * * * | * * * * * |
Failed     |             |         |           |

Voltage margin: nominal;  Clock margin: nominal

              CLU Status    PM Status   CLU POST
UGUY LEDs:     ***_____     ****        _____

                          | Parity  | Connected  | Location       |
Flex connections | Connected | error   | to cabinet | (Upper/Lower)  |
+----------------+----------+---------+------------+----------------+
  XBC [7-0]      | YYYYYYYY  | NNNNNNNN | 11111111  | N/A            |
  RC [7-0]       | NNNNNNNN  | NNNNNNNN | 00000000  | LLLLLLLL       |

PM  firmware rev 14.4, time stamp: FRI APR 25 14:33:38 2003
CLU firmware rev 14.4, time stamp: WED JUL 09 14:57:57 2003

MP:CM>
```

This output produces a wealth of information about the system. For example, there are two cabinets and four I/O chassis in this Integrity Superdome system. The **ps** command provides a good rundown on your system hardware. To return to the *Main Menu,* issue the **ma** command.

I issue these commands on a running system configured with four nPartitions. To create the first partition, called the *genesis* partition, issue the **cc** command from *CM*. Before creating the genesis partition, save all nPartition-related information with **parstatus -V -p** *partition* in order to have all the information that you need to rebuild nPartitions. The genesis partition is created only at the time of initial installation and information related to other nPartitions in the MP is destroyed when the genesis partition is created. After you determine the components that you want to be part of the genesis partition, issue the **cc** command from the *CM* prompt and select the *g* option for genesis. You then have the genesis partition created and you can boot the instance of HP-UX that will run on it.

Next, I cover issued HP-UX nPartitions commands using the *Consoles* area of *MP Main Menu.*

HP-UX nPartition Commands Using *Consoles* Area

Selecting *Consoles* from the *MP Main Menu* allows you to get console access to a specific nPartition. Through this menu, you can create additional partitions provided that the genesis partition has already been created and booted. (See the end of the previous section for the **cc** command with the *g* option for genesis at the *MP: CM>* prompt.) This section covers HP-UX nPartition-related commands on an HP Integrity Server. The commands issued are identical on HP 9000 (PA-RISC servers) and Integrity Servers, but the output varies based on the configuration of the server on which the command is issued, such as the number of processors.

The parstatus Command

After HP-UX boots you can log in to the console and issue HP-UX commands as you would on any console. The first command that I issue is **parstatus -P** to get some high-level information about the nPartitions in our system:

```
# parstatus -P


[Partition]
Par                     # of  # of I/O
Num Status              Cells Chassis  Core cell  Partition Name (first 30 chars)
=== ============        ===== ========  =========  ================================
0   Active              4     1         cab0,cell0 nPar0
1   Active              4     1         cab0,cell4 nPar1
2   Active              4     1         cab1,cell0 nPar2
3   Active              4     1         cab1,cell4 nPar3
```

This output shows that we have four nPartitions on this system, all of which have four cells in them.

To determine the local nPartition on a system, we issue **parstatus -w**, as shown in the following output:

```
# parstatus -w
The local partition number is 1.
```

Let's now get some details on nPartition _p0:_

```
# parstatus -V -p0
[Partition]
Partition Number      : 0
Partition Name        : nPar0
Status                : Active
IP Address            :
Primary Boot Path     : -
Alternate Boot Path   : -
HA Alternate Boot Path : -
PDC Revision          : 1.258
IODCH Version         : ffff
Cell Architecture     : Itanium(R)-based
CPU Compatibility     : BCB-0
CPU Speed             : 1500 MHz
Core Cell             : cab0,cell0
Total Good Memory Size : 30.0 GB
Total Interleave Memory: 30.0 GB
Total Requested CLM   : 0.0 GB
Total Allocated CLM   : 0.0 GB


[Cell]
                              CPU       Memory                                      Use
                              OK/       (GB)                            Core        On
Hardware      Actual          Deconf/   OK/                             Cell        Next  Par
Location      Usage           Max       Deconf    Connected To          Capable  Boot  Num
==========  ============  =======  =========  ==================  =======  ====  =
cab0,cell0 Active Core    4/0/8    8.0/0.0    cab0,bay1,chassis3    yes      yes    0
cab0,cell1 Active Base    4/0/8    8.0/0.0    -                     no       yes    0
cab0,cell2 Active Base    4/0/8    6.0/2.0    -                     no       yes    0
cab0,cell3 Active Base    4/0/8    8.0/0.0    -                     no       yes    0

Notes: * = Cell has no interleaved memory.


[Chassis]
                                    Core  Connected  Par
Hardware Location    Usage          IO    To         Num
==================  ============  ====  ==========  ===
cab0,bay1,chassis3   Active         yes   cab0,cell0  0

#
```

This listing shows that _p0_ has four cell boards configured in it and one I/O chassis. The paths for the components are shown as well.

The next command that I issue is **parstatus -C** to get details about the way in which the cells are configured, as shown in the following listing:

```
# parstatus -C


[Cell]
                          CPU      Memory                                      Use
                          OK/      (GB)                           Core         On
        Hardware  Actual  Deconf/  OK/                            Cell         Next  Par
        Location  Usage   Max      Deconf   Connected To          Capable Boot Num
        ========  ======  =======  =======  ===================  ======= ==== ===
        cab0,cell0 Active Core     4/0/8    8.0/0.0  cab0,bay1,chassis 3  yes      yes  0
        cab0,cell1 Active Base     4/0/8    8.0/0.0  -                    no       yes  0
        cab0,cell2 Active Base     4/0/8    6.0/2.0  -                    no       yes  0
        cab0,cell3 Active Base     4/0/8    8.0/0.0  -                    no       yes  0
        cab0,cell4 Active Core     4/0/8    8.0/0.0  cab0,bay0,chassis1   yes      yes  1
        cab0,cell5 Active Base     3/1/8    8.0/0.0  -                    no       yes  1
        cab0,cell6 Active Base     4/0/8    8.0/0.0  -                    no       yes  1
        cab0,cell7 Active Base     4/0/8    8.0/0.0  -                    no       yes  1
        cab1,cell0 Active Core     4/0/8    8.0/0.0  cab1,bay1,chassis3   yes      yes  2
        cab1,cell1 Active Base     4/0/8    8.0/0.0  -                    no       yes  2
        cab1,cell2 Active Base     4/0/8    6.0/2.0  -                    no       yes  2
        cab1,cell3 Active Base     4/0/8    8.0/0.0  -                    no       yes  2
        cab1,cell4 Active Core     4/0/8    8.0/0.0  cab1,bay0,chassis1   yes      yes  3
        cab1,cell5 Active Base     4/0/8    8.0/0.0  -                    no       yes  3
        cab1,cell6 Active Base     4/0/8    8.0/0.0  -                    no       yes  3
        cab1,cell7 Active Base     4/0/8    8.0/0.0  -                    no       yes  3

Notes: * = Cell has no interleaved memory.
#
```

This output shows that we have 16 cells in the system, 8 in each of the 2 cabinets. All the cells are *Active* at this time. The headings indicate that we are provided with a lot of information about the physical aspects of the cells, such as their location, hardware paths, and so on, as well as configuration information, such as whether they are *active* or *inactive*.

Now I issue **parstatus -I** to list all the I/O chassis on our system:

```
# parstatus -I

[Chassis]
                          Core Connected  Par
    Hardware Location  Usage      IO   To         Num
    =================  ==========  ====  ==========  ===
    cab0,bay0,chassis0  Absent     -     -           -
    cab0,bay0,chassis1  Active     yes   cab0,cell14 1
    cab0,bay0,chassis2  Absent     -     -           -
    cab0,bay0,chassis3  Absent     -     -           -
    cab0,bay1,chassis0  Absent     -     -           -
    cab0,bay1,chassis1  Absent     -     -           -
    cab0,bay1,chassis2  Absent     -     -           -
    cab0,bay1,chassis3  Active     yes   cab0,cell0  0
    cab1,bay0,chassis0  Absent     -     -           -
    cab1,bay0,chassis1  Active     yes   cab1,cell14 3
    cab1,bay0,chassis2  Absent     -     -           -
    cab1,bay0,chassis3  Absent     -     -           -
    cab1,bay1,chassis0  Absent     -     -           -
    cab1,bay1,chassis1  Absent     -     -           -
    cab1,bay1,chassis2  Absent     -     -           -
    cab1,bay1,chassis3  Active     yes   cab1,cell0  2
#
```

This output lists everything related to I/O on our system. There are four I/O chassis in this system, one for each nPartition. The remaining I/O chassis are *Absent*. A minimum of one chassis is required for each nPartition because a Core I/O card is required for each nPartition.

The **parstatus** command without any options produces a more detailed list of results, as shown in the following output:

```
# parstatus
Note: No action specified. Default behavior is display all.
[Complex]
   Complex Name : Complex 1
   Complex Capacity
     Compute Cabinet (8 cell capable) : 2
   Active MP Location : cabinet 0
   Original Product Name : superdome server SD64A
   OEM Serial Number :
   Current Product Order Number : A5201A
   OEM Manufacturer :
   Complex Profile Revision : 1.0
   The total number of partitions present : 4
```

```
[Cabinet]
```

			Cabinet Blowers OK/	I/O Fans OK/	Bulk Power Supplies OK/	Backplane Power Boards OK/	
Cab Num	Cabinet	Type	Failed/ N Status	Failed/ N Status	Failed/ N Status	Failed/ N Status	MP
===	============	=====	=========	=========	==========	============	======
0	8 cell	slot	4/0/N+	5/0/NA	6/0/N+	3/0/N+	Active
1	8 cell	slot	4/0/N+	5/0/NA	6/0/N+	3/0/N+	Backup

```
Notes: N+ = There are one or more spare items (fans/power supplies).
       N  = The number of items meets but does not exceed the need.
       N- = There are insufficient items to meet the need.
       ?  = The adequacy of the cooling system/power supplies is unknown.
       HO = Housekeeping only; The power is in a standby state.
       NA = Not Applicable.
```

```
[Cell]
```

		CPU OK/	Memory (GB)			Core	Use On	
Hardware Location	Actual Usage	Deconf/ Max	OK/ Deconf	Connected To		Cell Capable	Next Boot	Par Num
==========	============	=======	=========	====================		=======	====	===
cab0,cell0	Active Core	4/0/8	8.0/0.0	cab0,bay1,chassis3		yes	yes	0
cab0,cell1	Active Base	4/0/8	8.0/0.0	-		no	yes	0
cab0,cell2	Active Base	4/0/8	6.0/2.0	-		no	yes	0
cab0,cell3	Active Base	4/0/8	8.0/0.0	-		no	yes	0
cab0,cell4	Active Core	4/0/8	8.0/0.0	cab0,bay0,chassis1		yes	yes	1
cab0,cell5	Active Base	3/1/8	8.0/0.0	-		no	yes	1
cab0,cell6	Active Base	4/0/8	8.0/0.0	-		no	yes	1
cab0,cell7	Active Base	4/0/8	8.0/0.0	-		no	yes	1
cab1,cell0	Active Core	4/0/8	8.0/0.0	cab1,bay1,chassis3		yes	yes	2
cab1,cell1	Active Base	4/0/8	8.0/0.0	-		no	yes	2
cab1,cell2	Active Base	4/0/8	6.0/2.0	-		no	yes	2
cab1,cell3	Active Base	4/0/8	8.0/0.0	-		no	yes	2
cab1,cell4	Active Core	4/0/8	8.0/0.0	cab1,bay0,chassis1		yes	yes	3

```
cab1,cell5 Active Base   4/0/8   8.0/0.0   -                    no    yes  3
cab1,cell6 Active Base   4/0/8   8.0/0.0   -                    no    yes  3
cab1,cell7 Active Base   4/0/8   8.0/0.0   -                    no    yes  3

Notes: * = Cell has no interleaved memory.


[Chassis]
                                     Core Connected  Par
Hardware Location    Usage           IO   To         Num
==================== ============    ==== ========== ===
cab0,bay0,chassis0   Absent          -    -          -
cab0,bay0,chassis1   Active          yes  cab0,cell4 1
cab0,bay0,chassis2   Absent          -    -          -
cab0,bay0,chassis3   Absent          -    -          -
cab0,bay1,chassis0   Absent          -    -          -
cab0,bay1,chassis1   Absent          -    -          -
cab0,bay1,chassis2   Absent          -    -          -
cab0,bay1,chassis3   Active          yes  cab0,cell0 0
cab1,bay0,chassis0   Absent          -    -          -
cab1,bay0,chassis1   Active          yes  cab1,cell4 3
cab1,bay0,chassis2   Absent          -    -          -
cab1,bay0,chassis3   Absent          -    -          -
cab1,bay1,chassis0   Absent          -    -          -
cab1,bay1,chassis1   Absent          -    -          -
cab1,bay1,chassis2   Absent          -    -          -
cab1,bay1,chassis3   Active          yes  cab1,cell0 2
cUnable to get read lock for cell.
May not be able to display complete information.


[Partition]
Par                  # of  # of I/O
Num Status           Cells Chassis  Core cell  Partition Name (first 30 chars)
=== =============    ===== ======== ========== ==============================
0   Active           4     1        cab0,cell0 nPar0
1   Active           4     1        cab0,cell4 nPar1
2   Active           4     1        cab1,cell0 nPa
r2
3   Inactive         4     1        cab1,cell4 nPar3
#
```

This useful summary of the system shows the capacity of the system and which cell boards and chassis are devoted to which nPartitions. This is an ideal output to keep up to date as you modify the nPartition configuration of your system.

The olrad -q Command

Next, let's look at detailed information for the local nPartition. We're interested in all the components of our local nPartition and a detail of PCI I/O. The following listing shows the PCI detail with the **olrad -q** command:

```
# parstatus -w
The local partition number is 1.

# olrad -q
                                                     Driver(s)
                                                     Capable
Slot          Path       Bus   Max   Spd  Pwr  Occu  Susp  OLAR  OLD   Max    Mode
                         Num   Spd                               Mode
0-0-1-1       4/0/1/1     21   133   N/A  On   Yes   No    Yes   N/A   PCI-X  N/A
0-0-1-2       4/0/2/1     42   133   N/A  On   Yes   No    Yes   N/A   PCI-X  N/A
0-0-1-3       4/0/3/1     63   133   N/A  On   Yes   No    Yes   N/A   PCI-X  N/A
0-0-1-4       4/0/4/1     84   133   N/A  On   Yes   No    Yes   N/A   PCI-X  N/A
0-0-1-5       4/0/6/1    105   133   N/A  On   Yes   No    Yes   N/A   PCI-X  N/A
0-0-1-6       4/0/14/1   234   133   N/A  On   Yes   No    Yes   N/A   PCI-X  N/A
0-0-1-7       4/0/12/1   212   133   N/A  On   Yes   No    Yes   N/A   PCI-X  N/A
0-0-1-8       4/0/11/1   190   133   133  Off  No    N/A   N/A   N/A   PCI-X  N/A
0-0-1-9       4/0/10/1   168   133   N/A  On   Yes   No    Yes   N/A   PCI-X  N/A
0-0-1-10      4/0/9/1    147   133   N/A  On   Yes   No    Yes   N/A   PCI-X  N/A
0-0-1-11      4/0/8/1    126   133   N/A  On   Yes   No    Yes   N/A   PCI-X  N/A
#
```

olrad displays information about all the On Line Addition and Replacement OLA/R slots in nPartition number 1. A more detailed discussion of OLA/R appears in Chapter 6. There is a lot of detail in this output that is not as easy to understand as the **parstatus** output, so let's take a closer look at a couple of these fields.

The first field of the **olrad** output is the slot information, which is in the following form:

```
Cabinet-Bay-Chassis-Slot     such as 0-0-1-1 for the first entry
```

This example shows that the first card is in cabinet 0, bay 0, chassis 1, and slot 1. The hierarchy is such that the cabinet is the overall enclosure, the bay holds two I/O chassis, and there are slots within each I/O chassis.

The second field, which is the *Path*, contains the following:

```
Cell/SBA/LBA/Device     such as 4/0/1/1 for the first entry
```

For this entry, the cell board is 4, the System Bus Adapter (SBA) is 0, the Local Bus Adapter (LBA) is 1, and the device is 1. All the cards in this nPartition are connected to cell 4 because the **parstatus** output showed that I/O chassis is connected to cell 4.

As with Virtual Partitions (vPars) covered in Chapter 16, you need to know something about the structure of your system in order to work with nPartitions. The System Bus Adapters (SBAs) and Local Bus Adapters (LBAs) are not components that you would typically worry about if you were not working with partitions. For the purpose of working through the information in this chapter, it is sufficient to know that there is a hierarchical I/O structure on servers in which the SBA exists at a higher level than the LBA and there are typically several LBAs per SBA. That is why for the second field, SBA of *0,* for example, you see several third fields, which are many LBAs per SBA.

The ioscan Command

Next, I issue some **ioscan** commands to see various components in nPartition 0. The first command shows the processors. These were not shown in the **olrad -q** output produced earlier because, at the time of this writing, they are not OLA/R components. The following **ioscan** output uses options to produce information about the processors in nPartition 0 that are configured into the kernel:

```
# ioscan -fnkCprocessor
Class      I  H/W Path   Driver     S/W State H/W Type  Description
===================================================================
processor   0  4/120      processor CLAIMED    PROCESSOR Processor
processor   1  4/121      processor CLAIMED    PROCESSOR Processor
processor   2  4/122      processor CLAIMED    PROCESSOR Processor
processor   3  4/123      processor CLAIMED    PROCESSOR Processor
processor   4  5/120      processor CLAIMED    PROCESSOR Processor
processor   5  5/121      processor CLAIMED    PROCESSOR Processor
processor   6  5/122      processor CLAIMED    PROCESSOR Processor
processor   7  6/120      processor CLAIMED    PROCESSOR Processor
processor   8  6/121      processor CLAIMED    PROCESSOR Processor
processor   9  6/122      processor CLAIMED    PROCESSOR Processor
processor  10  6/123      processor CLAIMED    PROCESSOR Processor
processor  11  7/120      processor CLAIMED    PROCESSOR Processor
processor  12  7/121      processor CLAIMED    PROCESSOR Processor
processor  13  7/122      processor CLAIMED    PROCESSOR Processor
processor  14  7/123      processor CLAIMED    PROCESSOR Processor
```

This output shows 16 processors in the nPartition that are on cell board 0.

This **ioscan** output produced information about the cell boards that are configured into nPartition *0,* but there are 16 cell boards in this system. To see information about a specific cell board in the system, issue **parstatus -c***cellboardnumber* such as **parstatus -c3** for information about cell board 3.

To see all the components in your nPartition, issue the **ioscan -f** command. The following listing shows only the first six lines of this output because it is long:

```
# ioscan -f

Class    I  H/W Path      Driver    S/W State   H/W Type      Description

==========================================================================

root     0                root      CLAIMED     BUS_NEXUS
cell     0  4              cell      CLAIMED     BUS_NEXUS
ioa      0  4/0            sba       CLAIMED     BUS_NEXUS     System Bus Adapter (127b)
ba       0  4/0/0          lba       CLAIMED     BUS_NEXUS     Local PCI-X Bus Ad (122e)
tty      0  4/0/0/0/0      asio0     CLAIMED     INTERFACE     PCI Serial (103c1048)
lan      0  4/0/0/1/0      btlan     CLAIMED     INTERFACE     HP PCI 10/100Base-TX Core
                               .
                               .
                               .
```

All components in nPartition 0 would be shown in this output. Because I did not use the *-k* option, all component are listed, not just those built into the kernel. This **ioscan** output includes all components in nPartition *0*. The form of the **ioscan** output for an nPartition looks like the following:

```
    Field 1          Field 2      Field3      Field 4   Field 5   Field 6

Global cell no./proc, mem, or SBA/LBA/Card address/Function/dev addr
```

It is not immediately apparent from an I/O listing in what slot a card is located. Chapter 6 covers identifying the LBA and slot number for cards in detail, so refer to that chapter if you want to know the nuances of this mapping, but I give a short overview of this mapping here.

You know the LBA from the **ioscan** output but you don't know the slot number. (Remember that the **ioscan** output is in the form of *Cell/SBA/LBA/ Device.*) The I/O cardcage itself sometimes has on it the mapping of slot and LBA. Table 17-2 shows this mapping for an Integrity Superdome.

Table 17-2   *SLOT* Versus *LBA* Information Shown on Integrity Superdome

SLOT	11	10	9	8	7	6	5	4	3	2	1	0
LBA	8	9	10	11	12	14	6	4	3	2	1	0

This information is for a 12-slot I/O cardcage on an Integrity Superdome.

The LBA numbers and slot numbers do not correspond to one another in the table. The LBA number is the same as the "rope." The rope is an internal connection to the slot. In the case of some LBA slots, such as 4 through 7, there are two ropes connected to the slot thereby doubling its speed. The LBA number for those slots is the first of the two rope numbers of the slot.

Modifying and Creating an nPartition

Now that I've covered the basics of some HP-UX commands for working with nPartitions, I put a few of these commands to use by modifying and creating some nPartitions. The example in this section uses a PA-RISC system (HP 9000) with four cell boards. The same commands apply to working with an Itanium (Integrity) server.

I start this work on the system with four cell boards that have been used in other examples in this chapter. In the following listing, I issue **parstatus** with the *-P* option to see what partitions exist, of which there are two, issue **parstatus** with no options to get an overall rundown on the partitions, and finally, run **parstatus -I** to see the I/O that exists in the complex:

```
# parstatus -P
[Partition]
Par                  # of   # of I/O
Num Status           Cells  Chassis  Core cell   Partition Name (first 30 chars)
=== ============     =====  ========  ==========  ================================
 0  active             1       1      cab0,cell0  Partition 0
 1  active             1       1      cab0,cell1  Partition 1


# parstatus
Warning: No action specified. Default behaviour is display all.
[Complex]
   Complex Name :
   Complex Capacity
     Compute Cabinet (4 cell capable) : 1
   Active GSP Location : cabinet 0
   Model : 9000/800/S16K-A
   Serial Number : USR414203J
   Current Product Number : A6093A
   Original Product Number : A6093A
   Complex Profile Revision : 1.0
   The total number of Partitions Present : 2

[Cabinet]
                 Cabinet    I/O        Bulk Power   Backplane
                 Fans       Fans       Supplies     Power Boards
                 OK/        OK/        OK/          OK/
Cab              Failed/    Failed/    Failed/      FAILED/
Num Cabinet Type N Status   N Status   N Status     N Status       GSP
=== ============ ========== ========== ==========  =============  ======
 0  S16K-A       21/ 0/ N+   6/ 0/ N+   6/ 0/ N+    N/A            active

Notes: N+ = There are one or more spare items (fans/power supplies).
       N  = The number of items meets but does not exceed the need.
       N- = There are insufficient items to meet the need.
       ?  = The adequacy of the cooling system/power supplies is unknown.

[Cell]
                            CPU       Memory                              Use
                            OK/       (GB)                        Core    On
            Hardware  Actual  Deconf/ OK/                         Cell    Next Par
            Location  Usage   Max     Deconf   Connected To       Capable Boot Num
            ========= ======= ======= ======== ================== ======= ==== ===
            cab0,cell0 active core 4/0/4  4.0/ 0.0 cab0,bay0,chassis0 yes    yes  0
            cab0,cell1 active core 4/0/4  4.0/ 0.0 cab0,bay0,chassis1 yes    yes  1
            cab0,cell2 inactive      4/0/4  4.0/ 0.0 -                 no     -    -
            cab0,cell3 inactive      4/0/4  4.0/ 0.0 -                 no     -    -
```

```
[Chassis]
                                    Core Connected  Par
Hardware Location    Usage          IO   To         Num
==================== ============   ==== ========== ===
cab0,bay0,chassis0   active         yes  cab0,cell0 0
cab0,bay0,chassis1   active         yes  cab0,cell1 1

[Partition]
Par                  # of  # of I/O
Num Status           Cells Chassis  Core cell  Partition Name (first 30 chars)
=== ============     ===== ========  ========== ===============================
  0 active             1     1       cab0,cell0 Partition 0
  1 active             1     1       cab0,cell1 Partition 1


# parstatus -I
[Chassis]
                                    Core Connected  Par
Hardware Location    Usage          IO   To         Num
==================== ============   ==== ========== ===
cab0,bay0,chassis0   active         yes  cab0,cell0 0
cab0,bay0,chassis1   active         yes  cab0,cell1 1

#
```

These outputs indicate that I have some challenges on my hands to create a new nPartition. There are two nPartitions on the system and two I/O chassis on the system, both of which are in use. In order to create a new partition, I must delete nPartition *1* and then re-add it.

I first delete nPartition *1* in order to free up *cell1* and *chassis1* so that these components will be available. (You may want to move a cell board out of an nPartition with **parmodify -p 0 -d 1** to remove cell 1 from partition 0.) After shutting down nPartition *1,* I go to the *MP:CM>* prompt and issued **rr** on nPartition *1* and then in nPartition *0,* I issue **parremove -p 1**. I then issue the following **parstatus** commands to see the resources that I want for nPartition *1, cell1* and *chassis1* are now available. Before issuing any of these commands, I run a **strings** on **/etc/lvmtab** so that I know the boot device that is used in nPartition *1* that I'll use when the new partition is created:

```
# strings /etc/lvmtab                       <-- View boot devices
/dev/vg00
/dev/dsk/c0t6d0

# parstatus -c 1            <-- Confirm that cell1 is available
[Cell]
                  CPU     Memory                           Use
                  OK/     (GB)                    Core     On
Hardware  Actual  Deconf/ OK/                     Cell     Next Par
Location  Usage   Max     Deconf  Connected To    Capable  Boot Num
========= ======= ======= ======= ================ ======= ==== ===
cab0,cell1 inactive 4/0/4  4.0/ 0.0 cab0,bay0,chassis1 yes    -    -

# parstatus -I            <-- Confirm that chassis 1 is available
[Chassis]
                                    Core Connected  Par
Hardware Location    Usage          IO   To         Num
==================== ============   ==== ========== ===
cab0,bay0,chassis0   active         yes  cab0,cell0 0
cab0,bay0,chassis1   inactive       yes  cab0,cell1 -

#
```

This listing shows that *cell1* and *chassis1* are now available for use.

You can create a new partition and specify the boot device in the **parcreate** command, or create the nPartition and *search* for boot devices at the time the nPartition is started. I create the nPartition without specifying a boot device and then *search* for devices at the time of boot. The following is the **parcreate** command:

```
# parcreate -P marty_npar2 -cl:base:y:ri
Partition Created. The partition number is: 1
#
```

Implied in the creation of this nPartition is *chassis1*, which is connected to *cell1*. All devices in *chassis1* are part of nPartition*1*. Now that the partition has been created, I reset it in the MP:

```
MP:CM> rs                                        <-- Reset partition with rs

This command resets the selected partition.

WARNING: Execution of this command irrecoverably halts all system
         processing and I/O activity and restarts the selected
         partition.

  Part#  Name
  -----  ----
    0)   Partition 0
    1)   marty_npar2

  Select a partition number: 1                   <-- Select partition 1

  Do you want to reset partition number 1? (Y/[N]) y

  -> The selected partition will be reset.
MP:CM>
```

After this *rs* is issued you can monitor the progress of tests run at the *VFP*. At the *console* for nPartition*1*, I issue the **search** command as shown in the following example:

```
---- Main Menu -----------------------------------------------------------

     Command                         Description
     -------                         -----------
     BOot [PRI|HAA|ALT|<path>]       Boot from specified path
     PAth [PRI|HAA|ALT] [<path>]     Display or modify a path
     SEArch [ALL|<cell>|<path>]      Search for boot devices
     ScRoll [ON|OFF]                 Display or change scrolling capability

     COnfiguration menu              Displays or sets boot values
     INformation menu                Displays hardware information
     SERvice menu                    Displays service commands

     DIsplay                         Redisplay the current menu
     HElp [<menu>|<command>]         Display help for menu or command
     REBOOT                          Restart Partition
     RECONFIGRESET                   Reset to allow Reconfig Complex Profile
----
```

```
Main Menu: Enter command or menu > sea <-- Search for bootable devices

Searching for potential boot device(s)
This may take several minutes.

To discontinue search, press any key (termination may not be immediate).


    Path#  Device Path (dec)                  Device Type
    -----  -----------------                  -----------
    P0     1/0/0/2/0.6                        Random access media
    P1     1/0/0/2/1.2                        Random access media
    P2     1/0/0/3/0.6                        Random access media
    P3     1/0/8/0/0.8                        Random access media

Main Menu: Enter command or menu > bo p0         <-- Select p0 for boot

 BCH Directed Boot Path: 1/0/0/2/0.6


 Do you wish to stop at the ISL prompt prior to booting? (y/n) >> n

Initializing boot Device.


Boot IO Dependent Code (IODC) Revision 0


Boot Path Initialized.


HARD Booted.

ISL Revision A.00.43  Apr 12, 2000

ISL booting  hpux

Boot
: disk(1/0/0/2/0.6.0.0.0.0.0;0)/stand/vmunix
```

The boot from the device at *p0* progressed and nPartition*1* is now running. The following **parstatus** command shows the makeup of this nPartition:

```
# parstatus
Warning: No action specified. Default behaviour is display all.
[Complex]
    Complex Name :
    Complex Capacity
      Compute Cabinet (4 cell capable) : 1
    Active GSP Location : cabinet 0
    Model : 9000/800/S16K-A
    Serial Number : USR414203J
    Current Product Number : A6093A
    Original Product Number : A6093A
    Complex Profile Revision : 1.0
    The total number of Partitions Present : 2

[Cabinet]
                    Cabinet    I/O        Bulk Power  Backplane
                    Fans       Fans       Supplies    Power Boards
                    OK/        OK/        OK/         OK/
Cab                 Failed/    Failed/    Failed/     FAILED/
Num Cabinet Type    N Status   N Status   N Status    N Status       GSP
=== ============    =========  =========  ==========  ============   ======
 0  S16K-A          21/ 0/ N+  6/ 0/ N+   6/ 0/ N+    N/A            active
```

```
Notes: N+ = There are one or more spare items (fans/power supplies).
       N  = The number of items meets but does not exceed the need.
       N- = There are insufficient items to meet the need.
       ?  = The adequacy of the cooling system/power supplies is unknown.

[Cell]
                           CPU    Memory                             Use
                           OK/    (GB)                        Core   On
Hardware    Actual         Deconf/ OK/                        Cell   Next Par
Location    Usage          Max    Deconf    Connected To      Capable Boot Num
==========  ============   ======= ========= =================== ======= ==== ===
cab0,cell0  active core    4/0/4  4.0/ 0.0 cab0,bay0,chassis0  yes     yes  0
cab0,cell1  active core    4/0/4  4.0/ 0.0 cab0,bay0,chassis1  yes     yes  1
cab0,cell2  inactive       4/0/4  4.0/ 0.0 -                   no      -    -
cab0,cell3  inactive       4/0/4  4.0/ 0.0 -                   no      -    -

[Chassis]
                                   Core Connected  Par
Hardware Location     Usage        IO   To         Num
===================   ============ ==== ========== ===
cab0,bay0,chassis0    active       yes  cab0,cell0 0
cab0,bay0,chassis1    active       yes  cab0,cell1 1

[Partition]
Par                   # of  # of I/O
Num Status            Cells Chassis  Core cell  Partition Name (first 30 chars)
=== ============      ===== ======== ========== ==============================
 0  active            1     1        cab0,cell0 Partition 0
 1  active            1     1        cab0,cell1 marty_npar2
#
```

From this **parstatus** output, you can see that nPartition*1* has *cell1* and *chassis1* in it.

I now modify nPartition*1* to include the path of the boot device with **parmodify -b**:

```
# parmodify -p 1 -b 1/0/0/2/0.6
Command succeeded.
#
# shutdown -R now
```

I shut down this nPartition (with the *-R*) option to see if the primary boot path specified with the *-b* option to **shutdown** would work. You can specify the primary boot device with *-b*, the alternate boot device with *-t*, and the secondary boot device with *-s*. These options work with both **parcreate** and **parmodify**. This chapter also covers setting the *PathFlags* in such a way that you can control what devices are used in what sequence during the boot process. Now that the primary boot device is specified, I can issue the **boot pri** string at the *Main Menu* as shown here:

```
# shutdown -R now

---- Main Menu ----------------------------------------------------------

    Command                          Description
    -------                          -----------
    BOot [PRI|HAA|ALT|<path>]        Boot from specified path
    PAth [PRI|HAA|ALT] [<path>]      Display or modify a path
    SEArch [ALL|<cell>|<path>]       Search for boot devices
    ScRoll [ON|OFF]                  Display or change scrolling capability

    COnfiguration menu               Displays or sets boot values
    INformation menu                 Displays hardware information
    SERvice menu                     Displays service commands

    DIsplay                          Redisplay the current menu
    HElp [<menu>|<command>]          Display help for menu or command
    REBOOT                           Restart Partition
    RECONFIGRESET                    Reset to allow Reconfig Complex Prof
----
Main Menu: Enter command or menu > bo pri

    Primary Boot Path:  1/0/0/2/0.6
```

Next, I add cell*2* to nPartition*1* by using the **parmodify** command:

```
# parmodify -p 1 -a 2:base:y:ri

In order to activate any cell that has been newly added,
reboot the partition with the -R option.
Command succeeded.
#
# shutdown -R now
```

The command **parmodify -p 1 -a 2:base:y:ri** adds cell board 2 with options *base* (*base* cell is the only valid type at this time), *y* (which means that the cell will participate in the reboot), and *ri* (which is *reactive with interleave* which is the only valid value at this time). I left *cell3* unused by not including it in nPartition*1*. The *-R* option is required when making a change to an nPartition to set the ready-to-reconfigure flag. I could run a **vparstatus** when this nPartition reboots to confirm that both cell boards are in the nPartition; however, I don't have to wait that long and can use *VFP* to watch the boot status, as shown in the following output:

```
         PARTITION STATUS:  E indicates error since last boot
              Partition 1  state              Activity
              ------------------              --------
              Starting                        Cell PDH platform register operat    3
Logs

         #  Cell state                        Activity
         -  ----------                        --------
         1  Cell has joined partition
         2  Cell has joined partition
```

Now the two nPartitions are set up as I want them to be. The second nPartition requires a manual boot, and I'd like to have it automatically boot from the boot device that I specified. This requires some BCH interaction. The next section covers resetting a partition.

As a side note, be careful of the order of cells on systems. Cell 1 is the primary cell on a two-cell board system, so a single DVD in a system is probably connected to cell 1. On a Superdome and four-cell system, it is cell 0. On a two-cell system that consists of one nPartition, I have inadvertently split the system into two partitions and then was unable to boot because both the DVD and boot disk were connected to cell 1. In this case, I had to use **cc** to modify the complex configuration, **g** for genesis, and specified partition 1 so that I could boot from nPartition 1 components.

The following **parstatus** listing shows that partition 0 consists of cell board 1 and partition 1 consists of cell board 0:

```
# parstatus
Warning: No action specified. Default behaviour is display all.
[Complex]
    Complex Name : Complex 01
    Complex Capacity
      Compute Cabinet (2 cell capable) : 1
    Active GSP Location : cabinet 0
    Model : 9000/800/rp7420
    Serial Number : USE4440F97
    Current Product Number : A7025A
    Original Product Number : A7025A
    Complex Profile Revision : 1.0
    The total number of Partitions Present : 2

[Cabinet]
                    Cabinet    I/O        Bulk Power  Backplane
                    Fans       Fans       Supplies    Power Boards
                    OK/        OK/        OK/         OK/
Cab                 Failed/    Failed/    Failed/     FAILED/
Num Cabinet Type N Status    N Status   N Status    N Status        GSP
=== ============ ========= ========= ========== ============  ======
  0  rp7420       4/ 0/ N+  6/ 0/ N+  2/ 0/ N+    N/A          active

Notes: N+ = There are one or more spare items (fans/power supplies).
        N  = The number of items meets but does not exceed the need.
        N- = There are insufficient items to meet the need.
        ?  = The adequacy of the cooling system/power supplies is unknown.
```

```
[Cell]
                          CPU     Memory                            Use
                          OK/     (GB)                     Core     On
Hardware    Actual        Deconf/ OK/                      Cell     Next Par
Location    Usage         Max     Deconf   Connected To    Capable  Boot Num
==========  ============  =======  =========  ==================  =======  ==== ===
cab0,cell0  active core   2/0/8   8.0/ 0.0 cab0,bay0,chassis0  yes      yes  1
cab0,cell1  active core   2/0/8   8.0/ 0.0 cab0,bay0,chassis1  yes      yes  0

[Chassis]
                                   Core Connected  Par
Hardware Location     Usage        IO   To         Num
===================  ============  ==== ==========  ===
cab0,bay0,chassis0   active        yes  cab0,cell0  1
cab0,bay0,chassis1   active        yes  cab0,cell1  0

[Partition]
Par                  # of  # of I/O
Num Status           Cells Chassis  Core cell   Partition Name (first 30 chars)
=== ============     ===== ========  ==========  ==============================
 0  active             1      1      cab0,cell1  Partition 0
 1  active             1      1      cab0,cell0  nPar1cell0
```

Summary of HP-UX nPartition Commands

The commands that I issued in the previous sections have produced a lot of useful information about the way in which nPartitions are configured. There are also many commands that you can issue to create, modify, remove, and manipulate nPartitions in other ways. Table 17-3 summarizes some of the commonly used nPartition-related commands.

Table 17-3   Commonly Used nPartition-Related Commands

Command	Description
ioscan	Scans system hardware and produces results. This command is context sensitive in that it produces output based on the *local* nPartition.
olrad	Performs online addition and replacement-related tasks. Provides a detailed hardware summary when issued with no options.
parmgr	Graphical interface for configuring and managing nPartitions.
parcreate	Creates a new nPartition.
parmodify	Modifies an existing nPartition.
parremove	Removes an existing nPartition.

Command	Description
parstatus	Shows nPartition information.
parunlock	Unlocks profile data.
fruled	Blinks attention indicators.
frupower	Reads status and control power for cells and I/O chassis.

Using *CM*, *VFP*, and *CO* to Reset a Partition on Integrity

When you're new to *CM*, *VFP*, and *CO*, it is sometimes difficult to determine which of these to use for what function. A good example of using all three of these menu areas is to reset a partition. This demonstrates the level of functionality that each menu area provides. This is a three-step process as outlined here:

1. Use *CM* to reset a partition.

2. Use *VFP* to see the partition progress through various stages of the boot process.

3. Use *CO* to search for bootable devices, select one, and boot the partition.

You can issue an *rs* command to reset the partition from *CM*, as shown in the following example:

```
MP:CM> rs                            <-- Reset partition with rs

This command resets the selected partition.

WARNING: Execution of this command irrecoverably halts all system
         processing and I/O activity and restarts the selected
         partition.

  Part#  Name
  -----  ----
     0)  Partition 0

  Select a partition number: 0     <-- Select partition 0 for reset

  Do you want to reset partition number 0? (Y/[N]) y

   -> The selected partition will be reset.
MP:CM>
```

Although this is a one-nPartition system, you are asked which nPartition you want to reset. After specifying that partition 0 is to be reset, you can view the progress at the *VFP*, as shown in the following example:

```
#  Partition state                  Activity
-  ---------------                  --------
0  Cell(s) Booting:                                         443 Logs

#  Cell state                       Activity
-  ----------                       --------
0  I/O discovery      IODISC_SBA_CONFIG_START               102 Logs
1  I/O discovery      IODISC_SBA_CONFIG_START               105 Logs
2  Memory discovery   MEM_TEST_WRITE                        118 Logs
3  Memory discovery   MEM_TEST_WRITE                        118 Logs
```

At this point, the *VFP* shows that memory discovery is taking place.

Next, I switch to *CO* so you can see that you have control of the HP-UX boot process through the console. I specify the **search** command to search for bootable devices in the following example:

```
MP> co                                    <-- Select Console with co

    Partitions available:

  Part#  Name
  -----  ----
    0)   Partition 0
    Q)   Quit

    Please select partition number: 0


        Connecting to Console: Partition 0

        (Use ^B to return to main menu.)



EFI Boot Manager ver 1.10 [14.60]

Please select a boot option

    HP-UX Primary Boot: 0/0/0/2/0.6.0     <-- Select boot off Primary
    Acpi(000222F0,0)/Pci(1|0)/Mac(00306E4B9AD9)
    Acpi(000222F0,100)/Pci(1|0)/Mac(00306E4BAA28)
    EFI Shell [Built-in]
    Boot option maintenance menu


    Use ^ and v to change option(s). Use Enter to select an option

Loading.: HP-UX Primary Boot: 0/0/0/2/0.6.0
Starting: HP-UX Primary Boot: 0/0/0/2/0.6.0
 - - - - - - - - - - - - Live Console - - - - - - - - - - - -
(c) Copyright 1990-2003, Hewlett Packard Company.
All rights reserved

HP-UX Boot Loader for IPF  --  Revision 1.73
```

```
Press Any Key to interrupt Autoboot
\EFI\HPUX\AUTO ==> boot vmunix
Seconds left till autoboot -    0
AUTOBOOTING...
AUTO BOOT> boot vmunix
> System Memory = 65407 MB
loading section 0
........................................ (complete)
loading section 1
........... (complete)
loading symbol table
loading System Directory(boot.sys) to MFS
....
Loading MFSFILES directory (bootfs) to MFS
......
Launching /stand/vmunix
SIZE: Text:23228K + Data:5560K + BSS:7905K = Total:36694K

Console is on a Serial Device
Booting kernel...




                          .
                          .
                          .
```

Many options are available for booting, and I select to boot off the *Primary* device. The full HP-UX boot takes place.

This example shows using *CM, VFP,* and *CO* to reset a partition on an Itanium-based HP Integrity Server.

Using *CM*, *VFP*, and *CO* to Reset a Partition on PA-RISC

When you're new to *CM, VFP,* and *CO,* it is sometimes difficult to determine which of these to use for what function. A good example of using all three of these menu areas is to reset a partition. This demonstrates the level of functionality that each provides. This is a three-step process:

1. Use *CM* to reset a partition.

2. Use *VFP* to see the partition progress through various stages of the boot process.

3. Use *CO* to search for bootable devices, select one, and boot the partition.

You can issue an *rs* command to reset the partition from *CM*:

```
MP:CM> rs                              <-- Reset partition with rs

This command resets the selected partition.

WARNING: Execution of this command irrecoverably halts all system
         processing and I/O activity and restarts the selected
         partition.

  Part#  Name
  -----  ----
    0)   Partition 0
    1)   Partition 1

  Select a partition number: 1   <-- Select partition 1 for reset

  Do you want to reset partition number 1? (Y/[N]) y

  -> The selected partition will be reset.
MP:CM>
```

After specifying that partition 1 is to be reset, you can view the progress at the *VFP,* as shown in the following example:

```
PARTITION STATUS:  E indicates error since last boot
    Partition 1  state              Activity
    ------------------              --------
    Partition Booting:  310  Logs

  #  Cell state                     Activity
  -  ----------                     --------
  1  Memory discovery               Physical memory test          310  Logs


MP:VFP (^B to Quit) >
```

At this point, the *VFP* shows that memory discovery is taking place.

Next, I switch to *CO* so you can see that you have control of the HP-UX boot process through the console. I specify the **sea** command to search for bootable devices in the following example:

```
MP> co                                  <-- Select Console with co

     Partitions available:

   Part#  Name
   -----  ----
     0)   Partition 0
     1)   Partition 1
     Q)   Quit

   Please select partition number: 1    <-- Select partition 1

        Connecting to Console: Partition 1

        (Use ^B to return to main menu.)

        [A few lines of context from the console log:]
- - - - - - - - - - - - - - - - - - - - - - - - - - - - - - - - -
     SERvice menu                     Displays service commands

     DIsplay                          Redisplay the current menu
     HElp [<menu>|<command>]          Display help for menu or command
     REBOOT                           Restart Partition
     RECONFIGRESET                    Reset to allow Reconfig Complex Profile
   ----
Main Menu: Enter command or menu >

- - - - - - - - - - - - - - - - - - - - - - - - - - - - - - - - -

Main Menu: Enter command or menu > sea <-- Search for bootable devices

Searching for potential boot device(s)
This may take several minutes.

To discontinue search, press any key (termination may not be immediate).

     Path#  Device Path (dec)                  Device Type
     -----  -----------------                  -----------
     P0     1/0/0/2/0.6                        Random access media
     P1     1/0/0/2/1.2                        Random access media
     P2     1/0/0/3/0.6                        Random access media
     P3     1/0/8/0/0.8                        Random access media

Main Menu: Enter command or menu > bo p0 <-- Select boot off of p0

  BCH Directed Boot Path: 1/0/0/2/0.6


Do you wish to stop at the ISL prompt prior to booting? (y/n) >> n
```

```
Initializing boot Device.

Boot IO Dependent Code (IODC) Revision 0

Boot Path Initialized.

HARD Booted.

ISL Revision A.00.43  Apr 12, 2000

ISL booting  hpux

Boot
: disk(1/0/0/2/0.6.0.0.0.0.0;0)/stand/vmunix
10403840 + 2019328 + 1340376 start 0x1f2a68
             .
             .
             .
```

In the previous listing, you can see that the **sea** produces several devices. I select one of the disks off of which to boot and do not want to stop at the ISL prompt. The full HP-UX boot then took place.

This example shows using *CM, VFP,* and *CO* to reset a partition on a PA-RISC HP 9000.

Using Partition Manager (parmgr) to Modify and Create nPartitions

As an alternative to performing all our work at the command line, we could have used the Web-based tool **parmgr**. **parmgr**, with a full path of **/opt/ parmgr/bin/parmgr**, can be used to perform most nPartition-related functions. **parmgr** is invoked in a browser window with the following command:

```
https://hostname:50000/parmgr
```

You can use either the *hostname* or IP address of the nPartition on which you want to run **parmgr**. At the time of this writing, this command brings up HP Servicecontrol Manager (SCM).

I now perform a simple example using **parmgr** on an Integrity server. In an earlier example, I modified a PA-RISC system at the command line by freeing up some resources and using them to create a new partition. The **par- modify** and **parcreate** commands are issued when using **parmgr** in the upcoming example. I now perform some similar tasks, freeing up some resources and creating a new nPartition, using **parmgr** on an Integrity server. Figure 17-4 shows nPartition0 of the **parmgr** screen on an Integrity server.

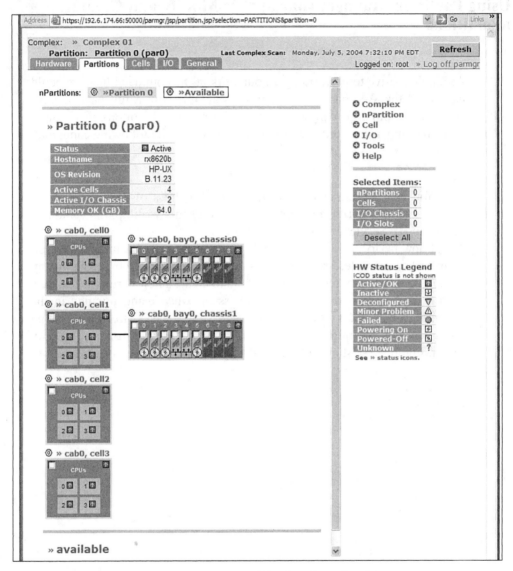

Figure 17-4 **parmgr** Main Screen Showing One nPartition

Figure 17-4 shows that only nPartition0 exists because there is only one nPartition from which you can select at the top of the screen. There are four cell boards and two I/O chassis in the system. This figure shows that all the components are devoted to nPartition0. I can confirm this by selecting *Available,* as shown in Figure 17-5.

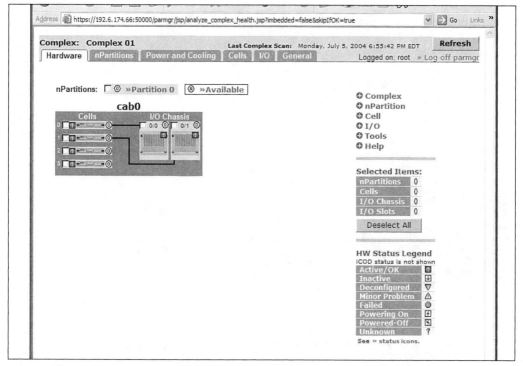

Figure 17-5   **parmgr** Showing No Available Components

No available components exist on this system because all the cell boards and I/O chassis are devoted to nPartition0. Available components would have been shaded differently than used components, as you see in an upcoming figure, on the *Available* screen. Because no components are available, I free up cell 1 and the I/O chassis connected to it and create a new nPartition. Figure 17-6 shows selecting the two components, as denoted by the box checked in the upper left of the two components, and then selecting Unassign Cell(s) on the right of the diagram.

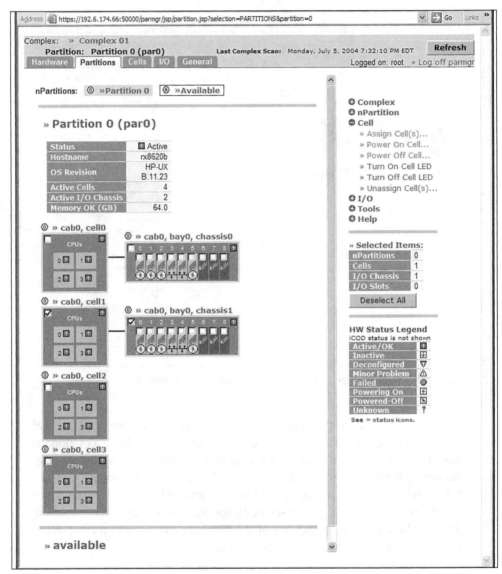

Figure 17-6   Unassigning Components from nPartition0

Unassigned cell1 and the I/O chassis connected to it gives me available components to use for a second nPartition. Several Windows appear, including one that shows the command being issued to unassign the cell which is as follows:

```
/usr/sbin/parmodify -p 0 -d 1
```

I could issue this command at the command line as I did in the previous example. This line modifies nPartition0 (-p 0 on the command line) and deletes cell1 (-d 1 on the command line) from it. When cell 1 is deleted from nPartition0, the I/O chassis connected to it also becomes available.

I am comfortable removing this cell board and the I/O chassis connected to it because the boot device for nPartition0 is not connected to the I/O cards in the chassis.

The cell board and I/O chassis now appear as available components. To create the nPartition, select *nPartition* and *Create nPartition...* from the *Hardware* screen, as shown in Figure 17-7.

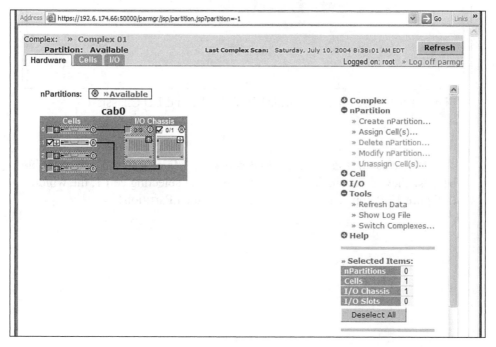

Figure 17-7   *Hardware* Screen Showing the Menu Pick *Create nPartition...*

After making the *Create nPartition* menu pick, Figure 17-8 shows creating the new nPartition, nPartition1, with cell 1 and I/O chassis 1 available to add to nPartition1. The box in the upper left of cell 1 is checked, which indicates that it will be added to nPartition1.

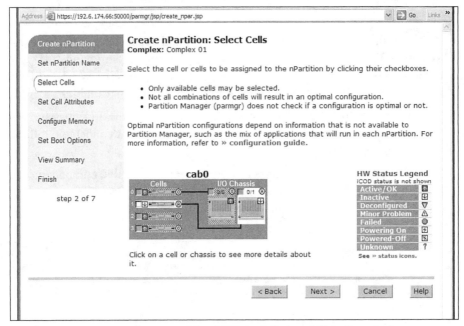

Figure 17-8   Creating nPartition1 With Cell 1 and I/O Chassis 1

It is clear in this diagram that cell1 and I/O chassis 0/1 are available because they're not shaded in Figure 17-8. After selecting cell 1, the window in Figure 17-9 appears showing attributes of the nPartition1.

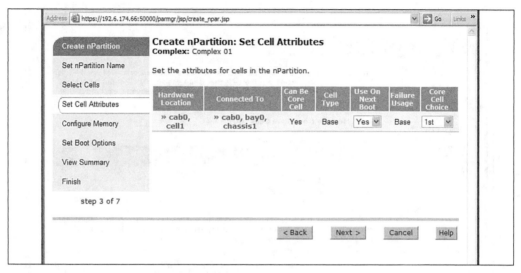

Figure 17-9   Attributes of nPartition1

The cell attributes include cell1, chassis1 which is connected to cell1, and the fact that this is a core cell. Figure 17-10 shows the memory configuration, including the option for Cell Local Memory (CLM). All 16 GB of memory are used in the nPartition configuration.

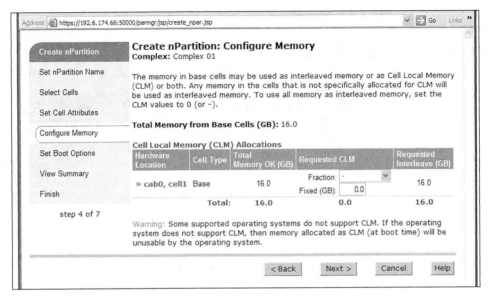

Figure 17-10   nPartition1 Memory Configuration

I have not selected CLM in this example, but all 16 GB of RAM on the cell board are interleaved. With all 16 GB of memory selected and interleaved, the next step is for boot options, as shown in Figure 17-11.

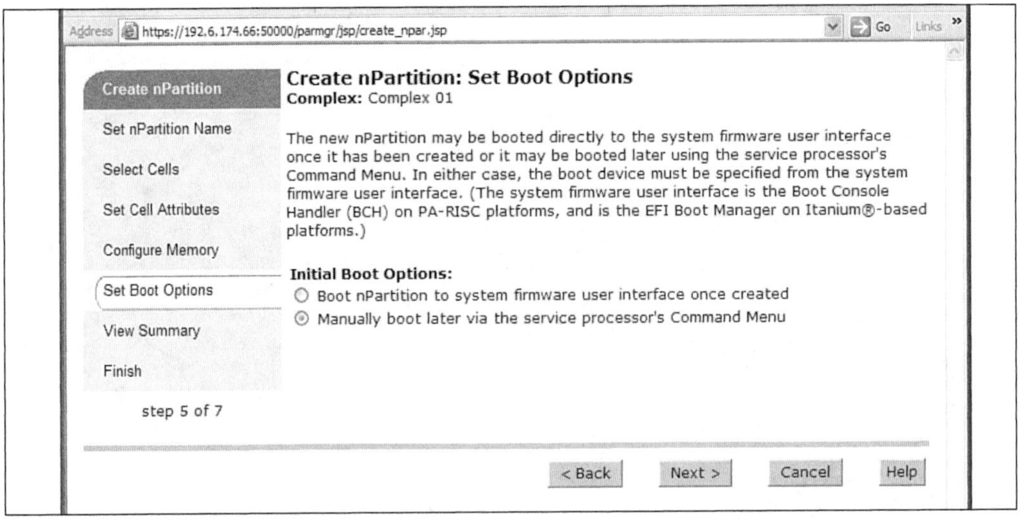

Figure 17-11   nPartition1 Boot Options

I select *Manually boot later* from the Command Menu. The summary screen shown in 17-12 appears.

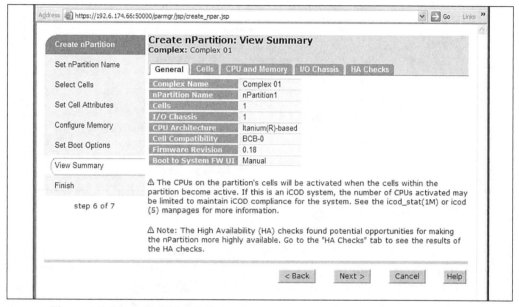

Figure 17-12   nPartition1 Summary

At this point, **parmgr** is ready to finish the operation, as shown in Figure 17-13.

Figure 17-13   nPartition1 Final Creation Screen

This nPartition is now ready to create. The **parcreate** command shown in Figure 17-13 will be issued, which I could have issued at the command line to create the partition. The *Finish* command is shown here:

```
[Finish]: /usr/sbin/parcreate -P nPartition1 -c 1:base:y: -r 1
```

The earlier **parmodify** command combined with this **parcreate** command would have accomplished the same outcome of modifying and creating the partition that was performed graphically in **parmgr**.

Now that nPartition1 has been created, I reset it from the *MP:CM>*, as shown in the following listing:

```
MP:CM> rs

This command resets the selected partition.

WARNING: Execution of this command irrecoverably halts all system
         processing and I/O activity and restarts the selected
         partition.

    Part#  Name
    -----  ----
       0)  Partition 0
       1)  nPartition1

    Select a partition number: 1
```

```
Do you want to reset partition number 1? (Y/[N]) y

    -> The selected partition will be reset.
MP:CM>
```

Through the virtual front panel, I observe the nPartition1 progress through the boot process. Because manual boot was selected at the time I created this nPartition, I select a boot device for nPartition1.

Chapter 18

Future Directions for HP-UX System Administration

Introduction

The last few years have resulted in quite a bit of change for anybody involved in the world of IT or IT management. There has been a lot of the usual technology change, for many business has gotten more dynamic than ever and management expects IT capacity to change overnight. There is also increasing pressure to reduce IT operating costs with all kinds of options being considered. The September 11, 2001 attack has forever changed how we think about security. On top of all of that, auditors are giving advice based on different interpretations of the Sarbanes-Oxley Act.

We can only expect more change in the future. We can also expect that Hewlett-Packard and other technology companies will race with each other to provide IT management with the technology solutions to address this changing world. This chapter describes the major driving forces and technology adoption trends and discusses the implications for HP-UX system administrators going into the future. Some of the major topics discussed include server consolidation, virtualization, configuration standardization, and multi-OS automation.

Driving Forces

The primary force driving IT change usually comes down to increasing service levels and reducing operating costs, although this takes on many faces. There are a number of strategies that IT management in different companies have taken over the last few years, but one of the most common initiatives, especially for larger enterprises, is some form of data center consolidation. The first step is usually to consolidate the number of physical locations into as few as possible. This in itself results in some increased operating efficiencies. However, at this stage, management starts asking some good questions about server utilization, service level management, and disaster recovery strategies.

Also, it never hurts to throw in a few new government regulations to keep life interesting.

Need to Increase Server Utilization

Many larger enterprise customers have already consolidated their physical data centers and are currently in the process of figuring out how to make the best use of the IT resources that have been consolidated. In fact, many systems are under-utilized while many others are too often near 100% utilization; those are the ones constantly having problems delivering required service levels. Because these data centers are usually centrally monitored, upper management has better visibility to the actual utilization of the hundreds of millions of server assets within those glass-enclosed data centers.

Need to Increase Service Levels

The more IT systems get embedded into businesses processes, the more important it is that IT systems enable business opportunities rather than inhibit them. A clear example of a company with computers embedded throughout its process is Amazon.com. One real challenge is how a data center manager explains to a line of business managers that the data center needs a larger budget to meet service level agreements when the majority of existing resources are already under-utilized.

High availability is another aspect of service levels and is especially important when more and more workloads from various business units are stacked onto fewer servers. Any system faults need to be addressed quickly and application failover solutions need to be robust and scalable. Unfortunately, with some of the ugly realities in today's world, disaster-tolerate data center strategies are becoming the norm.

Even planning downtime for maintenance becomes all the more challenging when a window of time needs to be negotiated among multiple business units.

Heterogeneous Operating System Administration

Another consequence of data center consolidation is many of the old silos around different operating systems have been broken. Now, many data center managers are responsible for administration of multiple variants of UNIX and Windows as well as various Linux Distributions, BSD UNIX, and a host of legacy proprietary systems. There are certain fundamental differences in how some of these systems are managed. However, it is easy to understand why many centralized IT organizations would desire a single security management tool that simply makes sure that all systems are in compliance, regardless of operating system.

Affects of Sarbanes-Oxley Act

The Sarbanes-Oxley Act is also having an impact on how systems are managed, accessed, and audited. IT management is being forced to institute more formal processes.

Virtualization

Virtualization technologies have the potential to finally meet the often conflicting requirements of increasing service levels while reducing cost. This an area where many IT operations started playing with the idea of virtualization in the storage context first. Because of continuous and often unpredictable growth, storage was usually over-provisioned. With networked storage arrays, for the first time IT managers could share a large pool of storage resources across many servers. The storage arrays need to have some extra head room available, but the individual servers don't need to be over-provisioned for growth. The overall utilization of the storage is significantly improved by allocating storage from a shared pool when it's needed. Moreover, there will always be storage available to individual servers that really need it, so this also helps maintain high service levels. Another benefit of having a virtualized storage pool is that it much easier to new applications provisioned with storage. Instead of having to procure dedicated storage for the application, you simply get some LUNs assigned and you are off and running. Think about how easy it would be to create a temporary development environment where you *borrow* from the array for a few weeks. Think about how nice it would be if other resources could be shared among servers in this same manner. Hold that thought.

Current HP-UX Partitioning Technologies

HP-UX has been the target operating system of many server consolidation projects going back to V-class systems, which were very scalable in their time. This continued with Superdomes, and today, we have a wide range of HP Integrity Servers that are ideal consolidation platforms not only for HP-UX, but also for Linux and Windows. HP has supported a range a technology solutions to address different customer needs around resource optimization, resource sharing, fault isolation, and manageability.

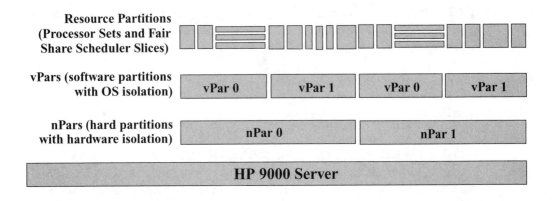

Figure 18-1   HP-UX Partitioning Technologies

Today's technologies range from nPars with complete electrical isolation, to vPars based on software partitions with isolated operating system instances, to resource partitions which allow CPU and memory to be selectively allocated to various workload processes running in a single OS instance (see Figure 18-1). Note that the management of resource partitions requires the optional HP Process Resource Manager (PRM) or HP Workload Manager (WLM) product. The two types of resource partitions are those created using Processor Sets (psets) and those creating using process groups with time slices of CPU allocated by the UNIX Fair Share Scheduler (FSS). A fairly logical trade-off needs to be made between sharing resources and isolating faults associated with those resources. nPars and vPars were designed to provide fault isolation and do not allow sharing of I/O cards. On the other hand, resource partitions allow I/O cards and even CPUs and memory to be shared depending on configuration.

When it comes to resource optimization, resource partitions using the FSS are the most efficient because of the ability to allocate resources at sub-CPU granularity. nPar and vPars can only allocate resources at the whole CPU granular level. In fact, without iCAP (instant Capacity) CPUs, entire four-CPU cell boards is the finest granularity for allocating CPUs in nPars. Processor sets are allocated in whole CPU increments so the granularity is the same as vPars. For this reason, resource partitions using FSS are an ideal solution when you want to stack similar, well-behaved workloads into a single OS instance. However, keep in mind that a single run-away process associated with one workload could still negatively affect other workloads running in the same OS instance. For this reason, vPars are often the ideal solution where a certain amount of isolation is desired between different OS instances. Another thing to keep in mind here is that the more OS instances you have, the more management effort is required.

It is also important to keep in mind that these technologies can also be used together in a mix-and-match way to meet the needs of different workload profiles. For example, you could have resource partitions running inside of vPars, which are running inside of nPars, as shown Figure 18-1. You could also have resource partitions running directly in nPars or any combination in between. It should also be pointed out that only larger cell-based HP 9000 and Integrity servers support nPars. In the case of non-nPar systems, vPars or resource partitions would run directly on the non-partitioned hardware.

To reiterate, HP-UX provides a range of partitioning technologies because each has some trade-off and the best one depends on the many factors.

Integrity Virtual Machines

HP recently announced the future availability of Integrity Virtual Machines (Integrity VMs) on the HP-UX 11i version2 operating system. The Integrity VMs design is based on virtualizing CPU, memory, network, and storage resources. This allows expensive resources to be shared between multiple VMs. Each VM runs its own copy of the operating system, so VM benefits by having OS isolation from each other. Moreover, unlike vPars, resources such as CPUs can be allocated with fine granularity at the sub-CPU level. This allows a number of smaller workloads to share resources on a moderately sized system. Just as important, resources can be dynamically reallocated between VMs with fine granularity. By sharing the pool of resources between mixed workloads with different demands, extremely high levels of resource utilization can be achieved.

Another unique feature makes Integrity VMs even more interesting: They support HP-UX, Linux, and Windows guest operating systems on 64-bit Integrity servers. Different guest operating systems can even be hosted on the same host system. For example, this allows resource balancing across multiple instances of Linux running web servers, multiple instances of Windows running application logic servers, and one or more instances of HP-UX hosting database servers in a multi-tiered application. It will also be conceivable to mix enterprise applications, messaging, and various development and test environments on the same system.

Tools to Make It Fool-Proof

There are clear benefits to virtualizing resources, but one of the challenges of virtualization is in understanding the critical relationship between the virtual hardware world and the real hardware world. Fortunately, HP has much experience in this area and HP's Partition Manager, which is already being used today to manage nPars on HP-UX 11i version2 systems, highlights the kind of progress that has been made.

Partition Manager is a web-based application that makes extensive use of graphics and colors to show the relationship between partitions and the underlying hardware resources that are associated with each. Figure 18-2 shows the relationship between various Superdome partitions and the associated physical cabinets, I/O bays, I/O slots, and cell boards. Think about how difficult it would be to reconfigure memory or I/O cards without knowing their relationship to partitions, some of which might be running mission-critical applications.

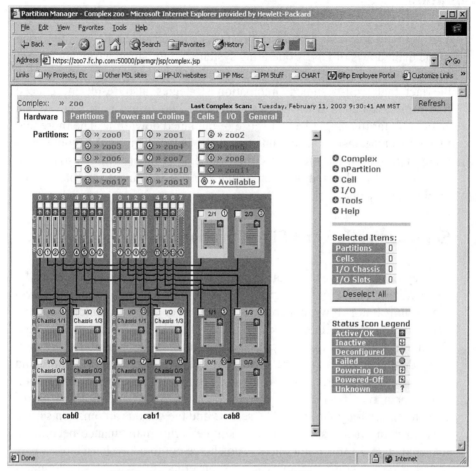

Figure 18-2   HP Partition Manager Screen Shot

Partition Manager was used extensively in Chapter 17 covering nPartitions.

Automation

The ability to automate administration tasks with scripts and cron jobs is one of the main draws of UNIX operating systems. Automation has the benefit of significantly improving administrative productivity, but just as important is the fact that well-designed automation strategies also result in reduced downtime associated with failures caused by human error. In fact, human error is by far the single largest cause of unplaned downtime. The more that manual routine tasks can be automated the better. This will become even more important in the future as virtualized environments allow resources to be dynamically allocated between online workloads to meet variable service level requirements.

Standardization and Simplification

The key to an effective automation strategy is to simplify the environment by standardizing on as few configurations as possible. It is common for a system administrator to write a comprehensive set of scripts to automate many configuration-management tasks. Often, Ignite-UX servers are implemented for automating cold installations and custom depots created for efficient patch deployment. At first, the strategy works fine, but over time, more and more new systems are added to the mix, each with a unique configuration *tuned* for a specific task. Before you know it, there is a proliferation of golden images for your Ignite-UX servers and the various automation scripts have so many if-def statements that simple script maintanance becomes a real challenge. At this point, there is no choice but to take a hard look at why different system configurations can't be converged into a much smaller number of standard configurations.

Automated Configuration Management

Recently, there has been an rapid emergence of tools and platforms from multiple management vendors that specifically address the problem of automated configuration management. These tools provide comprehensive solutions for cold installing, updating, patching, software inventory, and compliance monitoring. These tools generally require a fairly significant investment up front, but the payoff comes later when the environment can be efficiently and reliably maintained. Another benefit is that most of these tool vendors support a wide range of operating systems so that management consoles and configuration expertise can be leveraged across all the systems that need to be managed. Some other benefits in deploying these types of solutions is that security is designed in and, most importantly, tool maintenance is the job of the software vendor rather than the IT staff.

In early 2004, Hewlett-Packard acquired one of these management vendors called *Novadigm*. This company coined the term *Desired State Management* to describe how its Radia product lines approach the problem of automated configuration management. The Radia line includes modules for OS management, application management, patch management, software inventory, and more. Naturally, these tools support the usual assortment of operating systems, including HP-UX, Linux, and Windows. The acquisition was recently completed, and you can expect healthy cross-pollination between native HP-UX tools, such as Ignite-UX, and the Radia suite of tools over time.

Policy-Based Workload Management

HP-UX has a long history of providing leadership workload mangement tools going back to Process Resource Manager (PRM), which has been supported on HP-UX for several releases. PRM is bundled with the HP-UX Enterprise Operating Environment. Workload Manager (WLM) was introduced with HP-UX 11i version1, and was the first goal-based workload mangement solution on UNIX. WLM is bundled with the HP-UX Mission Critical Operating Environment. With WLM, you establish policies for how resources are dynamically allocated between workloads to meet service level goals, such as maximum transaction queue. WLM works with PRM to dynamically re-allocate CPU resources between resource partitions and can also move CPUs between online vPars. It was discovered early on that many customers simply did not feel comfortable having a tool make changes to online production systems, so WLM also provides the option of an advisory mode that describes the action WLM would take without actually making the changes. This allows administrators to *test drive* the tool within their comfort zone before actually going into a fully automated mode.

Hewlett-Packard has again raised the bar with the recent introduction of gWLM (*global* Workload Manager). gWLM takes many of the concepts of WLM and extends its capability to the management of multiple servers. In addition, gWLM is also supported on Linux and made a number of significant improvements to *ease of use*.

Virtual Server Environment

Virtual Server Environment is the term Hewlett-Packard uses to describe a set of technologies that have been tightly integrated to deliver a comprehensive solution around high availability, virtualization, automated workload management, even hardware provisioning through iCAP (instant Capacity program for CPUs), and utility pricing programs. Here is an example to demonstrate the level of integration between vPars, WLM, and Serviceguard. By the way, Serviceguard is the high availability clustering software for HP-UX. If a failure causes the workload in one vPar to go down, Serviceguard immediately fails over the package for the workload to another vPar. However, WLM has established policies such that on the event of a failover, the new vPar is allocated additional resources to handle the additional load. Also, because WLM is integrated with iCAP, WLM could even trigger the activation of iCAP CPUs to provide the additional resources needed by the new vPar.

One variation of the Virtual Server Environment is especially interesting and has actually been implemented in production by a number of leading-edge customers. The basic idea is to combine clustering with virtualization in a way that provides high availability and resouce utility with flexibility to dynamically shift resources between different workloads based on business priority. For example, BEA has a Java Application Server product called WebLogic Server (WLS). BEA also has a clustered version of this software that supports load-balancing across multiple instances of WebLogic Server. These clusters enhance scalability and availability. The most common model is for this clustered version of WebLogic Server to scale horizontally over a number of smaller two-way servers. However, the interesting variation on this theme is when the various instances of WebLogic Server are hosted within partitions on more than one large server. On HP-UX, the partitioning scheme would most likely be resource partitions or vPars because they both support automated, dynamic resizing via WLM. This hybrid clustering and virtualization model provides the same or better scalability and high availability as traditional horizontal scaling models. However, this hybrid model providesmore flexibility to dynamically shift resources to address changing business requirements. The hybrid model can also provide much higher resource utilization depending on the mix of workloads and granularity of resource allocation between the workloads. One nice thing about WebLogic Server is that multiple instances running within a single instance of HP-UX behave very well. The advanatage of having mutiple instances of WebLogic Server in the same instance of the operating system is that communication between the BEA instances is much better than going over a network.

Looking Forward

The Virtual Server Environment clearly demonstrates how the integration of critical technologies can result in a solution that is more powerful than the sum of the parts. The evolution of HP's Virtual Server Environment over the next few years should bear some interesting fruit. The value proposition around the Virtual Server Environment is already compelling. However, a number of recent announcements by Hewlett-Packard give clear indications of how the Virtual Server Environment will evolve over time.

The first is the announcement of Integrity Virtual Machines. The benefits of Integrity VMs have been previously described. In many ways, virtualization is the foundation of the Virtual Server Environment, and the availability of Integrity VMs will provide a big boost in resource utilization and application isolation. Also, because Linux will be supported as guest operating systems on Integrity VMs, the Virtual Server Environment can be extended to Linux. Note that HP's industry-leading Serviceguard high availability clustering has been available for Linux for some time now.

The second is the announcement of gWLM (global Workload Manager), which has also been previously described. gWLM supports automated workload management across many servers. gWLM also improves ease of use and extends these functionalities to Linux in addition to HP-UX.

The third recent announcement is around agreements between HP and Veritas to strengthen the partnership and provide high levels of integration between Veritas' storage management suite of products, which includes the Cluster File System (CFS) technology. These Veritas technologies will help improve the manageabilty, performance, and scalability of Serviceguard clusters. HP will be OEM'ing these technologies, which means that HP will deliver these products with the same level of integration and quality as HP-developed products.

At the same time as the HP/Veritas announcement, HP also announced the future availabilty of cluster-management tools in what it is calling *Single Virtual View (SVV)*. The idea behind SVV is to provide a set of tools to allow any cluster of sysems to be managed as much as possible as if it were a single system. These clusters could be Serviceguard clusters or they could just as easily be a group of mostly unrelated servers that need to be managed more efficiently. The goal of this tool is to improve system administrative efficiencies and increase availability through automation. Some of the tools described include a utility for sychronizing critical configuration files across systems in a cluster, a command fan-out utility, a cluster-wide log viewer, and a high availability assessment tool. These tools couldn't be more timely. The implementation of Integrity VMs will most likely result in a proliferation of operating system images that need to be managed. These SVV tools should help make that management more efficient and reliable.

In summary, it is the integration of many new and exciting technologies into the already powerful Virtual Server Environment value proposition that will bring many new capabilities to the data center. Sure, like any new new technology there will be an adoption curve, but I can't think of a more exciting time to thinking about what is over the horizon.

Index

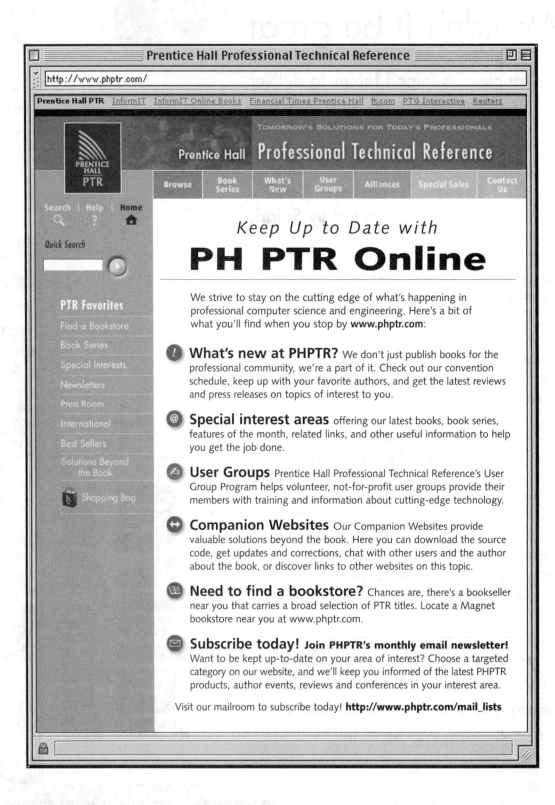

Prentice Hall Professional Technical Reference

http://www.phptr.com/

Prentice Hall PTR   InformIT   InformIT Online Books   Financial Times Prentice Hall   ft.com   PTG Interactive   Reuters

TOMORROW'S SOLUTIONS FOR TODAY'S PROFESSIONALS

Prentice Hall **Professional Technical Reference**

| Browse | Book Series | What's New | User Groups | Alliances | Special Sales | Contact Us |

Search | Help | Home

Quick Search

PTR Favorites

Find a Bookstore
Book Series
Special Interests
Newsletters
Press Room
International
Best Sellers
Solutions Beyond
the Book

Shopping Bag

Keep Up to Date with
PH PTR Online

We strive to stay on the cutting edge of what's happening in professional computer science and engineering. Here's a bit of what you'll find when you stop by **www.phptr.com**:

What's new at PHPTR? We don't just publish books for the professional community, we're a part of it. Check out our convention schedule, keep up with your favorite authors, and get the latest reviews and press releases on topics of interest to you.

Special interest areas offering our latest books, book series, features of the month, related links, and other useful information to help you get the job done.

User Groups Prentice Hall Professional Technical Reference's User Group Program helps volunteer, not-for-profit user groups provide their members with training and information about cutting-edge technology.

Companion Websites Our Companion Websites provide valuable solutions beyond the book. Here you can download the source code, get updates and corrections, chat with other users and the author about the book, or discover links to other websites on this topic.

Need to find a bookstore? Chances are, there's a bookseller near you that carries a broad selection of PTR titles. Locate a Magnet bookstore near you at www.phptr.com.

Subscribe today! Join PHPTR's monthly email newsletter! Want to be kept up-to-date on your area of interest? Choose a targeted category on our website, and we'll keep you informed of the latest PHPTR products, author events, reviews and conferences in your interest area.

Visit our mailroom to subscribe today! **http://www.phptr.com/mail_lists**